Diary of
Kenneth A. MacRae

Diary of Kenneth A. MacRae

A record of fifty years in the Christian Ministry

Edited with
additional biographical
material by

Iain H. Murray

The Banner of Truth Trust

THE BANNER OF TRUTH TRUST
3 *Murrayfield Road, Edinburgh* EH12 6EL
PO Box 621, Carlisle, Pennsylvania 17013, USA

The Banner of Truth Trust 1980
ISBN 0 85151 297 6

Printed in Great Britain by
ROBERT MACLEHOSE AND CO. LTD.
Printers to the University of Glasgow

Contents

Illustrations

Acknowledgements
7 By courtesy of the Rev A. MacDougall
11 By courtesy of *The Ayr Advertiser*
15, 20, 21, 24. By courtesy of Edwin Smith
22 By courtesy of William McLauchlan
31 By courtesy of W. G. Lucas

Introduction

It was my privilege to have known Kenneth A. MacRae for seven years before his death on May 5, 1964. At the invitation of Mrs Catherine MacRae, his widow, another form of acquaintance with him was to begin unexpectedly in November 1966. At that date, on a visit to Stornoway, I first saw the large boxes of personal manuscripts and notebooks which he had left. The majority of these manuscripts proved to be diaries, varied in shape and size, with entries covering most years from 1912 until 1963. I was at once convinced that there was a purpose in the survival of these diaries. They belong to that category of Christian literature which appears but rarely in any century. Probably nothing comparable to them has been published in the United Kingdom since Andrew A. Bonar's *Diary and Letters* in 1893.

Eleven years have now elapsed since I began work on the diaries with a view to their publication. Of necessity, my attention to it has been intermittent but the chief reason for this lengthy time-factor has been the sheer size of the work involved. In an appendix I have listed the forty-one diaries and journals out of which this volume has been formed. This alone will give some indication of what was required. To have printed the original diaries *verbatim* would have meant over a dozen volumes of the present size! Selection and abridgement were essential and yet to do this while preserving an accurate balance of the originals was exceedingly difficult. At the same time there were letters, notebooks and other records to be consulted. This was necessarily the work of years rather than of months.

Opinion on the value of keeping diaries has passed through many changes. In 1898 Joseph Parker expressed what was to become the common twentieth-century view when he stated his belief that to keep a diary is 'often a dangerous and still oftener a silly practice'. Contemporary fashion had already turned away from the practice before Kenneth MacRae began his record of more than fifty years. In this instance, as in many others, his actions were not guided by current opinion. He took up and maintained the practice for one reason only, namely, because he believed in its value. Although his entries were often made at the end of a very full day, he never abandoned his early conviction that his diary was too valuable to be given up.

But what gave the diaries this value in his eyes? It was certainly not the thought that they might one day reach a wider readership. Such a possibility he would have treated with utter incredulity. Literary ambition was no part of his make-up and he lived and died altogether unconscious that his thoughts might be laid open to the world. The truth is that he valued a diary for its spiritual usefulness. In his judgment it could play a significant part in the fulfilment of duties which belonged to him as a Christian. This statement may require some explanation.

Biblical religion asserts the reality of the presence and providence of God in the lives of His people. Moses at the end of his days could say, 'O Lord God, thou hast begun to shew thy servant thy greatness, and thy mighty hand' (Deut. 3:24), and the same is true for all Christians. Their lives are spent under the blessing and care of their Redeemer. But the enjoyment of God, begun in this world, is not an end in itself. The end is that God may be praised; hence it is obligatory for Christians to remember what they have received and how they have been led. The experiences of the past are to remain as subjects for praise in the future. 'The Lord hath made his wonderful works to be remembered' (Psa. 111:4) and, accordingly, the right use of memory and the glorifying of God belong together. A diary may therefore become a practical help in the fulfilment of 'man's chief end'. Such was the chief reason why it was advocated in the Puritan tradition of England and Scotland. 'We must use diaries,' urges Paul Bayne, the Cambridge Puritan leader. 'Observe and lay up God's dealings,' says Richard Sibbes. 'Let us keep a catalogue of God's blessings.'

Sibbes gives an additional reason why such a 'catalogue' should be kept and it was also one in which Kenneth MacRae believed. 'It will serve', he writes, 'to establish our faith the more, for God is Jehovah, always like himself.' The clear memories which the pages of a diary may revive for its writer, long after they were first recorded, can be a source of encouragement second only to the Bible itself. In days of trial they will help the Christian diarist to take a wider view and to say with John Newton:

> His love in time past
>   Forbids me to think
> He'll leave me at last
>   In trouble to sink:
> Each sweet Ebenezer
>   I have in review,
> Confirms His good pleasure
>   To help me quite through.

There is a final reason why a diary can be of much spiritual value to a Christian and it is well-rooted in Scripture. The Christian is called to cultivate self-knowledge. He is not to be as those who, in John Owen's phrase, 'live in the dark to themselves all their days'. Self-examination and self-judgment are Christian duties, to be exercised with a conscience open towards God and the standards of His Word: 'Let a man examine himself . . . For if we would judge ourselves, we should not be judged' (I Cor. 11:28–31). Sincerity is of the essence of the life of godliness and it only thrives when men consider that all their thoughts and deeds lie open to God. Those who, with Paul, believe that 'We must all appear before the judgment seat of Christ: that every one may receive the things done in his body, according to that he hath done, whether it be good or bad' (2 Cor. 5:10), will not live purposelessly or merely to please men. They know that in a very short time nothing will be of any consequence except the approval of God.

For this reason also Kenneth MacRae valued a diary. It became an aid to spiritual watchfulness and single-mindedness. His diary was a reminder that his life must not be a whirl of activities and events which he had no time to stop and consider. It helped him to learn the benefit of the psalmist's testimony, 'I thought on my ways, and turned my feet unto thy testimonies' (Psa. 119:59). The witness of his conscience, when it testified against him, he would often record as a spur to greater obedience. Self-examination, prayer, and new resolution were thus all aided by the practice which he began a few years after his conversion and continued until he was eighty.

It must be borne in mind that this volume is in no sense a biography. A spiritual diary reveals a man's inner springs, and in so doing it reveals much of the real man, but it has limitations which need to be understood. There was much in Kenneth MacRae's life of which there is little trace in these pages. Many things which were true of him may here be scarcely mentioned – his close bond with his wife and daughter; his cheerful presence (which his twinkling eyes often announced even before he spoke); his ability to lead and to command – these, and many other things, do not fall within the scope of a diary. At the same time a diary may give prominence to features of which even those closest to the writer may see little or nothing. Christians of the apostolic age did not observe in Paul the struggle which often made him cry, 'O wretched man that I am'. Christians of Boston, New England, did not see why Cotton Mather had to complain so often of pride in his diary.[1] Marjory

1 The words of Jonathan Edwards should also be remembered: 'The Christians that are really the most eminent saints . . . are astonished at and ashamed of

Bonar says of her father's experience, 'Deeper waters crossed his pathway than even those nearest him ever knew. They only heard the song with which he praised Him who had delivered him from all evil'. So it was also with Kenneth MacRae. On this point his daughter, Mrs Mary MacLeod, writes:

'In our homes we can all see the faults of our nearest and dearest, but we overlook these just because we love them. In the case of my father I could see no faults to overlook. His sense of the sinfulness of the human heart and of the holiness of God caused him to mourn much over his inward sins, but to me, who had to judge by outward appearances, his life was most impressive – in its meticulous honesty which extended to the minutest details, in his unbroken control over his temper no matter what he felt, in his charity which manifested itself in refraining from talking about the faults of others, and even in his rebukes, which were given in such a Christian and fatherly spirit that they drew one yet closer to him, and made one admire him more than ever.'

It is also necessary to speak briefly of the method I have used in making the selections which have gone into this volume. Mr MacRae's daily life as a pastor and preacher underwent no major changes from 1915 until near his death. Accordingly there is much which appears in his early diaries which is re-echoed in all the diaries which followed. Instead, therefore, of merely giving short extracts from consecutive years, I have sought to introduce variety by highlighting certain periods or particular themes. Sometimes I have concentrated fuller extracts around certain years or have grouped diary entries of a particular kind under a general subject. Thus, the entries given here for the years 1940–42 are not to be understood as though the Second World War then excluded all else from his thoughts. The usual subjects were all to be found in his diaries at that time, but I have purposely selected the entries dealing with the War. Besides showing an aspect of the author's character they give a vivid impression of how a Christian reacted to the news upon which the nation hung in those critical years.

The reader should therefore bear in mind that, if a volume of this size was to be produced at all, abridgement and the selection of material were essential. In following this method I have constantly sought to retain the balance of the original but inevitably there are gaps and

---

the low degrees of their love and their thankfulness, and their little knowledge of God . . . eminently humble saints, that will shine brightest in heaven, are not at all apt to profess high' *The Religious Affections*, 1746, Part III, Sect. 6.

omissions, and it may be that the names of friends who meant much to him scarcely appear in these pages.

While the responsibility for this selection belongs to myself I am much indebted to Mr MacRae's family for the help they have provided. In the first place Mrs Catherine MacRae, who died in January 1976, has supplied material from her own pen which no one else could have done. I shall ever treasure the memory of her friendship. Miss Ida MacRae, who still survives her brother, has contributed a valuable glimpse of his boyhood. Especial thanks are due to Mr MacRae's daughter Mary, and her husband, the Rev Norman MacLeod. The hospitality of their home, their encouragement and their help with many particular items, have meant much to me.

At various points I have had the ready help or advice of ministers and friends in the Free Church of Scotland. A complete list would be long and I will confine myself to the names of those who have finished their course since the preparation of this volume commenced – Malcolm Galbraith, John M. MacLennan, Peter W. Miller, and Roderick Cameron. Mr S. M. Houghton of Oxford, my friend and colleague in the work of the Banner of Truth Trust, in checking the manuscript, and in providing an Index, has once more contributed a vital element in the final result.

This volume will naturally be of much interest to those who knew Kenneth MacRae. That is not, however, the reason for its publication. Those who knew him have their own memories of him. Concerned as he was with the past, Mr MacRae's chief interest lay in the future. There was perhaps no single item more repeatedly in his public and family prayers than the petition that the young might become 'witnesses on the Lord's side in another day'. It is for the young, chiefly, across the world that these pages are published and especially for those who have been or will be called to the happiest of all work, the preaching of the gospel of Christ. If such are helped by these pages, as I am sure they will be, then one of the author's prayers will have been answered and in a way he never anticipated.

As Kenneth MacRae looked and prayed for the future there was one text to which he repeatedly referred. It was the triumphant declaration of the Prophet Isaiah, 'A little one shall become a thousand, and a small one a strong nation: I the Lord will hasten it in his time' (Isa. 60:22).

IAIN MURRAY
Edinburgh,
December 7, 1978

As the world hurtles on through time, to those who live in it its pace seems continually to increase. Changes, which in former times would require a generation for their full development now take place in the course of a few years, and what would create the greatest controversy then fits into place now practically without comment. Those of us who can look back over a range of 50 years have the feeling that the world which we then knew was an altogether different one from that in which we live today. It had its shadows and its toils no doubt, but as compared with the hectic, fevered, distraught sphere which is now our abode it was a care-free world. The sun shone then and the birds sang.

K. A. MacRae
'Fifty Years of Religious Life in Scotland –
A Retrospect'

In *The Monthly Record* of the Free Church
of Scotland, 1950

1 The Son of the Army

In the year 1883 the Recruiting Officer of the Seaforth Highlanders arrived with his wife and their two small boys in Dingwall, the county town of Ross-shire. In earlier years Murdo MacRae had served with his famous regiment in Canada and Gibraltar, but he was at this period settled in Fort George, on the north-east coast of Scotland, in quarters provided by the army. For the next three years this home was left for Dingwall, a better centre for the recruiting work to be done throughout the North, and consequently it was here on November 4th, 1883, that the third child, Kenneth Alexander MacRae, was born.

Most of Kenneth MacRae's own earliest memories were of Fort George, a place which in the early nineteenth century was regarded as one of the strongest defensive fortifications in Europe.[1] The massive architecture, and expansive parade ground, often crowded with Highland troops, were enough to feast the eyes of a child, and it may have been his father's voice, as a Regimental Sergeant-Major in the Seaforths, which he sometimes heard bringing the ranks into line.[2] 'Being born in the army I have a kinship with these people', he wrote in later years after a meeting with soldiers. The setting of Fort George was also full of appeal to one who had the native romance of a Celt in his blood. It stands on the low promontory of land dividing the southern shore of the Moray Firth from the quieter waters of the Inverness Firth; adjacent to it, looking westwards about a mile across the water, is the medieval town of Fortrose on the Black Isle – a name given in antiquity to that rich portion of land which lies between the Inverness and Cromarty Firths. And beyond the Black Isle, as it is viewed from Fort George, there rises in the distance the grand panorama of the mountains of Ross and Sutherland. At times when the Garrison School, which Kenneth joined in 1888, was closed for holidays, one of the earliest treats of childhood was the short ferry-crossing to the Black Isle, of which district both his parents were natives, his father from the parish of Knockbain and his mother from the farm of Glenurquhart near the old-world port of Cromarty. Before her marriage in 1876 Mrs MacRae,

1 It was built in the years 1749–1763 after the Jacobite rebellion of 1745, and garrisoned by troops from 1770 onwards.
2 Murdo MacRae appears to have served in both the 3rd and 4th Battalions of the Seaforths. The regiment itself was formed out of the 72nd and 78th Highlanders – the latter, the Ross-shire Buffs, being raised in 1793.

then Alexandrina Mackenzie, had served as Lady's maid in the ancient Cromarty house of Ross, fulfilling this position at one time with Louisa, Lady Macdonald of the Isles.

On the Black Isle there were the homes of several relatives, including those of his aunt and uncle at Cromarty, and another uncle who had succeeded to his maternal grandfather's smithy at Davison, where there were also cousins with whom to play. For Kenneth the green hills across the water from the grey walls of Fort George remained the happiest memory of his childhood: the glen and burn of Ethie, Ord Head above Cromarty, the rocky shores with their breaking waves and the call of gulls and peewits – these were all scenes which to life's end made him love his native Ross-shire. Outdoor adventures were many, including the near-disaster of one hot August day, when the MacRae brothers were swimming with a friend who collapsed and was brought home only with difficulty. Then, in the long evenings on the Black Isle, there was the often fascinating conversation of the elders to be overheard. We may surmise some of the things to which Kenneth listened in his aunt's house at Cromarty from some of the words in her obituary which his younger brother George was to contribute to the *North Star* on her death in 1912: 'Away back in the days of long ago she lived, and her mind was full of the simple pictures of her childhood. With a hard and bitter resignation she saw the changes which science and industry had wrought even in this far-off spot, and when the gloaming would steal over the land she would slip away out to commune with herself on the days that were...'

Murdo MacRae retired from the army in 1892, and it is a comment on the peaceful years of the Victorian era that he had never been engaged in action. The decision necessitated a move south to Edinburgh, and on 5th September 1892, Kenneth MacRae's name was entered on the roll of Sciennes School, with the note attached, 'from the Military School' and with his home address given as 12 Drumdryan Street, Tolcross. Shortly changes came. Duncan, the eldest brother, was soon away from home and as Alfred (the second boy) had died in childhood, Kenneth became the acknowledged leader, with twins George and Vic three years younger, and a second sister, Ida, the junior member of the circle. Recalling her first memories of Kenneth, seventy years later Ida wrote:

His inventive powers produced some wonderful games for us children, some too hilarious and dangerous to be approved of by our elders, but which filled us with great excitement and enjoyment. Often, too, on upturned table we travelled with Ken as Captain to various ports all over the world discharging and loading cargo. (This had been encouraged by our father, who often on a Saturday took us by train – sometimes travelling 1st class as a great treat – to Leith, to wander through the docks, gazing in awe at ships which had voyaged over many seas, and at the sailors, who to us were exclusive foreigners).

At the end of each month, too, the four of us (the second oldest having died in boyhood), gleefully and proudly wended our way down town – hand in hand – in charge of Ken, to spend our allowance, which though only 2d each was burning a hole in our pockets, and most economically it was spent, leaving the remainder for another day, – an unforgettable thrill and adventure as we returned home with a 'bouncer' price ½d, bulging in each cheek.

Kenneth left school on 26th March 1899 at the age of fifteen, and began training for the civil service at the General Post Office in Edinburgh. In connection with this work he obtained a first-class certificate in electricity in 1907 and in telegraphy the following year. Vacations and holidays were spent as much as possible in the open air and preferably in walking or mountaineering. Twice he climbed Ben Nevis, Scotland's highest mountain. With friends he walked over many parts of the country, and exuberant spirits sometimes overflowed as when, in 1906, the party went down the main street in Lochgilphead balancing upon their hands! One summer with friends he was as far afield as France, Switzerland and Italy. Nor did such athletic activities terminate with the coming of winter; sometimes he was to be found in the early morning climbing in the area of Arthur's Seat – the rocky crag overlooking Edinburgh – practising for 'putting the shot'; at other times he would, as his youngest sister recalls, erect muscle-building apparatus indoors. 'He was always', she writes, 'methodical and disciplined, full of enthusiasm; whatever Ken tackled was done with terrific concentration and enthusiasm.'

Along with these energetic recreations there was almost equal enthusiasm for literature. The English classics, Nature and History were his favourite subjects, and as far as the history and geography of the Scottish Highlands were concerned, his interest, fully shared by his brother George, amounted to a passion. The various clans and their battles, the Jacobites, the evictions which dispossessed a noble people of their Highland homes and scattered them across the earth – all such themes were pursued through books and folk-lore with unwearying persistence. Among the papers which Kenneth MacRae left at his death

[3]

there are four exercise books from these early years filled with composi-
tions about the Highlands both in prose and verse. Volume One of these
books, entitled *Heather Bells*, dates from his early teens, as is evident in
his boyish attempts at poetry with themes such as 'Glen Dorch', 'Back
to the Highlands', and 'The Jacobite Exile'. But the writing of poetry
was not a passing experiment and with the years his verse improved
both in quality and depth. Occasionally subjects were suggested by his
Edinburgh environment, 'Sunset from Arthur's Seat', or 'Blackford'
(a hill where he often went, overlooking the city); but for the most part
the scenes which rose before him when he took up his pen were those
of the mountains and glens of the North, the shore at Cromarty, the
burn at Ethie. These, and kindred subjects, fill up his pages. Though
only nine when he left Fort George and the Black Isle that region was
ever to remain his 'home'. Characteristic of his later verses is his poem,
'The Scattered Children of Kintail' which was adopted by the Clan
MacRae Association, set to music, and published:

> There are many, many weary hearts,
>   And feet are bleeding sore,
> But still our steps are further turned
>   From Duich's lonely shore.
> On a thousand plains our clansmen roam
>   In exile's bitter pain,
> And eyes are dim with longing tears
>   To see Kintail again.
>
> Oh! often in our dreams we see
>   The day fade in the west,
> And watch the glory lights of eve
>   Flash o'er Loch Duich's breast;
> In a distant land we hear once more
>   The heron's wistful cry,
> And live again a fleeting space
>   In days forever by.
>
> But a silence dwells upon our land,
>   And broods in every glen,
> And never shall we gather round
>   The ceilidh fires again.
> The red deer sleeps in sheltered nooks,
>   Where homes were wont to be,
> And those who loved and laboured there
>   Are exiled o'er the sea.

Though our restless feet have wandered far,
  And severed wide we be,
The children of a common stock,
  A clan till death are we.
Yet the hills we loved shall ne'er resound
Our slogan's thrilling peal,
Nor catch the tumult of our march
  Come throbbing down Glenshiel.

For reasons shortly to be stated Kenneth MacRae's secular poems were soon to come to an abrupt close, whereas his brother George was to continue writing, and in a large volume of 'Cuttings', bound in a once rich-green cloth, there are some forty pages of poems from his pen which were published in various Scottish newspapers.

To Kenneth's poems there is also another side which ought to be mentioned. A natural sense of humour was a life-long part of his temperament, and in these early years, with nothing to disturb fun and high spirits, he would not infrequently turn subjects into verse for the amusement of his Post Office companions. In one poem, 'The Heavy-weight's Domain', his friends are delineated, in another a 'Lament' is expressed for Miss Robb on her departure to Glasgow, while the talkativeness of one of the young ladies who worked with them became the subject of a thirteen-verse epic entitled 'The Transmigration of a Soul'. The soul in question was that of an African parrot whose 'din was so preposterous' that at length Khama, its owner, had to bring its days to a violent end with a club. But the bird's soul escaped:

Then far behind that parrot's soul left Afric's sunny clime
And cleft three thousand miles of space, one hundred years of time;
Towards the north it took its flight where midst the billow's roar
Old Scotia frowns out o'er her seas and spurns them from her shore.

It chanced that while that homeless soul roamed through Dunedin's
  towers
In wand'ring mood, contented thus to while away the hours,
It came upon a slumb'ring child whose soul was out at play
And that sly wicked parrot's soul usurped the one away.

The child grew up, her tongue waxed long, she chattered night and day,
And never once in all that time a word of sense she'd say,
Until at length they were compelled to tie her tongue to weights –
But even then she strove to speak and fought against the Fates.

And then her tongue became so strong, with every word she spoke
Those weights went whirling through the air and dealt a frightful stroke,

Three men she killed and stunned a cat and wrecked the household gear
Until her folks and all around were paralysed with fear.

The tale ends:

I know the chap who walks her out – How they enjoy those walks!
He takes her arm and smiles ahead, she holds his arm and TALKS;
For many years he's waited now but chance had ne'er the ghost,
I think if he is really keen he'd best propose by post.

Day after day she sits and talks into my weary brain,
I feel my reason tottering beneath the awful strain;
Oh would the past were come again and she a parrot green,
Had I a club I'd re-enact old Khama's tragic scene!

These notebooks surviving from MacRae's youth convey much of
his mood in the early years of this century. His vivid awareness of
nature, his nostalgia and plaintive dreams, his commitment to the
Highlands and joy at traversing her hills with light-hearted companions
– all these things still live in the black ink of his faded exercise books.
Interspersed among the leaves of these books there are even yet some
loose Post Office Telegraph forms, incompletely used for their original
purpose, and bearing on the back in Kenneth's hand perhaps a neat
sketch-map of a mountainous area or a poem recalling some favourite
scene. In short, he doubted not the pleasure which life held out to him.
The past was romantic and the future bright.

We cannot tell whether this outlook ended suddenly, or by what
precise means it occurred. It is clear enough that by the year 1908 he
had met with some painful disappointments and that the hopes which
once charmed him could do so no longer. New subjects – sorrow, despair, death – now surge through his poems. Even Edinburgh's scenery
takes on another hue. Once he had written joyful verse on Blackford Hill
but now 'On Viewing the East Lothian Coast from Blackford Hill on a
Stormy Morning' he writes:

> A silvery streak on a wandering sea,
> A low dusky shore on the edge of the scene,
> A rock and a hill 'gainst a passionate sky,
> And a pain in my breast for the days
> that have been.

In twelve lines, written in pencil on a scrap of paper, his feelings overflow on the subject of 'Sorrow':

[6]

It does not ebb nor flow
  For it is constant woe;
Nought can its pain assuage,
  Its spears strike with each breath;
Its heaviness is more than life,
  Its bitterness, than death.

Amidst such verses as these there also appears for the first time a cry heavenwards. Among verses written on 7th July 1908 the following lines occur:

The gath'ring clouds are creeping o'er the sky,
  The solemn calm foretells the storm is nigh,
In lurid copper gleams the cloud-framed west
  And trailing mists sweep o'er Ben Arthur's breast;
The voice of nature now is hushed and still
  And fleeting shades come gliding o'er the hill;
    O God, 'tis night.

The clouds of sorrow darken o'er my life,
  The darkness round bespeaks the coming strife,
When woes and trials shall my soul beset,
  When friends shall seek to snare me in their net;
No radiance breaks the blackness of the sky,
  No star of hope my searching eyes espy;
    O God, 'tis night.

O Lord, Thy might controls the rolling storm,
  Thy hand alone those cloudy wastes did form;
Thy pow'r is over earth and air and sea;
  Thy hand may stay the night now threat'ning me.
Then if it be Thy will, O God, I pray,
  Repeat the words that once made darkness day,
    'Let there be light!'

Although these were perhaps among the first of MacRae's real prayers it would be wrong to conclude that spiritual influences had not touched his life until now. From his infancy he had received a religious upbringing from his parents who were at that time connected with the Dingwall congregation of the Free Church of Scotland. Dr John Kennedy, the minister of that congregation, would have baptised him had it not been that he left the town for convalescence in Italy just twelve days after Kenneth's birth. On Sundays in Fort George the child would sit with his parents facing the massive pulpit which occupied the whole eastern end of the garrison church, and during the week the first hour of every day in the Garrison School was devoted to Religious Instruction, with Saturday, from 9 a.m. till 12 noon, spent on revising the biblical knowledge imparted during the week. At Sciennes School, also, Religious Instruction occupied the first half-hour of each day. In later life, recalling the strength of Christian influence in the Scotland of his youth, MacRae wrote:

Fifty years ago the Sabbath was universally observed throughout Scotland, and whatever desecration there might have been was furtive and shame-faced. This being so, church-going was the order everywhere. The writer remembers as a little boy how both sides of Earl Grey Street and Lothian Road in Edinburgh from 10.45 till 11 o'clock every Sabbath morning were thronged with a double stream of worshippers, the one stream flowing contrary to the other, but all the units comprising those streams converging upon their respective places of worship. Then, with the cessation of the church bells, a strange hush fell upon the city, and on the streets not a single person was to be seen except perchance a straggler hurriedly pursuing his way to the house of God. Such an order of things may appear incredible to the city-dweller of today, but it was literally true. In the country districts a similar sight was to be seen, the roads being almost black with people as practically the whole community exercised their privilege of waiting upon God in the courts of Zion . . . In the evangelical districts of the Highlands at any rate, family religion in those days was a reality, and the daily worship of God was a permanent feature of most homes.

Yet even at this period the influences which were to bring sweeping changes across the face of Scotland were already well established. First in theological colleges, and then, more hesitantly, in traditionally Calvinistic pulpits, voices were to be heard which would in time transform both the church and the day school. It began with professors of divinity tentatively questioning the historicity of the Pentateuch, and this was coupled with theories as to the authorship of portions of the Bible which assumed errors in the Scriptures' own testimony. We must return to the rise of these ideas later. All that needs to be added at this point is that the same school of thought which urged a less 'rigid' view of doctrine was often equally strong in asserting that a personal *experience* of Christ would not be undermined by this approach. The need for an evangelical faith remained unquestioned and if the Bible required in some measure to be re-constructed it would only result, it was said, in establishing its authority on a truer and firmer basis. It is difficult today to understand how this assumption was possible, but the

[8]

fact is that the new religious outlook – for the present at least – inspired enthusiasm and offered re-assurance in a century which believed it saw so many proofs that 'truth' cannot 'stand still'. The claim was that with this new outlook the church would retain her credibility in the face of modern scholarship and thus extend her influence in the contemporary world. She could, it was also urged, do this all the better if denominational divisions within Presbyterian Scotland could be healed, and a major step towards this end took place in 1900 when the majority of the Free Church joined with the United Presbyterian Church to form the United Free Church. The excitement and almost festive spirit which accompanied the Union of 1900 was all part of the larger hope which had captured the imagination of so many ministers as they crossed the threshold of the new century.

At the time of the Union Kenneth MacRae was only sixteen years of age, but with his parents he was involved in the event. On coming to Edinburgh the family had joined the Free Church congregation of St David's, Morrison Street, whose minister for many years had been Dr Jacob Alexander, an eloquent evangelical Irishman. This congregation went into the Union. The need of conversion was not unfamiliar to Kenneth in his youth and it was perhaps about this time that he experienced what he later was to call his 'first conversion'. Since the 1870's, evangelistic campaigns had been widely introduced in the South of Scotland. John McNeil led such a campaign in Glasgow in 1898, and great attention was paid to the campaigns of R. A. Torrey in Glasgow and Edinburgh in 1903. Kenneth MacRae, while not mentioning the speaker, records that it was through the kind of evangelism exemplified in these meetings that he first came to regard himself as a Christian.

As this is so important to an understanding of MacRae's later thought, Dr Torrey's manner of dealing with anxious inquirers should be noted. One writer, who heard the American evangelist in Edinburgh and 'in general approved of his preaching', gives this narrative of how Torrey would close a meeting:

The following was the exact method that he pursued: (1) He invited all who wished to be saved to come forward to the front seat. (2) After which he read John 1:12 'As many as received him, to them gave he power to become the sons of God'. The Dr then asked them if they were willing to receive Christ, and they replied in the affirmative. (3) Next he read Romans 10:9 'If thou shalt confess with thy mouth the Lord Jesus, and shalt believe in thine heart that God hath raised him from the dead, thou shalt be saved.' Again they replied in the affirmative that they believed with their hearts, when he commanded them to turn to the audience and confess him with the mouth. This was all.[1]

The Monthly Record of the Free Church of Scotland rightly commented, 'Dr Torrey's methods of constraining faith and urging men to confess Christ are mechanical to a degree'. While there was enough gospel in Torrey's preaching to be blessed to the conversion of souls, the tendency of his procedure was to hasten some to 'conversion' who did not know the divine work of regeneration, and thus to encourage 'results' which might well prove to be temporary rather than permanent. Kenneth MacRae's 'conversion' belonged to this latter group. The influence of his own heart and of the world remained the strongest factors in his experience, and when, in time, he was exposed to the growing influence of 'Higher Criticism' within his denomination, his convictions – like those of so many of the youth of that period – went through a revolution. 'The teaching in the United Free Church', he later wrote, 'the literature of professors of divinity and the walk of communicants brought me to consider Christianity a farce and the Scriptures an imposture. If the Scriptures were not authentic there could be no God of whom I could get any certain knowledge. My creed then was to walk uprightly – if there was a God he would acknowledge me, if not I would be no worse than others. But he proved Himself to me and then I began to seek Him.'

The 'proof' to which he refers was probably the broken plans and grievous disappointments which in the providence of God he had experienced by 1908 – the year in which his poems first contain the cry to heaven which we have already noted. With Augustine he would later be able to say, as he thought of that time, 'I had been undone if I had not been undone. I had been ruined if I had not been ruined. God orders lesser afflictions that we may escape greater.'

Seeking a personal knowledge of God he now began to visit other places of worship in Edinburgh: 'I went from Church to Church and got nothing. He took His own way of liberating me.' The occasion was a summer's afternoon in 1909. Sometimes in after years he would speak of that joyful day to close friends, and amongst his papers there is a reference to it written as late as 1st January 1964: 'I hereby put on record that since the Lord in his sovereign mercy entered my heart on the lonely summit of Bell's Hill in the Pentlands on that memorable afternoon – 9th August 1909 – I have ever sought to serve Him as my

1 The Monthly Record, 1903, p 98.

only Lord'. The deliverance was evidently sudden. Until the time it occurred, notwithstanding his distress of spirit, rebellion and unbelief were still his masters: 'I was in extremity, but instead of calling upon God I was only railing against Him; yet in the twinkling of an eye, my will, my affections, my mind – the whole outlook of my life was changed.'

This, then, was the beginning of MacRae's spiritual life. A short time later another event decisively changed his Church connection and determined the sphere of his future service. Following the turning point in August, 1909, he began, he says, 'to seek bread but could not get it'. The end of this search came on a Sunday in the November of this same year. Where the western end of Edinburgh's ancient High Street rises towards the hill on which the Castle stands, a road – Johnston Terrace – turns off and down beneath the southern walls of the Castle. Here, scarcely to be noticed in an area replete with ancient buildings, stands the church of St Columba and into it Kenneth MacRae first came at this time. The preacher was the forty-year-old minister, Donald MacLean, and the congregation – perhaps 250 strong – was not of the Church of Scotland, nor of the great United Free Church; instead, they adhered to the old Free Church. The preaching of that day not only won MacRae back to the Church of his childhood, it satisfied his soul, and confirmed him in the resolution that henceforth he, also, would say with Paul, 'I count all things but loss for the excellency of the knowledge of Christ Jesus my Lord'.

On Hogmanay, 1909 – the last night of the year in which the new life commenced – Kenneth wrote what was probably the last of his secular poems, 'The Home of the Years'. A chapter in his life had closed and as he thought over that chapter another poem was written which summarized it all:

> I have seen the roses blooming on
> their swaying boughs of thorn,
> I have seen the heather blushing 'neath
> the rosy smile of morn:
> I have seen the green leaves quiver
> where the summer zephyrs strayed,
> But I've seen the summer dying, and
> the roses droop and fade.
>
> I have seen the bright sun shining on
> a waste of cloudless blue;
> I have seen his parting glory taint
> the sky a ruddy hue;

I have felt the peace of ev'ning and
    the hush of shadows grey:
But I've seen the morrow dawning in
    a weeping, windswept day.

I have seen life bright before me, down
    the flow'ry glades of youth;
I have seen the sunlight shimm'ring
    on the tideless sea of truth;
I have heard the distant future call
    me laughing o'er my way;
But I've seen my dreams all vanish –
    One by one, they died away.

I have seen the roses fading and
    the leaves fall from the tree,
I have seen the cankered russet where
    the green was wont to be:
I have heard the storms of winter,
    snowy-plumed, go whirling by;
But I've seen the snowdrops springing
    where I saw the roses die.

I have seen the night close round me
    like a drift of blinding cloud;
I have felt the silence creeping, as if
    'twere with life endowed;
I have heard the voice of waters moaning
    hungry for their prey,
But I've seen the heavens brighten with
    the coming of the day.

I have seen my life lie blighted, and
    my dearest visions dead;
I have dared the bolts of fortune to
    descend upon my head.
I have lain, and wept, full weary,
    longing, yet afraid to die:
But I've seen the One whose solace
    wipes the tear from every eye.

The late Dr Kennedy, Dingwall, preached in 1881 at Fearn, Ross-shire, from Isaiah 26:20, 'Come, my people, enter thou into thy chambers ...'. In applying the teaching to his own time he said that judgment was fallen upon the church in Scotland. It was a judgment within the church and would manifest itself in five ways. (1) The Lord would remove most of his living witnesses and great blanks would be left unfilled in the church. (2) False teaching would take the place of the Gospel. (3) Spiritual discernment would leave the people, and under their darkened under-standing they would swallow new teaching as a blind man would swallow a dish of water whether clean or unclean. (4) A spirit of worldliness would fill the minds of the people, and they would forsake the means of grace. Where hundreds once attended, they would soon be counted only by tens. (5) The Lord would deny to Scotland the work of the Holy Spirit. Though He promised to leave a seed to serve Him, He did not promise that Scotland would continue to enjoy this favour. As in days of old the worldliness entering in would grieve Him and cause His Holy Spirit to be withheld and then His true servants and people would be few.

2 Joining the Remnant

Kenneth MacRae's attachment to the congregation of St Columba's, Edinburgh, brought him, as we have already said, into the fellowship of the Free Church of Scotland. He probably became a communicant member of that Church in 1910, and that year – at the age of twenty-six – he was accepted as a candidate for the ministry in the same denomination. Next to his conversion, MacRae considered this change of denomination to be the most important event in his spiritual life, and unless we pause, in this chapter, to explain his reasons for this belief, a great deal of the meaning of later pages may be lost upon readers unacquainted with the Church history of Scotland.

At the end of the nineteenth century there were three leading Presbyterian denominations in the country: the Church of Scotland (the National Church), the Free Church and the United Presbyterian Church. All three owned the Westminster Confession of Faith as their doctrinal standard. The Free Church of Scotland had seceded from the Church of Scotland in 1843 in order to free the cause of the gospel from an unscriptural interference on the part of the secular authorities. In this event, known as 'the Disruption', the Free Church had taken with her by far the largest part of the evangelical witness which, prior to that date, had dramatically revived in the National Church. But after twenty years of spiritual expansion, both at home and in foreign missions work, the Free Church had entered a period of increasing controversy.

First, a proposal to unite the denomination with the United Presbyterian Church was urged but successfully resisted by the more conservative leaders in the Church. They considered that the ministry of the U.P. Church – a grouping originating in 1847 from secessions from the National Church in the eighteenth century – was not wholly consistent in their declared adherence to the theology of the Westminster Confession.

Secondly, the form of worship practised in the Free Church became a subject of repeated debate. Hitherto a plain simplicity, based on the principle that worship should include only what God himself has authorised in Scripture, had prevailed since the Reformation. Psalms, and occasionally paraphrases, were the only form of praise in public worship. In the 1870's, however, hymns and, subsequently, organs, were authorised notwithstanding opposition – especially from the Highland section of the Church.

A third area of controversy we have already touched upon, it concerned the whole question of the reliability of Scripture.

In 1881 Dr Robertson Smith, a young Free Church professor in the denomination's theological college at Aberdeen, was – after much hesitation – removed from his post by the General Assembly for advocating opinions on the origin of the Old Testament inconsistent with its divine inspiration. But while such Higher Critical views as Robertson Smith's were not common in the Free Church ministry in the 1880's there was a growing readiness to believe that the Higher Critical view of the Bible did not necessarily affect the substance of the Christian Faith.[1] In 1883, as Moderator of the Free Church General Assembly in the year of Kenneth MacRae's birth, the aged Horatius Bonar considered it necessary to warn the Church that 'Fellowship between faith and unbelief must, sooner or later, be fatal to the former'. Others of Bonar's contemporaries repeated the same warning. The day of the older leaders was, however, almost over, and when, in the 1890's, a charge was levied against two Free Church professors, A. B. Bruce and Marcus Dods, on the grounds that their teaching was undermining the New Testament, it was put aside by the General Assembly even though confirmation of the charge could be drawn from their writings. Speaking of Dods' role in the Free Church, C. H. Spurgeon wrote, 'That Church in which we all gloried as sound in the faith and full of martyrs' spirit has entrusted the training of its future ministers to professors who hold other doctrines than those of its Confession. This is the most suicidal act a Church could commit'.

Underlying to some degree all the above controversies was a growing unwillingness on the part of ministers to preach, and indeed to believe, the full Calvinistic theology of divine grace as set down in the Confession to which they had subscribed at their ordination. While it was not yet

1 An example of this occurs in Norman L. Walker's *Chapters from the History of The Free Church of Scotland*, 1895, p 355, where he writes: 'Of one thing we are assured, that among the highest class of our rising men there is no disposition to forsake the old evangel. Dr Denney's recently published *Studies in Theology* introduces us to one who holds very advanced opinions about inspiration, but who tells us what is the gospel which he believes must be proclaimed to men.' Of the same spirit was Alexander Whyte who defended Robertson Smith, and yet as an old man in 1920 he could plead for a return to Puritan preaching – 'such preaching will alone rally Scotland round the pulpit' – apparently unconscious that he had been a party to the removal of the *foundation* for such preaching. Whyte was representative of the spirit of many who went from the Free Church into the United Free Church in 1900.

1. The three brothers (from left to right), Kenneth, Duncan and George, with their parents, Dingwall, 1884.

2. George and Kenneth as teen-agers.

3. March Past of Indian Troops in Princes Street Gardens, Edinburgh, 1902, an occasion which the eighteen-year-old Kenneth was not likely to miss.

4. Kenneth (second from left standing) in the uniform of the Royal Scots Territorials, part-time army duties were a major interest of his early manhood.

openly said that these doctrines hindered evangelism it was observable that the kind of evangelism which had become so popular and apparently successful since D. L. Moody's visit to Scotland in 1874 had small doctrinal content. The 'old-school' evangelism exemplified by such figures as Robert Murray McCheyne, had been firmly founded on a clearly recognisable doctrinal position; the new evangelism, in so far as it was doctrinally orientated at all, leaned more to Arminianism than to Calvinism. For the first time in Scottish Church history a comparative disinterest in doctrinal purity was found in alliance with evangelistic endeavour and this explains why men who were adopting Higher Critical views could be found engaged in evangelism alongside others who still retained the orthodox view of the Bible. The latter were still the large majority and perhaps their very numbers served to blind them to the danger. They believed that a toleration of different views of Scripture and of a modified Calvinism would do no harm to the evangelical witness of the Free Church.

The first formal step to make allowance for an Arminian understanding of the gospel within the Free Church came with what was known as the Declaratory Act passed by the General Assembly in 1892. Hitherto commitment to the whole doctrine of the Westminster Confession had been required of all office-bearers, but the Act, with its preamble, 'It is expedient to remove difficulties and scruples which have been felt by some in reference to the declaration of belief', now permitted such a latitude of interpretation as would prevent disciplinary action ever being taken against men who had abandoned Reformed and Puritan theology. Toleration of Arminianism was thus one practical result intended by the Act, another was the lessening of differences with the United Presbyterians who had passed their own Declaratory Act in 1879.

Though the best-known of the old-school leaders of the Free Church were all dead by 1892 a minority voiced their strong opposition to the Declaratory Act and several thousands in the Highlands, led by two ministers, seceded to form the Free Presbyterian Church. Undeterred, however, by such protests, which they regarded as coming from a dwindling school of traditionalists, the leaders of the Free Church pressed on to accomplish the union they had long desired. In May, 1900, the General Assembly, led by Dr Robert Rainy, agreed to union with the United Presbyterian Church by 586 votes to 29. They were not, it was professed, abandoning their Free Church position but simply furthering such union as Scripture requires. So general was the enthusiasm for amalgamation that it was commonly doubted whether any would be found standing apart when 31st October 1900, the date set for the consummation of the union, was reached. But there were those prepared to deny that the Free Church amalgamated into a new denomination – to be called The United Free Church – would still be the same Free Church as was constituted in 1843. On the contrary they believed that the only way to preserve the original testimony of the Free Church from extinction would be for a remnant to remain where they were. Thus when the Assembly met to carry through the final arrangements for union on 30th October, there were twenty-seven who recorded their refusal to go with the majority who were to unite the next day with the United Presbyterians in a great public gathering in the Waverley Market, in Edinburgh. Instead they indicated their intention to meet in the Assembly Hall of the Free Church at the same time when elsewhere in the city the formation of the United Free Church was being celebrated. They were not, however, permitted so to meet, for on the morning of 31st October the gate of New College, with its historic Assembly Hall, was locked against them.

This action was the beginning of the policy which was followed by the United Free Church in respect to the minority. In their judgment the only Free Church which had any existence was the one which had entered the Union. The one option for anyone who refused to unite was secession, with a consequent loss of claim to any property or funds formerly in the name of the Free Church. The old Free Church, as such, no longer existed! This was the argument of the majority but it was denied by the remnant. From among their own number on 31st October 1900 they re-constituted the General Assembly, and made plans to continue a separate testimony in the name of the Free Church and on the basis of her original constitution.

Over 1,100 ministers went from the Free Church into the Union while a mere 25 remained to face the future together. Outside the ranks of the ministers, however, support for a continuing Free Church was considerably stronger. In the Island of Lewis, for example, while only one minister remained with the Free Church, eleven congregations declined the Union, and in Skye, where two ministers stood firm with their congregations, another three congregations forsook their United Free ministers and refused to accept the Union. The combined strength of these congregations ran into many thousands.[1] In all, some 95

1 The congregation at Knock, Lewis, for example, numbered over 2000 souls.

congregations, remained in the Free Church.[1] One United Free Church writer, in 1902, estimated that the continuing Free Church had meant to Dr Rainy the loss of at least one-third of those who formerly constituted the Free Church. Speaking of the Highlands he referred to congregations which 'have almost entirely left the Church' (that is, refused to go into the U.F. Church), 'and in very few of them does one-half of the former congregation meet'.[2]

Nonetheless, compared with what she had been, the Free Church of 1901 was a remnant. All three theological Colleges, and all the foreign missionaries of the Church – with the denomination's overseas assets – went with the majority. The disadvantages of the minority were altogether more serious than those which had been faced in 1843 and, among those disadvantages was the fact that their geographical spread was very uneven. By far the greater part of the strength of the continuing Free Church lay in the Gaelic-speaking Highlands. In large areas of the Lowlands not a single congregation declined to enter the Union: and of the two congregations which remained with the Free Church in Edinburgh, and the four in Glasgow, the majority of the people were natives of the North of Scotland. It thus became possible for the Free Church to be viewed as a Highland rather than a national Church.

On one significant issue the position of the minority in 1900 differed from that of the fathers of 1843. As already stated, the action in 1843 had been a secession; in 1900, in contrast, the minority were faced with eviction from the properties of the denomination to which *they* were adhering. The majority claimed the entire resources of the Church from which – as the minority argued – they were departing. When the continuing Free Church went to the Court of Session, Scotland's highest judicial body, for a ruling on this procedure, the United Free Church was upheld and the Free Church minority treated as virtually having no case. But when the Free Church appealed to the House of Lords against this verdict the outcome was dramatically different. The Lords' judgment, announced on 1st August 1904, was that the U.F. Church was not the Free Church, and that it had no right or title to any

---

1 These are the figures according to *The Monthly Record of the Free Church of Scotland*, November, 1901, pp 190–191. In 1905 the Free Church claimed that the number of their members and adherents stood at 70,000.

2 *The Monthly Record*, 1902, p 81. This same writer reported that only six out of the twelve Highland U.F. Presbyteries gave a return of members and adherents in 1902. In the six Presbyteries which did report, only 60 out of 130 congregations provided figures. These sixty reported a total of 26,293 as against 66,288 in 1897.

B

of the property held by the Free Church prior to 31st October 1900!

The principal reason for the difference between the decisions reached by the Court of Session and the House of Lords was that the latter took doctrinal questions into account. They ruled that the rightful claimants to the name and property of the Free Church were those who adhered to the doctrine of the Church's original constitution, and in this connection the Declaratory Act of 1892, which the U.F. Church had made part of her constitution and which the Free Church minority rejected, proved of major significance. Prior to the Lords' decision, Marcus Dods of the U.F. Church, foreseeing the possibility of a major reversal, protested against a State being able to prevent a Church from revising her belief. To this the Editor of *The Monthly Record* replied: 'No one hinders Dr Dods from changing his creed; the one thing which the law of the land happily prevents is that Dr Dods will appropriate the funds destined for the promotion of the doctrines of the Westminster Confession of Faith and use them for the promotion of doctrines of an opposite character. It is a pity secular judges should need to teach doctors of divinity elementary morality'.

Scotland, as a nation, was not unused to religious controversy, yet there was no precedent for the excitement and the storm which was to break after the Lords' decision of August 1904. While the Free Church after 1900 had faced her situation in comparative silence, the astounded U.F. Church of 1904 began an outcry which was soon to polarise strong feelings throughout the land. By means of public meetings, sermons and the lobbying of members of Parliament, their leaders proclaimed the hardship of their predicament. At the same time they asserted the spiritual incompetence of what, in disparagement, they now called the 'legal Free Church', or the 'Wee Frees'. The U.F. Church was represented as a great Church, faithful to the 'theology of John Bunyan, Thomas Boston, Thomas Chalmers and Charles Spurgeon', and yet advancing and progressive – unlike the reactionary and traditionalist remnant. In particular, it was loudly urged by some U.F. spokesmen that the Free Church, by rejecting the Declaratory Act, was unable to preach a 'free gospel' – thus implying that all who had held to the un-modified theology of the Westminster Confession from 1647 to 1892 were hyper-Calvinists! 'The long oppressive nightmare of Calvinism', some said, was over, and the cause of the U.F. Church, in its difference with the Free Church, was the cause of the gospel.

The outcry against the Free Church was taken up by secular papers and it was not difficult for the U.F. authorities to convince the government that, as they could command far more votes than the Free Church, they must be heard. Accordingly, Parliament appointed a Royal Commission to examine the U.F. claim that the Free Church could not administer the funds and assets to which she had legal title. There followed an Act of Parliament in 1905 which superseded the decision of the House of Lords and placed all the property in dispute in the hands of an Executive Commission. This Executive Commission divided the properties and funds between the two denominations. Such was the national disfavour with which the Free Church was viewed that not a single member of Parliament coming from the Scottish Highlands spoke on her behalf.

It should be said that the bitterness exhibited by some U.F. spokesmen was not characteristic of the whole denomination. Though the number of genuine Calvinists who went into the Union was small, the majority of the ministers were of evangelical sympathy. Their hope was that the union of two large denominations would be a means of advancing Christianity both at home and overseas. It was an illusion, and for the very reason which Horatius Bonar had pointed out in 1883: unbelief, left unchecked, would grow and nullify historic Christianity. The striking thing is that whereas most evangelicals in the U.F. Church failed to recognise the inevitability of such an outcome, it was recognised by the liberal leaders who were now in a majority in her theological colleges. In a letter to a friend, dated 8th January 1902, Professor Marcus Dods wrote:

I wish I could live as a spectator through the next generation to see what they are going to make of things. There will be a grand turn up in matters theological, and the churches won't know themselves fifty years hence. It is to be hoped some little rag of faith may be left when all's done. For my own part I am sometimes entirely under water and see no sky at all.[1]

In another private letter Dods expressed his concern over what could happen when the conclusions which he and other leading theological professors had reached became more commonly known. Speaking of his belief that Christ was ignorant of some things (as, for instance, the authorship of various parts of the Old Testament) he declared: 'I dread the turbulent panic which shallower natures will occasion when we can no longer avoid the open discussion of such themes'.

But the Free Church leaders saw the real direction in which the

1 *Later Letters of Marcus Dods*, selected and edited by his son Marcus Dods, 1911, p 67.

U.F. Church was moving. The Rev. Ewan MacLeod – one of the '25' of 1900 – was reported in 1906 as saying, 'With regard to the Colleges, he was within the truth when he said that what was taught in these three Colleges now was diluted rationalism . . . The Colleges were likely to be hotbeds of rationalism and such teaching in time to come'. The speed with which this process of theological change took place can be seen by the fact that Marcus Dods' letters could be published by his family without any embarrassment in 1911.

Certainly Kenneth MacRae had been exposed to the disbelief of U.F. ministers before 1909. In later life he explained his change of denomination in these words:

When the Lord in mercy opened my eyes I was an adherent of the United Free Church. Very shortly afterwards I came in contact with Free Church preaching and studied the position of those whom I had been taught to believe were a small body of ignorant Highlanders. On the one side I had the preaching of Christ crucified which was as honey to my soul, on the other I had that hateful and soul-destroying thing called Higher Criticism. Which was I to choose? I did not hesitate for a single moment. For ever I turned my back upon a Church which so dishonoured my Lord.

☐   ☐   ☐

After Kenneth MacRae's conversion some of his old interests remained. His enthusiasm for walking and hill climbing he never lost. His sense of attachment to the army also lingered. While working with the Post Office he had joined the 9th Battalion of the Royal Scots – a battalion of territorial soldiers – and in 1911 he still attended occasional training exercises in the uniform of this historic regiment. But it was his new interests which now absorbed him. He was never missing from the services at Free St Columba's, and he also joined in the activities of the Telegraph and Telephone Christian Association. Next to the Scriptures themselves Church history began to stir him deeply. Old places in Edinburgh previously passed by, he looked at in a new light, and in the Highlands his awakening to the spiritual significance of the past was still more profound. From childhood he had always returned regularly to his 'home' in the North but after 1909 these visits were attended by a new joy. His native Ross-shire possessed no less than thirty-four Free Church congregations and in them he found a type of Christianity far different from that which was popular in the South.

In part the difference between North and South was physical and cultural. The Highland Gael, bred through centuries of hard experience, accustomed to solitudes and a majestic creation, was both stern and sensitive. While familiar with strong emotion he did not easily show his feelings and, in particular, he shunned a glib familiarity with spiritual things. If he had to choose between a religion spoken or *seen* he would choose the latter. In these characteristics, and others, natural temperament played a prominent part. Yet, allowing for this, the main difference between religious conditions in the North and South of Scotland has still to be explained. The truth is that until late in the nineteenth century the pulpit had exercised the controlling influence upon large areas of the Highlands – controlling because the message it gave forth was the Word of God, delivered with unction to a people often characterised by spiritual hunger and spiritual zeal. Under the representatives of this preaching – among whom one of the last and greatest was Dr John Kennedy of Dingwall – a multitude of common people were grounded in the doctrines of the gospel. Untravelled and unlettered as most of them were, their minds were 'in the heavenlies'. They knew their Bibles, and their simple homes would be sure to have some shelves of well-studied volumes from the Puritans to Spurgeon.

More important still, it must be said that this school of belief had come into existence as the result of widespread revivals. Unlike the Lowlands of Scotland there were many parts of the Highlands and Islands which were not evangelised until the eighteenth or even the nineteenth century and at the end of the nineteenth century there were still people alive who remembered the state of their locality before the power of the Holy Spirit was known in their midst. They were certain that the change had not come by human energy, and they learned to distrust all religion in which the Spirit of God was not evidently present. Conviction of sin, reverence, holy joy, spiritual conversation and fellowship – these were the characteristics of Highland religion in its best days. To which must be added the importance attached to prayer and especially to such prayer as has 'the breathing of the Holy Ghost' in it.

Certainly Highland piety was not without defects. At times it was distrustful of false assurance to a degree which blurred the triumphant note of New Testament Christianity;[1] it had a tendency to give perhaps too much place to the sayings and doings of the first-generation 'fathers';

---

1 This, in part, explains the disproportion which existed in Highland congregations between baptised adherents and communicant members, the former generally outnumbering the latter by about eight to one in 1900.

and yet, taken all-in-all, the period in which this piety took such deep roots among the mountains and moors of the North was one which has seldom been excelled. It was scriptural, Christ-centred religion, not in form only but in power.

When Kenneth MacRae first began to explore the spiritual heritage of his native Ross-shire in 1910, the opinion he met among the Free Church Christians was that the 'glow' which still lingered in the churches was like the glow lingering in the sky after a beautiful sun-set. They mourned a change in the times, and the change which they witnessed at the sight of three denominations – the Free Presbyterian, the U.F., and the Free Church – where formerly, in many districts, there had been only the one. And yet he saw and heard enough to appreciate what the past had been; in some homes and pulpits its warm atmosphere could still be felt, and as he joined in open-air gatherings at communion seasons, at such places as Creich in Sutherland and 'the burn' at Ferintosh in Ross-shire, it was a visible reminder of how these scenes had commenced in days of revival.

Among the older Free Church ministers of Ross-shire whom Kenneth MacRae met at this period were William Fraser of Strath-peffer, William McKinnon of Gairloch, and Donald Munro of Ferintosh whose name occurs so frequently in the following pages. Donald Munro, had settled in his bachelor's manse at Ferintosh on the Black Isle in 1894. Born in 1860 he was old enough to remember the former order of things, and so great had been his youthful attachment to Dr Kennedy (of whom both then and later he often spoke) that when a student at Aberdeen his fellow-students used to refer to him as 'the Doctor'. As a young man he was often in the homes of the godly people of an older generation for the benefit of their conversation and in later years he always sought to use his own home for the same purpose. Probably Kenneth MacRae first met him in 1910 and it was in the Ferintosh manse – on visits to Ross-shire – that he was to spend some of the happiest days of his early Christian life. John MacLeod has well described Donald Munro's spirit in the following words: 'He was eager to draw and arm recruits for the Christian warfare. The secret of it was that he was wide awake with his eyes on the future. For he knew that the young who are won for the Lord are those whose influence will tell in the days to come. They will serve to pass on the witness to regions beyond and to others yet unborn. Thus though he lived very much himself in the past and judged things by the gauge of a bygone order, yet he went out in thought to the future, and in his aspirations he had a

[24]

high ambition not only for his young friends themselves but for those on whom the impact of their lives should tell.'[1]

There is no record of how Kenneth MacRae was brought to the conviction that God was calling him to devote his life to the ministry of the Word. It seems to have come to him as an urgent persuasion soon after his conversion, and when, at about the same date, he was offered a higher position in the Telegraphic service overseas, he knew that it had to be declined. Although he was accepted for the Free Church ministry in 1910 formidable difficulties remained in his way. The long-established academic standard for admission to the ministry was a three-year Master of Arts degree, followed by three years' theological study. In addition, he knew scarcely any Gaelic, the language indispensable to an effective ministry in many parts of the North. His first hurdle was to gain admission to Edinburgh University and this he surmounted with the aid of the correspondence classes of Skerry's College which he commenced in April 1911. He obtained entrance to the University in September of the same year. The Training of the Ministry Committee of the Free Church meanwhile reached the unusual decision that he should be allowed to take his Arts degree and his theological studies in the Free Church College concurrently in four years. As J. M. MacLennan, one of his fellow-students recalls, it was a 'real feat', and the more so as his M.A. degree included the Gaelic language (in which he was to be the 'prizeman' of his year before his University days ended).

In 1911 the Free Church was still struggling to survive as a spiritual force. Certainly the acuteness of the problem she faced in 1900 was over, and instead of her original 95 congregations there were some 162 congregations and preaching stations where services were regularly held. A large part of this increase was due to causes resuscitated in the name of the Free Church after 1901, or to congregations and groups which, after the Lords' decision of 1904, decided to stay with the Free Church. Increase due to these reasons was most noticeable in the South. By the end of 1909, 17 new Church buildings had been opened or were in the course of being built. To meet this situation there were some 72 ordained ministers or missionaries, and 5 professors set aside for the College in Edinburgh, which meant 'a total of 77, or as nearly as might be, one ordained man, fit for active duty, to every two congregations or stations'.

These figures, however, were not as encouraging as might first

1 *Donald Munro*, A Memorial Volume edited by John MacLeod, 1939, p19.

appear. As the years passed the ordained missionaries, who had played a vital part in supporting the 25 ministers of 1900, became harder to replace, and in her need to supply her pulpits the Free Church had also some ministers within her ranks who were not to prove equal to the task of evangelizing and standing by the old faith in the face of widespread opposition. A letter in *The Monthly Record* in 1913, from the lawyers of the Free Church, noted that 'some half-dozen ministers' had left the Free Church ministry in the preceding twelve months, one of them describing the Free Church as 'a ruined temple'. The Church's ablest ministerial recruits had come from the Free Presbyterian Church – these were George MacKay, John MacLeod and Alexander Stewart, who had left the Free Church at the passing of the Declaratory Act and who returned in 1905 after that Act had been rescinded by the continuing Free Church. An initial hope of a complete re-union with the Free Presbyterians was not, however, realised.

As Kenneth MacRae prepared for College in the summer of 1911 – a summer memorable for its many days of sunshine – Archibald McNeilage, the Editor of *The Monthly Record*, wrote in the August issue of the magazine:

If there was sufficient reason for the stand which the Free Church minority made in 1900, there is greater need for maintaining that stand in 1911. The intervening decade has shown a rapidity of backsliding from the high evangelical standpoint of the Disruption which could scarcely have been anticipated when the breach occurred on 31 October 1900. Godlessness as illustrated by Sabbath desecration, worldliness, frivolity, and every kind of superficiality, is on the increase. The sanctuary is being deserted, and the outward ordinances of religion are being despised.

In the September issue he pointed to the Free Church's own need:

Spiritual deadness reigns in many parts of the land. The Free Church is not exempt from the blight. Those who have been visiting or labouring for any length of time in some of the vacant congregations of the Church have seen enough to convince them of the crying need for spiritual and moral quickening.

In response to this situation *The Monthly Record* consistently advocated one supreme solution. It urged the necessity of the kind of revival which Scotland had known in the days of Whitefield and the Haldanes, and at the same time insisted that preaching is the divinely-appointed means for the recovery of the Church. 'The only hope, humanly speaking, for this land is a religious revival, and the human instrumentality in such a revival has invariably been a faithful Gospel ministry'. According to this standpoint the future of the Free Church depended upon her being given a 'Gospel ministry divinely called and divinely commissioned'. This was conceived of as far more important than any benefit received from the House of Lords' decision. 'Man-sent messengers ruined the Free Church, and the sure token of a Divine gracious return will be the appearance among us of a Spirit-baptised ministry.' 'The noblest gift the Most High has to bestow on fallen men is the gift of preaching the Word. An essayist is not a preacher, although many essayists occupy the places where preachers ought to be.'[1]

The outlook of *The Monthly Record* was thus far from that of a passive waiting for a future awakening. McNeilage, himself a layman, constantly stressed the primacy of preaching. The Church needed men who would give their all to the preaching of the Word: 'May a layman appeal to the ministry of the Free Church to magnify their office? The ministers who gave their strength to pulpit preparation and pulpit ministration are the ministers who live in the memories of men and the ministers whose work has a measure of permanency in the lives of men.' In an editorial on the same subject in 1910, in the course of an appreciative comment on an address by the Rev. J. H. Jowett of Birmingham, McNeilage underlined the same point:

The drivelling interests, which swallow up so much of the modern minister's time, and leave him no leisure for the hard work of the study, have not escaped the notice of Mr Jowett. He told his hearers that 'they sought refuge from the difficulties of thought in the opportunities of action.' A truer witness has never been borne to an outstanding baleful characteristic of the present day. Ministers are perpetually on the move. There is no limit to the number of engagements some men will undertake provided they furnish an excuse for not spending toilsome hours in the fellowship of one's library and the exercise of prayer. There never was a time in the history of the Church when truth had greater need to be studied in the harmony of all its matchless parts, and yet there never was a time in which 'opportunities of action' more seductively presented themselves. A minister should spend the major portion of his time in his study. He cannot read too much, pray too much, or think too much;

1 One characteristic of the 'essay' style was that it encouraged ministers to read their sermons – a practice which has never prevailed in the brighter periods of church history. 'None of them read their sermons', reported R. M. McCheyne of the men who occupied his pulpit during the revival of 1839. 'Though all are not to be condemned that use Notes', observes White-field, 'yet it is a sad symptom of the decay of vital religion when reading Sermons becomes fashionable where *extempore* preaching did once almost universally prevail.'

but he can very easily travel too much, gossip too much, and do too much purely ecclesiastical work. In proportion as truth presents itself to the mind in its deeper and more awful significance, will the soul desire spiritual fellowship with the unseen. What men seek after in their theological studies is a sure index to their spirituality.

Kenneth MacRae entered the Free Church College as a student on Wednesday, 18th October 1911, and the opening address of the new session, given by the Principal, the Rev. James Duff McCulloch, struck exactly the same note as McNeilage was sounding in the magazine. The address, on 'The Church and Social Work', was intended to demonstrate that the social reform which was then being emphasised in so many Churches as the best means of 'elevating the masses' was no substitute at all for the preaching whereby man himself is changed. 'Have faith in God, trust to His appointed means and methods', was the exhortation with which the address concluded. It was a lesson which Kenneth MacRae sought to practise all his days.

From 1846 to 1900 the Free Church College in Edinburgh was located in what was best known as New College – a magnificent building, at the head of The Mound, overlooking Princes Street, erected by the gifts of several Free Church laymen after the Disruption. With the General Assembly Hall as part of the same complex of buildings, New College was virtually the home of the Free Church itself. New College was lost by the continuing Free Church in 1900, regained for two years after the Lords' decision, and lost again when the denomination's property was re-allocated by the Executive Commission. Consequently after 1906 the Free Church College was finally housed in the eighteenth-century block of tenements, adjacent to New College, which had been reconstructed by the Free Church after 1843 for her church offices and for the Edinburgh Presbytery Hall.

There were 24 other students either beginning or already studying at the College when Kenneth MacRae entered in 1911. In the hope that the College would regain the influence of earlier years a Faculty (Senatus) was appointed with a numerical strength out of proportion to the number of students then in attendance. Something must here be said about the men who made up its number. The first professor appointed by the General Assembly after the troubles of 1900 was Dr W. M. Alexander who occupied the Chair of Apologetics, Natural Science, Homiletics and Pastoral Theology until his death in 1929. Along with temporary helpers he was responsible for Free Church theological students until 1905 when the Rev. James Duff McCulloch

(1836–1926) was appointed to the Principalship. The Rev. Colin A. Bannatyne was appointed to the Chair of the Church History and Church Principles and the Rev. Robert Moore to that of Hebrew and Old Testament exegesis. Principal McCulloch was, in MacRae's opinion, 'the life of the Church' in the crisis of 1900 although, even at that date, he had reached the age when most men retire. Combining his Principalship with the pastoral charge of Hope Street Free Church in Glasgow, McCulloch nevertheless gave enough time to the students to lead them to believe they could always depend upon his ready friendship and counsel. As one of them later recalled, 'He made the youngest minister or student feel at once at home with him; and he talked as freely as if they were his equal in ability, position, and experience.' Certainly Kenneth MacRae, when his College days were over, seldom passed through Glasgow without calling at the home of 'the Principal'.

Colin Bannatyne, the first Moderator of the Free Church after the breach of 1900, had entered New College in 1870 along with a group of men who were to become prominent in the U.F. Church. George Smeaton was at that date giving his best in the Chair of New Testament exegesis, yet with diminishing appreciation among the student body. Norman C. MacFarlane in his biography of another member of the incoming class of 1870 writes of Smeaton: 'His students would have prized the slightest suggestion of heresy such as they found in his successor [Marcus Dods]. But Dr Smeaton held on like a full moon slicing its way through the clouds. His lectures were like golden paths which his students found richly monotonous. Older men kept on their shelves his books on the *Atonement* and his Cunningham lecture on *The Holy Spirit*, but the younger men gave them no place.'[1] Bannatyne was an exception, and years later the same writer noted him as a man who 'sticks very close by the old landmarks'.[2] Bannatyne had begun his ministry as the assistant of the aged Dr A. Moody Stuart, of St Luke's, Edinburgh, who forty years before had been the friend of R. M. McCheyne, and it was the spirit and outlook of those men that he brought with him to the College in 1905.

Robert Moore came from the Presbyterian Church in Ireland with high credentials for the Hebrew chair gained from earlier study in Ireland, Oxford and Edinburgh.

The Senatus of the College had been completed in 1906 with the addition of the Revs. John MacLeod and J. Kennedy Cameron to the

1 *Rev Donald J. Martin*, 1914, p 34.
2 *Ibid*, p 43.

Chairs of New Testament Exegesis and Systematic Theology respectively. John MacLeod, then thirty-four years of age, was destined to be one of the best known of the Free Church leaders of this century. Recalled to the pastorate in 1913 he was not to be at the College throughout all Kenneth MacRae's student days. In 1927 MacLeod succeeded James McCulloch to the Principalship and the reader will thus find affectionate references to him as 'the Principal' in later pages of this volume.

The appointment of J. K. Cameron to the teaching of Systematic Theology was regarded as the most important of all the appointments in the re-constructed College. Some of Professor Bannatyne's words at the Induction of Professor Cameron are worthy of quotation:

The number of years that have elapsed (14) since I had the pleasure and privilege of first standing by your side in the fighting line, and the fact that since that date – the disastrous day of the passing of the Declaratory Act – we have been often and closely associated in hours of crisis and conflict for the principles our Church holds dear, make me feel I may be permitted to say it gives me no ordinary pleasure to welcome you as my colleague, and personal feeling apart, no ordinary satisfaction that the Church has intrusted a position vitally connected with its future efficiency for good to so able an exponent, and so well tried a champion of Confessional Doctrine. In the past we have been painfully taught that defection begins in a Church not so much by overt teaching of error, not by want of ability to unfold nor even reticence regarding truth, but in the want of whole-hearted loyalty and absolute sincerity in regard to the doctrinal testimony for the truth. Hence I read in your appointment – the appointment of one who stood the test and made the sacrifices and ran the risks of 1900 – a conspicuous evidence of the resolve of the Assembly so far as in them lay to secure that the Free Church shall be indeed the Free Church dominated and permeated by the doctrines and principles of 1843. Need I say more than that your brethren confidently expect you to vindicate this their expectation and to endeavour to train our students to be what the Disruption Fathers were – earnest, disinterested and loyal upholders of the whole doctrine of the Westminster Confession, notwithstanding whatever trouble or persecution arose.

I cannot suppose in appointing one who had your term of experience in the practical work of the ministry, and in whose ministrations lucidity in doctrinal exposition was so well-known and characteristic a feature, the Church had not specially present to her mind the great advantage such qualifications would be in enabling the occupant of the Chair of Systematic Theology to give such direction to the studies of those committed to his charge that they would be able at the close of their

[30]

course not merely *ex animo* to sign the Confession of Faith and prove earnest and well-equipped defenders of its contents in after life, but to be in their pulpit ministrations eminently *doctrinal* preachers. The absence of this valuable element in modern preaching had been so conspicuous as to excite amazement among intelligent men of the world. Thus a British statesman of the foremost rank in recent times is said to have remarked, 'one expects at least a little Christian doctrine in the discourses of professed divines.' But for the Free Church, that the doctrinal element predominates in her pulpits is surely vital, and as your position is pre-eminently fitted to secure that result its attainment will doubtless be to you an object of unwearied and prayerful effort.[1]

Of all the professors of his student days Kenneth MacRae seems to have owed most to J. Kennedy Cameron. He was to write of him as one of the three men who had most influence upon him in his early years.[2] As Cameron was also an elder in St Columba's, where he took a Sabbath Bible Class, he also frequently met MacRae in the life of the congregation where, as will be seen, he gave the younger man helpful criticism with respect to his preaching.

The strength of the Senatus of the College reflects the sense of purpose possessed by the Free Church at that period. The leaders were far from having the mentality of a remnant. They viewed themselves as the stewards of a great spiritual tradition, a tradition belonging as much to the Continent, to England and to America, as to Scotland, and they considered there was nothing more important than to secure, under God, increasing numbers of spiritually-minded men who would be thoroughly grounded and trained in the biblical principles of the Reformed and Puritan school.[3] Accordingly they were not prepared to lower the standards of theological training.

It was also a characteristic of the leaders of 1911 that they saw themselves as part of the Reformed cause as a whole. Professor John MacLeod, for example, made one of a number of visits to the Netherlands in the summer of 1911. It was also his practice to address the

1 *The Monthly Record*, 1906, pp 131–2.
2 'As a young man I was largely moulded by the influence of the 1900 worthies, especially Dr Munro, Professor Cameron and Mr. Fraser, Strathpeffer'. The University of Aberdeen conferred the degree of doctor of divinity on Donald Munro of Ferintosh in 1924 in recognition of his activities as a genealogist.
3 *The Monthly Record*, 1911, p 101, reported 40 undergraduates preparing for the ministry. The number of vacant charges tended to produce a danger, long present in Scotland, that men might be accepted for the ministry without sufficient proof of the presence of those gifts which are indispensable in preaching elders.

students on some of the older leaders of American Presbyterianism.[1] Archibald McNeilage frequently drew attention to the English Puritans,[2] and James McCulloch visited both South Africa and Princeton, New Jersey, within the first decade of his Principalship.

When the reader comes to the next chapter, which covers in MacRae's own words his student years from the Spring of 1912, it will be found to read much more like the diary of a preacher than of a student. This was not simply due to the fact that preaching was his first love. At this date there were still many more Free Church congregations than there were ministers to supply them, and consequently theological students were required from the start of their College course, and long before they were licensed, to take a full share of pulpit work. As these duties could include travelling to distant parts of the North of Scotland College lectures were not given on Mondays.

McNeilage, with his usual discrimination, saw and spoke of the dangers of this policy. In an editorial entitled 'Good Advice to Students', in 1912, he comments on the remarks of an Aberdeen professor of divinity who was advocating that ministerial students should be more involved in regular practical Christian work. He approved of this advice but with this qualification:

If this means that the student, as soon as he enters the Divinity Hall, is to begin preaching, we scarcely approve. During her difficult middle passage to a better order, the Free Church is forced to avail herself of the services of young graduates, but this is felt to be an anomaly and a risk. The experience may certainly avail to benefit the young man himself by painfully discovering to him the limits of his knowledge and the interval that separates him from Spurgeon, but the Scripture, we are well aware, indicates a danger on the other side. We think, however, that aspirants to the sacred calling should in every case serve an apprenticeship in the Sabbath School. A Sabbath School teacher of the thorough kind purchases to himself a good degree.

Another issue of *The Monthly Record* in the same year quoted the words of James Durham, 'If I had ten years to live I would study the nine, and preach the tenth'.

Without question, the amount of preaching MacRae had to undertake in his student years was undesirable. One of his fellow-students, Peter W. Miller, remembered him as 'a strong athletic man, endowed

1 For example, in the opening address for the session 1909–10 he spoke on Archibald Alexander, 'A Nestor among Theologians'.
2 The amount of space given to the *English* Puritans in the early years of McNeilage's editorship of the *Record* is remarkable.

with tireless energy', but as the Diary entries show he was sometimes very tired indeed. With his University work, his College studies and his week-end preaching he was engaged simultaneously on three fronts. The result was a monumental amount of work compressed into the years 1911–15 and this was certainly not accomplished without strain. It shows itself in the bouts of depression and the undue degree of self-examination which tend to recur in his diary during this period.

Those who heard Kenneth MacRae preach in his undergraduate days had little conception of what it was costing him. They saw only the preacher and what they saw was to remain a memory with many throughout life. Writing in 1971, the late Roderick Cameron of Inverness recalled the first time he listened to Kenneth MacRae (on 2nd February, 1913):

He was advertised to officiate at the Sabbath morning English Service in the East Fountain Bridge Free Church. Some of us who attended that church were most anxious to see and to hear the young man who had refused the offer of a most lucrative post in the Civil Service abroad and instead decided to enter the ministry of the Free Church – a Church whose testimony at that time was not popular – indeed one thought of the Free Church then as those described by the Apostle Paul in the closing verses of the last chapter of the Acts of the Apostles as being 'everywhere spoken against'. We were not disappointed. He gave us an excellent discourse. His introduction was a most vivid and telling description of the Burn at Ferintosh – in some respects bordering on the poetic. About the same time another outstanding student – Mr W. M. Cameron – who was afterwards settled in Resolis in the Black Isle – conducted the Sabbath morning service in Fountain Bridge and preached an excellent sermon on the text, 'But the natural man receiveth not the things of the Spirit of God; for they are foolishness unto him; neither can he know them, because they are spiritually discerned', 1 Corinthians 2:14. The preaching of these two young men at once won the admiration and respect of the then younger generation of the Free Church and confirmed them in the belief that the teaching in the Free Church College was fundamentally sound in doctrine and pleasing in diction.

Principal Peter W. Miller, also writing more than half-a-century after this period, has set down the following record of the impression which MacRae's preaching made when it was first heard in Edinburgh:

His natural, fine preaching gifts burst dramatically on the local Church congregation and especially on the student population. His slightly greater age gave him perhaps greater confidence in putting over his message to that notoriously difficult audience comprising so many well-known faces. On the lower level his immediate and memorable appeal lay in his well-projected moral earnestness, his self-forgetting absorption in his theme, and his easy command of an English that was crisp and vivid, with the apt use of figures of speech betokening the poetic mind. At the very outset he caught the ear of his hearers and their attention was heightened as he developed his subject, often to an almost painful intensity of listening. Phrasemaking he did not attempt, and he was content to set forth the lively oracles of God in simple, telling and awesome terms. At times the listeners felt carried away as the speaker's strong resonant voice took on a rarer more melodic quality that brought home to heart and conscience the Word of the Cross. At the same time, a serious and even sombre vein ran through his exposition of divine truth. He would say, 'You are sitting at an open window on a fine summer evening as the dark comes on. A moth flies past – that is life'. Again, he would compare human existence to a mountain. A great light burns on the summit, drawing upwards the eager feet of the young and strong and aspiring. Ere long the ascent grows more arduous, more toilsome, more lonely, and to the now lagging climbers the jagged runnels of the mountain slopes seem brimming with the tears of sorrow and distress. Having been moved himself he moved his rapt audience with a sense of the weariness, pain and vanity of life. (Doubtless the *lachrymae rerum* of the Classics, the 'tears of things', were in his thoughts.) Anyway the futility and distresses of human life became urgent pleas for the acceptance of the One Saviour and for following on to know the Lord.

To these and other scenes of more than sixty years ago the Diary itself will now take us.

THE LONELY WAY

Where there gleams no ray of splendour, nor blares forth the
    trump of pride,
Where the sea of vain ambition never rolls its pearly tide,
Where there rings no laugh of pleasure, in the gath'ring night
    I sigh,
Waiting till the flash of glory flames athwart the murky sky.

Here, in pain and tribulation, jeering laugh and biting scorn,
Life seems but an endless struggle, driving through a brake
    of thorn;
But the bloodstains dark before me on the bush where'er
    I stray
Check the moan of protestation – Lo, the Lord has passed
    this way!

Be it so then, Saviour Jesus, let the lowly path be mine,
Let my days be spent in shadows, never summer on me
    shine;
Lead me through the mists of sorrow where Thou passed
    Thyself before –
Such to me is more than honour, I would seek, would ask no
    more!

KENNETH A. MACRAE
in *The Monthly Record*, April 1911

What a student is in his first public services, that he is likely to be through
life; and if there be no earnestness then, there is likely to be little afterwards.

JOHN ANGELL JAMES
An Earnest Ministry the Want of the Times, 1858, *p.* 329

3 The Student-Preacher

When I first entered the hall I felt that my discourse was altogether out of place, so few were present and those few were elderly; yet ultimately more gathered and a fair proportion of them young so that I felt encouraged to proceed. Still I thought the attendance much poorer than when I was here last year, amounting only to about twenty-five. Preached from Proverbs 23:26, but although had reasonable liberty was as cold and heartless as ice.

Evening – preached from Psalm 50:15. Attendance miserable = 14, equal to my Fortrose prayer meeting, but ah, how different was the atmosphere. Feel as if I could give it all up and hide myself. Certainly I had my portion of blessing tonight but it was not the abundant fare to which I have been accustomed of a Sabbath evening. I had not the same pleasure in developing the text as has been my wont. Surely it is not that I am becoming like so many preachers, hardened and careless, prosy and profitless. May I be kept from this above all things! If I were to know that such was to be my future I would not ask to live a moment longer in the world. A minister spiritually dead is the most pitiful creature in God's earth. But why should I be cast down? I cannot expect all sun and no gloom, I shall have my seasons of depression as have others; the day of gladness shall be but the brighter because of them. God will not leave me; God will not desert me. He will finish the good work which He has begun.

Ah Grantown, Grantown, you are a town to give a Christian a sore heart and surely indeed must the Lord's heart be sore when He looks upon such a godless people!

What a sweet night! I shall never forget it, for the Lord was with me and He fed my weary soul. I had not cried upon Him in vain during the long hours of the afternoon. Then I was miserable in spirit and ill in body but when the Lord opened my mouth all was forgotten and oh it was precious to me! The congregation was splendid and was specially encouraging in view of the large proportion of young men and women in its composition. I could not but notice the essentially Scottish type of feature in the faces before me.

But if Satan kept from me during the service he soon made up for his absence. I see plainly that I care more for the delivery of my sermons than for any results which might be to the glory of Christ and the salvation of souls. May God have mercy upon me!

19 MAY: GRANTOWN F.C.

Attendance again very small in evening = 16. Preached from John 1:36 and experienced blessing especially when dealing with the purity, the patience and the tenderness of Christ. Still the Gospel appeal seemed to lack fire, I suppose because there was no need for it. Still I must not take anything for granted, I cannot see into the hearts of my hearers and I must not lose sight of the preacher's golden rule: 'Never preach a sermon which has not sufficient in it – used of the Spirit – to lead a soul to Christ'.

I fear there are not many who think of upholding the preacher in prayer in this place. Sometimes one would wish there were more young people in our congregations but here I could wish there were a few more old folks, for then there would be more prayer and more blessing.

2 JUNE

In afternoon cycled to Drumwillie near Boat-of-Garten. Small old-fashioned hall but people turned out very well. Real country style, rough and ready, collection taken in a soup-plate, and people just the old simple country style too. Only about eight miles from Grantown, yet what a difference. They listened well. There was no inattention. Pleaded with them to take Christ. Oh that some would! that they all would!

I shall not forget Drumwillie. It is a warm little place and there is an added zest in proclaiming Christ there to such a simple kindly people. It is a rough bare hall, with the ooze at places green on the walls, with no place for a fire but a recess in the wall, yet to me it is a place of beauty, for Christ was with me there.

At Aviemore I found a very fair congregation gathered in a corrugated-iron church. Preached from John 6:67 and was given fair liberty.

Struck with what one of the elders at Aviemore said to me re smooth-mouthed preaching. While commending the full-orbed proclamation of the Gospel he deplored the fact that in cities such was an offence to some people and drove them to other churches. Had never thought of people being offended at my preaching but from personal experience I know how such offends the unconverted, and I must not be surprised if in some cases the effect of my preaching is the opposite of what I would wish. While recognizing this, yet I still adhere to my belief that what is urgently required is even this old 'offensive' preaching. If the Gospel were faithfully proclaimed throughout the land I believe that in a month's time we would be a changed nation. Anyway, offence or no offence, I shall not cease to proclaim what God has given me. I would rather see a soul leave me because offended at my words than that he should drift calmly into hell without a word of warning from me.

9 JUNE: PERTH

Surprised and pleased at the fine interior of the church which is especially striking because of the contrast with the plain and insignificant exterior. The congregation was bigger than I expected, as was the church, but I am afraid that here I have reached the limits of spiritual deadness. How different are these Lowlanders from our reverent Highland people! I found afterwards that my distaste of the choir was not altogether unfounded. I was told that the attendance of male voices was generally poor in the morning; further, that if the evening were fine, there usually were very few of the choir present at all. These things speak for themselves and I have often noticed that this laxity is a common characteristic of choirs. After service I was thanked for my address: I was told I would make a fine minister. Aye, people will praise men so, but never yet has anyone told me of a single conversion brought about by God through the medium of my preaching: and if it be not so used then is my preaching vain and the sooner I give it up the better. Would that He would give me the knowledge of at least one! Hope to preach from Romans 10:21 in the evening. Very suitable for such a people: let them be offended as they may.

To me they appear on the whole to be careless, a people that would grieve a man's heart. Yet God in His mercy can change this and it may be that He has in the bosom of His Providence a time of rich blessing for this very congregation.

23 JUNE: BURGHEAD

Degree work seems to destroy all spirituality.[1] My frame of mind this morning brought me to the verge of despair, so full was it of worldliness, vanity and the whispers of Satan. Preached from Psalm 50:15. Received more blessing from it than I had any right to expect.

1 A passing reminder that at this date the greater part of his time was being given to his studies in the University of Edinburgh as well as at the Free Church College.

Oh that I might realise the intensity of eternal things! Yet how can I until I make them of paramount importance in my thoughts! A man cannot feel deeply about anything until he has given to it long and earnest attention; how then can I expect to realise the importance of such until I give them chief place in my meditations?

Although the congregation was thinned by the absence of many of the younger people at the fishing, still there was a very good turn-out, gallery and down stairs being fairly well filled. It is strange what an effect the singing has on me when I am in the pulpit. When in the pew it usually is a matter of no great concern, but when in the pulpit somehow it seems to me as if this were the voice of the people whereby I can judge their spiritual condition. If the singing is heartless it makes me heartless; if it is time and measure, as at Perth, it makes me long to get away from the building; if it is slow, reverential, yet withal hearty, as at Resolis, it makes me promise my soul 'a good time here'.

One striking feature of the people here is their unfailing punctuality; so different from Saltcoats. The service starts at the hour punctually and there are no late comers. I think and I trust that more than I got blessing tonight, for when I went out to the vestry the tongues of these fishermen seemed to be loosened and they spoke as godly men only can speak. Said burly Mr Main to me, 'I suppose you have heard of the dove that had one foot black and the other white?' 'No,' I said, 'I never heard that one'. 'What!' and he looked surprised, 'and she is continually mourning over that black foot'. Then it broke on me and he must have seen it on my face for he laughed pleasedly. 'My mother', he said, 'used to tell me of a woman who had a black side and a white side, the black was always turned to God but the white was towards the world'. Then he gave me good and salutary advice, advice which I am conscious I greatly need even as I enter into the immediate future. 'You are young', he said, 'remember that example is better than precept'. I thank that fisherman for his advice.

They gave me praise, these gentle simple men, the praise I estimate, not the unguarded praise of Perth which was a whetstone to my pride, but the praise which they only can give who know the deceit and vanity of the human heart. Mr Hendrie is fortunate in having such a charge and such office-bearers under him. This place seems to be altogether different from the rest of Morayshire, and I notice with pleasure that it is the only place in Morayshire which has a Free Church congregation worth speaking about. Verily the labours of God's servants live after them. In the seventies Burghead enjoyed the ministry of a faithful and godly man, Mr Walters, a man who, be it noted, was strenuously opposed to that motion which culminated in the union of 1900. The congregation to whom I preached this day live to bear testimony to the influence of his work. What a great encouragement this is to a minister to go on toiling faithfully, but ah what a warning to the careless and negligent when they see what might have been the outcome of their ministry had it been faithful to the Lord!

2 AUGUST: FORTROSE PRAYER MEETING

Received somewhat of the wonted liberty I used to have when in Fortrose. My soul was sore needing such a time and greatly I appreciated it. It was certainly far and away the sweetest time I have had in the Black Isle since I left Edinburgh. Preached, or spoke rather, from Isaiah 64:1 – Cry of church upon earth.

1 Cry implies:
  (a) Loneliness (b) That godliness is declining (c) That ungodliness is advancing.
2 That Thou mightest rend the heavens,
  (a) To make Thyself known (b) To make Thy glory to be seen (c) That Thy mercies may descend,
3 That Thou mightest come down
  (a) Mercies not enough (b) Descent of the Holy Spirit (c) Love-cry of spouse.
4 That the mountains might flow down at Thy presence
  (a) Mountain of infidelity (b) Mountain of popery (c) Mountain of indifference.

11 AUGUST: DINGWALL

Preached from Isaiah 2:10. I had more liberty and blessing at the end than at any other part; but woe is me, how my vain soul panted after praise! Sandy Clunas, worthy man, knew well how to meet me. No indiscreet words did he utter, but words of encouragement such as a father might give. There are not many like him. He is left among us, one from the old days among a backsliding people. He must, for all his cheerful ways, be oftentimes cast down because of these days.

Ah well, how strange are the workings of God! I remembered today how I used to sit in that very church an innocent little boy.

25 AUGUST: DINGWALL

Preached here at night. Felt the church even larger than last time and myself smaller. Think I was even also more self-conscious, for I felt my knees quiver once or twice in an unusual way, at least nowadays. I got gracious liberty and an earnestness in impressing the Gospel that alas I have too seldom. Sandy Clunas did not give me a single word of praise except to compliment me on my punctuality. He is a wise man.

27 SEPTEMBER

Today, despite my disagreement with the strictness and indeed unreasonableness of some of Miss Kemp's views, it has been brought home to me that entering for the ministry means something more than merely preaching the Gospel; it means also a consecration of the whole life to the service of God, it means a holiness of walk and conversation far exceeding that expected of a Christian in a less responsible sphere.

28 SEPTEMBER

Feel in a strange mood tonight. Am now beginning to realise that I shall really have to depart from Resolis on Monday, and downright sorry I am to do so. I wish I could feel the responsibility of preaching here tomorrow for the last time.

6 OCTOBER: NAIRN

Beautiful church from outside and very nice and compact inside. Gallery unopened, waiting brighter days. Congregation pretty fair, perhaps about sixty, but proportion of young people rather low, of young men very much so. Indeed felt that perhaps I would do better to give them doctrine than the bald Gospel; but then if there be one unsaved soul in the place, and I have no doubt there is, the preaching of the Gospel is not out of place. After the service was over Sheriff Lightbody stayed to shake hands with me and passed a few words commending my discourse – said it was what was needed in these days and exhorted me to continue as I had begun.

9 OCTOBER: EDINBURGH

A few days make a vast difference. Away from the North I seem to be another person leading another life altogether. I seem to have been plunged into a chaos of new interests, cares, temptations, in the midst of which I almost lose sight of what was uppermost hitherto.

20 OCTOBER: URRAY

Somehow despite my late hardness of heart I became conscious that the

Lord was drawing near to me yesterday and I began to look unto a time of blessing today. Nor was I disappointed. Preached from John 14:31 and had gracious liberty. In evening was driven to Marybank School-house four miles away. Preached from James 4:14:

1 Uncertainty of life
   (*a*) Assurance of men as manifested in plans
   (*b*) A groundless assurance
   (*c*) Tomorrow
2 Its shortness – a little time
   Comparatively (*a*) A little time to prepare for eternity (*b*) A little time to serve the Lord (*c*) A little time to weep.
3 Its instability – a vapour
   (*a*) Life's realities as phantoms (*b*) Vapour – nothing tangible
   (*c*) Vanishes away – no trace.

This week-end has indeed been a time of quickening and reviving for me. Lord grant that I return not to yon deadness of soul which was mine when I left Edinburgh!

23 OCTOBER: EDINBURGH

I have need to take to myself the words that Mr MacLean said at the Prayer Meeting tonight regarding seeking popularity. I am afraid that when preparing and preaching I think more of giving the people a 'good sermon' than of anything deeper and more to be desired.

25 OCTOBER

When I worry, as I am prone to do when I feel myself becoming swamped by the excessive amount of study I have to undertake, I should remember that in view of the fact (1) that in the ordinary course of nature, in three years such will be a thing of the past and (2) that these my studies may finish for ever at any day, worry not only is sinful but it is positively foolish. If I would but keep in mind, too, what I clearly realised at the outset, that this is simply a means to an end, and that the One who has called me to the ministry will bear me safely over all obstacles thereunto, I would be less prone to vexing thoughts.

6 NOVEMBER

If sometimes I am cast down at College and University, yet in another sphere I have what makes up for it and comforts me. Tonight's letter from Mrs Ross, Fortrose, and Mrs MacLean's present, certainly encourage me.

[43]

19 NOVEMBER

Have today experienced the blessedness of that plan which I found myself constrained to adopt last session – that of devoting five minutes of every hour of home study to reading some book dealing with spiritual matters. Found Spurgeon today as a balm poured upon my restless spirit.

20 NOVEMBER

Today I have been a good deal exercised with a question which presented itself as the outcome of observing the high standard of Christian life required by Spurgeon of the believer. This is a feature characteristic of the more modern English writers. I find that the great men of the North laid claim to nothing save their own sinfulness and the efficacy of Christ's sacrifice. This comforts me whereas these English writers make me despair. Perhaps it is merely another illustration of the difference in national temperament.

30 NOVEMBER

For the first time for many a long day I am at home on a Saturday night. I do not know what has come over me this last day or two. Somehow I have gone back to my old dreams, the melancholy of the Celt has come drifting into my soul.

1 DECEMBER

I know now why it is that I have been left at home this week-end. Mr MacLean had got a message for me if ever there was a message for anyone. How solemn were his words, 'There is never a sin that you commit but is done despite the pleading of Christ; never a temptation confronts you, but Christ comes between it and you, holding out His pierced hands'. How earnestly he implored to flee from temptation and that which would occasion it!

4 DECEMBER

As I rose in the morning a petition came to me with wondrous clearness. It came to me again during the day. Finally in the meeting, I had glorious liberty in prayer; I have never so prayed in that hall[1] and I know it was re-echoed because I heard Mr MacLean's deep undertone of approval. This shows me (1) that that prayer was given me of a purpose, (2) that it is not wrong to ponder over a prayer before-hand, (3) and that

1 *ie* the hall of St Columba's church.

the Lord has removed His anger from me else would He not give me a token such as this. This gives me renewed confidence in view of tomorrow's exam. The same Lord will be with me there and despite my unpreparedness I shall be sustained.

5 DECEMBER

I feel I have made a sad mess of that exam today but the issue is in the Lord's hands.

18 DECEMBER

Only one exam to go now and soon I shall have forgotten all the worries entailed in this last fortnight's work. So time goes and bears with it those petty troubles over which foolish souls so often vex themselves.

22 DECEMBER

I am too faithless in prayer. I fear I think my prayers so wretched, so sinful, cloaked with pride and sown with self-conceit, that even Christ cannot present them unto the Father; but ah, let me remember His eternal power and realise that He can cleanse even the prayer that arises from my lips.

3-4 JANUARY 1913: FERINTOSH

Now that my visit to Ferintosh is over I can plainly discern that it has been to my spiritual benefit. The society of that heavenly-minded and warm-hearted man has affected even my hard heart, and I can perceive that I am somewhat softer and less given to these vain dreams of worldly desire than was I when I came North. I have indeed reason to be grateful to the Most High that instead of leaving me to the consequences of my sins, as I well deserved, He prepares an experience for me which drives me back once again upon Himself.

21 JANUARY: EDINBURGH

I have been but seldom troubled with fits of depression since I left the Telegraph service, but assuredly there has been a cloud upon my spirits during these last two days. The reasons are various, perhaps not one singly able to cause such a gloom but in concert very depressing. They are (1) Not enough sleep and too much work (2) Irritation at Prof. Moore's senseless and slave-driving policy (3) The present renewed attacks upon and misfortunes of the Free Church and (4) Troubles re preaching and my duty in the difficulties which confront me and which seem to defy solution. Yet after all, in spite of this formidable list, if only I would trust God, I need not allow one care to rest upon me. Ah that I had faith!

23 JANUARY

Because of work and its monotony I feel rather discontented and depressed at times. Oh that I might remember how it has been with me, how it is with others even now, that instead of complaining so I might be thanking God that I am not broken under one or other of life's sorrows!

Was angered by Miss M's letter this morning in which she said that J. had told her that he would go to Canada if he got the chance, angered because neither Church nor Highlands can spare him and because the time has now come when the action of every Gaelic-speaking person in leaving the Highlands is paramount to signing his or her name to the death-warrant of the language. The Gaelic can only hope to live in the Highlands.

Feel as if I am turning over a new leaf today. I am going to be so easy-going no longer. That Exit Exam has taught me a lesson. I must be firm. I'm afraid that with an exaggerated notion of the sin of discord I have overstepped the other bounds. And those letters I have sent to the papers re Hogge and the Free Church are the first evidences of the change. After all it is folly always to shrink from the battle. There are some things worth fighting for. Had the leaders of our church not fought and endured much bitterness in 1900 there would be no Free Church today.

26 JANUARY: SABBATH, EDINBURGH

In the evening Prof. Cameron dealt with 'God requireth that which is past'. I felt my soul moved within me. What a spiritual man Prof. Cameron is! His preaching tastes like ripe fruit. I could almost have groaned when I heard him conclude. His remark that there is no past nor future with God, that all unto Him is present, combined with the manner in which he dealt with the text, almost awed me. Would that I could be, not almost, but altogether awed!

It is only of late that I am beginning to discover my painful doctrinal ignorance – and yet I essay to teach others.

Tomorrow is coming and I am afraid of it – that long busy worldly week; the very thought depresses me.

2 FEBRUARY: FOUNTAINBRIDGE, EDINBURGH

With great trepidation I entered this pulpit but I found it to be a pulpit of liberty to me. I had been uneasy because of the many students I should have to face, but soon I forgot them. Preached from Cant. 3:3 and had great liberty. The people listened most attentively and there were some faces most eager, most earnest. On going out, the men of the church were very kind to me. Mr Sinclair told me that I had struck a lost chord and I knew then that I had won the great critic's favour.

But night was the time of the full cup for my soul. Because my discourse was a new one I was afraid I would be slow and hesitating with it, but never had I more liberty. If they listened well in the morning they listened better at night. Preached from Luke 24:29, 'It is toward evening and the day is far spent'.

  1 The Necessities of the evening:
    (a) A Light. (b) A Shelter. (c) A Bed.
  2 The Characteristics of the evening:
    (a) Darkness. (b) Coldness. (c) Weariness.
  3 The Opportunities of eventide:
    (a) Same as midday. (b) Of finding Christ. (c) Of prevailing with Him.

3 FEBRUARY

All day long has my pride been feeding itself upon its memories of yesterday as if I, a frail vessel of clay, had anything to do with it at all. And it is always so with me. I am continually taking to myself the glory which pertains unto the Most High because of what He has done in me, this miracle of opening my stammering lips to give utterance to the Gospel. Nevertheless my pride got its own rebuke in that in its hungering after praise, all it got in this house was criticism. Oh pride, pride, would that I could kill you! I feel languid and depressed. I was terribly tired last night and I have not got back my usual energy.

14 FEBRUARY

It was good for me to pay that visit tonight. I felt so drawn to that godly, affectionate old woman that it was not in the same state of coldness I left as had been mine on entry. Such a visit I feel to be a good preparation for a profitable Sabbath. Let me take notice of this: Ere I went I prayed with some measure of earnestness that my visit might be unto my spiritual quickening – and as I prayed so it was.

[47]

SABBATH, 23 FEBRUARY:[1] FOUNTAINBRIDGE

This second Sabbath at Fountainbridge was a repetition of the first –
the same liberty, the same tense silence, the same unknown power. If
there is a night I shall never forget, this is it. Preached from Matthew
22:25 and indeed was upheld of God. When I got out Jim MacIver was
waiting for me. All the way home not a word passed between us. The
silence remained unbroken until we reached the upper side of Brunts-
field Links where our paths diverged. 'Come to my digs, Kennie,' said
Jim in a low tense tone, 'I want to speak to you'. His lodging was only
about 50 yards from where we stood, and feeling that this was no
ordinary matter I willingly went on with him. Nor was it. He gave me a
full account of his spiritual experience leading up to the present, and
now the whole gist of his difficulty was 'What must I do to be saved?' He
had been well and religiously brought up, and religion he respected
although he knew not its power. He had come to Edinburgh full of
hopes and with the ambition to make a name for himself in the University – and well he might, for he had talents of no mean order and his
educational successes up till then were second to none. Naturally
sociable and a keen lover of music, besides being himself a musician and
singer of outstanding talent, his natural proclivities tended to take him
into a faster company than that to which he had been accustomed, but
his association with the two Free Church Divinity students who were
his fellow-lodgers served to act as a wholesome restraint upon him. Not
only so, but there he saw as never before the difference between the
world and the Lord's people, and he realised that he must make a choice
as to with whom he was to throw in his portion. With a deepening
realisation of the seriousness of life he had gone to Fountainbridge that
first Sabbath when I stood up, the trembling occupant of that austere
pulpit. That very day and at the first service the truth gripped him.
The evening service deepened it and he went out into the night at the
close under the deepest conviction of sin. He strove to cast it from him;
he was young and fresh, he wished to enjoy life a little, and taste all that
youth craves for, and he was not willing yet to forfeit all this for peace
with God – but his conscience would not be still. The wrath of God
seemed to seize his very soul.

1 This memorable date – the first occasion when MacRae was aware of his
preaching being used in the conversion of a soul – is unusual in that there are
no less than four separate accounts of it in his diaries and papers, one written
as late as 1924. In the entry here given it has been necessary to conflate these
several accounts. Jim MacIver was a native of Elgin; Annie Munro was a
daughter of the home where he lodged; she professed faith and joined the
Fountainbridge Church later in the same year.

Jim was a different being when for the second time we both appeared in Fountainbridge, I to speak, he to listen, and the Word that day, especially that night, finished what it had begun. Poor Jim was crushed and broken, he had no strength left.

After unitedly seeking Divine guidance, it seemed so easy sitting there at the fire to explain the way of life to him. I had no experience in such cases and little would have confused and rendered me helpless, but the Lord must have made teacher and taught suited for each other. In any case Jim seemed almost at once to grasp – and this was his chief difficulty – the difference between faith and feelings, and after a few words more of prayer I left him, as I have every reason to believe, a changed lad, a humble, rejoicing believer in Christ.

I thought I had reached the finish of this wonderful soul-stirring day when I left him sitting staring into the red glow of his bedroom fire, but about half an hour after my entry to my own home, I was surprised by a ring at the door-bell. Who was this but Jim, with a strangely excited yet awed expression upon his face! 'Kennie, come and help Annie', he panted, 'She is as I was'. Out I went without delay, feeling myself absolutely helpless, yet unable to resist such a cry. I found that she too was under deep concern and would give anything to have peace of mind, but she seemed to be unable to grasp the truth which had set Jim free. At last after prayer with her I had to go, but on the door-step she entreated me to remember her and to try to help her. I sought my own door exulting at such signal tokens of the Lord's power, yet feeling humbled to the dust. This is an encouragement to me to preach the Gospel.

I MARCH: LOCHGILPHEAD

Despite the fact that I have had more social intercourse tonight than usually falls to my lot I have such a measure of the Lord's presence as gives me to hope for a sweet day tomorrow.

2 MARCH: LOCHGILPHEAD

While here in Lochgilphead I cannot but contrast my present with what I was when here last in 1906. What a difference! Well do I remember the happy harum-scarum band that came tramping down Argyll Street. Who would ever have thought then that one of them would return to preach the Gospel? What a wonderful thing conversion is! How gracious is the Lord that He should have wrought this miracle!

Undertook the Gaelic service, although of course preaching in

English, and had fair liberty and some little blessing. The congregation numbered perhaps close upon forty and I was pleased to see some children present. What struck me most was the heartiness of the singing. Nevertheless it was different from the Gaelic singing of the North, being on the whole faster and having fewer grace notes. The variants too were a trifle different. Preached from Psalm 51:3. In the afternoon there was a much better congregation but perhaps not as large as I expected. Preached from John 14:31 and had great liberty and no little blessing. In the evening the people were all gathered downstairs which made the meeting more compact. I had not the liberty of the afternoon, but still I had in no wise less blessing and I felt in earnest.

The people here bear the impress of Mr Watson's personality. Argyllshire material is hard to work upon but he has succeeded in moulding them after the Ross-shire pattern.[1]

SABBATH, 16 MARCH: ABERFELDY

I plainly see that I must give more time to prayer and devotional reading, and I must forthwith arrange a scheme which shall do justice to my studies and at the same time allow me to give an hour to the Lord in the mornings. At the same time I hope to purchase one of Spurgeon's weekly sermons every Thursday[2] and to read it duly through the week.

SATURDAY, 22 MARCH: FORTROSE

As I walked along the Rosemarkie beach today and gazed across at the old grey bastions of Fort George I could not but marvel at how wondrously the Lord had dealt with me. Who would have thought in the old childhood days that in years to come, I as a young man should stray along the opposite shore deep in preparation for the proclamation of the Gospel? That sent me to dreaming of the past, and as I looked at the Fort I realised that I had forgotten a whole world of what had once been my primary interests and circumstances. Further than that, it seemed to me as if that were a different life altogether, and then came a stinging pain, and I would have given all I possess to be once again the little innocent child that knew no more of life and the world than what the eye scanned from the old grey ramparts.

1 Angus J. Watson, a native of Ross-shire, was minister of the congregation from 1896 until June 1904 when he died at the early age of forty. From that date the congregation had been without a settled minister.
2 Spurgeon died in 1892 but his publishers continued to issue a weekly sermon until 1917, using records of his sermons which had been taken down by shorthand. Spurgeon's name was a household word in the Scottish Highlands at this period.

And then after that, on the other side of the Point, the sight of Fortrose with the background now become so familiar to me, bade me make the most of my present, for the time would yet come (D.V.) when I felt I would look back to the days of my sojourn here with such feelings as a little before I looked across at Fort George.

SABBATH, 23 MARCH: FORTROSE

I am beginning to think that the reason for my inability and lack of power in prayer is that I have lost sight of the holiness of God. I do not estimate it a serious matter to enter in before Him, and so there is no sense of awe upon me, nor of the reality of the solemn thing I am performing. How then is this to be rectified? Evidently the remedy must lie in the deepening of my sense of the majesty of God, but how this is to be accomplished, as yet I see not.

THURSDAY, 27 MARCH: FORTROSE

I never went to any public exercise in such an unprepared state as I went to the Prayer Meeting tonight. Just as I was about to leave Dingwall after sitting my Undergraduate's Bursary examination there, I noticed a nail through my bicycle tyre. Fortunately just round the corner, although it was the half-holiday in the town, I found a bicycle shop, and speedily got the machine set aright again. Yet the delay was such that despite all my efforts it was ten minutes before the prayer meeting hour when I rode into Fortrose, and time for preparation I had none. Nevertheless the Lord prepared me and a sweet night was granted. Lesson: Trust implicitly to the Lord in an extremity.

TUESDAY, 15 APRIL: EDINBURGH

Back to the University and back to my godlessness. Perhaps have no specific sins upon my conscience but feel far out of touch with things spiritual, I am so busy that I have no time to think of God. Poor wretch! Yet I felt worship tonight with Jim MacIver to be to the help of my soul. I am very pleased with him. If he is spared he will be a preacher who will satisfy hungry souls.

FRIDAY, 25 APRIL

Pride has been terribly in evidence today. Because of the results of my three class examinations I have been contemplating the possibility of my getting one or two second class merit certificates and from that I have gone on to dream about the M.A., and I have been taking to myself the glory which is due to the Lord alone.

c

SATURDAY, 3 MAY

I felt all of a sudden this afternoon that the spiritual bonds in which I had sat were broken asunder. I have experienced such before. It seems that the Lord will not utterly forsake those whom He has sent out to preach the Gospel; that despite all their ill-desert, for His own glory's sake He will prepare them to deliver His message.

SABBATH, 11 MAY: LOCHGILPHEAD

Had fairly good Gaelic congregation with a good sprinkling of children. Preached fron Cant. 3:3. In the afternoon I had a fine congregation, and, I must confess, a happy time. Preached from Isaiah 60:20, had ample liberty and was enabled to put some life into it. In the evening preached from James 4:14 and had both liberty and blessing. The people listened very well indeed, and I found the service sweet to my soul. It is more than strange that the house in which I now am is the very house in which I lodged – although then on the lower flat – when first I came to Lochgilphead long ago, a merry, irresponsible youth upon a walking tour. Had I then been told that my next visit to Lochgilphead would be to preach the Gospel I would have considered the very idea the extreme of madness. How truly wonderful are the workings of the Lord! His ways are past finding out. Lochgilphead! Lochgilphead! thou hast not a few happy memories for me and I am beginning to have a love for thee.

MONDAY, 26 MAY

I am becoming more and more convinced that my ways must change, that I must not quietly pass what I know to be out of accordance with God's laws. There is a method which cries 'Peace! Peace!' where there is no peace and I fear that that is the method I am adopting. I shall have to abandon this method when I am settled D.V., else it will ruin my ministry, but it would be folly to carry on with it until then. I must part with it now and be remiss no longer in faithfulness to Him whom I profess to serve. I must be prepared to endure for Christ's sake.

SABBATH, 15 JUNE: KIRKCALDY

Nice church, but oh what a miserable time I had in it! The elements contributing to my misery were: (1) A scanty congregation – about fifty (2) A listless auditory (3) A choir (4) Standing at singing and sitting at prayer (5) Collection before the closing psalm (6) A heart harder than any rock. The Lord manifestly was not with me, there was nothing but sound and formality. Nor did the atmosphere of the place help me in any wise. In Mr Gilfillan's day there were 230 members here, now there are about 120. Out of these 120 *members* there is an attendance of fifty, some of whom, of course, are not members. Surely such in the Free Church is a tragedy indeed.

MONDAY, 16 JUNE

Although I dropped one question at the examination today I felt that I had done a good paper in Logic and I was beginning to have visions of a degree after all. This impression was intensified and I felt quite jubilant as I engaged myself upon the fourth question in the Philosophy section of the paper, but I crowed too soon. The remaining three questions were altogether beyond me, being based upon the lectures I had missed on Monday mornings while away for the week-ends. Strange that I should have 'come down' through having gone out to preach God's Word. Yet I do not regret it. He knows best and this is done for the best.

THURSDAY, 19 JUNE

My degrees are over at last, but I do not yet feel free, and no doubt I will not do so until I get rid of the Greek exam which yet awaits me. Nevertheless I have much reason to feel grateful to the Most High for the way in which He has borne me in health and strength through this session.

MONDAY, 23 JUNE

There is no doubt about it; these present are happy days. Let me appreciate them while I have them!

MONDAY, 30 JUNE

Am greatly gratified at my sister's success but was for a time rather downcast at my own failure in Logic. Still I was given grace to save me from undue depression. I found my consolation in the reflection that the Lord is ruling all for His glory, and that this, although the reason is hidden from me, is for the best. I have accordingly resolved (D.V.) to return to Edinburgh at the beginning of September and to study for the October exam.

TUESDAY, I JULY: STRUAN

Left Edinburgh this morning on the bicycle en route for Glenurquhart, crossing the Forth by the Granton-Burntisland Ferry. I had meant to stay overnight at Pitlochry but reaching my proposed destination at about 3 p.m. I felt that it was too early to call a halt and pushed on as far as Struan. I overdid it, however, for I felt that the last few miles of the journey were taxing the last remnants of my strength. Arriving at the hotel I found it full up. In my dilemma I fell back upon the Post Office people who had assisted us in our walking tour several years ago, and was recommended to try a certain Mrs MacPherson's on the hillside. At the same time they did not appear very sanguine of my admittance. But the Lord was good to me. Mrs MacPherson, an active pleasant-faced woman, at once admitted me, and from the appearance of the room and bed I might have thought that it was just waiting for me – everything was ready, and fresh and clean. What confidence I should have in the Lord who thus proves His interest in me!

I find that Gaelic is generally spoken here, a fact which agreeably surprised me, but I do not appreciate the frequent interjection of colloquial Englishisms or Scotticisms, such as 'gey hard lines', in their Gaelic.

WEDNESDAY, 2 JULY: KINGUSSIE

Had a splendid day for crossing the Grampians and despite my feeling rather fagged out when I started in the morning, by the time I reached Kingussie felt in very good form. Arrived in the early afternoon and very much enjoyed my stay in the Manse.

THURSDAY, 3 JULY: GLENURQUHART

Had a swelteringly hot day which tired me very much, and added to this, just when I thought that I had got the worst past, I got a puncture. Trusting in the fact that my bicycle was quite new I had omitted to bring a repair outfit with me, and here I was, apparently in a most lonely spot, for not a house was visible, and hopelessly punctured. Ruefully I wheeled on my machine, when, coming to an unexpected dip in the road just about a quarter of a mile further on, I saw at the foot of the hollow a house, and hard by a shed over which the words appeared 'Cycle Repairs'. I rejoiced at this signal piece of good fortune, and, getting the puncture repaired with all speed, soon was in the saddle again. At Daviot while navigating the big dip there I felt very tired but after that had a clear run down to Inverness which I reached about 4 p.m. The last part of the journey – out to Glenurquhart, where Donald Smith was waiting me – I accomplished in the cool of the evening and very much enjoyed.

MONDAY, 14 JULY: GLENURQUHART

Now that I am with Dolly[1] and find how often downcast and depressed he is through questionings as to his being in the right way, I see what great reason I have for thankfulness in the measure of assurance granted me. But my entrance into the kingdom entailed such a rough tossing about the bar; and the difference which a moment's flash of heavenly light into my soul wrought in my life is still too obvious to admit of any serious doubting as to the reality of what took place that memorable Sabbath evening four years ago.

Was surprised and comforted last night when that godly man Peter MacDonald confessed to often wondering whether he has ever really prayed in his life. His answer to the travelling evangelist who asked him whether he was converted was characteristic: 'Oh well, that's a hard question, and a question you have no right to ask, for that is between myself and my Maker'.

SABBATH, 20 JULY: KILTEARN

Felt with a new force today that I ought to begin to plead with God for souls. It is not presumption after all for such as I to ask this, since the glory of such redounds unto Christ, and yet even here I am confronted with the dread that I am seeking this, not for His glory, but for my own name as a preacher.

THURSDAY, 31 JULY: FORTROSE

Visited Dingwall today with at least this result: – a further bearing in upon me of the necessity of a more sanctified walk, and this the Lord brought before me by means of Mr Cameron's Gaelic sermon this forenoon.

SABBATH, 3 AUGUST: FORTROSE

Preached from Job 30:26 with ample liberty but was distressed at my lack of earnestness. In the evening preached from Hebrews 10:16–17 and feel that I never want to preach again. I went to the church in a much more spiritual frame of mind than in the morning. I received liberty in prayer, but when I turned to my sermon I found that I was in bonds and that all my preaching was but weariness to the flesh. For all its disappointment this day has not been without its profit. It has been a day of humiliation, and my pride requires that, and it has caused me to feel an increasing appreciation of the solemnity of the course upon which I have entered in devoting my life to the Gospel ministry.

1 The nick-name of his friend and fellow-student, Donald Smith.

FRIDAY, 8 AUGUST: FORTROSE

Attended the Ferintosh Fellowship Meeting in the Burn today. The question which was based upon Romans 5:1 was given out by Farquhar MacLennan, one of the local elders, opened by Rev. A. Stewart, Edinburgh, spoken to by ten men (not including any of the local speakers) and closed by the minister, Rev. D. Munro. There were some very heavy showers.

SATURDAY, 9 AUGUST: FORTROSE

I believe that, however much I fear that craving for and love of romance which ever and anon cries yearningly through my soul, my most dangerous foe is pride – simply because it is most insidious. I cannot escape it. I am attacked of it in most unexpected places – in the pulpit, on my knees, everywhere, and it wearies me terribly. Oh that I were not such a vain wretch!

THURSDAY, 14 AUGUST: CREICH

Arrived here last night with two fellow-students, Donald Smith and John MacLeod, for the Communion services. We came by the last train, which does not run further than Tain, and from there we had to cycle. Darkness latterly made our progress slow, since we had no lamps. I have tender sweet memories of my own connected with this place, but somehow, the memories of days before my days, the memories which are still lurking fondly in the minds of those who have seen these days, have crept into my mind and heart also, and when today Rev. George MacKay of Fearn in his closing prayer in referring to those former days broke down as he uttered the words 'Send us such days again!' I almost broke down with him.

Have been exercised today over my lack of holiness. One thing I clearly see – that any measure of holiness is not attained without self-denial and striving.

SABBATH, 17 AUGUST: CREICH

Went to the Table today but not to behold Christ, nay, only to see what a great sinner I am. I am tired of myself. The Communion is past, the season is well-nigh over, and I am not yet quickened. I do not know what is to become of me. Principal McCulloch, Glasgow, took the Action sermon in English and preached from John 17:4, 'I have glorified thee on the earth; I have finished the work which thou gavest me to do'.

There was an amazing amount of doctrine in the Principal's discourse, and to appreciate him one would have to give the closest attention, but I do not think that the Principal can be regarded as a popular preacher. His mind is the mind of the abstract theologian and soars above the common throng.

I thought I was to get no blessing at all – until evening came. Then the Lord in His goodness gave me my portion. Mr Munro, Ferintosh, preached an earnest, beautiful sermon from Psalm 2:12 which softened my hard heart and gave me the peace I longed for. In it he quoted the late Dr MacKay of Inverness to the effect that these distressful lamentations because of the smallness of our love for Christ come not from the Enemy of our soul, but are an evidence of grace. This was for me.

So ends a blessed day. I am tired. I would wish to rest here always. The Lord is good!

SABBATH, 24 AUGUST: FORTROSE

Tonight an idea came to me which I would do well to keep in mind. If ever I be settled in a congregation and there be any non-church-goers there, I shall make a point of asking permission to have a cottage-meeting in their house. If they won't come to the Gospel, I must take the Gospel to them.

THURSDAY, 28 AUGUST: FORTROSE

Was very much upset by a card which came today advising me to proceed to Dornoch for Sabbath for I had arranged to cycle to Elgin on Monday, but I do not feel disposed to decline to go for I could not look for blessing in a place where my own will had dictated my remaining. I see nothing for it but to take my cycle with me and ride all the way from Dornoch to Elgin; for owing to delay at connections I can make nothing of it by train.

SABBATH, 31 AUGUST: DORNOCH

One of the elders took the preliminaries at the Gaelic service but I was expected to give an English address. This I did from Hosea 13:5, 'I did know thee in the wilderness, in the land of great drought', and was enabled to speak with fair liberty. At the English service I spoke from John 2:5, 'Whatsoever He saith unto you, do it!'

The Dornoch hall in which the evening service was held is a sweet place to me. I spent a happy, happy night in it last year and on this occasion I was no less happy. Although I did not finish writing my sermon until 11 o'clock last night, I was given all the liberty I desired, while the deepest solemnity rested upon my spirit. Spoke from Psalm 1:5, 'The ungodly shall not stand in the judgment, nor sinners in the congregation of the righteous'. I do not think it was all without effect for I never saw people go out from a service more gravely. The Lord has been gracious to me here and I would fain lengthen the day if I could. I came grudgingly and I shall go grudgingly. I feel somewhat sad to realise that this must be my last Sabbath in the North, at least in the meantime – perhaps for ever.

MONDAY, I SEPTEMBER: ELGIN

Cycled down early this morning the seven miles to the Ferry across to near Tain. Very tired and hungry after battling against the wind, I at last reached Fortrose. I had no option but to set out again and cross the Fort George Ferry with as little delay as possible. As I drew near the shore after a rough passage, was relieved to see Jim MacIver waiting for me on the beach. I had a look through the Fort, but it seemed all so changed, and it made me utterly heart-sick to look upon the school, the church, the square and the old home, and to realise that they were all in the hands of strangers, and that I indeed was the stranger there. There was not one individual there whom I knew in what had been once my home. I was glad to get away and to resume our journey on to Elgin. I was tired enough ere we reached our destination.

FRIDAY, 5 SEPTEMBER: EDINBURGH

Left Kingussie yesterday and came on as far as Bankfoot when I sought out the little inn in which Willie Miller had lodged on our walking tour some years ago. When I reached Perth today I felt that I had gone over the Edinburgh road so often that since I had the long day before me I would prefer to press round by Stirling and Falkirk. This I did but I was glad enough to get home.

Although I love cycling I fear it is not conducive to spirituality. After five days awheel I feel that the change in my feelings since Sabbath is more like that of five years than of as many days.

SATURDAY, 6 SEPTEMBER: DUMFRIES

My completing my sermon in one day upon the same plan as I adopted last Saturday serves to convince me that the whole can be most expeditiously done by going over the discourse mentally first and noting down the leading thoughts, afterwards enlarging from them at length. Came on to Dumfries this afternoon.

SABBATH, 7 SEPTEMBER: DUMFRIES

Being in straits was forced again to take up John 2:5. Got abundant liberty of utterance but my heart was little moved. The congregation numbered seventy. Felt disappointed in the evening when found only forty-two present, for formerly found that the evening attendance was better than the morning one. I could only account for it by the prominence I gave to the law in the earlier part of the day. Dr Moody Stuart used to drive people away by his law preaching, and I have been told that Lowlanders will not suffer it; therefore I believe that this indeed is the reason. Well, let it be; it will not alter my preaching. God helping me, to the last my preaching will be Calvary, judgment, and hell. Preached from John 3:2.

MONDAY, 8 SEPTEMBER: EDINBURGH

In the forenoon, ere leaving Dumfries, cycled out with Mrs Stewart, the minister's wife, to Irongray to see the Covenanting relics there. Found the parish minister, Rev. Mr Dunlop, very friendly and most interested in Covenanting lore. I was no little surprised to find that the old-fashioned collecting-ladles are still in use in his church. He showed us several specimens of 'Old Mortality's' work.

On our homeward journey we visited the parish church of Troqueer, the minister of which, Mr Campbell, kindly allowed us to see the interior of the church and the tablet erected in 1902 to the memory of the Rev. John Blackadder,[1] once minister of the charge. I copied the inscription:

To the glory of God and in memory of the Rev. John Blackadder, born 1615, ordained minister of the parish of Troqueer 1653, extruded 1662, outlawed for preaching in the fields 1674, imprisoned on the Bass Rock 1681, died there after cruel confinement, 1685.

Faithful unto death
Erected A.D. 1902.

TUESDAY, 9 SEPTEMBER

Being asked to give the marks of the Lord's people today, gave the following to one exercised about her state: (1) A certain love for God's Word, house, and day (2) A desire for holiness (3) A longing to be able to pray (4) A mourning over a carnal heart (5) A desire to love Christ (6) A desire for fellowship with Him (7) A fear lest, these evidences being so faint in us, we lack them altogether (8) A belief that if Christ

1 See *Memoirs of the Rev John Blackadder*, Andrew Crichton, 1826.

be not for us in eternity then we are lost (9) A belief, founded upon the free invitation extended in the Gospel and in virtue of His work on Calvary, that He will be for us and will be our Surety.

WEDNESDAY, 1 OCTOBER: EDINBURGH

Yesterday and today I have been busy over my Logic exam and already Badenoch[1] has shrunk into the background. I feel that I have done pretty well and I shall feel deeply disappointed if I do not get through. A load has gone from my mind.

MONDAY, 13 OCTOBER

Am exceedingly thankful to learn that I have got through my Logic examination. It is a great weight off my mind.

FRIDAY, 17 OCTOBER

Started College Classes today, taking Junior Greek and Senior Hebrew with Prof. Moore and Junior Church History with Prof. Bannatyne. Do not anticipate much pleasure in the two former classes for I do not appreciate Prof. Moore any more as a teacher than I do as a preacher.

TUESDAY, 21 OCTOBER

Have taken Dr Chalmers' *Select Sermons* for reading in any spare moments I may have at my disposal.

WEDNESDAY, 22ND OCTOBER

Was called upon to pray at the meeting tonight but was in such a wretched state that could scarcely pray at all. Felt I could go out of the place. I am really getting into an awful condition and this study is killing my soul.

FRIDAY, 31 OCTOBER

This afternoon we held our first weekly prayer meeting in the College. Owing to the meeting of a special class on Church Principles at the same hour the attendance suffered considerably. Still, eight of us turned up. Somehow a very frolicsome mood had prevailed all day in the College and I went to the meeting in anything but a fitting frame of

1 The name of the mountainous area south of Kingussie in Inverness-shire. He had supplied the congregation at Kingussie from September 13th to the end of that month.

mind; yet I was not there long ere I lost it all. It was a warm meeting and I felt the better for it.

SABBATH, 9 NOVEMBER

Prior to the evening service in St Columba's I was sore put to it, and when I appeared before the people it was in much trepidation and trembling. There was a splendid gathering. Spoke from Psalm 1:5 and this was the sweetest portion of a sweet day.

MONDAY, 10 NOVEMBER

Went out this morning in rather a depressed state of mind. I was still tired, I was still somewhat agitated, and the apparent uselessness of yesterday's efforts was weighing heavily upon me. I met Donald Polson sheltering from the rain at the Library door. After a few commonplaces he said, 'I was greatly impressed with your sermon last night, Mr MacRae', and then to my unutterable amazement he burst out crying. I looked at him, scarcely able to believe my eyes. I could not understand how he, one of our most promising young men, should be so perturbed by a sermon which had been preached *in toto* to the unconverted. But he told me his troubles. His past was troubling him: 'You do not understand in the North' he said, 'but it is different in the town. I went to an office when I was fifteen and a half, knowing nothing about sin'. He said no more, nor did he need, for well did I know from my own experience what he meant. I remembered how I too at the same age was cast into the swirl of commercial life in innocence and utterly unwarned, and how, were it not for God's grace, I would have found it the gates of hell for my soul, and I could sympathise. He declared that these things were so troubling him that he could do no studying and that he seriously thought of giving up the church altogether. I tried to comfort him by telling him that Satan had tempted me in the same way, and to re-assure him by pointing out that were he to give up studying for the church then he would only gladden the Enemy. I besought him to let the past lie since Christ has promised never to unearth it. Heard of the above discourse being blessed to a soul (Mary Bain of Glenurquhart).

SABBATH, 23 NOVEMBER

Not being engaged today – and owing to my low state, felt relieved that I was not – heard my fellow-student John MacLennan at the three services. In Gaelic he spoke from Matthew 12:50 to an audience of 35, but of course I could make practically nothing of him. At 2.30 heard him again from John 10:27. He was very good.

[61]

THURSDAY, 4 DECEMBER

Got postcard today for Campbeltown but owing to my Scottish History exam being due on Wednesday got exchanged for Leith.

SATURDAY, 6 DECEMBER

Professor Cameron asked me to take his Bible Class for him. How I am to manage it all I do not know. At present I have nothing for it.

SABBATH, 7 DECEMBER

Preached in Leith in the morning from Ruth 1:21 to a congregation of eighteen. At 2.30 preached in St Columba's from John 10:42 and had a grand afternoon. In the evening preached again in Leith from John 2:5 to an audience of twenty-five. Hurried up from Leith for Professor Cameron's Class. Surprised to see fully forty waiting in the Hall. Felt rather nervous at first but soon forgot everything in speaking from John Chapter 2 on the miracle at Cana.

WEDNESDAY, 10 DECEMBER

Sat my Scottish History Class exam today. There was a very good attendance at the Gaelic Prayer Meeting tonight. Mr MacLean spoke from 2 Corinthians 2.

THURSDAY, 18 DECEMBER

Got card today from Supply Office instructing me to give supply to Fortrose on the 21st inst. and 4th prox., and Elgin on the 28th inst.

FRIDAY, 19 DECEMBER

Sat my exam in Economic History and think I did fairly well. Got maximum marks in my Scottish History exam. Travelled North by the night train.

SATURDAY, 20 DECEMBER

Reached Fortrose this forenoon. Got letter from Mr Munro asking me along to Ferintosh on Tuesday by the 9 a.m. train.

TUESDAY, 23 DECEMBER: FERINTOSH

Came on to the Ferintosh Manse today for tuition in Gaelic.

WEDNESDAY, 24 DECEMBER: FERINTOSH

Mr Munro today was strongly condemning the growing tendency in the North to observe the Popish festival of Christmas. I feel very happy in this quiet house.

WEDNESDAY, 31 DECEMBER: FERINTOSH

Visited Dingwall and got tea and warm welcome in the Manse. Like to be in that home. Afterwards went to Prayer Meeting. The attendance was poor. Mr Campbell spoke from Psalm 38:9 and in the course of his remarks said 'The groan or sigh is the prayer most pleasing to God, for there is the least of self in it'.

Another year over!

MONDAY, 5 JANUARY, 1914

Returned to Edinburgh but somehow did not feel as I usually do when returning to the City. Felt as though I were only going for a short sojourn.

THURSDAY, 8 JANUARY

Got card notifying me St Columba's next Sabbath.

Had a solemn talk with Calum Galbraith after the Greek class this afternoon in which we compared our backslidings and then engaged in prayer. We agreed to have prayer daily at this time. Felt greatly the good of the exercise. Resolved also to read the Scriptures oftener – every working hour for five minutes, if possible.

MONDAY, 19 JANUARY

Went up with several other students to Professor Cameron's for tea. Later in the evening one or two of the girls present regaled us with a few Scotch and Gaelic songs. Could hardly bear them and felt that I would have to leave the room. The Gaelic airs seemed to tear at my heart-strings and wakened a passion of longing for I know not what. What mysterious power is in Gaelic melody?

TUESDAY, 20 JANUARY

With Callum Galbraith visited a most interesting old couple of the old school – Mr and Mrs Charles Lyon. Mr Lyon is a man of meekness, yet in religious things of a good deal of discernment. His wife is of strong mettle and uncompromising. She is a typical product of the Dr Kennedy school, having in her young days enjoyed that favoured ministry. Both condemned in unreserved terms modern revivalism.

Felt great liberty in worship and enjoyed the visit immensely; and to sit yonder in the deepening shadows singing Psalm 103 to the wail of 'Coleshill' with those two poor helpless old creatures was good for my soul.

FRIDAY, 6 FEBRUARY

Mr Sutherland gave a very good paper tonight [in the College] on the 'Men of Caithness'. Would like to have more of such papers.

1 MARCH: ST COLUMBA'S 11 A.M. HALL

Preached from Psalm 45:15 to a congregation of twenty.

6.30 *pm.* Preached from John 15:2 to a very good congregation. This has been a night of especial blessing to me. Oh sweet are the evenings I am having in St Columba's! The Lord is indeed gracious to me. I did not have great liberty tonight but I had what is better, I had earnestness and I was really pleading with souls. If I had without cessation what I had tonight it would be like heaven to me.

Jim [MacIver] was my precentor and I never enjoyed the singing so much in St. Columba's as I did tonight.

7 JUNE: ST COLUMBA

Preached from John 6:2 before a good congregation. The service became sweet to me in the Psalms and I had a night that was good to my soul. After the service, however, Prof. Cameron warned me of the danger of being led away by my imagination. He said that the grand principle was never to read anything out of the text, only to bring out what was in it. I have been exercised about this matter of imagination, but I find that thus only can I preach, and if I adopt that principle I must stop preaching.

28 JUNE: LOCHGILPHEAD

11 *am. Gaelic*

2 *pm.* Found a very good congregation awaiting me. Preached from John 19:5. Had earnestness at times but in the main was vexed with my want of life.

6.30 *pm.* Considering the weather, the congregation again was very good in the evening. Preached from John 18:40. It was far and away the best service of the day, for I had some earnestness. Indeed because of it I go away from Lochgilphead much happier than I did last time. I only pray that my visit here may be blessed to some poor soul. After the discourse was over I became conscious of a strange yearning coming over me as I looked upon the people and somehow they came in close to my heart and I knew I loved them. This is a strange feeling but I once felt it before in respect of the St Columba people.

23 AUGUST: RESOLIS

11.30 *am*, *Gaelic*. Pleaded with the Principal to take this service but it was no use, he was determined to make me face it. He however took the first prayer for me. Preached from Isaiah 62:6 and got on reasonably well. After the service, asked the Principal to tell me without flattery whether or not he would advise me to go on with my preaching or wait until I was more proficient in the Gaelic. He strongly advocated the former and encouraged me by telling me that every word I said was quite easily understood, my only faults being in my vowel qualities. I am very glad and should be grateful to God.

1.10, *English*. Preached from Psalm 60:3 to a splendid congregation. Some of the hard things shown the Lord's people: (1) The awfulness of the wrath and curse of God (2) Their own hearts (3) The indifference of the impenitent (4) Providential dealings (5) The spiritual desolation of the land (6) War.

Some considerations regarding this last: (*a*) Some scourge inevitable because of the nation's departure from God (*b*) Some hope yet for Britain (*c*) But not unless she repents (*d*) Prayer therefore necessary (*e*) Urgency of seeking the Lord at this time.[1]

6 *pm*, *Church*. I went in a very depressed frame of mind. I felt I had nothing for the people. What I had would be soon exhausted and there was nothing in it. Yet I had not been long in the pulpit ere I became aware of the fact that I was greatly moved. The whole night was blessing to me. Preached from Romans 1:20 and if ever I felt in earnest it was tonight. The singing was beautiful. Rory MacKenzie led and he had the taste of the Gaelic, but as I sat and listened after the sermon I felt I had never heard anything so beautiful in my life. I felt almost lifted to the gates of heaven.

The night was beautiful and still when I came out and as I walked home quietly there was a song in my soul. The Lord has been good to me this day but oh that some soul may be led to Christ!

4 OCTOBER: ST COLUMBA'S, 6.30 *pm*

I found myself back at my old station at last but, ah, my heart sank within me as I stood looking out from between the lamps upon the meagrely-filled pews. It used to be so different, so many young people. I enjoyed the service tonight. My discourse was clear cut before my mind and I had no hesitation in delivering it. When I was reading out the last

1 The First World War had started for Britain on August 4th when German troops marched into Belgium.

portion I suddenly remembered that I had omitted what I regarded as the most important side issue in the whole sermon, that dealing with the nation's lack of repentance and continued and increased provocation of the Most High.

11 OCTOBER: ST COLUMBA'S, 6.30 *pm*

In the evening the congregation was considerably improved from what it had been last Sabbath. Preached from Hebrews 1:1-2. As usual the audience was most attentive. In the course of the discourse I pleaded for better attendances both at the services and the prayer meeting, and in concluding I said that I seemed only able to preach harsh sermons, yet it was only the outcome of my experience, especially as regards formal Christianity. However, Mr MacLean said there was one young man there who would have taken it all to himself, and with good reason too, as he has not been at the church for a year.

25 OCTOBER: ST COLUMBA, 2.30 *pm*

Before the usual congregation preached from 2 Timothy 3:15. Was rather disheartened when I saw the gathering. Foolishly had thought I might have a few more than usual but I believe if anything I had less. I am evidently under the impression that I shall make this congregation grow. Lord, forgive me for my pride. And yet on the other hand if I have no expectation I shall become a poor dead creature with no energy and no hope. I have a right to expect my prayers to be answered and I pray for this, not for my own glory but, I hope, for the cause of Christ.

8 NOVEMBER: ST COLUMBA'S

6.30 *pm*. Preached before a pretty good congregation from Luke 16:31 and had an exceedingly good evening. Today somehow I have felt less under the awful influence of that indifference which has so long sat upon me. I was sitting nearer to holy things. Prayer today has been no task for me; I have not shrunk from it as my wont. I may even say it has been attractive to me and today I pleaded specially for a blessing because it is the anniversary of a Sabbath evening I shall never forget.[1]

After the service Mr MacLean complimented me on the discourse. Prof. Cameron also commended it, but his praise hurt me more than flattered. He said I should continue on these lines, keeping my imagination well in check.

1 The Sunday evening in November 1909 referred to on p 11.

[66]

22 NOVEMBER: ST COLUMBA'S HALL, 11 *am*

Preached from 2 Timothy 3:16–17. The attendance was exceedingly poor, only fourteen being present,[1] but somehow I did not feel discouraged. I realised that the work was the Lord's. My discourse was severely practical. I made some remarks at the outset about the young people of the Free Church forgetting for what our church stood and also referred to so many of them from the North deserting us when they come South. Also said I was surprised at the opinions I found sometimes held by Free Church people.

6.30 *pm*. Before a pretty good congregation preached from Isaiah 59:21. In my discourse I had liberty, but it was the last that was the crowning portion. The Bible was closed, the sermon was over, but still I continued and this that came to me then was worth the whole prepared sermon put together. I was never so earnest in pleading with sinners to come to Christ. I felt possessed of some strange awful Spirit; I began to feel my knees to shake under me, my eyes became suffused with tears and I was just on the very brink of breaking down utterly. If I had uttered another sentence I believe I would have crossed the limits of my endurance and wept before the people. Ah, perhaps what my words failed to do my tears might have accomplished and I would be willing even to weep if thereby I might have won some soul to Christ.

Oh that this may be the beginning of better days for me! How happy the Lord has made me! I believe He has called some soul to Himself or He would not have moved me so.

20 NOVEMBER: ST COLUMBA'S HALL, 11 *am*

Preached before congregation of sixteen from 1 Corinthians 14:40. The weather was wild and wet and I felt terribly depressed. Yet I felt as I sat there at the singing that perhaps, after all, such discipline was good for me. Certainly these hall services are a good antidote to pride.

1 Corinthians 14:40. Breaches of this rule: (1) Beginning to pray *after* we have embarked on a project (2) Beginning to work *before* called to it (3) Expecting success *before* making preparation for it (4) Expecting blessing in the House of God although we are not improving our privileges (5) Seeking to be sanctified *before* we are justified (6) Seeking things of this world *before* Christ.

2.30 *pm*. Preached again in the afternoon. I had prepared this sermon

1 This was an English service held in the hall at the same time as the greater part of the congregation (largely Highlanders) were meeting for worship in Gaelic.

for the evening but for some reason or another Mr MacLean transferred our services. I must say I was disappointed. I like the evening service. The attendance of course, as the afternoon usually is, was poor. I preached from John 6:45 with a fair measure of liberty and enjoyment but, ah, today has been a poor, poor day as compared with last Sabbath. If I am not as happy as I was last Sabbath I am a long way humbler. Blessed be the name of the Lord! He sees fit to give the lean day as well as the day of liberty. He does nothing in vain.

27 DECEMBER: ST COLUMBA'S, 6.30 *pm*

Before a fair congregation preached from Ruth 3:1 and had a very disappointing night. I was not at home in my subject, I was too ill prepared. I was glad when I was through. This I think is the most disappointing night ever I have had in St Columba's. Cathie was present.[1] This was the only sermon I felt I could preach, and when it came to the point – I could not even preach it.

3 JANUARY, 1915: GLENURQUHART, 11.30 *am*, GAELIC

The roads being covered with ice the congregation was not very big. Preached from Proverbs 23:26 and felt it most painful; felt like running away altogether. Yet the Lord brought me through and the people professed to be pleased.

1 *pm, English.* This congregation was yet smaller. By this time was beginning to feel the cold so much that I was shivering. Preached from Matthew 5:18.

31 JANUARY: SHISKINE, ARRAN, 11.30 *am*, ENGLISH

Although it was fair at church time, this morning had been exceedingly wet and none save the local people were able to attend. The congregation, I was told, was less than half what it was last Sabbath. It appears that the people are pretty faithful to the means but I am afraid there is a coldness and hardness among them. I preached from John 5:46 with liberty and some measure of enjoyment. While I was preaching I glanced out through the window before me. The sun was shining amid the grasses and somehow it seemed to me that the summer had come, and not only that, but that the old blessed days when Arran was rejoicing under the outpouring of blessing from on High were come again, and oh the warmth that came over me! It was all the experience of an instant. I halted not for a moment in what I was saying nor did I

1 Cathie Matheson, his future wife.

turn my thoughts therefrom, yet I was conscious of feeling that since this had come I had no desire ever to leave them. Alas, alas, it was all the fancy of a moment and Arran and I are dead and cold and lifeless still.

6 *pm*. A very good congregation awaited me in the evening and practically all of young people. Preached from John 5:39 and had liberty and earnestness.

14 MARCH: LOCHGILPHEAD

11 *a.m.*, *Gaelic*. Preached from Ruth 1:21 but am afraid did not get on very well. Latterly almost gave it up in despair. Still the Lord brought me through. These Gaelic services are terrible ordeals to me.

2 *pm*, *English*. Preached from 1 Corinthians 14:12 and had a measure of liberty and enjoyment.

6.30 *pm*. Preached from Philippians 4:5 and had one of the best nights ever I have had. Although I kept command over my voice, in the prayer the tears came and ran down both cheeks: never before in public have they come so unrestrainedly. How full my heart was! Poor people, they listened intensely, eagerly. At such moments as I paused for an instant not a stir could be heard. I know the Holy Spirit was working; I felt it in my own soul. How intently some listened! Dear Lochgilphead! I love this place and its people. Happy are the days I have spent here.

21 MARCH: KILDONAN

Found a wide barn of a church with a congregation of about fifteen. It made me sad. The empty pews spoke to me of other days and I seemed to see them full again – alas, those days are gone! The sight of the tiers of empty seats was sad enough, but the feeling of desolation was yet increased by the broken windows and the crumbling roof. It made me realise very vividly the terrible change which has come over our dear land when I heard that tiny congregation singing in the midst of that waste of pews. Nevertheless I enjoyed the service fairly well and was given good attention. Preached from 1 Corinthians 14:12.

4 APRIL: ST COLUMBA

11 *am*, *Gaelic*. Preached from Jeremiah 50:6. Felt this an awful ordeal as the sermon was entirely new. This was the first attempt to preach in Gaelic without having first given the discourse in English. Owing also to having all the services of the day with the Sabbath School

besides, while also being engaged all week working at top pressure for my exams, I felt very nervous about it. At the outset I was really afraid that I would break down, yet I never found the Gaelic so easy. How marvellously does the Lord sustain me! I have never found Him to fail yet. Blessed be His name for all His goodness to me!

2.30 *pm*, *English*. The congregation was miserably thin. Preached from 1 Peter 3:18 and enjoyed it fairly well. Was vexed to see so many sitting silent at the singing.

6.30 *pm*, *English*. Preached from Philippians 4:5 and had a night full of blessing. After the service that dear man from Leith (MacLeod I think his name is) waited for me, saying that he could not go home until he had seen me and wished the Lord to bless me, and he added, clapping me on the back affectionately – and with that he was gone – 'You're the only man that ever makes me cry in the church'. I only wish some Christless soul would weep because of fear of a lost eternity. This has been a hard day but a day not without blessing. I should be grateful to the Lord.

2 MAY: ABERDEEN

6 *pm*, *English*. At this service the attendance was slightly augmented but some who were present in the morning were absent. Preached my sermon which I have to prepare for licence, 1 Thessalonians 1:5, and got on pretty well with it. Had liberty and earnestness and the attention was markedly better than in the morning. After the service was over Mr MacKay made some complimentary remarks about beginning at the right place and preaching on Effectual Calling. I would, however, that I would hear about some soul being led to Christ. Set forth the present deplorable state of Britain and the responsibility of the church in the matter.

16 MAY: TARBERT, LOCHFYNE

11.30 *am*, *Gaelic*. Preached from Psalm 1:3 and with much more liberty than last Sabbath.

2 *pm*, *English*. Preached from Acts 15:16 and with a good deal of freedom. Acts 15:16
  1 An inquiry into the prevailing desolations
    (*a*) What they are (*b*) Are the ministers responsible? (*c*) Are the people responsible?
  2 An examination of the promise vouchsafed
    (*a*) He will return. (*b*) He will build up again. (*c*) He will set it up.

3 Our duty in respect of it

   (*a*) To hope for it. (*b*) To pray for it. (*c*) To work for it.

6.30 *pm*. Preached from Jeremiah 12:5 and had a night which made my very heart to rejoice. Oh how happy I was! I do not think ever I have felt so uplifted since I came home rejoicing in the gathering night of yon quiet autumn evening when last I preached in Sage's old church. I feel this joy yet.

30 MAY: ABERDEEN

2.30 *pm*, *Gaelic*. To my consternation I found the hall full of soldiers of the Camerons and Seaforths but there was nothing for it but to appear before them and face the ordeal. I explained to them my position and asked for their patience and then I spoke on Psalm 1:3. I am sure they could make little of my Gaelic. I must really set to the language in earnest once my degree is past (DV).

For the benefit of Southern readers, it may perhaps be advisable to explain that in the Highlands the services of the Communion season are continued over five successive days. Thursday is the Fast Day and is observed as a day of humiliation and prayer. Friday is the day for self-examination, and in the forenoon the service is held to which frequent reference is made in the following pages – the Fellowship Meeting. At this service a passage of Scripture is given out, generally by one of the local elders, in the light of which the characteristic marks of the Lord's people are to be traced. This is called 'the Question', and the duty of the senior minister present is to 'open' it, that is, to explain its setting and import. Then the 'men' present are called upon in succession to 'speak to the Question', after which all is summed up by the other minister in his 'closing of the Question'. As the text is not known beforehand, the exercise is a rather severe test, not only of readiness of mind and speech on the part of those who engage in it, but also of their theological knowledge and spiritual experience. Saturday is the day of preparation. Sabbath is the great day when the Lord's Supper is dispensed with a simplicity and solemnity seen nowhere else; while Monday concludes the season as a day of thanksgiving. Such seasons are frequently times of reviving and refreshing, even in these present degenerate days, when the glory has so largely departed.

K.A.M. in a Foreword to
Records of Grace in Sutherland, Donald Munro, 1953

4 Lochgilphead

As the previous pages reveal, Kenneth MacRae, in the course of a number of visits to the Free Church congregation in Lochgilphead, Argyll, had become especially interested in the needs of that vacant charge while the congregation, on their part, had developed an affectionate esteem for his person and ministry. Consequently in July 1915 the Presbytery of Inveraray moderated in a call to him from the Lochgilphead congregation which he gladly recognised as the guidance of God. The call was supported by 289 signatures – 66 members and 223 adherents.[1] Accordingly he was inducted to his first charge on the 28th of that month. A newspaper announcing this news reported:

About five years ago Mr. MacRae turned his thoughts from the Civil Service to the work of the ministry, and when in 1911 he was offered an important post as telegraphist in a foreign country, the higher call urged him to abandon this service, with the result that in April of that year he began his studies for the ministry by correspondence classes with Skerry's College. In September of the same year he had the striking success of a pass in all his preliminary subjects, and a few months later he commenced to study concurrently in Arts and Theology, finishing his double course as M.A., and licentiate of the Church last month. This completion of study in so short a time has not many parallels. In addition to his other gifts, he has poetic talent of no mean order. He is a most popular preacher, who brings the resources of a sanctified imagination to the service of the Gospel. He is well-equipped religiously and educationally to carry on the splendid tradition of the Lochgilphead pulpit for evangelical preaching.

For his first year in Lochgilphead MacRae was dependent upon a housekeeper for the running of the Manse but in August 1916 his bride, Catherine Matheson, joined him and there began nearly 48 years of a very happy married life. Cathie Matheson, born on 3 October, 1893, was the daughter of Mr and Mrs Robert F. Matheson of Kirkton, Dunvegan, Skye. Although it anticipates to some degree the Diary's chronological account, her narrative of their courtship and of her coming

---

1 There is a tendency in Scotland when a call is given to a new minister for a number who have only the loosest connection with a congregation to rank temporarily as adherents. This seems to have been the case in the present instance. In 1900 the congregation had gone with the majority into the Union but at a crucial meeting of members and adherents on December 16, 1904, while 74 supported a motion for adhering to the Union, 122 voted for an amendment committing them to the Free Church.

to Lochgilphead, is most appropriately introduced at the beginning of this chapter:

'In 1912 the time came for me to leave home in Skye to pursue studies, and my preference was towards Glasgow where we had several friends, but my mother, who herself had studied in Edinburgh for the teaching profession, wished me to go there. So to the Capital city I went about the age of 19, always trusting to the wisdom of my dear mother's advice. I stayed in a Y.W.C.A. Hostel where I met several fine young women students who were my good friends for many years afterwards. With one of them one evening I attended a social meeting of the Ross and Cromarty association and enjoyed making the acquaintance of a few people from the Highlands, among whom were Mrs MacRae, her two daughters, Vic and Ida, and her youngest son, George. They very kindly invited me to their home where I subsequently found a warm welcome. I loved to listen to their many interesting tales of the Black Isle where all the family used to spend their summer holidays with relatives. From time to time I would visit them, or Vic and Ida would call to take me out, and a strong friendship was formed between us. Later on I met their older brother, Kenneth, who used to be either steeped in his studies or away from home so that I seldom saw him.'

Catherine Matheson's first memory of seeing her future husband was in the congregation of St Columba's where a friend had taken her to hear a visiting Free Church minister from Dingwall. During the service she was conscious of the strong singing voice of a man sitting at the end of a pew and enquiring afterwards from her friend who he was she learned it was Kenneth MacRae, sitting beside his brother George. In this congregation Cathie in due course first professed her faith in Christ. Her spiritual experience had been a gradual one. She had first known a deep concern about the age of 12 when the learning of Isaiah 53 had been part of her lessons at school.

Mrs MacRae's narrative continues:

'In Edinburgh I was studying for Civil Service Examinations and after sitting my finals I returned to my home in Dunvegan to await results. The good news that I had passed was followed by a posting to a Government Office in London. Once there I grew to like that great city until the outbreak of war in 1914 changed conditions in the South and my parents urged me to return North. Ken and I had already become interested in one another and our friendship now developed into mutual affection, which led us both to consider matters prayerfully. According to God's plan I became his wife, our marriage taking place in Kyle of

Lochalsh on 15 August, 1916. Ours was a quiet wedding owing to the clouds of war. The Rev. Donald Smith of Kiltearn, who was a fellow-student of my husband's was best man, and my sister, Meta, was bridesmaid. My father and mother were able to be present. George, Ken's brother, a Lieutenant in the Seaforth Highlanders, and my only brother John, a Lieutenant in the Cameron Highlanders, could not be with us, but both sisters of my husband attended. Jim MacIver to whom there is reference made in my husband's early diaries, was one of the company on that happy day.

'We spent two days in Edinburgh with my parents-in-law before proceeding to Lochgilphead by train through Glasgow to Wemyss Bay and from there by steamer to Ardrishaig. I shall never forget the beauty of that first voyage to our first home.

'Lochgilphead is a neat little town nestling by the shores of Loch Gilp, an arm of Loch Fyne, amidst beautiful scenery. The fishing industry was well established there at one time, but by 1916 very few boats were to be seen and herring fishing was almost at an end there, although in other Loch Fyne parts it still goes on. The Free Church of Lochgilphead stands on the corner of Lochnell Street and Manse Brae. Shortly before my husband's settlement the inside of the Church was skilfully re-planned and beautifully remodelled by Mr Ronald Carswell, architect son of a highly respected elder who died previous to the new minister's settlement.

'In the congregation my husband had the support of praying men and praying women. There were sixteen men upon whom he could call upon to engage in prayer in public – fine, humble, earnest, intelligent, spiritually-minded men, discerning in the Scriptures. There was a Gaelic and an English prayer meeting on alternate Wednesdays. The English meeting attendance increased greatly; young people came, many being lastingly impressed. Usually there was a short exposition given in English from one of the Epistles, and from the Psalms in Gaelic. There were three services each Sabbath in Lochgilphead congregation – Gaelic at 11 am: English at 2 pm and 6.30 pm. To this (owing to scarcity of public supply during war years, and until his departure) my husband added an afternoon service in Tayvallich, North Knapdale (12 miles distant) and in Kilmartin (8 miles distant) on alternate Sabbaths, having been fortunate enough to secure a hired car for this purpose. Cars were few in those days. These services were greatly appreciated. In the Lochgilphead congregation the singing of Psalms in English was the heartiest we had ever heard. Everyone sang, from the young children upwards, and no wonder! With such a leader of the Sanctuary's praise as worthy Alexander MacColl (one of the elders), who himself sang lustily with appropriate feeling and splendid time, the congregation sang in harmony. There certainly was life there! The minister enjoyed lively singing and always joined in heartily.

'Lochgilphead Manse was one of the old type, a square double house consisting of ten spacious rooms besides kitchen premises – a large house to keep, but pleasantly situated on Manse Brae. To the front were two public rooms which had fine oriel windows commanding an extensive and lovely view of the town below, with the Crinan Canal in the background cut against the wooded grounds of Achandarrach House with more distant rising slopes of fertile farmland surrounding the whole. On each side of the Manse front gate there was a lilac bush prolific in summer with sweet-scented blossom.

'As I have already mentioned, during the years of World War I the travel route to Lochgilphead from Glasgow was by train to Wemyss Bay and from there by steamer through some of Scotland's most superb and varied scenery – sailing down the Clyde, passing through Rothesay Bay, and on to the narrow Kyles of Bute, calling at various ports en route. After entering Loch Fyne, which washes the shores of Argyll, the steamer makes its way to Tarbert and from there sails on to Ardrishaig which is the port of call for Lochgilphead, two miles distant by road.

'In more recent times (since World War II) the main route to Lochgilphead has been by road. Buses run from Glasgow through to Lochgilphead and on to Tarbert, Clachan, and further on south to Campbeltown in Kintyre. This route is said to be one of the finest, even in Scotland, for magnificent and varied scenery. It skirts scenic lochs, thickly-wooded slopes and glens, stretches of green pasture lands, and the rising slopes of great mountains, until it approaches Inveraray, where the road winds by the shores of Loch Fyne and leads on past many noted beauty spots to the shore of Lochgilp.'

☐   ☐   ☐

I AUGUST, 1915: LOCHGILPHEAD

6.30–8 *pm*. This my first sermon as settled minister caused me no little anxiety. The church was simply packed (except the gallery which was not open). The first singing almost moved me to tears, there was so much meaning in the Psalm (27:7–11), and the voice of my people

[76]

affected me. Preached from 1 John 3:4. Had not much liberty save towards the end. The evening was cloudy and I could scarcely see my notes, so this in itself hindered me. Was afraid also that I was offending some. Nevertheless my gospel appeals were very sweet to my soul and I am thankful to the Lord for that. I finished with a feeling that I had set the people against me. I was relieved therefore to find how hearty were the handshakes of the men, and especially that Mr Cameron who was in the pulpit with me was highly pleased.

8 AUGUST, GAELIC 11 *am*

Was surprised and somewhat agitated to see so many present at the Gaelic service. I am sure there would be about sixty present. Preached from Psalm 1:1 and I do not think that ever I had so much liberty in the Gaelic. I even enjoyed it instead of its being the nightmare it usually is to me. Before the service I was in a way despairing of ever being able to make much of the Gaelic and half wishing that I could give it up, but if the Lord will continue so to deal with me as He has since I came here it will soon lose its terrors for me. How good He is to me!

6.30 *pm*. The evening turning out somewhat wet I by no means expected such a congregation. Preached from Revelation 3:20 and oh what an evening of blessing I had. Sometimes when I stopped for a moment I could not but notice the tense stillness. How they listened! Oh that some may have been led to choose Christ as their portion! My poor people, how my heart yearns after them![1]

29 AUGUST

What is lying sore upon my spirit today is the desire for fruit. I feel I have poured out my very soul to my people and yet it all seems in vain. What more can I do? What more can I say? Will I not get one soul?

8 SEPTEMBER: ENGLISH PRAYER MEETING

Spoke from Romans 1:7-15 and enjoyed it very much. The attendance, however, was down to thirty-six. Mr MacColl and Mr MacLean prayed, both very earnestly, the former in particular. I like the tone of his prayers; there is unction in them. He made me catch my breath at one expression when he said it was time the Almighty was beginning to

---

1 It should be borne in mind here and in the following pages that as these entries are only selections from the writer's original diaries there were generally more services on a Sunday and during a communion season than are recorded here. Throughout the Lochgilphead years there were afternoon and evening services in English.

work, for His name was beginning to be held in disdain. Then he strikingly referred to our own unbelief hindering the blessing. I don't think a North country man would have used such an expression even though it is scriptural.

12 SEPTEMBER: EVENING

There was a very fine attendance. Preached from Psalm 1:6, 'The way of the ungodly shall perish'. I had wonderful power and I have hope that the Holy Spirit was at work among my people. I never saw a congregation so gravely leaving the church. No one spoke, I saw no smile on any face.

5 OCTOBER: CAIRNBAAN

Spoke from John 3:2–3, continuing from the last evening. The meeting was held in Mrs MacLachlan's house which was packed, twenty-eight being present. It was very encouraging. A Miss Gilchrist asked that the next meeting should be in her house for the sake of her old mother. This means a move into an established house.[1]

2 NOVEMBER: CAIRNBAAN

Spoke from John 3:4–5 and enjoyed the meeting very much. There would be about twenty-five present. The meeting was held in the house of the Gilchrists. Was very much interested to learn that old Mrs Gilchrist, ninety-three years of age, had heard Dr MacDonald of Ferintosh[2] preach at Lochgilphead.

5 DECEMBER: GAELIC

On account of the snow the attendance only reached forty-four. Preached from Psalm 67:20.

Afternoon. Preached from 1 John 5:18. Was disappointed on the whole. Had not much liberty, and vexed at my lack of life. Yet the Word is the Lord's and I must not complain if He does not acknowledge it. If it be to His glory that I labour fruitlessly here so be it, I must not complain, but oh that He would honour His own great name in our midst some way or another, for I long for times of quickening. I feel it to be my life.

1 *ie* a house belonging to members of the Church of Scotland.
2 John MacDonald was minister at Ferintosh from 1813 until his death in 1849. His life, entitled *The Apostle of the North*, was written by Dr John Kennedy in 1866.

Evening. The attendance, considering the evening, was wonderfully good. Preached from John 3:3. Some nights, despite an evening of great power, I would be terribly downcast feeling that all was in vain. Tonight I do not feel so, for I seem to realise more that the power is in the hand of Another and if it seems good to Him He will work. Thus I know not what will come out of today's services and consequently I have hope.

12 DECEMBER: EVENING

Before the sermon, was feeling very far down; felt that it was all useless, that the Spirit was away and that I would never see any fruit for my labours – and oh the weariness of that feeling! But may the Lord be praised, He lifted me from that.

1 JANUARY, 1916

11 *am, New Year's Service.* Was quite pleased at the attendance. For some unaccountable reason I was strangely moved at the singing of the first psalm (Psalm 76, 1–7). In the prayer the tears rolled down my cheeks but I kept control of my voice. Preached from Luke 15:18 and enjoyed it. I was glad to see so many of the young people present.

2 JANUARY

Afternoon. This being the day set aside for national prayer my discourse bore upon national sin and the need for national repentance. Conjoined with these points I treated upon our need as individuals and as a congregation for the same.

9 JANUARY

I am tired of preaching, preaching, and all to no purpose. All my efforts in this direction seem to be like trying to dig a hole in a bog.

SATURDAY, 5 FEBRUARY

Blessings Received[1]: (1) Improved health (2) Undisturbed day with power to concentrate (3) Guidance and light in skeletonising next week's sermons, especially Matthew 12:34 (4) Consciousness of His favour.

1 During this period in 1916 it was his practice to note each day, 'Blessings Received'.

SABBATH, 6 FEBRUARY

A good Sabbath, especially in the evening.

Rays of Light: The Lord has some whom He sends forth, not to win souls, but to prepare a people for Him when He comes in the power of His Holy Spirit, perhaps through some other instrument, Luke 1:17. In my preaching have not emphasised the doctrine of repentance sufficiently.

SABBATH, 20 FEBRUARY

Evening. Was more uneasy at the outset of this service than before a Gaelic service. It was a children's service and I was altogether uncertain how I would get on. I feared lest I should talk above them, I feared that I would tire them, I feared a thousand things, but the Lord unto whom I had committed all things took me through and gave me a night, perhaps not of power, but of exceeding sweetness and tenderness. As it was a children's service they were all gathered at the front, but I never saw such a gathering since my first evening here. There were some earnest little faces looking at me, particularly the Fergusons, especially the elder, Mairi MacGregor and the dark MacColl girl. Oh Lord, I thank Thee for such a night. Oh that there may be fruit! Blessed Lord, Thou hast filled my cup with gladness!

SABBATH, 27 FEBRUARY

Blessings Received: Taken through sermons and given a night of great blessing. Have sense of His favour and presence.

MONDAY, 28 FEBRUARY

Blessings Received: Able to cycle to Tarbert and back despite faulty chain. Palpitation removed on my crying to the Lord. My prayers were sweet to me and easy in my visiting. Protection from prevailing influence.

THURSDAY, 9 MARCH

Blessings: Told about keeping prayer meetings too long.
Sins: Irreverence – wandering mind while others praying.

SABBATH, 12 MARCH

Met Miss Beaton from Gairloch and had a profitable hour with her, including worship. Stirred me up in respect of my unfaithfulness, especially regarding my failure to urge them to have family worship here.

[80]

FRIDAY, 17 MARCH

Blessings: Enabled to finish sermon on Revelation 22:17.
Sins: Said nothing to Mrs Bruce about her soul.

SABBATH, 16 APRIL

Evening. Considering the steady downpour the attendance was very
good. Preached from Mark 8:36 and had a pretty good evening of it.
Certainly in this sermon I have cast more upon Him than ever before,
simply trying to show the sinner how helpless he is unless the Lord has
mercy upon him. May He bless and acknowledge His Word! Satan may
tell me that the Lord is so grieved by me that at last He is beginning to
withdraw such preaching gifts as I possess, but I'll not give heed to him.

SATURDAY, 29 APRIL

Very much of the Lord's presence all day.

SABBATH, 30 APRIL

Evening. Preached from Ephesians 5:6 to an excellent congregation.
I had been afraid that I was going to have a miserable evening, for it is
long since I have had such a poor sermon, but the Lord shows me that
the blessing does not depend upon my sermon but upon His power. Oh
what a glorious night I have had! What joy, what delight, what
glimpses of the beauty of my Redeemer! I got very great liberty in the
prayer, and then, how the dry sermon was transformed for me! The
insipid parts became quite fragrant and as for the portions better
favoured, they became wells of water brimming over. But above and
beyond everything in sweetness was the offering of Christ to the sinner.
It was then I saw something of His glory. Oh I pray that this blessed
and comforting frame of spirit may not depart from me, for in it is
power – and oh how I thirst for the salvation of my poor people!

TUESDAY, 9 MAY

Blessings: Nice weather for George's coming. Opportunity for preparation of Gaelic sermon.
Sins: Hardness of heart.

WEDNESDAY, 10 MAY

Cycled over and stayed with Mrs MacTaggart, the Manse. George came with me to within three miles of destination and we parted on shores of Loch Sween.[1]

Sense of the Lord's favour in the evening when in the beauty of the fading day by the sea shore.

11 MAY: TAYVALLICH [FAST DAY]

Gaelic 12 noon. Preached from Psalm 13:1 with unwonted liberty. I was very much afraid of this service because I was responsible for everything and because I have come very low in my experience.

5 pm, English. There was again a fairly good attendance in the evening when I preached from Luke 19:41. I had liberty but it was that awful mechanical, icy liberty which distresses me more even than stammering lips. Again they listened very well but who can expect any blessing to attend what came from a heart hard as rock and cold as death. I have marred and ruined this whole day, whereas I should have come here with a longing after souls, since never before have I been privileged to preach the Gospel in this place. I feel in despair. What a terrible downcome this is after the glorious and exhilarating experiences which but lately were mine! The singing was miserable, the time being lamentable.

SABBATH, 14 MAY: LOCHGILPHEAD

Afternoon. Preached from Psalm 66:16. I had no liberty whatsoever and frequently I felt as if I could sit down in despair. I cannot understand it. At Tarbert and Tayvallich while my heart was hard and puffed up I was given great liberty, yet this mechanical liberty so grated upon me that I was conscious of a desire that the Lord would take that mechanical freedom away. He has done so and my heart is certainly not so hard, but now I feel that unless I am to get some power I would rather not be preaching at all – and if I can't get to preach I don't want to live.

Evening. I got more liberty in the prayer this evening which in itself was a good token. Then just before beginning the sermon the closing notes of the psalm came with great comfort to my soul. It was as if it were no longer the congregation who were singing it but angels, and it thus came upon me as a great promise:

> Thou shalt Jerus'lem's good behold
> Whilst thou on earth dost dwell;

1 This was to be his last meeting with his brother George to whom he was so attached.

Thou shalt thy children's children see
And peace on Israel.

It was sweet. Oh that I might see that peace on Israel! When I had
finished the sermon I could raise my heart with a song of thanksgiving
to the Lord who had dealt so bountifully with me. I leave it with Him
to give fruit unto the harvest.

Communion in Arran, June 1st-5th[1]

Arran has seen great days in the past but like many another place is
seeing changed days in the present. One of its own native preachers
described the influx of summer visitors as a plague and the truth of that
remark cannot be questioned when one looks at the religious life as it
now is in the eastern and more fashionable part of the island; but yet it
appeared to me that something of the old spirit lived yet in the secluded
south-western extremity. At least that was the feeling which came over
me as for the first time I stood in the pulpit of Sliddery; somehow the
old days, the great days, were called back irresistibly to my mind.

There had been one or two signs prior to my visit that the Lord had
not entirely veiled His favour from Arran. A Shiskine lad had come
home from the battlefront and it was current that a 'change' had come
over him. Besides this, at the Shiskine Communion in May of the
present year, a woman had broken down on the Saturday under the
ministrations of the Rev. John MacLeod of Inverness.

Mr MacEwan, the minister of Southend, had long been exercised
about his lack of fruit. So much did this weigh upon him that he
announced to his office-bearers his intention of throwing up his charge,
that the Lord might send some other whom He would acknowledge, but
of course his devoted staff would not hear of it.

In announcing the approach of the yearly communion to his people
Mr MacEwan pleaded with them that they would entreat the Lord that
He would send them a messenger who would be blessed unto them in
causing an awakening in their midst. At that time, of course, he did not
know who was to come to his communion, but shortly after, he wrote
me. Since the request was from a Lochgilphead man, and from one for
whom I had a great respect even the very first time I saw him, I was
only too pleased to meet him in his desire.

---

1 This account of his visit to Arran was written subsequent to his diary entries
for the same days and in a separate note-book. The spiritual condition of
Arran was transformed by remarkable revivals in 1804–5 and, more especially
in 1812–13.

I came home from the Assembly[1] in a particularly barren state of soul and had a miserable Sabbath in my own pulpit. On the Tuesday I set out for Arran and reached my destination in the early afternoon of the following day; but that day had not gone out without a decided improvement in my spiritual condition. One could not help feeling strengthened in the company of such an earnest-minded, sincere, simple Christian as Mr MacEwan. How I envied him his sincerity and his deep spirituality!

On the Thursday morning we set out for the church which was about a mile away and situated on a high plateau on the other side of Sliddery Water. The night and morning had been stormy and wet. It was fair when we left the house but we had just climbed the brae at the other side of the burn when the rain came on in torrents. I felt my heart sore for the poor people, not a few of whom were out without coats or umbrellas. The church I found to be a nice well-furnished little building and very easy to speak in. Considering the day, and considering the fact that Southend has not the status of an ordinary congregation, I was not prepared to see so many present. I preached from Proverbs 20-4, 'The sluggard will not plough by reason of the cold, therefore shall he beg in harvest and have nothing.' I enjoyed the service pretty well. I felt the place warm – spiritually warm – and that made all the difference for me.

At the close of the service Mr MacEwan made an earnest appeal that any who had already engaged in the ploughing spoken of, but yet had not found their way to the Lord's Table, should now come forward and interview the Session at the close of the service or at the close of the service on Saturday.[2] While speaking, the good old man became so overcome with his emotion that he could no longer control his voice and was constrained to stop for a few moments. This was the first evidence I had of anything of unusual life in the place. Yet despite his emotion and his earnestness no one came forward.

We were staying in a good home. There were but the three of them – Mrs MacAlister, her son John, and Bessie MacKelvie, a local girl who was serving with them. There was also another son away in Ecclefechan and one who had been with them on the farm had died only six months before, a pious lad and one whose loss was deeply felt. The next morning

1 *ie* the General Assembly of the Free Church of Scotland which meets annually in May.
2 None can come to the Lord's Table for the first time in the Free Church without first being examined by the minister and elders of a congregation. At every communion season the Session meets for this purpose after the preparatory services.

[84]

I was wakened from sleep by the sweet strains of one of the songs of Zion. I was bewildered. I looked at my watch; it was only half past seven. For a moment I felt angry with myself at having slept in, yet I had been told that the breakfast would not be till nine o'clock. Then I felt vexed – to think that I should be lying in bed in sloth and the others up worshipping the Lord. I wished I was with them. Last of all I lay quietly and listened, and I shall never forget what I heard. I shall never hear that melody without that little bedroom rising up before the eyes of my memory, I lying in bed and the sweet notes rising and falling down below. After that I heard reading and then the voice of prayer. After that, again I fear I fell asleep.

At breakfast Mr MacEwan gave me the explanation. The preceding day being the Fast Day there was no work done on the farm and the family had just come in to worship with us but on other mornings, since they required to begin work early, they had worship by themselves, John reading and the mother praying.

In the forenoon, the weather having improved somewhat, Mr MacEwan proposed that we should go and call on one of his elders who lived at Torrylinn about two and a half miles away, and who was pretty well disabled with a swollen knee. Nothing loth I at once fell in with the proposal and in due course we reached the farm. Mr MacKinnon was a tall elderly man yet quite erect, and it was not hard to see that the account I afterwards heard of him as being one of the strongest men in the district in his day had even yet its witness in his appearance. Mrs MacKinnon was a kindly body with a pleasant way and a hearty welcome. We had not been long in the house when Mrs MacKinnon rose and called in her two daughters. The younger of the two, Jessie, was an exceptionally tall, strapping girl, one who would not be passed without notice. Her sister Katie was of ordinary size. They were both striking girls, strong, hardy and intelligent, and as they sat there just as they had been called in from their work, I could not but contrast them with the poor, weakly, dressed-up things I am so accustomed to see nowadays.

I did take notice of them – I couldn't help it – but I certainly would have taken more notice had I known then what Mr MacEwan told me after we got outside. Two years before, Katie had been awakened under the preaching of Mr MacLeod (Inverness), yet she never had made any profession, and in that some of the Lord's people were a little disappointed. Certainly Mr MacEwan was, and it was for her more than for anyone else that he had been looking to come forward at this time.

[85]

That she had not gone wholly back was evident from the fact that, a fortnight before, she had travelled to Shiskine to be present at the Communion that she might hear Mr MacLeod again.

But I have omitted to mention the service of the previous evening. Then my subject was more topical, being founded upon Genesis 10:20–21 and entitled 'the Cry of Sodom'. The day having continued unfavourable the congregation was a little smaller. Nevertheless I did not enjoy the service any the less but felt even more warmth than in the morning. Towards the end of the service, a woman in the front seat, a member and a good woman, burst out crying so unrestrainedly that her sobs were audible even to myself. This was the second evidence of life.

All Friday afternoon I was busy working out the text which had come to me the previous day, 'The hearing ear and the seeing eye, the Lord hath made even both of them' (Proverbs 20:12), and in the evening I preached from it. This was still sweeter than anything that had gone before. I enjoyed it immensely and was given an earnestness which is not often mine.

Next forenoon (Saturday) I preached another topical discourse on 'the Dew that descends upon Mount Zion' (Psalm 133:3). This was a theme I had worked out in my own mind one dark evening, coming home from the Cairnbaan meeting some time before, yet I never had had time to shape it and preach it until now. I do not know when I enjoyed anything so well. Tears were frequent. The two poor old women in the front seat were weeping. Jessie MacKinnon was with her mother and sister near the front. If ever I saw distress I saw it in that poor girl's face.

At the end Mr MacEwan again gave an invitation to those who wished to partake of the Lord's Supper for the first time. After the benediction the adherents left the church, the members remaining for their tokens.[1] To my amazement, as the people were moving out, who stepped up on to the platform and crossed to the vestry door but Jessie MacKinnon. The tokens were all given out and the members departed.

'There's one in the vestry', said old Mr MacAllister the elder, and there was a strange gentleness in his voice and a softness in his eyes. I could have shouted for very joy, but I lost that when I saw the poor girl in the vestry. She was weeping and yet she was calm. I could see that her soul was face to face with eternal realities; nothing else mattered to

1 A voucher made of lead inscribed with the name of the church and admitting a qualified communicant to the partaking of the Lord's Supper.

LOCHGILPHEAD | AGED 32

her. Mr MacEwan was weeping too, but he gently led her to a chair and sat down beside her.

'Tell me Jessie', he said, 'What has led you to this?'

Her answer came low, clear, terribly in earnest, half like a sigh or a gentle wail, yet without a sob, 'To be saved from my sins'.

The scene will ever linger in my memory. The weeping girl, the old man struggling with his emotions and striving in vain to control his voice seated beside her, and the old elder at the other end of the table with a great tenderness upon his face.

Mr MacEwan strove to direct her to the One who alone can save, and explained that neither he nor admission to the church could do anything for her salvation. Then he asked if I had anything to say. I simply told her to look to Christ for everything, and her trust would not be brought to shame, to look to Him – in obedience to His word – to save her soul.

'And have you anything to say to her, Mr MacAlister?' asked Mr MacEwan.

For answer the old elder began one of his innumerable anecdotes concerning the rich days in Arran. There was one, he said, who came before the session and the answer he gave as to why he sought admission to the Lord's Table was that he had met his Redeemer as he was driving the cow into the byre on the previous day. Jessie was admitted a member of Christ's visible church and then, still weeping, she took her departure. Perhaps the most touching scene took place after that, as poor old Mr MacEwan tried to express his gratitude to the Lord for all that He had done. It was so wonderful; he had hoped for Katie, but he had no thought whatsoever of Jessie, and the poor old man broke down altogether. It was a moment of great stress. I could neither restrain my tears nor my smiles of joy and was constrained to cover my face with my hands. Thus we were, till Mr MacAlister broke the silence by beginning again one of his stories, to which for once I did not listen.

That evening I stood at the door gazing out upon the vast expanse of water before me. It was a lonely scene but one which appealed to me. The sea is always lonely but I think that that loneliness is enhanced if away on the horizon there be some dim, stretching ridge of land. That was present in the scene before me, for across the waters to the west lay the dark hills of Kintyre and the rocky island of Sanda, while far, far away and vague in the distance I could just discern the Irish coast. It was the Firth of Clyde but it was deserted; nothing was to be seen out upon the waters save the towering bulk of Ailsa Craig. The clouds were heavy but the prospect certainly appeared better than it had been all day, only there was an ominous shifting of the wind to the South-West which did not augur well for the morrow.

I was thus standing surveying the prospect when Mrs MacAlister joined me. She was a soft, gentle woman whose very look was love; one of the Lord's poor ones whom suffering has made meek. She spoke of the evening and the weather prospects for the morrow. She spoke of the dews of Zion and how she had enjoyed the morning's discourse. Still the quiet voice went on beside me, and then it was the old days in Arran that were uppermost, until soon the tears were welling up in my eyes and flowing from hers. Last of all she began talking of her son John and what a comfort he had been to her since his brother died. He seemed to have changed and it made her heart glad. That morning he had broken down. On his return from church he began telling Bessie MacKelvie about Jessie MacKinnon going forward, but it proved too much for him and he could not continue.

John was an exceedingly shy lad yet he had stepped forward and offered his services as precentor when the ordinary precentor had been called away for service in the army. Mr MacEwan called him in for a little, and we had a talk dealing more or less with spiritual things, but John was very quiet; he was not to be drawn.

The next day was Sabbath and a wild morning it was. Yet it cleared off a little before church time and we got over dry. My usual complaint is that I cannot preach Action sermons but I got ample liberty on this occasion when I based my discourse on Matthew 27:46, 'My God, my God, why hast thou forsaken me?' Despite the unfavourable weather conditions the attendance was very good and I was afforded a most attentive hearing. Yet there were two young girls who vexed me with their inattention and restlessness.

To me the serving of the Tables was the sweetest of the lot. Jessie was weeping, Mr MacEwan was weeping, one poor woman made no secret of her tears; I could see them streaming down her cheeks and her black bodice shining wet with them. There was also weeping throughout the church, Katie MacKinnon and a married sister, I afterwards heard, quite breaking down. The Lord was very near to me and oh how precious it all was! I do not think that ever I came nearer to being carried away altogether while speaking publicly. It took me all my fortitude to control my voice.

After I had served the English Table, Mr MacEwan took the Gaelic Table and afterwards addressed a short exhortation to the people.

Being in Gaelic, it was not so clear to me as it would have been had it been in English, but I could not help admiring the fine spirituality of the man.

The evening service soon came round, for owing to the prolonged service of the earlier part of the day the interval was short. I felt perhaps more of the Lord's presence than ever I have felt when going to a service. I preached that evening from 'This is the will of him that sent me, that every one which seeth the Son, and believeth on him, may have everlasting life; and I will raise him up at the last day' (John 6:40). From the very outset I felt a power and solemnity descend upon me which made me seem to lose sight of self, and all I knew was that I was preaching Christ to sinners. Almost at the very outset, poor Jessie MacKinnon bent her head and leaned forward upon the pew before her, and it was not long till Katie joined her and thus they remained throughout the whole evening. And they were not the only ones. Throughout the church here and there, there were bent and averted heads, and a stillness and solemnity prevailed, the like of which I have never before experienced. Awe seemed to be written upon many of the faces which were turned towards me. As for myself, I was conscious that some mysterious Power was constraining me to preach as I never had preached before.

We concluded by singing the closing verses of the second psalm. In reading out the verses to be sung, something constrained me to repeat twice over the lines:

'Kiss ye the Son, lest in His wrath
Ye perish from the way',

and that of itself seemed to increase the solemnity prevailing.

John MacAllister in the precentor's desk below the pulpit was hidden from me, but he arose and began the psalm. He had not completed the first line, however, when he ceased singing. Under the impression that his throat had failed him I sang as loudly as I could, and at the same time I heard the powerful voice of Sandy Robertson, the Shiskine precentor, come in to keep the singing going. But I was soon conscious that there was something more wrong than I had expected, for John was not singing at all, and Sandy Robertson from his seat had to take his place in leading the congregation. The perception of this almost overcame me and for the second time that day I almost broke down completely. But I would have been worse still had I been able to see what the congregation saw. The poor lad, after he had uttered the first few notes, broke down completely. He did not sit down. He simply stood there before the congregation trying in vain to sing. That sight, of itself, the precentor standing up thus weeping before the people, should have gone home to many hearts and I have not the slightest doubt but that it did. Were it not for Sandy Robertson the singing would have failed altogether, and even as it was it almost did for he too was so overcome that he came near to breaking point.

Of course, all this was hidden from me but when, upon the departure of the people, I left the pulpit, Mr MacEwan was waiting upon the platform. He did not say a word, his eyes were brimming with tears; he simply motioned me to look to the precentor's box. To my mingled amazement and joy I saw there poor John sobbing like a child. I threw my arm round him and tried to comfort him, but it was long before he could check his emotion.

Mr MacEwan sent the two of us on together on our homeward way, he bringing up the rear with Mr MacAllister. I thus had the opportunity of talking freely to poor John. I tried to show him that there was nothing for him but to leave everything with Jesus, and to trust to Him and to Him alone to save him. He told me that he had been in exercise ever since the death of his brother.

As we ascended the brae we met Peter MacKelvie, Bessie's brother, on his way home after saying good-bye to his sister, for on the morrow he departed for France. He was in the Royal Engineers and was home for a week's furlough. As he came nearer I saw that he was unwontedly moved. He shook hands with me and wished good-bye, but I shall never forget the earnest look in his eyes and the evident sincerity in his voice as he twice repeated: 'I'll never forget the sermons I heard from you when I am out yonder' (i.e. in France).

The family worship was very solemn and filled with a strange unction. Oh what glorious days were these! We seemed to be away from everything except the things of the soul, and the Lord was very evident in our midst. Could those days have continued it would have been heaven upon the earth. We read verse about, but we were not half way through the chapter when John broke down again and Mr MacEwan considerately finished the reading himself.

I did not sleep much that night. I was too happy; too roused, but I had no wish for morning, for morning would witness my departure from a place which had become sweeter to me than any place on earth. Still, time will not tarry and the morning came. I would have given anything to stay for the Thanksgiving service, but I had to be at

Minard on the following evening for the moderation in of a call to the Rev. John MacLeod, and that meant departure that very morning.

Worship was again very solemn and when we rose from our knees everyone in the room was in tears. Shortly after this old Mr MacAlister came up to pay my expenses. I had purposely avoided expense by taking my bicycle with me, for the congregation was not a fully-equipped one. I thus was due only seven shillings, but nothing would satisfy them but that I would accept two pounds. Eventually, sorely against my will, I was obliged to give way to their wishes. Yet their kindness touched me. We enjoyed a little conversation together and Mr MacAllister gave me something else to cheer me, and that was that he was of opinion that his own son Charles had become impressed.

Then there came a heavy knock to the door. It was the driver of the motor car which the people had sent to take me up to Pirnmill, cycle and all. The parting came terribly suddenly. It was cruelly abrupt, but what amazed me was the feeling the people displayed. Both Mrs MacAlister and Bessie were in tears and as for John, he was sobbing helplessly again.

I went away with a strange mixture of sadness and gladness in my breast. To be leaving the place was tearing my heart strings, yet I could not help feeling a great gratitude to the Lord for His goodness to me during those few never-to-be-forgotten days in Sliddery. Soon I was out upon Kilbrandon Sound and it was not long before I had landed at Carradale upon the Kintyre shore and was cycling laboriously up against the wind on my way homewards. For the first fifteen or sixteen miles my way led along the shore and somehow I did not feel so downcast as long as I had the big Arran hills on the other side of the water from me, but when once I had climbed the long ascent above Claonaig, and the hills of Jura opened up before me, I felt a great loneliness enter my soul as I cast behind me a last look at the land I had come to love. But the brae was sloping before me. I free-wheeled down it and I saw the Arran hills no more.

Thus ended the most blessed time I have ever had in my life. I got a taste then from the Lord that was worth waiting for for a hundred years, yet after it I can never rest content until I get another such. It has come not only as a blessing to me but as a lesson. I had been inclined to think that the Lord was so grieved away by the sins of the people that He had ceased to evidence Gospel power in any marked degree, but this came to show me that He is as willing and as able to save as ever He was, and that those who pray for it will get the blessing. This is its great lesson to me – the power of prayer. I believe that if the people of my own congregation would stir themselves up to plead for a blessing, as did the people of Sliddery, they would get it too. Blessed be His name for giving such a wretched sinner such a sight of His power.

□   □   □

WEDNESDAY, 28 JUNE: DUNVEGAN, ISLE OF SKYE

In meeting had Cathie's Testament and found the words of Psalm 25:17 underlined [in the Psalter]. They came with such power to my soul that I was constrained to praise the Lord for it. In the evening, on passing through the kitchen after the others had retired, found Mr Matheson[1] upon his knees. These two things sent me to bed with a full heart.

SATURDAY, I JULY: DUNVEGAN

Spent the forenoon among the woods preparing for the morrow.

SABBATH, 2 JULY

Preached at Lonmore from Psalm 133:3. Congregation appeared somewhat listless.

MONDAY, 3 JULY

With Mr Matheson visited Dunvegan Castle. Most interesting. Saw dungeon in which the 19th MacLeod starved his wife, and the banqueting hall where fifteen of the Clan Campbell were slain. Saw the Fairy Flag, the Fairy Tower, and the Fairy Room in which Dr Johnson slept – also Prince Charles' waistcoat, Rory Mor's sword[2] and many other interesting relics and curios. Taken up to the Tower, from which a superb view was obtained.

At 5.30 motored over with Cathie and her mother to Portree. Lovely evening and most enjoyable run. Shall never forget it.

SABBATH, 9 JULY: LOCHGILPHEAD

Greatly enjoyed the singing which sounded very refreshing to me after the poor singing of the last two Sabbaths. Also felt warmer in my own congregation than in any I have visited since I left Arran. The Lord has been wonderfully good to me in everything today, but oh, I wish I had more life.

1 His future father-in-law.
2 Rory Mor's two-handed sword, said to have been captured from the Saracens during the Crusades.

TUESDAY, 11 JULY

Wrote Mr Munro asking him to marry us. Wrote Dolly[1] asking him to be my best man, failing George. Also wrote George to similar effect. Wrote home.

SATURDAY, 15 JULY

Got letter from George in which he said that he was not likely to get leave. Spent the whole day in sermon preparation. Felt rather depressed in studying 2 Chronicles 30 in connection with the events of our day.

I feel that it is the Lord's mind that I stay here despite my lack of fruit.

SABBATH, 16 JULY

Evening. Preached from Luke 14:16–24 before a fairly good congregation. Had earnestness in this sermon and pointed out how that there was no result of a year's labours, yet I do not feel that tonight is any more potent than the nights that have gone before. My soul is therefore cast down in me and I am distressed. I cannot but feel that I am labouring in vain. Something must happen. I must get relief. There is dryness both among the people and in myself. I felt terrible in the prayer tonight. I was like a wizened stick in whom there was no sap. May the Lord bless His own Word. I must leave it with Him.

SATURDAY, 22 JULY

Spent whole day at my sermons but miserable; fidgety over trifles connected with my marriage arrangements and the new permit requisite to get beyond Inverness. That of course drove me away from all spirituality, and naturally, then I felt miserable.

SABBATH, 23 JULY

Evening. Before an excellent congregation preached from Psalm 17:15. There were quite a number of strangers present. For the first time since I came to Lochgilphead I had a sermon for the Lord's people in the evening. Had liberty but did not enjoy it so much as usual, and noticed that the people were not so intent as they usually are in the evening, that they were more as they are in the afternoon service. My very last point, however, was an appeal to the unconverted and both the people and I myself woke up at that. I have great reason to thank the

1 Rev Donald Smith, his friend of College days, at this time minister of Kiltearn Free Church and later at Govanhill Free Church, Glasgow.

Lord for such a day, especially when I consider how I grieved Him away from me during the last two days through my faithless worrying over worldly cares.

SABBATH, 30 JULY

Gaelic. Wet morning; only forty-three present. I noticed Mrs Robertson going away to some other church and that spoiled me, for it worried me. I remember that I had noticed her on the road on the evening of the last Gaelic prayer meeting, although she was present at the English last Wednesday. That showed me then that it is my Gaelic which drove her away and that took all the heart out of me. Yet it intensified my resolve to make Gaelic the home language when Cathie comes.

Evening. Preached from Isaiah 4:2 and enjoyed it. The evening being still wet the attendance was down. Had good liberty and clearness but again noticed that I was afforded best general attention when I was concluding and pressing the Gospel invitation upon the unconverted. The service left me with a desire to get up my Gaelic as rapidly as possible and flee away to Skye or Lewis, or somewhere where I shall not have the carelessness in attendance to vex me which I have here. I feel much discouraged in my labours here. A humbling day. I won't be so ready to believe people when they praise my preaching after this.

SABBATH, 6 AUGUST

Gaelic. Preached from Ephesians 1:15–19 with exceptional liberty. If I was cast down last Sabbath I was exalted today. These things are strange, for spiritually I was in a very unfit frame of mind today. Besides I had taken less trouble with my preparation than I had last Sabbath, yet I had a freedom altogether unusual.

THURSDAY, 10 AUGUST: FERINTOSH FAST

Beautiful day and excellent attendance. Gaelic: Prof. MacLeod, John 3:10.

FRIDAY, 11 AUGUST

Ferintosh Question Day. Question, 2 Corinthians 8:17 given out by Alexander MacKenzie. Opened by Rev. Prof. MacLeod; closed by Rev. D. Munro. Ten spoke.

SABBATH, 13 AUGUST: FERINTOSH COMMUNION

Beautiful day. Preached in church in English. Absolutely packed. Action

Sermon Luke 22:42. Got liberty and enjoyed it. After service went up to Burn where Mr Campbell was preaching in the Gaelic, and communicated there.

MONDAY, 14 AUGUST

Preached from Isaiah 4:2 in church and got on very well with it. After service went up to Burn where Mr Campbell was again preaching. Felt very sad when the Communion finished. In bidding good-bye to old Duncan MacRae, almost broke down utterly.

Caught 3.30 train. Mr Campbell left us at Dingwall but Dolly Smith joined us, while Ida and Katie Ann went in with Vic in another carriage. Jim McIver joined us at Achnasheen. Felt the solemnity of the step I was about to take weighing so much upon me that I did not sleep till 6 o'clock in the morning.

TUESDAY, 15 AUGUST: KYLE

Married at 1 o'clock in Kyle Temperance Hotel by Rev. D. Munro, Ferintosh. Left 5 pm and stayed overnight in Strathcarron Hotel. Beautiful place.

WEDNESDAY, 16 AUGUST

Left again by 12 noon train. Got into Edinburgh at 9.30.

THURSDAY, 17 AUGUST

Had our photos taken at Drummond Studios. Visited Mathesons, Braid Road, in afternoon. Attempted to go to Fountainbridge Prayer Meeting but found the doors locked.

FRIDAY, 18 AUGUST

Left Edinburgh by 6.25 train.

SATURDAY, 19 AUGUST

Spent day in composing and preparing Gaelic sermon on Psalm 107:43 but made very little of it.

SABBATH, 20 AUGUST: LOCHGILPHEAD

Gaelic. Was wretchedly unprepared for this service and it was with feelings somewhat akin to despair that I entered the pulpit. That I should be unprepared at such a time was no wonder, since one cannot do much by way of preparation in the week of one's marriage, but still

[95]

that did not help me much. Spoke from Psalm 107:43 and floundered through it somehow. I was comforted somewhat at the conclusion by my new Gaelic tutor saying that I got on better than she had expected.

Afternoon. Preached from Luke 22:24 but felt very mechanical and heartless throughout, so that I left the church quite downcast in spirit and afraid that the Lord had utterly forsaken me to a barren Sabbath. He has brought a great happiness into my life, but it would seem as though that happiness was engaging my affections and interests too much, with a consequent loss of spirituality.

Evening. Before a fairly good congregation preached from John 7:37. I was dreadfully afraid of a barren evening. I had no liberty, but soon I became conscious of a strange softening, and that was more precious than jewels to me, for it was that for which I had been sighing all the day. Blessed be His name, He did not leave me to my fears but took away the spirit of heaviness and gave me the garments of praise. Once again, I am given to see His wonderful goodness to me.

TUESDAY, 29 AUGUST

Congregational meeting in evening. Cathie presented with silver tea service and I with roll top desk, clock and two vases.

SABBATH, 24th SEPTEMBER

Gaelic. Don't think that ever I went into the pulpit in a worse frame of mind. I felt as if I should throw up the ministry altogether. Were I not a married man, perhaps I should have been seriously tempted to do so.

4 OCTOBER: PRAYER MEETING (ENGLISH)

Spoke from Romans 8:7–11 and greatly enjoyed the meeting. I felt as though the late dryness of which I have been complaining was about to depart. There was a good attendance.

SABBATH, 8 OCTOBER: KILMARTIN

Gaelic, 12 *noon.* Before a very small congregation, preached from John 10:11. Since this was now my third time at this discourse I had exceptional freedom – and indeed I enjoyed it very much. What was giving me most anxiety beforehand was the opening prayer, but as usual the Lord was at my right hand and I had little more difficulty in it than though it were English. It is wonderful what power of expression He gives me in the pulpit in a language in which I am really very lame, and in which I could not carry on five minutes' conversation.

[96]

I made no break between the two services but simply carried on in the English whenever I had finished the Gaelic. After the sermon, explained to them the difficulty of supply owing to most of the students being away upon military service, but asked them to try to struggle on till the war should be over, for then, should the Lord continue to preserve and protect our students as He has done, our position as a Church in this respect will be the most favourable in the country. Pointed out that the responsibility would be theirs if the testimony of a pure unpolluted Gospel were removed from the district.

SABBATH, 12 NOVEMBER

Gaelic: Philippians 3:3, 55 present. *Afternoon:* John 9:39; 98 present. *Kilmartin:* John 9:39. *Evening:* Romans 2:4; 97 present. Promised to give Kilmartin a service once a month.

Had a night which was a comfort to my soul, although at the same time I feel my heart very sore because the Lord is not acknowledging me. Spoke out my heart. Some looked very solemn under it, others unmoved. Yet they were very grave on the whole. May the Lord have mercy upon us all!

FRIDAY, 24 NOVEMBER

Visitation. Oakbank – Mrs Campbell very far through. Read Psalm 103 to her. On Saturday she had almost gone; the family were all gathered round her. But she rallied and opened her eyes after a time; 'Oh, you're all round me', she said, 'but I was far away and oh it was sweet, very sweet. I'm not afraid to go now.' Tonight's scene was very touching. She was so weak that she had to be held up in bed. It makes me realise the nearness of eternity as I never did before.

SABBATH, 26 NOVEMBER

Gaelic – Acts 13:39, fifty-five present. *Afternoon* – Lamentations 3:33, a hundred and five present. *Evening* – John 12:21 & Matthew 8:34, 120 present.

In my evening discourse went out upon the sinner under concern seeking guidance from the Lord's people and said that since I had come to this place I had never heard one say – apart from the Lord's people – that there was anything wrong with his or her soul. After the evening service Mr MacColl told me that a person had said to him, 'Why does the minister never say anything to me about my soul?' I could easily show this to be unreasonable, but nevertheless my conscience pricks me.

[97]

If I have gone into the ministry, assuredly it is mine to be on the look out for souls, to take people as I find them and to leave no stone unturned to bring them to Christ. Manifestly this is my duty, and in the light of it I stand condemned. Apparently, too, it is expected of me on the part of the world. May the Lord help me to begin anew, and when I am at it I require to bestir myself in respect of another thing, i.e. in rebuking sin.

MONDAY, 27 NOVEMBER

Mrs Campbell still in life and still conscious but terribly weak. Read part of John 14 and expounded it – received liberty in doing so. She was not afraid to go, for she was looking to Jesus to take away her sins and she had got an assurance that all was well. She bade me good-bye for the last time. Formerly I used always to get a warm firm grasp, no matter how ill she might be – indeed, I was often astonished at her grip. Now all that was gone – a poor tired helpless thing was in my hand. I almost lost control of myself. My utterance was choked, the tears were flowing down my cheeks. Her poor husband was bending down over her to catch her words, precious as gold to him now, bending down and weeping. Thus I came away. Oh for a death-bed like hers – not afraid to go! My heart is sore at losing her. I don't expect to see her in life again.

Got a sweet sense of Christ's favour going down the brae tonight.

WEDNESDAY, 29 NOVEMBER

In preparing for meeting got great blessing, especially in realisation of the blessed truth that a holy walk is not the outcome of discipline or will power but of looking towards the Lord. In striving against sin let me look to Him after this, instead of to self. The whole portion, Roman 8:12–25, was exceedingly sweet. I had been a little downcast through reading the disappointing state of the Sustentation Fund, but that was taken away by this blessed portion. I was led to look at the glory to follow. I do not think I ever had a sweeter prayer meeting. They were very attentive. Forty present.

FRIDAY, I DECEMBER

Called on Campbells. Mrs Campbell a little stronger. Felt pretty cold all day. Yet in the evening the Lord answered my mourning cry. Poor little Flora[1] asked me to help her as she was in distress about her soul. Three

---

1 Flora MacLullich – a maid living with the MacRaes. She afterwards became a nurse and spent her life, along with her missionary husband, on the foreign field.

temptations seemed to be hers: (1) that she was too young (2) that her impressions would wear away, (3) that she had not enough love for Christ. Tried to explain the matter to her – she seemed to understand. Gave her *Grace and Truth* to read. Left her with prayer.

Oh Lord, put some warmth into my heart. Here my prayer has been answered, the prayer that I thought was not answered, and yet I am as unresponsive as a stone. But oh, blessed be His name that I have got proof of my ministry at last in this place. May it be but the beginning!

SABBATH, 3 DECEMBER

Flora told me that she had read the chapters I pointed out in *Grace and Truth*, and had given herself to the Lord. I gave her *Holding On* to read as a protection against the fear of falling back.

MONDAY, 4 DECEMBER

Called on Mrs MacGregor. Was enabled to talk more freely and pointedly than ever I have done. She seemed to follow in all things and to agree.

WEDNESDAY, 6 DECEMBER

Gaelic Prayer Meeting. Psalm 7:10–17. Had exceptional liberty and greatly enjoyed the meeting. The Lord is giving me sweet waters to drink just now; I hope I'll not soon lose the taste of them. I was wondering today at the littleness of my love to Him. That was the result of my discovery in the meeting that I had love for Him, and then, after, I discovered that I could not help wondering at how little it was.

THURSDAY, 7 DECEMBER

Attended funeral of D. Crawford, whose remains were brought down from Glasgow.

Still feel sweet sense of divine favour. Long may it last! Makes visiting and speaking much easier for me.

TUESDAY, 12 DECEMBER

Spent morning gardening. Cairnbaan meeting. Spoke from Exodus 5:8. Had greater liberty than expected since I had made no attempt at writing it. Meeting held in Mrs MacVean's – only twelve were present. We are beginning to get worn down to my own people now. For their sakes I will still go on; the work is the Lord's. Feel inclined, however, to depart from these 'Cries of Scripture' now that I have reached the end of the year and have the notion to draft out a scheme of elementary subjects covering the whole of next year. I think it well to set before them the fundamentals of the Christian faith with a special view to showing them the way of salvation.

WEDNESDAY, 13 DECEMBER

Considerably relieved to find that £103 has been gathered for the Sustentation Fund.

SABBATH, 17 DECEMBER

On the whole I have had a happy day. Oh I wish the Lord would work among my poor people!

MONDAY, 18 DECEMBER

Began sermon on Romans 8:1 but did not get on well with it. Worried in morning by discovering that, of £80 received at beginning of November, £40 of it has gone. Worried at night by Cathie turning ill again.

FRIDAY, 22 DECEMBER

Still very dry but feel that part of my weariness in prayer is due to a lack of the realisation that I am speaking to the Most High and that He is hearing me. Was ever one of the Lord's servants as helpless in prayer as I?

SABBATH, 24 DECEMBER

Had a happy day. Seemed to get more of the Lord's presence and to be able to speak to Him in prayer.

Flora told Cathie tonight that she was first impressed on the last Sabbath of last year. I find that I preached then from Matthew 3:1 and had an evening of evident power. It is encouraging for me to learn this as there may be others in a similar position. She has been struggling in concern for almost a year. Perhaps there are others also. May the Lord grant it!

SATURDAY, 30 DECEMBER

Feel terribly dry and hard, and shrink from the intimation re catechising which I must make tomorrow. May the Lord give me grace lest I fail, for I am conscious that little would turn me from it.

SABBATH, 31 DECEMBER

Felt pretty miserable all day despite rather comfortable services in God's house.

Thus ends my year. I would I were happier and more spiritually minded. I have had a sore experience of the power of sin during these last few days. I trust it will be a lesson to me.

A Song of War

Hark! I hear the pibroch sounding
  Over hill and over dale:
Warlike music swells the breezes
  As they sweep across the vale:
Slogans sounding on the mountains,
  Marches reaching o'er the plain:–
'Tis our warrior Chieftain's signal –
  We must up and march again.

Ha! we see the glorious muster:
  Brawny sons of lone Kintail:
Stalwarts who have fought in battle:
  Heroes who will never fail;
Each a clansman, each a soldier,
  Each a warrior staid and brave;
Loyal to their Chieftain's summons,
  Loyal even to the grave.

Standing there in martial grandeur,
  Eager for the coming fray;
Thirsting with a soldier's keenness,
  Proud to bear the name MacRae.
We had left our homes and children,
  Left our pastures, left our all,
We must up and fight for freedom
  Fight and live, or fight and fall.

Draw your broadswords, then, my children:
  Fight for kinship, love, and home;
Death and danger now despising,
  Surging through the blood-red foam:
All is won! – our slogan rises
  Clear, triumphant o'er the field,
But our ranks are sorely broken
  For our clansmen ne'er would yield.

In the clachan's lonely silence
  Sobbing mothers mourn their slain,
Sons, who joined their Chieftain's summons
  Now lie lifeless on the plain:
But they fell as heroes, fighting,
  And the death gleam in their eyes
Told a tale of dauntless courage
  And of strong men's brave demise.

GEORGE P. T. MACRAE, C.1912

5 The Shadow of Death, 1917–1918

Echoes of the First World War have already been heard in the preceding pages, but in 1917, with that War in its third year, the Scottish High-lands were passing through horror which was unimagined in the days when the sun had shone on quiet hills and straths before the breaking of the storm in August 1914. Prior to this time no British army had been in France for a hundred years. The desolating effects of conflict which had been felt in Scots' homes from the 'small wars' of the intervening century were to be as nothing compared with what was to come after 1914. For now nine million men across Europe were in arms, and before those arms would be laid down, almost every family fireside in the Highlands would mourn its loss.

The decision which in God's providence Kenneth MacRae reached in 1911 to take his Arts and Divinity courses concurrently in four years had one unanticipated outcome. Had he followed the normal procedure his Arts degree course would have finished in the summer of 1914 and it is unlikely that he could have remained a civilian for a *further* three years thereafter. It is equally unlikely that, if he had gone to the battle front as an infantry officer in a Highland regiment in 1914 or 1915, he would have lived to see the end. As it was, he was ordained within a year of the outbreak of War. There is 'a time to every purpose under the heaven'.

His brother George's verses, 'A Song of War', appear to have been written in 1912. They exemplify the patriotic instinct and the martial spirit which two years later led thousands to enlist long before they were conscripted. Kenneth was not immune to that same spirit and yet he viewed the War at a deeper level than his brother. The cause of the War was not simply German militarism, it was divine judgment. As Archibald McNeilage wrote in *The Monthly Record* in September 1914, 'Though we may descend into the arena with a clear conscience of the rightness of our case against the Kaiser William, our relations to the God of Heaven are by no means so untroubled. For long years the British people have been provoking the God of their fathers. . . . War, no matter how just soever it may be, is a national calamity and a divine judgment. It is placed by the Holy Spirit on the same plane as pestilence and famine. All these are the servants of the Most High to punish men for transgression and forgetfulness, if not open denial, of God.' Among the causes of God's wrath with Britain, the same writer listed pride, luxury, and the spirit of unbelief entertained within the church itself. On the latter subject he writes:

An awakening consideration with regard to this German menace is the German Higher Criticism that has so long been patronised and imbibed by many leaders and schools of religious thought, especially in Presbyterian Scotland and Nonconformist England. For years past nothing would serve our aspiring youth and men of culture but a term in some German University, there to assimilate the godless learning of Harnack and Wellhausen. But God is now showing us that the haunt of a godless culture is also the land of barbaric militarism, and that Krupp's cannon factory is a related phenomenon to Pfleiderer's infidel lecture room. This lesson is being taught, but whether it will be learnt is another matter. However, a more spiritual generation yet to come will easily discern that the quenching of the Holy Spirit, implied in the admired disquisitions of Harnack, or some other idolised exponent of a godless criticism, is justly followed by the hardness of heart which breeds war and destruction.[1]

This was precisely the view of the cause of the War in which Mr MacRae shared, and, consequently, while he often felt like joining the river of men which flowed from Scotland to the battlefields of France he believed that as a servant of the Word of God he had first to answer a higher call and discharge a higher duty. The survival of the country depended upon more than patriotism.

From the outset of the War, the Highlands were one of the most important sources of men for the army and the navy. 'Recruiting proceeded with a numerical success that was not exceeded, if (in proportion to the population) it was equalled, in any other part of the United Kingdom'.[2] By November, 1914, the Free Church had over 4,000 men in the Forces. 173 congregations or stations had men away at the Front or in the Navy, and from six congregations more than 100 men had gone. One entire company of the famous Seaforths – 8 sergeants and 100 men – was made up of Free Churchmen coming from the congregation of Ness, Lewis. The parish of Knock, also in Lewis, gave 500 men. Even before the end of 1914 it was clear what a high percentage of loss the Free Church would be likely to bear before the conflict was over, for the Highland regiments were among the first to be decimated in Flanders. In one day's fighting at Cambrai,

1 *The Monthly Record*, 1914, p 182.
2 *The Highlands and Islands of Scotland*, A Historical Survey, W. C. Mackenzie, 1949, p 287.

'of 800 men of the Gordons who entered the battle, only 170 answered the roll call when the day was over'.

The present writer has not seen figures of the total losses suffered by Free Church families in the First World war. It is known that from the Isle of Lewis alone more than 1,100 men died, a large majority belonging to Free Church. Even from such a comparatively small congregation as Shettleston, in Glasgow, 37 men went to the army, of which number, nine – including, a minister, the Rev. J. B. Orr – were killed. Ten divinity students from the Free Church College were lost and there were more who went straight from University to the Forces. Many were the tributes to the calibre of these men. A high-ranking naval officer, wrote Donald MacLean, 'gave the unsolicited testimony that husbands and sons of the storm-swept Isles of Scotland, reared in the alleged gloom and severity of Calvinistic preaching, formed the rallying centres of staggered crews by the example of their physical endurance and the influence of their moral character and devotion to duty.' But when the strife was over, and War memorials arose all over the North, the Church had suffered a loss from which, in some areas, she did not recover.

In the following chapter I have concentrated largely on Diary entries relating to the national struggle. The homes and firesides of Lochgilphead accurately represent the sorrows which afflicted the hearts of a nation, and from which there was no relief save in the gospel of Christ.

☐   ☐   ☐

MONDAY, 1 JANUARY, 1917

11 *am, English service, Psalm* 84:7. The attendance was very good. Had liberty and greatly enjoyed the service.

A dull and dreary day of rain; no one stirring and dreadfully quiet. Did no visiting.

TUESDAY, 2 JANUARY

Spoke to Mrs Crawford about her soul but she shrivelled up and appeared, I am afraid, to resent it. I shall have to resort to a more subtle method. Think I will give one of Ryle's tracts to every household in the congregation with a private message written on the back.

FRIDAY, 5 JANUARY

Got salary, Nov. 1st–Dec. 31st, £26-13-4.

TUESDAY, 9 JANUARY

Got letter from 'Polly' specially to thank me for my letter. She had been returning from a sorrow-stricken home when she seemed to be overcome with anguish because of the hideous desolation caused by this war, and with anxiety on account of her own sons, and cried out asking the Lord if He had forgotten all. On her way home she called at the Post Office and got my letter, and she said it brought peace to her troubled heart. Wonderful are the ways of the Lord.

WEDNESDAY, 10 JANUARY

Cycled in for prayer-meeting and got a proper wetting. Visited Mrs MacGregor and spoke to her about her hope. She said that she could only look to Jesus, that no one else could do anything for her. Was very glad to hear so much. Not so wet going home, but the package of sugar resting on my thighs when cycling quite exhausted me so that felt done out ere I got back to Minard. Was dreadfully hungry.

THURSDAY, 11 JANUARY

In forenoon had a ramble through wood. Greatly taken with it.
Got Hodge on Ephesians, Flavel's *Works* Vol. I, Owen on Psalm 130, and *The Scripture Treasury* from John.

FRIDAY, 12 JANUARY

Returned home. Found Mrs Mitchell had passed away at 12.45 am today. Her last words were *Moladh Mor do Dhia* ['Great praise be to God']!

TUESDAY, 16 JANUARY

Had very little time for preparation for Cairnbaan, but was given abundant liberty of utterance and enjoyed meeting very much. Held in Mrs MacInnes' house – good attendance. Began first of my lectures on the fundamentals of the faith: 'The Total Depravity of Man as taught by the Word of God'.

WEDNESDAY, 17 JANUARY

In forenoon, visited Mrs MacGregor. Found her very low. Told her my remarkable dream of two nights ago. Dreamed that I was visiting her and that she was dying. I asked about her hope for eternity and she told me, but it seemed to me that she was basing it upon her own efforts to prepare herself while upon her bed of sickness. I therefore tried to make the way clear to her by showing that all trust must be in Christ and in Him alone. Now there was another woman with her, lying at the outside of the bed, a hard-faced, wicked-looking woman, and she was urging me to go away, that I was only worrying Mrs MacGregor and that she was too weak to bear it. Seeing, however, I would pay no heed, she turned to Mrs MacGregor and told her to pay no heed to me, that what I was saying was error and that I was telling lies. But Mrs MacGregor ignored her also, and presently her face lit up and she said, 'Oh I have it. I understand now'.

Told this to her and again emphasised necessity of trusting in Christ. Said many trust in themselves, 'But that is a great error', she said.

Mrs MacKellar asked her for her hope–said it was in Jesus.

THURSDAY, 18 JANUARY

Called on MacGregors, but only to find, as I expected, that the change had come. She passed away at 6.30. Poor woman! I am glad that I was enabled to talk to her of eternal things at the last, and that she did not leave us without hope.

TUESDAY, 23 JANUARY

Heard that John MacEwan was terribly upset about his soul and had been crying out for me all day. Went down in afternoon. Found him very depressed and declaring that he was without hope for eternity. He said that he had been professing Christ for years, but that now every-thing had been taken away from him. I asked him what had taken away the hope that he had. 'Oh', he said, 'my short-comings!' The fear of man has always been a snare to me and I have not lived as I should, I have not been visiting the sick as I should'. So terrible was his concern that he had not slept for five nights. I tried to show him that his eyes ought to be directed to Christ and His work, and not to ourselves and our miserable doings. But he would not be comforted. He said his day of grace was past. I said that, if that were so, there would be no concern in his soul. I left him wishing that he could trust Christ and asking for grace to do it.

Mr MacGregor pretty low too. Read him something to comfort him. Was weeping – Oh Lord, help me in my work! It is more than I can face.

THURSDAY, 25 JANUARY

In afternoon visited John MacEwan – again very low. Will not be comforted because he cannot get a sense of the divine favour. Said that he had to confess that during his years of profession he had never lost his desire for private prayer, and said that sometimes when he was lively he would be on his knees as often as five or six times in the day.

FRIDAY, 2 FEBRUARY

Today, determined to fix daily upon some subject for meditation upon which to strive ever to centre my thoughts. Today took, as my theme for meditation, the forgiveness of my sins. Going out to Badden especially it brought peace to my soul and made the world wonderfully bright. In great measure got my old joy restored to me. Isaiah 43:25 came to me very forcibly, and with great comfort, while out on the road.

SATURDAY, 3 FEBRUARY

Theme for meditation: God as the disposer and controller of my time. Found my theme very comforting. It seemed to stave off all worry and brought with it a quiet peace. Time is in the hands of the Most High. He will give me enough of time for all the work which He has for me to do and what more do I want than this?

SABBATH, 11 FEBRUARY

Gaelic: Hebrews 10:20, 55 present. *Afternoon:* Isaiah 35:8, 109 present. *Kilmartin:* Isaiah 35:8, 19 present. *Evening:* John 14:6, 109 present.

The sun of favour is shining upon me again. Today I have had the best Sabbath of the year. First of all I had liberty at the Gaelic. Then the afternoon in both places was sweet to me. But the treat of the day was the evening service. It was a veritable feast for my soul; I was at the King's Courts.

MONDAY, 12 FEBRUARY

Cairnbaan meeting – in Mrs MacCallum's. 20 present. Subject, 'Man's Depravity' proved (1) from Scripture (2) Experience (3) Conscience. Enjoyed meeting. Am surprised that I should enjoy these doctrinal meetings so well.

THURSDAY, 1 MARCH

Bible Class. Spoke on Conviction of Sin. After meeting, Miss Dewar came up with Flora. Also under concern. Flora persuaded her to come in to see me. Wish I could feel as grateful to the Lord as I should. How wonderfully is He working and acknowledging such a poor wretch as I am.

TUESDAY, 6 MARCH

Students not now protected from military service. College to be closed and students posted in congregations as having a better chance of exemption before local tribunals.

SABBATH, 18 MARCH

Gaelic: Hebrews 10:19, 53 present. *Afternoon:* Psalm 45:15, 109 present. *Tayvallich:* Psalm 45:15, 41 present. *Evening:* Hosea 6:4, 100 present.

Enjoyed the day throughout. Feeling the Gaelic much easier. Enjoyed the afternoon discourse, especially in Tayvallich. Felt a drawing while in the pulpit there towards the people, as though I would fain be used for a work of grace in their midst. In the evening, again had a good time. Mr Dewar the tailor was out at every service today. I never saw him at the Gaelic before, and when I see this and remember that he was at the prayer-meeting last Wednesday, I begin to wonder what is going on in him.

MONDAY, 19 MARCH

Heard from Flora that her sister in Tayvallich is under concern. That explains the drawing I felt yesterday while in the church. How wonderfully the Lord is working just now!

FRIDAY, 23 MARCH

Cathie went to Glasgow to see John[1] on his way through to France. Had some pleasant communings with my Redeemer tonight while out on the road.

SABBATH, 1 APRIL

Beautiful frosty day. Lacked earnestness and spirituality. Felt ere the evening service was over that prayer was not getting the place in my life which it ought, and resolved once again – and oh I hope this won't also come to nought! – to give half an hour daily to the Lord in prayer – this half an hour to be given in the evening, immediately after tea. The following commends itself: Monday, for my congregation; Tuesday, for my church; Wednesday, for my people; Thursday, for my country; Friday, for my home; Saturday, for my soul.

John Matheson, Mrs MacRae's brother.

SABBATH, 8 APRIL [Communion]

11 *am, Gaelic.* Rev. Roderick MacLeod,[1] M.A., Matthew 22:4. 2 *pm, English.* Self, Isaiah 53:11. 6.30 *pm.* Rev. R. MacLeod, M.A., Luke 9:57-62.

Day of drenching rain, and attendance accordingly suffered. Could not follow in Gaelic very well today.

In the afternoon, however, I found it better. Got much enjoyment in my sermon – came near to breaking down several times. Poor Miss Dewar was weeping copiously, especially when I was describing the sufferings of Christ. The sight of Flora weeping in the gallery just before the communicants came forward nearly unsettled me also. Did not get so much liberty at the Table, although it would appear that my precentor was weeping all the time. I have to thank the Lord for those tears, for I often complained of the hardness of my people. I hope that there has been some working of the Spirit along with the tears.

MONDAY, 9 APRIL

This Communion season has been very pleasant and very profitable. Attended Mr MacLeod's funeral today, but did not go all the way on account of the vain Masonic ritual at the grave.

TUESDAY, 10 APRIL

Roddie went home today. Feel much the better for his sermons. I got a real feast and I can honestly say that Christ is nearer to me than He has been for long.

FRIDAY, 13 APRIL

Miss Maggie MacFarlane came up tonight to see if I could help her. She has lately been very troubled about herself. Told her she must cease considering self, and must turn away at once from every troubling thought, looking ever to Christ and resting peacefully and satisfied upon Him. Gave her *Grace and Truth* asking her to read two of the chapters which I thought might help her. Felt very sorry for the poor girl.

Heard from Flora that her sister had now got the peace which she had been seeking. Very thankful. Truly, the Lord is working in wondrous ways.

1 His great friend Roderick MacLeod, a native of Balallan in Lewis, was minister of Tarbert some 12 miles from Lochgilphead. This was his only charge. He died there as a comparatively young man in 1928.

SATURDAY, 14 APRIL

The blackest day of my life, but the Lord has not left me without consolation. Got word today that my darling brother George was killed in action on the 9th in the advance at Arras while leading his platoon.[1] A thousand times over I wish that it had been I myself who had been taken and George left. Oh I wish that I knew that his soul was safe! Then I would not sorrow so much. But I must leave that with the Lord, who does all things well. May He comfort my poor stricken people! As for myself, He has given me strength to bear it. To His name be the praise!

SABBATH, 15 APRIL

Had no heart to count today's attendances. Felt the Gaelic service keenly. The Lord was with me, helping me, for the sermon never came more easily to me.[2] Kept up all right till last prayer, when broke down. Again broke down in reading Psalm 118. Was enabled to get through the other services without giving way. Felt greatly moved down by Loch Sween, for there I parted with my dear brother almost a year ago. I feel sometimes an overwhelming longing to get away from here back to the dear North-land, where I used to be happy and where I can get away among God's own warm people. How are my dear ones bearing it! What a Sabbath this must be to them!

THURSDAY, 19 APRIL

Got letter from Vic which greatly comforted me re George. What gratified me most was that when they went over to see him at Dunfermline, in a public tea-room full of soldiers and their friends, he said grace before beginning their food. He also mentioned in a letter home that he could not understand how men could live out 'here' (France) without God, and in an article he spoke of serving a Higher than King George.

SATURDAY, 21 APRIL

Read George's last notes home, written on the eve of his death.

1 The Battle of Arras opened the Allies' offensive on the Western Front in 1917. It was hoped that this combined action might end the war, but the British army suffered 150,000 casualites and no such hope was realised. Perhaps a million Europeans had died in 1916, and 1917 was to prove yet darker.
2 Visiting Lochgilphead in 1976 the editor of this volume found one older member of the congregation who remembered this sermon.

Dear Mother and Father,

The end of all war is peace and I am going to sleep often to the sweet music of that. I will write you at the first available opportunity. Till we meet again in the beautiful land of Dream and of Love – au revoir.

Your affectionate boy,
George.[1]

Am exercised today concerning my duty as to putting my name in for a chaplaincy. Certainly I cannot see how I can well be spared here, and I cannot go unless some provision is made for Kilmartin and Tayvallich; yet despite all, something is calling me away, away to the chalk plains of France and the torn fields of death.

WEDNESDAY, 25 APRIL

Letter from Vic enclosing one from Sarah Grant to my parents. In this letter got a full and final answer to my prayer. She says that, more than once, George in answer to letters of hers had mentioned his faith in a Saving Redeemer. I can now think of my darling brother in glory and my pain is gone. I no longer think of that grave in far away France, but of his glorified soul rejoicing with the saints of God who gather about the throne.

FRIDAY, 27 APRIL

Letters of sympathy from Jim McIver and Calum Galbraith. The former stated that he had seen one of George's fellow-officers who had told him that he had met his death while endeavouring to help another who had been hit.

TUESDAY, I MAY

Travelled through to Edinburgh.

WEDNESDAY, 2 MAY: EDINBURGH

Read many of the letters received about George. 150 such came. These letters made very pathetic reading and wrung my heart. Although my parents bear up well, they have aged very much since last I saw them, although that was not a month ago.

1 George wrote a number of letters from France for publication in various Highland newspapers. In the last paragraph of his last published letter he said: 'Who of us would not be home again, idling on the green, green braes that are now so far away? Of a night as we huddle together in our dug-outs, we will often go back to the quiet hush of the gloaming, glamorous and peaceful, and find there the knowledge of our dreams . . . Happy shall those of us be who go back to the rest of it all'.

Was out in the forenoon with Dunc[1] and could not help noticing that there was not such a fine soldierly figure to be seen anywhere, although we were meeting with soldiers everywhere.

As I left to return to Glasgow my poor mother broke down. 'It will be a dull house when you come again', she said. I could not answer, my heart was too sore.

THURSDAY, 3 MAY: GLASGOW

On going to St Enoch's Station in the morning I found that Arran sailings were suspended until further notice on account of mines or submarines in the Clyde.

SATURDAY, 5 MAY: GLASGOW

In the evening felt dissatisfied that I had no new sermon for tomorrow, and sketched out a discourse on Isaiah 45:15. Wrote nothing of it apart from the skeleton.

SABBATH, 6 MAY: GLASGOW, BARONY COMMUNION

Was dreadfully cold in the morning and felt that I was coming to church without Christ. In the afternoon I was not much better, but I enjoyed the evening fairly well. Otherwise it would have been a miserable day. Mr MacKay, though suffering very much, was out in the afternoon and evening. He is a typical Sutherlandshire man and the backbone of the congregation. I felt exceedingly sorry for him. He told me that he expects soon to be called away – indeed he said he knew it. Last Monday night, in the midst of great pain, he suddenly had a half hour of wonderful sweetness and pleasure and found himself singing the Lord's praises at the top of his voice.

There was a lad from Appin, a sergeant in the Seaforths, who favourably impressed me. He had been wounded in France. He had been in the original Gairloch company, which he said was a treat, as you would not hear a wrong word in it all day long. The same applied to the Ullapool company, but alas, the older men are gone now.

MONDAY, 7 MAY

Returned to Lochgilphead. Saw twelve minesweepers getting to work down the Clyde. Letter from Mr MacLean[2] saying that if another chaplaincy were asked for, if there were no volunteers who could be

1 His elder brother, Duncan, then on leave and soon to return to France.
2 The Rev Donald MacLean, responsible for liaison between the Free Church and the chaplaincy departments of the Army and Navy.

more easily spared than I, then I would be called upon. Letters from John.[1] He fell through an abandoned dug-out in an advance and is now in hospital. Of a battalion of 700 men only 120 men and 3 officers came out of the fray.

FRIDAY, II MAY, TAYVALLICH

Mrs Maclachlan told me that, of all the sermons ever she heard, the one I preached on the Friday last year on Proverbs 20:4 was the one which made most impression upon her. She could give most of it even yet. Felt much encouraged because I think I preached that sermon then with a sinking heart.

SATURDAY, 19 MAY

Got letter from Ida which made me weep bitterly, yet my heart was rejoicing within me, for it is evident that the Lord has used this great sorrow for the blessing of my sisters. Further she told me of George pressing men to serve Christ.

TUESDAY, 29 MAY

Beautiful day. Left for Arran.

WEDNESDAY, 30 MAY

Reached Sliddery about 3 o'clock. I was very glad to get into this warm corner again.
Prayer Meeting 7.00 pm – I took this for 35 minutes, then giving place to Mr MacEwan who had a baptism. I spoke from Hosea 6:1 and to my amazement, before I had spoken for five minutes, tears were flowing copiously from all parts. I am indeed astonished at the liberty I got here.

THURSDAY, 31 MAY: FAST DAY, SOUTHEND

All day long the rain came down without cessation. Yet at both services the attendance was very good, poor Mr MacKinnon tramping all the way from Tor Luin with his bad leg. At both services I had liberty, especially in the evening, and tears were abundant.

FRIDAY, I JUNE: SOUTHEND

Weather improved but still showery. Went for a walk along in Shiskine direction in forenoon. In afternoon visited the MacKelvies and enjoyed it. Miss MacKelvie in bed 54 years.

1 John Matheson, Mrs MacRae's brother.

Service at 7.00 pm – attendance only four less than forenoon yesterday. Spoke from Romans 8:6 (last clause) and had an evening remarkably sweet to my soul. After the sermon was over I would like to have shouted out for very joy. Mr MacEwan, in giving the intimations, pressed upon believers their duty in respect of the Lord's Table.

SATURDAY, 2 JUNE: SOUTHEND

Had service today at 11.30. Preached from Isaiah 45:15. Again had power, and again many tears. The attendance was no less than usual and numbered about 70.

I thought then that only John MacAlister was to come to meet the session, but the door opened and in came Jennie Piper, Mrs Cook and Mrs Ferguson, all in tears. When Mr MacEwan saw them he broke down weeping also, so much so that he had to come over to me and ask me to speak to them for he couldn't. But I could no more speak than he, for I felt so overjoyed that I could not keep my happiness from breaking forth into a smile. I accordingly prayed until he should recover.

In the evening another person, Donald Stewart, came in also with a view to communicating. A very worthy man. What reason for thankfulness. Five new communicants!

MONDAY, 4 JUNE: SOUTHEND

Thanksgiving, 11.30 *am*, Isaiah 35:8. Still very wet. Yet weather did not keep the people back, nor James Cook from walking in his five miles. Wonderful meeting. From the very outset people seemed to be strongly impressed – a very solemn spirit pervaded the church. At the second singing (Psalm 84:3–7) the precentor broke down and it was only with the greatest difficulty that the singing was kept going at all – there was weeping all over the church. I never saw a congregation so moved, nor felt an assembly so softened and solemnised in my life. May the Lord grant that it is not the goodness which vanishes away as the morning cloud.

After the service Mr MacEwan asked Charles MacAlister why he had not helped John when he broke down, to which he replied softly, 'There was more than John broken down'. Then on chancing to visit a neighbouring house Mr MacEwan put the same question to the head of the house. The man tried to answer, but couldn't speak. The tears stood in his eyes. In a moment he seemed to have broken down, and his wife was in a scarcely better case. He would hardly let go my hand when I wished him good-bye, although he could not utter one word.

E

FRIDAY, 8 JUNE, LENIMORE

Finished *Life of Robert Finlayson*. Very helpful book. Note from it
(1) To urge the people to catechise their children on the Sabbath
evenings as to the sermons they heard. (2) To begin diets of catechising
(3) To try to be a *loving* minister.

THURSDAY, 21 JUNE: CAIRNBAAN

Was shocked to see in the *Oban Times* about death of Mrs MacLeod's
brother Farquhar in Mesopotamia. Was also very grieved to see in the
Record that poor Roddie Finlayson fell in action. Truly the Lord has a
controversy when such lads of promise are being cut away. A finer lad I
never met. But he is happier now and in the very presence of the King
whose name he loved. I shall not readily forget the sweet summer day
when he sat beside me on the slopes above Loch Migdale at the Creich
Communion. Who next? What awful times!

SABBATH, 24 JUNE

Enjoyed Gaelic service and had more than usual freedom of expression.
Am beginning to feel that my fullest joy is in showing forth Christ. When
I get a text dealing with Him my heart warms within me.

There was a sprinkling of strangers both in the afternoon and in the
evening. Another day done. Will there be any fruit of it?

TUESDAY, 26 JUNE

Meeting of the Presbytery 11.30 am, Tarbert. Beautiful day. Sent p.c.
to Mr Miller[1] saying that I did not wish mention to be made in the press
of my having offered my services for a chaplaincy.

MONDAY, 23 JULY

John MacLeod called.[2] Seems to be passing through what is my frequent
experience – discouraged and disheartened by the carelessness of his
people and their evident disregard for what he says – in the case at least
of some.

THURSDAY, 26 JULY

Self-Examination. (1) Worldliness (2) Lack of care over tongue
(3) Faithlessness – omitted to say something for my Master in saying

1 The Rev. Peter W. Miller, presbytery clerk and minister at Campbeltown.
2 As minister in Minard, John MacLeod was MacRae's nearest colleague.

'Good-bye' to Annie and May Carsewell who leave for Glasgow on Saturday (4) Pride in measuring myself with others and in listening critically to a man's prayer instead of helping him in it.

FRIDAY, 3 AUGUST

Letter from Edinburgh Highland Societies re necessitous soldiers or dependents – also re knitting for soldiers. Very sorry to see in *Scotsman* Jim McIver's name in the wounded list. Hope it is not serious.

WEDNESDAY, 8 AUGUST

Travelled North to Ferintosh with Mr Munro, leaving Edinburgh at 9.50 am. Very glad and thankful to be in this quarter again. Feel my mind easier, although I do tremble at the thought of all that is before me and my inability to get prepared. But the Lord will help me as He always has done. I trust I shall have a blessed time here!

THURSDAY, 9 AUGUST: FERINTOSH FAST DAY

Good day and excellent attendances. Was greatly taken with the spirituality of Mr Cameron's[1] prayers. His discourses were logical and doctrinal and showed a mind unaccustomed to the superficial. Feel very happy at being here again and to see such concourses of people. My desire for my home country seems but to increase.

FRIDAY, 10 AUGUST: FERINTOSH QUESTION DAY

Question: Ephesians 2:5. Given out by F. MacLennan. Good congregation. Felt it a trying ordeal, but as usual the Lord brought me through. How I enjoy this life! There is a taste here which I cannot get in Argyllshire.

A letter from home states that a very bitter letter has appeared in the local paper against me in reference to what I said in respect of visitors and the Sabbath.

SATURDAY, 11 AUGUST

Very wet in the forenoon and showery later. Very sorry for poor people in the Burn. The attendances, despite the rain, were very good. Saw William Murray and dear old Duncan MacRae[2] in the Burn. The latter looked love.

1 The Rev. William M. Cameron, minister of the Free Church at Resolis (Black Isle) from 1916 to his death in 1950.
2 A godly elder from Elphin in Sutherland-shire.

The sight of Dingwall, quiet, lying in its peaceful valley across the water, has brought much back to me. Well may I say, 'As for me, my feet were almost gone; my steps had well nigh slipped!' But the Lord was watching over me. Blessed be His name!

SABBATH, 12 AUGUST: FERINTOSH COMMUNION

Attendances very good – church crowded. Received liberty and had a very sweet day. Saw many in tears at the Table. Oh how I prize such gatherings and such softness. Communicated myself in the Burn. Mr Munro served the Table (the 2nd). That dear old man Duncan MacRae stood behind me and rested his hand on my shoulder all the time of the Table addresses.

MONDAY, 13 AUGUST: FERINTOSH THANKSGIVING

Showery day but got good weather during the services and attendances were good. Had great liberty in the church and enjoyed the service exceedingly. Thereafter proceeded to the Burn. Five of us in the 'Tent'.[1] Duncan MacRae returned with us to the Manse where he is staying overnight.

Enjoyed this communion season exceedingly and vexed that it is now over. What reason I have for gratitude that the Lord is so dealing with me. May there be fruit from this time!

Mr Munro gave me the *Life of Moody Stuart* to read.

THURSDAY, 16 AUGUST: CROMARTY

Crossed with Father to Glenurquhart in the forenoon. On the way home, sought out Roddie Finlayson[2] at the Camp. Found him taking the Gaelic service. When I came in he was reading a chapter. He insisted on my addressing the men. Not having sufficient confidence in myself to start off in Gaelic without forethought, I spoke in English from Psalm 40:17 and enjoyed it exceedingly. The company was very warm (about thirty-five men). Felt parting with Roddie very much. Oh that the Lord would spare him from this awful war for we need him greatly!

WEDNESDAY, 22 AUGUST

Another letter appeared in the local paper criticising my preaching, and since the tone is in no wise improved with the change of editorship I sent down to the newsagent cancelling my order.

1 A covered, wooden pulpit used for outdoor services, cf. illustrations 5 and 6.
2 Afterwards Professor R. A. Finlayson.

SATURDAY, 25 AUGUST

Today I pleaded as I never did before for the guidance of the Holy Spirit in the sketching out of the three subjects given me to work upon next week – Matthew 6:34, Psalm 46:10, Jeremiah 12:1. Desired that I might be directed so as to meet the needs of actual cases in my congregation. Have been led so to plead through reading the *Life of Dr Moody Stuart* and realising that I am not as dependent on the Holy Spirit as he was and therefore a stranger to much of his blessed experience. May the Lord make me to depend more and more upon Himself alone, not only in preaching but in all things!

SABBATH, 26 AUGUST

Today, while yet exercised by the book I am reading, I endeavoured to do as Dr Moody Stuart did, to throw myself upon the Lord and to preach in dependence upon Him, and what a blessed day it was! I have not had such a day since I left Arran. Enjoyed the Gaelic and got liberty in it. This liberty and enjoyment was yet increased in the afternoon, and the evening was best of all. The house of God was very sweet to me today and seemingly it was also sweet to others. Some were visibly affected. Oh that there may be good of it! How thankful I am that He has given me another drink in the wilderness and that He has put this helpful book into my hands!

SATURDAY, I SEPTEMBER

Work of week: Visitations = 22; Meetings = 4; Letters etc. = 16; Tracts, etc. given away = 4; Sermons composed = 4.[1]

FRIDAY, 14 SEPTEMBER

Spent the evening trying to write poor Jim McIver's obituary.[2] Feel very sad after it all. This is an awful world. I seem to be moving in a very atmosphere of death. One is taken away after another, and oh my poor people! How my heart mourns for their sorrows. Oh how softly I should walk!

THURSDAY, 20 SEPTEMBER

I was feeling today that I should be accepting more directly, as being for myself, the Lord's promises. Oh to be close friends with Him!

1 This entry is representative of many others which indicate the nature of his usual weekly labours in Lochgilphead.
2 In this he wrote: 'Only five years intervened for him between the strait gate and the gates of glory – a short race, but a blessed one'.

Spent most of the day shifting my study to up-stairs as the room below is very damp, and bound soon to spoil my books.

WEDNESDAY, 26 SEPTEMBER

In the afternoon went out to see poor Mrs B. whose son was drowned on the 21st on the minesweeper 'Grenadier', blown up by mine. Very dark house and ignorant of the Word.

SATURDAY, 29 SEPTEMBER

A gift of £1-10 received today has provided quite enough to tide us over till November and got full and abundant answer to the prayers of my need. What a gracious Lord He is! Why should I doubt when I so see His goodness to me time and again. This is by no means the first time, for I have seen it repeatedly in my life. 'Seek ye first the kingdom of God, and *all these things* (temporal necessities) shall be added unto you'.

SABBATH, 30 SEPTEMBER

The attendance was very good, and I was given great warmth in setting forth Christ as the Saviour of sinners. Whether I have love for Him or not, this I know, that it is very sweet to me to preach about Him and to point poor fellow-sinners to Him.

TUESDAY, 2 OCTOBER

Letter from Alice Maclachlan asking for disjunction certificate in order to join Partick. Wrote a very nice letter in which she said: 'I can never quite thank you sufficiently for the help you gave me. When I first came to Lochgilphead I liked your preaching because you really seemed to care whether I came to Jesus or not. Often after the sermon I met you and meant always to ask you how I could come to Jesus. I was very anxious and unhappy in those days.' Little did I suspect it when I used to meet her on the road. Here is a lesson not to judge by appearances.

SATURDAY, 6 OCTOBER

Had a very happy evening. Christ drew near to me and I saw something of His beauty.

SABBATH, 7 OCTOBER

Have been a good deal turned in thought today towards the days of other times, to the early days of my student career. Then I was able to say that I lived only to preach the Gospel. I tried to face that question today again. I am bound now with ties which were not upon me then, and these ties naturally cause me to have more regard for this world, but how much hold have these ties got upon me? Have they made me ready to live in the world apart from preaching the Gospel and solely for their own sake? After facing that question honestly, I am thankful that I am still able to say that I would not wish to live a day longer in the world if I were able no more to preach the gospel. May the day never come when I shall be of a different mind!

FRIDAY, 12 OCTOBER: GREENOCK

In the afternoon I walked out to Gourock and visited Captain Shaw. He has a good library. Showed me a book which he greatly appreciated and I think it would be very helpful to myself: Octavius Winslow's *Personal Declension and Revival of Religion in the Soul*. Must try to get it from the College Library. I cannot help noticing how well read our leading laymen are. People of some other churches who are leaders in their own way have their bookcases stored with novels and worldly books, yet who more loud and sweeping in their denunciation of the 'old ways'! The truth is that, despite this pride, their attitude is the fruit of ignorance.

WEDNESDAY, 5 DECEMBER

Letter from Ida enclosing two from Dunc. Seemingly he has had marvellous escapes. On two occasions his section was practically wiped out, on the latter of which he was the only man unhurt after a shell burst only a yard from him and killed 17 men. He attributes this to his mother's prayers; otherwise, he says, he cannot account for it. This made a great impression on me. I was enabled to write him very plainly pressing Christ upon him.[1]

TUESDAY, 1 JANUARY, 1918

Today having been appointed as a Day of Humiliation and Prayer by our Church, it more resembled a Sabbath than a New Year's Day, and therefore to me it was the happiest New Year I have spent. This appointing of New Year as a Day of Humiliation was, I thought, a happy venture. It would test the people. Would they be willing to sacrifice the usual festivities of the day or not? I confess that I was curious beforehand as to how the test would prove my people, but now that the evening has come I think I have every reason to feel satisfied that

---

1 His eldest brother, who served with the Australian Expeditionary Force, survived the War but died as a result of wounds in Perth, Australia.

although they have been weighed in the balances they have not been found wanting. Cumming, Mrs Drysdale's nephew – winner of the military medal – was present in his hospital clothes. Poor fellow, he seems badly wounded. What a big, strong man he is!

THURSDAY, 3 JANUARY

After a feverish night, spent most of the day in bed. In bed worked out my Gaelic sermon on Matthew. Managed to get out in the evening to the Class when I spoke on 'The Covenants and the Covenanters'. Nineteen were present. Enjoyed it fairly well. Am thankful that I am so far recovered.

SATURDAY, 5 JANUARY

Another Sabbath, and a very solemn one, is again at hand. Although I do not feel quite up to normal, yet with God's blessing I think I shall be able to face the strain of the morrow without much hurt. I only wish my spiritual health were as good. When I was a student I called my studies a wilderness because of their chilling effect upon my soul, and I longed for the advent of my ministry that I might be free from all such, so that I could enjoy my soul to the full. But now, in the course of my ministry, I see that even sermon-making may become a wilderness to me and that in providing for the souls of others I may have no time to bethink me of my own poor, starved soul.

TUESDAY, 8 JANUARY

Had some freedom in composition of discourse upon Micah 7:19, when I attempted to give some signs which will precede the coming of a day of favour, whenever that will be. All the signs go to indicate that it will not be for a long time yet, and certainly that is my own opinion, although I would like to be wrong.

Before going out to visit this afternoon, sought the blessing of the Lord upon each visit I intended making and found that I enjoyed my visiting much better than usual, and also that my prayers were not hard, formal and meaningless, as they usually are.

The cold is very severe today and it is impossible to find a warm corner in the house. The hot water pipe is at present frozen and there is no sign of the frost relaxing its intensity.

I believe I have enjoyed a little more of the Lord's favour today than I have for some little time, but still I have to complain of coldness and a sad failure to realise that standard of spiritual-mindedness rightly expected of a minister of the Gospel.

WEDNESDAY, 9 JANUARY

Composed Gaelic sermon on Jeremiah 9:24. Today has witnessed a complete change in the weather. The morning dawned wild and wet. Through the day weather conditions improved, but in the evening the wind again rose and by prayer meeting time the night was as wild and wet as the early morning. The attendance accordingly suffered, being as low as twenty-five. Messrs. MacLean and MacColl prayed. The former asked that preachers might be raised up in the church to meet the present supply difficulty. May that prayer be answered! Enjoyed the meeting pretty well. Spoke from Malachi 3:2 on Christ as a refiner's fire (1) As separating the dross from the metal (2) As testing the works of His people. Appealed to the people for a greater earnestness and seriousness as to our own lives and the use to which we put our time.

THURSDAY, 10 JANUARY

After dinner went down to Paterson Street and visited old Mrs C. Found her up again and somewhat better. Read to her and Mrs M. Genesis 3 and briefly touched upon man's lost condition by nature and indicated the only way of escape. I had a struggle to bring myself to say anything at all, and once I had said my say I was anything but satisfied with it. I greatly fear that it is a very dark home. Yet the Lord's mercy can reach even there.

At the Class I took up the Revolution Settlement and traced out the growth of Moderatism, halting on the threshold of the Ten Years' Conflict which (D.V.) I shall take up next week. I enjoyed tonight's discourse perhaps better than any since this present session began. There were twenty-two present.

Of late I have been dwelling in a favoured corner; I have been getting a little more of the 'sun' than usual, and consequently the chill of which I have been lately complaining has in a measure been removed.

SABBATH, 13 JANUARY

Gaelic: Jeremiah 9:24; *Afternoon:* Micah 7:9; *Evening:* Luke 13:24.

Satan troubled me early today. During worship he continued his onslaughts so that I began sorrowfully to fear a barren day. Even the shutting of the pulpit door after me did not shut him out. If anything, he troubled me only worse, filling my mind with dark, harsh thoughts towards certain before me when I should have been wholly taken up with love and pity for my poor fellow-sinners.

Between the Gaelic and the afternoon Satan found another occasion against me. Chancing to notice how the mould was gathering on certain books in the study owing to the damp, I began to worry about the preservation of my library in this damp house. However, once out and once embarked upon my theme – the better day which is coming when the Spirit of the Lord shall be outpoured upon us – I found a freedom which I enjoyed very much.

Although the snow lies almost two inches thick, the afternoon and evening were fine and the attendance at night was good.

MONDAY, 14 JANUARY

Never felt such cold as experienced this morning. Was perfectly benumbed. Fortunately I had taken the precaution of letting the taps run overnight, but even so, the cold water tap in the wash-hand basin was frozen stiff. About 10 o'clock snow began to fall, fine and powdery, and driven with such a wind that there was scarcely a window in the house but had a snow heap below it. As to the doors, the snow was simply drifting in under them.

Worked out a sermon on John 1:16 but was not very well pleased with it. In the afternoon made some calls. The snow was drifting badly and was in places from six inches to a foot in depth. Called at Erskine Villa and found that the baby is not getting on at all well. Certainly this awful weather won't help it. Poor little thing! Called on MacGilps and Finlay. Was pleased to learn that he had won the D.C.M.

TUESDAY, 15 JANUARY

Composed sermon on John 6:27 and enjoyed it pretty well.

While down in Ardrishaig Jeanie Campbell came up with *Grace and Truth*. I was very disappointed that I missed her. At Ardrishaig I found little Archie still in the same critical condition. On my way home my conscience began to check me for not having spoken to him plainly enough yet and I determined to have the matter out on Friday, (D.V.). It seems so easy to imagine myself doing such a thing, but it is altogether a different matter when it comes to reality. Yet I must look to the Lord, else I shall not be free of his blood. Oh that He may preserve him till I see him again (D.V.) and that I may be given grace then to do my duty. What a poor wretch I am who cannot talk even to a child about his soul! – and yet I presume to be a minister.

WEDNESDAY, 16 JANUARY

Worked out Gaelic sermon on Jeremiah 10:23. At Gaelic Prayer Meeting I gave an address I had intended giving a fortnight ago on Psalm 14:4–7 and was given such liberty that I enjoyed it very much. Felt grateful to the Lord for giving me strength to deliver my message tonight.

This forenoon, after finishing my sermon, certain aspects of the text which I had omitted came up before me, aspects which would, if applied, have made the text more personal and, I believe, more helpful. This led me to the conclusion that it would be a wise thing on my part before beginning a sermon to take the text to the throne of grace with a view to seeing what might be given me out of it suitable to my own case. What is suitable to myself is bound to be suitable to others and therefore helpful.

THURSDAY, 17 JANUARY

Spent forenoon reading up the Disruption Period for the class. Very much moved by many incidents in the history of that stirring time and by the unflinching testimony borne by our fathers to the principles and contendings of the glorious Church to which we belong. Felt not only edified by what I read, but strengthened and quickened. Those were glorious times!

Enjoyed the class pretty well. Eighteen were present. Wish I could imbue these young folks with a passion for the principles of the Church. Feeling a little liberty these days, but kept so busy that no time for the nourishment of my own soul. It is awful to be starving among the means. It is like a man starving in a cookhouse.

SABBATH, 20 JANUARY

Went out this morning as hard as ever and got no relief in the church. Had liberty neither of language nor of spirit. In the afternoon fared, if anything, worse and felt weary of myself and that I might as well give up preaching altogether. It is long since I have had this feeling, and a miserable one it is.

MONDAY, 21 JANUARY

Composed sermon on Isaiah 1:18. Engaged upon it with more than usual earnestness, endeavouring to keep before me all the while as vividly as possible the fact that I was God's ambassador, and that I was sent with a message to the poor unsaved who would be listening to me.

TUESDAY, 22 JANUARY

In the morning received terrible news that John MacEwan died suddenly this morning or last night. What awful blows our Church is getting – one after another! On every side I see my friends cut away, old and young. I seem to be spared as a soldier in the battle who escapes the bullets which have slain his companions. Yet how long shall it be so? I feel I may be cut off at any moment. Oh how my affections and interests should be set upon eternity! I might have known that Mr MacEwan was near his end, he was so mellow and ripe. His congregation will be distracted, for they simply adored him. I pity them in their grief How wonderful it was that his last two communions should have been such rich ones! In a ministry of twelve years he had only one new communicant. Then two years ago he got another in Jessie MacKinnon, and last year he got five. Poor old man, I shall ever remember how he wept when they came in before the Session. But his work is over and he is happier now. He has crossed the Jordan and dwells in the Promised Land, and no doubt he will be waiting somewhere near the entrance to see, sooner or later, one of his own flock from Sliddery coming in.

WEDNESDAY, 23 JANUARY

In the afternoon had a visit from three MacNeill lads, Archie, Angus and Donald. Thought a great deal of them and my heart went out especially to the two going to France. At the door Angus said that eternal things came home more to a man out in France than at home. Said he was not afraid for himself but he didn't like Donald having to go.

Donald was out at the Prayer Meeting. I think he is feeling leaving very much. Oh that the Lord would take care of these dear boys!

MONDAY, 28 JANUARY

Walked down to Stronachullin in the afternoon and saw the Shaws. On the way I was turning over Matthew 11:30 in my mind in preparation for tomorrow. Seemed to get some light upon it. Also had one or two sweet moments there in the gathering night as I walked along by the lashing sea.

THURSDAY, 31 JANUARY

Today I have again had a painful experience of that dreadful formality to which I am so prone, both in my pastoral visitation and in family worship. What grace I require to keep me from this sin, which I so much hate, yet to which I am so prone. Yet it has its own lesson, and that lesson is a sad one – too little feeding upon the hidden manna.

SATURDAY, 2 FEBRUARY

Have been very much troubled all day by thoughts leading me away from the solemn and responsible work of preparing for the duties of the Sabbath. First of all my mind was agitated on the arrival of the *Record* by the leading article, which, in dealing with the recent secessions from our Church, assumed a mildness of tone which rather nettled me. The breaking of ordination vows is not a matter for anything but plain speaking – and the plainer the better. I am grieved when I see how lightly this sin is regarded even by some of whom I would have expected better.

The second matter which took up my mind at the cost of my work was the shifting of the study downstairs again in view of the damp which is also apparent upstairs, and which is spoiling my books and rendering my roll-top desk practically useless through the swelling of the wood. How I wish I could get away from all these things, that I might have the Lord with me and enjoy His presence!

WEDNESDAY, 6 FEBRUARY

The attendance at the Prayer Meeting was exceptionally low, only twenty-three being out, yet I enjoyed it very well indeed. I took up the first clause of 2 Samuel 23:4 'And he shall be as the light of the morning when the sun riseth, even a morning without clouds'.

Feel sad as often as I think of leaving home tomorrow. I have no great desire to visit cold, inhospitable Islay; indeed I have no desire at all, and home appears to me very sweet at present, but go I must and I must go willingly too, for this is Christ's service. I pray I may be blessed in my mission and that I may have souls for my hire.

FRIDAY, 8 FEBRUARY

At West Loch Tarbert, en route for Islay, I saw 100 American troops who had come ashore on the Islay coast from the torpedoed troopship 'Tuscania'. It was with powerful feelings I surveyed them, more especially since I supposed that these were the only survivors out of a complement of about 2,500 men. My relief was therefore great when I learned that the death-roll, in spite of the earlier reports, was comparatively light, 210 being the present number missing.

The wind having increased considerably since yesterday and still continuing from the S.W., I could do nothing but look for a bad passage. And indeed it was bad, but I wasn't sick, for which I was and am very thankful, else I would not have been fit for what was to follow – our eight miles tramp on foot. The door of the hotel was opened to us by two American soldiers and I was informed by a lady that a bed had been reserved for me by Mr Ross's landlady as the hotel was completely occupied by the troops.

SATURDAY, 9 FEBRUARY: ISLAY

In the afternoon the weather unfortunately broke, and during the first part of the great funeral of forty-eight American soldiers the rain was very heavy. Yet there was a large concourse of people gathered from all parts of the island. I was exceedingly sorry for the Americans who were paraded without greatcoats or any protection from the rain. The men were buried above the sea near the place where the survivors came ashore. And there they shall rest, on that grim height, overlooking the hungry sea that beat them to death against the rocks ere it would part with them – the poor brave lads from over the sea.

MONDAY, 11 FEBRUARY: ISLAY

In the afternoon with old Calum Taylor I went visiting round the Cladich district. I must confess that I am taken up with the Cladich people. They appear to be an intelligent class and possessed of a greater love for the truth than I would have supposed could be found in any part of Islay. One man, Ferguson to name, who has been confined to bed for two years, began to talk about MacRath Mor,[1] and it would appear that his name is still familiar in the district. He also told me that Mr Campbell, minister of Portnahaven before the Disruption, used to have Dr MacDonald, Ferintosh, every year for his communion. I cannot find this love of the old ecclesiastical tradition at all in Lochgilphead so I am more than surprised to find it in Islay. My conception of this quarter is completely changing.

---

1 The Rev. John MacRae, 1794–1876, affectionately known in Gaelic as MacRath Mór (Big MacRae) who ministered in Lewis, in Knockbain (on the Black Isle), in Greenock and in Lewis again. At the time of the revival of 1859–60 in Lewis it is said that 40 young men joined the membership of his congregation at Lochs. In a short account of his life, written in 1895, the Rev. Nicol Nicolson, who had heard all the leading Highland preachers of his day and Spurgeon in English, said, 'in our opinion he surpassed them all in point of substance, animation, power, fulness, and impressiveness', *The Rev. John MacRae, A Short Account*, 2nd edition, 1924, p 30.

WEDNESDAY, 13 FEBRUARY, ISLAY

Today another dead American soldier was found among the rocks about two miles away. The body was removed this evening to Port Charlotte. Heavy firing was heard this afternoon to the South.

WEDNESDAY, 20 FEBRUARY: LOCHGILPHEAD

At the English Prayer Meeting twenty-seven were out, the evening being wet. Spoke from 2 Samuel 23:4 (latter clause) about Christ being like the tender grass which springs up by clear shining after rain. I may say that it is long since I had such a night. The 72nd Psalm reached my heart. Oh the glory of it! I could almost have shouted out for very joy when in singing the last verse we came to the words 'Let all the earth His glory fill'. There is no end to the desire of grace for the glory of Christ. All the way home I was simply in raptures. Oh what a sweet experience! It was just like what I used to get long ago – at first. More, Lord, more!

THURSDAY, 21 FEBRUARY: MINARD

John[1] gave me my choice of various books which he is leaving behind him besides an almost complete set of Calvin's *Commentaries* and *The Works of Jonathan Edwards*. He made up in all sixty-three volumes.

FRIDAY, 22 FEBRUARY

Another wild day. Got down from Minard in the car with my cargo of books.

While visiting in Ardrishaig and being engaged in prayer in Oakbank I had occasion to plead as a warrant for our coming again to the door of Christ the kindly treatment which we had before received there, even as the beggar returns to the door of the one who has shown him kindness. While in the midst of the prayer a knock was heard at the door. Mrs Campbell at the conclusion ran down stairs only to find a beggar at the door. It was very singular.

TUESDAY, 26 FEBRUARY

I again got liberty in working out a sermon on 1 Samuel 22:23 which I think of preaching in Southend.

1 John MacLeod had lost his wife suddenly the previous October at the time of their daughter's birth. Shock and poor health combined to make it impossible for him to continue his ministry at Minard and he had now decided to leave. Thereafter he served congregations at Lochcarron and Barvas (Isle of Lewis), dying in 1963.

Went down to Archie MacEwan's and got my choice of his brother's books. I was overjoyed to get *Dr Kennedy's Sermons*, *M'Cheyne's Sermons* in Gaelic, David Brown's *Life of John Duncan*, and Duncan's *In the Pulpit and At The Communion Table*.

FRIDAY, 1 MARCH

Started off again for Arran. Beautiful day. On arrival at Glasgow had a search for the George Hotel but in the darkness could not find it. However, I came across the 'Ivanhoe' and got the only available single bedroom. The shortage of food was much more apparent than in Islay. Called on the Principal in the evening.

SATURDAY, 2 MARCH

Was rather staggered to find my hotel bill to amount to 9/6. To pay 1/6 for three slices of bread, two cups of tea and a little butter and jam, and 2/6 for the same plus a little bit of fish is sheer extortion.

We got a lovely crossing. I walked about half way across from Lamlash before the mail-gig overtook me.

SABBATH, 3 MARCH: ARRAN

11.30 *am*, *English*: Isaiah 43:20. *Gaelic:* Genesis 6:8. 6.30 *pm:* 1 Samuel 22:23.

The morning dawned crisp and keen with the ground frozen hard. I was surprised at the size of the congregation which I understand was abnormal. I was very anxious about the service as I feared that, now that Mr MacEwan was away, my former liberty would forsake me, but it was not so. I had not long started before tears were in evidence in various parts of the church. I enjoyed the evening even more than the morning. The attendance again was large and the service was very solemn. What a great treat it is for me to be in this place.

MONDAY, 4 MARCH

Left by steamer at 2.15 and got to Glasgow at 6.17. At Glasgow I went with Mr MacLeod to his sister's at 8 Bute Gardens where we had tea. We reached Edinburgh at 10.5 after a tiresome journey. I have to thank the Lord for His great goodness to me during all this day. I feel tired. All looking well at home except Dad, who is very much thinner.

TUESDAY, 5 MARCH: EDINBURGH

Spent the whole day in Committee work and felt rather weary of it before the end of the day. I find it exceedingly easy to get out of touch with my Maker in the routine and heat of ecclesiastical business and debate.

THURSDAY, 7 MARCH

John saw me off at the Central Station and helped me along to the platform with the pile of books I was taking home. Had a good passage.

Was astounded at what I saw in the *Bulwark* re a book recently issued under the joint authorship of Dr Norman MacLean of St Cuthbert's and Dr Schlater of the U.F. North Church, *God and the Soldier*. In the book not only is it declared that we should pray for the dead, but for the dead in hell, for God is there ultimately calling His children to Himself. Usually error takes a long time to work itself out, but I who am yet a young man have to confess that in the short space of my life I have seen the transition from orthodoxy to the most deplorable heresies conceivable.

THURSDAY, 14 MARCH

Spent forenoon in working out for the Class. I dealt with doctrine – Calvinism versus Arminianism – and found it very edifying.

Felt very discouraged at the Class tonight. Only thirteen turned out. I cannot help seeing that there is no great zeal for Free Church principles among my people. It is not a good sign.

THURSDAY, 21 MARCH

Felt as though the ill-will of the community were resting upon me and I longed to get away to some more congenial sphere. It was a wicked frame of spirit, because my lot is apportioned by the Lord and I ought to leave it in His hands, but I have no doubt that my depression arose from my physical condition, for I feel perfectly listless and worn out.

In the evening had my class. Subject was Purity of Worship and I enjoyed it fairly well.

FRIDAY, 22 MARCH

Today the news has come of the great German offensive having begun at last. It seems to be a stupendous effort. Certainly not since the early stages of the war have we been in such peril. May the Lord enable our armies to stand firm against this awful rush! and oh may He stretch His covering wings about my dear brother!

SABBATH, 24 MARCH: TARBERT

In the afternoon 108 were out. I got fair freedom and excellent attention; wherever I looked I saw attentive faces turned towards me, yet somehow I felt that my discourse was growing wearisome and stale to them and therefore I unduly hurried over the closing portion of it. I should remember that the message is not mine, which would be a poor pitiable message indeed, but Christ's and invested with all His authority.

In the evening I preached from Luke 13:30 and apparently the message was blessed to a young soldier on the eve of returning to France.[1]

WEDNESDAY, 27 MARCH

In the morning I got up a little earlier than usual and had a little time for private reading which I put in at Marshall's *Sanctification*[2] and at prayer. Found liberty before a throne of grace and felt in better trim all day. I trust I may be able to continue this, for it will be worth my while getting a private hour to myself if it will make me fresher and stronger for the day. It certainly keeps my soul from being utterly dried up, as is the case when I am swamped with overwork.

At the Gaelic Prayer Meeting, at which eighteen were present, I took up Psalm 16:2–3 and enjoyed it pretty well. The meeting past, a great cloud darkened upon my spirit because of the dreadful battle now being waged upon the Western Front and of the inevitable slaughter. How is it with my dear brother? Oh God of Battles, protect him and cover him with thy wings! Oh for his conversion!

THURSDAY, 28 MARCH

George has been very much in my thoughts lately and I have been feeling my grief more sore than at any time save at the beginning. Mingled with this is a great apprehension because of Dunc. News came today of the first from the village to fall in this great battle and it is Sergt Archie Orr of my own congregation. I fear that this is only the first.

SATURDAY, 30 MARCH

Was inexpressibly relieved today to hear from home that Dunc is in hospital. It seems that he has diphtheria, and that is bad enough, but it

1 A margin note in the Diary adds, 'Informed of this, 8th November 1924.'
2 Walter Marshall, *The Gospel Mystery of Sanctification*, 1692, and many later editions.

appears that he has now got past the worst of it, and oh I am thankful that he is out of this awful battle. I hear that Dugie MacGilp is wounded. I am thankful that it is no worse.

WEDNESDAY, 3 APRIL

Called on poor Mrs Lambert today who yesterday received word of the death of her son in France. She is bearing up wonderfully well. She is sustained from on high. She said that yesterday the message that came to her with power was 'Be still and know that I am God'.

Further vexing news came today. Poor Willie Carswell is missing; last seen he was slightly wounded. I am deeply grieved for the Carswells. The suspense incidental to this news must be excruciating.

FRIDAY, 5 APRIL

There is still much anxiety in the village respecting some of the lads at the Front. The Carswells are still without further word about Willie[1] and so far nothing has come from Donald MacFarlane. His wife is beginning to worry terribly. Nothing has been received as yet from George MacKenzie but his sister seems to be less alarmed than some of the others. I trust that the poor boys are well and that word will soon come from them, for this suspense is cruelty itself to their people. I spent most of the day going from one place to another enquiring about the lads. The battle has again been resumed and the fighting is very fierce. What fearful havoc! What devastation! How is it all going to end? May the Lord have mercy upon us as a people!

Am still pretty dry, yet I must confess that the morning private hour is very sweet to me. I trust that it will become a means of blessing to me yet.

WEDNESDAY, 10 APRIL

Disturbed at the appearance of Parliament's Military Service Bill calling upon ministers for military service. Prepared to resist to the utmost.

THURSDAY, 11 APRIL

The text of the Military Service Bill appeared in the *Scotsman* today. There is no mention in it about consulting denominations. Every minister under 51 is deemed to be enlisted on a certain date and is forthwith called up; then he is offered the choice of combatant or non-combatant service. On the way home from the meeting tonight I felt

1 Confirmation of his death came on April 9th.

my heart going out to Christ, and I thought, 'Oh what a sweet thing to die in defence of the crown rights of such a glorious Redeemer'.

TUESDAY, 16 APRIL

Cycled down to Tarbert. Lovely day. Presbytery meeting. To my great relief I had both my resolutions passed (1) Respecting the invitation of Father Collins to the Ardrishaig Induction[1] (2) Asserting the freedom of the Church of Christ from the control of the civil power in respect of things spiritual, especially in connection with the calling up of ministers for military service.[2]

After the meeting, it was reported in the press that the clause relating to clergymen had been dropped from the Military Service Bill. I am overjoyed that we were able to raise our testimony before this became known. The Lord indeed works for those who will dare to stand for the truth.

WEDNESDAY, 17 APRIL

I am perfectly overwhelmed with work consequent upon my having taken over the Presbytery Clerkship at a time of exceptional stress, but I am striving to fight against giving way to care, which of course would cost me the Lord's presence.

THURSDAY, 18 APRIL

Got up early and worked before breakfast in the garden, and felt the better for it all day.

SATURDAY, 20 APRIL

Archie McDiarmid told me tonight that the collection for last Communion was the best since the division in the congregation in 1904. Again I have reason to thank the Lord for this. It is not without its own significance. Both John MacLeod and Prof. Cameron spoke of warmth in the congregation. I have lately been feeling it myself. I never pleaded for better contributions, yet this increase coincides with increased warmth. It is ever so. Grace opens the purse-strings.

1 A Roman Catholic priest had been invited to the induction of a minister to the Established Church of Ardrishaig.
2 The Presbytery, whose resolution was given in full in the local press, declared that they could not 'recognise the authority of the State to interfere with any minister of the Gospel under its jurisdiction in the way of removing him from the charge to which he is bound by solemn ordination vows, and thus suspending him from the due performance of the duties pertaining to his office'. Unknown to the Presbytery, Parliament had, in fact, dropped this clause in the new Bill the previous evening.

SABBATH, 21st APRIL

I heard today that Duncan MacLullich had died of wounds received on the 21st and I went to call on his poor mother ere I came home from the morning service.

MONDAY, 6 MAY

Today in the service I could not help marvelling at the wonderful goodness of the Lord in having made a minister of the Gospel of me – truly, a brand plucked from the burning.

THURSDAY, 9 MAY

After the service I visited Ann Graham who lost her son in France recently. I prayed in Gaelic. She evidently understood, for she wept. Poor creature!

FRIDAY, 10 MAY

Spent the forenoon in preparing Sabbath's Gaelic work and got some liberty in it. In the afternoon did a little visiting, and then met John MacLeod who came in the car. He brought news that cast a gloom over my spirits, namely, that Mr MacColl died last night. It was not altogether unexpected, nevertheless it was a sore blow. It leaves us very weak. Lord how long! The walls of Zion are crumbling and where are the witnesses for the years to come? Those to whom we looked are falling upon the field of battle. Only today I also heard of the death of John Munro, the Lewis student, who was killed in action. I wonder that when death is so busy I myself am spared. It makes me afraid. I am afraid of death. This world is too sweet for me to consent willingly to leave it, and yet in honesty I must confess that it is only the Cause that is making it sweet. Oh that the Lord would revive Zion! It is for that I long! All else is nothing.

SATURDAY, 11 MAY

Lying upon my spirit is the thought that I am not ready to die. I fear and shrink from death, whereas I feel that, were I as I should be, I should not have such a fear, but should be able to look forward unto the Promised Land with joyful anticipation. I too must die. Oh that I were prepared for it and were rid of all fear of it, content to serve my Redeemer either in time or eternity just as His will ordered it!

I long for a day of power on the morrow.

SABBATH, 12 MAY: TAYVALLICH COMMUNION

I have to thank the Lord for a very blessed day. He heard my mourning

1918 | DIARY OF KENNETH MACRAE

cry and raised me up from my despondency, giving me a sweet sense of His favour.

Coming along the road to the church I was glad that I was a man and not an angel, because I have a blessing which is denied even the angels, the privilege of preaching the Gospel to my fellow-sinners.

SATURDAY, 18 MAY

Felt very unsettled and unfit for work. Satan also was trying me sore. I took my case to a throne of grace, but it seemed as if I were not to make better of it and Satan only got more power over me, until I began to fear that I would soon have no strength to keep him off any longer and that he would ruin my Sabbath for me. But while yet I fainted, his assaults seemed suddenly to fail, and I got a gracious sense of the Lord's favour which cheered me greatly and which has given me hope for the morrow. Blessed be the Lord who hath not given me over into the hand of my Enemy! Oh to live for His glory alone!

TUESDAY, 21 MAY: EDINBURGH

Opening day of the General Assembly. Rev. John MacLeod, Urray, the Retiring Moderator, preached from Zechariah 4:6. Rev. Donald Munro, Ferintosh, in his opening address, dealt with 'Evangelical History in the Highlands – its growth and character'. It was splendid and went straight to my heart. It was as much as I could do to preserve my composure under it.

THURSDAY, 23 MAY: EDINBURGH

At about 5.30 the Assembly had a visit from Lloyd-George.[1] He gave us a fine speech. Apparently he had been told that we were practically a Highland Church, for he began at once talking about Wales and the Welsh. He seemed to lose himself in it all, for he spoke four times as long in our Assembly as in any of the others. He indeed stirred me.

MONDAY, 27 MAY

Left home en route for Arran. On the way I fell in with Gillespie Campbell of Inveraray who was most pressing that I should enter the fold of the Established Church. I told him that I would do so when the Church of Scotland returned to her ancient testimony.

1 The British Prime Minister.

FRIDAY, 7 JUNE: LENIMORE, ARRAN

In the evening I had a most enjoyable time with Mrs Kelso. She is a very exercised woman. She mentioned that one of the old divines had said, preaching at Catacol, that the time would come, although he would not see it, when people profaning the Sabbath would be as numerous on the hills as were the sheep then.

TUESDAY, 11 JUNE: LENIMORE, ARRAN

In the forenoon I went away up the hills with Cook's sermons.[1] I got down into the dell worn out by a burn in the course of its many centuries of flowing, and felt quite happy there – it was so beautiful, so still, and so peaceful. Since I have come to Arran I have had some beautiful walks and there is a freedom of access to hill and glen which reminds me of old happy days in the North. This lack of liberty I feel very much at Lochgilphead. There are very few bye-paths and one has to go miles before one can take to the hills.

SATURDAY, 6 JULY

When I was having supper with Miss Scott on Thursday she told me that she asked Mr Livingstone at the time when the letters were appearing in the local paper condemning myself, as to why none of the other ministers said a word in my defence. 'Oh we don't like controversy' was the reply. What the people think of such is reflected by the answer she got to the same question put to a Baptist woman in the town, 'Oh they are afraid of their people'. 'I would rather be a tinker's dog', said Miss Scott.

THURSDAY, 11 JULY: ISLE OF SKYE

At Staffin I found Mr MacLeod, Duke Street, in charge. He is at present home in his native place for a rest. When I got into the pulpit I found myself in an awful quandary. I had brought in my sermon wallet, but the Gaelic sermon I wanted was missing.[2] I had left it out in my overcoat pocket. There was nothing for it but to go on as I was. I preached from Isaiah 59:19. The attendance was very good and the people listened well. I had dinner with Hugh Thomson, the missionary, and then set out for Kilmaluag. The schoolhouse was packed. I preached from Romans 7:4.

1 Probably, *Sermons in Gaelic and English by Archibald Cook*, 1907, edited by J. R. Mackay. Archie Cook (1788–1865), and his brother Finlay (1778–1858), both natives of Arran, were eminent servants of Christ.
2 He carried notes of the main heads and sub-heads of various sermons in this wallet when away from home.

FRIDAY, 12 JULY: KILMUIR, SKYE

The Question Day unfortunately turned out to be so wet that neither the Kilmaluag nor the Staffin section of the congregation could get over. I went to the church in fear and trembling. For me to close the Question was indeed an ordeal and I did not know how I was to manage. Should it ever have been said while we were in College, that the time would come when Calum [1] and I would preside at a Question Meeting, I would never have credited it.

SATURDAY, 13 JULY

At 12 noon Calum preached from Exodus 32:26. At the close of the service the Session was constituted. One man came forward. He seemed to be in a very exercised way, the tears streaming down his cheeks and falling on the floor. At this meeting also – as Calum afterwards told me – the elders expressed their desire to give me a call. Calum said that they would be better to hear me oftener that they might know whom they were getting. The Staffin elder, Mr MacLeod, replied in a way which made me wonder, after my miserable plight in going into the pulpit without my notes. He was quite satisfied to go upon what he had heard. This brings the whole matter to an issue, for it was resolved, in order to save expense and since the people would be gathered together, to have a congregational meeting on Monday at the close of the service. It is a very serious matter for me and I can only pray the Lord for guidance. I do not feel that I shall dwell here. When I look out on hill and sea I have no feeling that the landscape will become very familiar to me, but yet I feel the people drawing my heart. Oh for guidance!

SABBATH, 14 JULY

The great day came at last. Calum took an English service in the Manse at which only eight attended and all these had Gaelic. I went out to the church with a great dread upon me. What a congregation! The day was beautiful and there was a great gathering; the church, which would accommodate about 750–800, was packed. I preached my Action sermon from Isaiah 40:11 and was thankful to get along comparatively easily in it. By the time the Table Service came on I felt much more at my ease.

Calum preached again in the evening when again there was an enormous congregation. When I looked out upon that sea of faces and

1 His friend of student days, Malcolm (Calum) Galbraith at this time minister in Duirinish, Skye.

realised that these were immortal souls; when I saw so many young people present and realised what an influence our Church has got in this place; when I thought that to conserve this with all its clinging to the old customs and traditions was surely more profitable, more beneficial to the Church, and more my duty, than to try to turn a community to ways which they have forsaken and that in a district where our cause is comparatively weak; I saw it, I felt it, that I ought to come here.

At times I felt that I must rise and rush from the pulpit, or else break down altogether there in the presence of that throng – oh the singing!

MONDAY, 15 JULY

Preached from Hebrews 11:16. There was a wonderful attendance for a Monday, about 500 being present. What impresses me most about this people is their subdued looks in the house of God.

After the service the congregational meeting was held. The outcome was that the whole congregation (amounting to about 400, for all strangers had to depart at the close of the service) voted in favour of the call. Calum called upon anyone who might be against it to rise, but there was none. I cannot treat this lightly; I fear I cannot go past it.

I felt very sorrowful leaving Kilmuir. The people were coming to their doors and waving to us as we were driven past. At present I feel that I must accept this call. Not to do so would be like cutting off my right hand. Is the ordering of my mind in such a way not of the Lord?

THURSDAY, 15 AUGUST

Mr Roy came with a wire intimating John's death from wounds on Tuesday. It was awful, but my poor little Cathie stood it wonderfully. I am anxious because she has wept so little. I trust she will get relief. I wish I could bear her burden for her. I am also very anxious about her mother. Oh what a stroke is this! It has taken all the strength out of me. Have mercy on us, Lord, and spare us! Oh for grace that affliction might bring me nearer to the Redeemer! Black is the night over me, mournful my rest. When will this horror of war cease? Are there none to be spared?

MONDAY, 19 AUGUST

A woman in Ayr was heard to declare that her household was in receipt of £27 per week and that she was at a loss as to how she was to spend it. I am afraid that a very black day is yet to come even after the war is over.

People look for a much better world after the war. Unless there comes a change I fear that what will follow the war will be worse even than the war, gigantic tragedy though it be.

THURSDAY, 29 AUGUST

I somehow find, whether it is a good sign or not, that the preaching of consolation is becoming sweeter to me now than the preaching of warning. To console rather than to warn seems to be the tendency of growth in years, although I would not be prepared to say that this is the tendency of advancing in grace. Instead I would be inclined to say that when there is a falling away in zeal and faithfulness there will be a turning away from the note of warning.

MONDAY, 2 SEPTEMBER

Spent the day as a day of self-examination and improvement and must acknowledge that I felt the benefit of it.

I have been led to see that the failure of my ministry is in large measure the outcome of my lack of faithfulness in my private dealings with my people, that is, in my pastoral visitation. It is there that I fail, and I fail sadly. I ought to have had a list of every individual in my congregation and made a point of dealing with each separately, but I have not done this and hence my failure. May the Lord pardon me and help me to improve in the future as the fruit of failure in the past.

MONDAY, 9 SEPTEMBER: STRACHUR [LOCH FYNE]

Spent the day in visiting and enjoyed it pretty well. Must admit that I am enjoying the little change very well. The scenery is such as pleases my eye and thus I find the place agreeable to me; but, alas, the blight of Moderatism is everywhere present. It matters not whether the people belong to Established Church or U.F. or Free Church; for the most part the only religion they have is sheer Moderatism.

To such a desolate region would it not be a great privilege to bring the Gospel. Assuredly it would and I would esteem it so, but what takes my heart from me is the fact that I cannot get them to listen to the Gospel. Not only are they hindered by ecclesiastical prejudices, but their indifference is such that it is well-nigh impossible to get a gathering of any size. A preacher of the Gospel may come to this district, but what can he do when he cannot get a hearing? This is a very difficult problem, so difficult that I know not how to solve it, but assuredly it is not to be solved by ordinary means.

[140]

TUESDAY, 10 SEPTEMBER

I am feeling today what a terrible thing this Moderatism is, over-spreading the country like a blight, which takes it for granted that everything is well with everyone who is at all respectable. Wish I could cry out loud against it, but how to do so I know not.

THURSDAY, 19 SEPTEMBER

At night felt very happy. Had more of the presence of Christ than I have had for a long time.

TUESDAY, 1 OCTOBER

Today I heard a tale which has encouraged me and made me thankful to the Lord for His goodness to me. A certain Miss MacKay, a teacher in Oban and belonging to the Established Church, there met Mr Robinson, an Australian. He happened to mention myself, and she, when in the neighbourhood of Lochgilphead last summer, took the opportunity to come to hear me. Her portion has been a very sorrowful one. She lost a brother and her fiancé in the war, and her other brother, also as the result of the war, is confined in the Asylum here. I knew nothing of all this, but it happened that I had as my text, 'This is my comfort in my affliction', Psalm 119:50. She told Mrs MacKellar that the sermon seemed to be for her, that she never heard such a strain of preaching in her life, and that she would never forget that sermon. She had never been in a Free Church before and had been accustomed to believe what she generally heard as to the Free Church people being queer, prejudiced and narrow-minded. This case is all the more wonderful when I find that this sermon was taken after I had discarded the one upon which I had been working.

SABBATH, 10 NOVEMBER

I had hopes of getting out to the church today[1] but the weather was so awful – sweeping blizzards of rain and sleet – that to my great disappointment I had to abandon the idea. Instead spent most of the day reading *Grace Abounding*, and I hope not without profit.

My perusal of this book has made me realise in some measure the deadness of that state into which I have come. I live as though Satan were a myth. Is it not high time to bestir myself out of this spiritual sloth lest I become a castaway? May the Lord have mercy upon me!

1 He had been suffering from influenza.

Vexed to hear that Calum MacEwan has died of influenza in France. How sorry I am for his poor mother. May the Lord strengthen her in her trouble!

MONDAY, 11 NOVEMBER

Felt decidedly stronger today. In afternoon went down with Cathie and visited the MacEwans. Mrs MacEwan is bearing up wonderfully well. Poor soul! this is the sixth of her family she has lost.

At mid-day news came that peace had come at last. The first we learned of it was the pealing of the church bells in the early afternoon. Poor Cathie was sadly affected and broke down crying. As for myself I utterly fail to grasp it. That this report was authentic I was persuaded by the portion of Scripture which came strongly upon me, 'There arrows of the bow he broke, the shield, the sword, the war' Psalm 76:3. This I have taken as a text for one of my discourses on Sabbath (DV) and spent some time looking into it.

I feel strangely unmoved regarding the news which has come today. I wonder at myself. I feel more crushed than anything else – very sad and pensive. I look back and count the cost, and the reckoning crushes me down. I fear also for the future. Colossal questions must now be faced. Tremendous issues are now involved. Will it yet be said of us, 'Oh Israel, thou hast destroyed thyself'? God forbid!

SABBATH, 17 NOVEMBER

Last night Satan tempted me sorely. He strove to spoil me in two ways: (1) by putting me in a bad temper and (2) by denying me my night's rest and so reducing my strength. But blessed be the name of our Lord, his efforts came to nought and instead I was left with the comfortable hope that I was to get a good day, since the enemy had made such determined attempts to spoil it. And so it was. It is a long time since I have had such a happy day. In the morning, in view of the conclusion of the war, I preached from Psalm 46:10. I never had such liberty in the Gaelic – nor anything like it. In the afternoon I had as my text Psalm 76:3, 'There brake he the arrows of the bow, the shield and the sword and the battle'. Miss Dewar, Balliemore, was present and early gave way to tears. She is always very much exercised in the house of God. Later on, when I spoke of those who shall never return from the war, tears were wetting many a cheek, but these were the tears of natural affection and so far as spirituality is concerned count for nothing.

In the evening preached from Acts 28:24, 'And some believed the things which were spoken and some believed not'. Did not get the liberty of the earlier part of the day but, at finishing up, got such a lovely view of Christ as made my heart leap within me. And can I praise Him enough for such a day!

In the year 1805, when living Christianity was scarcely known on the Island of Skye, the preaching visit of a Mr Farquharson (a native of Tyree, Argyllshire) led to the conversion of a blind fiddler by the name of Donald Munro. Through Munro's subsequent witness the church at Kilmuir became the first effective gospel witness in the Island and it was in this parish that a remarkable awakening commenced in 1812. Opposition from 'Moderate' clergy secured Munro's ejection from the parish (where he had worked as 'catechist') but it could not stop the revival which brought multitudes to the possession of evangelical Christianity. Munro's closest ministerial friends were John Shaw of Bracadale and his successor, Roderick Macleod, who was to be the foremost preacher in another extraordinary revival which began in 1840 and moved the whole Island from end to end.

Foremost characteristics of these years were the spirit of prayer possessed by so many Christians, an insatiable desire for Scripture, and the life felt and manifested in singing the praises of God – 'The assembled multitudes engaged in the duty as with "one heart and one soul" and often seemed as if they knew not how to stop'.

There were not a few in Skye for whom the memory of these events – and something of their spirit – was still alive in the year 1919.

6 First Days in Skye

The winter of 1918–19 proved to be MacRae's last in Lochgilphead as the call of the Kilmuir congregation on the Isle of Skye, recorded in the entry for 15 July, was to bring to a conclusion his ministry in Argyll. In the period, however, between July 1918 and 27 May, 1919 (when he left Lochgilphead) there were a number of difficulties which deeply exercised him. First, it was not until 22 October, 1918, that the Kilmuir call, signed by 434 (46 members and 388 adherents) was considered by the Free Church Presbytery of Inveraray, and prior to that date enquiries had come to him from three other vacant congregations. This occasioned him not a little perplexity. Then, when the call was dealt with by the presbytery, its members – urged by spokesmen from the Lochgilphead congregation – declined to place it in his hands. The Free Presbytery of Skye, on behalf of the Kilmuir congregation, appealed against this decision to the Synod, and on 1 April, 1919, the Synod supported their appeal so that, at last, on 30 April, 1919, the call from Kilmuir was placed in Mr MacRae's hands. The previous October he had indicated to his congregation that he believed a removal to Skye to be in the will of God, and it was painful for him when the matter became so long-drawn-out.

In MacRae's own mind several things inclined him to believe that he was being guided to remove from Argyll. By 1918 it was clear that there was a minority in the Lochgilphead congregation who had no heart for his ministry. One individual, in particular, was a sore trial to him and yet, strangely enough, this person was to be found arguing keenly in the presbytery against agreement with the proposed removal! MacRae felt that the opposition was deceitful rather than open and it hurt him all the more for that reason. His state of health in the autumn of 1918 also led him to consider a move desirable. With three regular Sunday services in Lochgilphead, besides other congregations for which he was also responsible and to which he had to cycle long distances in all weathers, he felt that the labours required of him were verging on the superhuman. Physical ailments with which he had not previously been familiar began to worry him. The Diary complains of 'tiredness' and 'exhaustion', while the influenza which he suffered in November 1918 was severe. Occasionally when his physical condition was low he even wondered if his usefulness was near its end: 'The thought that the seeds of death may be already in me is a very depressing one. I do not think I am afraid to die, but I wish to live to see something of the Lord's glory made manifest through the preaching of the Gospel'. This desire to see a true revival was a strong factor in his thinking. In his Diary for 22 September, 1918, in a day of discouraging circumstances, he noted how the words of Psalm 37:4, 'Delight thyself also in the Lord; and he shall give thee the desires of thine heart', had come 'like soothing balm' on his spirit: 'My heart's desire is to experience the delights of a spiritual awakening. It is for that I long, but I don't think it will be realised in this countryside.'

This last statement requires some explanation. While he had witnessed several conversions in Lochgilphead, and had received especial encouragement from the response of younger people to his ministry, he found that the spirit of the community as a whole was moving decidedly away from those convictions which had formerly been so predominant in many parts of the Scottish Highlands. Christian traditions had lost their power and respect for the ministry of the gospel and the means of grace was in decline. At times the consciousness of this fact greatly oppressed him and such entries appear in his diaries as, 'The worldliness, the materialism of Argyllshire is strangling me'. In part his burden grew out of the conviction that he was not doing his duty as a servant of Christ simply by preaching within the walls of a church: he had also to see that Christ's authority was made known in the community even if that meant incurring displeasure, and in such a small town as Lochgilphead there was indeed no way of avoiding the giving of offence. For example, at the end of the war, the Town Clerk arranged a united public service on 11 November and asked for MacRae's co-operation. It was not forthcoming; instead, MacRae records that he addressed his own people at a mid-week prayer meeting the same week on 'two things (1) that national judgment follows national sin and (2) that mercy follows such judgments; and I encouraged the people to pray for a time of spiritual awakening and revival on a scale unknown in our day.' Co-operation between denominations was also expected in Lochgilphead at funerals, but in October 1918 MacRae refused to attend a service in the United Free Church preceding the burial of a man of known ungodliness. A few months later the Established Church and the U.F. Church combined in a 'Mission of National Re-dedication' and, perhaps because evangelism was to be a part of this mission, one of the local sponsors felt it worth while to write to invite MacRae's participation. Noting the fact in his Diary, MacRae says: 'I wrote a pretty frank letter, pointing out that I regarded such a movement as quite futile until there should first be sincere repentance in the ministry for sins of frivolity and heresy'. His reasons for adopting this attitude were far from being uninformed. He knew that in the same year, for example, the Church of Scotland Presbytery of Aberdeen had moved that an appreciation of the late Bishop Chisholm, Roman Catholic Bishop of Aberdeen, be recorded by the Presbytery. The mover said in reference to the Bishop that 'they had frequently been golfing competitors and then it would have been difficult to find out there was any difference between them doctrinally'.[1]

This adherence to his convictions drew increasing opposition. Before the war ended some were suggesting that the Free Church minister should be away at the battle front, and he was – as diary entries in August 1917 have indicated – publicly criticised in the local press. While not shirking such controversies MacRae increasingly felt his isolation and loneliness as a minister in Argyll; he longed to be preaching in an area where there was a greater hunger for the Word of God and where there would be less occasion for the contentions which were necessary in Lochgilphead. In Kilmuir, in July 1918, he felt that he was in a different atmosphere. There he visualised the possibilities of a spiritual quickening in a way which he could not do in the South. From that time on the 'pull' of the North became irresistible – 'I have desire, so great that to reject the call would be like cutting my hand off'.

In the outcome, therefore, Kenneth MacRae left his first pastorate with mixed feelings. Often he felt as he did when, in anticipation of his departure, he wrote in his Diary for 1 April, 1919: 'I love my dear congregation, and to leave them tears at my heart-strings. Just now there are several interesting cases among them which makes it doubly hard, yet it must be.' These same feelings were evident in the congregation on the 25th May, his last Sunday with them. As usual he preached at Lochgilphead in the morning, at Tayvallich in the afternoon and in Lochgilphead again in the evening. The last of these sermons was preached from 2 Corinthians 13:11, 'Finally, brethren farewell' and he notes: 'Felt it a great ordeal. Tried to deal faithfully yet lovingly with them. The poor people were greatly moved.' And yet when the time of parting came on the Tuesday following, it was with a sense of the coldness of the place he was leaving behind and relief to be gone.

He did not return to Lochgilphead until more than three years later, on a 'dull, damp, and cheerless' day in November 1923 when 'the town

1 *The Scotsman*, 18 January, 1918

F

looked its worst'. As other engagements had necessitated his being in the neighbourhood he had offered to preach to his old congregation that evening. He had not forgotten the sadder experiences of his four years' ministry in their midst, but that night he knew afresh that the despairing feelings he had sometimes entertained were not to be trusted: 'The service was held in the church and I was amazed and touched by the splendid turnout, fully 140 being present, and not very many of them outsiders. I preached from Revelation 21:6 with a good deal of liberty. I had some thought of inviting to the vestry those who wished to see me, but I closed in the usual way and I am glad I did so because of the sequel, which was thus entirely spontaneous. As the people slowly passed out, first one and then another who were near the front came forward to the platform to shake hands with me, and then when the retiring congregation had cleared out of the building, the people who apparently had not gone further than the doors began to file back until an unbroken stream passed in from one door, came forward below the platform, and passed out by the other door. Some were in tears. What gratified me most of all was the way in which the young people came back; they were in the great majority, and some were among them whom I would scarcely have expected to see. It was a magnificent tribute of affection and it touched me to the very core. I did not think that they cared so much. I could have wept over them! How thankful I am for such an evidence that I did not labour in vain!'

☐ ☐ ☐

In recalling their removal to Skye Cathie MacRae writes:
'June 1919 was a month of wet boisterous weather, more like mid-winter, so that our first impressions of Kilmuir on a stormy wet day were anything but pleasant. The parish of Kilmuir and Stenscholl (as it is named) forms part of the extensive promontory of Trotternish in the North-East of the Island; it is high, windswept and treeless, but rich in agricultural land.

'The Kilmuir Free Church and manse stand by the main road on the east side of the promontory about three miles from the coast line and high above sea level. The manse, separated from the church by a garden, is a large building commanding a fine expansive view westwards of the little Minch with the Outer Hebrides, North Uist, Harris and the south coast of Lewis as a great breakwater in the distant background. In sunny weather we could see from our windows some of the rooftops in South Harris glittering in the sunlight, and at nights the Scalpay Lighthouse shone its three flashes into our bedroom. The distance across the water as the crow flies is roughly seventeen miles.'

The Gaelic-speaking parish of Kilmuir was made up entirely of a crofting population of about 945 persons over the age of 18. The boundaries of the parish extended from Kilmuir itself north-east to Kilmaluag and a slightly longer distance to Staffin on the Western side of the Trotternish promontory. Unless, however, a person walked – as the new minister was often to do – through the Bealach (a pass through the mountains) it was necessary to follow the indirect coast-road round the North-East of the Island. This extended the distance to some twelve miles and as some of his congregation lived as much as six miles beyond Staffin, visitation sometimes required him to be as much as 18 miles from home. Many of the homes were single-storied, heated by the burning of peat, and surrounded by enough land to sustain the needs of each family. Since the great revivals which had been experienced in Skye early in the preceding century Christianity in its Calvinistic and Evangelical form was respected by almost the entire population. Church attendance was practically universal, although a long-standing fear of a superficial profession of faith in Christ kept the number of communicant church members much lower than the number of adherents. In the days of controversy in 1900 more of the population had adhered to the Free Church than to any of the other Presbyterian denominations, and although no Free Church minister had been settled in Kilmuir from that date to the time of MacRae's coming, the 434 names appended to his call reflected the enduring influence of the Free Church cause. Cathie MacRae continues:

'After 19 years' vacancy there was much to be organised by the incoming minister, although in that pastorless period the congregation had served by loyal missionaries who, together with their own highly respected and beloved elders, conducted regular services in each section of the congregation. Immediately prior to my husband's induction Angus Macaulay was missionary in Kilmuir and Hugh Thomson in Staffin; both were highly esteemed, spiritually-minded men, who gave of their best to the people. Before our arrival Mr Macaulay was sent by the Church to Aultbea.

'Each Sabbath Mr MacRae arranged to take services in two of the three sections of the congregation (Kilmuir, Kilmaluag and Staffin). This was not easy, especially when the twelve miles to and from Staffin by horse and trap was involved. Roads in those days were narrow and rough-surfaced, with loose metal (not to be compared with the wide tar-macadam roads of today). For most of his mid-week journeys in the early years he was dependent upon a bicycle and later upon a motor-bike. I must also not omit mention of the townships[1] of Digg and Flodigarry which lie between Kilmaluag and Staffin. Digg is a Gaelic name for a hollow and this little hamlet nestles in a hollow on the side of a hill sloping to the main road There are good houses there now and the older thatched buildings – familiar in our time in Skye – are gone. below the road is the school, and hidden below a series of knolls is the township of Flodigarry. From both these places the people frequently attended the Kilmaluag services in the evening, but, as a rule, they were present at the Staffin Church in the opposite direction in the morning.'

◻   ◻   ◻

THURSDAY, 5 JUNE, 1919

Left Portree by motor at 9.30 and about two hours later reached Kilmuir. I could not help being displeased at the Interim-Moderator's utter neglect of any attempt to take in hand the necessary arrangements, with the result that it was simply a scramble through as best we could, with, of course, the minimum of comfort. I never saw such a poorly managed induction and it was altogether owing to his neglect of his duties.

The service, however, was more encouraging. There was a splendid congregation and the singing affected me.

After the service we had dinner in the Budges' house where Cathie and I are to stay.

FRIDAY, 6 JUNE

Did not do very much today. Felt time dragging somewhat. Shall not be right until get settled in Manse and better acquainted with people. Am feeling my weakness in Gaelic a great handicap. Felt a strange feeling come over me today when I thought of this place being my permanent home. Yet if I find the Spirit of the Lord working with me and blessing my labours it will be more than a recompense for everything. I believe my poor wife is feeling it lonely too.

SABBATH, 8 JUNE

With fear, yet with great hardness, went out to my first service in

1 A 'township' in the Western Isles is the designation for a group of crofters' homes.

Kilmuir. The day was very stormy although not so wet as yesterday. There was a good attendance of perhaps about 130. After the service the people got very wet going home, and although once again the evening brightened up, the attendance was down to about 70. This of course was only to be expected in any case, for the distant people could not come out on the two occasions. Preached from Rev. 3:20. Felt very cold and came home disappointed. Yet my coldness today may have been due to my lack of freedom in the Gaelic and to my inability to get the proper privacy requisite for preparation for the service of the sanctuary.

MONDAY, 9 JUNE

Did very little all day long and hence felt the time drag heavily upon me. I am tired of such idle, useless days. I wish someone would come to take me around the people, for as things are it is impossible for me to distinguish my own flock.

WEDNESDAY, 11 JUNE

This has been a day more to my liking. At the Prayer meeting which was held at noon 23 were present and considering the hour I thought this very good.

In afternoon, the day having cleared up, called on Norman Gillies. Found him in his mother's house but not at all well. Yet he came out with me, taking me to the house of an aunt of his own, a Mrs Beaton and an exercised woman. I enjoyed my visit there and I greatly enjoyed his company. If such are typical of my people, despite my weakness in the Gaelic I shall be happy here. All the time I was in Argyllshire I never met with a man – although I met with a woman – whose conversation was so much to my liking as was that of Norman Gillies today.

Further I felt my heart go out to the place today in a new and a strange way.

THURSDAY, 12 JUNE

Worked out discourse on Romans 12:2. Could not help noticing that in the working out of the sermon my thoughts and expressions seemed to be turned in a new and blunt, forcible way which would not be very acceptable in Lochgilphead, and this leads me to think that, despite my own deadness and desperate lack of feeling, the Spirit Himself is leading me even when I fail to realise it, and adapting the message for the different class of hearers who will now wait upon my ministry.

SABBATH, 15 JUNE

The night and early morning were very wild and wet, but ere we left for Staffin conditions had somewhat improved. The driver did not appear to be too keen upon going, for apparently in this part of the country the people are more considerate than those to whom I have been accustomed, and do not take it amiss if the minister, owing to stress of weather, fails to turn up. As far as Staffin I was able to manipulate the umbrella so that, although I had only a thin unlined summer coat, I was very little wet.[1] We arrived at about the right time, and after a hurried cup of tea I began the service and preached from Romans 12:2. Considering the day, the attendance was good, about 75 being present. I enjoyed it very well and got some liberty. After dinner in the Mission House I proceeded to Kilmaluag. I got the loan of a stout oilskin from Hugh Thomson, and very thankful I was for it, for as we proceeded the storm was getting steadily worse, until by the time we came to Kilmaluag it was blowing a hurricane. Nevertheless there were about 60 out at the service – most of them young people. I seemed to get something of the breath of heaven. How happy I was! How thankful that the Lord had brought me to this place! Preached from Matthew 7:14. Stumbled a bit at first but got on better later – a solemn service. Got it terribly wet on my way home.

MONDAY, 16 JUNE

After a long day of waiting the furniture came at last. The 'Dunara' rounded Waternish Point about 10 o'clock and about an hour later I got a telegram intimating her arrival at Uig. It was about 6 o'clock, however, before the first of the carts arrived. Fortunately there were enough carts to admit of their conveying all the furniture in the one trip and the whole was under cover, although not unpacked, by 8.30. Until 10 I spent the time unpacking. I found some of the things miserably wet, drenched through and through, especially the mattress – one quilt being completely ruined, but fortunately beyond some nasty scratches and other minor details there were no breakages, at least so far as I have gone.

TUESDAY, 17 JUNE

Spent an arduous day in putting everything in its own place in the manse and at the end of it all, we did not appear to be much further forward

---

1 The vehicle was an open 'gig' drawn by a single horse – either 'Nellie', a strong chestnut mare, or 'Maggie', a dark brown mare of slighter build.

than when we began. I shall be indeed thankful when everything is in proper order and I am able to turn to my work properly.

WEDNESDAY, 18 JUNE

Feel very much depressed about my Gaelic. I seem to be making no progress whatsoever in it and I very much question whether I shall ever be able to master it sufficiently to allow of my conversing freely with the people. Unless the Lord help me I shall prove a miserable failure, but was it not He Himself who brought me here? Therefore I am constrained to believe that He will help me.

FRIDAY, 20 JUNE

Today went up to the Manse and worked out discourse on Luke 24:28. In afternoon went out to see a sick woman, a Mrs Mackenzie who wished to see me. Found her a greatly exercised woman with a mind only for the things of the kingdom. Also called at several other houses.

Today, after my depression of yesterday, felt comforted. I seem to be better able to understand the people and to converse with them.

SATURDAY, 21 JUNE

Spent most of the day at the Manse trying to prepare for the morrow.

There is still no word of plumber, or anybody else. I am longing to get settled down, for until we do so I cannot really get begun to my work. I hope we shall not see another Saturday out of our own house.

TUESDAY, 24 JUNE

I walked out to Kilmaluag and took the prayer meeting. Did not get any great liberty of utterance but nevertheless enjoyed the meeting. Felt pretty tired on my way home although the walk was a very beautiful one.[1]

SATURDAY, 28 JUNE

The account for the removal came today. It amounts to £61 odd. In conjunction with the expenses connected with the Manse I fear that it will be a terrible burden upon the poor people.

MONDAY, 30 JUNE

Another long, wet, miserable day. Neither plumber nor painter came. I

1 The walk was six miles each way.

am quite tired of this waiting, and this incessant rain is terribly depressing. I never saw such weather. It is worse than winter. I do not think that we have had a completely dry day since we came, and the temperature is abnormal for June. Today in the Manse it was as low as 48, or rather, 47.75 degrees.

TUESDAY, 8 JULY

After considerable hesitation lest I should be leaving Cathie with too much work, set out for the Prayer Meeting at Kilmaluag and now I am very glad that I did so, for although I cannot say that I got much liberty in speaking yet I feel in a much healthier frame of spirit, and as for Cathie everything has gone well with her.

On my return found Cathie ensconsed in the Manse, and very comfortable it looks. This will be our first night here. May we have many a happy year together in it, if that be His will!

WEDNESDAY, 6 AUGUST

In afternoon with Norman Gillies went round some more houses in the Bornaskitaig district.

Feel somehow very happy and contented here. I am at home at last and no longer a stranger in a strange land.

Visit to the Isle of Lewis[1]

THURSDAY, 9 OCTOBER: NESS [FAST-DAY]

In morning Mr MacLeod, Carloway, preached upon the dry bones, Ezekiel 37:9–10. The pulpit is so large that when I was sitting directly behind him I was not catching everything he said. I was amazed at the size and beauty of the church. I had no idea that anything of such a pretentious nature existed outside of Stornoway. The singing was very slow, much slower than that of Skye, but it did not impress me as did the singing in Stornoway five years ago. Perhaps I am becoming used to the singing of multitudes now and therefore am less impressed by it. The cloaks and bonnets of the younger women, and the mutches[2] of the older, made a pleasing impression upon me. I like the native garb; it is modest – which is exceptional today – and becoming – which is also

1 As a student he had visited the home of his friend Donald Smith in Stornoway in 1914 but the present occasion seems to have been the first time that he preached in the Outer Hebrides.
2 Head-dresses made of white lace.

exceptional. The congregation was large, about 650. In the evening I myself preached. The congregation would now be nigh upon 1000.

FRIDAY, 10 OCTOBER

A great congregation of over 1000 awaited us in the church. The Question was based upon Malachi 3:16. Eight men spoke; one said that those who felt it long at a Question Meeting would feel it long in heaven.

In the evening we preached in various districts. Garrabost in South Dell, Carloway[1] in the church at Cross, and myself at Lionel. I found the building packed, about 350 being present. I enjoyed it fairly well but not as much as in Kilmaluag.

SABBATH, 12 OCTOBER

The Lewis singing today appealed to me very much. It was just glorious to hear that multitude sing, their voices slowly heaving and falling like waves in an ocean of melody. I do not suppose I shall ever hear anything so like the song of glory in this world.

MONDAY, 13 OCTOBER

Another magnificent congregation awaited us on Monday.

After the service the office-bearers assembled in the vestry. I was astonished at the size of the staff. I am sure there were 20 present. I was also amazed at the givings of the people.

As the car expected at 3.30 did not come, Garrabost and I went out to send off a wire to Stornoway. In the course of this outing we visited one or two houses. After all I have heard of the black houses of Lewis I did not think them so bad at all – not any worse in fact than many in Kilmuir and much better to my mind than many of the poorer houses in Lochgilphead.

TUESDAY, 14 OCTOBER

Although we rose early it was 12.15 ere we could get away, as for a long time the car defied every effort made to climb the hill before us. At last, however, when I was beginning to be afraid that I would never get away today either, we got started. At the same time I was sorry to leave Ness.

At first we were very much afraid that we might be brought to a

1 Garrabost and Carloway are not surnames but the names of districts in Lewis, in both places, however, the ministers were Macleods and it is the commonness of some surnames in Lewis which accounts for the necessity of additional form of designation being used as here, *ie* Garrabost=Mr MacLeod of Garrabost.

standstill upon some brae out on the moor, but everything went well, and at Bragar we got a fresh supply of petrol.

At Carloway, which I thought prettier than any part of Lewis I have yet seen, had dinner in the Manse. Felt very sorry to part company with Mr MacLeod here. The country in this part is more hilly than further North and I could see that over in Uig the landscape still more approximated to that of Skye. Hard by we could see the famous stones of Callanish and further on, and in the distance, the hills of Harris. Latterly it became very cold, but altogether it was a most enjoyable run of about 50 miles embracing the greater part of Northern Lewis. Had tea at Stornoway Manse.

WEDNESDAY, 15 OCTOBER

We left Stornoway about 2.15 am and had a very good passage. It was pretty rough for a while but I stood the test all right for which I was very thankful.

MONDAY, 27 OCTOBER: KILMUIR

Walked across to Staffin in the evening. Left at 3.15 and arrived at destination about 6.45. Took the short-cut over the hill[1] and for the first part of the journey enjoyed the excursion very much. At the Quirang the scene was wild and impressive. The sky was wild; the shadows of evening were beginning to darken upon the moor. High to my left the great heaving shoulders of the neighbouring mountains were white under a covering of new-fallen snow. I was the only living creature in the waste. The wild loneliness of it all was sweet to me. I felt something of what I used to feel long ago when I would wish that the mountains and glens of the Highlands might be found in heaven. I have less of that spirit now. The world is not so golden. I have learned more as to the desperate nature of sin. I could never be eternally content here now, no, not even if sin were taken away.

Ere I reached Staffin the darkness had fallen. I felt the latter part of my journey very long and my parcel of necessities for my sojourn became strangely heavy.

TUESDAY, 28 OCTOBER: STAFFIN

Set out visiting in the Valtos district in the company of Alister MacLeod. The day was cold, showery and windy, and the country beyond the townships scattered here and there looked very wild, especially towards

1 A distance of twelve miles.

the great snow-capped ridge of mountains which lies like a back-bone through the centre of the peninsula of Trotternish.

Visited nine houses. Found the people kind though rather shy. This district seems to be the U.F. stronghold, but at the meeting in the house of a Murdo Lamont, 21 in all turned out.

WEDNESDAY, 29 OCTOBER: STAFFIN

Had the prayer meeting at noon when 28 turned out.

In afternoon with Mr Thomson visited the families in Clachan, calling in all upon 12 houses.

We got a beautiful day and I enjoyed it very much, although latterly my chest was beginning to bother me. I don't know what is wrong; unless it is due to reading and praying so much in an atmosphere charged with peat smoke.

THURSDAY, 30 OCTOBER: STAFFIN

Left home after an early dinner and spent the afternoon in visiting in Flodigarry. I had no idea of the existence of such a sequestered, pleasant little township among the green knolls below the high road. It is wonderful how much arable land there is there, and good land too, for the people here were further on with their work than in any other place in the district. The houses, however, were somewhat scattered and we could not get on as rapidly as yesterday. Accordingly we were half an hour late for the meeting which was held in the house of Mrs Stoddart. It was crammed and oppressively close. After the meeting one of the Stoddarts said that there were about 60 present, the passage and the three rooms of the house all being full. Spoke from Matthew 3:9 with a liberty of expression which in view of my scanty preparation surprised me. There seemed to be a solemn spirit among the people. The eagerness to hear the Word is most encouraging and comforting. I was told that numbers were so afraid that they would not get into the house that to make sure of a seat they arrived there at 5 o'clock – an hour before the time. I was surprised at the feast we got after the meeting – a huge joint of roast mutton gracing the table at which eight sat. It was a very happy night and I am thankful. What zeal I find here after the deadness of Argyll!

MONDAY, 3 NOVEMBER: KILMUIR

In afternoon walked across to Staffin through the hill. The day was perfect and the scene, looking back from near the top of the Bealach in the light of the dying day, was perhaps the most exquisite ever I have looked upon. The sky was bright, almost flashing, with cloudlets of brilliant hues, the mountains black, sharply outlined against the sky, and the moor before me shadowy with the gloom of coming night. As I stood there, not a soul broke the stillness, not a bird cried, not a breath of wind ruffled through the silence. Nature herself seemed to be holding her breath at the beauty of the sight. I wished that by some means I might have been able to take away a reproduction of the picture to show it to the world, but I had to leave it behind me in the loneliness of the wilderness until night came and blotted it out.[1]

THURSDAY, 18 DECEMBER

This being the Staffin Harvest Thanksgiving, started out with Lachlan[2] on a very grey morning. We had not gone far when the rain began and the wind became stronger. At one particular corner the wind caught us side on, so that we were in imminent danger of being upset. At Staffin scarcely anything could be seen but clouds of rain driven before the wind. In such a day I did not expect anyone to be out, but 23 awaited me, including five from Digg. After service, weather conditions improved and we managed to reach Uig with a measure of comfort. At 6 o'clock went up to the church in the midst of a violent gale but this was nothing to the intensity of the storm which soon developed. Amidst the uproar it was very difficult for me to speak in such a way that my voice would be heard. I endeavoured to speak from Exodus 15:11, but at last there came such a terrific blast that I felt it useless to attempt to speak. As I stood thus silent there came the crash of breaking glass – one of the gable windows had been driven in – and in a moment the church was swept with wind and rain. Although the whole length of the church was between me and the window I felt the rain upon my face. Lamps were also extinguished. I felt it useless and also dangerous to try to continue, so abruptly closed my sermon, briefly engaged in prayer, and gave out one verse of a psalm. Outside, the storm and the darkness were awful, lightning flashed, and I was whirled about almost like a leaf. We stayed in Mrs Stoddart's[3] until 2.15 am when we ventured to leave. Trees and stacks were down, but we managed to reach Kilmuir after a most exciting ride. We could never have managed had

1 The visitation of the Staffin district was completed on 7 November, when the writer noted 65 homes connected with the congregation in that area, all of which he visited.
2 The owner and driver of the gig.
3 A sister-in-law of the lady whose home at Staffin is mentioned in the entry of October 30. Both were widows.

not the wind been almost dead against us. Arrived at the Manse we found it locked and Dolina[1] fled. While Lachlan went to seek her in Budge's I took refuge behind the little row of trees in front of the outhouse. I am sure I was there for an hour. It was weird there in the storm. I felt as though the world were coming to pieces. At last Lachlan appeared with Dolina who had taken refuge in MacNab's and I got to my bed at 4.45, thankful to the Lord for having taken me unscathed through such dangers.

WEDNESDAY, 31 DECEMBER

This has been a year of many and great changes – of great troubles, great joys and great sorrows[2] – yet all through there has been a sequence of great mercies so that, although I have to cry for pardon on account of misdeeds great and dark, and mis-spent days, yet there must be the note of thanksgiving that He has not dealt with me according to my desert.

1 Mrs MacRae's maid. Mrs MacRae was at Dunvegan.
2 Among these was the loss of an infant son at birth in August, at which time Cathie MacRae's own life was in danger.

It is most probable that no gift, no pains, a man takes to fit himself for preaching, shall ever do good to the people or himself, except a man labour to have and keep his heart in a spiritual condition before God, depending on him always for furniture and the blessing. Earnest faith and prayer, a single aim at the glory of God, and good of people, a sanctified heart and carriage, shall avail much for right preaching. There is sometime somewhat in preaching that cannot be ascribed either to the matter or expression, and cannot be described what it is, or from whence it cometh, but with a sweet violence, it pierceth into the heart and affections, and comes immediately from the Lord. But if there be any way to attain to any such thing, it is by a heavenly disposition of the speaker.

> John Livingstone, from his 'Remarks on Preaching and Praying in Publick', in *Select Biographies*, Wodrow Society, vol. 1, 1845

I realise very vividly today the necessity of personal holiness if I am to have fervour and warmth in my preaching.

K.A.M.

7 Prayer and Ministry in 1922

SABBATH, I JANUARY, 1922

The first day of the new year and a day of mercy. I began the year by rising earlier and seeking the Lord. Felt the benefit of it.

A night of squalls and fierce rains was succeeded by a morning equally wild. This tried my faith rather severely, for it is so hard to believe that one is sent with a message when there cannot be more than one or two to receive it. I comforted myself however with three reflections: (1) that the blessing is not bound to large congregations; that a sovereign Lord can work mightily in the little company; (2) that there were times when Israel was bidden to stand still, and so no doubt with His gospel messengers, and (3) that it is not for the servant to question the will of his Master but to know that divine wisdom directs all His doings.

About half an hour before the service the storm somewhat abated and, to my surprise, twenty-four gathered. I spoke from Isaiah 49:9, on Christ liberating the captives. In the light of the text I entreated the captives to come forth at the call of Christ to gospel liberty and showed the Lord's people how needless was all their anxiety. My poor people! May the Lord bless them and lead them to the Rock! Despite the unfavourable weather I have had a good day and am thankful to Him who has dealt so bountifully with me.

MONDAY, 2 JANUARY

The benefit of rising early to seek the face of the Lord I richly experience in a sweet nearness to Him that is very comforting to me. I also find it easier to write of Him when I use my pen, and I find increased refreshment in the Word. May the Lord give me grace to continue!

TUESDAY, 3 JANUARY

Last night I enjoyed great nearness to the Lord, so that my heart was lifted up within me in exuberant joy, and this spirit continued with me more or less all day. What a blessed season I got and how I rejoiced in the light of the Lord's favour! It was like one of the days of the first love come back again.

Being in such a spirit I anticipated a very sweet meeting at Linicro[1] tonight, and as I tramped down the snow-covered road I felt strongly that souls would be born again in that house before long. Yet when I actually engaged in the meeting, although I got a little liberty in the prayer, I felt very much bound and could get no measure of freedom whatsoever. This was very disappointing, but I attributed it to looking to my experience of joy rather than to the Lord as the source of blessing, or rather as my warrant to expect blessing.

I must confess to surprise at seeing Eliza MacDonald[2] from Totscore present. What gladdened me, however, was to hear that in going out she told Mór Bhochd[3] that it was what she heard on Sabbath (morning) that brought her out. How wonderful is His kindness! Is not this a token for good for the new year? The Sabbath morning was wild, unpromising; the attendance was small, and I did not get much liberty; and yet the Lord acknowledged the message. Should I ever again complain on a wet Sabbath?

WEDNESDAY, 4 JANUARY

This has been a long, trying, wearisome day, and the anxiety is by no means over yet. Our poor little Mary[4] had a very bad night and towards morning became feverish and delirious. I was somewhat comforted by Psalm 37:3–5 coming repeatedly to my mind, and then, on rising to go down for the nurse, by reading in the 71st Psalm, in which is that verse which my dear wife got when she lay nigh unto the gates of death (v. 20). Throughout the day she has been somewhat better and her temperature has gone down practically to normal, but I cannot help being anxious.

With a mind so troubled, to prepare for the prayer-meeting was no easy matter, and I was therefore relieved when Jonathan Campbell[5] arrived upon the scene and after some little persuasion agreed to take

1 A small village in Kilmuir.
2 A woman who had recently come home from America to look after her aged mother and until this time had shown little interest in the Gospel. This was the beginning of a real saving change. Eliza's niece, born and brought up in Africa, also came to Kilmuir at this time and found the Saviour.
3 This godly old lady who lived to be 100 and was then close upon that age wished to be known as Mór Bhochd (Gaelic for 'Poor Marion') because she was so conscious of her failure to attain to the Christian perfection to which she aspired.
4 Their only child who was by this time a member of the family circle.
5 A young man from Kilmaluag who was then a divinity student. Later he was minister of Corpach near Fort William. His father, Ewen Campbell, a worthy elder in Kilmaluag, is often referred to in the diaries under his Gaelic name, Eoghann.

the meeting. I very much enjoyed my time of fellowship with him in the afternoon, although I regret that, despite the admonitions of a voice within, I neglected to ask him to join with me for a few minutes at the throne of grace. I have been feeling this of late, that when any of the Lord's people meet together, they should not neglect the opportunity given them for social prayer. I was interested and gratified to hear him say that he was of the opinion that something was brewing in Kilmaluag, that the Free Church section of the community seemed to be unusually seriously-minded. May it be so, oh Lord, and may it be soon! Oh that Thou wouldest visit my poor congregation!

And now the night is before us. Oh, help, Lord, help! Heal our darling little one! May joy come in the morning!

THURSDAY, 5 JANUARY

The joy I desired came in the morning and we found our little one greatly improved. What reason I have for thankfulness!

Spent a most enjoyable day in visiting in Totscore. Gave a brief exhortation in every house upon a text which I judged to be suitable to the state of each family, and thus was enabled to bring the truth to twenty-three individuals capable of comprehending it, nine of whom either cannot or will not go out (to the church) to hear it. What reason I have to mourn my formality and the readiness with which I lose the spirit of earnestness! On the other hand, let me praise the Lord for having given me the opportunity to proclaim His Word in every house, and let me look to Him to water and bring to fruition the handfuls of precious seed cast out by the way. There is life in that township; it is certainly in an interesting way. Oh that the light may burn there soon so that the glory of it may flare even to the heavens!

FRIDAY, 6 JANUARY

I have today sadly experienced the poisonous effect of giving place to the cares of this world. What troubled me were mere petty matters, but their occupancy of my mind for five minutes robbed me entirely of that sweet sense of the nearness of the Lord's presence which I have lately been enjoying.

Got reports today from Lewis as to the state of spiritual life in the congregations of Stornoway and Carloway which were very encouraging. Things there are promising and hopeful. This is in marked contrast to the state of matters when I was last in Lewis (November 1920) and when I found the ministers mourning over the frivolity and decadence of the young people. The conviction is growing upon me that we are upon the eve of a wide-spread revival and that I shall see it in my own congregation.

SATURDAY, 7 JANUARY

A day of much farness from the Lord and deadness of soul. Tomorrow is my day for the Staffin-Kilmaluag round, but prospects are not favourable. A good day has been succeeded by an unsettled evening, with rising wind and falling glass. This also is depressing me, yet the Lord can give me a good day, and if He does not, last Sabbath ought to show me that I have no cause for complaint. The Cause is His and He can work without me. He will not lose His glory although my lips should be closed. Have mercy upon me, a miserable sinner!

SABBATH, 8 JANUARY

Despite a stormy night the morning was good. My evil heart, however, was far from the Lord and this distance was intensified by my driver's lateness in putting in an appearance and slowness in driving over to Staffin. I got into church twenty minutes late, hurried and prayerless, and altogether in a most unfit condition for undertaking such a solemn duty. The attendance was much less than is usual in Staffin, about eighty being out, but no doubt the outbreak of measles in the district was the cause of this.

Despite the fact that the United Free's had a service in the Kilmaluag Schoolhouse immediately before us, I had crammed house (about 125), including five from Flodigarry. I spoke from Deuteronomy 30:19 on the Gospel being a setting before the people of life and death. It was a solemn meeting and I trust that it was not in vain.

MONDAY, 9 JANUARY

I am again beginning to be troubled with a light, unconcerned mind as natural to me. What an awful enemy it is! Oh that I could be serious at all times and that my speech were seasoned with grace!

I feel the need of being more systematic in prayer, both in public and private, and to this end contemplate drafting out a scheme which will ensure more definiteness to my prayers and give to every desirable thing its due place in my intercedings.

TUESDAY, 10 JANUARY

Despite a very stormy day managed to get out to Kilmaluag. Was surprised to see an attendance of about sixty-five out at the meeting on such a stormy night. Spoke with great liberty from Isaiah 48:18–21 on revivals as a work of the Lord, their dangers, and our present duty in connection with them. I pressed the Lord's people to an increased earnestness in expectant pleading for a visit from on high and to more prayer in their social intercourse.

WEDNESDAY, 11 JANUARY

Like M'Cheyne, I am learning to fear Satan much more than I used to.

FRIDAY, 13 JANUARY

I am given to see that only diligent and regular cultivation of my own soul can sustain in me that frame of spirit which I feel so necessary to the effective prosecution of my work. If I lose that spirit all becomes mechanical, cold, and formal, and I have little heart in the performance of my various duties.

MONDAY, 23 JANUARY

The perusal of the *Diary of Dr Andrew Bonar* has made me aware of how much spiritual benefit may be derived from the keeping of a diary. Daily the soul thus is brought to a personal and present scrutiny of its own state and condition. Such an exercise, especially in the case of one such as I am, prone to be entirely engrossed with duties and pressing interests, is bound to be beneficial. I erred in allowing my diary for so long a period of time to consist of nothing more than a few scrappy notes of congregational or ecclesiastical interest.

A further lesson I have derived from that Diary, and also from M'Cheyne's *Memoirs*, is that one's own soul must receive the *first* interest, and then the congregation. Here I have been altogether wrong from the outset of my ministry. I have worn myself out labouring for my people, preaching, visiting, writing, without end, and I have starved my soul by my neglect to such an extent that I almost forget that I had one. And the result of all this feverish output of energy has been meagre in the extreme. My method has been all wrong and must be changed. More prayer, more personal soul exercise, more retirement, must be my method henceforth, and then haply I may look for more fruit in my public ministrations.

TUESDAY, 24 JANUARY

This has been a happy and refreshing day. I kept it as a day of prayer and soul exercise up till 7 pm and found it most profitable. Perhaps the most happy and profitable part of it was the season I spent in the Church in the afternoon. In the course of it, it was borne in very forcibly upon me that I had no right to engage in any duty pertaining to my office, without first entreating the Lord to come with me. How vain and presumptuous to work without Him! Praise be to His Name for a happy day!

WEDNESDAY, 25 JANUARY

Although I still feel something of the benefit of yesterday's exercise, I fear that I am beginning to fall away already. Oh for a holy heart, a heart set only upon God!

THURSDAY, 26 JANUARY

Just because I had purposed visiting today a district in which I have none who appear to me to be very promising in the way of godliness, felt such a shrinking from the undertaking that I had almost to drag myself to it. And yet, after all, I found the day to pass very pleasantly, I got liberty in prayer and in expounding the Word, and in at least two cases, if one or two furtive tears mean anything, my visits did not lack appreciation. I visited or called at seven houses and got the ear of ten souls. Let me learn from this not to shrink from any duty, no matter how unattractive it may appear; the Lord can make it profitable. And oh let me not keep away from poor and needy souls!

In this bright, beautiful, spring-like day the place looked perfectly lovely – the blue sky, the far-stretching sparkling sea, the great tawny, snow-flecked hills – and I could not but feel my heart go out in gratitude to Him who had cast my lines in pleasant places and who had given me health and strength to enjoy such a day. Somehow, too, the glory of earth served to bring the glory of Immanuel's Land nearer to my heart. One could almost forget that there was a death-passage between.

FRIDAY, 27 JANUARY

Have been asked to take part in a Gaelic service at the unveiling of the Clan MacRae War Memorial in Kintail in April. On account of the doctrinal abuse connected so often with such services and the absence of any Scripture warrant for making such functions an occasion for public worship, I have no difficulty in seeing my duty clearly to be in the direction of declining this request.

Got another promising report as to religious conditions in Lewis –

this time from Back. Only within the last three months have things in the Back district taken this colour. Oh that the Power would visit us here!

WEDNESDAY, 1 FEBRUARY

I used to think that 'watch' and 'pray' were synonymous terms, that the way in which 'to watch' was 'to pray', but now I see the difference; for I can pray now and perhaps experience some blessing in the exercise, and then come forth from my study and immediately fall under the influence of a light and unsanctified mind. Watching, I see, is just as imperative as prayer.

SATURDAY, 4 FEBRUARY

The reading in Bogatzky[1] today concerning the dishonour done to the Lord by our small expectations coincides with my experience. I cannot but see that I ought to expect; and yet for all my seeing, I know not how to expect. This, however, I do see, that the nearer I get to Christ the easier it is to expect Him to work. But to get near to Christ is in itself one of my soul's most serious difficulties, and yet this evening's quiet time for prayer in the church seemed to point to the solution, namely, strive after it, even with a heart which at the outset appears hopelessly stony and cold.

SABBATH, 5 FEBRUARY

The day was good but the attendance was affected by the prevalence of influenza colds presently among the people. The Kilmaluag representation (15) was good. I spoke from John 12:43, on the fear of man keeping from Christ, but did not get much liberty with it. Felt disappointed, but as I was leaving the vestry the question was as it were put to me, 'Can you see the hearts of the people? Your place is to go on with your work, not only pleading with sinners, but building up the faith of the Lord's heritage. The Day will declare the fruit'. With that I must be content, and learn more to exercise faith than rely upon outward signs of the power of the truth under my preaching.

THURSDAY, 9 FEBRUARY

I had to deal with my first request re the performing of a marriage ceremony since declaring my mind in public on the matter. I indicated that the wedding must be over by midnight and have no dancing and

1 *Golden Treasury of the Children of God*

such frivolity. I am told that such a policy, if I continue it, will cost me some of my congregation. Even that is a smaller price to pay than the peace of my conscience, and I look to the Lord to hold me up.

MONDAY, 20 MARCH

Although very cold, with occasional light showers of snow, a very good congregation assembled for the Fellowship Meeting (about 150). The Question was given out by John Gillies, Digg, on I John 5:21 and required the marks of those who had separated themselves from idols. John Graham, Kilmaluag, gave some reminiscences of his youth and compared the warmth of those days with the dryness which now prevails, and mentioned in particular a sermon preached by Christopher Munro which had such power that, he said, there was not a dry eye in the church.[1] I noted the effect which the recital of deeds of gracious power in past days had upon the attention of the people, and I felt it also in my own soul, and was led thereby to think that the very narration of such deeds woke such desires in the hearts of the Lord's people as constituted a prayer so powerful as to draw the Lord sensibly nearer to us. In connection with this I also remembered how often in Scottish religious history the narration of revival scenes in other places has been followed by similar manifestations of divine favour in the very spot in which such has taken place.

On my way home, held a Catechising Diet in the Flodigarry Schoolhouse. The place was full, about 70 being present.

FRIDAY, 24 MARCH

The Lord has given me to see that I have been too prone to rest content with such duties as may be required of me in public. I have rested satisfied with preaching, as though there were no other ways whereby I could reach the consciences of my people. I see it clearly my duty to enter personally and privately with each one of them into the question of his or her relationship to Christ, that the minister of the Gospel has the right to make such enquiry, and that nothing less will be accepted of him as a conscientious performance of his duty. And yet I sit appalled, unable or unwilling – although desirous – to obey. Oh Lord, give me strength for this, for nothing less than a special provision of divine strength will suffice!

1 Munro (1817–1885) was minister in Kilmuir 1864–70, cf. *Memorials of Rev. Christopher Munro*, 1890.

MONDAY, 27 MARCH

Preached from Job 13:15 mostly for the Lord's people, but also trying to meet the case of the seeker. In the course of the sermon I declared that in future I would wait for five minutes in the vestry after every service to give an opportunity to anyone who might wish to speak to me about soul matters. I am afraid that I did not expect anyone. To my surprise I had no sooner entered the vestry than I heard someone at the door. Who appeared but Mrs Ramage! She believes that Christ is willing to save her and she is willing to be saved by Him, but further than this she cannot go. I tried to set the way of life before her, but she did not seem to grasp it.[1] I felt it very difficult. Nothing is more difficult than this, and the fact that I had to speak in Gaelic made it all the more so. But I plainly see that I erred, and erred grievously. I began to speak first and then prayed – I tried my own strength first, and then when I saw that I had not prevailed, I cried upon the Lord. The way of success is to realise that without God I can do nothing, and that the first thing of all to be done is to seek His strength. It is here I err continually. If I were instant and persevering beforehand in seeking the Lord to be with me in proclaiming the message, I believe that my preaching would be more effective than it is.

TUESDAY, 28 MARCH

While out in the church this evening the case of Katie Matheson presented itself very forcibly to my mind, and on coming in I once again tried to present the truth to her and sent her some literature which I thought might be helpful. Oh that I had more wisdom in dealing with such cases!

FRIDAY, 31 MARCH

Reports continue to come to hand of revival activity in various English centres, also in Ulster, Edinburgh, Dundee, and Glasgow, but I increasingly fear the prevalence of emotionalism and artificiality. I read of hundreds visiting the enquiry room and there coming to 'decision', and knowing from sad experience that only the Holy Spirit Himself can open up to a soul the way of life, I very much fear that decision for Christ, which in many cases may mean no more than a pious resolution to lead a religious life, is being put in place of faith in Christ, i.e. that personal closing with Christ which is essential to salvation.

1 Not then, but she did shortly afterwards.

TUESDAY, 4 APRIL

Called upon Katie Matheson today and put the question point-blank to her as to her having Israel's hope. She looked at me earnestly for a moment and then answered solemnly in the affirmative twice over. A good feature about her case was that she seemed to be more grateful than ever I have seen her, and showed anything but the resentment which the natural mind feels when pressed into such a corner. I went away very much cheered and encouraged, and I trust that she may yet be a bright and shining light before she leaves the world.

THURSDAY, 13 APRIL

Spent the day visiting in Kilmaluag. Visited twelve houses and conducted worship with 38 individuals capable of profiting by it. May the Lord acknowledge it!

TUESDAY, 18 APRIL

Spent a season of personal exercise today in the church, and from it I derived some benefit. On considering my ministry since the last such occasion (24 January), while seeing much to humble me in the way of sins of unbelief, pride, unfaithfulness, deadness, levity and soul neglect, cannot but perceive how graciously the Lord has been dealing with me. Since that date the Prayer Meeting attendance has steadily increased, until now it is in a most flourishing condition.

THURSDAY, 20 APRIL

Got a beautiful day for visitation in Kilmaluag in the townships of Conista and Kendram and kept worship in ten houses, reaching thus the ears of 22 individuals able to profit thereby. Besides this, tried to get a word home in the way of expounding the truth and left messages in the way of tracts. I am thankful for such a favourable and happy day.

WEDNESDAY, 3 MAY

Illness made me drop off my seasons for prayer in the morning and I have never re-started them. My loss has been great. If I could only waken properly in the mornings I would begin them again.

SATURDAY, 6 MAY

I have not been interrupted today and yet I seem to have made very slow progress; and not only so, but I seem to have no clear, firm grasp of my discourses, especially of the evening one. Yet I trust that I shall be blessed. After a very dull, depressing day the Lord seemed to meet with me in the church when I went out there for a little in the gloaming. I think I saw a little of His glory, and that gives me hope for the morrow.

Was reading this afternoon a short account in the *Christian Treasury* of a drum-head service conducted in India, the congregation being 'Havelock's Saints' – the 78th Highlanders, my father's old regiment, the regiment of my boyhood – when suddenly I was overswept by such a flood of emotions that I was completely unmanned. And yet I cannot tell why. Whether it was the sad reflection that that religious type of Highland soldier is gone now, and gone I am afraid for ever, or whether it was due to old memories, belonging to a distant past and circling round that very regiment to which even in my boyhood's day something of the old, solid, God-fearing spirit still clung, being stirred up anew and pensively pulling at my heart-strings, I cannot tell. For the present Seaforth Highlanders I do not care much, but oh, deep down in my heart there is a regiment which I shall love as long as life lasts. I shall never see them again, the familiar stalwart figures of long ago, but oh, my regiment has still its old place in my pride and my affections.

THURSDAY, 18 MAY

On Tuesday night, just as I was preparing for bed, a message came from Eliza Matheson, Aird, wishing me to call. With as little delay as possible I drove out, reaching Aird about 1 am, but poor Eliza was struggling between life and death, and being in a sleep which was precious to her the nurse was afraid to allow her to be wakened. All I could do, therefore, was write a note which I asked might be read to her should she so far recover as to be able to comprehend it.

Yesterday, ere going in to the Prayer Meeting, I was informed of the sad fact that poor Eliza had passed away shortly before. I felt exceedingly moved, so much so that it was with the utmost difficulty that I could get through the Prayer Meeting. Spoke from 1 Peter 1:1-2 with much awe upon my spirit. Somehow I have felt no congregational death either in Lochgilphead or here as this one – this little girl struck down and carried away, and all within a week.

Today I was amazed at the spirit in which I found the family, sad yet rejoicing because of the glorious end of the one who had finished her course in a chariot of fiery suffering. The mother was there, sitting like a queen in the midst of her family, completely resigned to the Lord's will. The spirit displayed by the boys, especially Johnnie, made me wonder. Evidently this has brought out what had lain more or less hidden, and I rejoice to see such evidences of a work of grace upon these young lads. On Wednesday Eliza had said that she was glad to leave the world, that she was going to the House of many mansions. Christ was made very near and precious to her in her last hours, and her testimony was wonderful. *Sgioblaich mi! Sgioblaich mi!* (Prepare me! Prepare me!) was her frequent whisper. Exclaiming *Tha'n dorus fosgailte* (The door is open) she expired in Hugh MacKay's arms. Her jacket was found out in the byre where she had left it at the time she turned ill and in one of the pockets a small Bible was discovered. I conducted worship with them. It was painful, yet glorious.

THURSDAY, 6 JULY

I received two most interesting letters today, one from Effie MacInnes, Flodigarry, and the other from Alick Matheson, Kendram. The latter is one of the most striking letters it has ever been my good fortune to receive. The composition is most surprising for a Gaelic-speaking sailor laddie writing in English, but what is most surprising of all is the depth of his spiritual experience and the clearness with which he can survey and present it. The poor lad is evidently going through such depths as I myself went through when the wickedness of a great city, and the hollowness of the religious profession of those around me, made me question the very existence of God. He seems to have got past the atheistic stage, however, and now complains of the felt rebellion of his heart against God. I have tried to answer his letter, but well I know from my own experience that only the Lord Himself can take away that rebellion and give him the quiet spirit of grace which he would fain have.

SATURDAY, 15 JULY

Got another letter today from Alick Matheson. His case seems to be of such a type as *Grace Abounding* should, under God's blessing, be helpful to. All the old nature is up in arms against the Spirit's work in him and Satan is doing everything in his power to keep him from resting in Christ. He tells me in the letter about how, one Sabbath morning, his mother called him to get up for the service at Staffin. But he decided to sleep on and did so, only to have a terrible dream of death which wakened him in terror. His cousin then called on him that he might go with him to Staffin and he made ready and went. To his surprise the text was: *Agus gu'n saoradh e iadsan a bha tre eagal a'bhàis ré am beatha uile fo dhaorsa.* (Heb. 2:15) ('And deliver them who through fear of death were all their lifetime subject to bondage'.) My notes upon this service (cf. 24 July, 1921) are not without significance: 'Enjoyed liberty and was conscious towards the close that the truth was prevailing upon the people; there was such a hush in the church and such an intentness of listening among them'.

He declared that he was going ashore to post the letter and that he would then go out to the country – the port where he was lying (Avonmouth) being small – and get a grassy corner where he could read the book I sent him – *Grace and Truth* – in peace. The picture of a poor Skye sailor lad in far away England retiring in such a way with such a book open in his hand has a pathos of its own.

SATURDAY, 22 JULY

Weather prospects appear fairly favourable. I trust that there will be a good attendance tomorrow for (DV) I have several matters of much importance to bring before the people. May the Lord Himself be with me and give me freedom and blessing! Since I resumed my early rising again I am conscious of more liberty and spirituality. To His Name be the praise!

MONDAY, 28 AUGUST: UIG

After the service Jonathan Campbell and Peter MacKay, Kilmaluag – who has come home from Grangemouth – were waiting to speak to me, the latter apparently being under deep soul concern. It was this that drove him home from the South. He said he could get 'no rest'. I said a little to him by the way of showing him that the work being the Lord's implied the Lord's willingness and desire to save him, but he seemed to be in deep, hopeless darkness and I felt that only the Lord could bring him relief. Nevertheless I returned up the hill rejoicing and wondering at how the Lord was beginning to work among the young people of this island.

FRIDAY, 22 SEPTEMBER: CROSSBOST, LEWIS

I left home on Tuesday and crossed the Minch next evening. It was rough enough, but I was exceedingly thankful that the storm which had been raging had subsided ere we ventured out. At Kyle I found the Revs. MacIntyre (Stornoway), MacLeod (Harris) and MacDonald (Portree), all Free Presbyterian ministers, in the hotel at breakfast and they kindly took me up to a bedroom to have worship with them. I enjoyed it very much. My soul longs for these men to come in among us. How long will Israel and Judah be divided?

Lochs is a beautiful district much eaten into by the sea, which stretches inland in long winding arms, and studded with many moorland lochs. Our congregation here is a large and, on the whole, compact one. I was shown the spot, lonely and secluded and sheltered by an over-hanging rock, down on the sea shore near the Manse, which served as a praying chamber for saintly Mr Finlayson of revered memory. Oh that we had such men now! We have preachers, but men of prayer are pitifully few. No wonder there is so little fruit to so much preaching! The blight which has come upon my own soul I see to be general. On the Fast Day I preached from 2 Corinthians 1:7 on personal sanctification.

TUESDAY, 26 SEPTEMBER: GRAVIR

On Saturday Mr MacLeod, Gravir, preached to an excellent congregation. There was a good deal of thinking in his discourse and it was well arranged.

After a rather stormy and wet night we got a good Sabbath and the church, which holds 1700, was crammed to excess, even the outside stairs and the vestry being fully occupied. The gathering evidently was a record one. Mr MacLeod, Garrabost, took the action sermon preaching an original and striking sermon from Isaiah 63:3.

At night I took the church service and preached from Ezekiel 33:11. Although services were held in two other districts the huge church was again packed. I must say that I got great liberty in pleading with sinners and am thus encouraged to hope that the service was not in vain. I was given earnest attention. A most pleasing feature about the Lewis religious life is their readiness to attend the prayer meetings. The Saturday night meeting ran into hundreds and that of the Sabbath night consisted of the bulk of the huge congregation.

On Monday I preached again. I was astonished at the size of the congregation, the area of the church being packed and the galleries almost full. I have enjoyed preaching here so much that I cannot help believing that the Lord had something for me to do.

The elders approached me with the view of persuading me to consider a call to the congregation, but I had no difficulty in showing them that I could not think of leaving my present congregation without the Lord making His will known in that direction. The matter therefore thus took its end. Poor people, I am sorry for them, and I cannot but envy the opportunities of the man settled over such a vast congregation. On the whole, however, if this congregation reflects the present state of religion in Lewis, I do not think that we are a whit behind in Skye. Better attention seems to be given to the Gospel in Skye – the silence of the people in listening is sometimes most tense – and there is certainly more brokenness under the Word with us. Yet there are features in Lewis which I wish were with us in Skye.

FRIDAY, 29 SEPTEMBER: KYLE

On Tuesday, which was rather wet, I did little more than have a look about the neighbourhood of Gravir, but next day we went across to Lemreway. The day was beautiful and the wild moorland scenery no less so. From the road summit a beautiful view was obtained, obscured in a measure by haze, it is true, but in such a way as to enhance the romantic effect. Towards the South East I discerned the familiar outline of my own parish lying beyond a 24-mile stretch of sea. To the West lonely, quiet lochs ran in through the moors towards the great mountains of Harris upon whose long slopes the sun shone through a light vapour which veiled while it did not hide. Lemreway is a lonely sequestered township nestling about a hill-encircled inlet of Loch Sealg. Although the day was a tempting one for harvest work, the hall and kitchen beyond were literally crammed and the atmosphere was very oppressive. Still I enjoyed the service. The singing was hearty and I got liberty in addressing them from Acts 14:22 on there being no easy way to heaven. The walk home in the moonlight was really exquisite only I felt tired enough to be glad when we reached our destination.

Yesterday, (Thursday) I left Gravir. The mail-car was an awful rattler, nevertheless I enjoyed the journey and reached Stornoway about 3.30. Mr Cameron[1] was not at home, being absent at the Back Communion but Mrs Cameron soon made me very comfortable. In the evening I had to take the prayer meeting. I was surprised and delighted at the attendance, and the singing was most hearty. I found the people most kind and felt quite sorry to leave Stornoway. My visit to Lewis has been a most enjoyable one and I trust that it has not been in vain. What a field these Lewis ministers have! I cannot but envy them. I got a beautiful passage across the Minch, for which I am very thankful. I long now to get home.

WEDNESDAY, 25 OCTOBER

At the Prayer Meeting tonight I spoke from 1 Peter 1:17 on spending our sojourn here in the fear of God. Enjoyed the whole meeting very

1 Kenneth Cameron, Minister of the Free Church in Stornoway.

much, but my sweetest time was when the meeting was over and ere I
left the church. I had a sweet, sweet visit from my Saviour then; it was
easy when I so felt and saw Him and had my spirit so bathed in His love,
to call Him 'my Saviour'. Oh that such moments would continue; then
would heaven be begun on earth! But I am thankful for such visitations,
for, short though they be, they wonderfully revive the drooping life of
my soul.

FRIDAY, 29 DECEMBER

Today the Enemy well-nigh overwhelmed my soul and ruined all my
Sabbath work. Engaged as I was upon the preparation of my sermons,
he would not let me rest, but continually cast horrid and distracting
thoughts into my mind, so that at last all liberty was gone and I feared
that I was to be left to darkness. Guilt on the conscience at first kept me
from seeking the help of the Lord, but, at last, realising that I had no
other refuge, in desperation I repaired unto a throne of grace. Blessed
be His name, it was not in vain, for when I turned to the sermon which
I was to prepare upon Isaiah 41:7, and which, because of my condition,
I was almost afraid to look at, I found my bands were broken, and the
very bitterness of my experience only enabled me the more feelingly to
enter into the case of 'the poor and the needy'. Thus was Satan foiled
and his very efforts to snare me and mar my work, were made to serve
to the Lord's glory and the furtherance of what he tried to destroy. May
this be a lesson to me to betake myself to the Lord when pressed by
Satan's temptations and to ignore the restraining influence of consciousness of sin upon the conscience which keeps me so often from
Him.

I think that no extensive awakening has ever been produced by preaching on the work of the Spirit, but rather by awakening the conscience and setting forth Christ.

Dr John Duncan, from one of
K.A.M.'s notebooks.

There is a kind of preaching which is peculiarly blessed to the awakening and conversion of sinners. I have often been much impressed with the statement that Paul preached the Gospel in power and 'in much assurance' (1 Thess. 1:5). When this expecting spirit, this assurance of success, is given, the blessing will surely follow.

K.A.M.

8 At the Gates of Heaven

MONDAY, 15 JANUARY, 1923

Have been in a dreadfully unspiritual state of late. I am ever living in the hope of a better season coming upon me, when I shall be able to live nearer to the the Lord than I at present do, and when that time comes I hope to have Gospel increase, but time passes and I do not earnestly seek what I long for: the best of my life is passing, and still I tarry and decline a resolute seeking of the Lord's blessing. Oh fool that I am! Oh Lord, quicken me! Baptise me anew with Thy Spirit! Save me from a formal, unspiritual ministry!

TUESDAY, 23 JANUARY

Held the Catechising in Kilmuir tonight and was miserably disappointed – only 16 were out. Truly this place is terribly dead. Oh that the Lord would come with awakening power! Were it not for the other districts I am afraid that I would lose heart.

SATURDAY, 27 JANUARY

Today felt that although the Kilmuir 'men' are more able and discerning than those of the other two districts, they are not so hopeful and thus lack the zeal and buoyancy of the 'men' in the other parts, and that this in measure is colouring this section of the congregation. I fear that they don't expect much and hence they don't get much. The other 'men' get more encouragement in their sections of the congregation just because they expect more, for 'according to your faith' is the rule of the Kingdom.

THURSDAY, 8 FEBRUARY

Yesterday the weather was exceedingly stormy and only had eight out at the Prayer Meeting. At night brought the Class to a close.[1] Spoke on holy living and, in finishing, pressed upon them the necessity of starting out upon the way of life. In preparing for this last meeting, through Dr Hodge's way of presenting the Truth got an insight into the doctrine of the believer's union to Christ which has been a great comfort and help to me. I see that I have been attempting the sancti-

1 A class for doctrinal instruction had been meeting in Kilmuir for a number of weeks.

G

fication of my soul in the strength of my own endeavours and I have miserably failed, just because I did not realise that the same helpless looking to Christ which is necessary to justification is just as necessary to sanctification. I seem to have caught sight of new power here, and to have come to see that the rising of the old nature within me is not mine, but pertains to sin which dwelleth in me and which I hate (Romans 7:20) and therefore that the guilt of it is not mine unless yielded to.

THURSDAY, 15 FEBRUARY

Yesterday had quite a good attendance at the Kilmuir Prayer Meeting (25). At night proceeded to Kilmaluag and gave a lecture (the first of three) on Dr Hodge's *Way of Life*. The evening was very wet yet about 110 were present, including a car-load from Staffin. I had no sooner begun the service than the atmosphere seemed to soften me, and during the prayer I could not keep the tears from brimming over my eyes and rolling down my cheeks. There was something, too, in the singing that touched me, a soft, gentle, broken note, as though there were a wistful longing among the people for the coming of Emmanuel to bless us. Hugh MacKay's gentle face, as he sat there before me with closed eyes, singing out – I believe – a Saviour's praise, somehow touched me also, and throughout the night, although I had no great liberty of utterance, I was repeatedly upon the borders of tears. These young people of Kilmaluag seem to draw out my very heart. Surely the steps of the Lord are sounding among us as He draws near to bless! I came home with a full and a happy heart.

Angus Ross called this evening for a little. He told me that, after the Union [1900], for three or four years he did not go to church, not understanding which side was right, and that when once he began to stay at home he soon lost all desire to go out.

WEDNESDAY, 4 APRIL

Today got a glad surprise in a gift of £7 mainly contributed by my own young people in Glasgow.[1] I value such on account of the source from which it has come and the spontaneous way in which it has been subscribed, more than if it were ten times its value, and I count it, together with the gift of the young people of Lochgilphead, as being more precious than any other gift which I have ever received.

1 That is, young people who had left their home congregation for work in Glasgow.

THURSDAY, 3 MAY

This morning, ere going out to visit in Kendram, asked that I might meet with something to hearten me and that prayer was answered. When I got near the house of Samuel Matheson I found him harrowing outside. At once he stopped work and came to me. After worship he came out with me and with the tears welling from his eyes asked me to remember him in prayer. He declared that he had no grace, that he still was as he had been when he came into the world, but that grace was speaking to me in that broken heart and contrite spirit was as clear to me as the noon-day sun.[1] When I suggested that it was possible for grace to be his without his knowing it, he admitted it. To prove grace in the soul to the one who has no assurance, I know no book more useful than Guthrie's *Saving Interest in Christ* and this I promised him. I could have danced with joy to meet such a case.

SATURDAY, 12 MAY

Have been feeling that we as a Church are keeping the Gospel far too much to ourselves, that we are not nearly aggressive enough. Feel a great longing in my own soul to go out thus upon Gospel adventures among those who seldom hear it. The chief difficulties are the methods and the finances.

FRIDAY, 18 MAY

Got a letter today from Morag MacKay in which she informs me that both Cathie MacKinnon and Katie Ann Ross are in a promising way about their souls. It is delightful to get such blessed news of my dear young people seeking Christ. May their number be increased!

MONDAY, 4 JUNE

Despite the fact that yesterday was the U F Communion Sabbath in Staffin we had a good congregation there.

In Kilmaluag spoke from John 12:21 on the desire of the seeking soul to see Jesus, and had a sweet night. I think the Lord was with us and I have hopes of lasting work having been done. All seemed to be solemnised and some moved.

MONDAY, 20 AUGUST

Crossed over to Staffin on Saturday, taking Spurgeon's *According to Promise* with me in my bag, and I do not cease to thank the Lord for

1 His life afterwards proved this to the full.

that book. It effectually showed me my sin and my folly in neglecting the promises, and taught me that I ought in a real, literal manner to take the promises, plead them, expect their fulfilment, and finally note their fulfilment.

The weather being beautiful I had splendid congregations both morning and evening (150 and 140). From Kilmaluag alone 30 were present and, of these, all remained for the evening service with the exception of a few individuals. In the morning preached from Psalm 51: 15 on calling upon the Lord in a time of trouble. Got unusual clearness of thought and utterance.

For the evening, contrary to my usual practice, I had another sermon for the saints (mainly) and I feared that I would not enjoy it as much as usual, but I took Spurgeon's advice and I pleaded Isaiah 62:7. I got my answer in as delightful an evening as ever I have had outside of Southend. Spoke from John 10:27 on Christ's sheep and, having especially in view these exercised lads from Kilmaluag, pressed home the marks and urged them to assurance's grip of Christ. Got great liberty both of speech and spirit, and there were visible tokens to show me that the message was holding the people. At the outset, in singing the closing verses of Psalm 119 just before the sermon, noticed that the brother of Myles MacInnes who has recently returned from America was furtively wiping away tears from the corners of his eyes and there were soon others in the same way. It was an evening at the gates of heaven.

TUESDAY, 25 SEPTEMBER

Yesterday was observed throughout the Presbytery as a Day of Humiliation and Prayer in view of the unfavourable harvest prospects.

In the evening went out to Kilmaluag where I got a good attendance, including four who had walked from Kilmuir. Spoke with a good deal of fire, and force, from Proverbs 30:6 on the sin of adding to the Word of God, and proved Britain to be especially guilty of it. Pressed repentance as the only remedy. The time for keeping silence because of the susceptibilities of a few of other denominations is past and if the country is to be saved from ruin there must be strong aggressive action upon the part of all Evangelicals.

MONDAY, I OCTOBER

Yesterday, having a baptism to perform in Kilmaluag, went there in the morning. The day was by no means promising but the meeting house was packed, almost 150 being present. I do not think that ever I saw it so full, with the exception of the opening day and the first Sabbath.

Was intensely gratified to hear from Eoghann that a certain girl gives evidence of having come under the power of the Gospel. I have observed how well she has been attending the means for the last two or three months. The Lord is wonderfully kind to motherless children – I have repeatedly observed it. I am exceedingly gratified for this fresh case for I am afraid that I was beginning to lose my keenness and expectancy. May she be brought to sure ground!

THURSDAY, 11 OCTOBER

On Monday evening, on my way home from Staffin, held a service in Digg Schoolhouse. Despite the very pressing concerns of a late harvest over 60 were present. Among those who assembled I observed three young girls from another part of the congregation all about 15 or 16 years of age. One of these was the girl of whom Eoghann spoke, the others were from Aird.

Preached from Revelation 22:17 and was given wonderful liberty, clearness of thought, and unction of spirit, and the breathless silence of my audience told me that the truth had completely gained the ascendancy over them. If ever I felt the Spirit I did so then. What soul-melting views I had of Christ, and how my lips seemed to be opened to speak of Him!

When the congregation were retiring, the girl mentioned above blurted out something about Christ and then fell a-weeping. As the people were pressing on, all desirous of shaking my hand in the passing, I told her that I would see her after the congregation had dispersed, and she passed out of the room. When I had shaken hands with all, to my surprise I observed some commotion at the door leading into the outer cloak-room through which the people were passing. One of the Stoddarts hurried in for a lamp, and, on my following him, there I saw the girl standing in the middle of the cloak-room, with eyes fixedly staring upwards and with a most heavenly look upon her face, yet unspeakably wistful. Miss Gillies, the teacher, had her by the arm, and behind among the throng one of her companions was convulsively sobbing. As I approached, and even when I spoke to her, her fixed look did not alter, and from her lips in most sad, yearning, appealing tones I heard the words, 'I want to see my Saviour! Oh Christ, reveal thyself to me!' The people were awed, my heart was so touched. I succeeded, however, in getting her calmed and taken round to the teacher's quarters, but she trembled all over and appeared to be so weak that she could scarcely walk.

At Duntulm, as we returned home, a storm of extreme fury suddenly struck us, and for a time progress was very difficult and dangerous, but fortunately the wind moderated somewhat soon after, and we got home in safety and naturally concluded that the tempest was all over. In this, however, we were sorely mistaken, for after midnight it rose again with the utmost fury and lasted without cessation until well on in the following day. Between the storm, and the sight of that poor girl's wonderful expression as I saw her at the schoolhouse door – a sight which never left my mind – I scarcely slept a wink all night. It was a wonderful and a most solemn night; a night which I am sure wil live in the memory of some for many a day.

I left for the Hope Street[1] Communion on Tuesday evening in a very strange frame of mind; very anxious, very much impressed, thankful, and sorry to have to leave home at this particular juncture. I fear that poor girl will not be able to control herself, and if she gives way in Kilmaluag, since a number there appear to be in an exercised way, I fear such a general outburst as will perhaps injure more than help the true progress of the work. I dread the effect of unrestrained emotion. When emotion is accompanied by reason it is good; when reason is thrown to the winds it can only be harmful. I have longed and prayed for a movement. Now, when it appears to be at hand, I dread it. Oh how anxious I feel about my poor congregation! But I must roll the burden of it all upon the Lord.

MONDAY, 22 OCTOBER

Although showery and threatening-looking, yesterday was a fairly good day and I got a good congregation in Kilmuir.

At night spoke in Kilmaluag from Luke 7:50 on the woman who was a sinner. Felt the atmosphere warm, yet did not quite get the liberty of the morning. Nevertheless I enjoyed the service. Felt after the service that I had come greatly to love that poor woman who had done such kindness to Christ. I would like to meet her in glory.

MONDAY, 29 OCTOBER

Yesterday was a good day despite some evening showers and the attendances were the best this year for Kilmuir – on an ordinary Sabbath – 115 being present in the morning and 85 at night.

1 A Glasgow congregation of the Free Church.

Visited the girl referred to above. She now appears much calmer and was able to speak very rationally. I was pleased with her intelligence. She, of course, is busy over heart work and has not yet grasped the fact that the door is open. Her difficulties are three:– (1) Atheistic doubts from Satan (2) She does not feel that she is lost (3) She lacks the Holy Spirit. I tried to meet these three points and to show her the folly of devoting her attention to such instead of to the acceptance of Christ's offer of salvation, but though we had quite a long talk I doubt whether I succeeded in making things any clearer to her. How helpless I feel! May the Lord give her light!

TUESDAY, 30 OCTOBER

Held the Kilmaluag Monthly Meeting tonight. Despite the stormy nature of the evening the hall was full, fully 100 being present. Spoke with some liberty from Proverbs 2:1–5 on how to get grace, but felt that I had not enough of Christ in my discourse to make it really sweet to me. Devoted my concluding remarks to those who were already seeking Christ, and strove my utmost to make clear to them that the message for them now was no longer 'Strive to enter in at the strait gate' but 'Believe in the Lord Jesus Christ and thou shalt be saved'.

MONDAY, 26 NOVEMBER

Tonight held a meeting in Bornaskitaig. Spoke from Isaiah 28:16 on Christ as the stone laid in Sion.

Things here are really in an interesting way and I cannot but perceive that the Lord is working. I am told tonight that at the Prayer Meeting at Kilmaluag last week the hall was full, although there was nobody present to conduct it but Eoghann himself, that is to say, that the Prayer Meeting, which at the beginning of my ministry here used to number 8 or 9, is now swelling up to ten times that number.

TUESDAY, 11 DECEMBER

On Saturday travelled over to Staffin and held Sabbath's services there. The morning being good the attendance was excellent, 140 being present, 30 of whom were from Kilmaluag.

Yesterday conducted the Harvest Thanksgiving services in Staffin and Kilmaluag. Unfortunately the day was very wet. Spoke to Staffin from John 6:27 on the vanity of labouring for the meat that perishes.

At Kilmaluag I had an audience of fully 100. I would willingly have excused the failure of the young people who had just walked back all the way from Staffin to appear. Wet, tired, and hungry, with barely time to get a cup of tea, I had no right to expect them, and yet, though they came in late, there they were, every one of them. I have never seen any like them. Then in speaking from Psalm 72:16 on the handful of seed sown on the tops of the mountains I got altogether exceptional liberty and power. It was a beautiful evening. I appealed for more expectation among God's people for great things. I cannot but hope that something blessed is hovering over Kilmaluag. May the floods soon be poured forth!

Today held the Harvest Thanksgiving service in Kilmuir.

Last night the beginning of the 60th chapter of Isaiah came home to me with wonderful power. I wonder whether I am really to have a fresh lease. I have felt a new preaching power – or a renewed preaching power – since Sabbath. Oh to be renewed and quickened and kept lively!

MONDAY, 24 DECEMBER

Yesterday was a very good day and the morning attendance was excellent (115), 35 being up from Kilmaluag. Spoke from Psalm 110:7 on Christ's war against, and ultimate triumph over his enemies. In the evening had an attendance of 75. Spoke from Hosea 14:5. Liberty was unequal, but towards the end I was conscious of an unwonted power, especially in declaiming against the despairing outlook which seems to be only too characteristic of most of the good people of the Kilmuir section of the congregation.

I am more and more of late seized with the longing to venture out upon new fields with the Gospel. I feel that we as a Church, and I as an individual, have not realised the imperious nature of the command to 'Go forth . . . and preach the gospel to every creature'. Simply to support our Foreign Missions when thousands are perishing at home for lack of the Gospel is not enough. Would that I could see my way clear to do something in this direction!

SATURDAY, 5 JANUARY, 1924

I cannot help observing of late what I have often observed before – that my freedom in public does not depend on my thoroughness in preparation but upon the spirituality of my mind. Is it not then my wisdom to give more attention to the preparation of the heart before services?

TUESDAY, 8 JANUARY

Spent today very agreeably in visitation. Once more found – what has been a comparatively frequent experience – that the visits from which I most shrink have given me the greatest satisfaction in the end. To my great surprise a girl in Herbusta thanked me in tears for what she called my kindness to her mother. I then ventured very half-heartedly to call upon a sick man at the MacMillans' who are said to be rather staunch U.F.'s. This poor man dissolved into tears during worship and when I rose to go, in very pleading tones he asked me not to be long in coming back. I felt more than repaid for both visits.

SATURDAY, 2 FEBRUARY

Peter MacKay told of a remark made by the late Peter Cameron of Staffin. Someone asked him, 'How thick is the clay in the miry pit (Psalm 40:2)?' 'Oh' said he, 'so thick that even the strongest horse in the place could not pull its feet out'.

MONDAY, 11 FEBRUARY

Kilmaluag Special Services. Yesterday was a beautiful day and the attendances were good. In the evening went down to Kilmaluag for the first of the series of lectures which I intend giving there on the Way of Salvation, and by way of introduction spoke from Isaiah 51:9. The hall was crowded, no fewer than 145 being present, and what with the heat and oppressive atmosphere I did not feel very comfortable. Tonight spoke from Romans 3:10. Got exceptional liberty. 115 were present, almost all being Kilmaluag people.

WEDNESDAY, 13 FEBRUARY

The Prayer Meeting at Kilmuir took away from my time for preparation and I had other hindrances to contend with. The result was a hastily composed and ill-prepared discourse for Kilmaluag. Although I reached the hall about the same time as last night I could see very few on the road and the fear possessed me that they were beginning to drop off now. To my surprise I found the hall well filled, and they eventually gathered to the number of 140. When I saw this and realised how little I had to give them, I felt a fear creep over my spirit and I became most miserable. Still I had to face matters and I tried to speak from Acts 16:30. I did not get liberty, I felt my lack of preparation, and I had not such a grip of my people as on the last two nights. Yet I felt more broken, more in earnest, and the bowed heads of Mrs Roderick and her sister told a tale. Morag Campbell does not often give way to tears, yet I observed her weeping. The Lord Himself knows what was done. Perhaps the message was more effective than when I had more liberty.

MONDAY, 18 FEBRUARY

The late afternoon and evening became very wet; notwithstanding, I had an attendance of 125 in Kilmaluag. Concluded my series of discourses there by speaking from Hebrews 2:3 and got the best night of a blessed season. I was given unusual liberty and power, and attention was rapt. How gracious the Lord has been to me! I could not but notice the visible effect which pointed, personal application had upon my audience tonight. These services have been a success.

TUESDAY, 11 MARCH

Conducted the Monthly Meeting in Kilmaluag tonight and enjoyed the service exceedingly. At present influenza is raging there and only 57 were out.

WEDNESDAY, 26 MARCH

Crossed over to Staffin on Saturday. Sabbath was a good day but illness affected the congregation. In the morning I spoke from Isaiah 31:1 on the folly of trusting in an arm of flesh. I was helped by an article I read on one of the old Welsh revivals, to realise more than ever I did that the only thing that can quicken my poor congregation is a visit from above. I went out more in the dependence of this in the evening, when I spoke from Psalm 94:14 on the perseverance of the saints. The article I had read gave as evidence of the Spirit's presence (1) warmth (2) the preacher feeling that he is only a channel for the expression of what is pouring out of him. If these be true evidences – and I believe they are – I had them both in measure towards the end of my discourse, especially when pressing the believer anew to renew his covenant with Christ.

MONDAY, 31 MARCH

Yesterday was a good day, but the influenza scourge seriously affected the Kilmaluag representation. In the morning preached in Kilmuir from Gal. 4:11. Applied it as pointedly as I could to the congregation (Kilmuir section) showing them very forcibly their indifference as to spiritual things and the ill-success of my labours among them.

SUNDAY, 26 APRIL

I have been ill, very ill, with influenza, and am only now beginning to recover. I needed this illness; it has shown me myself and the hollowness of my ministry – what pride! what self-complacency! what self-seeking! How little of the Spirit of Christ, of faithfulness, of true humility! The wonder is that the Lord did not cast me off altogether. Oh Lord, let me begin afresh by thy grace! I am trying to prepare a sermon for tomorrow but it is very questionable whether I shall have strength to deliver it.

MONDAY, 28 APRIL

Was enabled to crawl out to the church yesterday and despite great weakness to preach from 2 Kings 6:16.

MONDAY, 5 MAY

Crossed yesterday morning to Staffin in car and preached to audience of about 95 from Psalm 7:11–13, on God's anger with the sinner. Influenza still prevails in the district and this, combined with the calling up of the young men to the Clyde pleasure-boats, considerably thinned the congregation.[1] Got liberty of utterance, although my physical condition did not allow me to put much energy into it. In the evening preached in Kilmaluag and had an exceedingly happy night. Felt the divine dews fall upon my soul and my hearers seemed to be impressed. At the close baptised poor Hugh MacKay's little girl. The two standing before me – and the mother, I believe, in heaven – made a very pathetic picture and I think that many hearts were touched. I expect fruit from last night's meeting. I arrived home wonderfully fresh and with a full heart. How can I praise the Lord sufficiently for all His goodness to me!

MONDAY, 12 MAY

Rose early yesterday and benefited from it. At first had not much sense of the Lord's presence, but when I shut myself up in the study and began to seek Him, he proved His word to me, 'Draw nigh to God and he will draw nigh to you'. My cup simply overflowed, and so much did I realise His presence that for very joy I could scarcely contain myself. It was a sweet visit, like as in the days of my first love. The day was good, but the Kilmuir representation in the Church was not, only 65 being forward. In the evening asked them whether they were willing to hold Saturday evening prayer meetings, weekly, fortnightly, or three-weekly, to plead for a blessing upon the preaching of the Word and the revival

1 A large number of Skyemen left home annually at the start of the tourist season to form part of the crews of pleasure steamers on the Clyde and on Loch Lomond.

of the Lord's Cause among us, and to let me know if they were. I am more and more convinced that the only hindrance to a revival of religion is the unbelief and unspirituality of the Lord's people, and that the only progress towards it lies in their awakening to their duty, and their earnestly seeking the reviving influences of the Spirit. It is vain to look for a work of quickening among the careless till the Lord's people first be roused. Hitherto I have directed all my preaching towards the first – and with little success. I believe that to aim at the latter in the first instance would be more profitable.

WEDNESDAY, 4 JUNE

Held prayer meeting last night in Kilmaluag in view of the communion. The attendance was most encouraging, 70 being out, but long prayers are ruining prayer meetings in the Highlands today. They are a weariness to the flesh and they tire the people by their unfitness and selfishness.

MONDAY, 16 JUNE

Found the benefit of taking Spurgeon's advice re public prayer, namely, to think of the needs of the congregation beforehand and to ask definitely, remembering that the Lord has all blessings to bestow. To rush into His presence without forethought is not wise.

TUESDAY, 1 JULY

Conducted the monthly meeting in Kilmaluag tonight. Although got liberty of speech and close attention, felt that I was preaching self and not Christ. After the meeting I was vexed at an exhibition of temper on the part of one of my most valued office-bearers, which utterly marred all. Certainly he spoke under provocation but he has not a tithe of what I have to put up with from that very same source. How weak is man! In a month's time I have had more unpleasantness of this nature than during the whole of the rest of my ministry in Kilmuir. Surely a blessing must be near when Satan is so active; either that, or God is leaving us to our own devices.

MONDAY, 21 JULY

Last night I spoke from Luke 23:39-43 on the three figures on the crosses of Calvary and if ever I had a sweet night I had it then. My cup seemed just to overflow and I got lovely views of the glory of Christ. I could have lingered in that pulpit for another hour. Seemingly the experiences of those who sat in the pews – at least the exercised ones – was somewhat similar to my own. Oh how can I praise Him sufficiently for such a glorious night! May there be fruit!

WEDNESDAY, 30 JULY

Got a letter today from Angus Ross, Shulista, re his spiritual state and his desire to communicate. Within the last few years he says he has begun to think seriously about his soul and is aware of the striving of the Spirit with him, but he finds himself so weak, and the old nature so strong in him, that he fears Christ has not taken hold of him yet. Nevertheless he has a great desire to confess Him. Yet he is afraid to do so lest he fall away into sin again and disgrace the Cause. He asks my honest opinion of his case. I gave him some marks of the Lord's people and said that, if he found these in his own experiences, then my judgment was that he was a gracious subject.[1] This letter has given me great joy and encouragement, and just because there are so many in Kilmaluag like him, I am encouraged now to think that the good work is really going on in them.

THURSDAY, 31 JULY

Despite a rather showery morning a congregation of about 150 assembled for the Fast Day here. Reverend D. Cameron, Broadford, remained in Kilmuir, while Mr Chisholm (Coll)[2] took the Staffin-Kilmuir services. In the evening Mr Cameron spoke from Rev. 6:23. His arrangement was weak, but apart from this his discourse was full of Gospel sweetness and I got a feast for my soul. Apparently Mr Chisholm was also exceedingly good in Staffin and Kilmaluag; his prayer at family worship was beautiful.

FRIDAY, I AUGUST

Today was somewhat moist but, being calm and warm, attendances did not suffer. At the Fellowship meeting fully 200 were present, while at night the attendance mustered 150.

SATURDAY, 2 AUGUST

The earlier part of the morning was very wet but the Lord mercifully bound up the clouds and we had a gathering of about 130. Mr Chisholm

1 Angus Ross was to become a respected elder in the congregation.
2 The Rev. Peter M. Chisholm had commenced his ministry among the Free Church congregation on the Island of Coll in 1921.

preached a sermon of extraordinary power from Isaiah 4:5 on the words *thar a' ghlòir uile bithidh còmhdach*. I was amazed at such a sermon. I never heard such originality, such flashes of doctrine, such depth of experience, and such power. A number in the congregation were overcome, and he was overcome himself. I had to struggle my hardest to keep from betraying my feelings also.

MONDAY 4 AUGUST

Yesterday was very dull and threatening, but what rain there was did not much interfere with the gathering to the services. Mr Cameron took the English service in the school, where he preached to an audience of 10 from Hebrew 9:28. Mr Chisholm had a well-filled church before him, about 550 being present. He spoke from Psalm 24, and once again his treatment of it, and especially his grasp of doctrine and the originality of his handling of it, amazed me. Surely I saw the glory of the Lord in that sermon and throughout the whole of his services, and the melted state of many of the people showed that they saw it too. His fencing[1] was unique and just as wonderful as unique. The people were manifestly impressed under it. During the period when the people were partaking of the elements I could hear him praying where he stood. When my turn came to address the second table, I felt that I had nothing but the feeble utterance of a child. The concluding address was just as wonderful in its own way. What a service it was! I have never had such a happy time at my own communion. He himself confessed to having liberty and such a sense of the holiness of the Lord as almost took his strength away and occasioned him the purest sufferings mental and physical. The family worship at night was most sweet, but indeed this has been a feature of the whole communion. Oh how thankful I should be for such a day! Today we had a very good congregation of about 250. Mr Chisholm gave us another marvellous sermon from John 17:24. What glorious views he gave me of Christ and how he exalted Him in my soul! I do not think that ever I have had such a wonderful time under the preaching of the Word. I know not how to praise the Lord for all His kindness to us! I shall never forget this communion season.

MONDAY, 6 OCTOBER

Yesterday was a good day and congregations were good. In the morning we had in Kilmuir an attendance of 105. At night preached in Kilmaluag

1 Fencing: An exhortation given, with Scripture proofs, before the serving of the Lord's Supper to indicate who should and who should not partake of the sacrament.

to a congregation quite as large, from Jonah 4:7, on the worm that smote the prophet's gourd, and got freedom and deep feeling. It was a solemn and blessed evening. At the last singing I noticed Angus Ross's face; it seemed quite transformed in a wistful rapture of heavenly longing. How wonderful is the transforming power of grace!

WEDNESDAY, 22 OCTOBER

Every morning I have been spending some time in the church in devotional reading and prayer and it has helped me greatly. Brainerd's *Diary* I find most helpful.

MONDAY, 27 OCTOBER

My perusal of Brainerd's *Diary* has shown me where I am and the reason for my powerlessness. Oh that things eternal were more real to me and that I were able to live with singleness of eye to God's glory, especially to get rid of a cursed pride which corrupts all my spiritual duties, and to have my speech seasoned with grace! I long to have the natural set of my mind Godwards! In the evening spoke in Kilmaluag from Luke 14:22. The attendance was very good, reaching 120, and from the very outset felt the atmosphere warm and reviving. I could not but marvel at the contrast from Staffin. I can scarcely pray in Kilmaluag now without shedding tears and it was especially so last night. Surely the Spirit of God is at work among them. In the sermon got sweet liberty and my soul seemed to be drenched in heavenly dews. For the first time in my life I think I reached the point when I could honestly say that I would prefer to go away and be with Christ than remain in the world; not because the world of late had been made unusually bitter to me, but because of the glory of the One I saw and the longings of my soul after Him. Brainerd says that at such times as the preacher is so sensible of the gracious influences of the Spirit – and these he ought earnestly to seek after – he has an extraordinary power of reaching and handling the consciences of his hearers – a power he will have at no other time. This encourages me still more to hope that last night's message was not in vain. During the closing singing, too – Psalm 36:5–8 – my soul was in ecstasy and I think that there were others also who tasted what I got.

WEDNESDAY, 29 OCTOBER

In the evening cycled in to Uig to record my Parliamentary vote. For the first time on record, Socialism is receiving uncommon support in these parts, but this is mainly due to the activities of a few of the advanced type and to the fact that people here have not come in contact with the thing itself. It is a solemn day for the country. May the Lord save us from the hands of the godless schemers who are trying to seize the upper hand in the land!

THURSDAY, 30 OCTOBER

Today held the Harvest Thanksgiving, preaching in Kilmuir at midday and in Kilmaluag at night. The day was good and attendances were very good. Spoke in Kilmuir to an audience of 105 from Matthew 4:4 and brought it to bear so tightly upon the worldliness of some of the Kilmuir people as to rob me of my pleasure in the message. Yet it was greatly needed and I trust that it will do good. I do not suppose that ever they heard the truth concerning themselves more plainly put. Oh that the Lord would rouse them! I purposely intimated the evening service in Kilmaluag to see whether it would draw them to endeavour to go down there, but only one man – Charles MacKinnon – rose to the occasion.

At Kilmaluag had an attendance of about 115. Once again had a sweet, solemn, heart-refreshing evening. I felt that it was sweet to serve such a Master and to preach such a Gospel. Surely indeed there is something working in Kilmaluag. Last Sabbath evening I had wonderful liberty. On Tuesday I am told there was an unprecedented number of the young at the prayer meeting. Today 28 of them, not content with waiting for their own service, walked all the way to Kilmuir for the service there. Surely these are evidences of a gracious gospel work. Lord, increase and hasten it and subdue pride in me!

TUESDAY, 4 NOVEMBER

I was given an envelope containing money as the Kilmaluag share of the contribution towards coals instead of peats. I expected about 30/-, which would have been a reasonable contribution for this section, but on going home, to my astonishment found it amounted to £8.10. This is further proof of the fact which is almost daily becoming more evident, namely, that the Lord is working in Kilmaluag. I cannot shut my eyes to it.

SATURDAY, 8 NOVEMBER

On Wednesday conducted the Kilmuir Prayer Meeting and spoke from Mark 5:21–43, but was grieved at an expression used in one of the prayers wherein it was evident that there was no expectation of blessing in this present generation. Most of the Kilmuir men put all hope of blessing to a far future date because a godly man has said that the dawn of the latter-day glory would break upon the sword of the butcher, red with the blood of the saints.[1]

WEDNESDAY, 26 NOVEMBER

I see once again that high seasons are followed by seasons of terrible backsliding and soul trials, and therein I discern two facts which seem to be obvious enough:– (1) that high seasons are preparatory to fierce onslaughts by the Enemy, and mercifully bestowed for the upbearing of the soul during this dire period (2) that high seasons generate spiritual pride, which is very effectively humbled by these very dark times of the swelling up of the tides of the heart's awful corruption.

TUESDAY, 2 DECEMBER

Mrs Ross mentioned how much she had enjoyed the last Kilmaluag monthly meeting and commented on the stillness and solemnity of the service. She stated that a great change had come over the Kilmaluag people within the last few years.

THURSDAY, 18 DECEMBER

Gave tonight's lecture upon revivals by way of introduction to the subject which this winter I intend to take up, namely, 'Revivals in the Highlands and Islands of Scotland'.

THURSDAY, 25 DECEMBER

Was very pleased tonight to see the Class fill up to the measure of 40. Spoke on 'Revivals in the Celtic Church'[2] and enjoyed the meeting. Attention was close and I trust that the Lecture was not without profit.

TUESDAY, 30 DECEMBER

Today having to send up to Headquarters a report anent the state of religion and morals in the congregation, was compelled by the informa-

1 The reference is to a renewal of persecution inspired by the Papacy. The opinion here expressed was the view of Lachlan Mackenzie (1754–1819) who was commonly credited in the Highlands with prophetic powers. cf *The Rev. Mr Lachlan of Lochcarron*, James Campbell, 1928, pp 416–17.
2 Early in the Christian era the church in Ireland was known as the Celtic Church. Its first missionary to Scotland was St. Columba who came in the year 563. The new church in Scotland was also called the Celtic Church. Differing in many respects from the Roman Church it was later to be so influenced and absorbed by the latter that by the end of the 13th Century it had disappeared, apart from a few scattered remnants.

tion required by the schedule to survey and summarise the situation at Kilmaluag. The following facts emerge (1) that concerning seven, I have heard what encourages me to hope that within the last three years they have passed over from death unto life – (viz. Johnnie Matheson, Eliza Matheson, Jessie Matheson, Peter MacKay, Sammy Matheson, Mrs Roderick MacKenzie and Angus Ross); (2) that there are others whose zeal in attendance upon the means, and earnest attitude under the Word, are just as noteworthy as those mentioned, and whose cases therefore encourage me to hope that it is well with them, yet about whom I have heard nothing definite; (3) that the average attendance at the prayer meeting has risen from 7–9 in 1919 to 45–50 in 1924; (4) that it has been proved impossible to organise a vain gathering in the Kilmaluag district owing to lack of support among the young people; and (5) that the observant in the Kilmuir and Staffin districts repeatedly comment upon 'the change which has come over the Kilmaluag people'. Apparently therefore we have had what is undoubtedly a revival of religion without being aware of it, a revival which has been entirely lacking in the excitement usually associated with the idea of revival.

SABBATH, 11 JANUARY, 1925
Drove over to Staffin in morning, getting a beautiful day, and preached to congregation of about 100 from Psalm 9:12. At night had splendid congregation of about 135. Got liberty, earnestness, and unfaltering attention. I see that the Lord acknowledges hard, conscientious preparation. Felt very thankful for such a night and hope that that service was blessed.

Yet coming home through the night, and climbing up below the Quirang, I felt my heart very burdened with many questionings, the most insistent of which seemed to be: 'Is it true or is the grave the end of all, and the Gospel I have been preaching a beautiful dream?' Then the fact of sin, when committed, generating fear and dread in the heart of man, came in upon me as a most signal proof of God's existence and of the scriptural account of man's natural relation to Him; and as 'Rabbi' Duncan danced on the Brig of Dee when he became convinced of the existence of God, I almost danced then in the Bealach and praised God from the depths of my soul for His matchless Gospel and His wondrous love to my soul.

THURSDAY, 15 JANUARY
At the class tonight I had an attendance of 43 (including three from

Kilmaluag). Spoke of John Davidson's Overture of 1596 and the Revival in Ayr under John Welsh. These men shame me!

THURSDAY, 12 FEBRUARY

26 were present at the class tonight. Spoke of the Kirk of Shotts Revival in 1630 and the Revival at Ancrum in 1662.[1]

FRIDAY, 13 FEBRUARY

What ails our Church is that our orthodoxy is a dead one; we believe in prayer, but we don't put our belief into operation, and it is the same with all our other beliefs. Such faith is dead.

Was startled and shocked to receive a wire from poor, helpless, Mrs MacKinnon of Gairloch manse, to say that her husband passed away at 2.30 this morning. A prince has fallen this day in Israel, and I feel like one stunned!

MONDAY, 16 FEBRUARY

Left home at 4.45 am en route for Gairloch. At Portree Mr MacKinnon[2] joined me, at Broadford, Mr Cameron, and at Plockton Mr MacRae. We found poor Mrs MacKinnon wonderfully bright despite her helplessness. Mr MacKinnon (Aultbea), and Duncan Morrison, the missionary, were with Mr MacKinnon when he passed away. His last coherent utterances were: 'Into thy hand I commit my spirit! Lord, receive me to thy glory!' And again later with staring eyes he said, 'Do you not see the heavenly vision? I see Christ – all in white!' After that he was not intelligible, and at 2.30 on Friday morning, after two gasps, the brave spirit that feared only God forsook its labouring tenement of clay.

TUESDAY, 17 FEBRUARY

I was disappointed that only two other ministers appeared for the funeral today, namely Mr Campbell (Dingwall), and Dr Munro (Ferintosh). A Gaelic service was conducted in the church, which was almost full, while Mr MacKinnon (Portree) and myself conducted an English service in the manse. Afterwards we went out to the church.

1 These historical lectures on revival were continued in the autumn and carried into the following year, during which he covered most of the recorded revivals in 18th and 19th-century Scotland.
2 Donald MacKinnon, ordained and called to the Free Church, Portree in 1923 which he served for 19 years before his second charge at Kennoway (Fife). Died 1966.

What appalled me there was the coldness which overspread me, and which I cannot think came from myself, for I felt quite otherwise when in the manse. Throughout the service, and indeed throughout the funeral, I did not see a tear, which all the more amazed me when I contrasted it with the mere fact of my speaking about Mr MacKinnon's death drawing tears from not a few in my own congregation last Sabbath. The funeral was attended by about 800 people.

When I bade 'good-bye' to Mrs MacKinnon, as usual she had her Bible and her 'Spurgeon' there spread on the bed before her.

The glories of Scotland, when the trees are putting on their first tender green, when the last primroses still lurk in shady nooks, when the bog-myrtle and young fern are spreading their scented carpet, and the birch perfuming the air overhead, when curlews are calling all day long, when tern and gull, heron and rook, grouse and blackcock are devising artifices to decoy us away from their nests, when the sun is shining as, from an angler's point of view, it perversely does in the beginning of June all day and every day and far into the night, so that one might almost say: 'There is no night there', when long mountain climbs lead up to heights from which the dreamland beauties of the isles of the west coast seem little short, in their glory, of the very gates of heaven – these are memories which, to those who have experienced their beauty, are almost too sacred for words.

E. A. Knox, *Reminiscences of an Octogenarian,* 1934

9 Some Travels away from Home

Although MacRae's settlement in Skye in 1919 took him off the Scottish mainland, and further from the main centres of population, the constant invitations he received to preach in various parts of the country ensured that his ministry was not to be confined to the Hebrides. Thus his Diary for 1920, for example, reveals that while he made 438 pastoral visits at home and preached there 151 times, besides conducting 58 prayer meetings, he was also away for eleven Sabbaths and took some 65 services in other congregations. This proportion of time given to preaching in many other places increased in subsequent years.

The Diaries of the early 1920's contain practically no records of vacations apart from pleasant days spent at his wife's former home in Dunvegan; the only events in that period which resembled holidays were excursions with his friend Dr Munro to the South-West of Scotland where the Church had once been very strong, and where multitudes of men and women had suffered in the persecutions of the 17th Century. Also visited were the scenes of former revivals, as, for instance, Kirk o' Shotts, Cambuslang, and Ettrick where Thomas Boston ministered from 1707 to 1732. These journeys in the South, as well as providing some relaxation and exercise, gave an added stimulus to MacRae's practice of speaking regularly on important eras of church history in his own congregation.

Six days were spent in this way in 1921, of which the first three days are described as follows:

WEDNESDAY, 24 AUGUST

In afternoon came on to Newton Stewart which is to be our base for the rest of the week. It is a pleasant little town nicely situated in the Cree valley. The railway journey was very agreeable and opened up for us a rich, smiling countryside.

THURSDAY, 25 AUGUST

In the morning motored up Cree-side and visited Brigton, the home of Margaret Wilson. Pushed on to Glen Trool and saw the Martyr's Monument on the Farm of Caldons, afterwards venturing almost to the head of the loch. The scenery was wild and romantic and greatly resembled the Highlands.

In afternoon took train to Wigtown where saw (1) the Martyrs' Monument; (2) the graves of Margaret Lauchleson and Margaret Wilson and other martyrs, and (3) the stake at which the martyrs were drowned in the Solway.[1]

FRIDAY, 26 AUGUST

Took the train to Dromore and from there got motor mail to Gatehouse of Fleet. Visited (1) Rutherford's Monument on the Boreland Hills from which got a beautiful view. (2) Anwoth Church and Churchyard where saw John Bell's tomb and (3) Rutherford's Walk. Could get no one to give us any certain information re Rutherford's Witnesses.[2] Was charmed with the lovely woodland scenery of Anwoth. On way back passed Cardoness Castle. Just as we were waiting for the motor, rain began to fall and the evening turned out very wet.

The next year another visit was made.

WEDNESDAY, 6 SEPTEMBER, 1922: OLD CUMNOCK

Left home on Monday and after a long wearisome journey reached Glasgow last night. Today came out with Mr Munro and, with Muirkirk as our centre, visited Priesthill where we found John Brown's[3] grave in a most remote and secluded hollow in the midst of a trackless upland moor. In the early evening we motored out in the opposite direction and visited the monument on Airds Moss marking the scene of the conflict in which Richard Cameron perished. This also is moorland, but is more accessible and the ground is more level. At the end of a long and somewhat strenuous day we made our way to Old Cumnock where we have put up for the night. The quiet lonely moorland with its sacred pathetic associations of the past has its own peculiar attractions, especially upon such a day of sunlight as we today enjoyed, and I appreciated our outing.

THURSDAY, 7 SEPTEMBER: OLD CUMNOCK

Went out to New Cumnock and from there visited the Cairn Monument

1 Margaret Lauchleson, aged 63, and Margaret Wilson, aged 18, were sentenced to death by drowning in 1685. Several guides to the sites of the Covenanters have been written; probably the best is *The Martyr Graves of Scotland*, J. H. Thomson, edited by Matthew Hutchison, and published early this century. *The Homes, Haunts and Battlefields of the Covenanters*, by A. B. Todd, 1886, is also valuable.
2 Stones which Rutherford (minister of Anwoth 1627–1638) called to witness against some of his parishioners who were amusing themselves in a game among the hills on a Sunday. They were pointed out to Thomas Chalmers when he visited Anwoth in 1826.
3 John Brown was shot dead in the presence of his wife and her babe by soldiers on May 1, 1685, at the order of Claverhouse.

erected to the memory of George Carson and John Hair, two Kirk-connel men who were summarily shot there.[1] The old stone is not there having been removed by an impious wretch of a farmer to serve as a hearth-stone for his kitchen. That very night, however, the stone split into a hundred fragments. Unfortunately a heavy mist prevented us from enjoying what is said to be a view of some beauty. We waited till past midday in New Cumnock in the hope that the mist would lift, so that we could explore Glen Afton and visit the cave of Covenanting interest near Dalmellington, but in vain, and at last we had to return to our headquarters at Old Cumnock. In the afternoon however we drove out to Bellow Path, a beautiful and romantic pass, the scene of a thrilling encounter between the Covenanters and the dragoons. The latter were conveying one of the Covenanting ministers as prisoner to Edinburgh when they were ambushed in this thickly wooded glen and their captive taken out of their hands. In the evening we visited Peden's grave and that of the other Covenanters who were buried near, but this we had already done last year.

Despite all this, at times felt very idle. When a band of Plymouth Brethren began to sing at the street corner I felt a longing to go and join them.

MONDAY, 11 SEPTEMBER: GLASGOW

On Friday we took train to New Cumnock where we got a motor which took us to within three miles of Dalmellington. There at the base of Ben Beoch, after a run through rolling, bare upland, we left the car and climbed up to near the summit of the hill where on the face of a craggy cliff we found the cave of which we were in search. This formed the refuge of Paterson during the times of the persecution. The cave was about 6 feet in height but so narrow as scarcely to admit turning, and with an incline so steep as must have made it difficult for a sleeping man to rest without danger of slipping out at the mouth and falling down the rocks. Truly it was a most hazardous and uncomfortable hiding place, and illustrates most practically the heartbreaking hardships to which those faithful and steadfast men were exposed. From there we went to the summit of the hill which lay not far above us. From the breezy top we had an expansive view. To the East, and beyond the green valleys of the Nith and Lugar, vast clouds, indicating a coming shower, were darkening on the uplands and impeding the view in that direction,

1 They were caught, it is said, reading their Bible, which proved sufficient evidence against them in the eyes of their persecutors. An older stone commemorating their death was replaced by another in 1843.

but in the other directions the atmosphere was clearer. Goat Fell in Arran, the Holy Isle and Pladda were clearly visible, while beyond, melting into the distance, were the hills of Southern Kintyre terminating in the Mull, with the Irish Coast faintly discernible beyond.

THURSDAY, 14 SEPTEMBER

On Monday Mr Munro and I went to Wishaw and visited the Covenanters' Memorial erected at Dalmeid to mark the spot where Renwick, Cargill, and Cameron used to hold conventicles.[1] The stone is in a trackless moor and in a most secluded hollow and were it not for the kindness of a woman at whose house we enquired in guiding us within sight of it, we would have had considerable difficulty in finding it. To our grief and horror, on arriving at the place we found that the stone had been thrown down, and although an effort had been made to right it, the greater portion of the edifice lay in ruins at the foot of the small eminence upon which it had stood.

In 1923 two days were given to further visits, while the evenings were occupied by prayer meetings in Glasgow at which he preached.

FRIDAY, 31 AUGUST, 1923: GLASGOW

On Thursday went out to Kilmarnock where I met Mr Munro (Ferintosh), and Mr MacDonald (Rosskeen), and spent the day with them visiting places of Covenanting interest. First we motored out to Lochgoin, a lonely bare hilly district where corn is never sown because it will not ripen. There we obtained admittance to the old house – although owing to renewals it does not look particularly ancient. Many old relics of interest are preserved there, including Captain Paton's Bible which he handed over to a friend when upon the scaffold, and his sword, the Covenanters' Banner, the Fenwick Drum, some manuscript sermon notes of William Guthrie's, and coins of the period.

Outside, we visited Howie's monument.[2]

From there we motored in to Fenwick and were successful not only in obtaining entrance to Guthrie's church but also to his pulpit in which we stood. Except for the base, the pulpit was exactly as in Guthrie's day.[3] As I left the place I felt sad when I thought of the Moderate successors of these Gospel mighty ones.

1 Secret outdoor services held during times of persecution.
2 John Howie (1735–1793), author of *The Scots Worthies*, first published in 1775 and for long probably the best-known and most popular of all books on the Covenanters.
3 William Guthrie (1620–1665), author of *The Christian's Great Interest*.

Today we visited Douglas. After a good deal of searching and scrambling among rocks, trees, and ooze, discovered the hiding place of John MacGavin in a sequestered rock in a most romantic spot – hard by the waterfall in Carnsalloch Burn. In Douglas itself we saw John MacGavin's house, which bears an inscription, and Barony Court (now transformed into the Sun Inn) where Claverhouse frequently passed judgment upon the Covenanters arrested by his soldiers. In a corner of this apartment rested the head and hands of Richard Cameron after Aird's Moss.[1] Below was the dungeon, a place of exceeding strength which is now transformed into a bar – the house thus still serves the devil. Below this again is a large vault which runs up to St. Bride's graveyard. This we did not see as the air is foul.

No further visits to Covenanting scenes appear to have taken place until the end of August 1927, yet the passing years had done nothing to lessen the zeal of the two men to cover all the ground associated with the saints of an earlier day. Accordingly their explorations in 1927 included an ascent of one of the highest hills in the Pentlands. His entry for the last Tuesday of August reads: 'Motored to Dunsyre via Lanark and Biggar and climbed to the top of Black Law, one of the Pentland peaks, on the summit of which a stone indicates the last resting place of a wounded fugitive from Rullion Green who desired to be buried in sight of his native Ayrshire Hills. The place is exceedingly lonely and is very difficult to strike. The day was hot and the climb rather trying'.

On the next visit to the South-West – five days in August 1929, when Dumfries was their centre – their most arduous tramp was probably to Dob's Linn (waterfall), also remembered as the Holy Linn, near the head of the Birkhill Pass, in the vicinity of which Covenanters had scooped a cave out of the soft shaly rock. They found that this shelter had not survived the passage of time. On August 15, 1930, the same place was re-visited as part of a yet more strenuous day:

'Visited High Bridge of Ken where we saw "the College", a Covenanting rendezvous. About two miles beyond this, and on the Carsphairn-Moniaive road, we struck up a side-road which led up the valley of the Ken. The road terminated six miles up at a lonely habitation called the Lorg. By this time the rain had come on very heavily but eventually it cleared, and after some difficulty in finding a way over the Ken we

1 They were later fixed on the Netherbow Port in Edinburgh. Cameron, was one of nine Covenanters, killed by a party of 120 soldiers at Aird's Moss (or Ayrsmoss) on 22 July, 1680. Others were taken prisoner and subsequently executed.

scaled the Altry Hill in order to reach the Whigs' Hole, one of the hiding places of the Covenanters. The climb was very steep and tried us, especially the poor photographer whom Dr Munro had brought with us. Dr Munro took an easier gradient, but it was really surprising how a man of his age could manage such a climb. The hiding place was an ideal one and afforded shelter for quite a company, and while offering perfect concealment from below, allowed the concealed a perfect view of the glen below and of the only way of approach. On our return we went down again to the Holy Linn, last year's photos having been failures.[1] Then we continued on to Moniaive, the whole journey running up to 88 miles.'

These visits to the South were usually conjoined with preaching in Glasgow or with attendances at the Commission of Assembly which met in Edinburgh in the summer.

☐　　☐　　☐

By far MacRae's most frequent reason for being away from home was the call to preach at Communion services. For this purpose he was a regular visitor to scores of Free Church congregations – in Skye itself, the Outer Hebrides (Lewis and Harris), Arran, Glasgow, and across the Northern Highlands from Gairloch in Wester Ross to Lairg in the North and Ferintosh in the East. Two representative extracts from his Diaries will give an impression of such communion seasons. The first records a Communion of the Hope Street congregation in Glasgow where he met several of his former young people who had moved to the city for the sake of employment:

FRIDAY, 12 OCTOBER, 1923: GLASGOW

Yesterday was the Fast Day in Hope Street.[2] At 11 am I preached in Gaelic in the Hall from Psalm 119:176, but did not get liberty and did not enjoy the service. About 70 were out, which was more than I expected in the forenoon in the city. Mr — — took the English service at 2 o'clock and preached from Romans 11:20: 'Be not high-

1 Perhaps the climbing was too much for the photographer, as his work was no more successful on this occasion! This necessitated a return visit to the same place on 1st October of the same year, when two photographers 'took the utmost pains' in getting 'The Whigs' Hole', and 'The College' at the High Brig of Ken.

2 His friend the Rev. John MacLeod O.B.E. had become minister of Hope Street Free Church in 1921 as colleague and successor to the elderly Principal McCulloch. MacLeod died in 1939. At this period, and later, MacRae was very often invited to preach in the Glasgow Free Church congregations at communion seasons and there were many memorable services the records of which are not included in these printed selections from his diaries.

minded, but fear'. Apparent straining after fine language impeded his freedom and lent a stiffness and artificiality to his discourse which greatly spoiled it. There were no heads in his sermon, and although quite Scriptural and nice, very little real matter. Of dealing with heart and conscience there was none. At night Mr MacKay of Fearn preached to a larger congregation than ever I have seen in Hope Street, from 2 Corinthians 7:4, on glory in tribulation. It was a masterly production delivered in a masterly way, and simply rivetted the attention of his audience. Tonight Mr MacKay took 1 John 1:9 in Gaelic; he spoke to the heart and I felt the Lord enter my soul.

I feel very unfit to face the future services, more especially when I see that some individuals seem to expect something from me. May the Lord help me and keep me from trusting in my own strength!

SATURDAY, 13 OCTOBER: GLASGOW

Took the afternoon service in the Hall today and was surprised at the gathering, fully 250 being present. Spoke from Psalm 130:8 with a good deal of liberty and enjoyment. Got good attention. Saw Morag MacKinnon there and felt my very soul going out in love towards her. How wonderful is this love which binds me to those whom the Lord has given me as seals of my ministry! I feel exceedingly happy tonight and Christ is near. I hope all is well at home.

TUESDAY, 16 OCTOBER: GLASGOW

Mr MacKay took the Gaelic service in the church on Sabbath morning while I went down to the Hall for the English. The attendance there which could not have been less than 300 surprised me. At the close of the fencing we adjourned to the church, where the combined gatherings made a magnificent congregation of 700 or 800. Mr MacKay took the first table in Gaelic, I followed in English, while Mr MacLeod also took an English Table. At night I was again in the Hall which was densely crowded with a splendid Gaelic congregation, about 700 being present. It was a very happy night and I was thankful for it. Outside I fell in with some of my own dear young people and was in fact convoyed home by four of them. I was glad to see how established Chrissie MacLeod seems to be becoming in the faith, and I was unspeakably thankful to find that Annie MacKinnon (Kingsburgh) gives every appearance of being caught in the gospel net. After retiring that night I was so wonderfully exalted that I could not sleep for very joy and only with difficulty restrained myself from shouting out the Lord's praise upon my bed. I could have danced for sheer happiness. Oh what a blessed visit I had! Last night Mr MacKay took the English in the church while I went down again to the Hall. There I had a very good attendance of about 400 and had liberty in speaking to them from Revelation 21:6.

So ended a communion season which I exceedingly enjoyed, not only because I got liberty, but because of the Lord's presence being with me in public and, especially, in private. I cannot but think that eternity work was done. Yet the usual Monday heart-pain was there, especially when parting with the dear young ones of my own flock. May the Lord be with them and make them saints on earth!

The next extract records another such communion season but in a very different situation – the entirely rural parish of Rogart in Sutherland, birthplace of his friend, Dr Munro, who was also present to assist in the services:

WEDNESDAY, 15 JULY, 1931

Left home for Rogart Communion. Got very good day for travelling. Had company of Donald Campbell (Kinlochewe), from Kyle to Achnasheen, and from Dingwall thereafter had Dr Munro with me.

Shortly after our arrival in Rogart we went out to the Prayer Meeting which Dr Munro took. Got a very good address from Psalm 74:14, but was terribly plagued with sleep. Last night I only had four hours sleep and the preceding night only five.

THURSDAY, 16 JULY: ROGART FAST

At the Gaelic, which I took, only 21 were present. An old man, Donald Sutherland, who acted as beadle, told me that he remembered the time when the Gaelic congregation was 500 strong and when the English consisted of only two families. Such a contrast must be very saddening for these old people. Spoke from Hebrews 13:14. I expected about 70 at the English but to my surprise the congregation fully totalled 115. Dr Munro gave another very good sermon on Romans 1:16. Between services went out alone to the outdoor site of old-time communion gatherings. It is a beautiful spot and most suitable for the purpose for which it was utilised. Many great sermons have been preached there. The surroundings about this manse are beautiful and of the type to foster piety. A free run to secluded nooks and knolls undoubtedly is a great acquisition to any manse. A minister needs such more than a garden. In the evening 70 were out and once again Dr Munro preached an excellent sermon from Psalm 65:4.

FRIDAY, 17 JULY: ROGART

The question was given out by John Macdonald, one of the local elders, and based upon 1 John 5:19. I opened, 8 men spoke, and Rev. John MacLennan (Lairg) closed. 50 were present. It was quite a nice service.

In the evening Mr MacLennan preached in Rhilochan School from Isaiah 43:26. Rhilochan is up on a tableland, having all the appearance of a township in the Hebrides – crofts scattered about in an area of peat-lands. It was very hard for me to realise that the spoken language of those scattered home-steads was English and not Gaelic. The School was crowded, the accommodation being limited and the desks terribly cramped. Mr MacLennan preached a good sermon from Isaiah 43:26. It was orderly, well-arranged and very practical.

SATURDAY, 18 JULY: ROGART

At the Gaelic had an attendance of 21 and rather enjoyed speaking from Matthew 9:29. 54 were present at the English, and I again enjoyed preaching from Isaiah 55:10–11. Was rather interested to know that old Robert Sutherland, while professing appreciation of both discourses, expressed preference for the Gaelic. Felt much encouraged by this, for I am often afraid that my Gaelic is too wooden to have much power to reach the people.

SUNDAY, 19 JULY: ROGART

At the Gaelic had an attendance of 70, about half of them being strangers, mostly from Lairg, with a sprinkling from Dornoch. At the English, which began at 1 o'clock, 200 were present and I again enjoyed some liberty in speaking from 2 Samuel 1:26. At the Table, at which I got exceptional liberty, observed two of the old men shedding tears – and there were others. Only 20 communicated. The service finished at 3.30 pm.

In the afternoon the weather broke, but by the time of the evening service the rain was not very heavy. Spoke to a congregation of 125 from Matthew 11:30 with much liberty and earnestness.

MONDAY, 20 JULY: ROGART THANKSGIVING

The Lord's people seem to have appreciated the Communion and I have had a good time. May the Lord acknowledge His truth!

In the evening went over to the graveyard to see the grave of the famous Rev. Alex. MacLeod of the Uig Revival fame. The stone is in need of attention and the date of his death does not appear upon it. Near by, noticed the grave of Dr Munro's parents. The afternoon was warm and sunny and the walk was a beautiful one, although at times the countryside appeared rather sleepy.

Rogart Manse is in a beautiful nook but it is too much closed in by the hills for my taste.

☐ ☐ ☐

The great fall-off in numbers mentioned by the elderly Donald Sutherland in Rogart mirrored the common condition of so many Highland congregations. Kenneth MacRae himself observed a difference in several congregations between what he remembered of them before the Great War and what they were in the 1920's. It was not simply that the loss of young men and the general depopulation of the countryside had decimated churches: there had been a loss of spiritual warmth and power. At the end of a communion in Glenurquhart, Inverness-shire, in 1921, he noted: 'Considering the warmth I used to experience in this Glen before the war, I am much disappointed with the tone of the whole communion'. Speaking at a prayer meeting in the same place in 1929, to only eighteen people, he noted: 'Such an attendance does not indicate much life. Things have changed in Glenurquhart. In my student days three weekly prayer meetings were regularly held in the congregation'. After a question-meeting during a communion season in the once-eminent congregation in Creich, Sutherland, when eight men spoke, he recorded: 'Some of them seemed to have very little conception of what speaking to the Question means. I do not think that ever I heard such poor speaking, and when I remember what Creich was, even in my day, and the galaxy of speakers who were then present, I cannot but realise at what an extraordinarily rapid rate the Lord's Cause is decaying among us'.

MacRae gave a great deal of thought to the conditions reflected in these entries and he came to firm conclusions. He did not believe that the duty of the Free Church was to accept the situation and simply wait for the turning of the tide. He knew how God had honoured faithful, earnest preaching in the past and he had seen clear evidence that the power of such preaching did not belong only to the past. The result of this conviction was that he deliberately sought out opportunities for

5. A Communion Service at Ferintosh, Ross-shire. Dr John MacDonald, standing in front of the 'tent' is addressing those sitting at the Lord's Table. From a drawing by G. Urquhart, c 1846.

FERINTOSH BURN. F.C. COMMUNION. (2)

6. Approximately the same view as 5 early in the present century. In August 1935 MacRae wrote: 'The Burn is reaching the end of its day. It is questionable whether ever I shall sit there again, but it was pleasant to do so in the warm sunshine and in that place of memories.'

7. The Free Church Manse, Ferintosh, home of Donald Munro. This photograph was taken a few years after Dr Munro's death.

8. Dr Donald Munro of Ferintosh.

9. George MacKay, leader among the preachers of the Free Church remnant.

10. Remnant of the Free Church General Assembly, October 1900, who, upon declining to enter the Union, were locked out of the General Assembly Hall at New College where they had intended to meet.

11. The scene outside the Newton-on-Ayr Church, June 25, 1905. When the House of Lords upheld the case of the Free Church, the majority in a number of congregations, such as this one, found themselves excluded from the buildings which they had taken into the United Free Church. After some 130 people attended the Free Church service in this Ayr church on this date, they were met by a 'hostile crowd' of between 4,000 and 5,000.

12. Kenneth and Catherine MacRae, wedding photograph taken in Edinburgh, August 17, 1916.

13. The first home, Lochgilphead Free Church Manse.

14. Catherine MacRae, a photograph take[n] when she was still Catherine Matheson.

15. Loch Fyne, a familiar view during the Lochgilphead ministry

16. Map of Scotland, with particular reference to some of the places mentioned in MacRae's Diary.

17a Loch Gilp and Lochgilphead

17b Free Church and Lochnell Street.   North Lochgilphead

6877 The Winding Road through the Quirang, Isle of Skye

18. The road through the Quirang, Skye, a wild route many times walked and cycled over by the author.

19. The cheerful owner of his first motorised transport!

ST3302

20. A Skye croft at Torrin.

21. At the wheel of his first Jowett in the hazardous work of crossing by the primitive ferry at Strome.

22. The harbour, Stornoway, the tower and roof of the Free Church appearing on the left-hand skyline.

preaching in places where a new beginning was needed in gospel witness. One of his early 'tours' for this purpose was made in November 1922, when the last place visited was Stirling where there had been no Free Church minister settled since 1900. After a meeting of some thirty-seven people he comments:

'Small though the number was, there were some outsiders among them: Brethren, Salvationists, U.F.'s, and Parish Kirkers. I spoke from Acts 14:22 on there being no easy way to heaven, choosing that subject as being an apt one in a town almost wholly given over to religious formalism. My visit to Stirling was a most interesting experience and apparently I encouraged the little company there. May the Lord bless the Word spoken! I believe that, had we the man, Stirling is ripe for a Free Church evangelical movement. Was very glad to get back to my own dear home but am thankful for all the opportunities of my tour and am more than ever convinced that the best way to strengthen the Free Church is to send ministers preaching the Gospel through areas untouched by our Church. This would create an atmosphere favourable to us, and who knows what the ultimate upshot may be? It was thus Dr MacDonald of Ferintosh prepared the Highlands for the Disruption'.

The same theme often occurs in his Diaries in following years and he made a practice of preaching in struggling Causes such as Stirling and Dunfermline as often as he could. After the communion in Glasgow of October, 1923, recorded above, he went to help with special services which were organised by the small Dumbarton congregation as a means of outreach. In this connection he notes the following conversation with fellow-ministers:

'Discussed with Mr MacKay and Mr MacLeod, and afterwards with Mr Sutherland, the importance and urgency of aggressive action on the part of our Church in the immediate future, and suggested that Mr MacKay should call a meeting of those interested at the forthcoming Commission, and that a bond or union should be formed, membership of which would necessitate aggressive mission work in areas in which the Free Church testimony is either weak or non-existent'.

While it does not appear that this proposal was followed up, MacRae continued both by his testimony and his practice to urge the duty of stronger evangelistic endeavour. In this connection the following incident may appear incidental yet it illustrates the abiding cast of his thinking. Passing through Kinchillie (Lochaber) in 1925, he noted, 'The district abounds with Roman Catholics and the few Protestants

H

are mostly pretty indifferent'. With a Free Church friend who resided there he therefore arranged to hold an evening service in the Station Waiting-Room and thirteen people assembled, including four of the station staff. Of this meeting he writes: 'Spoke with fair liberty from John 6:37. Although it seemed so strange, the Waiting-Room proved to be quite a comfortable place. Felt that drastic methods are necessary in Lochaber; nothing less will penetrate the religious indifference of the people.'

Before we pass from the subject of evangelism a reference should be made to MacRae's views on the Foreign Mission work of the Free Church. On this subject he was involved in controversy on a number of occasions in the 1920's. He feared that the overseas missionary arm of his denomination was not proclaiming Reformed convictions distinctly enough and that it was in danger of being influenced by the drift characterising Presbyterian Foreign Missions in general. With this in view he attempted, unsuccessfully, to protest against the Church's participation in a Missionary Congress in 1922. The supreme need, as he believed, was for the Free Church to be zealously committed to her own biblical principles: 'More profitable by far than Pan-Presbyterian and Missionary Congresses would be a convention of the ministry of our Church for humiliation, heart-searching, and prayer'. When two of the leaders of the Church's mission in Peru left the denomination during the 1920's he saw it as an indication that the direction of the work – at least in Latin-America – needed re-examining. The policy in Peru was to put the main emphasis upon a school in Lima, the expansion of which required a considerable outlay of money in the late 1920's. MacRae, while thoroughly sympathetic with the need for Christian education, was against a large capital outlay upon an educational venture when, as yet, no strong indigenous congregations had been formed. In the 1929 General Assembly of the Church in Edinburgh he moved as an amendment 'that we get clear of the school and endeavour to start an Evangelical Mission'. But he only secured 16 votes in support. The general mood seems to have been full of optimism with respect to the measures being pursued. MacRae, on the contrary, was not hopeful. And he saw that ultimately all foreign mission work must dwindle unless the Church's base at home was preserved and strengthened. In a diary entry of October 30, 1928, he observed: 'Our leaders are dreaming fantastic dreams of Foreign Mission expansion while the Highlands are slipping from their grasp'. And, again, during the General Assembly meetings of 1930: 'At the Foreign Missions evening meeting the Hall was crowded out. I never saw so many. Was disappointed with Dr Mott.[1] Calvin MacKay excelled him as a speaker and I did not care for Dr Mott's outlook upon things. The tide is ebbing, not rising. I held my peace'.

☐   ☐   ☐

There is a lighter note which deserves to be introduced before this chapter is closed. As recorded in an earlier chapter, it was by horse-drawn carts that the MacRaes' furniture arrived at their Kilmuir manse in 1919. It was during the 1920's that motor-cars first came into more general use in the Scottish Highlands. After his bicycle, the gig and motor-cycle, MacRae had come to depend upon a local car and its driver who helped him to reach Kilmaluag and Staffin from Kilmuir. With the year 1928 a record of his own 7 horse-power car enters the pages of the Diary. His friend John MacLennan, minister of Lairg, seems to have preceded him in the use of a car and the previous autumn the two men had enjoyed one of the first of many drives together. In the last week of October 1927 he notes the following journey from Assynt to Lairg:

'We left at 3 pm, and after a cold journey, for the second car into which we transferred at Inchnadamph was open, we arrived in Lairg a few minutes before 6 o'clock. On the way, and near Altnacealgach, we saw marble used as road metal. A century ago the marble was worked, but now, owing to transport difficulties, such a source of potential wealth is ignored. Alas, our poor Highlands! How they are treated! Dr Munro proceeded South from Lairg by the 6.45 train, but I remained in the hospitable manse of Lairg.'

After the service at Lairg the narrative proceeds:

'On Wednesday John motored me to Dingwall. We left at 8.10 am. The scenery was magnificent. The morning mists in the valley below, the changing tints of the woods, the brown uplands, and before us the green smiling valley of the Oykell made a picture I shall not readily forget. At Ardgay and in the shallows near the entrance to the Kyle saw about 30 dead whales which had floundered too far inland. Wondered that some use was not being made of what whalers would have esteemed a veritable harvest. We crossed Struie Hill and all along old familiar

1 John R. Mott (1865-1955), American Methodist lay leader of the Student Volunteer Movement and well known for his ecumenical activities.

scenes awoke poignant memories of long ago. Oh how my life is flying! Near Ardross I saw fields of corn which had not even been cut. We reached Dingwall at 10.10, exactly two hours after leaving Lairg,[1] and soon I had to part with my kind and faithful friends at the station.

Some of MacRae's early experiences in his own car were far less pleasant. The 1928 diary contains not infrequent references to trouble with respect to almost all aspects of his car's performance in the rough and steep roads of Skye. Sometimes the wind literally blew the car to a standstill! At such times it was necessary to lower the over-head hood and sit, exposed to the elements, lest the car itself should be overturned. One drive home from Staffin on a Sunday, with Cathie and daughter Mary, reads as follows:

'In the afternoon the storm had so increased that I judged it better to run for home before night overtook us, leaving the evening service to the elders. At Kilmaluag lowered the hood in preparation for running the gauntlet at Duntulm. Descending the lower part of the brae, we found the strength of the wind to be terrific, and my light was so affected as hardly to be of any service. I was almost blinded by driving rain and at times it was only my knowledge of the road that kept me on it, for I could see nothing. The rest of the way was difficult enough but I encountered nothing like Duntulm. The Kilmuir service had begun at 5 o'clock but I entered at 5.30 during the second singing. Apart from Cathie and Mary the congregation numbered only 7. It was a trying day.'

About a week after this came another experience no less exciting:

'Was expected to preach in Staffin at 3.30. Took the Bealach road. After crossing the two rivers I ran into snow which, concealing ice, eventually became very treacherous. On venturing on to the upper slope of the Bealach where there was nothing but ice, the car simply skidded down and I lost all control. Norman Gillies was with me and in his excitement he seized the wheel and nearly turned the car on its side. I saw that the corner was impossible so I headed straight for a bank of loose metal and brought the car to a stop there. A little below us was the Doctor's car, also stuck. Very cautiously, between the four of us we got the Doctor's car down and then we followed with mine, but owing to the carburettor setting I could not get sufficient brakeage from the engine and again I had to drive off the road. However, by adjusting the carbu-

---

1 The two friends, making the same journey together in July 1960 – thirty-two years later – covered the ground in 1¼ hours which Mr MacRae considered 'too fast'!

rettor and tying old sacks to the wheels I managed to get down to a lower level and off the treacherous ice. It was a trying and dangerous experience. The Lord kept us.'

What seems to have been his first driving on the Scottish mainland with his own car was also memorable. With the family he left home on 10 August, 1928 for a month on the mainland made up of preaching engagements, with a holiday at Ardgay, Ross-shire. The first stage of the journey consisted of a drive at 18 mph through a heavy shower to the ferry-crossing from Kyleakin to Kyle. Driving on to the small ferries – which were little more than motorised rafts – was a hazardous business but, he writes, 'I had not much difficulty'. At Kyle the car was put on a train and only at Strathcarron station, where they left the train, did the business begin in earnest: 'By this time the weather was lovely and we very much enjoyed the drive for the first part of the journey. After that the pot-holes were terrific – mile after mile of them – with the result that a weak tyre collapsed with a bang beyond Achnasheen. The spare tyre was the one which had given way with me yesterday and it now only gave me about 6 miles when it too exploded. There was nothing for it but to proceed to repairs on the road – a process which was rendered agonising by the clouds of midges which enshrouded me. Three miles further on, near Lochluichart, the tyre let me down again and now I felt desperate, but, after another awful experience with the midges, we got away and crawled slowly on to Garve, fearful every moment that the tyre would burst. At Garve I got the spare tyre patched up and after about an hour's delay pushed on again. We travelled via Dingwall and reached Ferintosh at 8.5, feeling very thankful that the tyre I mended at Lochluichart was still serving us. We motored 72 miles in all.'

On the return journey to Skye on September 7, the aid of the train for the more mountainous part of the journey was dispensed with. It was nearly disastrous: 'The terrific hills at Keppoch taxed my driving powers, and coming down at Dornie Ferry we got a bit of a fright as I could not get my car to halt, so steep was the decline, until we had run right out upon the boat-slip.' They reached Kyle that evening and the next morning joined the queue of cars waiting to board the ferry: 'The car in front of us was a two-seater driven by a lady who appeared to be travelling alone. When her turn came she boarded the ferry boat without any difficulty but she must then have mishandled her gears for to our horror the car glided slowly on and then toppled down into the sea, only the back part and the back portion of the hood remaining above water. Fortunately a small boat happened to be in the immediate neighbourhood and the lady was got out in wonderfully quick time. She was deadly pale but did not faint. She was imprisoned by the hood but very fortunately her head was above water. Had the car not remained upright upon its nose the consequences might have been very serious. It was pitiable to see her effects floating about in the water and her beautiful car in such a plight.'

MacRae's first car, notwithstanding various repairs, did not last long and the Diary for 19 June, 1929, contains the entry: 'Inspected my new Jowett car which has come here by the "Hebrides". It looks rather slight for my rough work'. Initial misgivings were confirmed a few days later when, at the end of a communion season at Duirinish (Skye) Donald Munro was a passenger:

'Took Dr Munro over to Kilmuir in my new Jowett car. The gears are set in the reverse way from my old car and were very stiff and I found it very awkward. On three occasions Dr Munro had to get out and walk to the summit of the hill. Took from 7.10 till 9.55 for the 33 miles, i.e. 12 miles an hour'.

The Jowett, however, was to improve its performance. On the mainland, on July 12, 1929, its owner recorded with pride: 'Ran from the Lochcarron Manse to the Urray Manse in 2¾ hours, a distance of 54 miles.' Better still was a drive to Edinburgh, via Perth, in order to attend committees of the Church on 12 August. On that occasion the Jowett and the car of another minister set off simultaneously from Ferintosh: 'The day was beautiful but the pace was too hot to permit of much enjoyment. We left at 2.12 and reached the Royal British Hotel, Perth, at 8.22, a distance of 144 miles which, after deducting a halfhour spent in lunch on the Grampians, gave an average running speed of 25.4 miles per hour. At one lonely and dead straight section of the road I touched for a moment 46 miles per hour. I felt very tired but I could scarcely sleep when I retired, seeing nothing but a medley of roads slipping past me.'

The family vacation at Ardgay was repeated again in 1929 and the car's sturdiness was well tested on a day's outing in Sutherland. The objective was to visit Dr Munro's birthplace and the map marked a second-class road leading to it from Brora and past Loch Brora. But on taking this route they found that beyond Loch Brora the 'road became just a grassy track which came to a dead stop at a ford in the Black Water – an aptly named river'. Mr MacRae, never unwilling to face an adventure, did what perhaps few had done before him and took

[216]

the car successfully across the ford. Not far beyond this they came to the old house of Donald Munro's childhood.[1]

On the return journey to Skye, after this vacation, the Jowett did fail once, with what could have been very serious results:

'On reaching the further side of Strome Ferry I got a great fright. Just after leaving the boat, and on the steep quay, the engine failed and the brakes failing to hold the car I began to slip down backwards. Mercifully a log lay on the quay edge and I backed down on to this; otherwise I would have fallen into the sea. The Lord was good to me. I was now very much afraid that the car, being so heavy-laden, would not manage the slope up from the ferry but it ran up without any difficulty. We took the private road through the Duncraig grounds and were stopped by Colonel Kemble, but when he understood who I was he apologised and gave me full permission to pass through at any time. At the same time I felt inclined to tell him that he ought to be ashamed to stop anyone on such a miserable road. We got across the Kyleakin Ferry without further incident and then ran on to Broadford where I addressed the prayer meeting from Exodus 33:14.'

These car incidents of fifty years ago are not unworthy of a place in these pages. They reveal a side of Kenneth MacRae's character which might scarcely have been anticipated by those who seldom saw him except in a pulpit. From the beginning of his motoring days he had a practical interest in cars; he could handle their problems with his usual efficient determination and he enjoyed both proving and recording their capabilities. Then, and later, there was no recreation which he enjoyed more than that of driving through the magnificence of the Scottish Highlands.

1 When Dr Munro heard of this visit he was eager to have it repeated when he could be present. This was done a few weeks later with somewhat more risk at the ford, due to rain: 'The Black Water was so broad that we had grave doubts as to our crossing . . . although the water swept over the footboards, it did not enter the car'. It was characteristic of the driver that he accepted the challenge presented by this situation!

'Let us not be weary in well-doing; for in due season we shall reap if we faint not.' Galatians 6:9

We must abase ourselves indeed, but we must magnify our office. We must rise to the high and elevated character, which it impresses upon the spiritual pastor. It must take the lead of everything. It must occupy all our care, all our time, all our diligence, all the best and most persevering efforts of our minds and affections – all our exertion, and self denial, and study. The blessings we have to offer are the greatest; the woe we have to denounce is the most fearful. Every thing connected with our office partakes of the incomprehensible importance of the gifts of the Saviour and the Holy Spirit. Till our whole souls are filled with our sacred calling, animated, elevated, absorbed – till we see nothing to be important, compared with our work – till nothing satisfies, or can satisfy us, but success in it – till we look on the affairs of human pursuit, and human power, and human wisdom, and human glory, as the toys of children in the comparison – till the salvation of souls is the one thing we aim at, the one object of desire, the ruling passion of our souls, we can never expect a general revival of that religion, which can only spring, under the blessing of God, from such principles and impressions.

BISHOP DANIEL WILSON
Recorded in one of K.A.M.'s Notebooks

10 The Call to Stornoway

MacRae had been eight years in Kilmuir when he first considered the possibility that his work there might be drawing to a close. While preaching at Ness, Lewis, in October 1927, he was approached about the possibility of a call to that large congregation in which he had preached previously in 1919. It was not the first such approach from a Lewis congregation and the proposal had a real appeal. There was, firstly, the attraction of the spiritual warmth of the Island which he felt even more than in 1922, and he observed once more the wide field of opportunity open for preaching. 'This has been the best communion season ever I have had in Lewis', he noted at the end of his visit in 1927. As he drove back from Ness (on the Atlantic side of the Island) to Stornoway, to catch the boat home, the very terrain of Lewis, so different from the Scottish mainland, had its own impressive appeal:

'The long stretches of yellow corn stooks, sometimes as far as the eye could reach – for the afternoon was hazy – looked exceedingly pretty in the subdued sunlight, while beyond, the Atlantic heaved with an unrippled oil-like surface which reflected back the sun's rays like a vast mirror. There was a mystery about the day and surroundings which somehow touched my heart. The old tumble-down church at Barvas was a sad sight. I called at the Manse for a moment to see Mrs MacLeod who is in ill health, and then Mr MacLeod[1] came on with me to Stornoway. Somehow there is a subtle charm about Stornoway which attracts me. I have no such feeling about Portree.'

With respect to the enquiry from the Ness elders he wrote:

'I had been asked to consider a call to the congregation, and indeed, were I free I could come to it with my whole heart, but my way does not appear to be open in that direction.'

While he thus put aside the question of a call in 1927 the experience contributed a certain degree of unsettledness to his feelings. Commenting on this in his Diary in early November 1927, he wrote: 'I wonder what this means? Is it a temptation of the devil because he sees fruitful days are near? or is it the Lord's way of taking off my heart from my present charge and preparing me for some call in His providence?'

During 1928 he became convinced that as far as his own inclinations were concerned a move would be desirable. The deadness in Kilmuir

1 John MacLeod, formerly his neighbour at Minard in his Lochgilphead days.

contributed considerably to his view of the situation. It was a remarkable example of the sovereignty of divine grace that during the very period when Kilmaluag and also Staffin had been so spiritually refreshed, the church at Kilmuir, where the minister resided and spent the majority of his time, remained comparatively unblessed. Yet MacRae did not think that this situation was to be explained solely in terms of God's will. On the contrary he saw it as part of his business as a pastor to analyse the reasons for the relative unfruitfulness in Kilmuir and to seek out the appropriate remedies. To this he gave extended thought and prayer. He had observed, for example, in 1924, that there was a curious belief about unfulfilled prophecy in Kilmuir which had the effect of nullifying the Saviour's promise, 'According to your faith be it unto you'. Persecution, it was thought, would have to precede a great revival in the latter days and, as no such persecution had occurred, revival could not then be expected! This was an error he laboured to correct. But as the error had its source in the prophetical views of one of the revered leaders of an earlier generation it is doubtful if he had made headway against it.[1]

Another hindrance in the Kilmuir congregation seems to have been an element of Hyper-Calvinism. Because of the strength of MacRae's opposition to Arminianism this error was sometimes charged against him, but in Kilmuir, and indeed throughout all his ministry, he laboured vigorously against it. After a day's plain gospel preaching in Kilmuir in February 1928 he wrote in his Diary: 'Today's sermons were very elementary but I feel that this is very necessary in Kilmuir, where ultra-Calvinism has generated a mysticism and a drowsiness that is strangling the Gospel. May the Lord bless His truth!' He had no sympathy at all with the view that a minister should only tell sinners to 'Wait upon the Spirit' instead of preaching the command, 'Come to Christ'.

The people of Kilmuir certainly did not lack earnest preaching: they were nursed, pleaded with and warned. For a general work of conversion among them their pastor had constantly looked. Yet as the years passed and he went over their names and cases he had to write in his Diary: 'Exercised about the fact that working on the basis of new communicants since I came here, two out of every three of my hearers will be lost. It is a very solemn consideration'. At times, indeed, it seemed that a quickening in Kilmuir was imminent. At the end of 1927 he noted, 'Surely Kilmuir is looking up at last and the Lord is about to revive this long

1 See note on page 195.

[220]

barren section of the congregation'. But these periods of warmth and attention were not long sustained, and again such entries recur in the Diary as the following: 'Feel my responsibility towards them almost bearing me down. Spoke very solemnly and plainly to them; told them that their carelessness in attending God's house was breaking my heart.'

Health was another factor which led him to consider a removal. Though now well into his forties he had in no way lessened the exertions of earlier years, and such was the scattered nature of his charge that there was little possibility of his being able to do so. Spending so much time on hazardous roads in the long, cold months of winter was a heavy strain. Then his high view of the privilege of the ministry had led him to maintain a degree of labour which cannot often have been exceeded. When he had been a student in Edinburgh, Archibald MacNeilage had contrasted the old-style of ministers with the tendency of the moderns. From the old ideal Kenneth MacRae was never to swerve: 'The ministers whose work abides,' wrote the Editor of *The Monthly Record*, 'were those who spent and were spent in the service of particular congregations . . . Such men had small love for talk, and they had none at all for trifles. We live in a day when many ministers are extremely busy about trifles, and the thing they like least is the hard work of the closet, of the study, and the homes of their people.'

This is not to say that MacRae took no time for recreation. Cathie MacRae, in a brief note on their life in Kilmuir, gives one example of how much he enjoyed, and contributed to, the happy life of their home:

He tried to arrange his time in the home in the following way: the mornings for reading and correspondence, afternoons for visitation, and evenings – at least three times weekly – for meetings. On Monday evening he tried to relax and pass some time at play with his little daughter. On these occasions both delighted in building fortresses of wooden bricks and had the use of the large dining-room table. The child became an adept at the setting up of forts, battlements etc, and the supply of troops was not meagre. There were Seaforths, Camerons, Gordons, Black Watch and Argylls, all in their respective and colourful uniforms – these, of course, being kilted Highland regiments. There were also Grenadier Guards to take their place of duty, and alien soldiers, not at all of the smartest appearance, were also necessary to take their part in the battles. The principal ammunition in the warfare consisted of hard peas from the kitchen store which were aimed with remarkable precision by both fighters. There were always shouts of victory when a battle was won – usually by the 'kilties' – and a happy chuckle of triumph from the Commander-in-Chief when he saw the expression of delight in little Mary's face. Each time he visited the city he, as a rule, brought back an addition of tiny tin soldiers to fill the blanks caused by war.

Perhaps such intervals as these were too infrequent. It is clear that in the late 1920's he went through one of those comparatively rare periods in his ministry when his strength was worn down. In 1929 he was laid aside from his work from late January until the beginning of March. 'I cannot face another winter here under present conditions,' he wrote in his Diary on 9 March. Humanly speaking there was no reason why his pastorate in Kilmuir should not have ended in 1929, for he was, at this period, faced with repeated invitations from other charges. Approaches had come from Greenock, Duirinish, Gairloch and Ardgay. For many months Duirinish pressed their interest and, at first, he believed that this might be the call of providence; gradually and not without difficulty he came to the opposite conclusion.

In this same period, when these calls were before him, an unexpected issue arose which, as it required his presence in Skye, closed the question of his accepting a call away from the Island. Early in 1929 news was circulated that the London Midland and Scottish Railway Company was planning railway excursions from Inverness to Kyle on Sundays, so that trippers could cross to Skye. Immediately MacRae circulated petition forms against this proposal and set a target of 20,000 signatures – a large number – for that part of Scotland. The financial possibilities, however, were too attractive for the L.M.S. to pay heed to the protest. When, in June 1929, it became clear that they intended to proceed with the plans for excursions, MacRae originated a 'Skye Sabbath Defence League'. The condition for membership was that the members must be those 'whose action would be as good as their word' – the action in view being a boycott of the L.M.S. The Vice-President of the Railway Company, hearing of the disturbance its proposals were causing in Skye, expressed his inability to believe that any such action would be taken. He under-estimated the strength of the opposition. On July 3 MacRae noted:

'Wrote a letter to various papers today advocating the boycotting of the L.M.S. Railway and stating that steps were being taken locally to show how far the railway company err in supposing that Highlanders will not stand by their word.'

The previous day he had obtained his 'first four recruits to the Skye Sabbath Defence League' in Kilmaluag. To raise hundreds more he now travelled the length and breadth of Skye, organising and addressing meetings of the League. All thoughts of not spending another winter in Kilmuir were put to one side, and when the Colonial Committee of the Church proposed that he spend several of the winter months preaching in Toronto he promptly turned it down 'on account of the necessity of my being at home in Skye to conduct an aggressive campaign against Sabbath excursions'.

He found it a hard battle to raise the support which was necessary. Some ministers from whom he had reason to expect support seemed strangely lethargic, or at least unwilling to proceed to the length of encouraging a boycott. Of one such minister he writes with disappointment in his Diary: 'Had he as much zeal for the Sabbath as he has dislike for the Free Presbyterians he would be a most useful man'. Because of his determination to make a stand when he believed that principles were at stake, MacRae, at this time and later, was not without opponents, and some represented him as a man of contentious temperament. The truth is that he did not relish controversy. His zeal sprang from the conviction that the fourth commandment is as much the law of God for every individual as every other commandment and that Christians have therefore as plain a duty to resist Sabbath desecration as they have to resist the desecration of marriage or the unjust taking of life. If the Sunday excursions succeeded they would provide a constant temptation to the disregard of God's law in Skye, and he believed it was a sin for anyone not to resist the introduction of such a change in the Island. For himself he could write, 'I cannot bear to see the Sabbath murdered in it.'[1]

Nor was MacRae a man who relished the many extra engagements which the controversy entailed. He saw the spiritual danger: 'These things are necessary, but they dry me up. I long for peace to enjoy the things of God'. And he felt the loneliness which faithfulness can bring upon a minister: 'It seems to me,' he wrote on 19 February, 1930, 'that the more lax and inactive a minister is today, the better he will get on. Well, let me live more for the Lord and upon the Lord, and be less concerned to serve men even in spiritual things. Boston's troubles comfort me.'[2]

The issue was contested with the L.M.S. for more than a year when the end came suddenly on 6 October, 1930. MacRae had been away

1 This strength of feeling was by no means novel in Scotland. See, for example, the two letters of Robert M. McCheyne, 'I love the Lord's Day' and 'Letter on Sabbath Railways' in his *Memoir and Remains*, 1844, reprinted 1966.
2 Thomas Boston (1676–1732) of Ettrick. With Dr Munro he had visited Ettrick the previous autumn and he was currently reading Boston's *General Account of My Life* of which he says, 'It has been a blessed book to me'.

preaching on the mainland and returned that day to Skye. Of the day's events he writes:

'As I approached Skye, I felt the load connected with the Sabbath question again settling on my spirit. Felt the case very hopeless and much inclined to quit the Island altogether. At Portree interviewed Donald Nicolson of the Highland Transport Company. Had a talk with him which cleared the air. Found him ready to put his company on the panel of the League and felt inclined to press the boycott on the bus service. On my return home found a letter from Fellows, Vice-President of the L.M.S., which made me rejoice, for it actually pledged that the Sabbath excursions would not be run next summer to Kyle if our agitation in the Island would end. This is the doing of the Lord and wondrous in our eyes! A letter from the *Daily Express* also awaited me, stating that a public apology for the offence given the League would appear in next issue. We have triumphed all round.'

Cathie MacRae remembered how he almost danced for joy after opening the L.M.S. letter on that October day. It is true the letter reserved the Company's right to change their decision again in the future but MacRae rightly saw that such a statement was only an attempt to lessen their discomfort. The next day he records: 'Wrote Branch Secretaries of the League calling off the boycott and sent out press notices of our success.'

There were two important results from the work of the Skye Sabbath Defence League. The first was that the support from the population was so large that for many years to come it was to restrain railway companies, and other commercial concerns, from pleading that they wished to introduce changes in the facilities available on the Lord's Day 'in the interests of the people'. When, for example, air services to the Outer Hebrides were being discussed in June 1933 it was at once conceded that there would be no Sunday flights. MacRae wrote in his Diary at that time: 'No doubt the Skye fight has led many to be chary of ignoring the convictions of the people in these quarters, for in other areas they simply ignore such convictions.' Certainly there was widespread appreciation in Skye in 1930 for what he had done and one expression of that gratitude came from the people of Uig who presented him with a Remington type-writer. It was a valuable acquisition for until that time all his correspondence had been written by hand; thereafter his Remington produced most of his letters and sermon notes and it was only finally laid aside in September 1963 when he had no longer the strength to manipulate his trusted old model.

A second result of the League was that, as already mentioned, its struggle was a major factor in preventing him giving a positive response to any of the calls which he had received in 1929. But by 10 September, 1930 he felt that 'all his stakes' were uprooted. Yet he did not know which way his future path lay: 'I would no longer decline to consider Gairloch but they are taken up with another man. Why am I kept here? Let me wait patiently upon the Lord'.

The providence of God was now to reveal the meaning of this delay. During 1930 Kenneth Cameron, after 16 years as minister of the Free Church in Stornoway, Lewis, accepted a call to the Free North Church in Inverness, and the thoughts of the elders of the congregation turned to the minister of Kilmuir. In December 1930 MacRae received a letter of congratulations from the Lewis Presbytery with respect to the success of the Sabbath League. On 14 January, 1931 another letter invited him to preach at the Stornoway communion season in February. He had a premonition of what was to follow and wrote that day in his Diary: 'It is wrong to be outrunning Providence, but I cannot but think that the Lord's hand is in the matter and that it may mean the end of my ministry in Kilmuir. I wish I were a better man and a more spiritual minister. I am a secret grief to myself.'

In the weeks that followed, the question of Stornoway appears to have been little in his thoughts. He was as busy as ever in the three sections of his congregation. At the end of January, 1931, he noted that during the month he had preached ten times in Kilmuir, three in Staffin and five in Kilmaluag, and that the average attendance in each place respectively had been 54, 76 and 93. He also observed that he 'seemed to have more liberty in Kilmuir and Staffin.' When the communion season in Stornoway came it proved 'a soul-refreshing season': 'I have enjoyed much of the Lord's presence,' he wrote at the end of it. Congregations were vast, amounting to 1100 people on the final Monday morning. By way of contrast he found communion services that same month in Sleat, Skye, 'a misery. Felt quite forsaken and the atmosphere frigid'. On 19 March, 1931, word came from Stornoway that he had been unanimously nominated by the Vacancy Committee and the usual processes then began which terminated at a meeting of the Skye Presbytery on 24 June. On that date he wrote before retiring to bed:

'This day marks another turning-point in my life. At meeting of Presbytery, held at Kyleakin, accepted the call from the Stornoway congregation. Felt very sorry for the Kilmuir commissioners. Roderick Gillies's pleading especially touched me. The Lewis men spoke well. I felt it very difficult to keep myself under restraint and almost failed to conclude my speech. The cord is cut now, but I cannot realise it. Life is slowly but surely ebbing away. Probably this will be the last stage, oh to be more blessed in it than ever I have been yet!'

The call to Stornoway was certainly the most important event in Kenneth MacRae's ministerial life. Kenneth Cameron, the congregation's former pastor, had also been called from Skye to Lewis and it is interesting to note the arguments which the Lewis commissioners had used in 1913 at their first attempt to secure Mr Cameron. While it was undesirable, they said, to leave any charges vacant in the present circumstances, it was the Church's 'plain duty to apportion their best men to the most populous and urgent parts.' 'Stornoway,' they pleaded, 'was the commercial capital of the Western Isles, with a fluctuating population of 4000 to 7000 people; the finest school in the West, with about 800 pupils; and a secondary school with about 200 students, the majority of whom are Free Church. How were our Highland pulpits to be filled with ministers? Not from Canada or Ireland, but, as of old, from the homes of our Free Church people. In the interests of the Church as a whole, Stornoway offers a fine field for Mr Cameron's talents and piety – a splendid nursery to prepare Free Church students.'[1] These arguments were no less forceful in 1931.

The call to Stornoway did not occasion Mr MacRae the same personal exercise and difficulty as he had experienced in 1919. He believed that the way had been made plain; yet the pain at the prospect of leaving the people whom he had served for twelve years was severe. The Sabbath after his acceptance of the call he was due to preach in Staffin and Kilmaluag and, in his usual open way, he determined to tell the people how he had been led in the matter. His Diary reads:

'Sunday, 28 June, 1931: Got a showery day but attendances were good. In Staffin spoke from Hebrews 13:14 to an attendance of 120. Felt touched when I saw strong men like Neil Nicolson (Flodigarry) weeping as I spoke of my impending departure. At close declared my reason for accepting the Stornoway Call but could not lift my head to look at the people.

'At Kilmaluag 110 were present. Spoke from Hebrews 2:1 with liberty. Again felt very sore when saw such as James MacKay and Angus MacDonald weeping. Spoke at close re the Stornoway Call and the place became a Bochim. I almost gave way, but with a struggle managed to regain control of myself. Came home with a heart like to break. If

1 *The Monthly Record*, 1913, p 138.

the mere intimation of my departure causes such pain, what will the actual parting be? I shrink from the ordeal.'[1]

The following Sunday, after preaching in the Kilmuir section, he made a similar statement though with an added note: 'Spoke of the Call to Stornoway and told them that if they wished to keep a minister they must attend better. Some shed tears but felt hard as compared with Kilmaluag and Staffin.'

At the beginning of August, 1931, the last communion services of his Skye pastorate were held. The visiting preachers were Mr MacIver of Lochs and Mr Muirden of Maryburgh. To his great joy four came to the session expressing their desire to confess Christ for the first time. His diary notes on these four cases indicate something of what ministers and elders looked for in those days in those who wished to become communicant members of the Church:

'1. —— Felt satisfied with her, but she could give no details of her soul experience. An elder felt the necessity to giving a warning against gossip. Elderly cases are seldom so satisfactory as the young.

2. —— It was difficult to get anything out of her, but I rejoiced to see her there, for her life is her testimony.

3. —— Was awakened during the illness of her mother about two years ago and apparently found peace soon after. Felt some difficulty, as the girl is so young, but on the testimony of Ewen who witnessed to the change apparent in her life, admitted her.

4. —— She appears to be another fruit of the 1923 movement in Kilmaluag. In the Fall of that year she was awakened in the course of a sermon I preached down there, and in Spring she got peace when reading the text, "Believe in the Lord Jesus Christ and thou shalt be saved", in one of Spurgeon's sermons.

Felt very thankful for this, although there are still many whom I would like to see coming forward, especially in Kilmaluag.'

The following entries, concluding this chapter, speak for themselves:

MONDAY, 3 AUGUST, 1931

Mr Muirden preached today to a congregation of 175 from Romans 1:16–17. His sermon was as good, as weighty and as evangelical as usual.

At the close Cathie and I were made a Presentation by the Congregation of £48.10.0. In replying felt almost overcome. I do not suppose

1 'In his later years,' writes his daughter, 'he often spoke of Kilmaluag as "Goshen". Of all places in the world he loved it most.'

that ever again I shall have such an affectionate people. The sound of a significant sniffing[1] from the precentor's box, where sat two of the Kilmaluag men, almost upset me. In the evening Mr MacIver preached to a crowded house (130) in Kilmaluag from Hebrews 10:39. He gave a good sermon but in a low building it would have been far more telling had it been delivered in a less vehement key.

This has been a very happy communion. The weather was simply ideal and the preaching was good. It is hard to realise that it is my last here. May the Lord acknowledge His truth.

TUESDAY, 4 AUGUST

The ministers took their departure this morning. Wrote my last entry in the Kilmuir Kirk Session Records and felt very sad in doing so. Began sorting out my papers in readiness for our departure.

THURSDAY, 6 AUGUST

When I was packing my books today found myself wondering why I was taking them over the Minch. I don't suppose I shall take them back again.

TUESDAY, 11 AUGUST

Took Granny over to Dunvegan today. On my return found the house a desolation. I scarcely know where to turn or where to find a corner for study of any kind. The packers have pushed on wonderfully well with their work. I feel sad as I realise how soon now we must leave this dear old house of many happy memories.

SABBATH, 16 AUGUST

The day was beautiful and the people got every opportunity to come out. About 140 were present in Kilmuir. Spoke from Philippians 1:27 but did not make anything of it. At close gave them some very pointed advice. Bidding good-bye at the church door was a painful ordeal. Several times I was almost overcome. At Staffin at 4 pm had an attendance of 155. Spoke from Colossians 2:5 but without much liberty. The final ordeal was almost as painful as at Kilmuir. Parting with the office-bearers was very sore. Poor James MacKay was sobbing audibly as the people were filing out past me. It was a painful day but I was thankful to have been brought through.

1 An ineffective attempt to suppress visible emotion!

MONDAY, 17 AUGUST

About 9 am over 20 men assembled to help in the removal of the furniture. The day was beautiful, for which I was extremely thankful. Four lorries made two runs each and by 12 o'clock the whole was down on Uig Pier. After leaving the Manse had dinner with the MacLeods. Was amazed at the way in which Hugh spoke at the parting. Parted then with my office-bearers in Roderick Gillies'[1] house. Felt that I could bear no more of it. It was an awful experience.

☐ ☐ ☐

Lewis and Harris together make up one island, the largest in a one hundred and thirty-mile long chain of islands which form The Outer Hebrides – a breakwater to the Atlantic between thirty and fifty-four miles off the north-west coast of Scotland. Various factors caused the histories of Lewis and Harris to develop separately and this is the explanation why what is only part of one island is customarily known as 'The Isle of Lewis'. It has been conjectured that the original meaning of the word 'Lewis' or 'Lews' is 'a place abounding in pools'; whether or not that is correct, it is certainly an accurate description, for in addition to her 404,000 acres of land she has nearly 25,000 acres of inland water, not to speak of tidal fiords. With few hills, and virtually treeless, the brown rolling moorland contains little save peat bogs and rock with only small areas around the coast suitable for cultivation. Lewis has nevertheless maintained from antiquity a considerable population, and amongst the known waves of people to possess her rugged shores were the Picts, the Norsemen, and finally, the Gaelic-speaking Scots. Although the island's latitude is comparable to that of northern Labrador, with nights short in summer and long in winter, the influence of the Gulf-stream and of south-westerly winds, produces relatively high winter temperatures. Thus Stornoway has a higher mean-January temperature than Cambridge, England, many hundreds of miles further south.

1 Roderick Gillies – an elder from the Kilmuir section of the congregation – was a man of outstanding ability. When MacRae had occasion to be away from home, Gillies often conducted the services. After his minister had left for Stornoway Gillies remarked, 'In all those years of close co-operation not the slightest breath of disagreement ever came between us – no, not even as much as would cause the gossamer in the fields of rye to quiver.' When Gillies died in 1942 MacRae wrote, 'He does not leave his like behind, and the Lord's cause in Skye is greatly weakened'. The harmony that existed between minister and elder was but a feature of the general concord in the church courts in the congregation of Kilmuir and Stenscholl at that time. MacRae often spoke of the sheer loyalty and dependability of that particular set of office-bearers.

There are nearly a hundred villages of varying size situated in the coastal strip, with Stornoway providing the only town. Stornoway seems to have been the centre of Lewis as far back as the centuries of Norse rule, its name deriving from the Icelandic *stjorna* = to govern, and *vagr* = bay. But with its remoteness there were few reasons for development, and so as late as 1629, a report asserted that while it had the principal harbour of the island, it is 'a small village . . . it hath yet no traffic'. By the 19th Century, however, with a fishing trade stretching as far as Russia, Stornoway became a major burgh in the North of Scotland. While the rest of Lewis lived in the traditional 'black-houses' – low buildings with walls of uncut stone and roofs of heather and bracken – two-storied slated buildings of stone and lime were rising in Stornoway, and a population of tradesmen and merchants was becoming established.

It was also in the 19th Century that Lewis was swept by a great spiritual awakening. The Reformation in Scotland, which nominally ended Catholicism throughout the nation, had virtually left the spiritual condition of the Hebrides untouched. A visitor in 1630 wrote: 'In their religion they are very ignorant and have been given to the idolatrous worship of divers saints'. As well as 'Christian' saints, such pagan gods as 'Shony' (a sea-god or 'god of noise') continued to receive the reverence of many of the people. The custom was that at Hallow-tide Shony should be worshipped at night when a devotee was chosen to wade into the sea holding aloft a cup of ale with which the deity was invoked. Not surprisingly the morality of the people tended to be as low as their religious conceptions. Early in the 19th Century, Stornoway was said to have no fewer than eighteen licensed inns.

It was in 1824 that a new era dawned with the appointment of the Rev. Alexander MacLeod of Uig on the west coast of the island. By 1828 'the whole island seemed to be moved by one powerful spiritual impulse', and as many as 9000 were reported to be attending communion seasons. In 1834 MacLeod could write, 'Ten winters have I passed here, all wonderfully short, pleasant, and delightful'.

One result of this glorious revival was that when the Disruption occurred in 1843 practically the whole island sided with the evangelical testimony of the Free Church and new parishes and churches multiplied. A Free Church built in Stornoway was burned down in 1850, to be replaced by a yet larger structure in Kenneth Street capable of seating 1200. In 1855 the Rev. Peter MacLean was called to the Free Church in Stornoway; he lived in the large manse built on Francis Street in

1850 – the same house which Kenneth MacRae was to occupy for the rest of his life. It was when MacLean was preaching in Garrabost in 1859 that another revival period began in the island. In the same year a sermon preached by MacLean in the open-air on the Green in Stornoway was to be remembered and spoken of fifty years later. The text was Isaiah 44:22, 'I have blotted out as a thick cloud thy transgressions'. 'Zeal for the Lord,' it was said, 'burned in him like a fire'. As a result of his multiplied labours Peter MacLean's health broke down in 1861 and, after a resumption of work in 1863, he died in 1868, being spoken of as 'the father of thousands'.

At the beginning of the present century the population of Lewis stood at almost 29,000 and the extent to which a living Christianity had moulded the whole life of the community made a striking impression on all who visited the island. Prayerfulness, uprightness, and generosity towards the cause of the Gospel, characterised large numbers of the people. The Captain of a naval vessel, unaccustomed to this kind of Christianity, who called at a wood-yard in Stornoway to enquire concerning some repairs, reported how he found two men engaged in prayer. In witnessing their obvious abstraction and solemn impression of the presence of God he felt something which arrested him. 'They were,' he wrote, 'an extraordinary people here; one cannot but be struck with their honesty, kindness and sobriety. One *hears* of religion elsewhere, but one *sees* it here in everything'.[1] Another impartial observer, speaking in 1919, wrote 'If one were asked to point to a tangible sign of the vitality of religion in Lewis, one would direct the inquirer, not to its full churches, but to its empty prisons. It would be difficult to find elsewhere in the United Kingdom – or Ireland – a community of 30,000 souls with so clean a criminal record'.[2]

Kenneth MacRae's first visit to Lewis – unrecorded in his Diary – was with a student-friend in 1914. Between that date and his settlement in 1931 various changes were taking place in the island. Before the Great War he had seen Stornoway's harbour crowded with hundreds of fishing craft. There were at that date some 1000 fishing boats – 'wherries' – belonging to the island, besides steam-drifters which had started to come from the East Coast in 1912. Fishing was then a part-

1 Most of the information given here on the spiritual condition of Lewis in the last century can be found in the anonymous work *History of Revivals of Religion in the British Isles*, especially in Scotland, 1836, but it is singularly unfortunate that the records of the work of the Spirit of God in Lewis and Harris are so meagre.
2 Ian MacPherson, *The Book of the Lews*, 1919, p 152.

time occupation of many of the crofters whose small-holdings of not more than 10 acres provided an insufficient livelihood for a family. Another additional source of income was weaving, undertaken by many women in their homes on hand-looms. As in Skye, groupings of these crofts together were known as 'townships'.

In 1918 changes came when Baron Leverhulme bought the entire island.[1] The previous year he had motored all over Lewis and, says his biographer, 'he was enraptured . . . he realised that the backwardness of the island arose from lack of opportunity, and that opportunity he would do his best to provide'.[2] His aim was to work for a broader-based economy, though with fishing still as the mainstay. But difficulties soon arose. While he wanted farms for a milk factory near to Stornoway, servicemen, returning from the war, wanted crofts which they could work for themselves. When the fishing industry waned in the early 1920's Leverhulme's scheme for Lewis collapsed, and he abandoned his residence in Stornoway Castle which he had had restored in palatial style.[3]

One result of the failure of his enterprise was increased emigration from the island in the 1920's, so that the total population at the time of MacRae's arrival in 1931 stood at 26,000, the population of Stornoway itself being 3,644. The existence of two mills in the town for the production of Harris tweed was the means of preventing greater unemployment and depopulation.

Housing was improving in the 1930's with the traditional homes giving way across the island to white cottages of stone and lime with proper windows and an attic. Though Stornoway was, in this respect, well ahead of 'the country' it is recorded that, even in 1931, 44 per cent of the burgh's population lived in homes which possessed only one to three rooms.

Of major significance to Lewis between 1914 and 1931 was the coming of the motor car. In 1914 it was a day's journey to cross the island on foot; by 1919 a mail van was running once a day; and by 1931 Ford vans had brought all the scattered townships into comparatively easy reach of one another. The car also brought an important practical difference in the life of a Free Church minister of Stornoway. The

1 From 1610 to 1844 the island was owned by the Seaforths. At the latter date it was sold to James Matheson in whose family it remained until 1918. The crofters were only tenants, not owners of the land.
2 Quoted by Arthur Geddes in *The Isle of Lewis and Harris*, 1955, p 257.
3 When Leverhulme left the island he divided most of it into small estates which were sold. The nature of the land can be judged by the fact that his price per acre for some estates was as low as 2½d!

occupant of the Stornoway pulpit had always been in demand among the other congregations of the island, but with transport it was now possible to preach both in Stornoway and in any other part of the island in the same day, if occasion arose. This inevitably brought an increase of work.

It is difficult to conceive of a heavier charge than the one to which Kenneth MacRae now came. With about 650 homes under his care, he had the spiritual oversight of more than half the population of Stornoway.

The church on Kenneth Street was the centre of congregational life. Enlarged since its opening in 1851, it was capable of holding up to 1600, and here MacRae preached twice every Sabbath and at a prayer meeting on Thursday evenings. An additional church property, known as 'the Seminary' (rebuilt in 1899 to hold up to 300 people), had been used since the time of Peter MacLean for a Sabbath afternoon service in English for those who had too little Gaelic to profit from the regular services. By 1931 the need for such a service had increased[1] and accordingly MacRae, from the start of his ministry in the town, normally preached three times every Lord's Day. He also was to introduce a 'Lecture' in English on Wednesday evenings during winter months, an innovation which soon became an important part of the church's life.

A considerable portion of the Stornoway congregation belonged to six outlying country districts adjacent to the town, Culregrein, Laxdale, Marybank, Steinish, Sandwick and Melbost, and each of these districts had a meeting of its own one night every week. MacRae would be present and preach at at least one and sometimes two of these district meetings.

One of MacRae's younger hearers has recorded this memory of the town at the time of his settlement:

The harbour was the chief focus of activity, for everything that affected the town was dependent on the arrival of the boats. The mailboat arrived from Kyle of Lochalsh every evening around 8 pm, was unloaded and loaded again for departure at 11 pm. By this same means the daily newspapers came and were immediately on sale in the newsagents.

In summer, the herring fleet, newly painted, bearing attractive names came and left daily, selling their catches on the quayside to fish curers from the East Coast who had stations and workers all around the quay.

1 In 1931 Gaelic was the common language of 95 per cent of the people in 'the country', but in Stornoway the traditional language was only used by 70 per cent. Almost all Free Church families were, however, from a Gaelic-speaking background.

Herring was gutted and packed on the spot by girls from the villages and a small number from Stornoway. They were organised in crews of 3 (2 gutters and 1 packer) and supervised by a foreman from the East Coast whose language was not always delicate. So the general impression was noise, barrels, girls in oilskin aprons, wellingtons, bandaged fingers, and seagulls everywhere.

The other industry then expanding was the making of tweed.[1] People from the villages moved to the town to work in the mills and associated office jobs. Another field of employment was dock labour. Cargo boats from Glasgow came once a week and that cargo was distributed gradually throughout the week. The homes of the working people were situated around the shops in the centre and on the seafront. There were three banks. The shops, which traded in the usual commodities peculiar to an island agricultural and fishing community, were owned by sound business-men of integrity whose families have in several instances carried on their principles.

A minority who had wealth – reputedly acquired, in some cases, by their forbears in the Colonies – lived in fine houses. These were the coal and timber merchants, solicitors and mill-owners, and their homes could boast of having resident, uniformed domestic help from the villages. Almost none of these belonged to the Free Church! That is not to say that the Church did not have plain, astute and prosperous business men amongst its elders in 1931. They were a wise council and were all from 'the country' and Gaelic-speaking as were most of the congregation.

Doctors were less affluent because of their benevolence towards patients who had difficulty in paying the fees. The official fee for a doctor's visit to the home was 7/6 while a tradesman's wage was approximately £3 per week.

In 1931, on the outskirts, were about six or seven small dairy and poultry farms which supplied the town with its milk and eggs. The villages had their own milk supply – each home having one, two or three cows, depending on the size of the family.

A favourite 'outing' for children was to the grounds of Lewis Castle across the harbour. These grounds and greenhouses – which were open to the public for walks and picnics – were outstandingly beautiful and kept in perfect order by full-time gardeners. There are acres of trees and lush foliage, with rhododendrons in every hue growing in profusion in spring-time.

Stornoway's school, the Nicolson Institute, has always been a focus of activity in the town and in 1931 it stood exactly where it remains today,

1 A large number of looms for weaving belonged to crofters – men and women – and the work of weaving was carried out at their homes. The mills supplied the yarns for weaving, paid the weavers for their work and sold the finished tweeds.

opposite the Free Church Manse. Education was all-important and in most cases there was almost no limit set to the sacrifices made to educate one's family. This was the only secondary school in the town; there was also a primary school, and two more primary schools at Sandwick and Laxdale, two miles east and west of the centre. The Island's villages had their own primary schools and children there worked hard for the 'bursary' which would admit them to Stornoway. There were well-appointed hostels for these girls and boys from 'the country' and some were boarded in private houses. The rector and teachers at the Nicolson generally came from the Island or the Highlands and some belonged to the Free Church and taught in the Sunday School and Bible Class.

Tuberculosis was a scourge in the Lewis villages where housing was quite inadequate and control of infection impossible. A Sanatorium was situated about two miles from the town centre and it was always full to capacity with young people suffering from the various forms of the disease. The incidence was much less in the town.

As at the present time, the majority of town people, by far, attended the Free Church.

Kenneth MacRae was forty-seven when he penned the first pages of his Diary in Stornoway and to these pages of his narrative we now return.

My eyes have seen the beauty of the King. I anew realise that there is no work like preaching, and my heart is once more fired with the desire to make Christ known to perishing sinners.

K. A. M.

11 The Commencement of the Long Pastorate

WEDNESDAY, 2 SEPTEMBER, 1931

Was introduced today in the congregation of Stornoway. The church was packed, the aisles being thronged and even the outer stairs occupied. Mr MacIver of Lochs preached an excellent sermon from 2 Corinthians 5:20 and then inducted me as minister of the charge. Felt the vows as being most solemn; they made me afraid, as experience has shown me how I come short. Mr MacKenzie (Back) addressed me, while Mr MacIver (Shawbost) addressed the congregation. They did well. The service was followed by presentations – £50 to myself, £10 to Cathie, and a cheque to the Interim Moderator.

May the Lord bless and help me in my ministry here! Feel somewhat troubled when I consider my poorness of health.[1]

THURSDAY, 3 SEPTEMBER

Began to get the house in order. Got a willing band of helpers, and made good progress. By night things had taken better order.

Held my first prayer meeting here. Almost 500 were present. Spoke from 1 Peter 1:6–7 with some freedom of utterance, but no sense of power.

SATURDAY, 5 SEPTEMBER

Find it impossible to get proper opportunity for study and am very shaky as to tomorrow's discourse. I find that a great deal of supervision is expected of a minister here, there being from 10–15 services in the congregation per week. Mr Cameron reduced brevity to a fine art and got through an enormous amount of work, but I cannot do that.

At night welcomed Mr MacDonald (Rosskeen) who is to introduce me on the morrow.

SABBATH, 6 SEPTEMBER

In morning had a good attendance of fully 700 when Mr MacDonald preached from 1 Corinthians 1:17. At 2 pm he preached in English from Hebrews 2:1 to a congregation of 150. At 4.30 I conducted a service in the Sanatorium when spoke from Matthew 11:30.

1 He often suffered from a gall-bladder complaint and from duodenal ulcers.

At night had an enormous congregation, the church being full. About 1,700 were present. Spoke from Acts 10:29.

MONDAY, 7 SEPTEMBER

Got Mary enrolled in the Nicolson Institute today. This being the first Monday of the month had prayer meeting at 11 am.

At 7 pm we had another meeting and Mr MacDonald presided over a gathering of fully 300.

TUESDAY, 8 SEPTEMBER

Moved into the Manse today for which very thankful. Spent day in fixing up things and in overtaking correspondence.

WEDNESDAY, 9 SEPTEMBER

Longing to get things fixed up in the Manse so that I can begin congregational visitation.

THURSDAY, 10 SEPTEMBER

Did not feel too well today, but since I was able to do some congregational work felt easier in my mind. Attended funeral in Laxdale. The service was held in the house and was conducted as in Skye. There were not so many bearers as I have been accustomed to in Kilmuir, and the coffin was borne at the head of the company, not at the rear, but military precision was even more evident than in Skye.

At 6 pm I conducted my first marriage. The room was crowded with women and girls, and the bridal couple sat at the head of the table which was prepared for the feast. I waited to ask the blessing and then went out to see a poor old man in a neighbouring house who was very low.

At 7 o'clock conducted the Prayer Meeting. The attendance was again huge. Spoke from Mark 1:13 and enjoyed it. At the close the Deacon's Court met. Was pleased at the expeditious way in which business was transacted and the spirit among them. Feel thankful tonight to the Lord for all his goodness to me.

FRIDAY, 11 SEPTEMBER

Visited the Hospital today. Felt somewhat strange at first, but soon came to the work, and think I shall like it better than I expected. There are many poor creatures in there.

Composed discourse on 2 Corinthians 6:17 on Christian nonconformity to the world. Am interrupted here more than in Kilmuir. Studying is difficult.

SATURDAY, 12 SEPTEMBER

Find that I am continually interrupted and it is very difficult to find time for study.

SABBATH, 13 SEPTEMBER

Got a measure of liberty in preaching from 2 Corinthians 6:17. The congregation was huge. In the afternoon, at the English, about 180 were present. Visited the Sabbath School and said a few words to the scholars and to the teachers. There were over 100 children present.

In the evening conducted an English service in the Seminary. Long before the time the place was chock-a-block.

At the close of the morning service emphasised (1) that applicants for baptism for the first time[1] must appear before the Session, (2) that the sacrament is a public one. Spoke also respecting baptizing those who are seriously ill, and gave a warning as to the danger [of superstition].

Got a measure of liberty today for which I am thankful, yet feel that I lack power. This is what I long for.

MONDAY, 21 SEPTEMBER

Discovered today at a funeral at which I was present that the service is meant for the bereaved and their friends only, outsiders not being supposed to gather until the service is over. The Lochgilphead method is better in which there are two services, one for the bereaved and the other for the funeral company in the nearest church.

TUESDAY, 22 SEPTEMBER

Went out today to Melbost where visited 17 households. Found the houses much better than I had expected and the people very hospitable. At 7 o'clock had a meeting when spoke from Matthew 11:30 with some liberty. The house was quite full, 105 being present, some having walked out from town.

TUESDAY, 29 SEPTEMBER

Visited in Laxdale in the afternoon. Called upon 22 families. At 7 o'clock held a service in the Meeting House. The place was packed,

1 The reference, of course, is to parents seeking baptism for their first child.

fully 120 being present. Felt the atmosphere very warm and the singing was especially hearty. It was a helpful meeting, and came home feeling very thankful.

TUESDAY, 6 OCTOBER

Conducted meeting at Poorhouse tonight. Most of the audience were mental defectives. Felt very strange speaking to such an audience from Matthew 11:30. Some sometimes would smile inanely. Yet grace has a tremendous power and even these poor darkened intellects might be enlightened by Heaven's light. The thought encouraged me in the midst of the apparent hopelessness of my task.

MONDAY, 26 OCTOBER

Visited the Sanatorium today. How well many of the poor creatures look and how pretty many of the girls are! Were they not in bed one would say that they were the picture of health. Poor things!

Visited also in the poorer quarter of the town. How miserable many of the houses are!

THURSDAY, 29 OCTOBER: [FAST DAY OF GARRABOST COMMUNION]

The morning was wet and cold but about 425 turned out. Mr MacKinnon[1] preached from Micah 6:6–8. He is a good preacher, spiritual and experimental, with a homely, original delivery which reminds one very forcibly of the popular Highland divines of an earlier day.

FRIDAY, 30 OCTOBER

The day was cold but good and fully 900 assembled in the church. The question was a suitable one and was based on Matthew 5:6. I had a measure of ease in opening it. 13 men spoke and Mr MacIver, Lochs, closed.

SATURDAY, 31 OCTOBER

950 were present at the service today. Mr MacKinnon preached from Hebrews 6:17–19. Felt when he was in the pulpit that the Lord has not forsaken us as a Church, since He has given us a preacher of such an old-world and spiritual cast among our younger men.

Three new members came forward today.

SABBATH, 1 NOVEMBER

The morning turned out windy but fair. The church was quite full

1 Angus MacKinnon, Free Church minister in Aultbea, died 1958.

below, but there was room in the galleries for a hundred or two more. About 1500 were present.

At night went down to Aird where I had an attendance of 250. It has been a very happy day and I am thankful for it.

MONDAY, 2 NOVEMBER

Addressed a congregation of 1000 from Joshua 23:14 and enjoyed it very much indeed. It has been a very happy communion and felt quite sorry when it came to an end. Not only was the atmosphere in public helpful, but the company in the Manse was most agreeable.

At night the Prayer Meeting in Stornoway was very well attended, the Seminary being quite full. The Monthly meetings fall due today, but in addition this week is held throughout the Church as a week of humiliation and prayer on account of the state of the country.

WEDNESDAY, 11 NOVEMBER

Visited in Steinish. The houses out there are more comfortable than many in Sandwick or in the town. Held meeting at 7 pm when spoke with liberty from Revelation 21:6. The place was simply crammed, people having gathered from Melbost, Sandwick, Laxdale and Stornoway.

FRIDAY, 13 NOVEMBER

Had some pleasure in visiting today. Met some exercised characters with whom got liberty in prayer. Managed to get 50 visits put in this week which gives me a measure of satisfaction in feeling that I am making some progress in this the heaviest side of my work. Made little progress in sermon preparation.

SATURDAY, 14 NOVEMBER

Composed discourse on Jeremiah 32:27, 'Is there anything too hard for the Lord?' Feel somewhat impressed with our need of expectant faith.

MONDAY, 16 NOVEMBER

Spent the day in visitation in the Battery Park district.

TUESDAY, 17 NOVEMBER

Visited Holme. Found some superior houses there. Kept meeting in house at 7 pm. The place was thronged, some coming from Sandwick despite a very rough and wet evening.

People are everywhere talking about the Sabbath attendances as unusually large. Is there real desire at the back of this, or is it just the novelty of a new ministry? I am encouraged to think that there is something of the former in it, for were it the latter, attendances would be beginning to die away by this time, whereas they are increasing. Lord increase my faith!

FRIDAY, 20 NOVEMBER

Met a woman from Back on the street today who told me that a niece of hers had been savingly influenced – she hoped – by the sermon I preached here on Monday evening of the February Communion. This is good news. To the Lord be the praise! I long for many more such seals.

TUESDAY, 24 NOVEMBER

Visited in New Valley. The houses there are mostly poor and one wonders how they make a living at all.

Held a service in Laxdale. The place was crammed out, fully 160 being present. Liked the spirit of these meetings. I am told that the young in Laxdale never turned out as they are now doing.

WEDNESDAY, 25 NOVEMBER

Had a case of baptism tonight which gave me some difficulty. The father appeared very unwilling to promise that he would conduct family worship, and in a way I respected his straightforwardness, and could not but feel that the natural man cannot but have a very formal worship at the best. But why do these men want baptism when they stumble at their vows? Was glad to see him later at a Lecture on 'What our Church stands for' in the Seminary.

THURSDAY, 26 NOVEMBER

This being Harvest Thanksgiving had services just as on a Sabbath. Was glad to find shops and the school closed. Yet the scholars were too prone to regard it as a holiday and preferred to amuse themselves rather than attend church. Spoke of it in the afternoon. Felt that I had very little for the evening service, but got gracious enlargement in speaking from Psalm 68:9. About 500 were out. Am thankful for having been granted such liberty. It has been my best day in the pulpit since coming to Stornoway, and I think that there is some warmth among us. I am very tired.

FRIDAY, 27 NOVEMBER

Visited today. Found a young man who evidently was greatly blessed at the February Communion here. Feel very tired. I need more strength for this charge.

WEDNESDAY, 9 DECEMBER

Went through part of the School today. At night, despite a very wet evening, had an attendance at the lecture of fully 150. Spoke on 'Revivals of Religion' and enjoyed it. Oh that a revival would visit us here!

THURSDAY, 17 DECEMBER

There was a splendid attendance at the Prayer Meeting, fully 270 being out.

At the close held a Session Meeting for the benefit of parents desiring baptism. Found some difficulty in two cases. This is an aspect of my ministry here which does not appeal to me. There has been too much laxity in the matter of baptism.

WEDNESDAY, 23 DECEMBER

Had a record attendance at the Lecture tonight, almost 200 being out. The subject was 'The Way of Salvation' and I was pleased that such a subject should draw out a record attendance.

Heard that the Word is beginning to take effect – the case of a man, a proper rascal, who was seen in the Seminary on the evening of Sabbath, the 6th inst., with the tears streaming down his face. Should this man be brought in I am told that it will shake the town. May the Lord bring him in and shake many more! Another case is that of one who has been very indifferent in his attendance, being only occasionally seen in church; now he is at every meeting. This is the Lord's doing. To Him be the glory!

FRIDAY, 25 DECEMBER

Conducted a peculiarly touching baptismal service tonight–the children of two young widows, sisters, who both lost their husbands before their youngest were born. One lost her husband and older child in a car accident in Chicago. They were both very much overcome throughout the service. May the Lord bless their trouble to them!

THURSDAY, 31 DECEMBER

There was a large falling off at the Prayer Meeting tonight, only about 120 being present. Spoke from Mark 3:35 with a measure of freedom,

I

but feel very dead and formal. Long for a living breath. I seem to have lost all liberty, whether as the outcome of a legal spirit, the fruit of unbelief, or as the result of having grieved the Lord away from me, I cannot say. Probably both elements are present. In any case I am very low. May the Lord revive me in mercy and may I begin the New Year with Him!

This year has witnessed a great change in my life. Little did I foresee at the beginning of the year how I would end it – here as minister of Stornoway congregation. Who knows what next year may contain!

FRIDAY, I JANUARY, 1932

The morning was very wet and affected the attendance at the service which was held at midday. About 280 were out.

At night had supper in Domhnull Mhata's.[1] Enjoyed the Gaelic hymns which were sung there. It is long since I have been out anywhere on New Year's Day. At the outset of my ministry it used to be a very dreary day to me.

MONDAY, 4 JANUARY

Very much enjoyed the Monthly meeting today, especially the morning one. Felt it very warm. I like these Monday morning meetings.

Feel somewhat exercised at present at the poverty of my sermons. I am afraid that there is very little in them to meet the case of needy souls. I must try to get more time for them, and it would be wise to seek more earnestly from the Lord material for them.

WEDNESDAY, 6 JANUARY

Was very pleased indeed to get fully 180 at the Lecture tonight, especially when the subject had been intimated beforehand. A lecture on Church principles in Kilmuir generally fetched a very poor attendance. The audience gave very close attention. May the Lord make it profitable!

THURSDAY, 14 JANUARY

Seldom saw such rain as we had this afternoon down at the Newton Street fore-shore. It was literally hurtled along in sheets and the road-ways were simply streaming. The prospect seawards was exceedingly

---

1 *ie* Donald, the son of Matthew (Donald MacLeod), the senior elder of the congregation.

tempestuous. In the evening conditions improved and 130 were at the Prayer Meeting.

FRIDAY, 15 JANUARY

Apparently yesterday's rain was unprecedented and there was flooding in the lower parts of the town. The houses in Bayhead Street had 6 or 7 inches of water in them and the children returning from school to Laxdale had to be carried through the water. The Seaforth Road children were also cut off by a flood across the road which reached knee-deep upon those who ventured through it.

WEDNESDAY, 20 JANUARY

Visited in Sanatorium today. It is a sad place.

Very pleased to see another excellent attendance at the Lecture tonight, and so many of them young people. Spoke on 'the Witness of the Covenanters' and enjoyed it. Tried to interest the young folks in these things. 200 were out.

FRIDAY, 29 JANUARY

Made 78 visits since Tuesday which is a record for one week. Have finished the country visits with the exception of Manor Farm, and begin to feel that I have the back broken of the town visitation too. Were it not for the Communions I might expect to get finished by the end of March.

THURSDAY, 17 MARCH

Heard today that a Grimshader girl was awakened at the Gravir Saturday evening Prayer Meeting during the reading of the chapter, and that Miss MacSween, the Point girl, whose bonds were loosed after a period of great darkness, got relief on the Monday when I was preaching from Psalm 26:9. Her joy was so great that she could scarcely walk out of the church and she declared that every word of the sermon was for her.

THURSDAY, 24 MARCH

A busy day today, too busy for my soul's good. Had a funeral, a marriage, a prayer-meeting, submission of congregational Financial Statement for 1931, the presentation of Testaments to the children of the Sabbath School, and a Deacon's Court. Sandwiched in between the marriage and the Financial Report, the Prayer Meeting was bereft of all enjoyment.

[245]

SABBATH, 27 MARCH

Preached in the morning from 1 Peter 2:7 and enjoyed it very much. 650 were present at night. Spoke from Daniel 11:45. My subject was solemn and I got freedom of expression, but I sat down at the close with a feeling of disappointment and a deep-seated yearning for the conversion of sinners. Somehow there does not seem to be much satisfaction in the preaching of the law. Felt much exercised with the fear that I might be hardening the careless and starving the flock. Oh revive Thy Cause and revive me!

MONDAY, 28 MARCH

Motored out to Back for the Thanksgiving service. Mr MacQuarrie preached a very good sermon from Exodus 32:26.[1] It was well thought out, well arranged, evangelical and well delivered. It certainly had the law as its background and truth was declared with blunt faithfulness, but there was no harshness and the atmosphere was good. Almost 1000 were present.

Heard already of the appreciation of one of the Lord's people of last night's sermon. How good God is to me!

WEDNESDAY, 6 APRIL

Troubled today again over the baptism question. It seems that I have to choose between agreeing to baptise in the houses and losing families. The congregation has been accustomed to house baptisms and hence my trouble.[2]

THURSDAY, 7 APRIL

Finished the visitation today. Of course I have yet a few odd houses to look up, and I would like to reach all the servant girls, pupils and lodgers in the town; but still it is a great blessing to get the families done.

Spoke to the elders tonight on the question of baptism and was greatly encouraged to find that they were of opinion that very few would leave on account of insisting on public baptism and that those who might were better away.

1 Walter MacQuarrie, ordained 1917, spent his entire ministry at Knockbain on the Black Isle. MacRae was often in his bachelor's old-world manse and their friendship deepened with the years. 'In some respects he was unique,' *The Monthly Record* reported after his death in 1965, 'abrupt and stern; yet tender and kind; large of heart and of stature; hating what seemed to be shady, loving the truth, fond of his Church and her doctrine'.
2 'The Directory for the Public Worship of God', drawn up by the Westminster divines, stipulates that baptism is not 'to be administered in private places, or privately, but in the place of publick worship, and in the face of the congregation'.

SATURDAY, 9 APRIL

Heard today that two were awakened at the Monday night service at the Stornoway Communion last year (February). One was the Back girl of whom I heard before. She had to be carried out of the church. She is now serving in the Nurses' Cottage. The other is upon the staff of the Girls' Hostel. It is singular that that service was put upon me as an extra. I was preaching from Isaiah 40:4 and on consulting my notes it did not seem very like a discourse which would awake sinners. Yet I was aware of special liberty that night. I see that it is not the sermon that counts, but the power. Oh to have power on the morrow!

SABBATH, 10 APRIL

In the morning spoke with some liberty from 2 Corinthians 5:14. Yet at the close felt sorry that I had made so little of the love of Christ and that there was little warm heart-work in my sermon. Had a happy night in speaking from Psalm 102:17. When I gave out my text I wondered how such a text woud do in an audience in which the young so predominated. But got rapt attention.

Heard of another case to encourage me – that of a young man 'converted' either at Shawbost or the Barvas Communion. Truly the Lord is giving me to see that my labour is not in vain here.

SATURDAY, 16 APRIL

Was informed that quite a number of people are now regularly attending both the Sabbath and Prayer Meeting services who formerly were quite careless. That is very encouraging.

WEDNESDAY, 20 APRIL

At Lecture tonight dealt with 'the Drink Question'. Was very pleased with attendance which numbered fully 250, for tonight there were other matters which must have taken away some. Finished the lectures tonight. They were most encouraging and the attendance at the close was better than at the beginning, thus completely refuting the opinion of those who considered that the young people of Stornoway would not continue to come out to such meetings. For the summer I offered to give an English sermon at the same hour each alternate week if I could get an attendance of 50.

SABBATH, 22 MAY

Enjoyed morning service when addressed a congregation of 500 from

Psalm 73:2. In afternoon 235 were out, but felt cold and hard as I usually do at these English afternoon services. Yet attendances are steadily growing. At night spoke with liberty and earnestness from Daniel 12:10. There were fully 850 present. Surely the Lord will acknowledge His Word! I yearn for the salvation of souls. Surely that yearning is not for nought, but will be satisfied.

SABBATH, 5 JUNE

At night had English service in the Church for the first time, while the Gaelic went to the Seminary. Felt rather anxious as to the success of the arrangement, but very thankful to find that it worked out splendidly. 800 were in the Church while the Seminary provided ample room for the Gaelic. Some sailors from a warship and some East Coast fishermen were present.

MONDAY, 20 JUNE

Examined 7 classes in the Nicolson Institute today in Religious Instruction. It was well done on the whole but no better than in Skye.

TUESDAY, 28 JUNE

Spent the greater part of the day in getting Kirk Session Records, the Communion Roll and my Visitation List in order. So far I have a record of 340 families and I fancy that there will be another 200 more.

The weather is beautiful again, but people are troubled because of the poor fishing.

TUESDAY, 12 JULY

Spent most of the day painting my car and felt it a weariness. Yet it had to be done.

THURSDAY, 14 JULY

The Deacons' Court decided tonight to give me £7 for my car licence and £10 for vacation expenses. It is really very good of them and very considerate. When I think of so many other ministers situated as I have been until now, with little or no help apart from their salary, I feel quite ashamed. Yet I really need the money, for the furniture account incurred in furnishing this huge manse is not yet paid. God is good to me!

SABBATH, 21 AUGUST

In the morning had a good congregation of up to 560 and enjoyed preaching from Isaiah 44:3-4. Enjoyed the afternoon service also when

[248]

preached from 1 Kings 19:7–8 to a congregation of 210. At night there was an immense congregation present, even the spare seats outwith the pews being called into requisition down below. The gallery, however, was not quite so thronged as it was last Sabbath. One wonders what is to happen at the Communion, when such immense crowds are coming out on ordinary Sabbaths. Had a beautiful evening in preaching from 1 John 3:3. Felt quite overcome in the closing psalm. It was glorious. Very thankful for such a day. Surely the Lord is among us!

THURSDAY, 1 SEPTEMBER

Had a very good attendance at the Prayer Meeting tonight, fully 350 being present. Spoke from Mark 6:42 with fair measure of liberty.

SATURDAY, 3 SEPTEMBER

Feel my shallowness in my preaching material and the importance of giving the very best to preparation. There is much shallow, lazy preaching today, and I have not been careful enough in shunning this plague.

TUESDAY, 6 SEPTEMBER

Began my second year's visitation today. How quickly time has gone! Made 1103 visits for the first year. It is a big job to tackle all over again, but perhaps on the second round I may make better progress.

Heard that Norman MacLean, a Skyeman now living on Lewis Street, considered that I had unveiled his case as though I had been told everything, at the Prayer Meeting last night.

WEDNESDAY, 7 SEPTEMBER

John Livingstone says that a preacher must guard himself against two faults: an incomplete meditation by way of preparation, and an over-complete meditation, which latter would go to deprive him of a sense of need and dependence.[1] Of late I have been finding the value of unpremeditated utterance.

SATURDAY, 10 SEPTEMBER

Out on the hill alone this morning I asked the Lord to direct me as to the matter of sermon preparation which had been exercising me lately. I find that when I follow Livingstone's counsel, and leave opportunity

1 'Remarks on Preaching and Praying in Publick by Mr John Livingstone' in *Select Biographies*, edit. W. K. Tweedie, Wodrow Soc., vol. 1, 1845, pp 287–89.

for a sense of need and dependence upon the Lord, I get unwonted liberty, but Cathie's lack of appreciation of last night's sermon confused and puzzled me. The Lord is very gracious and I might well be ashamed of my unbelief. Before an hour had passed my wife told me that Ruairidh Beag[1] – a most competent judge – had expressed his very great appreciation of last night's discourse. This came so directly as an answer to my prayer that I cannot but accept it as the Lord's mind on the matter.

SABBATH, 11 SEPTEMBER

Went out, taking old John Livingstone's counsel, and looked to the Lord to help me. And He did. Spoke in morning from Exodus 8:30 with some liberty. In the afternoon addressed a congregation of 125 from 2 Kings 5:18 on bowing down in the house of Rimmon.

700 were out at night. I had a very good evening in speaking from Luke 14:17 on the Gospel Supper. I trust that eternity work was done.

SABBATH, 18 SEPTEMBER

The day was very wild, and together with the draw upon the congregation by the Gravir Communion, attendances were considerably down. In the evening 650 were present. Spoke with some force, earnestness and plainness from Luke 15:13 on the prodigal on the downward path and sought to warn the young.

At the close spoke about those who wish baptism in their houses, and afraid that I allowed myself to become too vehement and went too far. Came home troubled and restless. Had very little today for my soul. If I rebuke sin, my nature is such that I become roused and pugnacious, and that drives away the gentle influences of the Spirit; if I don't, my conscience reproves me. What grace I need to discharge my duties aright!

TUESDAY, 11 OCTOBER]

It is very seldom that I see tears after worship when visiting here. Today I had this experience, which used to be common enough in Skye, but the woman in question was a St. Kildan. The Lewis people never struck me as being emotional, they are too hard-headed for that.

SABBATH, 16 OCTOBER

In morning spoke to a congregation of 500, from John 11:6, on the Lord delaying to help in trouble and got a measure of clearness; 170

---

1 i.e. Little Roderick (Roderick MacLeod) – an elder in the congregation of Kinloch, Lewis, and brother of the Rev Roderick MacLeod, MacRae's great friend of Lochgilphead days.

were out in the afternoon when spoke from Psalm 37:5 on 'Commit thy way unto the Lord; trust also in him and he shall bring it to pass'. Felt very cold and mechanical.

The rain took the evening attendance down to 650. Felt somewhat happier in preaching on the Pearl of Great Price (Matthew 13:45–46). Both my afternoon and evening discourses stand in need of improvement. May the Lord bless His Word! Tried to urge them tonight to seek Christ but always feel that I fall very far short of what I aim at.

TUESDAY, 18 OCTOBER

Had a big day today, visiting in Laxdale. Had worship in 30 houses. Had two baptismal services in which I baptised five children and conducted the meeting in Laxdale. There was a record attendance. Extra seating was provided and yet the place was packed out to the door. Spoke from James 4:7 on resisting the Devil, and enjoyed it exceedingly. Oh to trust more upon the Lord!

SATURDAY, 22 OCTOBER

I see that this teacher MacDonald who had been writing against me in the *Gazette* has another epistle in this week's issue. I think it wiser to ignore him. The Lord can deal with him better than I.

SABBATH, 23 OCTOBER

Have reason for thankfulness for a good day today. Rain came on heavily and affected the evening attendance. Still there were 750 present. Spoke from Numbers 10:29 on Moses' invitation to Hobab, 'Come thou with us and we will do thee good: for the Lord hath spoken good concerning Israel'. Got freedom and force and had a happy evening. Surely some were persuaded to come. Would that my own daughter were persuaded to come! It troubles me very much to see her give no evidence of concern. Lord, bring her! Today again gives evidence of the fact that over-preparation gives less opportunity for the gracious suggestions of the Holy Spirit. He honours dependence on Him.

MONDAY, 24 OCTOBER

Today has been an upsetting day. A wire came from Dunvegan wishing Cathie to cross since her mother had become 'extremely weak', and tonight she has gone. I feel quite lost without her; she has taken my heart with her.

TUESDAY, 25 OCTOBER

Visited North Street, Sandwick, today. We have increased there from

20 households last year to 24. Rather enjoyed it. Missing Cathie very much and feel altogether out of my usual.

WEDNESDAY, 2 NOVEMBER

Enjoyed the day visiting the New Valley. The pure air, the tramping, and the manifest pleasure of the people in being visited made the day very pleasant and health-giving to me. Felt some liberty too in many of the houses.

MONDAY, 7 NOVEMBER

At 7 Mr Cameron preached in Stornoway to a magnificent congregation of 650. I was delighted that the people came out so well to welcome their old pastor and I hope all his suspicions as to their affection will now be removed. He preached from Mark 7:37 and gave the best sermon ever I have heard from him. I felt that my own efforts were just trifling in comparison.

I left tonight by the steamer and had a very smooth and comfortable crossing.

TUESDAY, 8 NOVEMBER

Reached Dunvegan at last and saw the poor invalid. Felt shocked at the change which has come over her. Her voice was quite strong and she talked freely, but she was only the shadow of her former self. She lay quite content and without pain. She said, 'God is very, very good to me. I am lying here in perfect peace resting on the finished work of Christ'. I seemed to see the shadow of death on her face and after worship I came away with a sore heart. I shall never see her again in this world. It was good to be with Cathie again but I got very little of her.[1] She has much before her. May the Lord give her strength for it!

FRIDAY, 25 NOVEMBER

Got letter from Cathie telling me that her mother was so low that it was advisable that I should make arrangements for Sabbath's supply. Went down to Point but Mr Campbell is none too well at present, so in afternoon went out to Back. Mr MacKenzie was out but left note for him explaining circumstances.[2] About 6 pm a telegram came saying 'Mother sinking fast, expecting the end every moment. Can you come tonight?' I then wired to Back and Mr MacKenzie kindly consented to take my

---

1 He had to leave next morning for services in Glasgow, after which he returned alone to Stornoway.
2 There were no telephones in Lewis manses at this date.

place so that I left with an easy mind. The night was wet and there was an occasional gust which indicated the possibility of a fresh night but I thought nothing of it.

SATURDAY, 26 NOVEMBER

The night was a stormy one and when I got up [on the ship] after leaving Glenelg and started to shave and dress I became quite squeamish and had to lie down. I meant to go ashore at Armadale but it was impossible for the ship to berth there. At Mallaig I ventured on deck but indeed I was not prepared for the stormy scene that met my gaze. The rain was sweeping along in torrents and the sea was dismally wild. Having the wind behind us on the return journey to Kyle we were steady enough but at Kyle it was miserable, the rain being swept into us in clouds. The Ferry was very stormy but I was thankful to get across and in the afternoon we left by bus. Ere we reached Dunvegan the weather had moderated and the night was fairly good. I found poor Granny still in life but quite unconscious.

MONDAY, 28 NOVEMBER

Granny passed away at 1.40 this morning without gasp or sigh. The breath simply grew faint and then stopped. Death had come as it were four days ago and therefore there was no change save the ceasing of the breath. The Lord's mercies are exceedingly clear at this time.

WEDNESDAY, 30 NOVEMBER: DUNVEGAN

Today was a painful day which will long linger in my memory. The attendance [for the funeral] was smaller than I would have expected and there were only the two local ministers between whom the service was divided. Grand-dad and Cathie bore up wonderfully.

Many a time I have set off on that very road on our way to Kilmuir, waving farewell to the happy home we were leaving behind. Never did I think of setting off in today's sad fashion.

SABBATH, 4 DECEMBER

The morning was good and a congregation of 425 was before me. Spoke with a measure of freedom from Mark 14:37 on sleeping Christians, but felt cold and hard. Truly I fear I am just such an one myself.

In the evening we had our monthly English service and fully 650 were assembled. Addressed them from Romans 10:3 on the sufficiency of the righteousness of Christ. Think I was enabled to set before them in clear terms the way of life and had some liberty.

[253]

Spurgeon says that we should always expect a faithful presentation of the Gospel, preached in dependence upon the Lord, to be blessed to some one.

MONDAY, 5 DECEMBER

In the morning had 44 out at the Monthly Meeting; at night 320 were present. Was very much interrupted and hindered today and my mind was so unsettled that got very little profit from them.

Two individuals called today at different times and both in connection with quarrels. Nobody comes to me about his soul. I am tired of their worldly errands and empty squabbles.

WEDNESDAY, 7 DECEMBER

In the evening had meeting down at Steinish. The place was full, the evening being so fine with moonlight. Spoke from Lam. 3:1 and enjoyed it very much. Felt that the gracious influences of the Spirit were among us. Light may arise upon dark Steinish yet. There is nothing more quickening than preaching on Christ crucified. We have the promise: 'And I, if I be lifted up, will draw all men unto me'. This has been a happy day and am very thankful for it.

THURSDAY, 8 DECEMBER

Finished the visitation in the Laxdale section today, getting a beautiful frosty day for the round. In the evening had a very good attendance at the Prayer Meeting, fully 250 being out. Spoke from Mark 8:3 and enjoyed the meeting very much. It was warm and hearty.

Relieved to get wire from Cathie to say that she will be home (DV) tomorrow night.[1] I do trust that this fine spell will continue another day so that she may get a smooth passage. Her poor father will feel parting with her. May the Lord hold him up!

FRIDAY, 9 DECEMBER

Cathie came home tonight. I am very thankful and thankful, too, that she got such a good passage. They will be very lonely, though, in Kirkton.

SABBATH, 11 DECEMBER

The day was favourable and attendances were good. In the morning I spoke from John 11:4, 'This sickness is not unto death but unto the

1 Mrs MacRae had remained with her father at Kirkton, Dunvegan, after the funeral on 30 November.

glory of God'. Enjoyed some liberty in the discourse. Noticed a young girl who appeared to be greatly exercised, and saw her departing from the church gate in tears after the service. 145 were present at the English service. Spoke from John 3:6 on 'That which is born of the flesh is flesh, and that which is born of the Spirit is spirit'. Again got a measure of freedom and was enabled to make the offer of salvation very free. The girl I had noticed in the morning was again present and in the same condition.

Had a splendid congregation at night fully 850 being present. Spoke from Jeremiah 4:14 'How long shall thy vain thoughts lodge within thee'. Had no difficulty of expression but felt hard and lacked unction unless towards the end. Felt crest-fallen, for my heart was yearning for quickening. Yet the Lord may bless it. Attention at any rate was good.

Was told about the girl whom I had noticed through the day. She is from Point and is working as a gutter at present in town. She was awakened at the Prayer Meeting on Thursday.[1] May the Lord bring this matter to a successful issue! I am cheered to hear of it.

MONDAY, 12 DECEMBER

Took Donald Munro with me to examine a house in Shawbost. He commented on last night's sermon and said that a young fellow remarked, 'Mr MacRae is often very heavy on us with the law, but that is what we need'. Felt much cheered to hear this and Donald's own appreciation of the sermon, for I had been very much cast down over it last night. I know that it was the Lord who caused him to say this for my comfort, for I have repeatedly found Him swift to comfort.

WEDNESDAY, 14 DECEMBER

Had first Lecture of winter on 'The Bible – the Word of God' and had very good attendance, fully 220 being present. Enjoyed it pretty well and was given good attention. May it be made useful, especially to the young, for there is much need today!

WEDNESDAY, 21 DECEMBER

I got a fairly good day for visiting in the Marybank and Castle Grounds

1 He later learned that while her concern had first become public at the prayer meeting, it was, in fact, at the Steinish meeting, the preceding evening, that she had been awakened. She had gone to Steinish at the invitation of a friend and 'those who knew her wondered what had brought such a light-headed character to attend a meeting'. The work of preparing fish for market was largely done by younger women, known as 'gutters'. At certain times of the year they left Lewis to do this work at fishing-ports on the east coast of Britain.

district. Had no meeting at night and felt rather lost in consequence. It does not suit me physically to sit in at the fire. Don't seem to have done much good today.

SATURDAY, 31 DECEMBER

So ends yet another year. How rapidly my life runs away, and yet I seem to make little of it! And yet I have much to be thankful for, especially for the fact that the Lord has not allowed my labours for the year go wholly fruitless. My record of work shows that I conducted 321 services, paid 1250 pastoral visits, attended 38 courts, attended 22 funerals, baptised 28 children, and performed 7 marriages – easily the heaviest year of my ministerial life; and yet I do not feel overtaxed. Blessed be the Lord for giving me such strength! May He lead me next year into more fruitful service!

FRIDAY, 20 JANUARY, 1933

Got a letter today which filled me with joy from a woman in the congregation who has been suspended on account of her having been found guilty in a slander case. I am so thankful that she took the matter in such a submissive, Christian spirit. It speaks well of her and I am glad that faithfulness has meant no loss.

THURSDAY, 26 JANUARY

Had a splendid attendance at the Prayer Meeting tonight. The Seminary was packed quite full right up to the front. Fully 280 were out.

MONDAY, 30 JANUARY

Visited today instead of taking Monday off, but don't think I am any the better off for it. There is work unending here for a man and it is wisest not to force the pace.

TUESDAY, 31 JANUARY

No new cases of spiritual concern to report during the month. Interest in the means is still manifested, and despite the counter influence of bad weather and 'flu', attendances continue encouraging.

FRIDAY, 3 FEBRUARY

Today I received a huge budget of legal documents from an individual in Kintail who has been engaged in litigation for the last 20 years, asking me to help him; although he had already enlisted the services of three M.P.'s and sundry lawyers! I don't think some people know what a minister's work really is.

TUESDAY, 14 FEBRUARY

Got a letter today which made my heart sing for joy; from a girl out at Melbost. She is in a state of deep concern. I am not surprised for I felt that there was something in that girl every time I met her. She tells me that her cousin is also troubled about himself. This is what I have been longing to hear – grace working among the young. May they both be drawn safely to Christ!

SATURDAY, 18 FEBRUARY: [STORNOWAY COMMUNION]

Mr Cameron preached today from Luke 2:25. He was very fine but I wondered where his brevity was, for his sermon lasted 1 hour 15 minutes!¹

After the Prayer Meeting at night we admitted five new communicants:

1 — — Her case was satisfactory although her experience lacked landmarks.

2 — — His change was so well known to us all that he scarcely needed questioning. I wish all applicants were like him.

3 — — She seemed confused and was not able to give us any great satisfaction, but she was very broken and had a heart knowledge of sin. Her ways, too, have been changed.

4 — — An old woman very strong in her assurance of having undergone a saving change, but with little knowledge of the heart's depravity. Admitted her on her own responsibility in virtue of her declaration and her life.

5 — — Wakened five years ago reading the Bible. Got relief from Romans 5:1. A young girl, but a most satisfactory case.

WEDNESDAY, 22 FEBRUARY

Had a lecture tonight on baptism. My elder, Angus MacLennan, expressed his gratification and stated that he wished all the people of

---

1 Lengthiness was very unusual in the preaching of MacRae's predecessor. On Kenneth Cameron's death in 1947 the tribute which appeared in *The Monthly Record* from MacRae's pen included the words: 'A deeply experimental preacher and an indefatigable pastor, he speedily won for himself a unique place in the religious life of the island . . . In his preaching he had a sweet, wooing note which made a wonderful appeal to the Lord's people, while the clear, terse and well arranged structure of his sermons, wherein no such thing as tediousness was ever suffered to appear, made him a preacher whom the younger element heard gladly'. His son, W. J. Cameron, was to be Principal of the Free Church College, 1973–1977.

Lewis might hear the lecture. There is much need indeed, for the views of the community respecting baptism are in general not over healthy.

SATURDAY, 11 MARCH: [PORTREE COMMUNION]

Dr Munro preached an excellent sermon today from Ephesians 2:18 which I enjoyed very much. He dispensed entirely with his usual allegorical style and in my judgment it was a decided improvement. Unfortunately only 25 were out to hear it. At the Gaelic I had an attendance of 52. A young lad of 26 years – a Kenneth MacLeay – came forward.[1] His case is an encouraging one.

In the afternoon we went out to Donald Munro's[2] grave in the old river-girt burial place at Skeabost. It is a peaceful spot and I enjoyed its quiet beauty. The afternoon was perfect.

MONDAY, 13 MARCH

Finished the Portree services today. Spoke in English from Matthew 15:32 with some liberty. My audience only numbered 23. Dr Munro had a much better attendance at the Gaelic. Thus ended the communion. I enjoyed it, but I cannot say I got much good for my soul. The spiritual life of Skye is less warm at present than that of Lewis. I did, however, profit from my perusal of the life of the Rev. Robert Findlater of Ardeonaig, a book from Mr MacKinnon's library which engaged so many spare moments as I could devote to it.[3]

In the evening went over to Dunvegan. Poor Grand-dad is becoming very helpless. I notice that he has become very spiritually-minded. He is fast ripening. I fear he will not be long after his beloved.

THURSDAY, 16 MARCH

Felt some difficulty today in getting back to the usual routine. Must try again to preserve some time for the interests of my own soul. Much work requires much prayer if it is to be at all productive.

FRIDAY, 31 MARCH

Got a wire today which shocked me very much. Mrs MacKinnon,

1 Notwithstanding the differences in their age, K. J. MacLeay – soon to commence preparation for the ministry – was to become one of his closest friends in later years. While a student he assisted MacRae in Stornoway in the summer of 1938, when the latter noted, 'by his warm, natural bearing he made himself a general favourite'. Kenneth MacLeay was ordained in 1942 and inducted to the Free Church charge at Lochinver.
2 The blind evangelist of Skye who died in 1830.
3 *Memoir of the Rev. Robert Findlater*, William Findlater, 1840. Ardeonaig, on Loch Tay, Perthshire, was the scene of a glorious revival in the years 1816–19.

Portree,[1] passed away this morning and I am asked to take the Sabbath services there.

TUESDAY, 4 APRIL

The funeral service of Mrs MacKinnon was held at 7.45 and was shared between Morrison (Duirinish), MacLeod (Bracadale) and myself. Felt heart sorry for the poor motherless little girl. We left Portree at 8.30 and reached Kyleakin at 10.10. We caught the 10.40 train and reached Achterneed at 1.20. There a large party awaited us. We walked down to the main road and then motored to Fodderty. The remains were laid there beside those of her father and mother. The service in the grave-yard was taken by three of the 1900 veterans – Revs. Dr Munro, Norman Campbell and Dr MacLean. Dr MacLean's prayer was beautiful and more than one was moved. Oh, it was a sad and a painful day and one I shall never forget.

I did not return to the West with the others but went down with Dr Munro to Ferintosh. Spoke at the Prayer Meeting, at which 13 were present, from Hebrews 11:16 and enjoyed it very much. Ferintosh is full of old touching memories and God always seems near to me in it. In all 23 Free Church ministers attended today's funeral.

SABBATH, 30 APRIL

Nothing to report concerning my own congregation this month, but felt refreshed at the Duke Street Communion (Glasgow). The atmosphere was very warm, attendances exceeded anything seen during the last 30 years and I had unwonted liberty in preaching. 11 new members came forward.

SABBATH, 7 MAY

The day was good and attendances were good. If only I could see the people taking Christ! but when I see them sitting there outwardly unmoved, and I have no evidence of Christ being received, I cannot help feeling wistful. Exercised too as to my duty in following up these services. Some promising cases have fallen away. Is it because they were neglected? Is it venturing into the realm of the rights of the Holy Spirit to do anything more than preach the Gospel? On the other hand are not *all* adequate means to be used? This is a question which has troubled me throughout my ministry and very especially when I am in any measure concerned about the unconverted.

1 The wife of the Rev. Donald MacKinnon and the only daughter of the Rev. and Mrs William Fraser of Strathpeffer. Her mother's death had preceded her own by just eleven days.

[259]

SABBATH, 14 MAY

It has been a good day and helpful to my own soul and I am thankful for it. In the morning was amazed to see Peter MacKay, Kilmaluag, in my audience. Felt my heart leap with joy to see him there. I could understand how MacColl wept after leaving Skye when he met a Duirinish man at one of the Glasgow communions. He was there with Willie Vander – they are upon steam-drifters come here for the fishing. They were out at the three services.

FRIDAY, 19 MAY

A dispute has broken out between curers and fishermen which threatens to have very serious consequences for Stornoway. Last night two trawlers and some of the drifters dumped their catch in the sea, a wicked act which is likely to bring its own punishment. Such a dispute in the present precarious state of the industry is suicidal. May the poor not suffer from it!

SABBATH, 21 MAY

The day was ideal and attendances very good. In the morning 500 were present when I preached with freedom from Psalm 125:4-5. The examinations in the school being just over, many of the country pupils had gone home for the week-end, and the English attendance was down to 135. Spoke from Psalm 119:8 but floundered a good deal and did not make much of it. At night had a splendid gathering of fully 800. Downstairs was almost completely full. Spoke from Isaiah 40:11. Got freedom and earnestness; was given perfect attention and felt thankful for such a good night – and yet somehow I was conscious of a feeling of disappointment and a great yearning for the in-gathering of souls. Oh that revival would come! And yet I know that nowadays a Sabbath scarcely passes without my being moved to the verge of betraying my emotion during the services of the sanctuary, either in the singing, the preaching or the praying, or in all – and this is characteristic of the week-day services too. This I cannot deny. And it was so during our best days in Kilmaluag.

WEDNESDAY, 24 MAY

130 were out at the English service this evening. At the close took the names of those who wished to become subscribers in the proposed congregational library and was considerably encouraged to get 64. Probably I shall get many more. Today I got word from a Leith second-

hand bookseller that he is willing to take up the matter and will furnish me with a list for my choice in a few days' time. Feel very much encouraged by such a response in this evil day.

SABBATH, 28 MAY

Today had the largest attendances of the year. The weather was good and Mr. Campbell (Knock)[1] being away at the Assembly, a number from the nearer districts of his congregation came in. At night my sermon was practical as distinct from experimental, and I felt before going out that there was very little in it, but was helped to say something which may have been of some service to some poor souls. My subject was based upon Acts 3:1. I have reason for thankfulness for a good day and I am thankful, but I long to be able to preach Christ more fully and I long for a day of God's power.

WEDNESDAY, 31 MAY

Cannot report any new cases of spiritual concern this month, but an unusual warmth seemed to pervade the services of the congregation, especially in the early part of the month.

THURSDAY, I JUNE

Shifted the Prayer Meeting tonight from the Seminary to the Church. It was certainly not so close but I much prefer the Seminary. 270 were out.

SATURDAY, 17 JUNE

Have had my time very much broken up and am not at all in good trim for tomorrow. Have had to meet Dr Money from Peru and to put him into a Barvas bus. That means that I shall lose my usual Saturday night reading which will be to my loss. Oh, Lord, revive and help Thy poor dead, unworthy, unfaithful servant!

MONDAY, 31 JULY

Had only two week-ends in Stornoway during this month. Have nothing to report of spiritual quickening or concern either here or elsewhere. Assisted at Communions in Grimsay, Alligin, Ardgay and Sleat, but in none of them felt any great liberty. The latter two congregations seem especially dead.

1 William Campbell, ordained and called to Knock in 1926, served the congregation there until his retirement in 1962. Died in 1967.

TUESDAY, 8 AUGUST

Got a telegram this forenoon informing me of Grand-dad's death. Had to break the news to poor Cathie. It was hard, but she got strength. Thankful that I was with her at the time.

WEDNESDAY, 9 AUGUST: DUNVEGAN

Left today for Kirkton. It is a sad house. Grand-dad could not live on without his beloved. It was a release for him, but it means the break-up of the home and the end of the old happy order of things which pertained to a better day. The whole house is full of that atmosphere. I feel very pensive in it and my own happy days of courtship here come very vividly before me. Good-bye, dear past! A long farewell! But I shall never forget.

THURSDAY, 10 AUGUST

Today buried poor Grand-dad. It was a sad day. We laid him beside his beloved. Felt tonight that I would like to die on the same day as my dear one and to be laid away in the same coffin with her.

SABBATH, 3 SEPTEMBER

In the morning had an attendance of close upon 500. Some habituals were missing, doubtless away at the Shawbost communion. In the afternoon 150 were out. At night had our monthly English service. 800 were present and had a splendid night (so far as my own feelings were concerned) in speaking from Psalm 143:9. Felt that surely the Lord would bless His Word. Very thankful for such a Sabbath. Felt that it has done more good to my soul than anything I have had for a long time. I always find that holiday time is a barren time for my soul and I am glad to get back to my work.

TUESDAY, 5 SEPTEMBER

Began my third round of pastoral visitation today and had a very busy day. Visited 22 houses in Battery Park besides other sick cases. Had a marriage and an evening meeting at Laxdale. The meeting house was packed out and was dreadfully close. I felt awful to begin with, but I lost sense of all discomfort when I became absorbed in my subject.

FRIDAY, 8 SEPTEMBER

Composed discourse on Colossians 3:1. Would that I could live it!

In evening went out to Kinloch where they have the Communion at present. Mr Cameron (Resolis) preached an excellent sermon from Luke 5:18–20. It was richly experimental and helpful to weak ones. It is the best sermon I have heard since Mr Cameron, Inverness, was here last spring.

TUESDAY, 19 SEPTEMBER

Put in a day of visitation although not too well. See many things to indicate that my visitation is not so useless as the Enemy would try to get me to believe.

WEDNESDAY, 20 SEPTEMBER

Was pleased to get a good attendance at the English service tonight and to see so many of the young. Over 160 were out. Spoke from Proverbs 3:6 and addressed myself mainly to young people. It is a great matter that they are willing to come out to a week-night meeting.

SATURDAY, 23 SEPTEMBER

Tomorrow I can only expect poor attendances. Fraser (Govan)[1] at Crossbost Communion, and Cameron (Inverness) at Carloway will draw away the best of my people. Yet the Lord can give me something for those who remain at home. This time last year I was at Carloway, the previous year I was at Crossbost. My heart is going out a good deal to these services. May they be blessed!

SATURDAY, 30 SEPTEMBER

Have reason for thankfulness. Attendances are still being sustained, the people indeed coming out in a wonderful way. I am told that some are coming in from the Aignish districts at night and people are coming to church who never used to come, for all which I would wish to praise the Lord.

The only new case of apparent soul exercise which this month has brought to my notice is that of Mrs Smith, Seaforth Road.

I feel in better condition than during the holiday season, but still I mourn my unbelief, my prayerlessness, and coldness. I have found Wodrow's *Biographies* very helpful.[2] These men and women knew a height of spiritual experience to which I am an utter stranger.

1 William Fraser, a close friend of MacRae's, was minister of Govan Free Church (Glasgow) from 1924 to 1938. From the latter date he served the congregation at Kiltarlity, Inverness-shire, for 15 years.
2 The two volumes entitled *Select Biographies*, published in 1845 and 1848 from earlier manuscripts and containing, chiefly, the lives of John Welsh, Patrick Simpson, John Livingstone, Walter Pringle and Robert Blair.

SABBATH, 1 OCTOBER

Despite Communion at Back, 500 were out in the morning. Spoke from Deut. 23:21 but had very little life in it.

In the afternoon, when 125 were present, spoke from Psalm 102: 12–13. Had clearness, but felt very cold. Longed for a breath of power.

In the evening we had our Monthly English service and had a congregation of over 650. Spoke with some liberty and force from Proverbs 13:4 and tried to show that Gospel success depends as much upon the pew as upon the pulpit.

At the close spoke to the young men against the suggestion in the local newspaper that the ministers should busy themselves in providing employment for the workless; showed its folly, and warned them against the modern conception of the ministry, emphasising that the legitimate duty of the ministry lay within the bounds of 'the ministry of the Word and prayer'.

MONDAY, 2 OCTOBER

Tonight the first batch of girls leave for Yarmouth.[1] I hope they will have a good season. MacRae (Kinloch) and MacIver (Crossbost) minister to them this year. They, too, leave this week.

SABBATH, 8 OCTOBER

Very much impressed today by a piece written by John Angell James inculcating upon ministers the duty of dealing individually with those who have been wounded under the Word – a most difficult duty, yet I feel it to be a real duty, and one which I too much neglect. Occasioned me a great deal of heart searching.

SATURDAY, 14 OCTOBER

Motored out in the evening to Crossbost for the services tomorrow which I take (DV) for MacIver who is away at the English fishing. Felt rather lonely motoring alone by night over that moorland tract but got out all right. Reading *Life of Whitefield* tonight. Would that I had his consecration, his faith, his humility, his selflessness and his power! May the Lord acknowledge me here tomorrow!

TUESDAY, 17 OCTOBER

Had a good day visiting in the Laxdale district and, despite my con-

1 They went annually to English fishing ports to gut winter herring. Ministers were released by their presbytery from congregational duties for approximately 3 months to go to these ports to look after the spiritual interests of the girls.

ducting worship with 28 households, felt better after it. But oh I long for a living breath! Would that I could meet with real living Gospel fruits of my ministry!

WEDNESDAY, 18 OCTOBER

Reading Whitefield's *Life* makes me long for days of power.

SABBATH, 22 OCTOBER

Spoke in the morning with a measure of comfort from 2 Corinthians 7:6 on the Lord comforting the cast down. 520 were present. In the afternoon emphasised the necessity of the new birth and the sovereignty of the Spirit from John 3:11. In the evening there was an immense congregation of fully 900. Felt very helpless in the presence of such a multitude. Spoke on congregational duties in respect of the spiritual side of the Gospel minister's work. Felt while speaking how holy a minister should be, and how absurd that his time should be taken up with worldly boards and committees. Spoke from Hebrews 13:7 with a measure of freedom. Invited anxious souls to write me explaining their difficulties and not necessarily revealing their identity.

THURSDAY, 26 OCTOBER

Felt the usual pensiveness when visiting the Sanatorium today. The poor things seem to be neglected spiritually. One little girl of 13 seems to have been very much affected by a Gospel book for children. The poor little thing seemed so earnest and showed me the book. It was a lesson for me not to overlook children.

Conducted worship at the Boy's Hostel tonight. Rather enjoyed it. Oh, that some young life may be savingly affected! Work among the young is fraught with great possibilities.

SABBATH, 29 OCTOBER: KINLOCH

All day got great freedom of expression but never felt melted. I got this, however, at evening family worship. Two girls waited for it, one of them the first fruit – so far as known to me – of my ministry in Lewis. In singing the 73rd Psalm and the words:

> Gidheadh 's e neart mo chridhe Dia,
> 's mo chuibhrionn bhuan am feasd,[1]

felt as though the Lord Himself was there with us.

1 'For of my heart God is the strength and portion for ever.'

TUESDAY, 31 OCTOBER

Visited in the Barvas Road district today. Have now visited 346 families since I started two months ago, which is good work. May the Lord acknowledge it! Some of the homes are dark enough.

WEDNESDAY, I NOVEMBER

Visited in Culregrein district today. Have thoughts of beginning services in the Township Hall there on week-days and perhaps a Sabbath School.

Began the winter's lectures tonight. Spoke on 'Religious Deceivers'.

THURSDAY, 2 NOVEMBER

240 were out at the Prayer Meeting tonight. Spoke with some freedom from Mark 15:31. Oh that I were able to live, and experience the power of what I preach! I wish I were not a sinner, or even such a sinner.

FRIDAY, 15 DECEMBER

Have been greatly hindered today in preparation for Sabbath. At night conducted meeting at Sandwick. Lacked time for preparation but was enabled to speak with some ease from Matthew 25:13. That Bayble girl was present and seems to be as broken as ever. I would be happier to see that phase pass. She is too long in that way, I am afraid. Relief is of the Lord, but — —'s¹ case makes me doubtful of similar ones. Oh that she might come to a happy issue!

WEDNESDAY, 20 DECEMBER

At Lecture tonight about 130 were present. My theme was 'Whither Bound?' and tried to show the dangers to which the present drift in the Church of Scotland exposes the religious future of the generation, and urged to constancy to principle and an intelligent interest in the religious life of the country.

At the close opened my congregational library and gave out about 70 volumes. The people seemed quite interested and eager.

SABBATH, 24 DECEMBER

Tonight struggled with an icy hardness from which I could not break away. There was no unction. Came home very sadly. I long with all my heart to see a work of grace break out among my people and yet my efforts are not acknowledged as I would desire. I feel that my own

---

1 The reference is to the young woman referred to earlier on pages 183–5, who despite much apparent concern and feeling did not come to a decided commitment to Christ.

prayerlessness has a lot to do with this, and yet I do not seem able to pray. I do try to pray, but my pleas are soon exhausted and I cannot continue long. Oh Lord, teach me the secrets of holiness and give grace to walk according thereto.

TUESDAY, 26 DECEMBER

Visited the Sanatorium today. Read some verses and gave a little exhortion in each ward, besides as usual engaging in prayer. Also gave out tracts. Felt my heart going out in an unusual degree to the poor creatures today and felt that I yearned for their soul's salvation. May He bless this day's work. Oh that I might never let a day pass without seeking the good of some soul!

WEDNESDAY, 27 DECEMBER

Sent a copy of James' *Anxious Enquirer* to Dolina MacDonald, Bayble.

Feel that it helps me to realise that I am here for the propagation of the Gospel. Too often I have simply striven to get through my duties as duties to be performed in connection with my office; but to view every duty as a fresh opportunity of furthering the Gospel and damaging the devil's kingdom adds a new zest. May the Lord Himself train me in this spiritual propaganda and may He acknowledge it!

FRIDAY, 29 DECEMBER

Tried to prepare for Sabbath today. Feel inclined to develop my themes less carefully than usual – as to details – and to look more for the quickening of the Spirit, but have I the faith to venture it? There is the rub.

Angell James says that ministers ought to try to find out the effect of their sermons, and I believe that it would be helpful to do so, but in practice how is it possible without giving those whom we may consult the impression that we are out for compliments? Would that I knew the effect of my poor sermons! I might know better then how to adapt them to the needs of actual cases in the congregation. To fire at random is not satisfactory, neither is it likely to ensure efficient campaigning.

SATURDAY, 30 DECEMBER

Another year almost gone. Youth has long since passed away, and still I am waiting for what I have not realised yet – a real and extensive work of grace. I have seen times of quickening in Lochgilphead, Southend and Kilmaluag, although I did not realise them as such at the time. Will

I ever see what my soul longs for? Life is passing, and it seems less likely now than ever it did, and yet His hand is not shortened that it cannot save. I still cleave to this hope, although well I realise that it is under a darkening sky.

I have been reckoning up my labours for the year and I find that I have conducted 321 services, made 1278 visits, baptised 29 children, attended 28 courts and 29 funerals and performed 8 marriages. I am amazed at how closely those figures correspond with last year's; these were 321 services, 1250 visits, 28 baptisms, 38 courts, 28 funerals and 7 marriages – the difference in the courts being due to the fact that I am no longer on the Standing Committees. May the Lord bless what I have tried to do in His Name!

I trust that I shall have a good day on the morrow – the last Sabbath of the Year.

SABBATH, 31 DECEMBER

Notes for year: Admitted 13 new communicants, which was only exceeded on two occasions during the last 24 years, ie. in 1921 when 22 came forward and in 1922 when 14 were added. There must have been a revival at that time.

The Duke Street Communion in April and the Fearn Communion in December were refreshing. The meeting in Hilton after the Fearn Communion ought not to be forgotten. There were evidences of the Spirit's power there.

FRIDAY, 5 JANUARY, 1934

Spent the day composing and revising sermons for Sabbath. One is on the new birth – John 3:3. May the Lord acknowledge it! This is the subject Whitefield plied so effectually, but in his day it was a new and startling doctrine to the people; here they have heard it from their youth up. It certainly is as needful as ever.

A heavy S.W. gale sprang up in the late evening and is still raging with some severity. Am thankful that I am not on the sea tonight.

TUESDAY, 9 JANUARY

While visiting today came in contact with a young woman who appears to be somewhat troubled. Apparently Sabbath night's discourse had some effect upon her, for she said that it was all for her. Feel encouraged to get another token for good and an evidence of the usefulness of preaching on the new birth.

Tonight we had our first meeting in the Culregrein Hall.[1] I think the Lord has smiled upon our venture in Culregrein and given us an evidence of His approval.

WEDNESDAY, 10 JANUARY

Tonight had lecture on 'Procrastination'.[2] Was pleased to see 180 present despite the rain.

THURSDAY, 11 JANUARY

The sick are very numerous just now and are, in fact, getting beyond me. 250 were out at the Prayer meeting tonight. At a Deacons' Court afterwards the proposal was made that we should have a bi-lingual missionary[3] but as the matter pertained to the Session it was not taken up. I wish I could get a good man, there is need for such.

THURSDAY, 18 JANUARY

Visited in Bayhead today and felt tired enough after conducting worship in 25 houses. Heard, however, what heartened me, as to how much my visits to the Sanatorium are appreciated by the patients there. As this testimony came from the male side, felt distinctly strengthened by it, for I was often tempted to think that as a minister I would be more or less of a bogy to the young fellows there.

SATURDAY, 20 JANUARY

Got a letter from Kilmuir today informing me of the death of another of the Kilmaluag 'crop' – Alick Matheson (Aird). His end evidently was a very remarkable one, and like his sister Eliza, what had been concealed under a quiet, reserved exterior, all came out with wonderful brightness at the end. Although he never made any profession, I had good hopes of Alick, and more than once in those quickening times in Kilmaluag I saw him with tears running down his face.

WEDNESDAY, 31 JANUARY

This month has been an encouraging one. Despite a good deal of broken weather which affected attendances there has been a measure of warmth in the congregation. I have come in contact with two cases of concern and have heard of one who was 'brought in' at the last Laxdale

1 See entry on p 266.
2 Other lectures given this winter were on 'Justification by Faith', 'Who ought to be at the Lord's Table?', 'Presbyterianism', and 'The Sabbath Question'.
3 That is, a non-ministerial assistant in the congregation.

meeting, for all of which I praise the Lord. May it be the beginning of of an even greater work!

TUESDAY, 13 FEBRUARY

One of my elders today made the statement that there were many in a promising way in the congregation at present, whether they came forward or not. Felt very encouraged to hear such a statement.

TUESDAY, 27 FEBRUARY

Heard what gladdened me greatly – of a Graham girl having been 'brought in' under my preaching at the Communion at Back, when I was there some years ago ere coming to Stornoway. It is good to hear of such cases, especially so long afterwards.

WEDNESDAY, 28 FEBRUARY

The congregation seems to be in a good way at present and a few appear to be under exercise; six came forward at the communion. Got in touch with Roderick Murray (Laxdale), who is seeking. One young man – and perhaps a very unlikely one – Alex MacLeod, has begun to attend the Prayer Meeting. Mrs Donald Munro (Laxdale), is also on the seeking list. Last Sabbath a girl walked up all the way from Bayble for the services.

SABBATH, 4 MARCH

At night felt especially happy in preaching Christ and holding Him up before poor sinners. If He gives me liberty to speak, is it not because He means to bless it?

MONDAY, 5 MARCH

Today had Monthly Meeting but cannot say I had much liberty. Am very much pressed at present. There is a great deal of sickness in the congregation and I have much urgent correspondence waiting upon me. I long to get clear.

Near midnight, the boiler burst, and I had to go out in search of the plumber. This has been a worrying day.

TUESDAY, 27 MARCH: GLASGOW

Bought a new car today – a Jowett demonstration model – for £122.10. It is a beautiful car but it has cleared out every penny I possess.

WEDNESDAY, 28 MARCH

Left Glasgow at 8.40 this morning. I was driven out as far as Anniesland Cross and then the car was left to my care. I very soon came into the four-speed gear work and was able to handle the car with an ease which surprised myself. At the same time I was glad to leave the traffic of Dumbarton and Renton behind. The day was beautiful and I enjoyed the run very much. Crossing the Moor of Rannoch, the speedometer touched 57 miles per hour.

FRIDAY, 30 MARCH

Motored down to Point for the evening service. Mr Chisholm preached from Judges 7:18. He was pretty much as he was in Kinloch, full of denunciations, stripping poor struggling souls of every comfort, banging and kicking the pulpit in a ridiculous fashion, and continuing inordinately long.[1] Felt that it was a waste of time to go down to Point to hear such a diatribe.

TUESDAY, 3 APRIL

Had meeting of presbytery today. Strongly protested against the new regulations which give the Pope and his nuncios naval salutes, and also agreed to approach Woolworth's in connection with the opening of their establishment in Stornoway, with a view to the prevention of any risk of Sabbath work, as has happened under similar circumstances elsewhere. It is high time that strong action was taken against the secret Roman propaganda presently going on in governmental departments.

THURSDAY, 12 APRIL

Feel somehow today somewhat homesick; at any rate I have strange longings for the beauties of my own country, and for faces that I shall see no more. I don't know what has caused it, but it makes this island seem very drab and dull to me.

FRIDAY, 13 APRIL

Am much exercised over a case of adult baptism. I have not seen the girl yet, but I am very much afraid that, like most, she has no adequate

---

1 This is in contrast to his words on Peter Chisholm's highly appreciated ministry in Kilmuir (see pp 191–2), but Chisholm was somewhat unequal in his preaching. Commenting on this in his diary in July 1936 MacRae wrote: 'When Mr Chisholm is in good trim he is a very helpful preacher and has rich food for the Lord's people. I find few so profitable – although when he goes off the rails he does so with a vengeance'.

idea of what baptism means and attaches a superstitious value to it. Baptism is almost as much abused in the Free Church as the other sacrament is in the large Church.

SATURDAY, 14 APRIL

The mother of the girl who seeks baptism seemed to think that she could take the vows, although her daughter is 18 years of age. She said that she had seen it done in her own native place in a case in which the person baptised had attained the age of 17 years. It is quite evident that this is another case of superstition. It is astonishing how ignorant they are in Lewis as to the meaning of baptism.

WEDNESDAY, 25 APRIL

Had a very narrow escape today from a serious motor accident at the Sandwick Cross roads. A lorry which was coming along the main road from the Point side at a great speed and without sounding the horn, nearly dashed into my car as I was crossing from North Street to Lower Sandwick. It was a matter of inches. I felt quite unnerved after it. How indebted we are to the preserving and protecting power of the Lord!

WEDNESDAY, 2 MAY

Had a letter from my cousin Johnnie today informing me that his father died on Saturday. Thus the last of my parents' family has passed away. Now I am without father or mother, uncle or aunt – a very marked intimation of the passage of time. The old happy days of my boyhood have been much before me, and in memory I have seen the world peopled as it used to be.

A Christian never falls asleep in the fire or in the water, but grows drowsy in the sunshine.

John Berridge

We should never see the stars if God did not sometimes take away the day.

From K.A.M.'s Notebooks

12 A Pause and Renewal in the Mid-Thirties

In the early summer months of 1934, following the closing entry in the last chapter, MacRae continued his usual full round of services and meetings in Stornoway. Among the encouragements was the special interest he observed at the Sanatorium – 'noticed an eagerness to hear the Word which I had never seen before' – but, on the whole, the degree of spiritual warmth in the congregation seemed to be lower than it had been in the previous months. In part this may have been due to his more frequent absence on other engagements. For the latter part of May he was away for the General Assembly and for services in Glasgow (where he found the weather 'tropical and the hard, burning pavements very sore on the feet'), while in June there were Communion Seasons to be attended in Staffin and Inverness.

Another distraction from his own pulpit work in Stornoway was public controversy on two fronts. The first concerned the preservation of the Lord's Day. In May the L.M.S. Railway Company announced their intention to run two Sunday Excursions to Skye in the summer. Recognising that if these went forward further developments of the same kind would follow, MacRae wrote to *The Glasgow Herald*. His letter caused more than usual attention and resulted in his having to deal with reporters from two other national papers. In consequence of this he sent an article to *The Daily Express* which was duly published. The second issue related to a growing willingness on the part of the Government to show deference to Roman Catholicism. Today it may seem a foregone conclusion that British dealings with the Vatican will not be in the spirit of the oath to support the Protestant religion required of British monarchs at their succession to the throne, but forty years ago Kenneth MacRae believed that the issue should be strongly contested and not allowed to go by default. The protest, already noted, which he raised in the Stornoway Presbytery in April on this subject duly went before the Synod, which supported it, and therefore it became a matter which led to public criticism and debate.

Such public controversy, and the time it could occupy, MacRae did not relish. Yet he felt obligated not to avoid it for the reason which he gives in a diary entry on 14 June: 'Am engaged in public controversy at present in relation to the firing of naval salutes to the Pope. It is undoubtedly a duty to contend earnestly for the faith once delivered to the saints, but it is a duty which most shirk, so that I get more than my fair share of it. It has a drying tendency which is not helpful to my spiritual interests.'

Whenever there was something of a lull in the spiritual progress of his congregation he looked first at his own condition. Diary entries at this time reveal that he felt his soul was parched. In addition, and no doubt related to it, was the cumulative effect on his health of all that he had undertaken in his new charge. Certainly in the Spring of 1934 he did not have his usual elasticity of body and spirit. Entries in May include: 'Don't feel too well these days. I think I am run down and in need of a good tonic . . .' 'Today has been a day of hustle so that I have had scarcely time to think . . .' 'Feel very dried up with all this work . . .' 'Had a very heavy day . . .' 'Very dull and dead'.

He was, in fact, on the verge of a serious breakdown in health. In the last two days of June, though running a high temperature which he assumed to be from a flu germ, he drove himself on. After the evening service on Sunday, 1st July, he recorded, 'I could do nothing but come home and tumble into bed right away.' Not for eight days (which included his first 'silent Sabbath' in Stornoway) was he up again, though 'very weak and fit for nothing'. The next Thursday he preached at the prayer meeting, presided at a deacons' meeting which decided to install electric light in the church, and 'felt very far through' before he could get to bed. The following week he was looking forward to an approaching vacation, and as he and Mrs MacRae were planning to spend their nights camping on the mainland they decided to test the tent by driving out into the moors one evening and remaining there overnight. But a drive of twelve miles revealed no place suitable for pitching the tent, and so, after watching the sunset over Loch Roag and Bernera they were back home by 11.25 pm. The next night another trial enforced a necessary lesson:

'Pitched our tent in the garden and settled down for the night but not to sleep. Between 12 and 2 am we were so cold that we had to come in. We took down the tent ere doing so, and it was as well that we did, for the rain came down in torrents all morning. Although the night was a failure, yet I am glad we went out, for we know now that we must take more bedding than we anticipated'.

It needs no entry in his Diary to tell us that he would have enjoyed the element of humour in this situation! The next Monday, 23 July, they left Lewis on the evening boat, with some of the congregation at the pier to see them off. A week's holiday followed on the mainland, including a day in Lochgilphead, where they received a great welcome, though he noted a decline in numbers: 'When I went to Lochgilphead I had 16 upon whom I could call to engage in prayer, now there are only three'. After this far-too-short break they reached their old manse at Kilmuir on Wednesday, 1 August, for the duties of another communion season. The Rev. Hugh MacKinnon had been inducted pastor of the congregation in 1933. After two nights' preaching, by Friday a pain which MacRae had been feeling for a while in his back and side suddenly worsened. On Sunday he had to preach sitting down, and on the Monday, he wrote, 'despite over-powering pain dragged myself out to the Church and preached from Matthew 5:6.' This was the last sermon he was to preach until 18 November. For weeks he was confined to bed in his former home at Kilmuir. First his pain was attributed to his appendix, then to pleurisy, and only after a blood-test was taken did it appear that he was, in reality, suffering from para-typhoid. It was this infection which had caused the temperature he had attributed to flu before leaving home, and a partial recovery had only led to this serious relapse in Kilmuir. By August 16, the Doctor expressed the hope that he might be able to return home in a fortnight, but the next day his condition deteriorated with the onset of thrombosis in his left leg which became hugely swollen and he was never more seriously ill. At the end of August, when he was once more able to lift his pen, he wrote:

'I have been very low and when the thrombosis laid hold of me I nearly gave up. It was very, very questionable whether I would ever rise again, and, in the midst of my pain, except for my dear wife and daughter I did not much mind. But the Lord has taken me out of that furnace, blessed be His Name! and I must now just exercise patience, waiting for the recovery of my leg.'

To this entry Cathie MacRae in later years appended a note of her own: 'May I add my word of gratitude and praise to the Most High for the wonderful strength bestowed upon me throughout my dear husband's prolonged illness. I did not go to bed for several weeks, yet received the strength (as of two or three women) to attend to all his needs. One week I wrote 60 letters in his bedroom! But to see him begin to improve was my reward, and delight. Truly God's mercy faileth never!'

It was not until 15 October that they were at last able to leave the old Manse at Kilmuir, but as the weather was too unsettled for an immediate crossing of the Minch they were welcomed to the home of Thomas and Isabella MacLeay in Portree. The previous year he had received

Kenneth, one of their sons, into communicant membership at Portree, as already noted.

On 17 October they were back at Stornoway, being welcomed at the pier by a great crowd, including most of the office-bearers: 'With my two sticks I hobbled through them as quickly as possible and was driven up to the Manse. How glad I was to get back!' The exertion of this journey led to another four days in bed, and then his own doctor ordered a further month's rest before he returned to work. This is the point at which the following record takes up.

As though to mark the event as a land-mark in his life, after his illness MacRae set aside the pocket diary he had been using for 1934, and started a new and large folio-size book in which he made weekly rather than daily entries.

☐   ☐   ☐

27 OCTOBER, 1934

I was never nearer death than during my late illness and I have reason to praise the Lord that He lifted me up again and has given me the prospect of being able once more to labour in the gospel vineyard. That it was not without its own blessings is evident, and yet in my pain and trouble I had very little of the Lord's presence. It is true that several times the words came vividly before me 'It is I; be not afraid', but I was afraid to build much upon them lest they should be the product of my own imagination, and not a message from the Lord. Nevertheless I had not much fear of death. I knew it was not very far away, and yet I had no serious fear of my rejection. In fact, there were times when, were it not for my wife and daughter, I would almost have preferred to go. No doubt excruciating pain brought me to this, but I never got nearer 'having a desire to be with Christ which is far better' than at that time.

The lessons learned upon that bed of suffering I might well commit to permanent record lest I let them slip:

1.   I saw the folly of wrestling against sickness when it comes. This, humanly speaking, was at the root of my sufferings, for had I been careful I would have escaped with the first light attack of my illness which came upon me ere I left home. I failed to see that sickness was God's will and an indication to me to submit. I thought my engagements in connection with the cause were God's will and that they must be discharged at all costs, and therefore I refused to submit. But this, I see, was self-will and rebellion – I was unwilling to give up that which

pleased me, for a phase of God's will which was distinctly distasteful to me. I see the folly of it now.

2. I saw how utterly foolish I had been in my ministry, working at high pressure all the time, and forgetting that all my efforts would be vanity were they not blessed of the Holy Spirit. This was what troubled me more than anything else in my illness. How I longed to be assured that I would yet return to labour in Zion, that I might be wise and that I might work aright, learning to take the Lord with me in every sermon and in every effort to advance His kingdom. And now let me not forget this most important lesson. One sermon preached in the power of the Spirit is better than 100 without. Time taken in pleading with the Lord for His blessing upon my endeavours is not time lost, but what makes my endeavours profitable. If I learn to work less and plead more, I will be able to accomplish much more. And that leads me to:

3. I saw how foolish I had been in being so neglectful of prayer. I saw it as a real duty to be performed – not slavishly, but as the exercise of sincere faith upon the Word of God. The promises were there, not to be admired, but to be pleaded, and, if they were pleaded in sincere earnestness, they would be fulfilled. I must use prayer as a means definitely provided by the Lord for the advancement of His cause and for the growth of grace in His people.

4. I have learned the value of intercession. Not only in Kilmuir and Stornoway were people pleading for my restoration, but throughout Lewis, in Glasgow, in Ferintosh, in Fearn and probably in many places – and that in public. This is what amazed and humbled me, that I should be publicly prayed for in so many congregations. At the same time it was a source of great comfort and strength to me.

5. I have learned the value of sympathy in a new way. I have been the recipient of extraordinary kindness and I felt my heart go out with gratitude to those of my friends who so remembered me, and especially to those who came to visit me. I can understand now, as I never could before, the value of a visit to a sick-bed and of a word of sympathy to those who are in trouble.

Death has been vested now with a new dread for me – not the dread of dying which is natural to all, but dread of the pains of the dissolution of the body. If the pains of death are worse than those I passed through they may well be dreaded. But with some the body dies easily.

2 NOVEMBER

Although laid aside from active duties I have tried not to be altogether

[279]

idle, and tonight I have finished the typing out of a piece of work which I began in Kilmuir – a booklet designed for the winning of the loyalty and affection of our young people to the Church of their fathers.[1] In it I have sketched out faithfully the fearful declensions of the Church of Scotland, which so reveal to what an extent that Church has got off the rails. I have been moved to do so, not only by the fact that our young people need a sound stirring up – and our older ones too – but by the withholding of all reference to the Church of Scotland at the Conferences recently held at Portree and Stornoway. These meetings were held presumably for the quickening of interest among our people in the testimony of our Church, but I fail to see how any testimony can be adequately set forth, unless what it testifies against is also declared. My booklet aims largely at amending this omission, which so characterised recent attempts to declare our testimony.

When I was ill, and at my worst, my mind was away back to my childhood, and I seemed again to be in a world peopled by those who have gone long ago. This made me think, perhaps more than anything else, that I, too, was soon to pass over to the other side. At nights in a half delirium I was conscious that the hymns of long ago were very frequently on my lips. I was away back again in Fort George, Dingwall and the Black Isle almost to the oblivion of everything else except my pain.

I fear that my profiting from that illness has been of no great depth. Oh Lord, hold up my goings so that my footsteps may not slide!

10 NOVEMBER

I have received an account of what has been transpiring at Carloway these last few months from the minister, the Rev. John MacIver. Indications of an awakened interest in eternal things became manifest immediately after the Spring Communion, and up to date 14 men and 8 females appear to have come under the influence of the truth. Some of the former were ringleaders in frivolity, with the result that concerts, etc. in that district cannot receive sufficient patronage to ensure their continuance. Besides, the effect upon the community is such as to discourage all such gatherings. These young men now are organizing and carrying on prayer-meetings among themselves. The movement is distinctly encouraging and there is much reason to plead that it would increase and spread.

1 Entitled *Sketching in the Background*; it was published in 1935.

17 NOVEMBER

Tomorrow I break my long silence. I am glad at the prospect of getting back to my pulpit once more; nevertheless I am troubled at the thought of it. A warm, spiritual discourse will be expected of me after being in the fire. I am afraid lest a cold, lifeless sermon chill and disappoint that expectation. I can only look to the Lord in my helplessness. He has never failed me yet, and He will not fail me now, ungrateful sinner though I be.

How prone one is to conduct services in a more or less mechanical way; as a duty to be performed and no more! How utterly I fail to realise that the Lord has promised to bless His Word (Isaiah 55:10–11), and how far I am from the eager expectation of fruit which such a promise warrants! And since the rule of the kingdom is that we shall have according to our faith (Matthew 9:29, Psalm 81:10), my barrenness is my own fault. Unbelief is rendering me unfruitful. And surely unbelief in the face of such unambiguous promises is a great sin. Oh Lord, keep me from sinning against Thee in this matter and give me faith to expect the Word to be blessed among us!

Have been somewhat impressed by reading Shedd on the place of fear as a motive to vital religion.[1] I am afraid that I have somewhat overlooked this in recent years. I have found it difficult to preach the sterner aspects of the truth in love, or without being myself somewhat hardened in the process, and I have tended more and more to neglect such subjects. But I am convinced that I have been in the wrong. I fear the deceitful heart prefers both to preach and to hear 'smooth things'.

24 NOVEMBER

A great congregation awaited my appearance on Sabbath night. I felt strangely weak as I slowly made my way up the pulpit stairs. I spoke from Genesis 6:9 'and Noah walked with God', but I had no sense of liberty and felt very disappointed. On my return home, however, a remark of Matthew Henry somewhat comforted me: 'When God's servants are bound, yet His Word and Spirit are not bound; spiritual children may then be born to them'. May it be so! I felt thankful that at last I have been able to make a start.

A thought occurred to me today which may not have been presumption. I had been disposed to look upon my recent illness as a chastisement for coldness and a generally backslidden condition, and I dare not say that I did not deserve it, but the thought flashed through my mind

1 W. G. T. Shedd, *Sermons to the Natural Man*, chapter 16.

today that perhaps, after all, the providence was of a preparatory nature, calculated to give me ballast and humility enough to make it safe for the Lord to bless my labours to this people. At any rate the thought encourages faith more than unbelief, and therefore I am not disposed to part with it.

It is curious how my mind has been so completely lifted from my former field of labour, despite the many happy and blessed days I have seen there. When I lay convalescing in Kilmuir I was longing to get away, and ministerial conditions there no longer appealed to me. I do not think that I could be happy there now – at least unless the Lord gave me another mind. That my mind is so set upon my present charge no doubt is an indication that the Lord sent me here.

I DECEMBER

We hear much today upon being filled with the Spirit, and those who make claim to this experience declare that it is a distinct and separate spiritual phase consequent upon, and analogous with, conversion, and that it gives triumph over and freedom from the vexing influences of indwelling sin, but so far as I can see, the more a man is filled with the Spirit the more he will be aware of and mourn over the vileness of his own heart.

I have been asked by Headquarters to give a year's service to the Geelong Congregation in Australia. An appeal for the services of a minister has come from Australia, and I have been suggested as likely to benefit in health by the change. I have thought over it and tried to pray over it, but I cannot find my mind going out to it in any way as a call from the Lord.

8 DECEMBER

I was able to take the three services on Sabbath, for which I was very thankful. The day was wet and attendances were not up to normal, but under the circumstances they were very satisfactory: morning 360, afternoon 110, evening 700. At the first service, spoke from Psalm 22:30 on God having a people in every age, and felt refreshed in my own spirit. Also enjoyed some liberty in speaking from John 13:15 on faith triumphing in adversity. At night we had our English service and I spoke forcibly and plainly from Hebrews 12:25 upon the danger of refusing to heed the gospel invitation. At the close of the evening service I made an appeal to the young men in connection with my lectures on the Shorter Catechism which I hope to carry on monthly throughout winter and spring.

On Tuesday the Quarterly Fellowship Meeting was held at Barvas. The day was good and about 600 were present. The Question was based upon Ephesians 2:1.

On Wednesday had my first lecture of the winter and was very gratified by the attendance. Saw many new faces there. Dealt with Catechism Questions 29 and 30 on the application of the redemption purchased by Christ, and enjoyed it. Well over 200 were present.

The Prayer Meeting on Thursday was well attended, fully 250 being out.

Got a letter from Mr Chisholm (Lochalsh) bemoaning the low state of religion both in our Church and throughout the country, and proposing that I should prepare an overture for submission at the forthcoming Synod, craving the appointment by the General Assembly of a week of prayer throughout the Church.[1] Three years ago I submitted such an overture and a week of prayer was appointed. I was disappointed with the result. The people came out all right, but the prayers at these meetings were just the usual round. The 'men' seem unable to concentrate in prayer upon a single, definite petition. All the place the purpose of our meeting together got in the supplications of those who engaged was a few words at the end, and oftentimes not even that. We seem so bound up in formality that it appears almost impossible to get rid of it. I think something should be done among the ministers themselves first of all. If we were only aroused, our congregations might follow suit. Oh to be awake myself! Find my mind inclining to the desirability of having ministerial meetings for spiritual conference and

---

1 Peter Chisholm had been called from Coll to the newly-formed charge of Partick Highland, Glasgow, in 1925, where he exercised a ministry rich in fruitfulness. His health deteriorating, he removed to the quieter charge of Lochalsh in the West Highlands in 1932 and, thereafter, as he tells in his book *Wandering In Fields of Dreams*, 1952, he came to entertain increasingly dark views on the prospects for the Cause in the Highlands: 'Long continued impenitence on the part of those who enjoy Gospel ordinances, without the power of "the Spirit of life in Christ Jesus", is the most fruitless and hardening evil that we know . . . A prolonged period of spiritual stagnation has dried up the very roots of our conservatism, where, in the past, by a full-orbed declaration of the prophetic, priestly and kingly work of the Redeemer, there flowed into the national life wholesome and varied streams of divine power and assurance, and a just balance between conservatism and reform in religion was admirably secured . . . It indicates and reinforces an attitude which, if persisted in, will allow the Church which adopts it to drift slowly away from having contact with the minds of men. So drifting it shrinks into a coterie, and its every activity becomes infected with the curse of futility' (pp 49 and 89).

MacRae's assessment of the spiritual need in the Highlands was similar to Chisholm's but he was more resolute in resisting the temptation to discouragement.

prayer. Once we finish our Presbyterial visitation of congregations, the evening of the Quarterly Fellowship meetings would furnish a good opportunity for the carrying out of such an idea.

A remark of Cecil's seemed to come home to me and not without encouragement – 'a stubborn and rebellious mind in a Christian must be kept low by dark and trying dispensations. The language of God, in His providence, to such an one, is generally of this kind: "I will not wholly hide myself. I will be seen by thee. But thou shalt never meet me, except in a dark night and in a storm". Ministers of such a natural spirit are often fitted for eminent usefulness by these means'.[1]

15 DECEMBER

Sabbath, for the third time in succession, was a wet day, yet the attendances were wonderfully good: morning 420, afternoon 135, and evening 800.

Worked out a text which Boston had handled and then compared the two. The comparison made me feel ashamed, but what I was interested to notice was that Boston sheared far closer to the conscience than I am wont to do, and did not deal out God's comforts with such a liberal hand. I find Boston's style very profitable to my own soul in wakening me up and disturbing my slothful spirit.

Conducted my first district meeting since my illness, on Tuesday when I went out to Laxdale. Addressed about 100 people from Romans 9:25. I am afraid that my discourse lacked logical connection and point, that, in fact, it wandered unduly from the text.

Felt that it is a mistake to handle two or more points of doctrine in the same sermon. A sermon, I think, should take aim and seek to drive home one great lesson. One point driven home ought to go deeper – humanly speaking – than two or three. To handle several points at once only distracts the attention and dissipates the effect. Boston, I notice, dealt with each point separately, and I think he did wisely. If a text raised two points of doctrine then he made two sermons of it. And I feel that I would do well to follow his example.

Modern religious books of the evangelical type generally make much of 'complete surrender', and they represent it as a spiritual crisis distinct from and subsequent to conversion, and fully as emphatic in its effect upon the life of the soul. It seems to answer to a second

1 *Works of the Rev. Richard Cecil*, arranged and revised by Josiah Pratt, vol IV, p 24. The best of Cecil's thoughts on the ministry are also to be found in the valuable volume, *Remains of the Rev. Richard Cecil*, arranged and revised by Josiah Pratt.

conversion and ushers the believer into a phase of experience in which sin is no longer the troublesome element in the daily life and private walk that it was. Boston, too, and many of the old divines, advocated a covenanting with God which in its terms went near to complete surrender. This is a matter that troubles me. I am aware of a will within which is not after the Spirit and which is ever striving for supremacy. I know that I ought to deny this will and give it no quarter whatsoever; and this is all my desire. But neither covenant nor surrender will eradicate this will nor change its nature. To covenant may indeed stiffen me in my struggle against it, but what I fear in respect of covenanting is that, owing to the strength of this evil will and my own weakness, it would very probably soon bring me under the power of a legal conscience – to which I have ever been prone – and usher me into great darkness of soul. I am therefore afraid of such resolutions, covenants or surrenders, and prefer simply to look to the Lord for grace to keep down the evil nature and to keep my feet from sliding. In 1909 I surrendered my will to the Lord, and I thought then, when I took Him to be my Saviour and King for ever, that I would only have the one will wholly for Him; but I was not long in learning that I had a will which could not be bound over to the Lord, the evil will of the old nature, and I have been wrestling against it ever since. I fear it and I dread it, but I trust the Lord to preserve me from it so long as it has power to vex me.

22 DECEMBER

On Sabbath had the second best attendance of the year – 450 in the morning, 145 at the English, and 850 at night.

I prepare one new sermon for every Sabbath; the others are old ones, and those which I am handling at present were composed in 1922. I find that I have to overhaul them and often to re-arrange them, and yet, after everything, I generally have little taste for them and find them disappointing in the delivery – although some of them were made of some service to poor souls when they were formerly preached. My mind seems somewhat to have altered, having a desire for pointed and clear reasoning which makes the more diffuse, wandering, and somewhat imaginative sermons of my early ministry less attractive to me. But that does not mean that I am a better preacher today than I was then. I am less earnest now, and earnestness gives power to preaching, and I often fear that I am in danger of drifting into the commonplace.

At the Prayer Meeting on Thursday the Seminary accommodation was exhausted except for the platform seats. Fully 310 were present, which constituted a record attendance for the year. Certainly the people are attending well at present, whatever it may portend, and I have much reason for thankfulness that it is so.

I am often in a dilemma between Antinomianism and Legalism. Sin often – too, too often – gets the better of me, and sometimes I consent to it with a deliberation which frightens me. When thus the conscience becomes clouded with guilt, and all liberty and joy in God's service are swallowed up in a chill apprehension of having offended Him, what am I to do? Were that question put to me by another I would at once reply: 'Flee to the blood of Christ, and, confessing your guilt and weakness, believingly plead its merits and seek to apply it to your wounded conscience'; but when I come to my own case I find it not so simple. I have come so often upon the same mission, having fallen by the same sin, that I feel that this process cannot continue indefinitely, and that to imagine that it can would be to cheapen sin. And yet I cannot promise the Lord that I shall put an end to it by refusing to yield to sin's wiles, for well I know that in my own strength I cannot do so for a single day. 'Oh wretched man that I am, who shall deliver me from the body of this death?' And yet, after all, there seems but the one way of relief; but God is not unduly hasty in lifting the burden of guilt from off an offended conscience, for the bearing of it is sore punishment to a gracious soul.

29 DECEMBER

This is the last entry of this year. What reason I have to be thankful that I am spared to see its end! No year ever brought such hazard to my life. Would that I could truly improve the season which, Hezekiah-like, has thus been added to my days!

On Monday counted the votes in connection with the election of office-bearers. About 190 voted and we took three hours to get through the work. The result was creditable to the discernment of the voters. The individual whom I feared might get into the eldership registered only 10 votes. I am very satisfied and thankful to the Lord for the outcome.

Went out to Culregrein on Tuesday for the meeting. The house was packed to capacity, fully 125 being present. Spoke on the two blind men of Jericho (Matthew 20:30) and from their case tried to present the Gospel as simply as possible. After the meeting I found that little Bayble girl weeping bitterly. Her case puzzles me. It is over a year since she was awakened and yet she seems to have got no solid ground of comfort yet. I have sent her *The Anxious Inquirer*, but apparently to no avail. I would like to have a private conversation with her to ascertain her difficulties, but that is not easily arranged. After I came home I felt that I could do nothing but pray for her, and definitely asked the Lord to give her peace.

I believe that I am happier here in this island than I would be in any place else in the world, yet were I deprived of my ministry I do not think that I could settle down either here or in Skye. I am a Mainlander and I can never feel as much at home in these bare Western Isles as in the wooded straths and green braes of my own country. Often I yearn for a sight of the old familiar mountains – none others can ever be the same to me – but, alas, when I go that way I always get a sore heart, for the old world I knew there has long since passed away. I am a stranger upon the earth. Oh for a heavenly spirit!

19 JANUARY, 1935

On Thursday ordained and inducted seven elders and eight deacons. Preached first of all to a congregation of about 450 from 1 Timothy 6:12, on witnessing a good profession before many witnesses. I am exceedingly thankful to get a difficult duty so smoothly discharged. May the Lord make them a blessing! How thankful we should be that we have such material.

26 JANUARY

Sabbath was a good day and attendances corresponded. 500 were out in the morning, 140 at the English, and 850 at night. The new staff of elders had difficulty in finding sufficient accommodation in the lectern.[1]

Legalism seems to be prevalent in our Church courts. Technical points receive altogether undue prominence in their proceedings. There seems to be a kind of pride in the knowledge of what they are pleased to call 'church law', and this 'church law' must stand, no matter what becomes of common-sense and Christian consideration. They seem to be utterly blind to the fact that most of what they designate 'church law' is simply church procedure, which is founded, not upon acts of assembly fortified by the Barrier Act, as true church law is, but upon use and wont. Sometimes I feel very tired of such a tedious and unsatisfactory way of doing business.

I am given to understand that my delivery has become monotonous, mournful and slow. I believe this is the result of my relaxing – as it

1 *ie* the platform below the pulpit where the elders sat during public worship.

were – in the pulpit under the impression that the Lord would help me. I see the danger of this – that it has a tendency to make me heavy and drowsy. I remember how sleepy and dull Mr — —'s delivery used to be, and how I wished that he would wake up; and here I have drifted unconsciously into the same fault, and were it not for my faithful wife I might have been allowed to remain in it until it had become a confirmed habit. It seems that I must not spare myself, but preach with energy and force, and then, having done all in my power, look to the Lord to bless my humble efforts.

9 FEBRUARY

All day on Monday felt a longing to have such a special meeting for the concerned as met with such success in Kilmuir, but have a shrinking from the idea of it being regarded as an innovation and as akin to the methods of modern revivalists. At the same time every legitimate effort should be used in the Lord's strength. To get into a rut is not helpful, and many, I fear, sleep because of it. If the Lord spares me till after the communion I may venture upon it.

On Wednesday had fully 150 out at the Lecture. Dealt with justification (Question 33) and rather enjoyed it. At close had a baptism at which I spoke of the failure of some parents to bring out their children to the public means of grace, and pointed out that the Sabbath School could never be a substitute, as it was not a divinely appointed means of grace. I trust that it may do some good, as few parents seem to realise their obligation to bring their family to public worship.

16 FEBRUARY

I note in the Life of Robert Blair[1] that it was law preaching that began the Ulster revival at Six Mile Water in 1624, but that it was judicious Gospel preaching that carried it on and gave it such a lasting character.

Corrected the proof-sheets of my booklet, *Sketching in the Background*, so publication draws near. I expect the book will make a bit of a stir and will make me the mark for many arrows, both without and within our Church, but the time for straight speaking has more than come.

23 FEBRUARY

I generally read when I visit the sick, but it occurs to me that it might be profitable to discourse on some passage read for two or three

1 *Select Biographies*, Wodrow Society, edited by Thomas McCrie, 1848, p 71.

minutes. At such a time people are more sensible to impressions, and such a method might extend my 'preaching' activities to some whom I could not otherwise reach.

2 MARCH

On Thursday there was a very good attendance at the Prayer Meeting, fully 250 being present. That morning got a wire from my old friend, Rev. Donald Smith, Govanhill [Glasgow], intimating the death of his mother and asking me to make local arrangements. The wire carried my mind back at once to 1914, when I paid my first visit to Stornoway and spent a very happy week in the Smiths' old home in Keith Street – a home which long since has been broken up. Who then would have dreamt for a moment that such as has taken place could ever be a possibility, and that I should later become the Free Church minister of Stornoway? Truly the ways of the Lord are passing strange!

23 MARCH

On Friday evening went over to —— and heard —— on Exodus 13:21-22. His matter was quite good, but felt angry with him for spoiling his discourse with a most abominable delivery and enunciation. Such a delivery would ruin the finest discourse. What makes it so annoying is that his extraordinary style is not natural to him. At times the noise he made in the pulpit made me think of the lazy droning of a bluebottle upon a windowpane on a hot summer afternoon.

30 MARCH

On Monday went out to Crossbost for the concluding services of the communion. Mr MacKay (Fearn) preached at night, taking as his text Ezekiel 9:4. He gave us a splendid discourse. Now I felt that we were getting real preaching, and yet it puzzled me to find the source of his effectiveness. He was very deliberate, clear and emphatic in delivery, and he held his audience, and when later on he warmed up and put pith and energy into the sermon one felt that he had power. He is a rare preacher.

20 APRIL

The Prayer Meeting on Thursday was well attended, fully 240 being present. At the Kirk Session which followed it was decided that we should apply for a congregational missionary and hold double services on Sabbaths, dispensing with the afternoon English service. This step has become necessary owing to the growing English element among the young of the congregation.

I have been sent for today to visit a poor dying girl (Flora MacIver) belonging to St. Columba's Established Church here, which is presently vacant. I found her in the last stages of consumption, but, although unable to speak, perfectly sensible. I told her to cast everything upon Christ, her sins, her soul and her every care. She could not reply, but the large, pleading eyes looked very earnestly into mine. Came away with a very sore heart. It seems that no-one has been calling upon the poor girl – that is, no minister or office-bearer. Surely that is a very strange state of affairs, since their Church has had a regular supply quartered in the town. I wish I had met with this case sooner. I fear that she cannot last over the week-end.

4 MAY

Only once was Sabbath's attendance exceeded this year. In the morning 450 were out. Spoke with some freedom from 1 Samuel 14:6. At the beginning of the service was very much troubled with worrying thoughts which cast me into an ill frame, until suddenly the thought flashed into my mind that, since I was going to preach against Satan and to incite believers to a greater and more practical zeal against him, this was his attempt to disarm me beforehand. That gave me some relief and some encouragement to look to the Lord for power. I believe that I am too often taking to myself the responsibility for what is really the work of the Enemy and thus I am bringing myself into bondage because my conscience comes to be burdened with the guilt of such. We are not half aware of the reality of the work of Satan and of his extraordinary subtlety – I am not at any rate!

11 MAY

Sabbath was good and so were services. Had the monthly English service at night. 750 were present which, with a good Gaelic representation in the Seminary, made a splendid congregation in all. Spoke from 2 Timothy 2:1 on being strong in the grace that is in Christ Jesus. At the close, and after a great fight with myself, intimated a meeting reserved to those alone who were interested as to their souls' salvation for Wednesday evening. Have long had this before my mind but always have been putting it off. After my late serious illness, I felt, now that I had finished the winter's series of lectures on the Shorter Catechism, that I dare delay no longer.

On Wednesday had the special meeting which I intimated on Sabbath night. Before going out felt very agitated about the matter and feared that there might be no response or only a handful – so few as to make the conducting of a meeting difficult. Felt thankful and encouraged to see seven individuals passing the manse on their way to the meeting. On going out, found 110 waiting me. Despite all I had said, 10 members also found their way in. No doubt there were some whose interest in their soul's salvation was only skin-deep, but, nevertheless, had great reason for thankfulness that there should be such great interest among my people in the great matter of their salvation. Was very gratified to see my own daughter and our servant there, although I asked neither of them to go. May the Lord bring them to make a definite choice! Tried to explain the scriptural answer to the question 'What must I do to be saved?' and asked them to settle the matter there and then. Oh that He may bless this meeting and that many may date their conversion from it! At the close, stated that I would be glad to answer difficulties at next lecture, if they would write them out and send them on to me.

Last night I left for the Croy Communion. I got a beautiful night for crossing, but the 'Lochearn' being on the run in place of the 'Lochness',[1] scarcely got a wink of sleep owing to the vibration and roar of her motor engines. Mr MacLeod met me in Inverness. By the time we got out to Croy, Mr Cameron [Ardersier] had begun the Gaelic service. Only 27 were present.

18 MAY

Rain fell during the night and the aspect of the weather was considerably changed. Fully 100 were present at the English service. About 36 communicated. At the Table service felt some evidence of softening. Noticed that Mr MacLeod, the minister, was in tears. When I saw that, I conceived a great respect for him, for I have never before seen a minister in tears under the Word.

At night we had an attendance of 110, which for this service apparently constituted a record.

On Tuesday the local schoolmaster motored me over to Ardersier. After considerable searching we found the Camerons' manse. Campbel-town – as we used to call it – has grown considerably since my child-hood's days, but the old thatch-roofed cottages are there still. Mr Cameron and myself in the late afternoon went down to Fort George.

1 The regular mail and passenger steamer plying daily between Stornoway and the mainland.

It is greatly changed. Palatial quarters have been built in another part. A hospital has also been erected outside the Fort, near the Ladies' Ramparts. The narrow slits in the outside of the ramparts, which used to give a ray of light as illumination to the 'bomb-proofs', have now been magnified into substantial windows, and the sergeants' mess too has been transferred to a specially constructed chamber within the ramparts. Within I found everything on a smaller scale than memory represented – the greens did not seem so large, nor the ramparts so high, and the whole area appeared shrunken to my eye from what it once was. The old 'Infants' School' has now become the Quarter-Master's Office; the church no longer serves as the 'Master's School', and all the children now have to go to Ardersier Public School. A daughter of Prof. Cameron, married to Dr Bissell, the Garrison doctor, is resident in Fort George and we found them living in what used to be the schoolmaster's house. It was very singular, and I felt touched when I was ushered into the room in which I used to play with the schoolmaster's boy, Vivvy Yaxley, long, long ago. I felt pensively sad at realising that when last I stood in that room I was a little boy of 9 years of age – 42 years ago! The view from the ramparts was magnificent, but everything was so changed and yet so familiar that I felt as though my heart would almost break. The past rose before me at every step, but what saddened me most of all was not the change which I saw about me, but the change which I felt within me. I was far more changed than the dear old Fort. Father, mother and three brothers were all gone, the old Ross-shire Militia of which we used to be so proud had vanished too, and I, a poor creature, with life well spent, had crept back to survey for a little the scenes of a happy past. Such is life!

At night we had a service in Ardersier with an attendance of 61. This was a very good representation. It served to confirm me in my opinion that, if only some East Coast ministers were a little less hidebound by custom and tradition, and if only they realised that our day calls for exceptional measures, they would not have to complain so much of the rising generation drifting away.

1 JUNE

On Thursday morning a woman of my congregation came to me in distress of soul. Years ago she had committed an error of judgment and she declared that for the last seven years, with the exception of the six months prior to last February, she had no peace and was persuaded that she could have no place in the kingdom of God – that she was lost.

The six months' peace she had enjoyed was consequent upon a sermon which she had heard from me in the Seminary. She was an interesting person and had been one of Spurgeon's hearers in her young days when she was employed in London. She seemed to be a truly gracious person, well acquainted with the depravity of her own heart. I tried to prove to her that this obsession was simply a temptation from Satan and that she must not give him credence in preference to God's Word. These cases are very difficult, and they are often partly physical in origin – Satan taking advantage of a weakened nervous system. Reasoning therefore goes for very little. The Lord alone can give light.

Flora MacIver seems to have passed into a more steady peace and a more settled condition. She told me that she is not afraid, that she is just trusting in the Lord Jesus. She appealed to me to come back soon,

29 JUNE

Monday evening, motored out to Kinloch and enjoyed an interchange of views with Mr Macrae[1] on matters relating to the spiritual state and prospects of our Church in view of present-day circumstances. He agrees with me as to the need for aggressive Gospel work and a fresh presentation of the principles for which we stand. He also desires to see more of what he calls 'team-work' among the ministers of our Presbytery, i.e., more Christian intercourse and united endeavour to advance the things for which we stand, and more meetings for prayer.

13 JULY

Sabbath was a good day and attendances were good. 480 were out in morning, and I got on better than I anticipated in speaking from Galatians 5:16 on walking in the Spirit. In the afternoon rather enjoyed speaking from Cant. 5:10 on the super-excellence of Christ. At night had our monthly English service and had an attendance above the average for English, fully 750 being present. Spoke from Genesis 41:56 on Joseph opening the storehouses, and enjoyed it. Thus I celebrated the 25th anniversary of my entrance into the Gospel ministry. How time passes! And how little I have done in all these years! How little progress I have made in grace!

14 SEPTEMBER

Began systematic visitation on Tuesday for the first time since my

1 The Rev. Murdo MacRae, minister of the Free Church, Kinloch, from his ordination in 1927 until his death in 1961 when he was rightly described as one of the Church's 'most highly regarded and outstanding ministers'.

illness and called upon 25 families at the Battery. Rather enjoyed it and my visits seemed to be appreciated. I do not feel equal to facing two days of such visitation per week as formerly was my custom, but if I can manage one day I shall be quite thankful.

5 OCTOBER

The wireless reported on Thursday night that war had broken out by the Italians bombing Adowa (Abyssinia). Apparently it was a sheer massacre on a tremendous scale, and considering what modern weapons are, if the war is to continue it cannot be anything else. If ever there was an unjustifiable war in history this is it. It will be a foul blot on the name of Italy for generations, and all to satiate the vain-glory of one ambitious, relentless despot! May Britain be kept out of it!

19 OCTOBER

On Tuesday finished my visitation in the first of my four congregational districts. In this district, which lies on the Inaclete and Battery side of the town and which includes the new houses built out in that direction, we have 156 families and 57 members. In the evening conducted the Laxdale meeting when spoke from Psalm 16:1.

16 NOVEMBER

Having promised Mr Macrae a Sabbath during his absence at the English fishing, came over to Kinloch in fulfilment of my promise. Did so, rather grudgingly, for I have to leave my own pulpit without supply other than the elders.

23 NOVEMBER: KINLOCH

Sabbath was a good day and people got out well from all parts of a particularly scattered congregation. Read a book by Dr D. M. MacIntyre on *The Hidden Life of Prayer* which made it well worth my while to come out here. Felt considerably helped by it, but am afraid to make any resolutions because of my lack of strength to keep them. Oh that the Lord would make me prayerful!

Bogatzky says that faith's most difficult exercise is to be penetrated both with a lively sense of our sinfulness and with a sense of absolute freedom from condemnation at one and the same time.[1] I know well how true that is. Felt the better for my visit to Kinloch. It has brought me somewhat nearer the Lord and delivered me from being altogether engrossed in my multitudinous concerns.

1 *Golden Treasury*: entry for 17 November.

30 NOVEMBER

Had a good day on Sabbath. A year ago I was just venturing to take two services after my long illness. How thankful I should be to be so much recovered! Fully 780 were out at the evening service. Dealt with the terrors of the law and spoke with a good deal of force from Psalm 18:41 on praying in vain. Felt that I lacked unction, yet I believe that the law must be preached. After coming home had a most comfortable sense of the Lord's presence with me and I sang the praises of the Gracious One. Just heard tonight that Dr Munro has accepted the call to Rogart. I never for one moment thought he would ever leave Ferintosh. This news comes home with something of a heart-pang. For me Ferintosh is a place of memories, many of them very tender. Once Dr Munro goes it can never be the same again, as his going marks the end of another passage in my life. The old people will feel it deeply.

4 JANUARY, 1936

New Year's morning (Wednesday) dawned very wet but about 11 am conditions improved and we had a very good day. Nevertheless the attendance was affected and the congregation which normally musters 300 at the New Year's service only totalled 250. Spoke with a good deal of liberty from 1 Samuel 7:12 'Hitherto hath the Lord helped us.'

My totals for the year just gone as compared with the two former years show the extent to which I have recovered my health:

	1933	1934	1935		
Services	321	222	327	Average Attendance for year:-	
Courts	28	37	38	Morning Service =	415
Visits	1,278	741	1,059	Afternoon =	112
Baptisms	29	31	75	Evening Service =	780
Funerals	29	22	37		
Marriages	8	6	12	Total =	1,307
New					
Members	13	8	10	Average prayer meeting attendance = 229	

25 JANUARY

The King yielded to a Greater on Sabbath, and Edward, the Prince of Wales, has been proclaimed King. This is now the fourth sovereign whom I have seen and it is likely to be the last.[1] One day death will come for me, too, and the world will go on just as usual. I fear lest it be soon made clear that the Romanists have been tampering with the Accession

1 Edward VIII abdicated on 11 December, 1936, to be succeeded by his brother, George VI.

Oath. I fear also that our new monarch will not be an influence helpful to true evangelical righteousness. Yet the Lord can change him.

8 FEBRUARY

Sabbath morning found the ground coated with snow and throughout the day there were showers. The frost was as keen on Tuesday evening as ever I have experienced it. I had to go to Kershader. When I went out to my car after the meeting I found the windscreen frosted up both inside and outside. It was only with the utmost difficulty that I was able to get the frost removed. I had hardly gone a mile upon the narrow, winding, dangerous road before it was almost as bad as ever, and, despite my good lights, I could scarcely see where I was going. At one particular corner the car refused to answer the wheel, and, continuing in the direction in which it had been travelling, went clean off the road. Immediately, however, the wheels got a grip of the heather it responded to the wheel which was now over to its fullest extent and dashed back to the road, crossed it, and left on the other side. Although I reversed the wheel as fast as I was able there was no response till I left the road. There I ran for three or four yards on the very edge of a declivity. I thought nothing could preserve me from plunging down, but I just managed, through the Lord's goodness, to retain my balance. As I regained the road I felt my nerves completely on edge and, what with the numbness of my hands, I felt as though I could give up the whole struggle. I was unspeakably thankful to get back to the main road again.

22 FEBRUARY

It is stated that a person from Point was awakened on the Sabbath evening prior to the Communion, that a woman from Back was brought under concern on Saturday, and that a servant girl in Keith Street came under the influence of the Word on Sabbath evening in the Town Hall. Such news is good news, but I have found out by experience that it is not wise to place too much reliance upon such. There are many awakenings in Lewis of which one hears nothing further. I cannot help, too, a certain amount of dubiety regarding the movement in Point. A work which spreads as an infection – from person to person – rather than from the influence or hearing of the Word, to my mind suggests animal magnetism rather than the work of the Spirit. I am fearful of being in opposition to anything that may be of the Spirit, but I cannot help recognising the wisdom of the scriptural precept to judge the tree by its fruits. It is wisest to say nothing and to wait and see. Time will tell. As for the movement in town among the school children inaugurated by the 'Pilgrim Preachers' I have no faith in it. It has resulted in additions to the communion rolls of at least two of the other Churches, but its products seem to be characterised by a cock-sureness and self-sufficiency that is very far removed from the humility and brokenness one associates with the genuine work of the Spirit. These young 'converts' were never heard of as being under concern and gave no evidence of any such thing, and even now, so far as those connected with the Free Church are concerned, have never put in an appearance at the prayer meeting, while such inconsistencies as attendance upon concerts and 'the pictures' mark them off as the victims of a religious delusion which is claiming only too many nowadays. I write thus, but, oh, my own religion is eminently unsatisfactory! And yet I can honestly say that, apart from the work of the ministry, I have no interest in life, and would not wish to live unless I could get to preach Christ to sinners.

29 FEBRUARY

It is reported that the movement in Shader, Point, has spread to Knock and Aignish and that a number of the young men have been affected. It is the young men who seem mainly to be visited. In Skye, too, recent cases of awakening seem to have been confined to the young men. Is this a token for good? Would that it would spread to Stornoway!

7 MARCH

The town is full of sickness, and flu, complicated by septic throat or pneumonia, is rife. May I be protected from it; for every day I have to go among such cases – and I am so susceptible to flu.

14 MARCH

Got word that John Weir Campbell[1] has been appointed as student-missionary to Stornoway for a period commencing on the 22nd inst.

On Friday morning I received a letter from Mr Muirden (Maryburgh) which troubled me. It acquainted me with the fact that the Ferintosh congregation wished to call me. Unquestionably Ferintosh makes a peculiar appeal to me, more so than any congregation in the Church, but I have no desire to leave Stornoway, nor do I see any reason for

---

1 Afterward minister of Perth, Brora, and Nairn. Died in the thirtieth year of his ministry on 18 December, 1966.

doing so. I would like to be where the Lord would bless me most, and I would like that His will should rule. If I were a little older I might have some reason for leaving Stornoway, for the charge is a heavy one.

Felt vexed today – as I often am – at my slowness of speech and my difficulty in expressing my feelings in ordinary conversation. A poor young man, bereaved of his wife, called here in connection with the funeral arrangements. It was after he had gone that I realised that I ought to have prayed with him, even though he is one who has not much interest in religion. Still, I missed my opportunity of perhaps influencing him for good and now I regret it very much. How prone I am to a kind of officialism in my ministry and to forget the need for the human touch! I fear that I am a poor failure both as a minister and as an ordinary Christian. Yet I have been greatly encouraged of late when I made up a list of those who had been influenced under my ministry during the last 21 years. Some were awakened under my ministrations, some brought to peace; other preachers and various providences played a part in the experience of some. Some never made a public profession, but their lives testified to the reality of the change. The list is summarised below. It is not drawn up for the glorification of self but for my own encouragement in times when hope may be low and my feet nigh to slipping:

(1)	Edinburgh (student period)	5
(2)	Lochgilphead and Tayvallich	15
(3)	Arran Communions	13
(4)	Kilmuir	6
	Staffin	8
	Kilmaluag	18
(5)	Skye Communions	5
(6)	Glasgow Communions	7
(7)	Other Communions	4
(8)	Stornoway	14
(9)	Lewis Communions	3
		––
		98
		––

Some of these have finished their course. No doubt there are others of whom I have not heard. To the Lord be the praise who hath so blessed the services of such an unworthy creature! Oh how this ought to enliven my faith and give me the spirit of expectation!

21 MARCH

It is reported that matters have been exceedingly bright in Breasclete ever since the communion. Up till then that village seemed to be unaffected by the revival. But strangely enough it seems to be the same sort of thing as is going on in Point – people affected by a strange concern which appears to bear no relationship to the truth. It seems to catch hold of those affected by it for no apparent reason. I would like to suspend judgment upon it in the meantime, but this is an aspect of the movement for which I do not care. I was also told that the movement had spread to Bernera and that 16 there had been 'converted'.

28 MARCH

On Monday went out to Crossbost and heard Mr Cameron, Inverness, preach from Galatians 1:24. After the service I ran him in to Stornoway and heard him again from Songs 8:5. Fully 600 were present. I felt the atmosphere distinctly warm. Mr Cameron gave us an excellent sermon, warm, experimental and loving. He seemed to be in his element. It is in the lack of the element of love in my preaching that I come short. Had a conversation with Morrison, Bernera, on the movement in his congregation. It seems to be a more rational work and to have more relation to the preaching of the Word than that of which I have heard in another area. I heard of no extravagances in connection with it.

While visiting on Tuesday in Culregrein came across an interesting case. This was Malcolm Chisholm who sent me the letter stating that Psalm 103:17 had been blessed to him at his brother's funeral at Gravir last year. Until May last year he never opened the Book in the family and had lived quite carelessly as to spiritual things. He appeared to be very broken and very humble and I have no doubt as to his being the subject of a gracious change. As I listened to his story, and surveyed him as I listened, I could not but marvel both at God's sovereignty and His power. He can soon make short work of the proud, rebellious heart and bring the sinner down. As I caught a glimpse of His power I realised in a new way the possibilities of a complete change in the present aspect of religion by a visitation of a day of power from on high.

18 APRIL

Sabbath was a beautiful day. Began our experiment of having double services morning and evening and felt very satisfied with it. I went to the Seminary in the morning for the English service while Weir Campbell, my student assistant, took the Gaelic in the church. Some of

[299]

the members of the session had expressed themselves as dubious as to our getting an English congregation in the morning but I was very gratified to have an attendance of 70.

220 were out at the Prayer Meeting on Thursday when I began to go through Colossians. Rather enjoyed the meeting. At Session afterwards interviewed 23 applicants for baptism. Thankful to get the 'Lochness'[1] petition away last night. It bore 10,251 signatures and formed quite a bulky parcel. May the Lord move the hearts of the Directors to grant the plea of the petition!

When in Glasgow Mr MacLeod of Hope Street informed me that his executive committee[2] had before them the proposal that the General Assembly should release me from my charge for 6 months and that I should be sent to try to stir up the vacant congregations. He asked me to consider the matter and to let him know before the Assembly meets. I find myself willing to go for three months on condition that Stornoway is provided with regular supply during my absence, and I have written Mr MacLeod to that effect.

25 APRIL

The Lord's favour was again manifested in answering our prayers for a good day on Sabbath so that the children to be baptised might be brought out in comfort. We have never yet been in difficulties upon such an occasion through unfavourable weather conditions. God's favours ought to be recorded and taken to heart. They ought to be an encouragement to expectancy in prayer. And is He not just as willing to bless us spiritually? Lord, increase my faith! Spoke in the church in the morning from Psalm 127:3 on children being God's heritage, after which I baptised eight infants.

2 MAY

Sabbath was showery but two of the three children who were to be baptised at the English service in the Seminary were brought out. Spoke from Luke 19:5 on Zacchaeus and think I was able to hold the attention of the very junior congregation I had before me. Although this new arrangement promises to make things difficult for us financially, yet when I saw such a congregation of young people – not fewer than 160 – on a Sabbath morning, I felt that it would be more than a pity to

1 The mail-boat which the owners proposed should leave Stornoway on Sunday evening. The petition, organised by MacRae, was successful.
2 The Public Questions Committee.

drop it.[1] Yet how to make it a really permanent feature is what baffles me. No doubt many were brought out from desire to see a baptismal service, but nevertheless it is quite evident that the material for a permanent and even substantial English congregation is present. Took the opportunity when I had so many young people present to condemn the use of the term 'christening', and to refute the Plymouthite statement that the baptism of infants was instituted by the Church of Rome.

Very much annoyed on Monday by a good woman, a member of the congregation, who came to the Manse to represent the enormity of Kenneth Street Church being closed at 2 o'clock on Sabbaths! It was a thing that hitherto was absolutely unknown and she abundantly strengthened her position by a profusion of Scriptural texts grossly misapplied. I could understand her position if she had been in the habit of attending the 2 o'clock service, but she can make nothing of English and the change does not affect the Gaelic services in any way. What it does is to give two services to the English section instead of one. But nothing mattered with her save the one thing – that Kenneth Street Church should be closed on Sabbath afternoons! I have no patience with that spirit which makes any change in connection with services or meetings a sin. This unreasoning, unreasonable spirit which refuses religion the right to adapt itself to the changed circumstances in which it may chance to find itself has done infinite harm in the Highlands. It seems to think that it is better to die in a rut than to try to get out of it. It is strange, too, how good people can be the main hindrance to every fresh effort to advance the Lord's Cause.

On Tuesday preached in English in the Seminary from Psalm 42:2 in response to an unsigned letter which I recently received in answer to the invitation I gave at the close of the Lectures to any who might have religious difficulties. Fully 160 were present. Enjoyed the service very much. Was pleased to see some present who did not usually come out to a week-night meeting.

Matters seem to be definitely improving religiously in Lewis. Carloway, parts of Point and Bernera, are the seats of revivals. There are certain features connected with these movements which, I must admit, make me somewhat dubious. Kinloch seems to be in a promising way, too, ever since the special meetings, and it appears that the Balallan meeting house is full up to the two front seats at the ordinary prayer meetings.

1 He was compelled by circumstances to revert to the former order in July; the main obstacle in the way of maintaining two English services every Sunday was his lack of a permanent assistant.

9 MAY

On Tuesday at English service took up the second question in the letter which I received, i.e., How may one know the true love of God's people for their Saviour? How may one be assured that one has it? Enjoyed the meeting and a few seemed to be somewhat moved. May the Lord acknowledge it! There is nothing like experimental religion.

23 MAY

Left for the General Assembly on Monday night and had beautiful crossing. We got in to Edinburgh at 3.17 and were able to present ourselves at 5 o'clock at the 2nd sederunt of the Assembly. I was on my feet almost right away in connection with an overture which asked the Publications Committee to publish cheap pamphlets in support of our testimony as a Church. The plea was successful. On Wednesday I registered my dissent against the wiping out of the Foreign Missions Committee debt of £7,000 by raiding the Reserve Fund; other three followed me. I seldom attend an Assembly without registering my dissent. On Thursday the proposal of the Public Questions Committee that I should be set apart for three months, beginning in September, to try to work up the vacancies was adopted. On Friday the Lord High Commissioner – Lord Kinnaird – visited us. It was a most wooden performance. He read every word of his speech, and read it nervously and badly. In doing so he confirmed what I had suspected – that he came in response to an invitation. We had been led to believe that the approach was from the other side and that it was our duty to receive the King's representative. Who invited him? There is no record of any Committee having done so. I seconded Dr Stewart in moving Peter Miller my old class-fellow and our Moderator, to the Hebrew Chair. No other name was proposed. Today went through to Govan and feel very thankful for the respite.

30 MAY

At the morning Gaelic service in Govan had an attendance of about 200. Spoke from 1 John 5:19 on the world lying in wickedness. Enjoyed the afternoon service better when I dealt with Ezekiel 9:4 on marking the sighers. The evening service was also in English. 400 were out, the church being almost full. Felt greatly comforted last week when Mr MacLeod of Hope Street mentioned in connection with my special appointment to work among the vacancies that my ministrations had been greatly owned in Glasgow and that there were several young men in his own congregation who were fruits of my ministry.

On Monday found my way back to Assembly. A report was given in by a Committee which dealt with the lapsing of youth, and in it there was a recommendation as to the forming of organisations to foster friendship among young people which I felt called upon to oppose. I gave warning as to the serious consequences of any attempt to introduce any such thing.[1] There was not much left for Tuesday, and in the evening we finished an Assembly which promised to be a record one in respect to controversy, but which actually proved almost a record for placidity and expedition, for which all felt profoundly thankful. Could not but feel sad, however, at the resignation of Prof. Cameron as Clerk.[2] We will never get another like him and without him the Assembly can never be the same. The old men are going. This was very obvious at the Assembly; only four of them were present. Only seven of the 25 stalwarts of 1900 survive.

20 JUNE

Since Saturday night I bore a burden of melancholy upon my spirit from which I could not get away, nor did I desire to get away from it. 'The days of old to mind I called', and the mystery of life, with its gradual ebbing away, its dreams and its unsatisfied yearnings, came in upon me and I felt oppressed. In youth I yearned towards the future for what I had not got, now I yearn in the self-same way for what I had in those days and for what I have lost in their passing. These longings are earthly, but they are pure, sweet and sad. Are they never to be satisfied, or are they longings which eventually will be met when the Lord creates the new heavens and the new earth? Who can tell? They are a mystery. Are others burdened by them as I am? The sad cadences of Celtic music rouse them at once in me.

On Wednesday evening conducted worship in the Girls' Hostel and read them one of McCheyne's letters. Took the names of Free Church

1 MacRae's views on this subject are given more fully on pp 465-7.
2 J. K. Cameron had been Clerk of the General Assembly since 1900. His resignation was accompanied by a strong expression of his fear that changes were taking place in the Free Church which were tending to give committees a position to which by Scripture and the law of the Church they had no right. Presbyteries, he protested, are 'the radical Courts of the Church . . . If adherence to Constitutional law is not to be strictly observed, the Church may as well scrap her whole Constitution, and be committee ridden'. See his book, *The Clerkship of the General Assembly of The Free Church of Scotland*. J. K. Cameron died in 1944 at which time he was Principal of the F.C. College.

girls who go South in October in pursuance of their studies. 280 were out at the Prayer Meeting on Thursday and rather enjoyed speaking from Colossians 1:4 on faith.

By natural talent and spiritual predilection he was fitted for evangelistic work. The tenor of his varied addresses, along with his pleading earnestness, proclaimed him to be *par excellence* the winner of souls. He would have freely admitted as the clear import of Scripture that ministers are fitted by the Spirit for most varied types of activity in the Church of Christ. Nevertheless, he illustrated in his own person the traditional and basically sound Scottish ideal of 'every minister his own evangelist'. By his own example, also, he demonstrated conspicuously that Calvinism has a message for the unconverted. These two lessons the Church might learn with advantage today.

Peter W. Miller in a note on K.A.M., May, 1969

13 A Three Months' Itinerary in 1936

As already recorded, MacRae was asked by the Public Questions Committee of his denomination if he would undertake a preaching itinerary in the more needy congregations of the Free Church if their proposal to that effect was approved by the General Assembly. The Assembly did sanction this unusual step and required him to labour 'principally among vacant congregations within the bounds of the Southern Synod and the Synod of Sutherland and Caithness, with a view to seeking to persuade the young people of the Church to a greater interest in and zeal for the message and testimony which has been given the Free Church of Scotland to declare.'

His itinerary, however, was arranged by the various Presbyteries concerned and he was to find that the arrangements made did not permit him to stay longest where he was most needed. He left Stornoway on 18 September, 1936, and, until the end of the second week in October, meetings in various congregations in the Glasgow area occupied most of his time, although 'outreach' meetings in Paisley and Renfrew were also included. At the end of each meeting a sheet he had prepared on the testimony of the Free Church was given out, and copies of his booklet, *A Word to the Anxious*, were made available but only to those who requested them. The purpose of the latter restriction was an attempt to assess any real spiritual concern among those who attended and it was made clear that none should ask for one unless they belonged to that category.

We continue from his Diary at the point of his visit to Arran – a return to the island after an absence of many years.

13–16 OCTOBER, 1936: SOUTHEND, ARRAN

Crossed over to Arran on Tuesday forenoon and had a beautiful day for the passage. At Whiting Bay I got the bus and enjoyed the drive round to Sliddery. I found quarters ready for me in Duncan MacAllister's Overdale Boarding House. At 8 o'clock had the first of our meetings. Unfortunately the evening was wet and only 29 were present. Mr MacRury came down from Shiskine, but surely they are dead there, for he was not able to get anyone to accompany him save the driver of the car. Felt very sad in that old familiar church. The fathers, where are they? What power I once felt there! Oh to feel it again!

24 were out on Wednesday night. Spoke from Psalm 26:8 but had no liberty. Apparently things have come to a very low pass in Arran and non-church-going has come in as a plague. In the other church here the average attendance on the Sabbath is about six, and at the Kilmory end a similar state of affairs prevails. Our congregation has not altogether escaped the contagion. Letting apparently has a great deal to do with it.[1] In the summer-time the people think themselves so bound to attend to their visitors that they have not time to attend church and consequently when the winter comes they have not the desire. Poor Arran! It once saw better days.

On Thursday conducted a cottage meeting in Kilmory. 24 were present. I felt almost a breath of the old Southend sweetness. The work here has been badly arranged; in fact there was no arrangement at all; everything was left until I arrived on the scene. The Interim-Moderator had advised me by postcard that he did not think it possible to have a meeting every night. To do the thing properly I should have been on the ground last Sabbath and should have had the whole week at my disposal.

Friday night unfortunately turned out rather wet but 31 were present and I somewhat enjoyed speaking to them from Psalm 60:4, 'Thou hast given a banner to them that fear thee, that it may be displayed because of the truth'. Pled with them not to let down the 'banner' in Southend.

From what I have seen in Southend I by no means consider the case hopeless. A fortnight's intensive, judicious work might work wonders under God's blessing. The revival in Southend 20 years ago threw up material which now is the mainstay of the cause there. Were it not for that movement I am afraid that our congregation would have gone under. What happened then might happen again and the Lord's Cause take a fresh lease of life in Arran. There is no need to despair, but there is much need for real, hard, earnest, prayerful work.

18–21 OCTOBER: RENTON AND HELENSBURGH

I left Sliddery at 10.30 on Saturday morning. The crossing to the Mainland was very rough. To enter Ardrossan was a hopeless proposition and therefore we made for the shelter of the Cumbraes and got ashore at Fairlie Pier. This considerably delayed my arrival in Glasgow and consequently in Dumbarton, but eventually reached the latter place at 7 o'clock. The wind was blowing half-gale force and I was

1 The reference, of course, is to the letting of rooms to holiday-makers which in many places had become a popular source of income.

very glad to get into the warmth of the hospitable Free Church manse. On Sabbath morning weather conditions had considerably improved, for which I felt very thankful as I had to walk 2½ miles out to Renton. 30 were gathered in the Church. Felt annoyed to see a vase of flowers on a table in the lectern and plants on all the window sills, but said nothing lest an unwary word should further reduce an already weak cause. Spoke from Psalm 110:3 and rather enjoyed it. 47 were out in the evening and I had a very good evening in speaking from John 6:37.

On Monday 40 were present and I spoke from Luke 15:18: 'I have sinned'. 37 were out on Tuesday including three from Glasgow. I think it a pity that the effort in Renton was not carried on longer. The atmosphere was very good, and despite the low numbers, I felt encouraged.

On Wednesday evening we held an experimental service in a new field – Helensburgh.

12 came down from Glasgow to encourage it, two were present from Dumbarton and seven came over from Renton. 48 in all were out, so that the local representation amounted to 27.

23–26 OCTOBER: STIRLING

Left for Stirling on Friday afternoon. Found comfortable quarters in Allan Park Lodge, a well-equipped hotel in the west end of the town. Held a service in the church at 7.30 pm. Only thirteen were present (including two from Edinburgh). The church is very fine inside, but the locality and the stairway entrance make it no bargain at the £1000 paid for it. And the congregation is a pretence, a shadow which may fade away at any time. To preach to such a handful in such a building is depressing.

It is long since I have seen such a wet day as we had on Saturday and the audience at the afternoon service only numbered 8, and of those only 5 were local people. Spoke from Psalm 63:5 but felt the service most depressing. When I was last in Stirling things were low enough, but they were quite rosy as compared with the present situation. I am afraid that the end is in sight.[1]

28 OCTOBER–2 NOVEMBER: DUNDEE AND PERTH

On Wednesday went on to Dundee and conducted service at 7.30 in the Hall. 41 were present and I had fair liberty in speaking from Psalm

[1] Further services on the Sunday and the Monday did not change MacRae's opinion and it was subsequently verified in the closure of the Free Church in Stirling.

110:3. Stayed in the Manse, a nice commodious building up on the hill, and here I was made very comfortable.

On Thursday climbed up to the top of the Law which is 572 feet above sea level. A thick, smoky pall lay over the city and obstructed the view Eastwards but to the West and North the outlook was rather pretty, although visibility was none too good. Afterwards we visited St. Peter's. It is a smaller church than I anticipated, being seated for 980. McCheyne's pulpit has been removed to the hall, but I stood in it and felt honoured for the privilege.[1] I left Dundee by the 4.9 train after quite a pleasant stay. The view of the upper reaches of the Firth of Tay as seen from the train was particularly fine in the gleaming light of a brilliant sunset. Arrived in Perth I found my way to the West End Temperance Hotel, quite close to the station, in which I remained during the communion season. At 7.30 I had a service out at Scone.

On Saturday forenoon walked out to Scone in company of a fine young man from Ard-Roag, a warder in the Perth Prison. His wife is one of my own old Kilmaluag flock. At 7.30 pm held a service in the Hall at which 24 were present.

Sabbath was showery and cold but the people got out comfortably enough. Was rather shocked to find only 30 before me on the morning of a Communion Sabbath in Perth. I had no idea that matters had reached such a low ebb. Spoke from Isaiah 53:10 with a measure of freedom. Practically the whole congregation communicated, only five remaining in their seats. In the afternoon went out to Scone and conducted another communion service there. The elders told me, to my amazement, that a young man had interviewed them with a view to 'coming forward' for the first time, and that they did not think it right, since he had the desire, to keep him back and that they accordingly had given him the token. I felt extremely displeased. I felt that these men had done what they had no right to do. I asked the elders whether they were satisfied with him, but from their answer I gathered – as I feared – that they had made little or no examination, and an old deacon who was present said 'He has been well brought up'. 'That may be', I said, 'but the question is, Has he been born again? If you are satisfied on that point, then it is all right'. Elders unfaithful to their duties are one of the banes of our Church. It is high time things were tightened up

1 Built in the 1830's, St Peter's, Dundee, was the scene of McCheyne's ministry from 1836 to 1843. See *Robert Murray McCheyne, Memoir and Remains*, Andrew A. Bonar, 1844 and currently published by the Banner of Truth Trust.

a bit in Perth. No wonder there are so many communicants. In the evening in Perth only 32 were present. Spoke with liberty from John 6:37 and then followed with a short Gaelic service. Felt thankful to get the Sabbath over. A communion in these lax congregations is disturbing and a Sabbath in a hotel is miserable.

On Tuesday left the hotel and went over to Perth Prison where the MacPhees put me up in their quarters. This they did in order that I might have an extra service and put before the congregation their duty in respect of the testimony of the Free Church. Spoke at the meeting from Psalm 60:4 and tried to meet their case as a congregation as well as I could.

7–14 NOVEMBER: FIFE

The train drew out from Waverley Station, Edinburgh, at 4.25 and we had not proceeded far ere darkness fell upon us and blotted out the countryside through which we passed. At Thornton Junction I left the Aberdeen express in which I travelled and after a short delay got into a train which took us down to Leven in 12 minutes. At the Station Miss Jessie Campbell from the Kennoway Manse met me and brought me out to where one of her fellow-teachers waited for us in her car. Thus I got up to Kennoway in the maximum of comfort. The Manse is one of the old country houses of a former age, dignified and pleasantly situated, but rather rambling within. Mrs Campbell, the widow of the late minister, is a stately, well-mannered lady of the old school, and she and her three daughters made me very much at home, so that I spent a very pleasant time in Kennoway.

Sabbath morning was fair, but no intimation had been given of my visit and only 40 were present. Apparently the evening service has been dropped in Kennoway – a fact which does not say much for their spirituality. I cannot understand students coming from Edinburgh and resting content with one forenoon service. I had an evening meeting, but owing to their having become unaccustomed to such a thing, only 28 were present.

On Monday evening had an attendance of 17 in the Hall. The people seemed pleased at the appeal to their loyalty.

Most of the Kennoway people appear to be miners. They seem to be a respectable, quiet people, but I don't think that there is much living religion among them.

I left Kennoway on Tuesday afternoon and a 30-minute run in the bus took me down to Sinclairtown where I found comfortable lodgings with Mrs Jack, 51 Roseabelle Street. 23 years ago I stayed with her during a week-end at Kirkcaldy in my student days, but now she is old, widowed and very lame. Apparently they have tried to do some advertising in this [Kirkcaldy] area, for not only are the meetings advertised in the local paper, but a paragraph had also been inserted, and little handcards issued intimating the meetings. Nevertheless only 28 turned up at the opening meeting at 7.30 pm, and, the service being held in the church, these showed up rather badly in such a large building. The church is a beautiful one, being little over 20 years old, but it is far too large for the little company who use it. The meeting would have been much better held in the Hall, but I did not know till the service was over that there was a hall. Spoke from Luke 19:5 with a measure of liberty but felt the atmosphere cold. Fife is full of self-righteousness, and sinners in this area do not seem to recognise themselves by their spiritual designation. Mrs Jack seems a true-blue Free Church woman, but some of the others connected with the congregation do not impress me favourably. The late minister was no friend to genuine Free Church principles, and those whom he has left behind him here appear to be no better.

On Wednesday I went up to Kinglassie to visit the young minister there. I had about an hour and a half with him and quite enjoyed my visit. The average attendance at Kinglassie is about 50 in the morning, yet the communion roll numbers over 100! Membership in Fife seems to be an ecclesiastical relationship and not a spiritual one – simply, as they put it, a case of 'joining the church'. At night, in Kirkcaldy, my attendance had increased to 43, most of whom were young.

38 were out on Thursday evening, most of them young. Spoke from Psalm 60:4, making special reference to their own duty of bearing the Gospel witness in Kirkcaldy. The address appears to have been appreciated. I think the people will respond all right when the real issues are put plainly before them. Their complaint is that they do not hear these things. I am quite pleased with my Kirkcaldy visit.

On Friday afternoon I proceeded by bus to Dunfermline. The first few miles were along a road which I had tramped one Saturday afternoon 25 years ago when, as a Territorial in the 9th Royal Scots, I set out to explore the neighbourhood of our camp at Balmule. Hungry as a hawk after my long tramp into Kirkcaldy I went into a tea-room and emptied every plate on the table! The bus ran below the green grassy hills upon which we used to manoeuvre in those far-away days and many a memory was awakened.

The Cause in Dunfermline scarcely survives. The hall used by the mission is quite a comfortable one and of a suitable size, but only 12 turned out to the meeting.

14–16 NOVEMBER: COULTER

I left Dunfermline by bus at 8.55 am on Saturday and motored to Inverkeithing where I entrained for Edinburgh, reaching Waverley Station at 10.57. I left by bus again at 5 o'clock and reached Biggar about 6.30. There I was met and conducted to my quarters, a little cottage a short distance outside the town. In the darkness, however, I could see very little of my surroundings.

Sabbath was a dreadful day of rain with a fairly stiff wind. Mr Gibson with whom I stayed had to tramp with me the two miles out to Coulter despite the rain. I thought it very poor of a congregation in which some of the farmers possess cars that the minister should be allowed to walk such a distance in such weather. It certainly would not be permitted in the North. Our legs and feet were very wet ere we got out, but I dried my trousers as well as I could at the vestry fire. No one came near me till the beadle appeared to usher me into the pulpit. Then when the service was over the congregation cleared off the scene at top speed as though I were a leper. Coulter really touches bottom level. It was the only place I visited in which there appeared no evidence of the slightest appreciation of my visit. I spoke from 2 Corinthians 5:17 on the necessity of the new birth, and once I began the beadle promptly fell asleep, and continued so despite the furtive efforts of his wife to arouse him. I do not think my doctrine was appreciated, but it is the very doctrine which they require rubbed well into them until they come to see the folly of their 'joining the Kirk' religion. I cannot understand why the people are allowed to sink into their present state of indifference. As long as Mr Clarkson had the health he tried to give them evening services, but now they have none and don't want any. Apparently the three Church of Scotland congregations in Biggar have a joint evening service, turn about, and most of our people in Biggar go there. I told my host that if they cannot get a small hall in Biggar for the evening service then they should meet in a house. He replied that they had not thought of that, but it came out later in the evening that Professor Cameron, when staying in Biggar some years ago, held evening meetings in the house in which he resided. Apparently he, my host, expected me, too, to go out with him in the evening to the Church of Scotland service, for he kept his boots on, until I made it clear that I had no intention of going. When he heard that, he took them off with the utmost despatch, although I did not ask him to stay in, nor object to his going himself. I cannot remember when I spent such a long and miserable Sabbath.

1–10 DECEMBER[1]: CAITHNESS

Mr MacLennan, being an assessor to the Presbytery of Caithness, which was due to meet at noon, motored me to Wick. I had never been further North than Helmsdale before and much enjoyed the run. The Ord of Caithness at Berriedale proved worse than I had anticipated but we mounted it without difficulty. Some distance North of Helmsdale a stone a little above the road marks the spot where the last wolf in Scotland was killed. In the hill sections north of the Ord snow lay on the road and we had occasional showers. The main north road through Caithness is a beautiful one and we made good speed, sometimes touching 50 miles per hour. My first view of Caithness reminded me very much of Lewis. The moorland, the rocky coast, and the green crofts bordering the highway were all there. We left Lairg at 9.30 and reached Wick at 11.50 which represented very good running. After a hasty cup of tea we hurried to the Presbytery which was attended by five ministers (including ourselves) and five elders.

I had an attendance of 46 at the meeting which was held in the church at 7 o'clock.

On Wednesday Henry Finlayson came in from Greenland and motored me over to Castletown. The intervening country is very flat and uninteresting. I was struck with the way in which paving stones placed on end are made to serve throughout Caithness as fences. Castletown is a decayed village on the coast to the west of Dunnet Head. Its prosperity waned with the passing away of the demand for the one time famous Thurso paving stones. I was driven to the Manse, a large, rather rambling house situated on the main road about the middle of the village, and there I found myself in what was once the centre of the ministry of the godly Dr Auld. In the afternoon we paid a flying visit to Thurso but it was bitterly cold and snow showers were fairly frequent. The billows riding in from the Northern ocean and charging

1 November 17th to 29th was spent in the Presbytery of Dornoch (Sutherland), the record of which is here omitted in the interest of space. His congregations in that Presbytery were as follows: Lochinver 48; Stoer 70; Drumbeg 48; Rosehall 45; Bonar-Bridge 110; Lairg 90; Rosehall (Sunday) 47; Ardgay (Sunday) 150; Elphin 11; Dornoch 120; Rogart 70; Brora 82; Golspie 35; Scourie (Sunday) 52, 75 and 66. His visit to Rogart provided his last opportunity for fellowship with his old friend Dr Donald Munro, newly settled in the manse there after his long years at Ferintosh.

up Thurso Bay were very grand. At night we had an attendance of 57 in the hall. The inclement weather affected the attendance of the older people, for most of my audience were young. The atmosphere was very good and I observed one young woman affected to tears.

On Thursday morning we found the ground coated with snow and prospects for the day appeared very unpromising. However conditions improved considerably as the day advanced. In the afternoon we went for a walk on the Dunnet Sands. The scene was particularly fine. The wind was strong and the billows sweeping in made a fine picture, while the rocky crags of Dunnet Head beyond us added to the general aspect of untamed nature. About 5 o'clock Mr Donald MacKay[1] of Watten called for me and duly conveyed me in his car to Shebster in which township the Free Church of Reay is situated. I was sorry that the journey was undertaken in the darkness for I could see nothing of the surrounding country. The Free Church of Reay is a huge double-roofed structure like the other Free Churches in Caithness, and the tiny audience of 21 made a very poor appearance in it. The wind was very high and the church very draughty; I made the service as brief as I could. The meeting began in Shebster at 6 o'clock; I was due in Thurso at 7.30 pm so that there was no time to lose. As we have no congregation in Thurso the meeting was held in the YMCA Hall, and I simply gave a Gospel address from John 12:21. 55 were present, including 24 who had come by bus and car from Castletown. After the meeting we had a very welcome supper from one of the local merchants who is connected with the Castletown congregation and who was mainly responsible for the organising of the meeting. It was about 11 pm before we reached Watten Manse. Although Caithness is practically treeless, it is not altogether so, and the Manse at Watten is ensconced in a bower of tall, well-grown trees. The wind was high all night and the sound in the trees made me think of the surge of the sea beating on the shore. But Watten is far inland.

Next afternoon Mr MacKay took me for a motor run to the famous John o'Groats. I got a very good view of the Orkneys. I was surprised to see how near they are to the Mainland. I thought the Pentland Firth was much wider. In their general appearance they are very like the Hebrides. They seemed to fill up all the horizon to the North and looked more like another mainland – or a piece of the mainland – than islands.

1 Ordained and inducted to the charge at Duthil in 1923, MacKay subsequently served the congregation of Watten and Bower (Caithness) for upwards of 34 years until his death in 1966.

Doubtless the wider view got on a good day would remove this impression. The coast scenery is wild and impressive, especially as I saw it under lowering wintry skies and enhanced by the majesty of the tumultous seas that rolled in from the cold North. In the evening we set out again for the meeting at Keiss but by this time the ground had got another coating of snow, and ere we reached the church it was snowing heavily. The congregation at Keiss is small but loyal and enthusiastic. 41 were present and they made hearty melody.

On Saturday we proceeded to Latheron for the communion there. In Latheron Principal MacCulloch, late of Hope Street, Glasgow, commenced his ministry, and therefore I was interested to see where he began his career. But, alas, things have altered much since his day and the once over-flowing congregation is a mere handful.

By Sabbath the snow had increased and showers accompanied with high wind were frequent. As the day wore on conditions became much worse until eventually a perfect blizzard was raging. Only 21 were gathered in the large, spacious church, and, there being no heating, the cold was intense. I got through the service as fast as I possibly could and finished five minutes under two hours, which was a record for me.[1] Only 5 communicated. On Monday morning my window was dark with the drift plaster outside and the thick frost films inside. Only 16 were out at the Thanksgiving Service, but I rather enjoyed speaking from Psalm 63:5. At the close gave a short account of my particular mission and gave them the same opportunity to get handbills and booklets as I had done in other places.

On Tuesday I got a phone message from Mr MacVicar, the Dunbeath missionary, to say that, owing to the state of the roads, he had cancelled the meeting which had been arranged for that evening at Borgue. I felt very disappointed, for a decided thaw set in and had the meeting not been cancelled I felt sure that I could have carried on all right. I tackled much worse roads in Lewis last winter. On Wednesday evening I travelled by bus North to Lybster. At the meeting 43 were present, most of them young. After the meeting we had supper in the house of one of the elders and then Mr MacKay of Watten called for me with his car and ran me out to his Manse again.

Thursday was the Watten Fast Day. In the morning I had an attendance of 57. I enjoyed speaking from Hebrews 13:14. At the close I made the usual statement as to my particular mission and distributed 27

1 i.e. for the 'Action' sermon, the 'fencing' of the table, and the two addresses given – one before – and the other after the partaking of the sacrament.

sheets and 15 booklets. It is true that the district is sparsely populated but there might have been more present.

Next morning left Watten Station by the 9.7 train and so my visit to Caithness terminated. I enjoyed it very much and I found matters religious in a better way than I had anticipated from all the doleful accounts I had heard concerning Caithness. Of course I have never seen its former glory.

11 DECEMBER

The abdication of King Edward is the topic of conversation everywhere and I feel quite tired of it. It is a great blessing and a merciful deliverance!

15–16 DECEMBER: THE NORTH COAST

We got away from Lairg shortly after 9 and were soon far into the desolate wilderness which forms the interior of Sutherlandshire. Ere we reached the summit (the Crask) it was snowing heavily and we had some anxiety as to what was to be the outcome. However, as we descended again towards the North Coast we left the showers behind us and the snow on the roads became much lighter; in fact when we got down to sea level it had almost disappeared altogether. Skerray is very isolated, but ought to make quite a pleasant field for a minister and the people appear to be of an attractive type. It is more than a pity that their present minister, Rev Norman Morrison, is so sadly ill. No doubt our visit will appeal to the loyalty of the people. It is to be hoped that the Presbytery will follow up by taking requisite and speedy action. The service was at midday in the church and 50 turned out. The more distant people, however, were hindered by the snow. In the afternoon, after a sumptuous repast for which we were very ready, we pushed on to Bettyhill. By this time the evening had become rather tempestuous but there was no rain. In a sheltered hollow towards the sea we found the Free Church Manse of Farr[1] and old Mr MacKay waiting to receive us. The wind increasing, we had an attendance of only 20 at the meeting which was held in the church at 6 o'clock; yet it was a good meeting and a fine spirit prevailed. At the close Mr MacKay got up and said he wanted to say a word. He expressed in warmest terms his appreciation of the address and said that he had heard nothing like it since his young days, when ministers were not afraid to speak plainly on ecclesiastical matters to their people; and then the poor man became quite soft as he bemoaned the fruitlessness of his labours in Farr.

1 Farr is the name of the parish, Bettyhill the name of the village in which the Free Church and Manse are located.

Next morning (Wednesday) we pushed on to Strathy where we had a meeting at noon. The day continuing very stormy, only 12 were out, but they seemed to be intelligent hearers. Part of the ridging of the church had been carried away by the gale. Both church and manse are in very bad condition and urgently require repairs. After the meeting we had dinner with the MacAulays and left about 2.30 pm. We got back to Lairg about 6 o'clock after a round drive of about 138 miles. The reports on the wireless regarding storms in the West were so disquieting that I decided to accept the invitation to wait where I was till Friday. Friday morning was calm and bright. I was motored in to Dingwall and enjoyed the run very much. About Strathcarron we ran into heavy rain but still the wind held off. I got a shock, however, when the ticket collector in the train told me that I would not get any further than Kyle that day, and that the sailings of the 'Lochness' were disorganised owing to the Stornoway Harbour being blocked by masses of tangled nets displaced by Tuesday night's gale.

A storm had been forecast for Saturday and sure enough we got it. The wind began to rise about 12.30 and by the time we got down to Kyle it was blowing a gale. Fortunately the wind was somewhat after us, W.S.W.; otherwise I do not think that we could have faced it, for in Lewis that evening the wind recorded a speed of 90 miles per hour. For the first two hours we had little to complain of, but after that things began to get lively. One particularly violent heave when we were off the Shiants tumbled over one of the chairs in the lounge – I have only once before seen that happen – and precipitated some of the steerage passengers on to the floor, where they began to scream under the impression that the vessel was sinking. We had left Kyle at 3.25 and we reached Stornoway at 9 o'clock. At Stornoway we had some difficulty in taking the pier. The spray was coming right over the side of the ship and wetting the crowd who waited our arrival on the pier. It was a wild night and I was glad to get on to terra firma and under cover. I have much reason for gratitude for all the care and goodness which was manifested to me in all wanderings and in bringing me safely home.

☐   ☐   ☐

In his itinerary Mr MacRae had preached in 38 congregations, the total number of services amounting to 84 and the aggregate attendance 5087. His handbills stating Free Church principles ran out before the end of November and a re-print was speedily executed by a printer in Golspie. 392 copies of *A Word to the Anxious* were given to those who asked for them, although in some instances he felt that enthusiastic church-officers had not heeded the restriction which he had wanted to observe in the use of this booklet.

The opportunity which these months gave him to observe the spiritual needs in many congregations made a deep impression upon him. Depopulation was certainly contributing to decline in Arran and in many parts of the North, but a not dissimilar weakness in congregations in the Lowland region pointed to the existence of other causes which were evidently contributing to the Church's lack of growth.

In reporting back to the Public Questions Committee MacRae endorsed the General Assembly's judgment that greater effort was needed to awaken interest and zeal for the Church's testimony among the young, and for the rest of his life he continued to act upon this conviction. In the course of the Report, which he wrote after his return to Stornoway he said:

'I approached my task under a keen sense of my own insufficiency for it but convinced me that the best way in which our young people could be led to take an interest in the testimony in their Church would be to preach the Gospel to them, and then, having shown the necessity for the continuance of such a witness in our day, to point out that that could only be through their own faithfulness and steadfastness to the truth once delivered to the saints. . . .

'Unfortunately the area allotted me was far too large to admit of the plan being systematically worked out, and in the Northern Presbyteries I had to content myself with holding one meeting in each congregation. Results therefore cannot but be superficial, but that does not mean that the experiment has failed; it only means that it did not have a fair trial. Where it did have a fair trial, as at Partick, the meetings were of such a nature that they could scarcely be deemed anything else but encouraging. There my stock of booklets (50) on the closing night was completely cleared out and not a few applicants had to go a-wanting. I would have been thankful to see three or four going and therefore such a response took me completely by surprise. My experience throughout practically the whole of my itinerary has confirmed me in the conviction that this idea should be seriously taken up and worked out throughout the Church. That our young people need such tuition is only too evident: and just as evident is the fact that, once they are reached, they respond to it. Repeatedly, in the course of my tour, appreciation was expressed of the effort made to enlighten them, and the complaint was more than once made that questions bearing upon the Church's testimony were never brought before them. Our young people require all they can get to give them stability in these present evil times, and if the Church fails to educate them as to the value of the great trust handed down to them through the years, their falling away will be the inevitable result of her neglect. The great mission of some churches would almost appear to be to amuse their young people, but to neglect them and allow them to go their own way is almost as fatal. For such work, then, there is a definite call today, but to appoint one individual for a few months to give attention to it is only trifling with the question. It is much too large for any one man. If it is to be done adequately, then it can only be by the Presbyteries throughout the Church giving their whole attention and energy to the matter . . .

'It would not be right to conclude this Report without expressing my most grateful appreciation of the kindness which I received every-where at the hands of my fellow ministers and other warm-hearted friends; their home was made my home and I sat at their table as one of themselves. This privilege of Christian fellowship was one which I shall ever treasure. To the Public Questions Committee I also tender my grateful thanks for their co-operation and forbearance, and I recognise that I am under a distinct debt of gratitude to the Conveners, past and present, for their warm and lively interest and valued help in my efforts.'

So ended three of the most memorable months in his long ministry.

Weimar. Hitler spoke about politics, the Idea, and organisation. Deep and Mystical. Almost like a gospel. One shudders as one skirts the abyss of life with him. I thank Fate which gave us this man.

Joseph Goebbels, July 1926.
(*The Goebbels Diaries*, Louis P. Lochner, 1948, p. xvii.)

On the return journey, Tom Johnston (Secretary of State for Scotland) dined us at the Station Hotel at Glasgow, and I sat next to Harry Hopkins (President Roosevelt's closest adviser and confidant), an unkempt figure. After a time he got up and, turning to the Prime Minister said:

'I suppose you wish to know what I am going to say to President Roosevelt on my return. Well, I'm going to quote you one verse from the Book of Books in the truth of which Mr Johnston's mother and my own Scottish mother were brought up: "Whither thou goest, I will go; and where thou lodgest, I will lodge; thy people shall be my people, and thy God my God".' Then he added very quietly: 'Even to the end.'

I was surprised to find the P.M. in tears. He knew what it meant. Even to us the words seemed like a rope thrown to a drowning man.

Entry for January 1941 in
Winston Churchill, The struggle for survival 1940–1965
Taken from the diaries of Lord Moran, p. 6.

14 Preservation from National Destruction, 1940–42

The pattern of the early years of MacRae's ministry in Lewis was to continue with comparatively little variation through more than three decades and in the remainder of this volume we will, therefore, confine attention to matters of more particular interest and not always take the selections from his diaries in their chronological sequence.

If all his entries relating to the Second World War were to be printed they would constitute a book in themselves. At first sight it may seem surprising that a hard-pressed pastor of a large congregation, in a remote part of the United Kingdom, should have kept such a detailed, and often day-to-day, record of the War. There were reasons for it. In the first instance, information from the news media was, of course, more readily available than it had been in the slow-moving world of 1914–1918 and, 'born in the army' as he was, MacRae could not do other than follow it closely. But, more important, his attention to the War was motivated by his realisation of the consequences which would flow from defeat. Though he was far from identifying Britain with righteousness, he believed that behind Hitler's lust for a 'Thousand-Year Reich' was a *blitzkrieg* of the powers of darkness upon the kingdom of God. If Nazi Germany triumphed there would be catastrophic spiritual evils inflicted upon the world. The War was, therefore, in the first instance, an occasion for prayer; conjoined with that was the duty of maintaining an intelligent watchfulness and it was from this stand point that he kept his own personal records.

At the time of Germany's threatened attack on Czechoslavakia in September 1938, MacRae was preaching at communion services in Portree, Skye. On 26 September 1938, the same day that the British Foreign Office warned that she would render support if any such attack was made, he wrote:

'I enjoyed the fellowship at the Manse. Everything, however, was darkened by the international situation. Tension was evident everywhere. On the wireless I heard Hitler's speech at the very darkest stage of the crisis. It was very evident that the whole thing with its tremendous and methodical cheering had been carefully arranged to impress the world. I could not understand a word of the speech but the voice sounded like the voice of a madman. I believe that the man is not normal. That night an extraordinary finger of light stretched across the

[323]

sky from East to West and combined with the speech to which we had just listened the effect of it was to infect us all with a certain inexplicable eeriness.'

Three days later, Neville Chamberlain, the British Prime-Minister flew to Munich and to the act of appeasement which surrendered part of Czechoslovakia to Hitler. After Bohemia fell to the German dictator in the following March he turned his attention to Poland which, though an ally of Britain, he invaded on 1 September 1939. At last convinced that the Nazis did intend to rule Europe, Britain and France declared war on Germany two days later.

The summer communion services in Stornoway, held traditionally on the last Sunday in August, were held in 1939 in the imminent prospect of the coming War, and the evening of that Lord's Day differed from anything ever before seen in the Island. The services of the day were solemn beyond description. After they were over, as naval reservists[1] filed to the steamer pier to board the 'Lochness', the harbour area – usually deserted at such an hour – was as full of people as if it had been a Market Day. The local press reported:

The crowd on the pier that night was probably the largest which has ever been gathered there in the history of Stornoway, and it was a strangely silent company. There was not even a hum of conversation ... There was a steady stream of reservists through the crowd and up the gangway, but their leave-taking with friends was also silent. A quiet handshake, at most a simple word of farewell, then up with the kit bag and away. It was eerie to see the deck of the ship filling up until there was scarcely standing room, and not a whisper rising from the crowd.

Then suddenly the silence was broken. At first a single voice rising tremulously in the air of a Gaelic psalm – a precentor giving out the line. Some of the crowd round about the Fish Mart door took up the verse and the solemn words of the 46th Psalm swelled out to the tune Stroudwater ...

That night, although war had not yet actually broken upon us, we felt that the scene was symbolic. It was not the 'Lochness' which was casting off her ropes and leaving the shelter of a quiet anchorage: man himself was setting out on a new voyage across seas uncharted except in the foreseeing Providence of the Almighty.

MacRae's diary for 1939 appears to have been lost and the following entries, therefore, commence in the fifth month of the War by which time from eight to ten per cent of the Lewis population was estimated to be on active service or under training.[2]

1 Men who did a period of training yearly in the Navy with the understanding that they would be the first to be 'called-up' in the event of war.
2 Commenting on the fact that the figure was lower than in World War I, a

MONDAY, 1 JANUARY, 1940

New Year's Day was bright and frosty. Attendances today were good – 240 at the service at midday and 230 at the prayer meeting in the evening. The year has come in amid the gloom of a colossal war which only seems to be beginning. How it will end who can tell? In the four months of war the Island has had its losses, but considering that over 2,000 of its young men are serving, these have been much slighter than might well have been expected, and for that we have great reason for thankfulness. Spiritually the outlook is not promising, but the darkest hour is before dawn.

WEDNESDAY, 3 JANUARY

Am kept busy trying to get names and addresses of service men, so as to forward them some good literature. So far have got 20 at sea – most on mine-sweepers – 2 in the Air Force, and 19 in the Army.

FRIDAY, 5 JANUARY

The frost has gone but the weather still continues quiet and favourable. Tonight over 100 Territorials and other service men return from their New Year leave. There are many sore hearts in the town tonight, for the leave presages their early transportation to France.[1] Was very pleased with one of them, Donald Macdonald, the son of one of my elders, who came to visit me tonight ere leaving. He requested a copy of the *Pilgrim's Progress*. From the accounts I get, the spiritual provision for these poor fellows is shocking. 20 minutes is the average length of their religious services when conducted by English chaplains. Fortunately, our boys, no matter how careless they may be, know better than to be deceived by such a travesty of religion.

SATURDAY, 6 JANUARY

Apparently yesterday a submarine was reported in the Minch and the 'Lochness' had an escort of four planes. One would almost be inclined

---

newspaper gave the estimation that probably only fifteen per cent of the population was of military age. The problem common throughout the Highlands had reached Lewis: 'The population contains a far smaller proportion than in 1914 of men in the prime, and a far greater proportion of those whose active years are passed.'

1 A British Expeditionary Force had been sent to France and placed under French command after the outbreak of war but, like the French forces, it remained stationary, awaiting German attack in this period which – on account of German inactivity – was called the 'Phoney War'.

to think that the enemy had some inkling of the fact that so many troops were to cross just now. These things bring the war very close to us.

MONDAY, 8 JANUARY

Mary left for Glasgow at 3 o'clock this morning. Conditions were perfect so far as the weather was concerned, mild and a dead calm, but the risk of mines out in the Minch weighed heavily upon my spirit. Had I been the traveller I would not have minded much, but to have Mary exposed to such risks was an entirely different matter, and the sight of so many life-belts laid out beside passengers made me very uneasy. But what could we do other than commit her to the Lord's keeping? We miss her very much and the house seems dull without her. May she be well and happy in Glasgow!

THURSDAY, 11 JANUARY

Wrote letter to *Glasgow Herald* tonight with reference to the Prime Minister's appeal to the middle classes to be prepared to do without their luxuries, and pointed out that Christian citizens would take such appeals seriously when the Government made an attempt to check the shocking financial and moral waste represented by the drink, betting and amusements orgies of the nation. Declared that our statesmen spoke as though there were no God, and that when Britain ought to be on her knees, frivolity, intemperance, and Sabbath desecration ran riot through the land.

THURSDAY, 18 JANUARY

The garden walk this morning showed a snow-fall of $4\frac{1}{4}$ inches, the deepest I have seen, I think, since we came to Lewis. A bright sun melted the more exposed surface of the snow, but at 5 pm 5 degrees of frost were registered in the summer-house.

TUESDAY, 6 FEBRUARY

Today has been a soldier's day. First of all I had a letter from John MacArthur from Catterick Camp. He remembers the approaching communion and feels lonely at the thought of it. Next I had a visit from Neil Campbell, at home on leave from France at present. After prayer I discerned some moistness about his eyes. Would that he were brought into the kingdom! I also heard that another lad, now with the remainder of the Battery boys[1] out in France, said to his mother on his return home from the Church on the Sabbath evening, when he was home on leave, 'I never heard a sermon until tonight', and then he went on to talk of the many privileges they had in Stornoway without being aware of it.

WEDNESDAY, 7 FEBRUARY

News has come of the mining and loss of the Liverpool-Belfast mail steamer. As the waters there are more sheltered than the Minch we cannot but feel uneasy about our own steamer.

TUESDAY, 19 MARCH

Felt very depressed all day at the international news. Italy seems to be about to enter the lists against us and there are indications which point to the ascendancy of German influence in Rumania. I wonder if our miserable Prime Minister[2] will think now that the time is opportune for the appointment of a Day of Humiliation and Prayer? What a tragedy it is for Britain that she has such a man over her! Few men in history have committed such a succession of gigantic blunders. He betrayed Abyssinia, Spain and Czechoslovakia, and helped our enemies to their present power whereby they are trying to crush us.

FRIDAY, 10 MAY

Today has come the tragic news that Germany has invaded Holland and Belgium. Now the war has really begun and soon death will take its dreadful toll. The French and British are moving northwards to their help.

WEDNESDAY, 15 MAY

Like a thunderclap has come the news of the surrender of Holland. The Dutch made much of their preparedness and resolutely refused help from the Allies. Their folly is now evident to the world. Five days was the limit of their preparedness.

1 The men of the Volunteer Force Artillery Company belonged to Ross-shire and formed the only artillery unit in North West Scotland. Before 1914 this force had changed its name to The Ross Mountain Battery and during the First World War it played a valiant part in the landings at Gallipoli. In 1940 it was part of the Highland Division serving in France.
2 Neville Chamberlain. He resigned as prime minister on the 10th May, 1940, and was succeeded by Winston S. Churchill. It is significant to note that, excepting Halifax – an Anglo Catholic – who gave inconsistent support to the policy of appeasement, the leading supporters of appeasement came from a religious background of liberal nonconformity. Chamberlain was a Unitarian, Sir John Simon the son of a Congregationalist minister and Sir Samuel Hoare a member of an anglicanized Quaker family.

SATURDAY, 18 MAY

Under the influence of the rapidly darkening international outlook and the amazing success of the German assault upon the allies in Belgium and Northern France, after midnight framed a fresh sermon on Abraham praying for Sodom (Gen. 18:33) and laid aside the discourse which I had prepared for the morning service.

SABBATH, 19 MAY

Preached sermon on Genesis 18:33 to congregation of 450 with a measure of liberty. At night when I took the service in the Church, had rather a grim subject – God's continual anger with the wicked – Psalm 7:11. These subjects I take to be necessary but there is no sweetness in them for my soul.

TUESDAY, 28 MAY

Left Glasgow at 7.20 am. At Fort William we were shocked to hear that the King of Belgium had surrendered with 300,000 of his troops, and had done so without any intimation to his allies. The result is that our army is in imminent danger of being surrounded, their Northern flank thus being left open. Only a miracle can save them.

SATURDAY, I JUNE

The impossible seems to have happened. Our army in Flanders together with the French have succeeded in reaching Dunkirk and with the aid of the navy evacuation is going on apace. The material loss is bound to be enormous but what a miracle it is that our army has not been destroyed! Is not this an answer to prayer?

MONDAY, 3 JUNE

The newspapers announce that the Dunkirk evacuation has been completed, 335,000 troops having been safely brought away. The loss, however, has been heavy – 30,000 men and the whole material, armaments and supply of the army. These have been made useless for the enemy, but still the loss is ours. The leader in the *Glasgow Herald*, in commenting on the evacuation, quotes as apt the opening verse of Psalm 124. I wonder how many recognise it as a wonderful answer to the Day of Prayer yesterday week? Despite the grave losses and the fact that in the first round the Germans have scored an astonishing success, the prowess of our troops during the last few days, when outnumbered 4 to I and out-gunned and out-planed, shows their superiority to the

Germans, and indicates that when supported adequately by tanks and planes they will give a different account of themselves.

WEDNESDAY, 5 JUNE

At 4 am the second great German onslaught began and a gigantic battle rages from West of the Maginot Line to the sea. The new French method now is to allow the tanks to pass through their lines and to close up behind them, thus cutting off petrol and other supplies, while anti-tank guns and planes deal with them further back.

MONDAY, 10 JUNE

Italy entered the war today and Narvik has been evacuated. The whole western seaboard from Abbeville northwards to within the Arctic circle is now in German hands. Events are moving with extraordinary rapidity and the outlook is daily becoming darker. What Italy will do remains to be seen, but her entry at this critical hour makes the situation still more desperate. Unless the Lord intervenes we are likely to go under, although the very thought is intolerable. Oh that Britain would repent!

THURSDAY, 13 JUNE

Today, in accordance with the Assembly injunction, observed a Day of Humiliation and Prayer.

Bad news still continues to arrive. A British division has been cut off in Normandy and 6000 prisoners taken. The Germans have crossed the Seine and the Marne and are only 11 miles from Paris.

FRIDAY, 14 JUNE

The Germans entered Paris at 7 am today. The French President has addressed an appeal to President Roosevelt for immediate help. People are now afraid that the French will capitulate.

Apparently the Germans have overwhelming air power. Returned soldiers from Belguim say that for three weeks they never saw the R.A.F. If America is to save the situation she must stop trifling and act at once.

MONDAY, 17 JUNE

Today came the dreadful news which stunned us all, that France had surrendered and that hostilities had ceased at 7 o'clock this morning. For the first time, admitted to my own mind the *possibility* of defeat – nay, it now amounts to *probability*. Life has suddenly gone grey and not worth living. It appears very likely now that the Christian Church in

[329]

Britain is once again to be thrust into the furnace of persecution. The prospects before us all are very dark and one shudders to contemplate the probabilities of the situation. Meantime what is to happen to our own troops in France? How is our own local unit hundreds of miles from the coast – East of Metz – to get clear? This is a sad day indeed.

TUESDAY, 18 JUNE

Churchill has declared that Britain will carry on the struggle, and in a broadcast tonight he sums up all that can be said in our favour. His words may rescue some from despondency, but they cannot improve the situation which appears pretty hopeless without God's help, and of seeking that help there seems to be no indication. The French have been refused any peace terms short of unconditional surrender and therefore they are fighting on, but their front is broken into four sections and their armies are in danger of being surrounded.

WEDNESDAY, 19 JUNE

Air raiding has now begun. About 100 German planes last night raided East Anglia and neighbouring coasts. 12 were killed and many injured, the most damage being done in a village in Cambridgeshire.

THURSDAY, 20 JUNE

Nearly 300 were out at the Prayer Meeting tonight when I spoke from Psalm 23:4. I am inclined to think that the seriousness of the war situation is leading to a betterment in attendance upon the means of grace.

Another raid was carried out last night, this time upon the N.E. counties of England. I am rather anxious about the local Battery lads who had been posted behind the Maginot Line east of Metz. Tonight a telegram has come to town stating that a certain gunner was missing. That seems to indicate that they have got through and are now in this country, or, at any rate, in touch with Headquarters.

SATURDAY, 22 JUNE

The French are still fighting but most of their country is in the hands of the Germans. The French cabinet meet tonight to consider the German terms. We hope that they will be such that they will feel constrained to continue the struggle from their North African colonies. If Germany gets the French fleet we may speedily expect invasion. May the Lord prevent this!

MONDAY, 24 JUNE

France has agreed to Germany's terms which include the giving over of her air force and fleet. To give over a fleet which has never been defeated, nor even injured, is surely a craven action on the part of any nation.[1] If the French navy meekly yields to the fiat of their politicians then let the patriotism of France be heard of no more.

TUESDAY, 2 JULY

Reports appear in the press of German troop concentrations in Norway. That means that they are preparing an invasion of Ireland and probably the Hebrides. I feel very uneasy about our unprotected state in this area. We have not a gun of any description, a search-light nor a soldier – except upon leave – in the whole Island.

FRIDAY, 5 JULY

By the action of the British fleet the strong French naval squadron at Oran has been prevented from surrendering themselves into German hands.

TUESDAY, 16 JULY

Began to go round the families of the local Territorials who are reported missing in France, prior to May 15, to instruct them as to how they might get a letter through to them if they be prisoners, by the instrumentality of the International Red Cross in Geneva. Felt the mission trying but at the same time felt that I was bringing a measure of comfort to the poor people.

SATURDAY, 20 JULY

Hitler today called upon Britain to surrender, offering her the option of peace or destruction, and declaring that common-sense could see no point in a continuance of the strife, and that he at no time sought to injure the British Empire.[2]

MONDAY, 22 JULY

Lord Halifax, the Foreign Secretary, answered Hitler's speech tonight. it was a splendid, high-toned reply, and the strongly religious note,

1 Britain was then unaware that, contrary to the terms of the Armistice, French naval commanders had received secret instructions to sink their ships rather than let them fall into German hands. This explains the action of the British at Oran recorded on 5 July.
2 At the same time Hitler had given orders on 16 July that preparations should go forward for invading Britain.

with its emphasis upon prayer, made every Christian in the country rejoice. From such a high source I am unspeakably glad to have such a speech.

FRIDAY, 26 JULY

Have spent most of the week visiting the homes of the missing Territorials and am glad to get the task completed. If only now we could hear from them!

During the week the enemy have been making sporadic raids upon us. Wick has suffered severely. Aberdeen, Peterhead, Leith, Port Glasgow and Greenock have all been visited. This seems like preliminary sparring. One only wonders that the waiting period is so long extended. America promises overwhelming help but it will be from two to four years yet before it can mature. It is hoped that the war will be over before then.

SATURDAY, 3 AUGUST

Today has brought the war closer to us. Last night German aircraft attacked an oil tanker near Cape Wrath and succeeded in setting her on fire. This evening she was towed in here still burning.

WEDNESDAY, 7 AUGUST

The lull in hostilities still continues, but I do not suppose that it can last much longer. That it is most useful to us is very evident from the fact that one of our young men in an anti-tank regiment told me that his unit which is stationed on the Dorset coast has only two old naval guns. However, equipment is coming in rapidly.

FRIDAY, 9 AUGUST

Reports have come through of a great air battle over the Channel which are distinctly encouraging. The Germans attacked a convoy with larger forces than ever they have used for such work.

MONDAY, 12 AUGUST

Another heavy raid has taken place over the week-end and the Germans have lost 60 planes. We have lost 26.[1] A troopship coming over with Canadians has been torpedoed with considerable loss.

1 This was part of a whole series of engagements – 'the battle of Britain' – for the control of the air over south-east England. The full attack of the *Luftwaffe* began on 13 August and extended to 15 September by which time they had lost 1,733 planes against an R.A.F. loss of 915.

WEDNESDAY, 4 SEPTEMBER

News of the captured Battery boys is now beginning to trickle through.[1] Tidings have been received of over a score of them up to date – news came today of eight – and parents and others who have not yet got word are becoming increasingly anxious. I trust that many more will yet be reported. Would that Donald MacDonald, my elder, got news of his boy![2]

MONDAY, 9 SEPTEMBER

London on Saturday evening got a very heavy raid in which over 300 were killed and over 1000 seriously wounded. The attack upon towns has now begun. Yesterday was observed throughout the Empire as a Day of Prayer.

FRIDAY, 13 SEPTEMBER

This week has been a week of heavy air raids upon London. Buckingham Palace has been twice hit. Churchill has given warning of German preparations for invasion, and the concentration of ships, barges and troops at certain ports on the coastline extending from France to Norway. These concentrations have been heavily attacked by the R.A.F. It is a solemn time when deliverance should be earnestly sought at the hand of the Lord.[3]

MONDAY, 28 OCTOBER

Italy attacked Greece at 6 o'clock this morning. This is in full accord with the acknowledged policy of the powers under dictatorships – to strike suddenly and with full strength. It is to be hoped now that Turkey will stand by her mutual defence pact with Greece.

THURSDAY, 7 NOVEMBER

The death list since the bombing started in September is very formidable – 8,000 in September and 6,000 in October. I feel increasingly anxious about ourselves in this town. We are between a seaplane base and a military aerodrome (for bombers) and there isn't a single anti-

---

1 They had been captured with the Highland Division at St Valery and spent the remainder of the war in prisoner-of-war camps in Germany.
2 He was later reported to be a prisoner and came home safely at the end of the war.
3 On 7 September British defence forces had been warned by the signal 'Cromwell' that invasion was imminent. On 17 September, as we now know, Hitler postponed it 'until further notice'.

aircraft gun or fighter plane to defend us. Defences should have had the first consideration, for as things are, if the enemy discover the base and the aerodrome there is nothing to prevent them bombing them to bits – and the town too.

WEDNESDAY, 13 NOVEMBER

A German raider is playing havoc with our shipping in the Atlantic. At the same time comes the news of the sinking of the crack German liner, the 'Bremen', by a British submarine.

SATURDAY, 16 NOVEMBER

Today at about 1.15 pm two German planes machine-gunned the aerodrome at Steinish and the wireless station at Ness, but fortunately there were no casualties. I suppose, now we are discovered, that we can look out for more. But who can excuse the criminal folly of building aerodromes and sea-plane bases before any defensive measures have been taken? Today those two Nazi machines could have done as they pleased. This is more Sassanach blundering; no Scotsman would be guilty of such folly. Coventry has had a dreadful raid – 1000 casualties.

TUESDAY, 26 NOVEMBER

Heard today that 'Lord Haw-Haw'[1] had been threatening the Stornoway churches with extinction. So another like him threatened Jerusalem long ago, but he was not suffered to shoot an arrow against the city.

THURSDAY, 5 DECEMBER

The Greeks are still pressing back the Italians, but our shipping outlook remains no brighter. American help at sea is becoming urgently necessary. Most of all divine help is needful. Prayer meetings in the air-raid shelters in Bristol – which has suffered heavily from aircraft – would seem to indicate that this at last is beginning to come home to the people.

TUESDAY, 10 DECEMBER

A letter from Dr MacLean informs me that I have been appointed Officiating Chaplain to the local R.A.F. Squadron. Received the information with rather mixed feelings. I don't know how it is going to work.

1 William Joyce, Germany's principal English broadcaster, who, though of Southern Irish parentage, had spent most of his life in England prior to August 1939. He was executed after the War.

MONDAY, 30 DECEMBER

Asked the R.A.F. Commanding Officer for a list of the men under my care, with their billets.[1]

TUESDAY, 31 DECEMBER

The year has closed in a mantle of white. Today has been a good winter's day – bright and with occasional showers of snow. The snow, however, does not lie to any depth. To many this year has brought sorrow, sudden and crushing. Who knows what awaits us in the coming year? Have visited two sorrowful homes today – one where a young widow mourned over her grief, the other where a young girl lay in the last stages of consumption.

WEDNESDAY, 19 MARCH, 1941

Details of the bombing of Glasgow last Thursday and Friday nights are now beginning to come through. 500 were killed and 800 wounded, and among the former are Mrs MacLeod, Dudley Drive, and two of her daughters. Felt very much upset by such ghastly news. How inscrutable are the divine providences! How devilish are the ways of man!

FRIDAY, 21 MARCH

Heard tonight that so many of the Grant Street congregation (Glasgow) were killed that poor Mr Sutherland[2] could not preach last Sabbath. Who can wonder at it? The poor man must be heart-broken.

SABBATH, 23 MARCH

The King desired that the day should be a special day of intercession for the country, and with that in view preached in the morning from 1 Peter 5:6 on humiliation as the way to ultimate exaltation. 270 were present. Made special reference to the increased wickedness of the town since the war broke out. In the afternoon spoke to a congregation of 60 from Genesis 13:5–13 on Lot's choice. In the Seminary spoke very directly and forcibly to the young from Ecclesiastes 12:1. About 110 were present. The School being closed greatly reducing the attendance. At the Gaelic spoke from Hosea 13:9 and pointed out how the

---

1 His spiritual responsibilities in Stornoway were never heavier than at this period. On one Sunday he speaks of taking five services!
2 Andrew Sutherland, minister of Duke Street Free Church, Glasgow, since 1921. He was shortly to accept a call to Tobermory. Ordained in 1910 he served several charges in his long ministry but the years at Duke Street were the most memorable.

wickedness of Cromwell Street was likely to bring divine judgment upon the town. My audience seemed to be impressed and the atmosphere was very solemn.

MONDAY, 7 APRIL

Germany has attacked Greece and Yugoslavia, and Britain has an army of 40,000 engaged. So far the attack has been held. The German-Italian advance in Libya has been held too.

THURSDAY, 10 APRIL

The news today is very depressing. In Libya we have lost 2000 taken as prisoners. In Greece the Germans have reached Salonica, have taken many prisoners, and cut up the Yugoslav army, isolating them in the hills. I am afraid that we have not yet mastered the Germans' mechanised technique. Things look very, very dark. The German military machine seems to be all-prevailing. Oh that Britain would look to the Lord! It looks very much as though we are to have a repetition of the collapse of France last year.

SATURDAY, 26 APRIL

The Germans state that the British are evacuating their forces from Greece, leaving only covering troops. I believe it to be true and so Hitler has blasted through another front. His next move appears to be Turkey and Spain. By failing to uphold Greece and Yugoslavia, Turkey has put herself in a hopeless position.

MONDAY, 28 APRIL

The evacuation of our troops from Greece goes on. The Germans claim to have entered Athens. I trust our troops and material will get away.

Yesterday, for the first time in its history, Stornoway witnessed a game of football on the Lord's Day. The offenders were naval men. Today, after praying that things might be made easy for me, I interviewed the Commanding Officer at the Base, Captain Wauchope, and was very much gratified at the heartiness of his response. He told me that these men had broken the regulations and must have smuggled the football on shore, and that he would signal from the Base at once that there must be no more such offences. He undertook also to notify the commanders of all the vessels that there must he no more football on the Sabbath. Felt infinitely grateful to the Lord for all His goodness and for answering my prayer.

[336]

SATURDAY, 24 MAY

At night was thunderstruck to hear on the wireless that HMS Hood, the largest ship in the British navy, had blown up in an encounter with the new German battleship 'Bismarck' off Greenland.

WEDNESDAY, 28 MAY

The adjutant of the RAF told me today that there are now 300 men of the RAF in the Island. Of these 255 are Church of England, 26 are R.C.'s and 19 of other denominations. Naval vessels are beginning to cluster here increasingly, so that the danger of an air raid increases every day.

WEDNESDAY, 11 JUNE

Lewis promises soon to be an area of first-class importance militarily. More airmen are arriving daily and the work at the aerodrome seems to be on the grand scale. Another aerodrome has been begun at Ness, and it is reported that huts for 300 men are being put up in Uig.

SATURDAY, 21 JUNE

Germany is heaping up forces on the Russian frontier from Finland to the Black Sea, and it begins to appear as though Hitler, shirking a direct attack upon Britain, seeks to strengthen himself before doing so by the subjugation of Russia, so that he can break right through to the Pacific and join hands with Japan. Russia's oil, grain and factories would help him immensely. Meanwhile Turkey has been adroitly bought over by a non-aggression pact. That seems to be his next move.

MONDAY, 23 JUNE

The Germans attacked Russia yesterday on a front extending from Finland to the Black Sea. They declared that Russia will be defeated in 10 days' time or at the most within a fortnight.

WEDNESDAY, 25 JUNE

Another German plane came over the town early this morning. It is difficult to understand the delay in sending on fighters when the runway has been ready for them for over a week.

FRIDAY, 18 JULY

The news from Russia is not too good. Slowly but surely the Germans seem to be smashing their way through the Stalin line. It is true that their progress is very much slower than was anticipated, but there are indications which show that the morale of the Russian troops is beginning to deteriorate. Yet the cost to the Germans may yet prove fatal to them. If only their way to the Caspian oil fields can be kept blocked while the Russians continue their air-raids upon the Rumanian sources of supply, lack of oil may prove their ultimate undoing. It is now four weeks since the Germans launched their attack upon Russia.

WEDNESDAY, 23 JULY

Was told today that the R.A.F. were playing football on Sabbath on the Melbost pitch. Wrote the Commanding Officer regarding the matter and asked him to act as the naval authorities have done in prohibiting games on the Sabbath. Perhaps the defence of the Sabbath furnishes another reason for my remaining in Stornoway.[1] In Glasgow the Sabbath is gone in any case. Here it is in the balance.

MONDAY 28 JULY

The Commanding Officer of the R.A.F., after plying the usual pretext that the arduous duties of the men allow them no other day free for recreation, has promised that there will be no more 'Sunday games'. I have told him that the people of this Island are too intimate with the fighting services to be impressed by such an argument, and that they recognise that the demand for 'Sunday games' arises from ignorance of Christian principles and consequent disregard for them. I suggested that the men might more profitably use up their surplus energies by walking in to the church services in Stornoway, and assured him that I would be delighted to see them.

THURSDAY, 11 SEPTEMBER

The war in Russia is as fierce as ever. The Germans are now investing Leningrad, but they seem to have a formidable task, and in the central front they are being beaten back by the Russians. Of late their progress has been very slow and at enormous cost.

FRIDAY, 19 SEPTEMBER

A soldier, a member of the Tanks Corps home on leave, told me that he had been twice in France recently – that our troops were making raids and doing what damage they could, and re-embarking before the enemy had time to strike back. He stated also that paratroops were used for the same purpose and that they were very successful.

1 MacRae was, at this time, under call from the Duke Street Free Church congregation in Glasgow. Shortly afterwards he stopped this call.

23. The old Free Church Manse, Stornoway, the right-hand window on the ground floor was the author's study.

24. Characteristic scenery on Lewis (Balallan).

25. The Free Church, Stornoway.

26. Stornoway Free Church Sabbath School in the 1930's

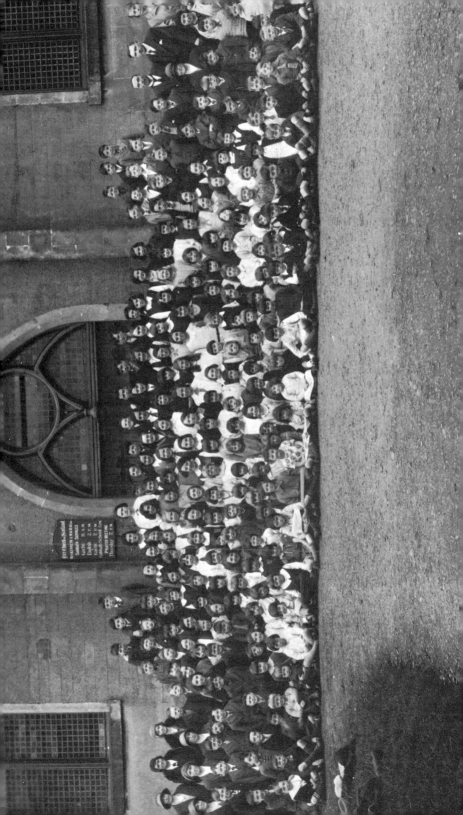

27. At Ardelve, 1953, with James Johnstone (an elder at Beauly) Norman Macleod (his son-in-law) and (seated) Kenneth MacLeay, holding Kenneth Macleod (his grandson).

28. Attending to sheep with his daughter Mary, at the Ardelve manse.

29. At Edinburgh, in 1955.

30. In his study, aged 78.

31. Catherine MacRae, taken a few weeks before her death.

32. The 600-yard-long procession, bearing the coffin to Sandwick Cemetery. This photograph was first published in the *Scottish Daily Express* on May 5, 1964, under the head-line 'Farewell to a friend'. The newspaper also reported that 'hundreds of women lined the streets, many of them weeping'.

ERECTED BY
STORNOWAY FREE CHURCH
CONGREGATION
IN AFFECTIONATE REMEMBRANCE OF
Rev. KENNETH A. MACRAE M.A.
THEIR BELOVED PASTOR FOR 33 YEARS
ORDAINED 1915
DIED 5TH MAY 1964 AGED 80 YEARS
A MAN OF GOD
WIDELY KNOWN AND HIGHLY RESPECTED
POSSESSED OF STRONG CONVICTIONS HE
HAD THE COURAGE TO CONTEND FOR THEM.
IN THE WORK OF THE MINISTRY – PULPIT
PASTORAL AND ADMINISTRATIVE – HE
ADORNED HIS OFFICE

"WELL DONE THOU GOOD AND FAITHFUL SERVANT".

MACRAE

"THEY THAT TURN MANY TO RIGHTEOUSNESS SHALL SHINE
AS THE STARS FOR EVER AND EVER".

33. The grave at Sandwick.

WEDNESDAY, 8 OCTOBER

The Germans have initiated another great offensive upon the Russian front under the direct supervision of Hitler himself, and backed up by all the psychological factors which he knows so well how to use. Apparently, if this fails, the Germans are doomed to a winter campaign in Russia, and their prestige in large measure will be gone.

THURSDAY, 16 OCTOBER

The Germans are still making progress and are within 70 miles of Moscow. In the South they are beginning to get within striking distance of the Caucasus.

MONDAY, 20 OCTOBER

Japan seems to be upon the edge of some drastic move. If she attacks Russia, will America act at last? The Germans are steadily drawing nearer to Moscow.

TUESDAY, 4 NOVEMBER

Today I completed my 58th year, but I feel that, could I live without going near a mirror, I could well believe that I was still a young man, for that is how I feel. But the mirror tells a different tale. How difficult to realise that it must all end one day!

MONDAY, 8 DECEMBER

For the past fortnight or more Japan has made a pretence of carrying on negotiations with America with a view to establishing good relations in the Pacific, and has sent two envoys to Washington to carry on the discussions. The move was a blind under which she planned to get in a heavy blow before her intentions were known. Today comes the news that she has cast off the mask, and simultaneously with a declaration of war on America and Britain, she has struck her well-planned blow. An island [Pearl Harbour] in Hawaii was heavily raided, with 3000 casualties; certain other islands belonging to America and forming part of her air defence were also attacked, as well as Hong Kong and Singapore. At the same time she landed troops in Thailand and attempted the same in Malaya.

TUESDAY, 9 DECEMBER

In these days the Psalms impress me as being peculiarly apt. There is no

M

hymnary suitable for such a day. At worship this morning the treachery of Japan was vividly set forth in the verses we sang:

The heathen are sunk in the pit which they themselves prepared,
And in the net which they have hid their own feet fast are snared.
The Lord is by the judgment known which he himself hath wrought;
The sinners' hands do make the snares wherewith themselves are caught.

There we have the forecast for Japan.

WEDNESDAY, 10 DECEMBER

Today has come the stunning news of the loss of two of our best battleships – the 'Prince of Wales' and the 'Repulse' – sunk by Japanese planes. Apparently the Jap air-force must be more efficient and powerful than has been bargained for. With Russia holding up Hitler and the situation in Libya looking more favourable, I thought we had turned the corner, but things now look blacker than they have done since long.

THURSDAY, 11 DECEMBER

2,300 survivors from the 'Prince of Wales' and the 'Repulse' have been rescued. American planes have sunk a Japanese battleship, a cruiser and a destroyer, but the Japanese have captured the Island of Guam, an advanced American base. They have also occupied Bangkok. Germany and Italy have declared war upon America, and America upon them. The Japanese landing on the North Malayan coast seems to be making some progress and their seizing the aerodrome there led to the disaster by which we lost our ships.

WEDNESDAY, 24 DECEMBER

Got a wire from Ness this evening asking me to give a service there tomorrow night. I am willing to go, but I have no petrol for such a journey. I have used all my supplementary coupons, and can get no more petrol until my basic rations become due next month.[1]

TUESDAY, 30 DECEMBER

Feel depressed. Although, considering all things, we have great reason for thankfulness that we have such peace in this Island, and that we have

1 It seems that he was trying to manage on around 10 gallons of petrol per month, which included an extra petrol allowance. In applying for the extra allowance he had stated that he had a congregation of over 2,000 souls, living in a wide area, that he required a car also for two district meetings each week and for communion and other services throughout the Island. Around Stornoway itself his car only averaged 20 miles per gallon.

passed through great perils from which we have almost miraculously been delivered, yet the blindness and the increasing wickedness of the people, combined with the dark aspect of affairs in the Far East, constrain me to the opinion that the end is not yet in sight. Along with all this, a terrible absence of the Spirit shows me that God's displeasure with this generation is to be manifested yet a while. I very much feel the removal of our young people to munitions and other government works. The services will be poor without them.

WEDNESDAY, 31 DECEMBER

So ends the year! May next year bring in better things and end this awful war! Since the year began we have won, lost, and again won Libya; Hitler has committed his greatest blunder by attacking Russia, and after initial successes, now he seems not only to be effectively checked but to be beaten back. We have had a wonderful period of relief from the dreadful air-raids to which we were exposed last winter, but Japan has come into the scene, deprived us of Hong Kong, and it seems to be only a matter of days till they over-run the Philippines. Singapore, then, will be next and Alaska.

SATURDAY, 7 FEBRUARY, 1942

Today got the best news in the world – that Mary made public profession of Christ at the Communion at Dingwall last Sabbath. This is what I have been praying for for many a day, and now that the Lord has answered me my heart is filled with gratitude and praise.

TUESDAY, 17 FEBRUARY

The news of the fall of Singapore with our whole army there consisting of 60,000 men taken prisoner, came as a dreadful shock. It is strange how the Japs are carrying everything before them, especially after making a rather indifferent figure in China during the last four years. It is to be feared that with Singapore out of the way they will be able to accelerate their conquests towards India and Australia. The Argylls and the Gordons are both among the captured troops.

THURSDAY, 26 FEBRUARY

The international outlook is very depressing. The series of retreats characteristic of the Malayan campaign has now set in in Burmah, and most serious of all perhaps is the announcement that the U-boat

[341]

campaign has again become a menace and that our recent shipping losses have been very serious. Russia remains the only bright spot in the picture. America still shows no sign of moving – she talks of her mammoth war programme, but that is all. Meanwhile the Japanese flood rolls on unabated.

THURSDAY, 2 APRIL

Last night we had an invasion practice in which commando troops tried to seize the local aerodrome and the radio location station at Shader. It would appear that their effort was regarded as unsuccessful and that the Home Guard were too many for them.

TUESDAY, 2 JUNE

After the meeting, heard the news that one of our most promising young men, Alistair Mackay of the R.A.F., is missing on reconaissance work over the North Sea. Feel very troubled about it, although I cling to the hope that he may turn up yet. But how often does it turn out that the best are taken and the worthless escape!

On two successive nights over 1000 British planes raided Germany, visiting Cologne the first night and then Essen. We lost 44 bombers on the first raid and 37 on the second. The tank battle in Libya still continues with great losses of material on both sides.

FRIDAY, 19 JUNE

The war news from all fronts is gloomy. Our army in Libya has been driven back to the frontier and Tobruk has again been isolated. We now occupy the position we had last November. No doubt our losses in men and material are heavy. The recent attack upon the convoy for Malta and Tobruk has cost us so heavily that nothing more definite than statements telling us so has yet appeared. The authorities appear to be afraid to tell the truth. In Russia the fall of Sebastopol may be expected any day. At sea the losses of the Allies are greater than the replacements. After a period when undue optimism appeared to prevail, our position seems to be becoming desperate. This is the gloomiest week this year. Our newspapers, under governmental direction, are tantalising. One would imagine on reading them that our defeats were victories. It gives one to fear that matters are very much worse than we know. Oh when will the eyes of this people be opened to their need of the help of the Lord?

MONDAY, 22 JUNE

News has come in today of one of the worst reverses of the war. Tobruk has fallen and 25,000 men have been captured with all their equipment. The explanation now is that the Germans have a super-efficient anti-tank gun, but there always seems to be something. The repeated surrender of such huge masses of men seems to suggest that Britain's soldiers in this war have neither the stamina nor discipline which carried their predecessors through many a hard-fought field, and that they simply cannot stand up to the Germans. At least that is what I fear. I never felt so much inclined to question our final victory as I now do, since we passed the dark days of Dunkirk.

TUESDAY, 23 JUNE

The Germans are gradually winning in upon Sebastopol and I expect that is the next reverse we must prepare for. I am afraid that Malta will follow at no distant date, and then the struggle for Egypt and the Caucasus will begin in earnest – the struggle that will decide the outcome of the war. The U-boat campaign begins again to assume alarming proportions on the American coast.

THURSDAY, 25 JUNE

The Germans have now crossed the Egyptian frontier and penetrated about 50 miles.

FRIDAY, 26 JUNE

The German advance in Egypt still continues. Sebastopol seems to be at its last gasp. By tank action at night the Germans seem to be making definite headway again on the main Russian front. Bremen has been raided by over 1000 of our bombers. We have lost 52 planes. Truly the news brings little comfort. America still talks of her vast production, but her troops have not appeared on the firing line yet – apart from the campaign in the Philippines.

MONDAY, 29 JUNE

The war news today is very bad. The Germans have taken Mersa Matruh, which was supposed to be very strongly fortified and in difficult tank country, together with 6,000 prisoners. Such surrendering never occurred before in British history. Surely our troops have lost the ancient stamina of their race. But it is not to be wondered at. With the present generation, principle has gone to the wall and the masses have been living with nothing higher in view than their own gratification. In the testing time such a nation fails and thus it is with us. Pleasure and drink have sapped away the iron out of our constitution. The situation is very grave. Will the country wake up at last? Troops are now being sent out in frantic haste, but as usual they will probably be too late. People are now beginning to suggest that we are being sold by traitors high in authority, but I cannot accept that.

THURSDAY, 2 JULY

Today the news of the fall of Sebastopol has come in – a sore blow for the Russians. Yet they have made the enemy pay very dearly.

FRIDAY, 10 JULY

The lull still continues in Egypt. Rommel is expected to strike again soon, and when he does it will be hard. In Russia the Germans have reached the Don and at one point crossed it, but the Russians are giving ground slowly and inflicting immense losses on the enemy. A year ago the Germans were driving forward at an irresistible pace and their propaganda machine declared that Russia would be defeated in 10 days or at most in a fortnight. Every boast in this war, on either side, has been falsified.

FRIDAY, 17 JULY

We are told that we have now reached the most critical stage of the war since the Battle of Britain, that Germany is exerting all her strength, totally regardless of losses, in an effort to break through the Russian defence, and that the next three months will decide the issue. Should she fail then, her failure no doubt will be final, for she will have spent her strength while her adversaries have only grown more powerful. May the Lord in His mercy avert the calamity we fear!

THURSDAY, 30 JULY

The German advance still continues. They are now far into the Caucasus and threaten to cut off the Northern Russian armies from their oil supplies. It is evident that reports of German oil shortage is a fiction; otherwise they could never carry on an offensive upon such a colossal scale.

THURSDAY, 27 AUGUST

The German advance in the Caucasus continues steadily and the fall of Stalingrad seems to be imminent. The chances of Russia's surviving until the winter are now very poor. If she collapses, then will come the dreadful time which we have been so long spared.

THURSDAY, 3 SEPTEMBER

Today was appointed by the King as a Day of Prayer, but so far as I could see, there was very little done about it. Business went on as usual. Had it been a day appointed for anything else there would be no end of stir and activity. The morning was wet but we had a congregation of 110 in the forenoon at the prayer meeting in the Seminary. About 400 were out at the service in the evening.

Today heralds the beginning of the fourth year of war. What will it bring? Our enemies show no sign of weakening yet. Russia is in the balance. If she does go down, the war will last for years, but if she can wear Germany out, perhaps this may be the closing year. May it be so! Rommel has again attacked in Egypt and has gained a little ground.

MONDAY, 7 SEPTEMBER

The news from Egypt is good. In some mysterious way our forces seem to have found out that they have emerged from the recent battles on top, and that Rommel has had to retire after a bad mauling. The movement seems to be just as unaccountable and unexpected as our own recent retreat from Libya. Quite evidently it is the direct outcome of our day of prayer.

TUESDAY, 15 SEPTEMBER

Today the distressing news came that the body of poor Alistair Mackay had been found upon the Islay coast. The remains are to be sent home. In spite of everything, I was very unwilling to abandon hope that he would eventually turn up somewhere, but that hope must be given up now. It is a great mystery that such a promising young life should so suddenly be cut away, but it is only a mystery as long as we are dominated by the feeling that this life is of more importance than the next.

FRIDAY, 18 SEPTEMBER

Alistair Mackay's funeral was held from the Free Church today. The service was partly in Gaelic (as Alistair himself would have wished) and partly in English. There was a large attendance, which included a detachment of the R.A.F., and the service was very impressive. I felt near to losing my balance myself. Poor Alistair! What a short course! Just like a bud beginning to open, but only to be cut away! How mysterious God's providences sometimes are! Felt very downcast after it was all over.

SABBATH, 20 SEPTEMBER

At night I had 420 in the Church and enjoyed some liberty in preaching from Psalm 89:15 on the people who know the joyful sound. After the service, said good-bye to Willie MacLeod[1] who leaves in the morning. He goes to the R.A.F. I shall miss him very much. We are being stripped of our best and left very bare.

FRIDAY, 2 OCTOBER

The Germans are now fighting in the streets of Stalingrad which is more or less a mass of ruins. The Japanese are being driven back by the Australians in New Guinea after advancing to within 30 miles of Port Moresby.

WEDNESDAY, 14 OCTOBER

The course of the war since the day of prayer has taken on a more favourable complexion, not that we can claim any victories for our forces, but a stop seems to have been put to the progress of our enemies throughout the world and our air supremacy is now beginning to show itself. Stalingrad still holds out, the Caucasus still remains an iron bastion against the German attacks, the situation in Egypt appears more favourable, and the Japanese still fall back in New Guinea.

FRIDAY, 16 OCTOBER

The lull at Stalingrad is now over, and the meaning of it now appears in an attack of overwhelming violence and force in which 3,000 German bombers were over the city. The Russians have been compelled to give ground and the end may indeed be near, but it is possible that this massing of bombers at one spot may prove the Germans' undoing. May it be so!

1 A teacher of classics (latterly principal of his department) in the Nicolson Institute, Stornoway. He was one of MacRae's elders.

MONDAY, 2 NOVEMBER

The news from Egypt is much better. After a stern battle lasting over a week the German lines have been pierced and Rommel is in retreat with the Eighth Army closely following him.[1]

SATURDAY 7 NOVEMBER

The Germans have been driven back 100 miles to near Matrah and so far they have attempted no stand. Prisoners now amount to 13,000.

MONDAY, 9 NOVEMBER

Things are moving fast in North Africa. Rommel is now back in Libya and six Italian divisions with their full equipment, abandoned by the retreating Germans, have been captured. American troops, with a strong British naval escort, and supported by the R.A.F., have landed at various points in Morocco and Algeria, and severe fighting is going on. If French North Africa can be secured Rommel will be between two fires. Hitler is beginning to fulminate again, a sign that he recognises the need of the Germans for some spurring up. He declares that he will never capitulate, a most significant statement, for it implies a very different outlook from that which was his when he began the war, and when in his view speedy victory was inevitable.

THURSDAY, 12 NOVEMBER

Correspondents with the forces are making out that of Rommel's army of 100,000 men and 700 tanks, only 20,000 men and 40 tanks remain, but I fear that such estimates are only 'wishful thinking'. We under-estimated his strength before, and to our heavy loss. I hope we will not do so again.

At present the general aspect of the war situation seems distinctly promising. Everywhere the trend of events seems to have turned against our enemies. The Americans are consolidating their position in Morocco and Algeria and have received permission from the Bey of Tunisia to march through to Libya. The German attacks upon Stalingrad and the Caucasus have all been halted. The Japanese are still falling back in New Guinea and seem to be getting the worst of it in the Solomons. Italy is as good as off the map. Hitler's horizon is darkening. May the Lord end it all soon!

1 This was the battle of Alamein, which commenced on 23 October with the British Eighth Army under the command of General Montgomery. In this prolonged action Rommel lost fully a half of his men.

FRIDAY, 13 NOVEMBER

Events in the war sphere are still moving quickly. Hitler has marched into and occupied Vichy France as a measure of defence against invasion from the Mediterranean. Rommel must have been badly smashed, for he has abandoned Bardia and Tobruk without attempting to stand.

An order has come out for the ringing of church bells on Sabbath in recognition of our victory in Egypt and to call the people to thanksgiving and continued prayer. The order – or recommendation – is well-worded, and stresses the desirability of thanksgiving in humility for mercies received.

THURSDAY, 19 NOVEMBER

The naval battle off the Solomon Islands has gone definitely in favour of the Americans, and the Japanese fleet has been driven off with heavy losses. Japanese air-power seems to be rapidly declining.

Axis troops are gathering in to Tunis by sea and air.

Before the First British Army landed in North Africa their commander, General Anderson, issued a service booklet for use of the troops which concluded with an appeal to ask God's blessing upon their enterprise, and on the day before they landed a service was held upon the ships.

TUESDAY, 24 NOVEMBER

The Russians have now to record a further victory, this time south-west of Stalingrad. The Germans lost 15,000 men in the battle in the Caucasus; in this latter battle they left 14,000 dead behind them and 13,000 prisoners.

FRIDAY, 27 NOVEMBER

The Russian offensive North and South of Stalingrad has now assumed immense proportions. The Germans are reported to have suffered over 200,000 casualties, inclusive of prisoners. Three German divisions, which were surrounded, have surrendered. The advance still continues but the Germans are rushing up reinforcements. Their forces in front of Stalingrad, said to number about 250,000, are now in increased danger of being encircled.

MONDAY, 30 NOVEMBER

So far as the war is concerned November has been a month of uniform good news. It came in with the tidings of the breach of Rommel's lines in Egypt. Since then the Eighth Army have chased the Germans back 800 miles, Northern French Africa has been seized by the Allies, and the Russians have begun their great offensive which is still proceeding.

THURSDAY, 31 DECEMBER

So far as the war is concerned prospects look much better than a year ago. The last two months have brought uniform good tidings. The Russian advance still continues and the position of the German armies becomes increasingly serious. In Africa in the meantime matters are hanging fire, apparently because of the massing of material and supplies for the offensive which will take place whenever we feel strong enough for it.

☐　　☐　　☐

MacRae's judgment that the decisive turning points in the War had been passed by the close of 1942 was correct. Nazi might was weakening under the impossibility of fighting world powers on two fronts – in Russia and North Africa. When their forces in Tunis finally surrendered in May 1943 the allies followed up by landing in Sicily; by January 1944 the Russians had pushed the Germans back across the Polish border, and in June 1944 the last act in the drama began with the invasion of Normandy.

All these events and others were followed closely by the diarist until the end of the War. The extracts in the preceding pages may convey to those who have no remembrance of these years some idea of how British Christians saw that conflict. Of course, in some matters of detail MacRae's record was inaccurate and yet it is noteworthy that as the War progressed, in his broad assessment of events, his judgment was clearer than that of the very leaders of the Third Reich. While he penned his diary in the Outer Hebrides, Joseph Goebbels, right-hand man to Hitler, was similarly employed in Berlin but how different are the two records! Ignorance of God's ways was the leading characteristic of the man whose charred diaries were to be found lying in the courtyard of the German Propaganda Ministry when the Russians entered Berlin.

'As always', Goebbels wrote on 31 January, 1942, 'the Fuehrer is at his post. As long as he is there, one need not worry about the future. As long as he can give us the strength of his spirit and the power of his manliness, no evil can reach us'. Again, on 8 May, 1943, he wrote: 'The Fuehrer gave expression to his unshakable conviction that the Reich will be the master of all Europe. We shall yet have to engage in many fights, but these will undoubtedly lead to magnificent victories. Thereafter, the way to world domination is practically certain. To dominate Europe will be to assume the leadership of the world.'

Blinded by confidence in man, he could not see what Kenneth MacRae saw before 1942 was over. In the summer of 1943 Goebbels still dreamed with Hitler of the peace that would come when they would be 'master of all Europe'. God was not in his thoughts, yet as the German North-African campaign finally failed Goebbels did write with respect to Rommel's troubles: 'We on our own part have also left nothing undone. But the forces of the elements are stronger than we'.

In November 1943 he ridicules, for his own satisfaction, a speech which George VI had delivered to Parliament in London: 'It is as inane as can be, and bubbles over with childish phrases. England, he maintains, has won victory with the aid of God.'

But a few days later, under a night sky which reflected the burning devastation of the German capital, he wrote: 'The sky above Berlin is bloody, deep red, and awe-inspiringly beautiful. I just can't stand looking at it . . . It seems as though all the elements of fate and nature have conspired against us to create difficulties. If only frost would set in, so that our tanks might move again in the East!'

The end came in May 1945. MacRae wrote on 3 May: 'The Germans now seem to be cracking on all fronts. Berlin has fallen to the Russians, the German army in Italy is smashed and in fragments and German troops are said to be evacuating Holland. The Germans say that Hitler has been killed in action in Berlin, but the statement is probably false. The probability is that Hitler left Berlin long ago. But how the tide has turned! This is the doing of the Lord and is wondrous in our eyes.'

The truth was that Hitler had committed suicide in the air-raid bunker of the Reich's Chancellery on April 30. Goebbels died by the same means twenty-four hours later.

German representatives signed an unconditional surrender on 7 May. Two days after this end of hostilities in Europe a special Peace Day was observed throughout the country. In the morning of that day MacRae preached to 290 of his people from Psalm 37:35–39 on 'The Triumph and Overthrow of the Wicked'. In the evening more than 300 gathered to hear him preach again. His notes of that evening sermon are as follows:

OUR GREAT DELIVERANCE

If it had not been the Lord who was on our side, now may Israel say,
etc.   Ps. 124:1–8

Intro This was the song sung in the streets of Edinburgh by the Covenanters
on their deliverance from the persecuting hand of the Prelacy. We
have reason to sing it today.

I OUR PERIL

1. Our enemies.

    1. They were strong.   2. They were prepared.   3. They were over-
    whelming.

2. Our weakness.

    1. We were weak.   2. We were unprepared.   3. We stood alone.

3. Their snare

    1. Their air-ships.   2. Their U boats.   3. Their plan of invasion.

II OUR DELIVERANCE

1. It was entirely due to the Lord being on our side – we could not save
    ourselves.

2. But how do we know that? Did our wickedness deserve divine
    assistance?

    1. How could He be on the side of such wickedness as the Germans
    perpetrated?

    (2) How could He be with those who persecuted the Jews?

    (3) Humanly speaking, gospel light was largely dependent upon
    Britain.

3. Its miraculous parts:

    1. Dunkirk 2. The Battle of Britain 3. The attack on Russia
    4. The difference re use of secret weapons on either side. The flying
    bomb was too late.

4. Its completeness – v. 7.

III OUR PROSPECTS

1. Surely we are not to continue sinning against our Deliverer.

2. Surely He should be our confidence.

3. And our praise.

4. We should never forget that He can cast us down as easily as He
    raised us up.

On the next day he noted in his diary, 'The prisoners of war from Germany are now beginning to come home. It is a happy time for them and their people, but a very sore time for those whose loved ones will never return'. By that date over a quarter of a million men from the United Kingdom had died in the conflict since 1939 and casualties were to continue for another three months until the war in the Pacific ended in August. 14 August, 1945 contains his last 'war' entry:

'Shortly before mid-night tonight the great news came through of the end of the great war and the surrender of Japan. Peace is now on earth, but what will come of it? We have reason to rejoice with trembling.'

Christians in consort are an abridgment of heaven, shining like a firmament of bright stars.

As sincerity is the heart of religion, so society is the breath of religion; it helps to preserve it alive. Christian conference is a great help to perseverance. The very countenance of a good man makes us cheerful; our sight of him is reviving to us. When Paul saw the brethren he blessed God, and took courage, Acts 28:15. When many mariners pull at a rope together, they strive with the more alacrity; therefore Christ sent his disciples by two and two, Mark 6:7. The great apostle expected comfort from the Romans' company, and hoped to confirm them by his, Rom. 1:11,12. The closer the stones of the edifice are joined together, the stronger is the building. Grace is the oil of gladness; and the more of this oil, the more of gladness. When Paul's faith and the Romans' met in one channel, such a river of oil would be a river of pleasure. The union of such flames could not but become a good fire, to refresh and rejoice their hearts.

Surely, of all fellowships, this is the only good fellowship. Next to communion with God, there is no communion like the communion of saints.

From George Swinnock (1627–1673), *The Christian Man's Calling*

15 A Collection of Memories

The Passing of Donald Munro and George Mackay

21 JUNE, 1937

On Saturday the 19th I motored to Dornoch after breakfast and preached in Gaelic from Romans 16:20 and then in English from the same text. Immediately after the service we left for the funeral of Dr Munro[1] at Rogart. The narrow entrances to the Manse were thronged with cars and there was much confusion. In the church there was a service, partly in Gaelic and partly in English, presided over by Mr Campbell [Dingwall], and in the Manse Mr MacKay [Fearn], conducted a service in English in which I was asked to take part. It was only when I entered into the Manse that I realised what had happened, and during the singing of the very appropriate verses of Psalm 107:29–31 I felt quite overcome. I felt then that I had truly lost my dear friend as far as this world was concerned. He was buried in a beautiful spot high up among the hills, not many miles distant from the lonely house at the head of Strath Brora in which he first saw the light. It would have been more appropriate had he been laid with his parents in the old graveyard of Rogart but there was no room for him there; but the new cemetery in which he – or rather his dust – was interred is not far away. There we left all that was mortal of dear Dr Munro and I came away with a sad heart and a feeling of loneliness which I could scarcely express. I felt that I was drifting out with the tide and that soon my course would be finished too, that already the order of things which I represented was out-of-date and ready to perish. Nineteen Free Church ministers were present at the funeral. Had it not been a Saturday the representation would have been even better.

14 JULY, 1945

In the afternoon visited the beautiful spot where lies the dust of my faithful old friend Dr Munro. The gates were locked and we had to climb over them in order to reach it. My mind was full of memories of

1 Donald Munro, had moved from Ferintosh to Rogart, Sutherland, in January 1936. After an operation which had to be performed in his manse he died suddenly on June 16, 1937. Manuscript records of Dr Munro's on some of the Christians of Sutherland eventually came into Mr MacRae's hands in 1946; these he edited in part, and they were eventually published by the Free Church Publications Committee in 1953 under the title *Records of Grace in Sutherland*.

the day when last I stood there – a sad, sorrowful day – now 8 years ago. He lies there; I come back. It may well be that I shall never return again. I have no expectation of it. How strange is life! How difficult to understand!

8 JUNE, 1942

Got news today that our good friend in Fearn has taken a slight shock. He lost his speech, but it has now come back to him and he can read. It will be a great loss to the Church if Mr Mackay's preaching days are over, for undoubtedly he was the Church's best preacher.

19 AUGUST, 1942

Mr Mackay is very much better, is going about and is able to converse quite freely. At the same time he complains of lack of power to transform his thoughts into accurate speech. Occasionally he uses a wrong word, generally a pronoun, but his power to recall names of persons and places is vastly improved. Yet I fear he will never be able to preach again, which will be tremendous loss for the Church, for there is no other preacher among us who can compare with him.

30 JUNE, 1943

Left Fearn at 8.30 am. Cannot say that I was sorry to do so. Find Fearn now fearfully depressing – everything is so changed and sad. What a terrible change has come over my old friend! He used to be so charged with vim and courage. Now it is all vanished, and he is a poor, little, old man. Poor George! He was a matchless preacher, and preaching was his glory, but he will never preach again.

25 MAY, 1944: EDINBURGH [GENERAL ASSEMBLY]

At the morning sederunt to my great grief intimation was made of the death of my dear old friend, George Mackay of Fearn. No doubt it is better, for he was simply eating his heart out at this enforced inactivity. He lived for preaching and when that was taken away from him he had nothing left to live for. Another master preacher has been silenced and I have lost a good friend.

'After Many Days'

26 SEPTEMBER, 1938

I was interested to learn that Jane Stoddart of Staffin had been savingly wrought upon through means of a sermon which I preached in Kilmaluag from Hebrews 2:3 on Sabbath evening 17 February, 1924. This sermon was the last of a special series of sermons which I had held during the preceding week and my notes certify that I had exceptional liberty and power that evening. What reason I have for gratitude to the Most High and what reason I have to be patient while sowing the seed! The results may be long in coming to the surface but the work will not be in vain.

18 APRIL, 1940

From Kyle to Inverness had the company of Katie Ann Ross of Kilmaluag (now Mrs MacKay of Staffin). Was very gratified to hear from her that the great crisis of her life took place in 1927 when I was at the Duke Street Communion.

2 NOVEMBER, 1940

Heard today of one case in which the Hospital ministrations seem to have been of definite value. A man in Culregrein told me that he got a blessing when a patient in the Hospital three years ago as I stood by his bedside when he was very low. It is most encouraging to know this, and it will help me to visit these institutions with a greater expectation of some good being achieved.

25 NOVEMBER, 1941

Heard tonight of a young woman – now the wife of a deacon in Habost – who was blessed when I preached at Lionel on the Sabbath night of the Communion in October, 1927. That was a service I shall never forget. I was sure that something was done then. Here is the evidence – after many days.

13 APRIL, 1942: LOCHGILPHEAD

Visited a great deal today and found that the old ties are still strong. I could gather from what was said to me that the Lochgilphead people were of the opinion that my ministry there had been greatly owned, and, indeed, although I knew it not at the time, I cannot but realise now in the light of its fruits that it was indeed so. The thought is an encouraging one. Perhaps it is fruit in later years that will bring to light what my ministry in Stornoway counts for. In any case, I shall hope so. But, oh I wish that I still had my Lochgilphead zeal and earnestness!

17 JUNE, 1943: KILMALUAG

The day was beautiful and I spent it very agreeably going through the old friends in Aird and Balmacqueen. Changes are many. Some have

[357]

gone, others have grown old, and the children of old time are no longer so . . . Dear Kilmaluag! What happy days I spent there! Felt, as I often have, that I would like it to provide my last resting place. I think I can see more clearly now than ever before, that the Lord did bless my labours in my old congregation for most of what is to the fore there now – and spiritually it is the richest congregation in the island – is the fruit of my ministry. This is acknowledged by the people and I cannot deny it. Although I often mourned, it is my encouragement now.

On Preachers and Preaching

On Friday morning Rev. Murdo Campbell of Partick Highland [Free Church, Glasgow] preached in Gaelic from Psalm 72-6. I was greatly taken with him. He preached a warm, orderly evangelical sermon, which bore a note seldom heard now-a-days i.e., that known as experimental. . . . [1936]

Mr —— said a great deal, but very little of it, except what bore upon the last clause, had any relation to his text. It was quite evident that he had not tried to get at the meaning of his text nor to study it. He shouted and banged, however, to such an extent, that he seemed to get the better of the nerves of some of the country girls. Fortunately they were able to control themselves, but I felt very displeased. . . . [1940]

Doubtless he regards himself as an expository preacher as he just gradually moves through a verse – or verses – saying whatever strikes him as he does so, but there is no attempt at orderly arrangement and the various steps of his progress are not marked off so that his listeners can appreciate them. The result is that although he has many good thoughts one finds difficulty in sustaining prolonged attention and to carry away a sermon from him is an impossibility even to the strongest memory. . . . [1940]

Learn: (1) When you have finished preparation of your sermon to fix hooks to it – hooks catch fish. Bait with love; (2) To appeal to the young – they are the hope of the Church; (3) To let yourself go as to speech – expect the words to be supplied as you need them. [1940 – a note at the end of the year]

I had the feeling today after both morning and evening services that it would be much easier to preach if only there were some way whereby the effect of our discourses were registered. When we engage in other things we see the effect of our operations, but after preaching, as a rule, there is naught but a death – like silence, and we have not the slightest idea as to whether we have done any good at all. . . . [1942]

I preached in Gaelic from Habakkuk 3:2. John MacSween followed in English and preached from Psalm 32:6. It was a remarkably able performance and I enjoyed it immensely – I do not remember when I heard anything so able. And ability was combined with rare spirituality. As I listened to him I thought that when the Lord is raising up such young men, He must surely have something to do with the Free Church after all.... [1943]

This has been a good day and I came home full of thankfulness and feeling that I would very gladly preach yet a fourth sermon. The Lord has softened my hard heart today and made me glad. I feel tonight that the gospel is the only thing that saves life from being a tragedy. ... [1944]

In the evening Mr F. preached from Hebrews 7:19. He was very good, especially in his presentation of the experimental effects of the law upon the heart of the awakened sinner. On the brighter side of his text he had less to say. That is where my weakness as a preacher also lies....

I spoke from Mark 5:17. Felt comfortable enough in expression but feel rather disappointed after it. The advice of one of the old divines (John Newton, I think) occurs to me: 'Catch them with honey'. Yet we cannot ignore the law.... [1944]

I spoke from Isaiah 2:10–22, but did not much enjoy it. Am doubtful if I shall carry on that exposition much further. I find that dealing with a text is generally more agreeable than dealing with a passage. Perhaps I ought to combine the two methods.... [1944]

I spoke from 2 Corinthians 13:14 on the blessing of the Trinity and enjoyed it. Feel greatly exercised as to the wisdom of giving sermons deeply doctrinal. I enjoy them exceedingly myself and I feel an unwonted warmth in delivering them. I know that a few will appreciate them, but the question is, can the bulk of the professing people follow them? Are they useless so far as most are concerned? On the other hand, how can a discerning people be raised up without such teaching? To be always dealing with the elementary things gives little prospect of rearing anything but spiritual dwarfs.... [1946]

At one time Kenneth MacRae gave a series of sixteen addresses on Homiletics to a number of the Church's 'Lay Agents' and other men in Stornoway. It is to be regretted that these lectures were never prepared for publication. Their nature will be seen from the following extract from the outline of the author's second address entitled 'Speech':

1. In preaching, speech is the vehicle of instruction.

(1) No matter how apt and virile the thoughts may be they must be expressed in requisite words. Speech is therefore supremely important.

(2) The voice is the vehicle of speech – use it – weak voices can be improved, good voices can be ruined – speak naturally.

2. Fluency – the faculty of ready speech.
   (1) Some have natural fluency – a great gift for a preacher, but not to be abused.
   (2) Some have not – but can be readily improved.
   (3) Helps to the attaining of fluency:
      (a) Reading aloud.
      (b) Impromptu private practice.

3. How to speak effectively:
   (1) See that you have something to say – something worth saying.
   (2) Arrange your thoughts clearly beforehand – clear thinking is necessary for clear speaking.
   (3) Speak out – watch to see that those at the back hear.
   (4) Avoid excessive and unnecessary noise.
   (5) Enunciate clearly.
   (6) Speak in an animated way. A heavy, listless delivery will spoil any address. Show that you *feel* what you say.
   (7) Don't be hurried. Don't pour out your sentences in a torrent.
   (8) Finish your sentences. Don't drop voice at end of sentences.
   (9) Avoid senseless repetitions. Repeat only for emphasis.
   (10) Try to make the people understand. Try to make everything as simple as possible.
   (11) Speak naturally and without affectation.
   (12) Don't think that words will cover lack of thought.
   (13) Don't imitate any other speaker. Be yourself. You were meant to be. But you can learn from a good speaker.
   (14) Accompany speech with fitting gestures. Don't be a wooden doll. But be careful re your gestures.
   (15) Don't weary your audience. A really effective speaker knows when to stop.

The Teaching of Church History

MacRae regarded the duty of instructing congregations on the work of God in past ages as part of the necessary work of a minister and he frequently gave courses of addresses on this theme in Stornoway. His attitude is well summarised by the following entry:

25 MAY, 1943

At lecture on 'The Struggle against Prelacy' tonight, felt and spoke very strongly as to the ignorance of the young people today and their indifference towards the history of the religious struggles of the past. Realised tonight how largely I am moulded by the past. The average person of today, knowing nothing of the past, is as flotsam and jetsam floating upon the waves of time, affected by every wind and current that bears upon him. I feel as though I am fitted into my place to bear my testimony, in my day and generation, for what bygone generations counted foundation and permanent truth. I have a connection with the past and have something to pass on. The average person today is content to have neither. If I did not know the history of the contendings of the fathers I am assured that I would be quite a different person from what I am.

In the spring of this same year, 1943, when MacRae was giving a series of lectures to his own congregation on the history of the Church of Scotland, his name was proposed for the vacant Chair of Church History at the Free Church College, Edinburgh. When the Assembly Report was published early in May, it indicated that he, and another candidate (William MacLeod of Dornoch) had both been nominated by seven Presbyteries and five Synods, and there was a strong probability that, if he did not withdraw his name, a majority of the forthcoming Assembly would vote for his appointment to the Chair. From the outset he had no inclination in the direction of this proposal, but there were ministerial friends who urged him to consider that his duty might well lie in this work. After receiving a letter from one such friend on 6 May he wrote in his Diary:

6 MAY, 1943

The letter threw me into much distress. I have no wish to leave Stornoway, and no desire whatsoever for professorial work in Edinburgh. The whole prospect is most distressing to me. Mr Maciver,[1] Carloway, took the prayer meeting for me tonight, when he gave an able sermon on Luke 24:32. As I sat there listening to the praise, looking upon the faces of the people, and noting the tears of at least two, I felt that to be taken away from my people to the uncongenial, frigid atmosphere of Edinburgh would break my heart. Oh Lord, guide me!

In the days which followed it became apparent that the hearts of

1 Rev. John Maciver. Carloway was his only charge. He died there in 1946 after a remarkably fruitful ministry.

others would be similarly affected if he left Stornoway, and on 18 May he wired the Assembly, which had already commenced, withdrawing his name. His Diary entry for the previous day, 17 May, reads:

This evening two of my deacons came up to plead with me not to leave the congregation: but my mind seems now to be pretty well settled. How can I leave the preaching of the Gospel to a congregation of well-nigh 1,500 for the giving of lectures on Church History to three students? – for war conditions have practically emptied the College. This seems to be the determining factor in the situation. McCheyne could not leave his 1,100 in Dundee for 300 in Stirling, even though he felt his own charge beyond his strength. How then can I leave 1,500 for three, even although they be sons of the prophets, and how can I exchange the ministration of the Word for College lectures?

Thoughts on Singing

19 JULY, 1943: BERNERA, HARRIS [THE MONDAY OF A COMMUNION]

Mr Shaw[1] preached at noon from Malachi 3:16 to a congregation of 57. Norman Morrison[2] [Scalpay], who was precenting, sang in such a feeling way that I felt sure that he was weeping, and his brother James[3] was weeping with him in the pulpit. The Scalpay contingent – twelve in all – left after dinner. Ere doing so, with Bernera friends they gathered on the rocky beach to the number of about 50 and led by Norman they sang the last three verses of Psalm 72 to the tune 'Torwood'. We went out from the dinner table when we heard the singing. There they were gathered on the further side of the bay about half a mile away. I never heard such singing in my life. It seemed to ring out over the whole island. I felt profoundly moved and could not command my emotions. It brought heaven near.

26 AUGUST, 1945

There was a good atmosphere. As I listened to the many voices on every hand the thought came to me – if this singing is so glorious, what must the song of the redeemed be like? And I felt quite unmanned.

SABBATH, 19 JUNE, 1960

Five hundred were out at the morning service. Felt greatly moved during the singing as I listened. It seemed to me that the singing here

1 Minister of Leith Free Church, Edinburgh.
2 Afterwards studied for the ministry and held pastorates at Stoer in Sutherlandshire and in Duirinish, Skye. Died 1972.
3 Minister at Bayhead in the Island of North Uist.

reflected the fact that they were an island people, for I could hear the sea in their singing – the great shuddering and swaying waves and the back surge sweeping back over the stones of the beach. Then I began to think of God's goodness in giving us so many sweet sounds and the gift of song.

Revival and Phenomena

As the preceding pages make clear MacRae had a deep interest in the subject of revivals from the first years of his Christian life and nothing was more pervasive in his life and ministry than the hope that God would grant a powerful spiritual re-awakening in the present century. While he did not minimise the more usual work of the Spirit of God in the conversion and sanctification of individuals, he believed that such were the prevailing conditions in the nation that only that unusual and widespread activity of the Spirit, witnessed in revival periods, would bring a turning of the tide. In one of many addresses which he gave on the subject he declared that revivals can be recognised by the following features:

(1) An increase of zeal and devotedness to Christ among believers. (2) The spread of conviction and alarm among the spiritually careless. (3) This change in spiritual conditions may come gradually or as suddenly as a thunderbolt. (4) The existence of numbers who are 'awakened': some of whom ultimately go back, while others try to drown convictions and fail. (5) Converts are established in a good hope of their salvation although the manner of their conversions differs considerably. Some are slowly brought to a sense of peace and cannot identify the time when they first came to Christ; others are suddenly changed and may experience immediate joy and ecstasy.

MacRae's reading of Church history and his own experience had led him to the conviction that careful discrimination needs to be exercised on this subject. Everything unusual in the life of the Church is not necessarily the work of the Spirit. Even great excitement and many *professed* conversions are no sure proofs, in themselves, that a revival is in progress. Accordingly when there were reported revivals in several congregations in Lewis in 1936, while he wrote that 'matters seem to be definitely improving', he was cautious in accepting these reports at face value, as his diary entries reveal.[1] These local revivals of 1936 were, however, to prove the precursor of a more general movement in Lewis. Recognising the existence of a wider work of true revival in 1939

1 See p 299.

MacRae traced its beginnings to three years earlier. Some put the commencement date further back. The Rev. Murdo MacRae of Kinloch, speaking in the Free Church General Assembly in 1939, said there was unanimity of belief among the Free Church ministers in Lewis 'that there is a deep and profound spiritual movement in the island', and that, in his opinion, it had 'been going on for a period of four or five years'. There was also a large measure of agreement between the Free Church ministers – and in this they differed with some Church of Scotland ministers in Lewis – that in 1938 certain features had become evident which were not beneficial to the work. Prior to that date, solemnity and spiritual concern, brought about by an uncommon consciousness of the presence of God, were the most prominent characteristics of the revival. 'Until recently', said Murdo MacRae in his speech already quoted, 'it was a profoundly spiritual movement revealing those tokens and evidences which one always expects to find when the Lord is effectively working in the hearts of men'. The nature of the changes seen in 1938 was pointed out by the Rev. M. M. MacSween, the Church of Scotland minister in Kinloch, who also spoke in Edinburgh in 1939 on the revival. He believed that in the previous year the district with which he was familiar had seen a quickening of intensity in the revival. A newspaper gave the following report of MacSween's address:

In a small village to the south side of Loch Erisort, Garyvard, unusual scenes were witnessed. A private house in which a meeting was being held, actually shook from its foundation, and many of those present felt an extraordinary Power present, and very soon a number of them were physically affected, and fell into what might be termed 'trances'. Those affected went off into these 'trances' quietly and without disturbance. Some of them, whom he saw in these 'trances', seemed to be transfigured and in a state of enjoyment. A few of them, who were ready enough to narrate their experience, told how they were conscious of unusual calm and peace, and some had heavenly visions. Others could give no account, and among those he found some who were quite prepared to admit that they had experienced no spiritual change.

From Garyvard, the movement spread out into the villages of Lemreway and Orinsay, where those influenced were not of the quiet variety. There were loud and appealing cries for mercy, as people became conscious of their need of salvation. At the same time the movement was being felt in Crossbost and Grimshader, on the north side of Loch Erisort, where it grew in intensity in March and April of this year. There again one found unusual and perhaps unprecedented – as far as Lewis was concerned – phenomena . . .

[364]

From Lochs the movement spread to the districts of Point and Barvas, where again these unusual symptoms followed it. He attended a few services in the Point district and admitted that there was a solemnity and a reverence which led one instinctively to believe that great and grand things were happening. There were undoubtedly elements of excitement and hysteria, but to say that that was all, would be false because there were clear evidences of lasting conversion . . .

The movement had many pleasing features. Many who were indifferent to organised religion, and men who, through having spent years abroad, had come to look upon church services as prosaic or even stupid, had come under the influence, and were among the most enthusiastic in their support of the things which they once condemned. Those influenced were ready to join the Church as members, and take an active part in witness and prayer.

From 1938 the phenomena of swooning, of outcries, of temporary paralysis of limbs and of muscular spasms or 'jerks' drew much attention and produced considerable excitement and debate. The secular press, prone to be disinterested in the spiritual, was quick to seize upon the phenomenal. A reporter of the *Scottish Daily Express*, after covering 70 miles in Lewis in May 1939, reported that the 'revival has its centres at four points of a square formed by Crossbost, Garrabost, Barvas, and Carloway', but his description was almost entirely confined to the 'extraordinary mental and bodily excitement', affecting, he believed, 'at least 200 people'. His narrative included the following:

At evening church meetings attended by ministers, which start at 10, there are few abnormal emotional experiences. At midnight, worshippers adjourn to private houses where prayer meetings go on for two or three hours. There may be 40 or 50 people present.

Each rises spontaneously and prays. Psalms are interrupted. As hour succeeds hour the 'atmosphere', I am informed, changes.

Sometimes a woman will collapse, others will rise simultaneously, weeping, call in Gaelic on their relatives. Some lose all power of their limbs, have to be carried into an adjoining room and laid on a couch until they recover.

It is expected that renewed manifestations of the revival will be shown this weekend, especially at Sunday's services.

The scenes associated with such phenomena inevitably brought controversy. Some ministers affirmed that the physical effects were a revelation of the same divine power which had brought the revival and were therefore subjects for praise: in their minds *all* the phenomena and the revival were one. Others were profoundly disturbed at this identifi-

[365]

cation and also lamented that what had been a quiet work of God was now 'being blazed across the skies by the public Press in Scotland'. Certainly the public reports and correspondence published in 1939 concentrate largely upon the issue of the phenomena and to this extent attention was turned away from what was of great spiritual importance. This is apparent in the columns of *The Stornoway Gazette* where the differing viewpoints all found expression. In the opinion of some 'the revival has followed a course so different to previous religious revivals in Lewis that they feel doubtful of its character'; others recalled that one great year of revival in Lewis – 1859 – had been known as *Bliadhna an Aomaidh*, 'the year of swooning'. Even medical opinion was divided. While it was reported that 'doctors on the island have disapproved of the developments', a Scots doctor wrote from Southern Rhodesia to warn against any judgment of the phenomena which would discredit the whole revival: 'To the stress of religious emotion, different temperaments react differently, and who shall say which is the wheat and which is the chaff? Time alone can tell . . . In all my experience of life, I have looked back with a loved regret which I would not willingly resign, to my association with the lovable personalities who were the products of a previous religious revival in my beloved native island'.

It is unfortunate that MacRae's diary for 1939, which would have given us his impressions of the work of the Spirit in that year, has apparently been lost. As it is we have only his judgment on the excesses of the movement, for in the debate which went on through the Spring of 1939 it was impossible for him to remain silent. Under the heading, 'The Lewis Revival, Rev. Kenneth MacRae's address to the Young', *The Stornoway Gazette* published a lengthy account of an address he gave on the subject and it is too important to leave unnoticed in these pages. The newspaper reported:

At a meeting in the Free Church Seminary, Stornoway, on Tuesday evening, Rev. Kenneth MacRae took as his subject, 'Unusual Features of the Present Religious Movement in Lewis'.

Mr MacRae first of all affirmed his opinion that a really sound religious movement had taken place in Lewis and was testified to by its fruits. The subject which he wished his hearers to consider that night was not so much the revival itself as some peculiar features of it . . .

He sketched the progress of the revival from its beginning in Carloway three years ago, and noted the first appearance of peculiar manifestations in the Park district last year, their progress to Grimshader, then Point, Shader (Barvas) and Carloway.

He drew attention also to the changing nature of these manifestations.

In Park they were more of the nature of convulsive fits; in Grimshader they took the form of tremblings or tremors, accompanied by a certain amount of crying out. In Point and Shader (Barvas) there were trances and also, it was said, certain irregularities in the meetings, such as women praying and exhorting, and a good deal of disorder . . .

He went on to consider various features of the more physical manifestations. He noted that they affected both believers and unbelievers: that they were not saving in their nature, that they were not accompanied by any sense of sin, that those affected could give no adequate explanation of their experience, and that they bore no relation to the preaching of the Word. Anyone who carefully considered these facts would surely have some hesitancy in ascribing these manifestations to the agency of the Spirit.

Rev Mr MacRae went on then to enumerate certain dangers which he thought were present. In the first place, the minds of people were distracted from the really important matter – the effectual work of the Holy Spirit as revealed in the new birth – and rendered apt to substitute this peculiar development for the 'one thing needful'. In fact, if these manifestations were not present, worshippers appeared to be quite disappointed, and to be under the impression that they constituted the hallmark of the Spirit's presence.

In the second place, he thought these unusual occurrences tended to minister to spiritual pride and to foster the idea that those who had been thus affected belonged to a superior order of Christians.

In the third place, he thought these manifestations had already led to unscriptural extravagances of various kinds and might yet lead to worse.

Mr MacRae considered closely and at some length the testimony of certain of the old divines concerning similar manifestations in connection with revivals in their own day. He quoted from the observations of such men as Robert Blair, the Covenanting minister, in connection with the Ulster Revival of 1630; James Robe, of Kilsyth, in connection with the Cambuslang Revival in 1742; and such others as Whitefield, Spurgeon, Dr Andrew Bonar, Dr Nettleton the American evangelist, and Dr Fish, an eminent Baptist minister who was well acquainted with the American revivals.

He also mentioned the experience of Mr MacRitchie, of Knock, concerning similar features of the Uig revival under Rev Alexander MacLeod.

All these divines, he said, made it clear, some of them very strongly, that they did not regard these things as being of the Spirit.

Having put forward the opinion of these men who had actual experience of such things, Mr MacRae said it would not be fair if he did not give his own opinion also.

[367]

'My opinion is,' he said, 'that these singular manifestations are not of the Spirit, neither yet are they of the Evil One, but that they are simply what is medically known as mass hysteria.'

In support of this view, Mr MacRae quoted from a medical textbook which he had brought with him, which gave the symptoms of hysteria as – (1) It is incident to highly-strung people, especially young women. (2) It is infectious. (3) It is frequently associated with convulsions, tremors and trances. (4) Attacks always come on in an audience, never alone. (5) Those affected declare that they cannot help themselves. (6) In spite of these declarations, by an effort of will-power they can control themselves. (7) They are subject to delusions and hallucinations. (8) Consciousness is not completely lost.

He then went on to consider the nature of the manifestations which had occurred in Lewis in the light of the definition of hysteria which he had quoted, and stated that the two were identical.

He pointed out that 80 per cent, or more, of those influenced were young women, and it was a singular fact that old, mature Christians of sound and strong judgment seemed to be unaffected. If these manifestations were of the Spirit, one would judge that such persons would be the first to be affected, but such was not the case. He had no faith, Mr MacRae said, in an aspect of the movement which for its driving force was largely dependent upon the nervous reactions of excitable young women of little or no Christian experience.

That the manifestations were infectious had been repeatedly noted, and also that they always took place in an audience. If they were of the Spirit, one would expect them, sometimes at least, to take place in private, for the deepest exercises of the human soul are experienced when alone with God.

Those affected declared that they could not help themselves, and that fact had been used by some to prove that these manifestations were of the Spirit, but as he had shown, that was one of the symptoms of hysteria, and it was clear that people could control themselves, as was proved by the response made to appeals on certain occasions by certain ministers.

From these facts, Mr MacRae said, he had reached the conclusion that the unusual features of the present movement in Lewis were due to mass hysteria, which was a natural reaction to strong religious excitement on the part of persons of a hysterical disposition.

He re-emphasised his belief that the Holy Spirit had been at work and that, therefore, strong religious excitement had been produced in certain areas in the Island. The history of former revivals showed that invariably where such excitement had been protracted, hysterical persons had manifested such features as had recently appeared in Lewis. He further expressed the fear that, although these manifestations were entirely

[368]

natural in their origin, they would be exploited by Satan to advance the interests of his kingdom.[1]

Towards the conclusion of his address, Mr MacRae said he was going to make a statement which he knew would be unpopular in Lewis, but which he felt it was his duty to make, and that was that late prayer meetings, protracted into the early hours of the morning, and repeated night after night, definitely did induce hysteria, and he suggested that consideration should be given to the wisdom of McCheyne who, at the time of the Dundee revival, resolutely refused to have any religious meeting continued later than 11 p.m., 'lest', he said, 'our good be evil spoken of'.

Mr MacRae expressed regret at the publicity which was given to the movement in the Press, because it might lead outsiders of various sects to come amongst them to exploit to their own advantage the very features which were causing uneasiness. He pointed out that the gravest danger of all was that unscriptural extravagances might grieve away the Holy Spirit and the whole revival end in smoke. That had repeatedly happened before in the history of the church and should cause them to beware. The great need was for a really solid work of the Holy Spirit, which would convince of sin, reveal the majesty and holiness of God, and send sinners in secret to a Throne of Grace for mercy.

In conclusion, Mr MacRae said he expected that his attitude would be misrepresented in the Island, but he considered that, believing as he did that there were serious dangers in the development which they had been considering, it was his duty to point them out. He considered that his young people stood in need of guidance at this juncture and he had endeavoured to discharge his duty towards them and to clear his own conscience.

The above address, it needs to be emphasised, contains his thinking only on the question of *excesses* accompanying revivals. He was not arguing that all unusual phenomena in revivals must be attributed to hysteria.[2] He knew that the existence of excesses was no proof that a true work of the Spirit was not in progress. At the same time he was alive to the danger of Satan making use of harmful enthusiasm and false fire to discredit the idea of revivals as God's work. It was because he

1 He was thinking, for example, of what had happened during the Skye revival of 1812 when offence was given by some who, after being awakened, 'became fanatical in the proper sense of the term. They pretended to *dreams* and *visions*, and to have received a spirit of penetration which enabled them to foretell who should be saved and who not'. See *History of Revivals of Religion in the British Isles, Especially in Scotland*, 1836, p 344.
2 Further on this subject see 'Bodily Effects of Religious Excitement' in *Theological Essays reprinted from the Princeton Review*, first series, 1856, pp 419–429. Also, Archibald Alexander, *Thoughts on Religious Experience*, 1844 (1978 reprint) ch 5.

believed in revival as strongly as he did that he was concerned lest men
were turned aside from its true meaning. This concern could not be
expressed without there being a danger of misunderstanding. When a
revival is in progress it is easy for people to assume that all phenomena
are so closely identified with the Spirit of God that to question them is
to hinder revival. Asahel Nettleton, for instance (whose experiences of
revivals Mr MacRae had carefully studied), found that when he
attempted to arrest excesses in one New England revival he was
charged with having 'put a stop to it. They seemed to be very much
grieved and shocked at my conduct'.[1]

The following Diary extracts will further illustrate his convictions
on this theme.

15 JANUARY, 1940

Began our week of special services tonight. A number of country people
were present and for a time felt afraid that we might be troubled with
some outbursts of the hysteria prevalent still in parts of the Island, but
fortunately we were preserved from any such disturbance.

8 APRIL, 1940: POINT COMMUNION

Principal MacLeod preached twice today. In the morning he had a
congregation fully 1,000 strong; at night he had 630. After the evening
sermon two girls were under the influence of the strange hysteria which
a year ago caused such a commotion in this place.

The Principal has failed very much in health. I am very afraid that
he has the early symptoms of paralysis agitans. I felt very sad on
parting with him on board the 'Lochness', and I felt that his foreboding
that this would be his last visit to Lewis would prove only too true.[2]

Enjoyed the Point communion and felt that I had a good deal of
liberty.

2 MAY, 1940: STORNOWAY

Had a very trying experience at the prayer meeting this evening. At the
first prayer I was conscious of the peculiar gasping sound characteristic
of the religious movement in Lewis, which has caused so much controversy and division throughout our congregations. Immediately all

1 *Nettleton and His Labours*, Bennet Tyler and Andrew Bonar, 1854 (1975
reprint) p 83.
2 Although illness necessitated John MacLeod's retirement from the Free
Church College in 1942 it was not until 1948 that he died at the age of seventy-
six.

liberty forsook me, and I felt that I could not pray. Throughout the meeting I was not conscious of any more of it, although it would appear that the person affected – a young woman from one of the country congregations – again gave way to it in the last singing. At the close I expressed my hope that we as a congregation were not to be troubled by what had caused such dispeace elsewhere. When the disturber discerned the gist of my remarks she completely abandoned herself to this strange influence, until at last she was bawling in such a stentorian voice that I had forthwith to pronounce the Benediction. There was almost a panic in the crowded hall and at least other two females subject to these attacks became similarly affected. One old woman, in her efforts to escape from the Hall, climbed over the back of her seat. Eventually the young woman was carried out and placed in a country bus which happened to be at the door.

If any think that this is the evidence of a revival among us, then all the other, ordinary evidences are absent. It troubles me very much, but I shall give the 'swooners' no latitude.

7 MAY, 1940

Gave a lecture this evening on 'Revival Dangers' and dealt with the history of the Davenport and Cumberland Presbyterians' movement in America[1] and pointed out that the essential features of these movements were currently present in Lewis. Warned my audience of the dangers of sectarianism and division. 135 were present, including, I was glad to see, some of those who are recognised as leading sympathisers with the new movement.

16 MAY, 1940

240 were out at the Prayer Meeting tonight. There was no 'swooning'. I think that matter has been effectively scotched in this congregation. I shall be surprised if it gives us any more trouble. Spoke from Psalm 27:1.

4 AUGUST, 1940, SABBATH

Took service for Mr MacKenzie at Back in forenoon. At night preached from my own pulpit and gave some plain hints regarding the strange religious features which have recently been disturbing congregations in

1 James Davenport (1710–1757) lapsed into fanaticism and supported excesses among his followers in the Great Awakening in New England, and the Cumberland Presbyterians acted similarly in the Kentucky revival of 1800–02. See W. B. Sprague, *Lectures on Revivals of Religion*, 1832, reprinted 1979, appendix, pp 30–35.

N   [371]

the island. Spoke from John 16:13 on the ministry of the Spirit with a good measure of liberty.

4 FEBRUARY, 1941

Was told today concerning one who is subject to these strange attacks, that she stated, when questioned, that she neither knew what the preacher said nor what she herself said, although in these fits she would lay off most vehemently. My informant told me that no softening could be observed after these turns, no appearance of heavenliness, but rather hardening.

14 FEBRUARY, 1941

At the Session we had Miss — —. I was very pleased. Although she was one of the 'swooners', her experience was clear and Scriptural, and had no relation whatsoever to these swooning fits. She was awakened three years ago while listening to a sermon at the Point Communion. Mrs——, another of the 'swooners', also appeared before us, but she was unsatisfactory. While her life appears to be changed, and while she appears to have some sort of knowledge of sin in the heart, she had no Scripture for anything and seemed most ignorant of the Word. We explained that on this score we were not satisfied and therefore, if she went forward, she would have to accept all the responsibility. To this she did not appear to demur.

15 FEBRUARY, 1941

After the evening Prayer Meeting, a girl came before the Session. She too was associated with these peculiar meetings, but I found her, after a most thorough examination, very clear and satisfactory, and basing nothing upon peculiar experiences, but everything upon Scripture. She was brought to rest on the Tuesday after the communion in her home congregation two years ago.

10 MARCH, 1941: GRAVIR COMMUNION

Preached to a congregation of 470 from Philippians 4:19 and enjoyed liberty. On Friday when two of the missionaries who favour the 'jerks' were speaking, hands were up in the customary style, but there was no more of it, and on that day I was not in the pulpit. I am inclined, therefore, to think that a great deal of this business is just a put on. I believe that there would have been plenty of it at this communion had I been one of the ministers who favoured it.

☐   ☐   ☐

After 1941 no further reference to unusual phenomena occurs in his diary until November 1945. These do not appear to have spread. Two years later there was another period of similar excitement about which he writes:

10 MAY, 1947

The excitement in connection with the movement in — — seems to be increasing. Buses are now going there, not only from Town, but also from Point; and late prayer meetings in houses seem to be the order of the day. The outcome of this will inevitably be another outbreak of the 'jerks', and to induce it seems to be the great object with some. Eight are said to have come under exercise of soul. It is difficult to conceive of anything worse for them, than their being made the centre of all this publicity and fuss. There is an element now in this island who would ruin any revival; they are far more dangerous to the interests of true, solid religion, than the careless and profane. To try to counsel them is worse than useless, for, conceiving that they are actuated and enlightened by the Holy Spirit to a special degree, all who do not agree with them they hold in contempt.

The Curse of Strong Drink

The abuse of alcoholic liquor was for long a traditional evil in the Scottish Highlands. After a period of improvement – due principally to the power of the gospel – the evil returned with new power in the present century, and in Lewis, as well as in other places, drunkenness ceased to be uncommon. MacRae was not of the opinion that the use of strong drink was so entrenched that nothing could be done about it. As he studied the problem he was convinced that the position had worsened, due principally to a change in public opinion under the influence of the massive promotion campaigns of the drink trade. 'Forty or fifty years ago', he wrote in the 1950's, 'Scotland was rapidly becoming a sober country; temperance societies were very active everywhere, especially among the young, and temperance as a principle and sentiment was gradually permeating the people'.

He also noted how the Government, who had formerly viewed the temperance movement with favour, were now indifferent. During the Second World War it had disturbed him deeply that unlimited quantities of free beer had been authorised for service men and women in Stornoway on Christmas Day.

Against this trend he used the Word of God in the pulpit. He also

[373]

gave strong support to a Temperance Committee formed by the Presbytery in 1941; he spoke on behalf of a Women's Temperance Association and took up the subject with school children on visits to the Laxdale school. Behind his burden to warn all age-groups against the use of strong drink lay his sad familiarity with events which revealed the appalling influence of alcohol. Some of his diary entries on cases known to him cannot be printed but the following two may be taken as representative:

17 JANUARY, 1944

Another black-out tragedy has taken place in this town and it is to be feared that once more it was largely due to the curse of this town – strong drink. The man, who was a careless character, nominally belonging to my congregation, went a-missing on Saturday night and has never since been heard of, but there is no doubt but that he has gone where all the others have gone – into the harbour. What an end! What an entrance into eternity!

30 AUGUST, 1947

After the Prayer meeting went to a sad home and conducted the meeting usually held in the house of mourning, but on this occasion the task was exceptionally difficult, for the deceased was a drunkard who had suddenly been cut away by a heart attack – the direct result of his intemperance. Too late he had begun to struggle against his enemy. It overmastered him and it killed him, just as it overmastered and killed his father and brother before him. What a curse drink is, and yet people seem to think very little of it! This is what I cannot understand.

One of his most powerful sermons against drink was preached in the later years of his ministry. He argued, firstly, that strong drink is a curse; secondly, that the support for the use of such drink alleged to be found in Scripture is unfounded: 'In the original languages there are 13 different words used for 13 different kinds of drink, ranging from the pure juice of the grape (Gen. 40:11) to strong drink of the most intoxicating quality (Prov. 23:31–32). Now in our versions of the Scriptures all these terms are translated "wine", and the distinction between what was harmless and what was hurtful is entirely lost . . . Were the wine consumed at the wedding at Cana ere supplies gave out according to our conception of wine, long before then the party would have degenerated into a drunken carousel. It is impossible to think of Christ creating anything that would harm or would in any way encourage drunkenness.'

Thirdly, he urged that resolute action was called for:

'What are we to do about it all? Are we to sit still and allow this curse to blight lives and homes without let or hindrance? There is no need whatever for such supineness, for there is a great deal that we can do about it.

'1. We can sweep the accursed thing out of our homes. You are justified in having a little brandy stored up in the home solely for emergency medicinal use, but nothing else. Let not your children be able to say that they saw a strong drink in use in their home.

'2. We can sweep drink clean out of our conventions and customs. New Year treating and wedding toasts are abominations — — Toasts force those to drink who have no desire to do so but who lack the courage to defy custom. Toasts should not be tolerated in any decent company. But so long as those who profess to be followers of Christ countenance these things what wonder if the thoughtless abuse them?

'3. We can refuse strong drink entirely. This is the only realistic policy. Let me appeal to the young people present to make this now their solemn determination that they will never from this time on allow strong drink to defile their lips. Thus you will be delivered from the great curse which has murdered more souls than any other engine in the Devil's armament.

'Are there any present who have become aware of a growing fondness for this accursed thing? Let them turn from it right away lest the beast be at their throats. Then it will be too late.

'There is nothing that so bestialises a man as indulgence in intoxicating liquor. I would a thousand times prefer a dog or a cat as a companion to a person under the influence of drink. It is a curse, a tremendous curse, and the sooner people come to realise it the more hope there will be of the deliverance of this community from its influence.'

1 JANUARY, 1960

My soul is filled with loathing at the evidences of the extent to which strong drink has demoralised this generation and affected both men and women. If ever there was a curse, strong drink is one, and yet few seem to view it so. I hate it with a perfect hatred in its every form.

When Mrs Alina Mackenzie, now with the Free Church mission in India, was in this country some time ago there was one particular day when she had a long wait at a railway station. Sitting beside her was an old man with whom she entered into conversation. Each soon realised that the other was a believer in the Lord Jesus Christ. The old man said, 'You'll be too young, lassie, to remember the minister under whose preaching I was converted long, long ago in the Island of Arran. His name was Kenneth MacRae and his charge was then in Lochgilphead'. 'Oh, but I do remember him', answered Mrs Mackenzie, 'and strangely enough it was under his preaching that I was converted too'.

Mary MacLeod (née MacRae) in a
letter to the Editor, 1978

16 Some Events in Post-War Years

TUESDAY, 1 JANUARY, 1946

Enjoyed the service, preaching from Psalm 39:1 to a congregation of about 250. The day was good, although the wind was chill. The duties of a new year have again been entered upon. What is to follow? Many questions emerge. Shall I see the end of the year? If so, will I still be in this charge? And if I still be here, will I witness anything in the congregation to warrant the belief that the tide has turned and that better days have already begun? Or shall it just be another year with nothing in it particularly outstanding? And what of international matters? Peace has come, but the nations are restless and uneasy. Politically and economically the year promises to be a very difficult one.

Prepared the Kirk Session's Memorandum re the Sabbath night sailings of the 'Lochness' for submission to the Ministry of Transport and also sent copies of Ryle's pamphlet 'Which Picture is Mine?' to the provost and to one of our bailies who is a great opponent. The Lord can bless what has been done with desire for the good of His cause. May He make such feeble efforts under such unpromising circumstances very effective!

WEDNESDAY, 16 JANUARY

In Dr Childs Robinson's *The Word of the Cross* the conviction is expressed that the secret of successful preaching is the exhibition of the cross. Perhaps it is, and perhaps it is there that I fail. What I delight in is experimental preaching, the application of redemption to the soul, the subjective side as opposed to the objective: and perhaps my partiality leads me to deny the preaching of the cross the place it ought to have in my ministrations.

THURSDAY, 28 FEBRUARY

Have been feeling much impressed with the need of issuing short, attractive and cheaply-priced apologetic books – after the style of the Penguin series – for the education of the rising generation in the verities of the Christian faith.

MONDAY, 11 MARCH

A week ago exactly I took my first trip by air. The wind was very strong but we got off the ground almost before I was aware of it. We circled over Aignish, which with the neighbouring parts of Point lay below us like a map, the houses appearing like little dolls' houses and the roads like ribbons through the dark moors – and then swept away out to sea over the Minch. The motion was fairly steady and there was no sensation of speed. What surprised me was that we kept a comparatively low level, not rising at any time higher than 200 feet above sea level. We crossed the Minch in 27 minutes. I soon was able to locate Achiltibuie and presently we were looking down upon Ullapool which appeared so close that I felt that I could throw a biscuit down into the streets. With the exception of the fore-shore all that region was heavily carpeted in snow. At the head of Loch Broom we began to climb up over the mountains and now torrents of wind blasting through those upland passes began to toss us to and fro like a leaf. While it lasted it was most disagreeable, and far more sickening than the motion of the Minch. The world below us was unbroken white and I could not but feel the desolation of it. When we reached Loch Garve things were easier and we soon sped down Strath Conon and over the Black Isle and the Beauly Firth, settling down on the Longman[1] exactly 65 minutes after we had taken off at Steinish. The normal time for the flight is 50 minutes.

SABBATH, 28 APRIL

The crowd in the Seminary tonight was even larger than last Sabbath, for there were chairs even in the passages. I am sure 420 were present.

We ought really to be holding our English services in the Church. Last week I brought the matter before the elders, but the usual man stood in the way. He stated his policy as being to leave things as we found them, but he appears to be blind to the fact that time will alter things in spite of us. I wonder that such an old man as he is does not see that his generation is all but out of sight.

SATURDAY, JULY 27

On Tuesday attended a meeting of the Presbytery of Chanonry which was held in Fortrose Church. This was my first visit since my student days to a church with which I was once very familiar and I felt as though my life had somehow suddenly lurched past in the interval. Everything about Fortrose was familiar as we passed over the bridge and I found myself wondering whether our initials were still visible on the tree near by upon which I carved them one fair summer afternoon 40 years ago.

1 An air-strip then in use on the edge of Inverness.

SATURDAY, 12 OCTOBER

260 were present at the Prayer meeting on Thursday when Mr Finlayson of Scalpay preached from Romans 8:16. At the close I delivered myself of an exhortation which I had prepared before I knew that Mr Finlayson was to be with us. Spoke against the divisive spirit which seems to be working in the congregation, and again appealed for unity.[1] While in tension during Mr Finlayson's address had a strange feeling. Felt that I was composed of three parts – there was the ego or personality, the nervous side of my nature, and then the physical. The first was grimly determined and afraid of nothing, but the other two were quaking and tottering and I felt as though I must give up ere I got opportunity to speak. I hope such straight speaking will prove effective. I felt better after it.

SATURDAY, 2 NOVEMBER

The Rev. James Morrison of North Uist took the service on Sabbath morning. He has a very original mind, and therefore he is an interesting preacher and commands attention.

At night we had our first English service in the church and I was delighted at the response, fully 580 being present. Surely this will convince even the most stubborn opponents.

SATURDAY, 9 NOVEMBER

Monday was both the day of the Monthly Meeting and my birthday – the completion of 63 years in the world. I am staggered every time I think of my age, for I feel still a young man. I feel just as I ever did, and my health is good. The only difference is that I seem to be continually more or less tired.

SATURDAY, 16 NOVEMBER

Began the Class for the winter, when we hope to go through Hodge's *Way of Life*, and was gladdened by an attendance of about 160. The Town Council at their meeting on Monday night agreed to go to the Free Church for their annual 'Kirkin', and since it offers me an opportunity to set before them their relationship as civic rulers to the law and

---

1 The reference is to an element which, having been in touch with a broader and Arminian evangelicalism in other parts of Britain, favoured changes in the traditional Reformed evangelicalism of Lewis.

sovereignty of Christ I have no objection.[1] The service will take place on the evening of Sabbath, the 24th.

I have just finished reading Abraham Kuyper's *Lectures on Calvinism*. Although I would hesitate to accept everything he says, yet he awakens in me the greatest admiration for his gifts. In many respects the book opens up for me a new world, especially in connection with his discussion of the operations of 'common grace'. The book is edifying and constrains lofty thoughts of God.

SATURDAY, 25 JANUARY, 1947

Sabbath morning was beautifully fine and we had a congregation of 410. Spoke from 2 Corinthians 5:14 on the constraining influence of the love of Christ and enjoyed it very much. Before going out felt concerned that I could get so little as to what really constitutes this love of Christ. However, the subject opened out to me as I spoke, although I am not yet satisfied that I have got to the essence of it. The love of Christ itself of course presents no difficulty, but that aspect which 'constrains' narrows the field to such an extent that few commentators really enter into the subject. While thankful for sweetness and liberty in the service, my concern now is that I myself know so little of this constraining influence experimentally.

14 MARCH [After eight weeks of wintry weather and heavy snow]

In the morning sunlight the view from my bedroom window was exceedingly pretty. The world looked so bright and so clean, and the houses stood out so clear against the snow that they looked as trim and neat as doll's houses.

22 MARCH

MacDougall of Ferintosh has accepted a call to Hope Street [Glasgow], and I am given to understand that feelers have been out in my direction with respect to filling the vacancy thus created. I have felt for some time now that I ought to consider a call, since the congregation here is getting beyond my strength, and at my age I cannot keep going much longer. May I have clear guidance if ever a call comes!

SATURDAY, 17 APRIL: SKYE

On Saturday night the wind rose but Sabbath was a good day and the

1 It was the custom for every new Town Council, elected to govern every three or four years, to attend one of the local churches in a body before they commenced their duties as councillors. The custom survived until local government was transformed into regional government.

little church at Carbost was well filled, fully 155 being present. Ere we went out to the evening service the skies had darkened and the aspect of the day was changed, but the rain did not begin until we were well through the service. Mr Macleod, Portmahomack, preached in Carbost while I went on to Portnalong. There I had an audience of 42 but I felt the atmosphere cold and dead as compared with Carbost, and like their compatriots in some parts of Lewis more than half of them sat throughout the singings with silent lips.

In the church on Monday morning I had a congregation of 82. Spoke from Numbers 6:26 and enjoyed it very much indeed. Thus ended a most profitable communion season – in fact the best I have had for years. I stayed in Sandy MacAskill's hospitable home in Drynoch. Tuesday was exceedingly wet all day long, but we spent it most profitably discussing theological, spiritual and ecclesiastical questions at the fireside. Was greatly impressed with Sandy's intellectual acumen. I felt that our discussions were sharpening up my own mind, and I found it most refreshing to find one who evidently was cast very much in the same mould as myself, and who was therefore able to understand and to sympathise with thoughts and feelings which seldom get expression because I find so few able to understand them. Had Sandy MacAskill been educated he would have made his mark.[1]

Very unwillingly left Drynoch on Thursday morning after a time of privilege I shall not readily forget. It was like leaving Elim and returning to the wilderness. I felt that I was being dragged unwillingly past the giant mountains of Skye, and my heart sank at the thought of what was before me, especially the duties which await me in my own congregation.

We left Mallaig at 1 o'clock, but at Fort William I transferred to a section of the train going to Edinburgh and there I got a comfortable carriage which I occupied alone. On the way I read Dr Kennedy's remarkable book, the loan of which I got from Sandy Macaskill. Such sublime theology transported me to the heavenlies, and the close of the book so moved me that I could scarcely refrain from weeping in the carriage. I got in to Edinburgh at 9.30 and found all well at Warrender Park.[2]

1 MacAskill (1873–1965), formerly a game-keeper and head stalker, had at this date retired to a small-holding at Drynoch. During the years 1900–1930, when the large and scattered parish of Bracadale had no Free Church minister, he had preached twice every Sabbath, cycling 26 miles in every kind of weather to do so. MacRae placed high value on the friendship of this old-school worthy. See *Alexander MacAskill of Drynoch*, K. J. Macleay, 1968, for a short memoir.
2 His old home.

SATURDAY, 17 MAY

On Monday felt troubled and sad. A letter came that morning asking me to the Ferintosh Communion, and I know well what lies at the back of that invitation. I have no desire to leave Stornoway, and Ferintosh has no great attraction for me, but I feel crushed by my burdens; my energy is ebbing away. Whatever I might do in a smaller charge I am no longer fit to carry on here and I would rather leave than allow the congregation to find it out. Soon, if spared, I shall be too old to expect a call anywhere, and I don't want to be left in incubus upon my people here. It is only the years that are crushing me out. The thought of parting with them is like to break my heart.

SATURDAY, 28 JUNE

As I came to the church a telegram was handed me containing the sad news of the death of my predecessor Rev. Kenneth Cameron, late of Inverness, at Burghead. Thus the old witnesses are being removed, one after another, and the Church is becoming very bare.

11 OCTOBER

On Tuesday had to leave a meeting of Presbytery in order to conduct the service at the funeral of a little tinker boy who had died in hospital. The service was conducted in one of the erections of beaten-out tins[1] which today are beginning to replace the traditional tents. Felt somewhat moved at the thought of the levelling power of death which at a stroke sweeps away all the distinctions of class and station. Felt also a great pity for the poor creatures who seemed so patient in their grief. As we returned, the Laxdale schoolboys were lined on both sides of the road to pay their respects to the dust of their little schoolfellow – the tinker boy. I thought the schoolmaster's gesture a very thoughtful and considerate one.

18 OCTOBER

A letter from Donald MacDonald, Urray,[2] awaiting me, which informed me that I had been unanimously elected by the Ferintosh congregation and that at the forthcoming meeting of the Dingwall Presbytery on the 22nd request would be made for the moderation of call on the 12th or 13th November. This news troubled me very much.

1 Huts built mainly from scrap metal. Tinkers were a wandering people of whom many are now permanently settled in Lewis.
2 A native of Ness, Lewis, Donald MacDonald subsequently exercised a long-to-be remembered ministry in Greyfriars Free Church, Inverness, dying suddenly on 15 April, 1977.

My mind of late seems to have receded from the idea of a transfer to Ferintosh. I would much rather remain yet a little in my present charge, but if I do so I may then be regarded as too old by any vacancies on the look out for a suitable minister. There lies my difficulty in the matter and I know not how to decide it. Oh for light from the Lord Himself!

I NOVEMBER

130 were out at the Prayer Meeting on Thursday. Evidently I was not expected to be present. On the pier that night one of my men, after referring to the blessed day we had on Sabbath, expressed his hope that I was not going to leave them. He would not blame me had I become tired of them, but I had many friends in the congregation who would be greatly grieved were I to go. 'Of course,' he said, 'some would be glad, but every good man has his enemies.' I felt the words cutting me like a knife, and my mind which had recently been hardening against the Ferintosh approaches, swung violently over in the opposite direction.

I reached Beauly at 9.50 yesterday morning and found Sandy MacAskill before me. I felt exceedingly glad to get into that hospitable Manse again where I feel absolutely at home.[1]

13 DECEMBER

On Saturday night I got little sleep, and, somehow, my mind went back in a strange way to the things of long ago. I seemed to survey my far past youth and the errors I had made – errors which I now see were entirely due to hurt pride, extreme sensitiveness and inexperience. I seemed to have a sense of missing happiness even when it was within my grasp. From it all I turned with a feeling of weary disappointment. Then I surveyed my ministry, and therein I felt the same feeling of disappointment. It was nearly over now, so that it could never be what I once hoped it would be. When I surveyed the case of my soul, it was worse still. The bright lights that once shone there were either dead or dying. I thought then of the world, its present position and prospects, and there was nothing there but gross darkness. These things all filled me with dismay, but sorest of all was the Lord's silence to my soul. I could not breathe out a sigh in the night, 'Lord, wilt Thou not speak to me again?"

1 The Beauly manse had become the home of Kenneth and Jessie MacLeay earlier in 1947, following their removal from Lochinver to the charges of Kilmorack and Strathglass. This was MacRae's second visit to them that year and it was to be a spiritual haven which he prized increasingly as the years passed. The MacLeays concluded thirty-two years' service in Beauly at the end of 1978.

[383]

On Sabbath night I had a strange experience as I again lay sleepless far into the night. It was not imagination, nor was it a dream for I was as wide awake as I now am. I am not going to record it fully, unless I get further light upon it, for I admit the possibility of its being the outcome of strained and distraught nerves, but it kept me weeping half the night, and I think I got a glimpse of the entrance to the Palace of the King. It seemed to be opened for someone – and the entry in was glorious; heaven was all rejoicing, while, without, I a spectator watched till the gates were shut. And the impress of the holiness and the mystery of it all was upon my spirit all the succeeding day.

In the morning I got a letter from the Clerk of Dingwall Presbytery intimating that he was forwarding the Ferintosh Call to the Lewis Presbytery Clerk. It was signed by 18 members and 291 adherents and was unanimous. The number of members is sad; the adherents are more than I expected. I wish that I knew what to do about it. At night I was visited by a deputation of four of my elders to try to dissuade me from leaving them. Tom MacKay greatly encouraged me by what he said as to the success of my ministry throughout the island – although unknown to myself – and as to the concern of the young people lest I leave them.

160 were present at the Prayer Meeting. Although we had no address felt liberty in the prayer and throughout the meeting. The experience I had on Sabbath night seems to have swept away that darkness which so long deprived me of any sense of God's Presence, and I feel an unwonted liberty in every spiritual exercise.

I have been trying all week to give expression to the strange experience of Sabbath night. I did not see nor here anything, but I felt conscious of an upward passage of invisible beings and of their entry into the Glory above and of the shutting of the gates after them. I could not see within when the gates were open, because of swirling robes of darkness which swathed down through the night towards me, but I sensed that there was joy of infinite holiness and songs of welcome which I could not hear; and the effect of it all upon me was not to cause any fear, but a deep heart longing that I might enter in too, and an unspeakable yearning that almost overwhelmed me. Awe filled my spirit, and a deep peace which still remains with me. The meaning of it all I cannot fathom.

SATURDAY, 3 JANUARY, 1948

New Year's Day was wet, raw and cold, and the rain reduced the snow which had fallen the previous day to slush.

I am greatly exercised over the Ferintosh call. Time is passing and I cannot make up my mind for or against. Sometimes I feel that I ought to stop proceedings, then shortly afterwards I find my mind working in the contrary direction. Oh that the Lord would give me light!

SATURDAY, 31 JANUARY

On Monday evening a young man called to plead with me not to leave.[1] He declared that he was getting great good from my preaching, and that it had made all the difference to him; and that many others were in the same case. As he made no profession but was just representative of the average adherent, I felt his visit weigh more with me than anything else so far.

On Thursday night spoke at the Prayer Meeting, some were out whom I never saw at the Prayer Meeting before, probably because of the intimation on Sabbath as to my call. After the meeting gave the annual Financial Report. The Report over, we came to the business that concerned me most – the appointment of Commissioners to next meeting of Presbytery. Gave the people my mind in the matter as freely as I could, and mentioned that the response of the young to the Gospel was what weighed most with me in the direction of keeping me where I am. My mind seems now pretty well fixed, for it seems to me that were it the Lord's will for me to go, surely the issue would have been made clear to me. I have no clear call to go. But I turn from Ferintosh with regret and wistfulness. I had a vision of rest which is not to be, and the secret call of the country of my youth and forebears must remain unanswered. In my congregational visits many express their desire that I would not leave them.

SATURDAY, 7 FEBRUARY

Sabbath morning was dull and raw but fair. The congregation numbered 315. In the afternoon rain came on and the wind got up. By evening the rain was coming down in torrents, and, driven as it was by a fierce wind I expected only a skeleton congregation in the Seminary. Was very pleased therefore to find up to 140 awaiting me. Spoke from Romans 8:5 and, because I knew many were very wet, tried to be as brief as possible.

Monday was better, but still very rough. In the afternoon motored over to Barvas in connection with the Special Services there.

Next day I took things very easy until night when I went to Shader

1 Other young people, on four different occasions, visited the manse for the same purpose.

and repeated Sabbath night's discourse in Gaelic. After supper had considerable difficulty in getting my car started after having been outside without shelter or cover the previous evening, so that I had almost concluded that I was to be another night in Barvas. However, at last I got it going, and, after an anxious run across the moors I thankfully drew up at my own gate at 10.30. Found that another young man had been up earlier in the day to plead with me, as representative of many like himself, not to leave them. These things both touch and encourage me; but they make my going away impossible.

SATURDAY, 24 APRIL

On Tuesday baptised two babies at Laxdale and preached from I John 1:9 on how to get rid of the guilt of sin. The last singing seemed to have some life in it. Felt somewhat puzzled by the problem: Is faith, when it is unaccompanied by feeling, dead? Faith without feeling tends to be purely intellectual; if it be only intellectual, then is it dead? But if it leads to *trust* in Christ it cannot be dead. Therefore faith without feeling may be bestowed by the Spirit. Further, faith plus feeling is something more than faith, and is not the instrument of salvation but faith alone? Consequently a faith which leads to trust in Christ, even without feeling, is not dead.

SATURDAY, 2 OCTOBER

On Friday evening went down to Tong and heard Mr Donald MacDonald, Urray, preach an excellent sermon from Acts 16:14 on the Lord opening the heart of Lydia. He was fluent, orderly and fresh – and earnest withal.

SATURDAY, 23 OCTOBER

On Thursday we had a Day of Humiliation and Prayer appointed by the Presbytery at the instance of the Commission of Assembly on account of the deplorable state of the world. At the morning meeting 76 were present. Conducted it purely as a prayer meeting and gave no address. Felt dead and heavy. One of the prayers was inordinately long, inarticulately uttered, and, so far as I could understand, had no bearing upon the matter which brought us together. A simple, direct little prayer would be far more to the point than a volume of divinity. These long, wordy, wandering prayers one hears so often in these quarters nowadays are squeezing the life out of our prayer meetings.

SATURDAY, 30 OCTOBER [EASTER ROSS]

On Monday when the special services began I preached in Tain church at 7.30 from James 4:7 on the duty of submission to God. The church was packed out, about 20 having to sit in the Hall where it appears they were able to hear reasonably well. Fully 270 were present. The day was sunny but a sharp wind blew from the North. We were not surprised therefore on Tuesday morning when we awoke to find the ground covered with snow. Fortunately it was not deep enough to hinder the buses and at Portmahomack where the service was held we had a congregation of fully 260. Here I preached from Hebrews 7:25 on Christ saving to the uttermost. This was the discourse which I most enjoyed of all I preached. The Presbytery ran free buses from as far as Beauly and others from Fearn, Edderton and Tain, the expense of which was to come out of the collections. The experiment was a conspicuous success and ere the week was ended double-deckers carrying 64 persons had to be employed on the main Dingwall road and these were packed to such an extent that many of the passengers got only standing room. In fact on Friday two double-deckers were on the road carrying a total of 150 passengers. The following evening at Fearn we had a congregation of 320 and I preached with some freedom my sermon on Revelation 1:7. On Thursday 40 folding chairs were brought in from Fearn and seating provided in the Tain church for 300 persons. Spoke from John 8:36, but did not get the liberty of the two previous nights. As it was anticipated that the church would never accommodate the attendance on the closing night the Town Hall was engaged. When the service began it was seen that the Hall was packed, some chairs having to support two hearers. Made a strong appeal to the young to rally round their ministers and to remain faithful to the testimony of their Church. After the meeting had a lively prayer meeting. Felt very sorry to finish these services for they were an inspiration and an encouragement to us all.

Beginning on Tuesday night at Portmahomack I intimated that those who were seriously seeking the salvation of their souls would get a copy of my booklet 'A Word to the Anxious' on asking either of the ministers serving as ushers at the door. At the same time I made it very emphatic that no believer nor indifferent person was to ask – they were to leave the booklets for those for whom they were intended. Knowing how difficult it is for East Coast Highlanders to do a thing of that nature I would not have been surprised even should none be asked for. My surprise and delight therefore were great when I learned that 41 were gone and that the majority of those who asked for them were young people. Next evening 24 went, on Thursday at Tain 23, and on the last night a stock of 6 dozen failed to meet the demand. In all 160 were taken. That there should be as many among our people really concerned to know the way of life was a tremendous uplift to us all.

The services were a great success and seemed really to rouse the people in a new way. All seem to be convinced that there will be lasting fruit. I think that this is only a beginning. To the Lord be all the praise!

SATURDAY, 13 NOVEMBER

200 were out at the Prayer Meeting on Thursday. That night I left for Croy and was fortunate enough to get a good passage. I reached Inverness at 10.20 am and found Mr McPhail awaiting me at the station.

Today we motored to Fort George and spent two hours roaming about the place. We found one of the church doors unlocked and we went inside. How changed! I felt very indignant. The massive pulpit which had occupied the whole eastern end of the church was gone and in its place was a low platform ascended by three steps. In one corner was a crow's nest pulpit ascended by steps from the back. Opposite was a reader's desk and behind, an altar and another article of ritualistic furniture, the purpose of which I could not guess. All the pews had been removed and chairs had replaced them. The church now no longer was as it used to be, a typically Presbyterian place of worship, but was completely transformed after the Anglo-Catholic pattern. It was a shame – the church of a Highland regiment!

My visit to the Fort filled me with wistfulness, and I would gladly have welcomed a corner in which to give vent to my feelings. I left when 9 years of age. I return 56 years later! The contrast between the two periods nearly broke my heart. How short life is!

SATURDAY, 11 DECEMBER

Went out this afternoon to see our elder at Laxdale, John MacLean, 'Shonnie Mor' who, I was told, was very low. I found him unable to speak, although I thought he was conscious of our presence. As I watched the wasted form lying there I felt that eternity was very near after all, and it appeared to me today that death was not an *end*, an entrance into rest eternal, but the *beginning* of a better and a sinless service. I did not feel at all that I was parting with my dear, faithful friend, but that I would soon meet with him again. There he lay till Christ would call him away, and it cannot be long now. I never saw death appear so little and the life beyond so real.

SATURDAY, 18 DECEMBER

My worthy elder, 'Shonnie Mor', passed away quietly at 10.30 on Sabbath night. On Wednesday on a day of storm and drenching showers his remains were interred at Sandwick. Fortunately the showers held off during the time we were carrying the bier, although the hearse was a good distance away – just at the top of Laxdale brae. Many a time Shonnie traversed that road on his way to God's house, but never again. He has gone to another Country. Despite the weather there was a very large turn-out at his funeral, fully 120 being in the procession. He was greatly beloved and I have lost one of my best friends.

FRIDAY, 31 DECEMBER

Today the last day of the year has been white. Snow or hail fell intermittently all day.

A year ago I thought I would be finishing 1948 in Ferintosh but I am here still. Life is swiftly ebbing away. But strange to say I feel as young as ever. It is hard for me to realise that my day must pass and that I too must leave the world. I wish spiritual things were more real to me and that I had more of the presence of the Lord and more zeal for His cause.

9 JANUARY, 1949

Thursday was milder but still stormy and wet. In the evening went out to a tinker wedding at Marybank. The road to the house was awful and the rain was just slashing down. The house was full, but what surprised me most was the nice appearance of many of the young girls. In their best clothes they would never be taken for tinkers. The bridegroom, a young fellow of 22, could not sign his name. This also surprised me. The best man signed army style – the surname first – in great scrawling handwriting. The bride, a pretty young girl of 18 with a delicate pink and white complexion, was of the Newmarket Camp. She signed very readily with a quick running hand as also did her sister, the bridesmaid. They were rather raw about matters and an onlooker no doubt would have seen much to amuse him, but they were very amenable to guidance and correction. I asked them to come to church, but I don't expect them. Somehow I felt very sorry for them all – outcasts, almost, from society.

SATURDAY, 22 JANUARY

It is strange how I very frequently enjoy the Gaelic services better than the English despite my limitations in the former language. Somehow there is a certain sweetness in the Gaelic which I cannot get in the English.

19 MARCH: NESS

Sabbath was an exceedingly stormy day. The Atlantic waves were running so high that they were sweeping right over the rocky headland in which is the famous 'Eye of the Butt'.[1] It was not simply a case of spray going over it, but whole waves in tumultuous masses of foam, to fall into the sea again on the nearer side. Then the rock discharged the waters left behind in scores of cataracts back into the sea. It so fixed my eyes in the morning when I got up that I could scarcely get on with my dressing.

SATURDAY, 7 MAY

When visiting the Hospital yesterday saw a retired policeman from Leverburgh – a native of North Uist – who told me that he heard me preach in Inverness from a verse in Romans 8 – which I forget – and that he could give me the whole discourse from beginning to end even now – and then he broke down. Apparently it must have been made precious to him. How long I have taken to hear of it!

Last night George Fraser left for Portree.[2] I was very sorry to part with him, for he has been an influence for good among us. He gave a tract – one of my 'Word to the Anxious' series – to a young man to whom he gave a lift, who passed it on to another, a Norman Campbell who happened to be concerned about his spiritual condition. Apparently the booklet proved to be the very thing for him and met his case. The booklet was not written in vain.

SATURDAY, 2 JULY

The fog still clung about on Sabbath morning but as the sun gained strength it soon dispelled it and we were favoured with a beautiful day. Preached to a congregation of 430 from 1 Thessalonians 2:13 and enjoyed it very much. Felt very much softened in spirit, and, in fact, for one particular moment was on the very verge of breaking down. Surely there was some power among us. At night had an attendance of 590 at the English service while the Seminary was absolutely packed. Spoke

1 A large hole in the peculiar rock formation which forms the northern extremity of the island said, by legend, to have held the chain which Norse sailors used to pull Lewis to its present position.
2 Subsequently George Fraser served as a Free Church missionary at Keiss and at Glenelg before his death in 1978.

from Ephesians 1:22 on Christ's exaltation in respect of the world and of the church, and again enjoyed liberty. The church was very close and preaching was very trying physically, but I was almost unconscious of it at the time.

15 JULY: SKYE

On Wednesday morning Kennie Macleay and his wife motored over to Drynoch and we all went on together to Glen Brittle. After a welcome meal from the MacRaes we set out by motor boat for the Island of Soay. The day was brilliantly sunny and on shore it was hot in sheltered places, but a stiff east wind which was blowing gave us rather an unsteady passage. We shipped much water, but fortunately we were sheltered by a canopy over which the waves washed harmlessly. We were landed at Soay after an hour's sail and it was a real treat on entering the nearest house to find a princely spread awaiting us, of such a nature as to excite our surprise that such provision could be made in such a remote place. There we rested for two hours and then set out again for Loch Coruisk – Coruisk, with the great black-brown Coolins towering over us; it was a grand yet gloomy sight. The rock around it is worn completely smooth and made walking very easy. We brought some small specimens of the black packed rock around us back with us as mementos of our visit. On our return we took the channel on the inward side of Soay. Soay took my fancy very much. I would like well to spend a month there. On our homeward way the wind blew behind us so that our progress was pleasant. The evening was beautiful and with the huge terrific Coolins towering over us the prospect was magnificent. In the far distance was Uist and the Outer Isles, nearer, Rhum, Canna and Eigg. We got home without incident after a wonderful day and one which I will not readily forget.

SATURDAY, 24 SEPTEMBER

We got our train at Invershin about 12.30 and reached Beauly about 2.20. I was glad for the respite there for I always feel the Beauly Manse a haven of refuge. At night I took the Prayer Meeting and addressed an audience of 18 from Hosea 5:15. Next morning we were advised that our train was an hour late at Inverness. While seated to a cup of tea we heard the train run into the station 20 minutes before we expected it. A mad rush ensued. We got to the station but just as I reached the bridge to cross to the other platform the train moved off. Back we dashed to our car and off we set to race after it to Dingwall. Although he had only a Morris 8 Kennie Macleay got ahead of it and reached Muir of Ord before it. We slowed down there to see whether the train would stop at the platform but it simply thundered through and dashed away ahead of us. Off we went once more and gradually overtook the iron monster. On a long straight run where road and rail were parallel I realised how fast the train was going. Very, very slowly we were drawing up passing carriage after carriage till at last we left the engine behind us – but our speedometer registered 60 miles per hour. I also saw what a good driver we had, for there were bends which would have cast less experienced hands – at such a speed – off the road. While negotiating such a bend which led the road over the railway the engine suddenly roared underneath us and with its rattling swaying carriages dashed away ahead of us again. At Conon Bridge Station it stopped, but we were afraid that it would be away again before we could reach it so we kept straight on. At Ferintosh Distillery it overtook us again and rattled into the station, but we knew that by this time we were quite safe, so we were able to take our seats in the train at our leisure. But it was an exciting race!

7 JANUARY, 1950

Last Monday got the stunning news that Mr Cameron of Resolis had suddenly passed away. In my opinion the greatest light in the Church has been removed. His remains arrived on Wednesday night, accompanied by his widow and son and daughter. It was a sad coming. Six ministers met the boat and three came with the funeral party. The coffin was carried by the ministers to the hearse which was waiting in Quay Street and then the whole party – exclusive of the local ministers – set out for Kinloch. The morning was very wet but ere we arrived the skies had opened up. The service began in the church at 12 o'clock and was conducted by the ministers of the Island. It was a solemn and singular coincidence that the table from which Mr Cameron had last served the Lord's Supper in September was now called into use to bear the burden of his coffin – for the Kinloch communion was the last he attended. The service was over about 1.10 and the funeral procession – fully 200 strong – set out for the Laxay cemetery. Just as we left, the skies clouded over again and we got a shower so heavy and persistent that some must have been soaked to the skin. The burial ground is up on a knoll above the main road and appears to be a very ancient place. There, beside his father, the Rev. Hector Cameron of Back,[1] we left the mortal remains of

1 The only minister in the Free Church in Lewis who did not go into the Union of 1900.

our dear friend and beloved minister in the Gospel, the Rev. William
Cameron of Resolis. He was a man of solid, massive intellect with a
wonderful grasp of truth, and one of the most humble and saintly
men that ever I have met. His removal is a sore loss to the Church and
to the Lord's cause in Scotland.

21 JANUARY

On Tuesday night with two of my office-bearers conducted a meeting
in a tinker's shanty on the Barvas road in which a death had taken place.
Felt somewhat moved in that strange company, especially when I
realised how these poor creatures had an equal claim with ourselves to
the blessings of salvation in Christ.

SATURDAY, 15 APRIL: LOCHGILPHEAD

The Lochgilphead congregation are greatly changed. My own-time
young people are becoming old and the then old are away, while the
incomers are nearly all Established Church or no Church at all. There
was no service on Friday – changed days! On Saturday evening I had an
audience of 25. On the Sabbath there were only 48 present at the
morning service of whom 32 communicated, but it is long since I saw
so many in tears as I saw at the Table service. At night there was a
congregation of 93. On Monday afternoon the Rev. Jack Morrison took
me over in his car to Tayvallich and right down all the way to the road
end at Keills. I was never there before and I enjoyed the visit very much.
The country down there is wonderfully pretty, but the very evident
depopulation is sad.

Next morning I left and the world was beautiful. I felt rather
pensive. I had left that once familiar countryside a young man – now I
had come back to it 30 years later probably to pay my last visit. 'The
days of old I called to mind'.

29 APRIL: SKYE TO MAINLAND

The crossing was pretty wild and when we reached Mallaig the scene
was one of tempestuous grandeur. Overnight snow had fallen and Skye
was white down to its shores. From the West the waves were surging
angrily against the harbour wall and every few moments sending showers
of spray right over into the inner harbour. The passengers from the boat
had to study the waves and run the gauntlet in the intervals in order to
get up to the station. I, however, took an unorthodox way and got the
shelter of some fishwagons between myself and the lashing sea and so
got up untouched to the train.

14 OCTOBER

At night weather conditions worsened and we had only about 390 at the Gaelic service. Spoke from Psalm 89:15 and enjoyed liberty. Was surprised and touched to see the poor old tinker woman, who lost her husband some months ago, present in a black dress with a young girl beside her. Oh if the gospel would take root out there, what a blessing it would be!

SATURDAY, 4 NOVEMBER

Left on Monday night for Mary's marriage and after a comfortable journey reached Perth next afternoon where I was met by Cathie and Archie MacDonald.[1] We proceeded up to the manse in which I felt very comfortable and after tea I took the Prayer Meeting at which only 12 were present. After that we went to Mary's hotel where we met herself and Norman[2] and also a number of the friends from the North who had already come for the marriage. Next day dear Mary was married and she was no longer ours. The marriage was conducted by Mr Fraser of Kiltarlity with Mr MacDonald of Perth and myself assisting and Mr MacKinnon of Kennoway precenting. There were in all 9 ministers present. The reception was held in the Queen's Hotel and was very pleasant.

SATURDAY, 3 MARCH, 1951

Arriving at Dingwall Station at 8.20 on Thursday I found a farmer from Ferintosh waiting for me with his car. Half an hour later I was sitting at a large wood fire in the drawing room in Ferintosh Manse – a room once very familiar to me and – like all that house – full of memories. While I was in that Manse I repeatedly had the feeling that I ought to see Dr Munro with his concertina trousers and leather-bound turn-ups stalking into the room.

On Friday forenoon I preached from 1 Peter 1:23 and was considerably surprised and disappointed to find that my congregation numbered only 26.

2 JUNE: VISIT TO ARDELVE, WESTER ROSS

On Monday night I closed up the Manse and left for a few days' holiday at Ardelve. Mrs Macleod of Barvas was also crossing on her way

1 Minister at Perth, a native of Uig, Skye, and well known to the MacRaes in their Kilmuir days.
2 The Rev. Norman MacLeod of Carloway, Lewis. Mr MacLeod had been inducted to the charge of Lochalsh in October and it was therefore to the Lochalsh manse (situated at Ardelve) that he was to take his bride.

to Balmacara and the car which met her at the pier took me right on to Ardelve so that I arrived at the Manse at 6.30. The morning was beautifully fine, so I loitered around till 7.45 before seeking admittance. The surprise of Mary and Norman was very great for they expected me to arrive by the mail bus at 3.45 in the afternoon. The weather was ideal. That evening I cycled over to Carn Dubh beyond Dornie. I had not been on a bicycle for years, and I felt very pleased to discover that I had not lost the art. The following evening cycled again to Bundaloch, the next township, and conducted a house meeting there.

On Thursday afternoon with Norman climbed the mountain at the back of the Manse – 'Meall Chonchra'. The panorama below us was magnificent, almost the whole of Loch Duich and Loch Long in their mountain setting being revealed. Our climb was unpremeditated and consequently we had not sufficient time to reach the summit, but we were up to nearly 2000 feet above sea level, and perhaps it was as well that we went no further, for ere we got down to the Manse again the strain of the descent was so severe that our thigh muscles were well-nigh giving out altogether. I could not have continued much further and Norman was not much better. Even now I cannot descend the stair without muscular pain. Notwithstanding all these I was very thankful that I was able to do it. I had concluded years ago that my climbing days were for ever over.[1] To find that it is not so makes me feel as though I had got a fresh lease of life. To the Lord be the praise!

Cathie arrived on Wednesday evening from Edinburgh and yesterday, reluctantly after a most enjoyable time, we left Ardelve by the 9 am bus.

28 JULY: ARDELVE

I left Ruarach at 3.40 and reached the Manse at Ardelve at 4.15. Past days were much before me and saddened me. 44 years ago I came down that glen for the first time with three of my old Post Office chums, and we saved ourselves a long detour of about two miles by wading across the shallows to below Clachan Duich. Little did I dream then that I would yet be a minister preaching in Gaelic in that very place. From Ruarach one has a much more extensive view than from the Manse and a more vivid impression of the magnificence of the scenery. Opposite our windows, Sgurr na Moraich, one of the Five Sisters of Kintail, rose

1 His illness in 1934 had caused permanent damage to his leg which was bandaged for the rest of his life. Yet he always walked with a brisk step and without any trace of a limp.

steeply to a height of 2850 feet, while to the left, and beyond the green tree-clad strath down which flows the River Croe, was the huge bulk of Ben Attow (Beinn Fhada) towering up to 3385 feet. In comparison, the sequestered and pleasant scenery around the Manse at Ardelve seemed quite tame. Yet I was glad to get there and to enjoy its peace.

(After another brief visit to Ardelve in the autumn of the same year he wrote, 'Felt sad and wistful at the thought of leaving such a restful and beautiful spot. I would fain have stayed. I love the hills, I love the trees, I love the quietness of country places'.)

28 SEPTEMBER, 1952

Today got the news that Donald Macleod ('White')[1] my dear elder and our Gaelic precentor, had passed away in the local hospital. For the last few days his condition was critical, but the long fight he had put up made us begin to hope that he was to pull through. But the Lord ordered it otherwise. His removal is a great loss to the congregation and I felt it keenly. He was a true friend, wise and reliable. He was one of those whom I loved and respected most in the Session. After the evening service, conducted the usual meeting in his home. It was a sad home. Who would have thought that 'White' was to be the first to be called away! A fortnight ago he was in his usual health. Then came the sudden turn, the rush to hospital, the operation, and now all is over, and 'White' has left us to be with his Lord.

30 SEPTEMBER, 1952

This afternoon we laid 'White' to rest down in the sands of Aignish burying ground where lie the remains of the two precentors who preceded him – Angus MacLeod[2] and Alistair MacLeod (the baker), and then with sad hearts we turned away and left him there – or what is mortal of him – awaiting a glorious resurrection.

1 So nick-named in his youth on account of his fair hair – 'white' being the Gaelic equivalent of 'fair'.
2 Of Angus MacLeod he wrote at the time of his death in 1938: 'He was a dear, affectionate, loyal friend. His death affected me more than I could tell, and till we left his body sleeping by the quiet waters of Aignish Bay my spirit remained under a dark and heavy cloud... Dear Angus!'

MacRae had declined an invitation to visit Australia in the 1930's yet in 1953, at the age of seventy, he agreed to a request that he should give a year to intensive preaching in that country. One factor which made the time opportune was that the close ties between the Free Church and the Presbyterian Church of Eastern Australia had just been cemented in 1952 by legislation establishing mutual eligibility between the two denominations. In addition, the union of the Presbyterian Church of Eastern Australia with the Free Presbyterian Church of Victoria which is recorded in this chapter, gave rise to new hope. Certainly in terms of Australian Presbyterianism as a whole these were small Churches but they had held on to their reformed testimony and looked to God to give that testimony new power and influence at a time when it was very little known. This was just the challenge to appeal to MacRae and it did not disconcert him that he was asked to give the majority of his time to the small Free Presbyterian congregation in Chapel Street, St Kilda, about three miles from the centre of Melbourne.

The reader will observe how the temptations to despondency which he felt in the first part of his visit were succeeded by confirmation that his preaching in St Kilda was not in vain. Indeed by the time his visit concluded he was ready to express the opinion that had he been a younger man the prospect of staying in Australia would have appealed to him.

There has been a considerable re-awakening to the doctrines of grace in Australia since the mid 1950's and it is interesting to note that the St Kilda congregation under the ministry of the Rev. Edwin Lee (1959–66) became one of the focal points for those who were coming to a fresh appreciation of true biblical preaching.

17 Australia: 1953-54

This being my last Sabbath here prior to our Australian tour a record morning attendance appeared at the Gaelic service, fully 550 being present. At the first singing felt so moved that I had to ask the Lord to harden me. Spoke from Acts 20:32 and gave a good warning as to 'grievous wolves' from without and party-men from within. At night the church was full, some even sitting in the passages. Preached in English from John 4:11 to a congregation of well up to 1300, but did not get much liberty. At the close many waited to bid me 'goodbye', but even then I failed to realise that I am leaving them for such a long time.

SATURDAY, 9 MAY: S.S. 'OTRANTO'

Yesterday – Friday – we left St Pancras London at 1 o'clock in a very crowded train which carried none save passengers for the 'Otranto', and a 70-minutes run brought us to Tilbury river-side. There we went through the process of embarkation, and a very harassing experience it was. I could not but feel surprised that, after all the experience which these people (The Orient Line) have had, they have not yet devised a more efficient and expeditious method of dealing with the matter. I was also very disappointed with the vessel; she is not nearly as up-to-date as the 'Loch Seaforth'[1] and our cabin has to be illuminated continually with artificial light. It never sees the light of day and is much smaller than I expected.

We sailed at 4.30 down the muddy waters of the Thames. The day was good and the wind easterly. Last night the towns on the South coast of England were a nest of lights, red, blue and ordinary.

Today we are out of sight of land, crossing the Bay of Biscay, but we are indeed fortunate for there is very little sea.

TUESDAY, 12 MAY

While outwardly perfect, Sabbath was rather a miserable day and I felt like the Pilgrims at Vanity Fair. In the forenoon there was a service which was conducted after the Church of England style. We did not go into it, but remained within earshot, and indeed, so far as I heard it, the service was mainly music and mummery. We went down below and had

1 Successor to the 'Lochness' between Stornoway and the mainland.

a short Gaelic service in our cabin and read a sermon from McCheyne. Once the ship's service was over, apart from a children's Sabbath School, there was no more mention of God and the remainder of the day was given up to every kind of vanity.

Yesterday we got a very good view of Cape St Vincent and later on we enjoyed a lovely sunset where the waters begin to narrow in between Europe and Africa towards the Straits of Gibraltar. About 10.30 we anchored off Gibraltar which, with its flaring lights shimmering all over the lower slopes of the Rock, made a wonderful picture.

We left again about 12.15 this morning and about 9 am today passed a huge mass in the haze which I understand was Cap de Gata.

THURSDAY, 14 MAY

On Wednesday afternoon passed another bulk in the haze which turned out to be the southernmost point of Sardinia. It was treeless, precipitous and wild. This morning we entered Naples Harbour at 9 am and got ashore shortly after breakfast, not without a good deal of preliminaries. We were unfortunate in our day, for it was a public holiday and all the shops were closed. However the street vendors were much in evidence and were very troublesome. I went ashore again after lunch and, taking a much wider circuit, got a better view of the place. What arrested my attention most was the size and magnificence of some of the buildings, combined with the primitive aspect of some of the country people who had come in to sell their wares at the way-side. Old-fashioned phaetons abounded, all regulated for hire, some of them driven by wild-looking fellows. The buses were good and comfortable looking, while electric trams clanged noisily along their rails.

We left at 5 o'clock and I was able to get a good view of the copious harbour. I have never anywhere seen such magnificent maritime buildings.

Shortly after I got back to the ship a drenching shower came on and the lightning flashed vividly. Mount Vesuvius appeared very grim amid its clouds. Thereafter the sea became rough and for the first time the 'Otranto' rolled.

It is very strange that in a country defeated in war, and bankrupt, there should be so many evidences of industry and prosperity, and I could not but contrast it with our own neglected Highlands.

TUESDAY, 19 MAY

During last Thursday night we got into quieter waters when we passed through the Straits of Messina. I was sorry that I missed seeing Sicily. Sabbath was a miserable day and I was glad when it was over. At about 4 pm we reached Port Said and once we were berthed a fleet of small boats laden with goods for selling came out to us, and soon there was a veritable pandemonium of bartering, buying and selling. I could not but think of Nehemiah and the heathen Sabbath vendors. But the people who bought were more guilty than the sellers, for they know that there is a Fourth Commandment; the Egyptians don't. Port Said is an exceedingly well-appointed town with a prosperous appearance, and the proximity of the Suez Canal makes it a very busy port.

Yesterday morning, on going up on deck before breakfast, I saw we were running through the desert and knew that we were well on our way through the famous Suez Canal. We reached Suez shortly before nightfall. It too is a wonderfully imposing place and much larger than I looked for. However we did not lie up there but slowly passed out of the Canal into the Gulf of Suez.

WEDNESDAY, 20 MAY

Up to this point the heat was bearable, but now that we are travelling southward through the Red Sea it has become most oppressive. One poor woman from the Isle of Man, who sat at our table in the Dining Room, was rendered quite prostrate, and tonight to my extreme grief I learned that she had suddenly passed away. She had a weak heart and the heat was altogether too much for her.

FRIDAY, 22 MAY

Yesterday morning I got a shock when I was informed that the burial of the poor woman who had died on Wednesday night had taken place at 6 am on Thursday. I felt so upset that I could scarcely take my breakfast. I am quite aware of the necessity for rapid burial in the Tropics, but surely, in the light of the advances of modern science, in a vessel of this kind which carries hundreds of passengers for a protracted period a mortuary fitted out with refrigeratory equipment ought to be made essential by law. To commit a body into the shark-infested waters of the Red Sea in the morning and to arrive in Aden the same evening is indeed a shame and disgrace.

Today I was informed that other two had passed away – an old man who was travelling out to Australia with three grandsons, and a young person. Concerning their burial I heard nothing. Apparently, as in the first case, the burial would take place in the early morning, conducted by the Captain, and in such privacy that the amusement of the passengers, which seems to be the only thing this Company think about, would not be disturbed. I have never heard of such callousness. Truly, 'the last times' are upon us.

During our passage through the Suez Canal we were accompanied by an armed patrol who kept pace with us in an armoured car. Things in Egypt are in a very unsettled condition. (On Monday a British soldier was stabbed in full view of pedestrians in a street in Port Said.)

I was informed that the magnificent harbour installations at Naples were the work of the Americans who during and after the war made Naples their chief Mediterranean base.

MONDAY, 25 MAY

After leaving Aden, which we reached under cover of night on Thursday, so that we saw very little of the 'Barren Rocks', our course took us out into the Gulf of the same name which is so wide that we could not discern land on either side. On Saturday the heat was very severe and our cabin was too hot to sit in. On Sabbath morning we attended the ship's service, but I shall never do so again. The service was conducted by the Captain, and apart from the reading of the Word the whole service was a piece of senseless mummery which must have been as obnoxious to God as it was repellent to common sense.

SATURDAY, 30 MAY

On Wednesday we drew into Colombo about 11 am. The approach was rather interesting – quite apparently a city of the East. We got ashore by launch after an early lunch, but once again we were unfortunate – another general holiday! The large and reputable stores were all closed, but the small merchants and hawkers seemed to be everywhere. The main streets are well built and the buildings imposing, but we did not get near the native quarters. A sudden, heavy shower drove us into shelter which fortunately was near, and there we waited impatiently until the rain ceased. We were glad enough to get back to the ship, but I felt disappointed that I saw so little of the place.

Although Ceylon has been granted independence, British influence is everywhere. All the streets we saw bore English names, as also did all the local craft, and all the advertisements in the passenger launches were worded in English. The people are small and slight and rather dark of skin.

What perhaps surprised me most was that in the harbour, instead of our graceful, white seagulls, there fluttered about continually an ugly evil-looking type of crow. I have not seen a seagull since we left our own waters.

We left Colombo on Wednesday evening at 7 o'clock and have been ploughing steadily on in a south-east direction ever since.

Was interested to see a very good example of a coral atoll the day before we reached Colombo. It surprised me to know that this island – Minicoy – supported a population of 3000. How do they live? The lagoon, with the still submerged coral arms over which the seas were breaking, was clearly visible.

TUESDAY, 2 JUNE

Ever since leaving Ceylon there has been more motion of the ship than up till now, and some of the passengers have been suffering from sea-sickness. At present we are 22 degrees from the Equator which we crossed at 3 o'clock on Friday morning. This trip from Colombo to Fremantle is the longest span of the voyage, being about 3,150 miles from port to port and taking 8 days for the passage. It is tedious, but we hope to make port on Thursday morning.

SATURDAY, 6 JUNE

Tuesday was coronation day[1] and a day of extra vanity. At the dinner in the evening it was expected that every person would drink to the Queen in a glass of port wine and then unite in singing the National Anthem. I declined the wine and walked out at the close of dinner and refused to wait for their nonsensical observances. It is extraordinary how completely this generation is given over to vanity. I felt exceedingly angry at the way strong drink was thrust upon young people without the option of lemonade or any such non-intoxicant. We retired early to bed, but the next day we heard that things went to a great length the previous night.

On Thursday at about 4 pm we reached Fremantle. Arrangements were most inefficient and dilatory, and the night was coming on ere we got ashore. This was most annoying, for we lost the shops again, and my hope of getting to Perth to see Dunc's[2] grave was completely shattered. Fremantle seems to be largely an industrial town with very large wool factories but the main shopping centres are well lit and of imposing appearance.

1 That is, the coronation of Queen Elizabeth II.
2 His eldest brother, see p 121n.

We left again about midnight and have been steadily ploughing our way Eastwards ever since.

TUESDAY, 9 JUNE

Today we are skirting the Victorian coast with a fresh breeze after us. Although there is a fair sea, conditions are pleasant and there is no swell.

SATURDAY, 13 JUNE

At 8 am on Wednesday we reached Melbourne and the end of our voyage. Mr Graham[1] and Mr Nicolson met us. The customs was a very slow business and we were held up for a considerable period.

At about 10.30 we got away and were driven swiftly into the city, where we left Mr Nicolson, and then out to St Kilda. The city streets, especially Collins Street, were very imposing. Traffic was heavy and very swift.

Our flat is a comfortable suite of rooms on the first storey, built in colonial style – a good summer house but not cosy enough for the winter. We have the use of three rooms, a kitchen and a bathroom.

On Wednesday afternoon Mr Graham motored us out to Mentone where we called upon two Stornoway families. It is a long way out, yet there is no cessation in the built-up area which constitutes the Melbourne suburbs. I felt that we would never reach open country.

Yesterday a 'welcome' dinner was given us, at which we had besides Mr Graham and Alvan McIntosh of Hamilton, two Reformed Presbyterian ministers – Mr MacEwen [Melbourne] and Mr Barkley [Geelong]. After dinner there were several speeches and then we went to the church – (the dinner was held in a Methodist Church Hall) – where I gave an address on 'Scotland Today'. They have given us an extraordinary welcome and showed such kindness that I feel altogether unworthy and ashamed.

Preached my first sermon in Australia today in the small church of St Kilda and to a smaller congregation – only 26. Spoke from 1 Corinthians 2:2. Cannot say that I got the close attention to which I am accustomed at home, and restlessness among children was a somewhat disturbing element. However, perhaps I shall feel more at home when I become used to my new conditions. It is apparent that this is a very godless city and that comparatively few attend church.

40 were present at the evening service. Preached from Revelation 1:5 and felt more at home.

1 Rev. Isaac Graham of St Kilda.

[404]

SATURDAY, 20 JUNE

Afraid I have spent rather an idle week. It is really extraordinary how the days can go in this city of distances and leave one with very little to show for it. Transport is most confusing and the city is so widespread that one can accomplish no more than one or at most two visits in a day.

Yesterday visited the Botanic Gardens. They are very fine and in their wooded spaces one feels very far away from the city and in a most peaceful atmosphere. The city itself is rather untidy. There are no boxes for used tickets in the trams and very few rubbish baskets in the streets. There is usually a litter of newspaper, leaves, etc., lying about which spoils the appearance of the place.

SABBATH, 21 JUNE

The morning was somewhat dull and very cold, but fair. Spoke to an audience of 28 with a measure of liberty from Genesis 6:13 on sin as a precursor of judgment. The evening was wet and stormy and I was rather disappointed that my audience numbered only 22. Spoke from Philippians 1:20 on the great reconciliation and enjoyed it better than any service since coming here.

TUESDAY, 30 JUNE

I read in the press yesterday that Rev. Crichton Barr of the Scots Church had said that he was not aware of any branch of the Christian Church which definitely condemned the practice of praying for the dead. I wrote a brief letter to the *Age*, pointing out that his own church did, and quoting the Westminster Confession of Faith XXI 4. I did not like entering into the Australian press, but this was too barefaced to be allowed to pass uncontradicted.

SATURDAY, 11 JULY

Last night went to hear Dr Carl McIntyre in the Brunswick Methodist Church. Was rather disappointed. First of all I was disappointed with the church. It was poorly lit and dingy, and the few electric radiators on the walls utterly failed to disperse the chill of the building. A light paint badly in need of renewal completely spoiled the appearance of the interior. Then the audience was disappointing. About 200 present, but I expected more than twice that number. I was also disappointed with the acoustics of the building. Although we sat half way down I made nothing of the other speakers and missed a lot of what Dr MacIntire said. Last of all Dr McIntire did not appear to be in his usual form. His address seemed to be somewhat disjointed. Yet he taught me again what I had forgotten, namely, that the secret of effective speaking is emphasis. The only thing which favourably impressed me was the singing, which was very hearty.

SABBATH, 19 JULY

Struck a new low-level today when my audience numbered only 14. Spoke from 1 Peter 2:9 and enjoyed some liberty in it. The evening attendance was even lower – only 12 – and of these three were strangers – two Dutchmen and a Skyeman. Spoke from Hebrews 9:14 but felt that I lacked clearness. Things are pretty depressing, but perhaps the coldness of winter may deter some of the elderly from coming out.

SATURDAY, 1 AUGUST

Felt very unfit yesterday morning to leave for Geelong for Mr Alvan McIntosh's induction. Mr MacEwen of McKinnon Reformed Presbyterian Church accompanied us, for which we were very thankful, for he served as a most interesting guide. The train left from Spencer Street Station and was different in type from the ordinary suburban electric trains and rather more like our home trains. Yet it was not at all so comfortable and well-finished, and for heating purposes it had lying on the floor one of the old-fashioned footwarmers which I have not seen for well-nigh half a century.

The country through which we passed was very flat and on the whole uninteresting. I was surprised at the extent and the manufactories of Geelong. It seems to be a rapidly growing town.

The morning was beautiful but I felt it bitterly cold. We were soon run out to a very pretty house in the high part of the town which was to be our headquarters during our stay. At about 10.30 we convened in the church vestry for a meeting of ministers.

At 2 o'clock we assembled again in the vestry, this time as a Synod. Then a meeting of Presbytery followed, at which it was decided that I go to Hamilton (DV) for October and November, and to New South Wales at the end of March. With difficulty we managed to get sufficient time for tea at Mr and Mrs Crocker's ere assembling once more at 6.45 for the Induction service. I was disappointed at the smallness of the congregation, only about 40 being present. I preached from 2 Timothy 2:15 and enjoyed it. Mr Graham conducted the induction and charged the minister, while I addressed the congregation. There was a very good atmosphere, of which Mr McIntosh said he was very conscious.

Today we left Geelong at 10.45 and got back to our flat in Melbourne at about 2 o'clock.

SABBATH, 2 AUGUST

We had an attendance of 24 this morning. Spoke from Hebrews 12:5 on chastisements, their purpose and profit. At night spoke from 2 Peter 1:11 to a gathering of 22 and followed up by a Gaelic service for which 20 waited.

SABBATH, 9 AUGUST

The day was beautiful. In the forenoon preached from Malachi 3:6 on the immutability of God. 20 were present. At night I had only 15. It is most depressing. Spoke from 1 Corinthians 16:13. Feel very far from God in this country and long for the atmosphere of home.

SATURDAY, 15 AUGUST

On Tuesday out in Mid Brighton visited a Miss Macpherson whose grandparents come from Aird, Sleat. Her grandfather must have been a man of some worth, for on the voyage to Australia he conducted Gaelic services on board the ship, for which he was presented by the grateful passengers with a Gaelic Bible signed by the captain of the vessel. I did not take the most expeditious way and had a walk of 45 minutes, but I did not grudge it, for my walk was so rural and the air so fresh that I much enjoyed it.

Yesterday Cathie slipped and wrenched her back and has suffered considerable discomfort ever since. I hope she has not displaced anything.

THURSDAY, 20 AUGUST

Despatched my booklet on *The Resurgence of Arminianism* by airmail yesterday for publication in Inverness.[1]

This afternoon went out to Royal Park to see the Zoo. The afternoon was beautiful and in the warm sunlight the grounds looked their best.

SATURDAY, 22 AUGUST

I sometimes feel afraid in this country, and at such times I long to get out of it and back to Scotland. I feel then, not only that the country is godless, but that it is God-forsaken. I feel this especially at the week-

1 This material, written on the voyage out to Australia, will receive comment in the next chapter.

ends. God seems to be completely forgotten. A terrible coldness reigns such as I have never felt in my own country, low though religious life may be in Scotland today. May the Lord in His mercy take us home again, and may He grant that my visit may not have been made in vain!

SATURDAY, 12 SEPTEMBER

Since my last entry I have been laid aside with rather a severe bout of influenza. Last Sabbath I spent in bed and I feel weak enough for the work of the morrow, more especially when I have a Gaelic afternoon service in addition to the ordinary services. This is my third illness since coming to this country and I feel that it has told on me and pretty severely taxed my strength.

TUESDAY, 15 SEPTEMBER

At the Annual Meeting of the Bible Union of Victoria which was held in the Hall of the Independent Church, Collins Street, I gave an address on the 'Strategy of Modernism'. All day I felt miserably weak and when I was called upon to give my address I wondered what would happen were I to collapse. But the Lord was good to me, and once I got started I was wonderfully sustained and given an altogether unusual measure of vigour and vim without feeling exhausted.

Pastor K. A. Macnaughton of Geelong Church of Christ also spoke on 'Communism, Modernism and Nationalism in the Far East'. He spoke rapidly and well. As I listened to him speaking of the fatuity of evangelists' methods, it struck me very forcibly as strange that the speaker himself did not see that the calling for decisions at the close of a meeting was a pure farce. He attributed the absence of permanent results to lack of what he called 'follow-up' work, as though the whole of conversion were the work of man.

FRIDAY, 18 SEPTEMBER

The Spring now has really come and the weather is ideal, and, through the day, quite hot – up to 72 degrees. I feel somewhat stronger but still am very languid and disinclined to exert myself.

SATURDAY, 19 SEPTEMBER

This is a strange communion – only one week-day service in connection with it and tomorrow three services, with the communion service in the afternoon! No matter what the difficulties may be owing to the scattered nature of the congregation, I think that they have done wrong in cutting down the services to such an extent. They are nearly all members here, but indeed they have need of a good shaking up. Things would not have gone so low had there been more life among them.

FRIDAY, 25 SEPTEMBER

Visited this afternoon Rev. John Noble MacKenzie out at Balwyn. He is a Plockton man who came out to Australia well-nigh 60 years ago. He served as missionary in the New Hebrides for 10 years but spent most of his life in Korea in connection with the Mission to Lepers. He is now 88 years of age and is more or less confined to bed, but mentally he is very alert, and despite his long residence away from home, he has never lost his Gaelic.

SABBATH, 27 SEPTEMBER

A beautiful day, but only 11 appeared in church. Spoke from Romans 8:23 on waiting for the redemption of the body, and rather enjoyed it. In the afternoon conducted the monthly meeting at the Melbourne Bible House but did not enjoy it. Was a good deal distracted by the divided attention of those who had to look after their very small children. Although one would not like to forbid the children, even at that tender age, it is questionable whether there is any profit in bringing them out. They are too young to understand, and they leave their parents too disturbed to enjoy the service, while the distraction caused by them may also mar the service for the preacher and others. Spoke from Judges 5:8 to a congregation of 34. At the evening service had only 9. Felt very discouraged. They could do better here than they are doing, and, unless they are prepared to put more heart into the matter, I do not see how they can expect to carry on much longer.

MONDAY, 28 SEPTEMBER

Today Norman MacLeod took us a long run in his car the full length of Mornington Peninsula. We left at 10 am and returned at 6 pm. The day was ideal and the country looked its best. This afforded us an opportunity of seeing a good slice of Australian fruit-growing country – mainly apples and pears – and then all the way to Dandenong we passed through a land of dairy farms. It was a most enjoyable day.

WEDNESDAY, 30 SEPTEMBER

Today we 'struck camp' and rather reluctantly took our departure from our flat in St Kilda. We left Spencer Street Station at 1.40 on the

6 hours' journey of nearly 200 miles to Hamilton. Fortunately Mr Graham, who had unexpectedly called in on a visit to Melbourne, travelled with us and made the way very interesting for us. We reached Hamilton at 7.45 by which time darkness had fallen and were soon in the Grahams' hospitable home.

THURSDAY, 1 OCTOBER

This afternoon we motored out to a farm 10 to 12 miles to the North of Hamilton. The run took us through a green, pleasant country altogether given over to sheep rearing. Apparently the wool industry alone counts here, for the returns are enormous. At £3 a fleece the owner of 1,000 sheep makes £3000 at every shearing. In all this area I did not see a single patch of cultivated land. The farm house was a modern building of the bungalow type and beautifully furnished. The old lady whom we went to see was typically Highland in her appearance and still retained a certain amount of the Gaelic of her youth. Our car was the congregational one and I drove it back, for the sake of getting to know it ere I submit to my test for an Australian driving licence.

SATURDAY, 2 OCTOBER

Hamilton is a clean, well-built and broad-streeted town situated in a very pleasant stretch of countryside. It has very good shops and has the aspect of a well-to-do, prosperous town.

In the afternoon held a service at 3 o'clock at which I had an attendance of 14. Spoke from Isaiah 12:3.

TUESDAY, 6 OCTOBER

On my way home from Saturday's service I suddenly began to feel unwell. Early on Sabbath morning it appeared very unlikely that I would be able to take the services of the day, but the Lord was good to me and by His grace I was enabled, despite great weakness, to preach the Action sermon from Colossians 1:14 with a measure of liberty. I was disappointed to see that the congregation only numbered 40, of whom 30 communicated. In the evening I got a still greater shock in finding only 12 in the church. Things seem to have drifted badly here also. Spoke from Acts 16:14 on the opening of the heart of Lydia. Thus I got through a very trying day with great thankfulness to the Lord who had dealt so wonderfully with us.

Last night we had only 12 at the Thanksgiving service. Spoke from Philippians 1:6 on the sure continuance of the good work. So we concluded a very strange communion season, but there is one thing for which I feel thankful – the influence of Mr Graham's company upon my own soul. He is an unusually spiritually-minded man and I feel the better of having been with him. Indeed I felt quite unwilling to terminate such a profitable season. But it had to be, and today we transferred our belongings over to the Manse which for the rest of our stay is to be our home. It is a large, old-fashioned Australian type of house.

Here we feel very lonely and cast down. The house has been well stocked for us and the people have done exceedingly well, but – we are lonely!

SABBATH, 11 OCTOBER

Owing to the fact that I had four services before me and was required to drive the car 52 miles, felt very anxious. Fortunately the day was good although very cold in the morning. In Hamilton at 11 o'clock I had an attendance of 26. Spoke from Proverbs 1:22 on man's inherent dislike of the Word of God as an evidence of original sin. We left for the second service in the country at 1.15 and drove over pleasant, open, green undulating country to North Byaduk where in a small freshly painted wooden church I conducted a half hour's service, 1.45 to 2.15, to a congregation of 6 people. I spoke impromptu for about 15 minutes from Malachi 3:16 and, strange to say, rather enjoyed it. I was due at Mount Eccles, my next preaching station, 16 miles further on, at 3 o'clock. At Macarthur, a pleasant little country village, we left the main highway, which continues on to the coast at Port Fairy, and branched to the West. After 4 miles of running on a second-class road we reached the little church at Mount Eccles. It stands in a picturesque, secluded spot and inside it is as nice a country church as I have ever seen. Here I had a congregation of 13 – some of whom were Methodists – and I somewhat enjoyed speaking to them from Malachi 3:7 on God's call to repentance. At night in Hamilton my congregation numbered only 10, which was very poor. Spoke from Romans 6:11. I don't know whether my audience were able to appreciate it. I fear that here in Australia, even in the Free Church, there is more profession than spiritual exercise.

SABBATH, 18 OCTOBER

Had 26 at the morning service today. Spoke from Judges 5:8 on apostasy as depriving us of God's favour. Somewhat disturbed, as I was when I preached this sermon in Melbourne, by young children distracting myself and my audience. In the afternoon motored out to

Branxholme, 16 miles away, and at 2.45 held a service for a congregation of 28. Spoke from Psalm 73:28 and enjoyed it. The weather was lovely, the drive was through green, beautiful, smiling country, and the church – which has many memories of the pioneer days – is in a particularly attractive spot. At night we had only 11 out at the service.

THURSDAY, 22 OCTOBER

In the newspapers today there is an account of heavy flooding in the Gippsland area. The newspaper states that the Melbourne reading for rainfall was the heaviest for any 24-hour period since 1869. In Warburton families had to flee, and Moe – where 'Dolly' Munro[1] lives – and Yallourn were badly flooded.

SABBATH, 24 OCTOBER

In this congregation as in St Kilda (at any rate in the evenings) there is no man to lead the singing – which I think is very poor. Mrs Graham usually performs this part, but being away with her husband at St Kilda today, Cathie took her place and got on very well. Preached in the morning from Romans 8:33-4. Owing to the shortness of the interval between services Cathie could not accompany me to Byaduk and I myself had to do the singing there and also at Mount Eccles. At the former place I had an audience of 7, five of whom came over from Branxholme. At Mount Eccles 22 were out and I spoke from Philippians 2:9-11. The day was good. I got back at 5.15, tired but thankful to get through so well. But such rushing is not good, either for people or for minister. In Hamilton in the evening only 10 were present. Spoke from Philippians 2:9-11. This is a poor place and badly in need of an awakening.

SATURDAY, 31 OCTOBER

Tuesday we left by the 8.20 train for Geelong. The day was good and the journey very pleasant. From Hamilton we travelled in a diesel train which was somewhat like a tram car in its interior and afforded excellent opportunity for surveying the surrounding country. Towards Dunkeld we got very good glimpses of the Grampians. At Ararat we changed into a steam train and travelled on to Ballarat, where we had a wait of over 3½ hours. We reached Geelong at 5.15 and were met by Mr McIntosh who has been presented with a car by his congregation.

The Manse is a much better house than the one in Hamilton, yet

1 A son of Donald Munro of Laxdale – one of the Stornoway elders.

here, too, one found, as so often in Australia, what strikes us as a survival of more primitive times – the huge ugly fireplaces, the absence of a proper hot water system, and other amazingly far-back contrivances. However we were made very much at home and I could not but wonder at the strange disposal of Providence when I remembered a day long ago in Spinningdale, Sutherland, where, when with Mrs McIntosh, then a young slip of a girl, and her sister, we explored Fairy Glen. I do not know whether I met with her again after that, but had we been told then that she would receive me in her home in Australia, how incredible it would have seemed!

On Thursday Mr McIntosh motored us to Torquay beach on the Southern coast, about 14 miles from Geelong, and there we had an outdoor picnic.

At night I gave my lecture 'The Strategy of Modernism', but if it was a success in Melbourne it certainly was a flop in Geelong. The meeting was held in the Baptist Church under the auspices of some local committee, but from the outset it was disappointing. The audience only numbered a few over 50, and in the collection plate which went round *before* the address there was a fair sprinkling of pennies. There were three or four ministers present besides those on the platform, and two of these are associated with the World Council of Churches. I did not get on at all, and found speaking most difficult. It ought to teach me, however, not to be dependent upon the sympathy of my audience, but upon the help of my Lord.

We left Geelong at 9 am yesterday after a very pleasant stay and after a quiet journey got back to Hamilton at 3.15.

THURSDAY, 5 NOVEMBER

Yesterday I attained my 70th birthday. My feelings are strange. For one thing I utterly fail to realise it. The ego of my inner being is just the same as ever – not one whit older than it used to be. I am thankful to the Lord for having spared me so long and given me such a measure of health, but it is evident that I am drawing near to the end of this life's tale, and that is the part which is difficult to take in. In spirituality I am not advancing. Age seems to bring a callousness and hardness with it which are not helpful, and a long experience of the fickle nature of much that passes for spiritual life makes it easier for the devil to tempt me by questioning the eternal verities. Life is almost done, and I have done so little. My longings for a better day in this world apparently are never to be realised. I must look elsewhere.

SABBATH, 8 NOVEMBER

Today was cold, but there were bright periods punctuated by showers. In the morning preached to a congregation of 26 from Genesis 26:15 on the Philistines filling up the wells. At Mount Eccles, in the afternoon, we had only 12 at the service. Spoke from Jeremiah 6:16 on the old paths. At the evening service in Hamilton the attendance was down to 9. Spoke from John 17:24 with more freedom than at the earlier service, but felt very discouraged. I seem to be wasting my time in this country and I long to get back to Scotland.

SABBATH, 22 NOVEMBER

Today was my last Sabbath in Hamilton. The last few days have been very hot, but today, although a bright sunny day, has been much cooler. In the forenoon had a congregation of 26 and addressed them from 1 Corinthians 16:13 and tried to exhort them to faithfulness. At Byaduk I had 7 and spoke impromptu from Malachi 3:6 on the divine unchangeableness. 10 – four of whom were children – were out at Mount Eccles. Spoke from 1 Thessalonians 4:16–18 on the second Advent and the Resurrection. Felt discouraged. My audience appeared so drowsy, and for the second time today a noisy child had to be ejected. I do not wish to complain of young children, but it really is very trying for a speaker, and such distractions would not be permitted in any other audience.

At night, however, I had my best service since coming to Australia. Spoke from Romans 15:13 with somewhat of the liberty I am accustomed to enjoy at home. Felt very thankful that I am not as I feared – so forsaken as to lose all power to preach. 15 were present.

TUESDAY, 24 NOVEMBER

Left Hamilton this morning at 8.20 a.m. Felt quite sorry to go, for we were just beginning to get to know the people.

WEDNESDAY, 25 NOVEMBER: MELBOURNE

Today a special meeting of the Synod of the Presbyterian Church of Eastern Australia met in St Kilda Church to receive 'the ministers, elders and congregations of the Free Presbyterian Church of Victoria'. Rev. Arthur Allen of Sydney preached from Isaiah 8:20 a sermon which for sound Calvinistic doctrine, combined with ability and a forceful, effective delivery, exceeded anything I have heard for many a day. I was delighted. Thereafter, in receiving into the Synod the representatives of the Victorian church, he gave a resumé of Australian church history from a conservative point of view which revealed how thoroughly versed he was in this particular department.

FRIDAY, 27 NOVEMBER: ST KILDA (MELBOURNE)

The Synod today sat from 10 am till 12.15 pm, and again from 1.30 till 6 o'clock, and then had to rise with its work still unfinished. The 'union' of course brought into being a great deal of extra work of an entirely new nature.

At 7 o'clock the special Conference which had been arranged between ourselves and the two ministers of the Reformed Presbyterian Church began by the giving of a paper by Rev. W. R. McEwen of the R.P. Church at McKinnon, entitled 'The Holy Scriptures – God's Word to Man'. It was good and to the point. A second paper by Dr J. C. Andrews, South Africa, on the Headship of Christ, followed. Dr Andrews, owing to the illness of his wife, was not able to be present, and his paper was read by Mr A. D. McIntosh of Geelong. It was a masterly production and in every way deserving of permanent record.

SATURDAY, 28 NOVEMBER

This morning at the first session of the Conference Rev. Arthur Allen of Sydney gave a most able paper on 'The Rule of the House', which was a vindication of Presbyterianism. He is a true blue Free Churchman and for that I am profoundly thankful. At the afternoon session I gave an address on the Perpetuity of the Moral Law. Afterwards the members of Synod and most of the audience repaired to the neighbouring park where we had afternoon tea prepared by the ladies of the St Kilda congregation.

MONDAY, 30 NOVEMBER

The Conference resumed at 2 pm with a paper on 'Man Ruined by the Fall' by S. N. Ramsay.

In the evening Mr Barkley of Geelong R.P. Church gave an address on 'Redemption through Christ', followed by Mr McIntosh on 'Regeneration by the Holy Spirit'. Both were delivered – not read – and both were excellent. Mr McIntosh was very lively and pleased me much by condemning the teachings of Finney and the Arminianism of the Keswick movement. Felt exceedingly thankful and uplifted by the realisation that such addresses could still be produced among us and appreciated in this untoward generation.

[415]

TUESDAY, 1 DECEMBER

Mr Harman gave an address this morning on 'The Work of the Ministry', which formed the basis of some discussion. At night I concluded the Conference with an address on Scriptural Worship, in which I did not hesitate to condemn the attitude of some of our own people, who seem to regard our stand for Scriptural worship as a matter of preference rather than a principle.

The Conference ended in an atmosphere of thankfulness and regret. Undoubtedly it proved a great success and revived in us a fresh conception of the importance of the testimony for which we stand. The meetings were warm and decidedly spiritual, and our only regret was that they had come to an end. To the Lord be the praise!

FRIDAY, 11 DECEMBER

Tonight at the Annual Meeting of the Free Bible Society of Victoria gave an address on 'The Message of the Bible for Today'. Felt dreadfully disappointed in the meeting. Including myself the attendance only numbered 25. Surely there is something very far wrong with the Melbourne churches when such a meeting cannot command a better attendance.

SABBATH, 13 DECEMBER

The attendance today at the morning service numbered 8 and two small children. Spoke from Malachi 3:10 and referred to the dying fires of the Christian world in this country, one of which was this congregation. They may not like that, but it is the case, and there is no good in trying to evade what is patent to every thinking person among us.

TUESDAY, 15 DECEMBER

We are now in the throes of another heat wave and tonight is very trying. In the afternoon went out to Mentone and called upon three families of Lewis stock. The older ones are not happy in this country. It is very wrong, I think, of young people who have emigrated to bring their parents out after them. In very few cases will they ever be happy. They pine for the old country all their days.

MONDAY, 21 DECEMBER

Last night I got no sleep until I entirely dispensed with all bedding. The heat was most oppressive. Then I had a dream which made an impression upon me. I seemed to be walking down the Middle Meadow Walk in Edinburgh and it was night. I was alone and there was no one to be seen. But I wept bitterly because I could not keep myself clear of the world's sin. I wakened with my face wet, sad and perplexed as to the meaning of these things.

WEDNESDAY, 23 DECEMBER

Ten were present at the mid-week meeting, but not a man among them. Spoke from Ephesians 1:5–6. Feel depressed. I seem just to be beating the air.

SATURDAY, 26 DECEMBER

A terrible tragedy has taken place in North Island, New Zealand. On Thursday night a train bound for Auckland was precipitated into a flooded swollen river by the collapse of a bridge over which it was passing and 166 lives were lost. A cloudburst had swept away two of the piers supporting the bridge just before the train arrived. Many of the passengers were coming to the celebrations in Auckland in connection with the Queen's visit.

After consultation, her advisers recommended that the Royal programme should remain unaltered, which included attendance upon a race meeting and a visit to a cinema. I am quite sure that had such a tragedy taken place in a heathen land such brutal callousness would not have been shown. That shows the kind of men we have in authority nowadays. No matter what may happen the engagements of sport and pleasure must stand.

FRIDAY, I JANUARY, 1954

In the afternoon we were motored over to Melbourne Cemetery to see Mr Robinson's grave.[1] The setting of the graveyard is beautiful, but I felt depressed to see so many Highland names among the tomb stones and to realise that so many lay there far from their home land and surrounded by strangers from every airt. I felt quite sad and was glad when we left the cemetery.

Truly this has been a strange New Year. The Lord has filled the year that has gone with tokens of His kindness. May He continue so to bless, and may He bring us back in safety to our own land!

WEDNESDAY, 6 JANUARY

Was encouraged tonight to get an attendance of 12 at the Prayer

---

1 The Rev. J. C. Robinson was minister of the St Kilda congregation from 1921 to 1952.

meeting. Spoke from Ephesians 1:9–10 and rather enjoyed it. Showed the difference between the true and the false in the religion of today. The former attributes its source and power to God, the latter to man.

WEDNESDAY, 13 JANUARY

Was greatly encouraged tonight to have 16 at the Prayer Meeting. Spoke from Ephesians 1:11–12 with some liberty.

SABBATH, 17 JANUARY

We had 21 and three small children at the service today. Spoke with some comfort from Hebrews 2:2–3 on the great salvation. In the evening 22 were present. Today has been rather more encouraging than usual and I am thankful for it. Apart from communion services I have not had so many present on one single Sabbath since August 2.

WEDNESDAY, 27 JANUARY

Tonight had a new record attendance at the Prayer Meeting, 18 being present. Spoke from Ephesians 1:15–19 and enjoyed it. It is wonderful how the Prayer Meeting is growing.

SATURDAY, 30 JANUARY

So far our summer has been the hottest since 1908, but yesterday was the coldest January day for 10 years the maximum temperature being only 62. Rain fell all day long and did wonderful good to the ground.

SABBATH, 7 FEBRUARY

The attendances are slowly beginning to increase and attention has become much more intent than it used to be. I am beginning at last to feel encouraged and I am thankful for it.

SATURDAY, 13 FEBRUARY: BAIRNSDALE

On Tuesday we had an early start, leaving the house at 7.30 to get our train at 8.35 at Flinders Street. About 30 miles past Dandenong we began to climb over a long low ridge of typically bush country which was pleasantly green, and on the further side found ourselves in a wide valley walled to the South by a low range of hills. Beyond that again the country was very flat, broken occasionally by a river which flowed down from the distant ranges to the North. Of agriculture there was practically none; as far as the eye could reach, right on to the mountains, nothing was to be seen but the far-stretching, dead-tree dotted plains characteristic of the Australian sheep country. Bairnsdale is 175 miles from Melbourne and we reached it at 1.40 p.m.

Miss M. A. MacRae, who sent so many parcels to us during rationing in Scotland, was waiting on the platform along with her nephew. The latter soon drove us in his car to 426 Main Street where our hostesses resided. I got a bit of a shock when I saw them, for the ages of the three sisters were 85, 84 and 80, and it seemed almost incredible that women of such an age could receive and look after visitors. Yet they did, and made us feel very much at home. They were distinctly old-world and their Highland origin often obtruded itself through their Australian exterior.

Bairnsdale is a pleasant open town with wide streets, the main one having gardens in the centre of the road. The population is a little over 5000, but it is increasing every day and is largely a new town. It is a great tourist centre.

That night we went to bed about 10 o'clock and I don't know when I had such a lovely sleep.

SABBATH, 21 FEBRUARY: MELBOURNE

Had 27 at the morning service when I preached from Genesis 26:15 on the stopping of the wells. In the evening again had 27, which represents the best day's attendance (morning and evening) we have had, with the exception of our first Sabbath in Australia.

WEDNESDAY, 24 FEBRUARY

The Queen and her husband arrived in Melbourne this afternoon by plane from Tasmania. She got a good day. There is great excitement, and decorations and illuminations upon a most elaborate scale.

THURSDAY, 25 FEBRUARY

Today Norman Macleod took us another motor run which was most enjoyable. The day was sunny without being too hot. He took us up by the boulevard at the side of the Yarra river, passing through several pretty nooks laid out for picnickers from the city. At one point Norman ran us up to the summit of a low hill overlooking the river, upon which was built a memorial cairn to mark the spot where the first white men came upon the river in 1805 – they were a party of four from New South Wales. We returned by a different road, passing through quite a number of pleasant mountain villages. In some of them, so embowered in trees were they, that one could quite forget the altitude of their site.

Life in these lovely communities must be very attractive. Eventually we came down to the Fern Gully National Park and there we had tea.

MONDAY, 8 MARCH

Visited the Fitzroy Gardens today. This was Labour Day, one of the many holidays observed in this city, and the Gardens were crowded. Saw Captain Cook's house which was transported from Yorkshire in 1933 and re-erected in the Gardens. Over the door the date 1755 is deeply cut in the stone. The kitchen has something somewhat like our *slabhraidh*,[1] with two forms on either side of the fire-place, while in the back part of the house there was a cobbled apartment which in its day must have been used either as a stable or a byre, like the old blackhouses in the Highlands in which people and cattle entered at the same door.

FRIDAY, 26 MARCH

Tonight conducted the Preparatory service, when I preached from Isaiah 40:31 to a congregation of 19.

SABBATH, 28 MARCH

Had an attendance of 21 at the morning service, when I spoke from John 6:30 on Christ as the Heavenly Bread. In the afternoon we had the communion service with an attendance of 49, of whom 35 sat at the Lord's Table. At night 34 were present, which was a record. Preached from Titus 2:13 on Christ's second coming and enjoyed liberty. I am thankful that I got a good day for our final here in the meantime, but I am beginning to realise already that parting with this congregation will be a very painful experience.

SATURDAY, 3 APRIL

Thursday afternoon we said farewell to our St Kilda flat for a time and left from Spencer Street station on our New South Wales mission.

At Albury we spent the night at a guest house or hotel kept by a Lancashire woman. Next morning we left Albury at 8.53. On this occasion our carriage was a long car carrying about 50 double seats, with an aisle down the centre and large observation windows. The seats were arranged to give the maximum of comfort for a long journey and although the day was very hot, the carriage was air-conditioned and comfortably cool.

1 An iron chain on which pots and kettles were hung over an open fire in the fireplaces of former times.

Darkness came on about an hour before we completed our journey – 368 miles from Albury, 560 miles from Melbourne. We disembarked at Strathfield, 9 miles from Sydney, where we were met by the minister, Rev. Arthur Allen, and his brother Mr Robert Allen. A short drive took us to the manse in Margaret Street.

MONDAY, 5 APRIL

A run of 9 miles by motor yesterday morning took us in to the City and to St George's Church in Castlereagh Street. Sydney on the Sabbath is a sad place; it seems to be even worse than Melbourne. The Free Church in Castlereagh Street is an old building of the rather stately stone style characteristic of an earlier day. I had a congregation of 90 and preached to them from Isaiah 11:6–9, but I did not feel at ease. At 3 pm I conducted a Gaelic service attended by about 130 people. Spoke from Matthew 25:3 on the foolish virgins but did not enjoy the service. The print of my Bible was very small, the place was very hot, and sweat bedewed my spectacles, so that I was most uncomfortable. I enjoyed the evening service better.

TUESDAY, 13 APRIL: SYDNEY

This forenoon we made our way to the buildings opened 15 months ago by the Maritime Services Board, where we had been invited to meet the Harbour Master, Mr Donald MacRae. He is a great big man, 6 ft 2 ins in height, and he still retains in great measure his Highland speech. We were given a most interesting cruise around the Harbour in the Harbour Master's own launch under the care of a Captain Craven. He took us right round the Harbour and showed us miles of wharves. We saw the 'Australia' which accompanied the Queen during her passage over from New Zealand, and also the 'Radnor', which the dockers refused to load because she is going to Indo-China with arms to help the French, and which is now being loaded by servicemen. Communism is active in Australia and the situation calls urgently for firm handling by the government. In the course of our round we landed at Fort Denison, a small fortified islet in the midst of the Harbour. The view from the top of the small tower was very fine. Within, the walls were 12 feet thick, and half way up the tower there was an emplacement in which four old-fashioned cannons mounted guard over the Harbour. The fort was built in 1857 as a means of defence, should the city be attacked by any foe. Below were the dungeons, dark, gloomy places, but the dwelling houses on the islet, despite a somewhat gloomy exterior,

[421]

were both commodious and up to date within. The trip was indeed a memorable experience. On our return Captain MacRae had us with him for lunch, at which we tasted a new fish – the John Dory. It was good.

SATURDAY, 17 APRIL

Our last night in Strathfield was a sad one. I did not like leaving such an hospitable home. At 7.25 am we bade farewell to the dwelling which had been our home for the preceding fortnight.

Being Good Friday, the Sydney Central station was crowded with holiday-makers, but, curiously enough, our train was not over-crowded.

We reached Gloucester at 3.20 pm, and were conveyed to the Alcheringa Guest House which is to be our abode till Monday. Gloucester is a beautifully situated little town with a population of about 2,000.

SABBATH, 18 APRIL

A car came for us this forenoon and took us out to Barrington four or five miles away. The church at Barrington, on the near side of the village, is a nice wooden creation, pleasantly situated and well looked after. There I had a congregation of 20, most of whom were descendants of the Skye pioneers. It is extraordinary to find the Skye stock every-where associated with the Free Church witness in this land. Without them there would be no witness. Preached from Matthew 24:14 on the Gospel message and its ultimate triumph.

In the evening our congregation numbered only 15, but the re-deeming feature of this charge is that, although small, the proportion of young men in it is relatively high, and therein lies the prospect of increase and promise for the future.

One woman, I was told, said that she would not have missed today's sermons for anything, and for that I was exceedingly thankful.

MONDAY, 19 APRIL

We left Gloucester today at 3.10 and arrived at Taree at 5 pm. The train was laden with people returning from holiday. Our journey took us through beautiful and mountainous country to begin with, and then we came down to cultivated areas through which rivers and streams meandered. There we saw some examples of the stockman's life – riders rounding up cattle, etc., and the horse very much in evidence.

WEDNESDAY, 21 APRIL

We were taken out in the afternoon by Mr King, one of the elders, and a teacher of mathematics in the local school. In his car he gave us some lovely views of the Manning River. I question whether I have ever seen such a large river. Taree is like Hamilton, a good shopping centre for the surrounding districts, and is extending rapidly. In the old days many of the Skye settlers who came out in the 'Midlothian', settled on the Manning River, and the old church at Tinonee was the scene of a remarkable revival, which proved thoroughly genuine, under Rev. Allan Macintyre in 1860.

WEDNESDAY, 5 MAY

We left Wauchope[1] at 4 pm and reached South Grafton at 9 pm where Mr Webster was awaiting us with a huge Ford Consul car with which he swept us down very speedily to Woodford Island to the house in which we are to reside during the stay in Maclean.

This morning I saw the beauty of our present abode. On the other side of the road in front of the house flow the broad placid waters of the Clarence River. The island upon which we are is 13 miles long by 7 miles wide and is said to be one of the largest river islands in the world. In the midst of it there rises quite a considerable hill. Close at hand are banana trees and fields of sugar-cane.

At night I began the communion services by preaching to a congregation of 48 from Matthew 24:11–13. The church is a nice one, although the pulpit is too deep for comfort, and is longer than the one at Wauchope. I was requested to meet the congregation as they retired, and I was surprised to find how many of them bore Highland – and especially Skye – names.

THURSDAY, 6 MAY

We left a few minutes after 10 o'clock this morning for a service on Chatsworth Island at 11 am. We crossed the large bridge over the Clarence which connects the island on which we reside with the Mainland, then passed on through Maclean, and followed on down the river until we reached the ferry over to Harwood Island. The ferry is worked by a half-hourly service in the form of a huge 'punt' – as is the local term. The punt is a wide flat-bottomed vessel with a ramp fore and aft,

---

1 After a week at Taree Mr and Mrs MacRae had spent a further week in the home of the Rev. J. A. Harman (1900–1976) at Wauchope. Throughout these weeks MacRae was, as usual, preaching both Sundays and weekdays whenever opportunity offered.

and broad enough to accommodate three cars abreast. In this ferry 30 cars can be taken across in each run. The propulsive power is steam, but the vessel is guided by a wire cable which normally lies on the bed of the river but is lifted up by special mechanism as the vessel draws along. The day was beautiful and these Clarence islands really were wonderful.

MONDAY, 10 MAY

At the request of Mr Webster I preached today the sermon which I preached a week ago at Wauchope – on Ephesians 1:11. Evidently it was appreciated here also. I feel that there is much need for Calvinistic teaching among our people in this country. Arminianism seems to have got many of them – especially among the young – in its toils. I feel that the needs of the situation justify my coming out to Australia.

After the service went for lunch to the Macswans', Woodford Leigh – a farmhouse on this island which suffered rather badly in the recent floods. The water was $7\frac{1}{2}$ inches deep throughout the house even though it stands upon blocks about 3 feet high.

FRIDAY, 21 MAY

We left Grafton by train about 12.45 and arrived at Lismore about 4.15. Mr Harman was on the train and his knowledge of the country made the journey very interesting.

Yesterday we went to visit ninety-five-year-old Hector Macpherson who lives 14 miles to the South of Lismore. He has failed a good deal since we saw him at St Kilda last November, yet he persisted in moving about and would not be satisfied until he took us to his former home at Wanga – a most isolated place among the trees which, when well-looked after, must have been a spot of haunting beauty. Opposite Hector's door was a tall tree upon which we found three koala bears drowsily ensconced.

I am afraid that Hector is nearing the end of his long journey. He is no longer the Australian, but the old Highlander, thinking always of the old days in his native land. His conversation nearly all the time was of Gairloch and Stornoway, in which he served in a shop for several years.

This morning we left by car at 9.30 for Mullumbimby, Mr Harman driving us.

SATURDAY, 29 MAY

On Wednesday, late in the afternoon, we motored down to Port

Macquarie. The evening was calm and beautifully fine and on arrival at the sea front we prepared for fishing. Old Hector[1] was given a box to sit upon while Mr Harman cast his line for him into the sea. Mr Harman himself also fished while the boys[2] tried for fish with the rod. The only success fell to old Hector who caught two small bream. I was amused at the eagerness with which the old fisherman drew in his struggling catches from the sea. Hector insisted that Cathie should cast a line, which she did with no success, but she had the thrill of fishing in the Pacific.

Yesterday morning we reluctantly left Wauchope. It was hard to leave old Hector for we shall never meet again. The old man was in tears. We got our train about 8 am and travelled till 3.45 until we reached Broadmeadow, a suburb of Newcastle, having covered in all 182 miles.

At Broadmeadow we were met by Mr and Mrs Beaton in their Holden car. We had some delay in waiting for the ferry across to Stockton. By this time dusk was creeping down, and the whole estuary, surrounded everywhere by wharves, factories, mills, and craft of every description, and twinkling with a multitude of glittering lights, became invested with a wonderful beauty. After the crossing our run of twenty miles was through the night and we could see nothing but woods on either side. The first person I met outside the little church at Anna Bay was Donald John Macleod of Manish who had come out with us in the 'Otranto'. He is now married and settled down at a place five miles beyond Anna Bay. We had a congregation of 23 and I preached to them from Psalm 25:10 with a measure of freedom.

This evening we visited Nelson's Bay, a beautiful coastal town on the southern shore of Port Stephens, another huge estuary reaching far inland and divided into different arms. From the high ground overlooking the beach we had a vista of superb beauty. The sun was going down in the West, and sky and sea took on the wonderful hues of its setting, and presented a picture which only a divine Hand could paint.

On our way back, at Anna Bay we called at Donald John Macleod's home, and Cathie took charge of a photograph of his marriage group which she is to deliver to his mother in Harris. I came away with a sad

1 Hector Macpherson had become so attached to Mr MacRae that he insisted on making several journeys with him.
2 Allan and George Harman. The former was later to be a student assistant to MacRae in the summers of 1958 and 1959 and Professor of Old Testament at the Free Church College, Edinburgh, from 1966 to 1974 when he returned permanently to Australia. The latter is now Dr G. S. Harman who holds a university post in Melbourne.

[425]

wistfulness in my heart, because of our young people who are scattered all over the world and our own old people who are slowly dying out in the glens and islands of our own land. Soon our race must disappear and their mountain land be left a desolation.

Today I overheard a gramophone record of some pipe band playing the 'Flowers of the Forest' and it upset me entirely. It is difficult enough at home to listen to this tune on the bagpipes without emotion, but to hear it in this far land was more than I could suffer. I had to go outside.

MONDAY, 31 MAY

Our train to Sydney was comfortable, but a little beyond half-way our engine snapped an axle and two of its wheels went off the line. Fortunately we were ascending a long incline at the time and our speed was slow. After a long delay another engine appeared and took us back beyond Woy-Woy station. Here we were in the midst of the scenic loveliness of the Hawkesbury River Estuary. We had tea in our carriage and in such a setting we enjoyed it very much. Another engine then puffed into the station by a branch line and at last, as the sun was beginning its wonderful display of sunset beauty, we got away. We reached the Sydney Central Station at about 6 o'clock instead of at 3.45. Mr Allen and his brother Bob were patiently waiting our arrival.

On Tuesday afternoon, by special arrangement, the ladies of St George's met us for afternoon tea.

Next afternoon Bob Allen took me a motor run and then at 7.30 I gave a lecture on Purity of Worship to an audience of 45 in St George's.

On Thursday morning we got our train at the Central at 8.15. This was the Riverina Daylight express and was of the comfortable type which we find in N.S.W. We travelled 399 miles to Albury, mostly through rain.

Yesterday morning we entrained on the famous 'Spirit of Progress' at 7.50. It ran non-stop all the way to Melbourne, which we reached after covering 192 miles at 11.30. This was remarkably good running.

And so we found ourselves once more safe in our flat in St Kilda after all our wanderings these last 8 weeks. The Lord has been good to us. Was glad to find a packet of my booklet, *The Resurgence of Arminianism*, awaiting me.

Today I went back to my old open-air study at the Botanic Gardens and felt very thankful to get back to that beautiful spot. I shall miss it very much when we leave for home.

SABBATH, 6 JUNE

Mr Graham has organised a 'special effort' in connection with our evening services. He has asked me to preach for the unconverted at these services and he and others have distributed 500 cards in the district, inviting people to them. I am unwilling to fail him, but I feel that now is not the time for such an effort – just when we are on the point of leaving. Had it been carried out before we left for New South Wales, I would be free now to terminate my visit with themes in keeping with the occasion. To conclude with a sermon for the unconverted is scarcely suitable. I would rather close my ministry in this place upon a tenderer note and one addressed more directly to God's people.

In the morning preached from Proverbs 11:30 on winning souls and enjoyed a measure of liberty. At night there were only 27 present. Three of these were strangers, but they turned out to be relatives or friends of Mrs Crawford, so that, although over 400 cards have been distributed, they failed to bring out a single person.

SATURDAY, 12 JUNE

Have been busy all week trying to get through pre-embarkation formalities. These take up so much time that there is little opportunity for packing.

SABBATH, 13 JUNE

This morning was fine but cold. Spoke from 1 Peter 1:23. In the afternoon preached from Ephesians 1:11 in the Bible House in the city.

At night had a congregation of 33, including a few strangers. This afternoon picked up another man who seems to be wandering about in search of the Word and he turned up again at the evening service. We are undoubtedly beginning to break fresh ground, but what is to become of it all if my place is not to be filled by some suitable man?

WEDNESDAY, 16 JUNE

Tonight I gave my address on Purity of Worship in the hope that it would give our recruits an intelligent idea of the meaning of our form of worship and would thus help to stabilize them. Without this there would be a greater danger of their drifting back again into their former course, once I am gone.

SATURDAY, 19 JUNE

This afternoon, in the same church hall in which we held our 'Welcome' meeting a year ago, we assembled for our 'Farewell'. There was a good

[427]

gathering, including four ministers. How quickly the year has sped away and how different were my feelings today from those of a year ago! The three St Kilda elders spoke very ably and warmly. Old Mr Smith also spoke for the congregation. Then Mr Mackechnie presented us on behalf of the congregation with two handsome pictures of the Dandenongs, a magnificent electric lamp carrying a kangaroo-ornamented shade, and a case of tea spoons, each bearing the crest of a capital city of Australia. Mr McIntosh followed with a pair of kangaroo book-ends from the Victorian Presbytery.

I felt bewildered and humbled, and to return thanks was no easy matter. I spoke on aspects of religious life in Australia and then dealt with the witness of our own church in this land. I sought to make it clear that the danger which threatened us was due to a lack of appreciation of the value of the Reformation testimony for which we stand, and which in time would lead, if unchecked, to the abandoning of our whole position. I reminded them that the Reformation witness was that for which martyrs died, and that it was as precious today as then, for truth never changes. This I emphasised was the duty that faced our ministers today, both at home and in Australia, if the church was to survive – the rousing of our people to an appreciation of the value of our Reformation testimony and to a sense of the responsibility the possession of such a testimony conferred upon them.

I felt thankful for many of the things which were said in connection with my ministry in this place, and I feel that it has not been in vain. But it was an ordeal to have to listen to everything. It made me feel so unworthy and ashamed. What have I done to deserve such kindness? Now it is all over and I feel very sad.

SABBATH, 20 JUNE

Today was sunny but cold. I felt in large measure rid of last night's depression, but realised the need for some hardening of spirit, without which it would not be easy to go through the ordeal of the services before me. As Mr Graham had arranged that my last three evening services should be addressed to the unconverted, I was under the necessity of giving my closing message at today's forenoon service. I spoke from Revelation 3:11 on holding fast the crown which God had given us – the Word of His patience as set forth in our Church standards. 42 were present which was our largest morning attendance since I came. I got liberty and enjoyed the service. I sought to give our newcomers an intelligent appreciation of our position, and to weld them into our

AUSTRALIA: 1953–54 | AGED 70

ecclesiastical body that they might abide with the little company here
after we take our departure. Warned them of the danger of our allowing
our light to go out. The message seemed to be appreciated.

At night we had an attendance of 57. I preached from Luke 15: 3–7
on the lost sheep. One stranger who was present, on leaving the church
told me that this was the second time he had been to church during the
last many years and that he felt that the message had been for him. He
was the lost sheep – and his eyes filled up with tears. May the Good
Shepherd bring him into the fold! For this, at the last service in
Australia, I am deeply thankful. May it be a token for good!

MONDAY, 21 JUNE

Ted Thelander and his sister, Mrs Crawford, came for us at 8 o'clock
this morning to transport us to the Melbourne Station Pier. And so
we left our little flat in which we spent so many happy days – never
more to see it again. The parting was sore, but nothing to what yet
awaited us. At the pier a number of friends gathered, including the
McIntoshes who had motored in. They gave us a great send-off and
loaded us with presents. At last the great ship – the 'Orontes' – began
slowly to move and I felt that I must needs break down utterly. Despite
me, the tears would steal down. Oh what that parting cost us! Who
would have thought that in the short months we have been in St Kilda
our hearts should have become so knit with this people? Surely there is
something in it which is above and beyond nature – something of the
love of the Spirit. How hard it is to leave these dear, warm-hearted
people behind us for ever! But there is consolation in it. Some of the
warmest and most utterly devoted are those who a year ago did not even
know our congregation existed. What will grace not do? And so tonight
we are out on the Australian Bight and my heart is very sore.

SATURDAY, 26 JUNE

We reached Fremantle at 8 o'clock this morning. At 11 am we set out
by bus to the Perth Cemetery at Karrakatta but we failed to find Dunc's
grave. The superintendent, who was a Scotsman, was very helpful and
looked up all the records of interments from 1920–1925, but without
success.[1]

We sailed again at 4 pm and ran into rough seas. We rolled badly and
at dinner time many dishes slipped off the table – even though the
dining tables had a fence around them – and were smashed to pieces.

1 A few months later MacRae heard from a friend who had located the grave
and sent a photograph of it.

[429]

MONDAY, 28 JUNE

Yesterday was the same miserable day that the Sabbath generally is upon these ocean liners – a formal pretext of a service, conducted according to the forms of the Church of England, and the rest of the day given over to organized vanity. As we advance Northwards the weather becomes distinctly hotter. Yesterday the noon temperature was 66, today it was 72. Today the swell and the wind continue unaltered, but the weather is good. Up to noon today we have covered 2573 miles since leaving Melbourne a week ago. The noon record today for the previous 24 hours was 428 miles, i.e. $17\frac{5}{6}$ miles per hour.

FRIDAY, 2 JULY

Tonight we crossed the Equator at 7.30 pm. I observed the new moon lying flat on its back. Whether that is normal for the Equator or not I cannot say. The sea has been comparatively placid, but the noon temperature rose to 90 degrees. Our mileage at noon for the 24 hours was 418 miles. From the Equator to Colombo takes, I understand, 36 hours sailing, so we should get in about 7.30 on Sabbath morning. I am weary of the frivolity and vanity of this ship.

SATURDAY, 3 JULY

This afternoon about 4 o'clock was surprised to get a marconigram from Rev. Clarence Van Ens of the Dutch Reformed Church asking me to preach for him at 9.30 tomorrow, after our arrival at Colombo. I was afraid to decline for it seemed like the doing of the Lord. How the news of my coming has preceded me is a mystery to me, but no doubt it will be cleared upon our arrival.

SABBATH, 4 JULY

We reached Colombo shortly after 5 this morning. According to the terms of his wire Mr Van Ens came aboard for us at 7.45. He is an exceedingly tall and handsome Dutchman, and he has a twin brother, also a minister in Colombo, as like him as he can possibly be.

Mr Van Ens had his car parked near the jetty landing place and by it he soon ran us out to his church. It is a large handsome building, built to give maximum entrance to air. He took the service while I preached the sermon from John 17:2 and enjoyed liberty. Apparently it was most providential that I preached on that particular passage, for recently the Church in Ceylon has had to dismiss one of its ministers in Colombo on account of his unsound teaching with respect to the doctrine of election. He taught that Christ died for all, but that His work was only made effectual for the elect.

The Dutch Reformed Church in Ceylon at one time was very strong, but with modernism among its ministers it fell upon evil days. It became weak in numbers and lax both in doctrine and practice. In their trouble the conservative section appealed to the Christian Reformed Church in America for 'a loan' of ministers, and it was in connection with this scheme that Clarence Van Ens and his twin brother John and certain others accepted congregations in Ceylon. Since their coming they have tried to give instruction upon the old lines, both by the distribution of sound literature and by the holding of special classes and lectures. In this they have been remarkably successful, and the moribund church has been invested with new power. I thought that we as a Church ought to take a leaf out of their book and devote more of our time and resources to propagating the testimony of our Church, firstly among our own people and then throughout the land.

After the service we visited one or two of the other congregations in Colombo and found Mr Van Ens' brother John, along with a Mr and Mrs Schuring, drinking coffee in the verandah of the former's house. We joined them and as we sat there in that lovely eastern setting, with its wonderful foliage about and over us, I could not but feel that it was all like a lovely dream from which I would soon awake.

Thereafter we drove to Mr Van En's for lunch and enjoyed a quiet rest afterwards. About 2 o'clock Mr Van Ens drove us down to the jetty, mainly through the native parts of the town. The streets were thronged with pedestrians and they seemed to have no respect for the motor traffic. We drove at such a rate that I was thankful when we reached the jetty without an accident.

The sail out to the liner was pleasant and we climbed back into our ship with hearts full of gratitude for such a wonderful day. We were sorry at one time that we were to reach Colombo on the Sabbath; now we are unspeakably glad.

We were due to sail at 6 pm but it was fully 8.15 ere we pulled out of the harbour and left the multi-coloured lights of the city and the vessels behind us.

MONDAY, 5 JULY

Today we have been steadily ploughing against a strong westerly wind. The sea is rough and the sky is leaden all round. Drenching showers are frequent, and the tossing of the seas and the whirling away of their tops by the wind presents a grand sight.

SATURDAY, 10 JULY

We reached Aden at 6 a.m. today. Going on deck, a very striking view presented itself. In the bay lay many huge ships, while ashore the frontage of the town presented quite a substantial appearance. Back from the shore the town was perched on dark barren heights upon which grew not a single blade of grass, while further back again a wild assortment of jagged peaks cut fiercely into the sky. It was a sight to be remembered.

I went ashore about 8.30 am and slowly strolled through the main streets. The heat was terrific and the shops were full of people, for the most part bargaining at their hardest. Strange-looking goats roamed about everywhere, but I saw only one camel – drawing a rather primitive vehicle. Natives of all hues swarmed on every side and the city had all the atmosphere associated with the East. But it was too hot to go far.

We left again at about 3 o'clock and should be in the Red Sea by tomorrow morning.

MONDAY, 12 JULY

Last night was a desperately hot night and our cabin was like the inside of a steam cooker. To make matters worse, two of our ventilation blowers went out of action, while my bed is situated immediately under the pipe which conveys hot water to the cabins. It was awful. About 2.15 I had to get up and prowl about the ship in search of cold water.

Today we have passed quietly on through the waters of the Red Sea. The noon temperature was 91.

TUESDAY, 13 JULY

Today our record was 417 miles. Both sides of the Gulf of Suez are absolutely barren, and to look at the sterile coast line and forbidding hills of the Sinai Peninsula, gave one a most realistic impression of the difficulties which met Moses when he had to lead his people through such a land.

THURSDAY, 15 JULY

When we arose yesterday morning we found ourselves slipping along the Canal at a comfortable speed. All the lakes were well behind us and for the most part the country was flat, desert and monotonous. At Port Said, however, which we reached about 11.30 a.m., matters brightened up. Several of the harbour buildings are most ornate, and near our berth there were streets of exceptionally good appearance, most of the establishments being British. I went ashore for some lemon juice, after which I returned to the ship again, on my way making a few purchases at the stalls on the wharf. There was little point in strolling around as I did at Aden, for I would be pestered with beggars and retailers of every description at every step. We left again at about 3 o'clock. In the late afternoon we reached the coast of Crete, which for the next three or four hours we skirted. The coast-line was mountainous and terribly barren and signs of habitation were very few.

The ship's announcer gave a talk upon Crete which appeared to be very interesting, but most of his audience, after listening for two or three minutes, seemed to have no interest in it, but returned to their ordinary loud-voiced talk. How different from a former generation who would listen with respect and give every opportunity to their neighbour to listen! Today's generation for the most part seem only interested in horse-racing and football results and such-like frivolity.

FRIDAY, 16 JULY

This evening we drew near to the Italian coast, which roused two young Italian women, apparently sisters, to a state of great excitement and they began to sing some of their national songs. Night darkened down as we approached the Straits of Messina. The sight presented by a full-orbed moon throwing a shimmering carpet of light upon the waters, while on either side a forest of lights showed where Reggio to the North and Messina in Sicily lay, was a sight to be remembered.

This morning joined with about a dozen others in a Bible study in a corner of the stern lounge. The part discussed was the latter part of the 9th chapter of the Gospel according to Mark. It was quite interesting and might be helpful, but I became rather tired of the discussion of points which were more or less speculative.

MONDAY, 19 JULY

We left Naples at midnight. The first part of our journey yesterday was pleasant. We got a good view of the Island of Elba where Napoleon was first exiled. It is mountainous but its arable land is well cultivated. Towards evening a strong westerly wind sprang up from which Corsica gave us good shelter but on rounding Cape Corse, the northerly point, we ran into a very bad sea. The villages clustered about the hillsides at the North of Corsica made me think of Lemreway and Gravir at home. We retired early and awakened this morning in Marseilles.

Marseilles is a rocky, uninteresting place, although it has its own history. The docks were badly smashed by the Germans in the last war and the marks of the bombing are still very evident. A bus took us from the ship to the city – a distance of five miles.

WEDNESDAY, 21 JULY

We arrived at Gibraltar at 9 o'clock this morning. I went ashore in the launch which came out to the steamer, and spent two hours wandering around. The day was very hot, and although a fresh wind blew outside in the narrow streets of Gibraltar, one felt little of it. The shops in Gibraltar are more like those of Britain than those which we saw in Marseilles and Naples, and British goods are in evidence everywhere.

I went right through Main Street, the principal shopping centre, which struck me as being remarkably narrow. But all the streets were narrow. I would not like to live in Gibraltar. I saw Government House and the military quarters, and just missed seeing the changing of the guard. Beyond the great old Moorish gateway with its massive doors at the far end of the Main Street, I left the streets and found myself looking down upon Trafalgar Cemetery. Here in a quiet shady nook many of the dead after the Battle of Trafalgar in 1805 were interred, and also other naval and military men who died or lost their lives about that time. I did not notice any stone with an inscription later than 1810. I continued on up the hill by Prince Edward Road, but the surrounding houses were so high that I could get no view despite my altitude. I therefore retraced my steps lest I should miss the last launch.

THURSDAY, 22 JULY

All day we have been ploughing steadily along the Portuguese coast, although not within sight of land, against a stiff north wind.

FRIDAY, 23 JULY

Truly our prayers have been answered! We are now nearing the end of our 25 hours' sail over the entrance to the Bay of Biscay and the stretch of sea we dreaded most has turned out to be the most favourable of our whole passage. This evening the sea was as flat as a park and glistened in the sun's rays like oil. I am indeed thankful to the Lord of providence who is also the Lord of grace, and as such graciously hearkens to the prayers of His people.

SATURDAY, 24 JULY

All day visibility has been restricted by fog, which made things rather tedious, and possibly may have delayed us. We passed Cape Ushant at 2 am and then made straight across for Devon where we began to skirt the coast of the South of England. But we could not see it owing to the fog. However, at sundown the sun broke through and the vapours became less impenetrable, and now at 10 o'clock we see the lights of what one party said was Margate. What thanks we owe our Lord for all His goodness to us and for bringing us safely home again!

At all times in the world, but especially in the Church at the present day, there is nothing so lacking as moral courage. Few men comparatively think for themselves, and still fewer dare to say what they think, or to act independently. They go in crowds, and simply float with the tide. They are most unwilling to hold their faces to any wind of opposition. As the tide brings in bits of cork and driftwood, and carries them out again, or leaves them high and dry, so it is with many modern Christians, and even with not a few Christian ministers. They quail before obloquy – cry for 'open questions', and terrified by the idea of fashion, fear every thing and every body except Him whom they should fear.

James Begg, from his pamphlet
Anarchy in Worship, 1875, p. 18

His nature was peace-loving. 'As much as lieth in you, live peaceably with all men,' was a precept he sought ever to honour and obey. We are in a position to testify that none grieved more deeply than he over the dissensions, the cooling of friendships, the strife of brethren within the borders of the Christian Church itself. Controversy was a positive pain to him. But when he believed that duty demanded it he would throw himself into it with all the energy and talent at his command. In that hour his balanced and sane judgment paid respect to another solemn and scriptural directive: 'First pure, then peaceable.'

James Morrison in a tribute to the late
K. A. MacRae, *The Monthly Record*, July, 1964

18 Leadership in the Policies of the Free Church

It will be clear from all the foregoing pages that Kenneth MacRae was primarily a pastor and a preacher. But he was also a leader in the Free Church as a whole and in this chapter some account must be given of this side of his work. In order to do so it is necessary to go back to the mid-1930's when he had been twenty years in the ministry and was supported by one of the strongest congregations in the denomination. By that time he had become convinced that a policy was being introduced into the Free Church which would ultimately lead to weakening of the Church's true strength. The Christian character and orthodoxy of those who gave support to this policy he did not doubt. Indeed one of the foremost among them was Dr Donald MacLean whom he knew so well from the days when he had been his assistant in St Columba's, Edinburgh. It was the judgment which lay behind the policy which he questioned.

For nearly three decades after 1900 the Free Church had been largely isolated from the religious life which lay beyond her own borders. In part that was due to the strength of the propaganda against her, for except for those areas of the Highlands where her representation was strong, she was literally 'sent to Coventry' by the rest of the country. At the same time this state of affairs was also the result of her own convictions. The Free Church believed that her non-acceptance of the union with the United Free Church in 1900, and her consequent absence from the greater union of 1929 – between the United Free Church and the Church of Scotland – was due to biblical principles, and that in her adherence to these principles lay the hope of both her own future and the evangelical future of Scotland. With the passing of the years, however, there was less confidence among the Free Church ministers on the question whether a denomination so small and showing so few signs of growth could be the means of undertaking so vast a need as the evangelization of Scotland. The fact was that in the Lowlands of Scotland, where all the major centres of population were to be found, the Free Church was probably as weak in the 1930's as the lost ground of 1900 had left her.

There was reason, then, after the passing of three decades, why Free Church ministers should look around them for aid in evangelical witness. Some tended to look South to English evangelicalism for encouragement, and the representation of that evangelicalism, which was to be found not so far south of the border at the Keswick Convention every July, was not without appreciative visitors from the Free Church. Nearer home, however, a more unexpected alliance occurred. The conviction formed in the mind of Dr Donald MacLean, who was Professor of Church History at the Free Church College, Edinburgh, from 1920 to his death in 1943, that a revival not simply of evangelicalism but of genuine Calvinism was occurring in the Church of Scotland itself in the 1930's. This offered, he believed, an opportunity both for the Free Church to influence others and for her to be aided in turn by men sharing a common vision. Consequently in the pages of *The Evangelical Quarterly*, a Reformed theological review of which he was the Editor, contributions began to appear from Church of Scotland ministers and in 1938, a Church of Scotland minister, Professor J. H. S. Burleigh, was appointed Assistant Editor.

This move towards broader links MacRae viewed with apprehension, not because he approved of any sectarian, denominational spirit – he could say, as Thomas Chalmers had said in 1845, 'Who cares about the Free Church compared with the Christian good of the people of Scotland!' – but rather because he believed that the bridge-building policy was not being matched by a continued bold testimony to the Church's distinctive principles. The evangelicalism of Keswick, whatever the measure of good it could do, was not the fuller reformed evangelicalism under which Scotland had prospered in earlier days; and he was unpersuaded that there was a resurgence of real, experimental Calvinism in the Church of Scotland. It was also apparent that it would be hard to maintain a public unity with well-known figures in the Church of Scotland unless censure of unfaithfulness in the ministry of that Church became a great deal more muted than had been the case in the Free Church formerly. In a 24-page booklet on the position of the Free Church, *Sketching in the Background*, A word to Free Church Young People, which MacRae wrote in 1934, he gave a whole chapter to evidence on the aberrations of a number of leading Church of Scotland ministers of that day from the New Testament faith. He did so in the conviction that unless Free Church young people knew why they were separate from the National Church, and how their own Church's message differed from the popular one, the reason for the denomination's separate existence must be in doubt. Tradition might hold people in the national church but the only thing to hold young people in the Free Church was *conviction*. In addition to saying this, he expressed a fear lest his own Church, instead of concentrating upon her true calling, should follow other denominations in such things as fund-raising by 'sales of work' and social activities to 'hold' the youth. He wrote:

The writer of this pamphlet is firmly of opinion – and the passing of years only goes to strengthen it – that secular means of raising money and the provision of amusements, or even recreation, whether for old or young, is no part of the commission of the Christian Church. The only form of giving recognised by the Word of God is free will giving . . . No fault can be found with that initial part of the sale of work which has to do with the free giving of articles by contributors; the fault comes in later, in the buying and selling, which in the very nature of things, cannot be anything but pure commercialism.

The Church certainly has her own effect upon the life of the community, but that effect is in exact proportion to her spirituality and devotedness to the great mission for which she is in the world, i.e., the preaching of the Gospel and the feeding of God's heritage. When she side-steps from her commission to directly engage in social work she forfeits the power of her testimony and a cloud obscures the brightness of her native glory. The provision of amusements, however harmless, or even of recreations, is not for her. She may well leave such to those who have never yet shown backwardness in such a service. Hers is to go on in the strength of the Lord, a faithful witness intent upon the one thing – her divine commission in a sinful world.[1]

In stating these views MacRae indicated his appreciation of their controversial character and pleaded for mutual tolerance within the Free Church:

To entertain such views as the foregoing, however, is not to condemn all those who do not hold them in their entirety. There are those who cannot agree and who maintain that their attitude is determined by the testimony of Scripture. To such and to their opinions due respect must be given and every appearance of a pretence to superior spirituality must be sedulously avoided; but, at the same time, we have a right to expect a like forbearance.

MacRae's call for more testimony to Free Church principles was not unwelcome to the denomination and, as we have already seen, in 1936 he was released from his charge by the General Assembly for three months 'with a view to seeking to persuade the young people of the Church to a greater interest in and zeal for the message and testimony which has been given the Free Church of Scotland to declare'. The conditions he found during those months of travel supplied new and convincing evidence that the distinctive position of the Church was not

1 *Sketching in the Background*, Arthur H. Stockwell, Ltd., London, p 19.

sufficiently known nor understood, even within her own congregations.

In the General Assembly of 1937 the policy of bridge-building with the Church of Scotland was in evidence. MacRae was not present, but after reading press reports he noted: 'Dr MacFarlane, the Moderator of the Church of Scotland and one of the greatest proselytisers in his Church, paid a visit to our Assembly and was apparently cordially welcomed. Changed days!' The next year matters went further. The new Free Church Moderator was John MacLennan of Lairg who in his opening address – as noted by his friend MacRae – was 'excellent' and spoke in 'downright style' on the drift in the Church of Scotland. But it had been arranged that the Church of Scotland should be represented at a special diet of the Free Church Assembly to commemorate the famous Glasgow Assembly of 1638,[1] and at this meeting Dr Thomson, the Moderator of the Church of Scotland, took the opportunity of attempting a reply to points made in MacLennan's address. By way of a protest Kenneth MacRae was absent from this meeting, but when Thomson's speech was reported in the press he wrote an answer to its controversial parts which was published in the correspondence columns. 'I never returned from an Assembly feeling so downcast regarding the future of our Church,' he wrote at the beginning of June, 1938.

In 1941 the same policy led to the appointment of two Free Church representatives to the Scottish Churches' Council. 'Years ago, and on two occasions, an effort was made in this direction,' he noted on 21 May 1941, 'but it signally failed. Now it carried an overwhelming majority. It only shows how the Church has changed in personnel and outlook since those days. Spurgeon's policy of separation from error is no longer popular in the Free Church. Our present leaders seem to have a mortal terror of isolation. They seem to regard our separate existence as a Church as extending only to the matter of public worship on the Lord's Day.'

He registered his dissent on the floor of the Assembly. Later in the same summer this issue of church policies had an important bearing on a decision he took to decline a call to the Duke Street congregation in Glasgow: 'In the coming struggle in the Church which, unless we be revived, I plainly see, I shall have much more weight as a conservative influence in the Church (DV) as minister of Stornoway, with Lewis behind me, than I would as minister of Duke Street' (July 25).

---

1 This was the Assembly which united the Scottish Church against any intrusion of episcopacy and which ushered in what was known as the 'Second Reformation' in Scotland.

At the 1942 Assembly the issue came up again in another form. Dr MacLean – at his last appearance at a General Assembly – proposed that in the Church's plan to commemorate the Disruption of 1843 invitations should be given to ministers of other churches, including the Church of Scotland. MacRae had lunched with his old friend the same day that this matter came before the Assembly and he did not find it easy to oppose his proposal, but he did so, lost, and recorded his dissent. When he was subsequently asked by the Disruption Centenary Committee to address the commemoration meeting he replied: 'After my opposition at last Assembly to the representation of the Church of Scotland at the celebrations it would be inconsistent on my part to take any share in the proceedings, or even to attend.'

Without question Dr MacLean's endeavours through *The Evangelical Quarterly*, and other means, to forge closer links between Reformed men in different churches and various lands did good. The high-water mark was probably the Calvinistic Congress in Edinburgh in 1938 which he had taken the initiative in promoting.[1] But the links with the Continent were broken by the Second World War and his hopes of a return to the Reformed Faith in the Church of Scotland were not realized. The overwhelming majority of Church of Scotland ministers were unwilling to make any stand for evangelical Christianity. The leadership of the Church belonged to liberals. Dr James T. Cox, for example, principal clerk to the General Assembly of the Church of Scotland, was reported in the *Scottish Daily Express* as affirming that, 'The Church has to get rid of creeds and beliefs which are no longer tenable'. Instancing the Apostles' Creed, Cox declared: 'Congregations when reciting it affirm their belief in the resurrection of the body, in which not a single member believes, not even the minister himself'. He placed belief in the virgin birth of Christ in the same category. The use of the Apostles' Creed, he said, 'ought to be discontinued for it tends to repel many educated people.'

Nor were such deviations from historic Christianity merely the personal views of certain individuals. The National Church itself authorised error as, for instance, in 1942, when a service book was published containing a prayer for the dead. In an 'Order of Service in Memory of those who have fallen in the War', the petition appeared: 'O Almighty Lord, the God of the spirits of all flesh, we give Thee thanks for all those who have laid down their lives for our sakes, and

1 This Congress is fully documented in a volume entitled, *Proceedings of the Fourth Calvinistic Conference*, published at the Congress office, Edinburgh, 1938.

who are now at rest. Fulfil in them, we beseech Thee, the purpose of Thy love, that the good work which Thou didst begin in them may be perfected unto the day of Christ's appearing . . .'

In MacRae's mind one of the greatest hindrances to evangelism in Scotland was the inculcation of unbelief by the Church of Scotland, and he saw no consistency in the Free Church opposing such unbelief while at the same time giving public recognition to leading representatives of the Church which had contributed so much to its existence. He regarded this policy as calculated to blur a proper understanding of the Church's position among the rank and file of Free Church members, and what he saw as a growing lack of discernment at the congregational level convinced him that this danger was not imaginary: 'It occurred to me today,' he wrote on 14 September, 1943, 'that a great change has come over Free Church congregations since my student days. Then in every congregation there was a discerning element who would not be satisfied with everything, and who esteemed the preacher, not for his gifts of address, but for the spirituality of his matter. Today that element seems largely lacking and what often counts is a lively, energetic delivery, coupled with precise and elegant diction.'

Controversy on this subject was renewed in 1949, when by a majority of 41 to 32 the Free Church General Assembly decided to receive a visit from Dr George S. Duncan, the Moderator of the Church of Scotland, and to consider for report the following year the question of mutual 'courtesy visits' on the part of the Moderators of the two Churches.[1] In 1955 a similar issue was debated in connection with the membership of the Free Church in the World Presbyterian Alliance. For eighty years the Church had belonged to the Alliance but at the Assembly of 1955 an overture from the Synod of Glenelg sought the termination of the Church's membership on the grounds that the Alliance was now positively committed to the ecumenical movement and to the World Council of Churches. MacRae spoke in support of this overture and the opposite view was urged by Professor D. MacKenzie of the Free Church College. MacKenzie's speech epitomised the policy which he and others had been advocating: 'Some people thought there was virtue in mere exclusiveness and isolationism. The fact that many

1 These 'courtesy visits', for the time being, do not seem to have been resumed and perhaps this was, in part, due to MacRae who made a fervent personal appeal to Professor D. MacKenzie (a leading spokesman for closer links), urging him to believe that if he persisted in his view he would split the Church: 'Divided, the Free Church will die! All out as a living body in the strength of Christ she can turn Scotland yet back again to the glory from which she has turned away'.

of its constituent Churches were Modernist was not relevant, as we had to deal only with the constitution and not with the views of Churches ... He found in the Council of the Alliance a readiness to listen to the views of the Free Church. . . . This was an attempt to put an Iron Curtain around ourselves on the assumption that we were holier than others. Exclusivism could end only in ecclesiastical extinction'.[1] The Assembly of 1955 was not convinced, and voted for severance from the Alliance by 45 to 38.

By this date, however, another and, in some respects, more serious issue, had come to the fore and to this we must now turn. It had to do with the *raison d'être* of the Free Church. Like Professor MacKenzie, MacRae did not regard the extinction of the Church as an impossibility, but he considered that, if such an event ever occurred, the chief cause would lie in a failure to believe that they possessed distinctive truths for which it was *worth* contending. If the Free Church was to be made up only of those who happened to be born in her, rather than of those who possessed earnest and enthusiastic belief in her testimony, then there would be no future for her.

There were two matters, in particular, in which in the mid-twentieth century the Free Church appeared quaintly 'Puritan' and out-of-date. First, she professed – unlike the vast majority of evangelical Christians throughout the British Isles – the full-orbed reformed theology of the Westminster Confession drawn up in London in 1647. All her ministers, at their ordination, have expressly to disown all Arminian opinions contrary to, and inconsistent with, that Confession. Not without reason, therefore, John Highet in a book entitled *The Scottish Churches*, published in 1960, says, 'Most Scots would also call the Free Church "Calvinistic" and would not mean this to be a compliment'. Secondly, she had retained the Puritan conviction that the contents of worship must be warranted by the Word of God, and that the Book of Psalms ought to have an exclusive place in public worship as the God-given manual of praise. By his ordination vows every minister and elder in the Free Church has not only to accept these distinctives but to promise, 'to the utmost of my power', to assert, maintain and defend them.

In 1950 an issue arose which served to test the resolution of the Church and it originated in the Island of Lewis. In the Free Church congregation of Knock, on that Island, shortly after the November communion season in 1949, a period of special spiritual concern appeared in the congregation and this was reported to the Presbytery by

1 *The Monthly Record*, 1955, p 126.

the minister, the Rev. William Campbell, as having all the evidences of real revival. Such seasons of conviction and ingathering were by no means unknown in Lewis, as we have already seen. Later in the same winter of 1949–50 the minister of the Church of Scotland at Barvas – another rural district in the Island – invited the Rev. Duncan Campbell of the Faith Mission to take special services. From this visit of Mr Campbell there originated what was to be made known across the world as 'The Lewis Awakening'.[1] The Free Church Presbytery in Lewis – representing by far the largest number of Christians in the Island – recognised no such general movement of the Spirit of God in the Island and called upon their congregations to be aware of the Arminian nature of Duncan Campbell's preaching.[2] This was not to say that they considered that no blessing could attend Arminian evangelism. MacRae, who took a prominent part, first in the Presbytery's action, and then in a resolution of the Synod of Glenelg on the same subject, wrote:

No person who knows anything of the history of religion would for a moment contend that because a man is Arminian in his theology he cannot have the grace of God in his heart, or cannot be acknowledged in his labours to the conversion of souls. The names of Fletcher of Madeley and John Wesley, remaining indelibly inscribed as they are upon the record of Evangelical history, would at once give the lie to such a contention.

But a good man can mingle the good that he does with harm should his teaching not be wholly sound. The Arminian who may be used of the

1 This was the title of a forty-four page booklet written by Duncan Campbell and published by the Faith Mission in 1954, and an earlier account, given at Keswick (*The Keswick Week*, 1952, pp 144–47), was entitled 'The Revival in the Hebrides'. In these the author speaks of 'hundreds that came to know Christ' and of 'an island in the grip of God', yet in so far as any documentation is given it relates only to a few places. The most prominent feature in the accounts is the phenomena – visions, prostrations, outcries etc – which Campbell constantly tends to treat as proof of the supernatural: Donald 'is not praying more than five minutes when God sweeps into the church, and there is the congregation falling almost on the top of each other; others throw themselves back and become rigid as in death'. Advice allegedly given to George Whitefield is commended: 'Let them cry out; it will do a great deal more good than your preaching'. The phenomena were much more localized than in 1939. *Duncan Campbell – A Biography*, Andrew Woolsey, 1973, gives no clearer picture of events but it does concede – too moderately – that Campbell's accounts 'sometimes left him open to the charge of exaggeration' p 145.

2 In reply Campbell writes that from opponents of the movement 'The scare was raised – "Arminianism" ' (*The Lewis Awakening*, p 30). But the 'scare' was well-founded; Campbell's own booklet advertises 'A Study in the Doctrine of Entire Sanctification as a definite Experience'. It is equally clear that the Faith Mission taught a universal atonement. These facts, and others, MacRae pointed out to his congregation in addresses on 'Why the Free Church cannot support the Faith Mission'.

Lord for the conversion of sinners is used, not because of his preaching of the peculiar doctrines of Arminianism, but because of his preaching the doctrines of grace with which these Arminian tenets are intermingled. The doctrines of Arminianism, apart from the doctrines of grace, cannot be to the salvation or spiritual profit of any soul, whatever harm they may do, for they are not the doctrines of truth.[1]

It can be seen from this that MacRae's belief was that while God may bless the Gospel though preached in an Arminian context, Arminianism in itself is harmful. He knew it had done harm in many parts of Scotland in the preceding eighty years and – remembering his own premature 'conversion' – he feared its proneness to treat a man's 'decision for Christ' as proof of the possession of the new birth. The object of the Presbytery's statement on Duncan Campbell's meetings was to prevent the large claims about what was being effected in such rural hamlets as Barvas and Arnol from weakening the allegiance of the Free Church people in those areas to the gospel preaching under which they had long been hearers:

After spending our lives in teaching our people, at their own request, the glorious doctrines of sovereign grace, I think that we Free Church pastors have just cause for complaint, when strangers come in who imagine that they have a God-given right to bid our people lay their principles aside and come out that they may be taught something different. To them the testimony of the Free Church of Scotland is nothing. Of the reasons she has for remaining separate from the Church of Scotland they are totally ignorant. Yet they imagine that they are entitled to come to a district and summon people and ministers to sink their differences and to come out together that they may be taught by them. The shepherd resents anything that may be hurtful to the flock; so do we resent most emphatically this attempt to sow Arminian doctrine among our people.[2]

In the Edinburgh Presbytery of the Free Church, however, the activity of the Faith Mission was apparently not viewed with the same concern. Proof of this appeared in the acceptance by one member of the Presbytery of an invitation to speak on behalf of the Faith Mission in Stornoway in June 1950. At the General Assembly in May, 1950, MacRae reflected critically upon the anticipated visit of this Free Church minister to Stornoway under the auspices of the Faith Mission, where-upon his comments were strongly opposed by some members of the Edinburgh Presbytery. MacRae noted in his Diary at the end of the Assembly, 'I left, feeling troubled at the deepening of the cleavage

1 *The Resurgence of Arminianism*, 1954, p 30.
2 *Ibid.*, 31.

between North and South which is now too evident to be hid any longer'. Early in June, while the special Faith Mission meetings were taking place in the Church of Scotland in Stornoway, MacRae was over in Barvas – the alleged starting-point of 'The Lewis Awakening' – where he preached on the subject of the dying thief to 200 at a mid-week service. He experienced particular liberty in showing 'how differently the text would be treated by an Arminian and a Calvinistic preacher'. In Barvas, Arnol, and other places spoken of as centres in revival, he observed no marked difference from the conditions with which he had so long been familiar.

Controversy over what should be the Free Church attitude to the Faith Mission was prolonged. In September 1951, when Dr A. M. Renwick, Professor of Church History at the Free Church College in Edinburgh, wrote to the Free Church minister in Ness, Lewis, urging him to hold special services and giving, as a reason, the advice of a Faith Mission preacher who was concerned for the souls of the young people, the minister of Ness referred the matter to the Presbytery and they instructed MacRae to reply. His letter, of 9 September, 1951, included the following:

Possibly, Dr Renwick, it may be news to you that the Presbytery of Lewis is the only Presbytery in the Church which for the last 10 to 12 years has been carrying on special Gospel week-night services in all their congregations every winter. We see no reason to scrap them in favour of your proposal, nor do we consider that the preachers whom you recommend are specially endowed to convert souls. We leave that to Him who can use whatsoever instrument He pleases.

Our considered opinion is that the sooner this interference with our congregations, which is being engineered from the South, is given over the better. Surely those responsible have more than enough to occupy them within their own bounds.

We dare not boast, and we have no desire to do so, but we think that we are justified in making the statement that religious life is more healthy in these parts than in any other area in Scotland. The main reason for this lies in the sound Calvinistic preaching which is being given to our people. Why do you wish to introduce the Arminianism of the Faith Mission?[1] That Mission long have had a special field for their activities

---

1 He does not mean that this was Renwick's intention but rather that such would be the *result* if Faith Mission preaching was encouraged in Lewis. The strength of the difference of opinion between the two men on this subject should not be interpreted in personal terms. They both esteemed one another. On one visit to Lewis when Renwick spoke at a considerable number of different places (repeating the same missionary address) MacRae was an appreciative listener on each occasion. At the last General Assembly MacRae

in Argyllshire, and what is the long-term result? Argyllshire today is religiously a wilderness.

We deplore the championing of the Faith Mission on the part of some of our professors and ministers who have subscribed to the doctrines of the Westminster Confession of Faith, and still more do we deplore the apathy of their presbyteries in permitting them to do so. Must the issue between Calvinism and Arminianism which came to a head in 1900 be fought all over again? The answer must lie with those who are responsible for all this trouble in our congregations.

We write this letter by instructions of the Presbytery, but its terms are our own. With all good wishes.

This same controversy was continued in the general assembly of 1952. An overture from the Skye Presbytery sought to prevent Free Church ministers taking services in unsound churches on the grounds that they could not, in these circumstances, fulfil their ordination vows respecting both doctrine and purity of worship. This overture was defeated, the principal argument against it being that ordination vows with respect to the exclusive use of psalms in public worship apply to ministers only when they are exercising their ministry within the Free Church. Another overture from the Presbytery of Lewis was, however, carried. It asked the Assembly to ordain that special steps be taken to enlighten the people in all the congregations of the Church as to the distinctive testimony of the Free Church, especially with respect to the Calvinistic doctrines of free, sovereign grace. Yet this overture, which was moved by MacRae, was not accepted without opposition. The wording of the preamble of the overture had contained statements as to the part which Arminianism had played in the break-up of the pre-1900 Free Church, and also on the contemporary weakness of emphasis on the doctrines of grace within the Church. Dr Renwick argued that neither of these statements should be accepted as they stood: they should be referred to a Committee who could examine their validity and, in the meantime, the petition of the overture should not be granted.

was to attend (in 1960) his Diary records his sadness at hearing Renwick speak as though 'his day was wearing to a close'. Though MacRae spoke plainly, as P. W. Miller says, 'he never cherished resentment against his opponents but maintained friendly relations with them'.

After student days together in Edinburgh, Renwick and MacRae had been led in different paths. Influenced perhaps by his Foreign Mission service in Lima (1926–44), Dr Renwick was concerned for outreach of an evangelical nature; MacRae gave greater priority to the need for Calvinistic evangelism. Renwick was Professor of Church History at the Free Church College from 1944 to 1964, dying the following year. Highly esteemed by all for his spirituality, he will be remembered for his two books, *The Story of the Church*, 1958, and *The Story of the Scottish Reformation*, 1960.

After this debate an Edinburgh elder who had taken the opposite side to MacRae wrote to him expressing his regret over the action of the Lewis Presbytery and arguing, as Dr Renwick had done, that the statements in the preamble – the premises of the overture – had been wrong. In the course of a reply to this friend MacRae wrote:

The second premise of the Overture which you question is that which states the need of the rising generation to be instructed in doctrine, especially in the department of sovereign grace, and you maintain that this is a reflection upon the people and ministers of the Presbytery of Lewis. I am sorry that I cannot follow your reasoning, for to my mind it is all to the credit of the ministers of Lewis that, when the flood of doctrinal ignorance which engulfed the Lowlands of Scotland years ago showed signs of seeping in among their people, they took practical steps with a view to stemming back the danger.

In 1936 I was released from my charge for three months in order to lecture upon Free Church principles among our vacant congregations. In the course of that tour it was repeatedly said to me 'We were never told those things before'. That circuit revealed to me very vividly how great was the ignorance of our people concerning the subject which I had been commissioned to bring before them, and without question the lowest level of ecclesiastical and theological knowledge was reached when I entered the congregations of Fife and neighbourhood, particularly Scone. If the standard of knowledge was low in 1936 – as undoubtedly it was – it is far worse in 1952. That statement in the Overture therefore is also correct.

Now I come to the most serious aspect of the case. When the Assembly receive an overture they do not adopt its premises. What concerns them is its prayer. The premises may be faulty or questionable, but if the prayer be reasonable and called for, and calculated to be beneficial to the Church, the Assembly receive the overture and grant its prayer. Speakers may indeed point out the fallacious premise should there be such, but this would never be made the ground of the rejection of a reasonable crave. Nevertheless this is exactly what Dr Renwick did, and in it he received your whole-hearted support. He flew to certain premises which did not commend themselves to him, and, by a rather adroit motion, he proposed that the Committee on Testimony be instructed to investigate the truth of these premises and that, should they not find them to be substantiated, they be permitted to drop the matter.

Now what was the reason at the back of this attempt to evade a most reasonable crave, namely, that our people receive special instruction in the distinctive testimony of our church? Surely the Professor of Church History and Principles should be the last man to act in such a way. The only answer that suggests itself to me, and it does so because I have been taking stock of what I see and hear in the Church, is that the crave itself is distasteful to those who opposed it. Else why oppose it? I cannot help noticing that whenever I range myself in the Assembly on the side of anything calculated to foster loyalty to the distinctive principles of our Church, it is the same men every time whom I find standing against me. I am not going to name them, but I think that by this time you ought to be able to know for yourself.

From your letter you seem to be of the opinion that Calvinism originated with John Calvin, and to be quite unaware that the teachings which are nowadays so named are as old as the Word itself, for they are the teaching of the Word; else why in your letter speak of preaching Calvin instead of preaching Christ? Such an expression seems to indicate a haziness in your conception as to what Calvinism really means. But I need not be surprised when I recall the statements made by some of our own ministers – not from this area – who imagine that they are Calvinists, and especially the effort made by the Professor of Church History some years ago to persuade the Assembly that the Faith Mission were Calvinistic in their theology! The theology of the Faith Mission is the theology of John Wesley – one of the most outstanding and pronounced Arminians that ever lived, and who has left upon record in his writing his detestation of the doctrines known as Calvinism.

Because my Presbytery were troubled over the activities of the Rev. Duncan Campbell of the Faith Mission among our people, they commissioned me to draw out the Overture, and when I had done so, they approved of it unanimously . . . With kindest regards, Yours sincerely.

In 1936 the only material which MacRae had to give out during his itinerary on the Church's distinctive principles was what he had written himself in a brief leaflet. Such material was still unavailable from the offices of the Church in the 1950's, and accordingly, with the foregoing controversy very much in mind, he took the opportunity which his four-and-a-half-week voyage to Australia provided in 1953 to prepare a booklet respecting the doctrines which, as the previous year's Assembly had agreed, required special emphasis.[1] Entitled *The*

1 It should be added that on one point he went beyond what the Assembly had approved, namely, on the question whether the vow taken by Free Church ministers with respect to maintaining purity of worship only applied to the exercise of their office within the Free Church. The Assembly in 1952 and in 1953 took the latter view. MacRae argued that, if vows are made on the basis of what God commands, then they bind the person concerned in all his duties, and that no other basis is strong enough to justify vows. 'If it be simply a case of Free Church people having a preference for the use of the Psalms in their public worship, their ministers can surely meet their desire without having to go under such solemn vows that they will do so. But, if the vows are required on the ground that the Lord has commanded it so, then we can see every reason for their imposition' *The Resurgence of Arminianism*, p 24. MacRae's conviction appears to have been held by the men who did most to prepare for the stand of the minority in 1900; see, for instance, James Begg's *Anarchy in Worship*, 1875.

Resurgence of Arminianism, it ran to thirty-two pages and was published privately in June 1954. The contents were divided into two sections, first, The Doctrines of Arminianism, and second, The Historical Aspect, which sought to explain how, in the last century, Arminianism was first introduced into the religious life of Scotland and how the Free Church of 1900 had stood against it.

Some ministers of the Free Church took the strongest exception to this booklet, not because of its doctrine nor because of its interpretation of earlier history, but because it broadcast to the world the author's doubt whether a vigorous and convincing testimony on these issues was still to be heard from all the denomination's pulpits. The paragraph which gave the greatest offence read as follows:

Over 50 years have passed since the stirring events of 1900 aroused the country, but these things now are little more than a faint memory, where they are remembered at all. The barren period of indifference and spiritual lethargy has again set in and with it the old Arminian tendency re-appears. True, it may not bear that label, but that there has been a definite drift in the direction of Arminianism is unquestioned. So far as some of the Free Church pulpits are concerned, a robust Calvinism has given place to a colourless presentation of the doctrines of grace, which will neither satisfy a Calvinist nor offend an Arminian. The associations of Keswick and certain other conventions are prized and treasured by many Free Church people, and the theology of these gatherings is regarded as above suspicion. To suggest that this theology is largely Arminian and alien to the standards of the Church is the way to arouse their ire, and their attitude seems to be that, if this indeed be so, so much the worse is it for the Free Church.

It was, of course, entirely undesigned that *The Resurgence of Arminianism* should be published in the same year as Dr Billy Graham's arrival to hold his first major campaign in the United Kingdom. When MacRae returned to Britain from Australia late in July 1954 the evangelist's 'Greater London Crusade' had ended two months previously, and yet news of what had happened at the Harringay arena during the ninety days from 1 March was still the subject of supreme interest in the religious press. A million-and-a-half people had attended the meetings, and 38,000 had 'come forward' and signed decision cards. Nothing so phenomenal could be remembered from any past era, and Billy Graham's parting words had been charged with the hope of yet greater things to come: 'I leave Britain for the time being with the belief that she is on the verge of the greatest spiritual awakening in her history'. Excitement and euphoria seemed to extend to all the major denominations in England – excepting the Roman Catholic – and church leaders who had never before been known to assert their faith in evangelism were amongst those joining in almost universal tribute to Dr Graham's ministry. As John Pollock writes in his biography of Billy Graham, 'The expectancy was prodigious'.

In the Scottish Lowlands, the reaction to Graham was generally no less sympathetic. During the last month of the Harringay campaign some of the Crusade meetings had been relayed to different parts of Scotland by means of the long distance telephone lines, and by the summer of 1954 the decision was reached that Graham's next campaign in Britain should be an 'All Scotland Crusade' for six weeks in March and April, 1955. 'For the first time,' says Pollock, re-telling the story, 'Billy Graham would come with the official endorsement of the churches to lead a united effort to reach an entire land – the land of his ancestors'.

All these events represented a striking change in the scene which MacRae had left in 1953 and part of the change – at least as far as it concerned Scotland – was in the response of the Free Church itself. With the exception of some short comment in 1952, *The Monthly Record* was silent on Billy Graham prior to Harringay. The first comment – in the April 1954 issue – announced the surprising statistics of the opening Harringay meetings in tones of qualified hopefulness: 'If the Lord should deign to use His servant in Britain as He has undoubtedly done in America, that should be enough to silence criticism and to awaken in us the spirit of prayer and expectancy'. The next issue of *The Monthly Record* went further. The Editor, Professor R. A. Finlayson, wrote of the assurance he had received from Free Church people attending the London meetings that Graham 'preaches only the Word of God' and that they 'can see nothing in his preaching that should not appeal to Free Church people'. In this same issue a Free Church minister wrote a wholly sympathetic account of his own impressions of Harringay. The size of the response to the evangelist's invitation for people to 'come forward and receive Christ' he attributed to three factors: (1) Tens of thousands of people have been praying. (2) Many at Harringay are hearing the Gospel for the first time. (3) The Gospel of Christ is still the power of God unto salvation.

When the General Assembly of the Free Church convened in May 1954 the London Crusade meetings were still in progress and, *The Monthly Record* reported: 'Perhaps no topic was so often discussed between sittings as the significance of the Billy Graham campaign in

DIARY OF KENNETH MACRAE

North London, and when the matter was brought up in the Assembly by an Overture from its members, there was no division of opinion as to our attitude as Christian brethren to these happenings, even when there may have been a reservation of judgment as to their solidity and permanence. Indeed the accumulating evidence seemed to tend to the removal of such prejudice as remained.'[1]

The Overture referred to in the above paragraph sent fraternal greetings from the General Assembly to the Directors of the Greater London Crusade, and recorded 'their gratitude to God for the quickening of spiritual life evident as a result of the evangelistic services held at Harringay', and their prayer that the crusade might lead 'to nationwide spiritual revival'. Support was apparently universal.

The July issue of the Church's magazine carried further news of Free Church enthusiasm for Dr Graham's preaching, as well as indications of hope that what had happened at Harringay could happen also in Scotland. One small Free Church congregation was pointed out which, having taken relays from Harringay, witnessed what was regarded as 'probably the biggest religious meeting that Dumfries has had in its history'.

Such were the feelings which were running high when Kenneth MacRae returned to Scotland. When a letter on the subject appeared from him in the columns of *The Monthly Record* in September, its theme was so out of keeping with the sentiments already expressed that it seemed like a communication from another age altogether. The letter, together with the Editor's caption and comment, read as follows:

THE GREATER LONDON CRUSADE - ANOTHER POINT OF VIEW

Sir, – While all true Christians ought to rejoice at every genuine outpouring of the Spirit of Grace irrespective of locus or circumstances, and while the recorded events of the Harringay campaign cannot but move the interest of all who deplore the present godlessness of our generation, yet, considering the chequered history of American revivalism, one may well be justified in questioning the wisdom of the precipitate action of last General Assembly in publicly indicating their approval of what is known as the Greater London Crusade. Some of us are old enough to remember the visits of former outstanding American revivalists, and also the most unsatisfactory subsequent conduct of many of their professed converts, and we cannot but think that a measure of caution was called for ere committing our church to any public statement of approval. The movers of the overture who introduced the matter into the Assembly had,

1 *The Monthly Record*, 1954, p 104.

of course, every right to their own opinion, but they had no right to seek to promulgate that opinion in the name of the Church. Of late years we are having too many overtures from members of the House. This is a course of action which requires careful scrutiny, lest the Assembly be rushed into decisions without sufficient time for considering the questions involved in all their bearings.

From Mr Larter's article in your columns we learn that Dr Graham preaches a moderate Calvinism. I am not quite sure what the expression 'a moderate Calvinism' means, but I should judge that it gives us to understand that he is a Calvinist in some doctrines but not in others. To say the least that is scarcely satisfactory. Whitefield could not work with Wesley because of the Arminianism of the latter. In America, Nettleton could not approve of Finney for the same reason. In view of the fact that the standards of our church are thoroughly Calvinistic it surely behoves us to make certain ere we signify our public approval of any preacher that he is in doctrine an unquestioned Calvinist. In the case of Dr Graham this has not been done.

We may contend for what we know to be according to the truth side by side with Arminians, and we may make common ground with them in offering resistance to Modernism, but to give them our approval in matters pertaining to worship and doctrine is in my judgment a betrayal of our testimony.

The action of the Assembly, I fear, goes to show that there is a serious danger of the old Arminian leaven which ultimately came to a head in the passing of the Declaratory Act and the Union of 1900 beginning again to work in the Free Church of Scotland. – I am, etc.,

KENNETH A. MACRAE

(While we joyfully concede to Mr MacRae the right to state his own opinion, even in a case that would seem outwith his personal experience, we cannot grant him the right to question the validity of a unanimous finding of the General Assembly. We do not agree that overtures from members of the House are increasing or that, in any case, they constitute a breach with time-honoured Presbyterian procedure. If the opinion of all members of General Assembly is out of step with Mr MacRae's personal opinion, it can be characterised as unfortunate but not illegal. – *Editor.*)

Until this point in time, although some thirteen columns of type had been given to Billy Graham in *The Monthly Record* between April and August, 1954, no discussion had appeared on where Billy Graham's message and method stood in relation to Arminianism. The Rev. R. B. Larter, to whom MacRae refers, had in an article entitled 'Dr Graham and Harringay',[1] based his assertion about the evangelist's moderate

1 *The Monthly Record*, 1954, p 130.

Calvinism on a previous statement by Professor Finlayson who had earlier written: 'We are told on the authority of no less discerning an observer than Dr Carl Henry that "Graham's theological sympathies are of a moderately Calvinistic frame-work, though not a Calvinism which erases the urgency of personal decision" '.[1]

The inaccuracy of this statement ought to have been clear to all during the course of 1954. On the twin points of Arminian evangelism – a universal atonement and the human will as the decisive factor in the conversion – Graham was in that succession of gospel preachers who belonged to the tradition of C. G. Finney. MacRae was certain of this when, subsequent to writing the above letter, he read *Peace with God*. His Diary entry on that subject reads as follows: 'On Thursday I did not go out, but contented myself by the fireside reading Billy Graham's *Peace with God*. It is the work of one who really knows what conversion means and who is sincere and earnest in the presentation of his message. He has the gift of handling his subject in an attractive and interesting way, but so far as theology is concerned he is a thorough-going Arminian.'

The Editor of *The Monthly Record* also read *Peace with God*, but, as he reported in the October 1954 issue, he knew no reason to justify standing apart from the evangelist's forthcoming campaign in Scotland; on the contrary, 'Christian men of deep conviction should rally round him from the start'. The only people who, he wished, would stand apart from the 'All Scotland Crusade' were liberals in the Church of Scotland – who were already conspicuous in the preparations for the Crusade – 'then those who are heart and soul with Dr Graham in his message could get on with the job'. These words set the tone for a number of similar remarks in the *Record* in preparation for the Crusade which began in Glasgow on 21 March, 1955, and ran for six weeks. The influence of these meetings extended to almost all parts of Scotland in a week of relays to thirty-seven centres, including Stornoway where the Town Hall was hired by congregations of the Church of Scotland.

In order to understand the traumatic outcome of this difference of judgment within the Free Church it is first necessary to make some comment on the policy which was being followed in *The Monthly Record*. The reason for the silence over that prominent aspect in Graham's theology which led him to call men to signify they were receiving Christ by walking to the front of a congregation is not readily apparent. No Calvinistic evangelist had ever employed it; indeed the

1 *Op. cit.*, 66. Carl Henry had spoken at the Free Church College in 1953.

campaign organisers were themselves initially very sensitive about it on the grounds that to invite public decisions 'had never been known' in Scotland.[1] This reluctance on the part of Professor Finlayson to raise a controversial issue was not due, however, to a concern to win any influence or popularity for his Church. *The Monthly Record* under his editorship had consistently disdained suiting its comment to popular opinion, and on evangelism, as well as on other issues, it had given forthright and, at times, unacceptable exhortation to some of its readers.[2]

If one can interpret the volumes of the *Record* for those years, at this distance in time, it would seem that a malaise within the Free Church was one of the main concerns of the Editor. No one spoke more bluntly on the state of the denomination. In an Editorial entitled, 'Is the Church Hindered' (February 1952) he wrote:

When one looks back upon the last fifty years and sees the state of religion today, even in those parts where our labours were most abundant, who can deny that there is much to dishearten and dismay? Not only have the truths we proclaimed made little or no impact upon the nation as a whole, but our purity of doctrine and worship has made amazingly little impact upon our own people to whom we ministered from Sabbath to Sabbath . . . May it not be that *we are evangelical but not evangelistic?* . . . Is it not possible that ours has been *a preaching ministry but not, in any adequate degree, a teaching ministry?* . . . May this not be why so many of our young people have sat loosely by the testimony of our Church and have been so ready to forsake it when the opportunity arose . . . The question must again be pressed home whether *we are conservative, yet not aggressive in the faith* . . .

The same writer spoke on the same theme in the General Assembly of that year, advising concern rather than optimism over the Church's relations with young people.

In another editorial, 'The Paralysis of Fear' (September 1952), Professor Finlayson, having earlier criticized modern trends in evangelism, went on to speak of the dangers equally pressing at the other extreme, namely, 'spiritual lethargy and supine inactivity'. 'It is probable,' he continued, 'that in the opinion of several within the Church and of many well-wishers outside, this is the peculiar peril that

1 *Billy Graham*, The Authorised Biography, John Pollock, 1966, p 190. This statement was inaccurate as the quotation already given on p 9 shows.
2 For example, 'Another Gospel' (1952, p 61), 'The Trend of Modern Evangelism' (1952. p 155), and 'The Lost Chord of Modern Evangelism' (1953, p 151).

confronts our Church, that of strangulation through half-heartedness and a vague sense that we can do nothing at all about our spiritual state'.

In an article 'The Church and the Masses' published in May, 1954 – the month before the General Assembly – he wrote again:

It is obvious, then, that indifference to the Gospel and to the ministrations of the Church is very widespread in Scotland today and that it is not confined to any one denomination. Certainly our own Church, in face of the disclosures made, cannot sit complacently and point the finger of scorn to less 'faithful' Churches. The rot of religious apathy has entered our own Church and is sapping at the vitals of our spiritual life . . . At the forthcoming Assembly, reports will be submitted on the state of our funds, on missions, on religion and morals, and, if they are in line with recent years, there will be scant mention of the 'dead wood' that constitutes so much of our membership, no analysis of the situation in some of our congregations where there is complete indifference to the Gospel, no sense of urgency regarding souls in Scotland who are more insensible to the claims of Christ than 'Hindus or Moslems'. Why should an assembly of Christian brethren spend a week of their precious time discussing the frills and trappings of a spiritual vesture that is little more than a shroud, when this decay and death is rampant around them? . . . It behoves us as a Church to take stock . . .

The Free Church, according to the view adopted by *The Monthly Record*, was in no position to stand critically apart from the Graham crusades. Graham was unambiguously evangelical; his avowed dependence upon the authority of Scripture distinguished him at once from liberals; he had drawn the attention of the nation to evangelism as it had not been drawn for long years, and who was to say that his coming to the United Kingdom was not to be God's means for the beginning of a new evangelical revival? The very possibility that 'we might be on the threshold of a great spiritual revival'[1] surely demanded Free Church support. It was not a suitable time, said Professor Finlayson, to grind 'a particular theological axe'; and he believed that any deficiencies in Graham's theology the evangelist would, in due course, be prepared to remedy 'with patient learning and faithful instruction'.[2] In a word, the policy was that the times were truly propitious for evangelical co-operation on the basis of fundamental truths. To refuse such co-operation because the evangelism was not distinctively Reformed could be disastrous not only for the Free Church but for the

1 An expression used in support of the Overture relating to the Greater London Crusade, *The Monthly Record*, 1954, p 121.
2 *Ibid.*, 199.

wider interests of the Kingdom of God.[1] The case for this policy seemed indeed to be so overwhelming that, as we have already seen, no one dissented from it at the 1954 General Assembly, and when MacRae's letter appeared in *The Monthly Record* he was quickly reminded by the Editor that it was 'unfortunate' he should be alone in his views.

Alone or not, Kenneth MacRae was convinced that his brethren who took the other side were making a mistake. He did not believe that what was happening was the beginning of a new spiritual era. He remembered the excitement of Torrey's 'revival meetings' in 1903 and of Chapman's and Alexander's in Glasgow in 1913[2] and saw no vital difference between them and Graham's except for the size of the organisation. While he was willing to appreciate all that was truly evangelical – as his diary entry on *Peace with God* shows – he did not believe that the Word of God allows those who find their Calvinism in the New Testament to assume silence for the sake of evangelism. In his sovereignty God might bless Gospel preaching even when attended by considerable defects, but the rule by which He calls His servants to act is His own Word. Further, in his own mind he contrasted the apparent success of 'decisionist' evangelism, not with the comparative failure of contemporary witness to orthodox Christianity, but with the God-given results which since the Reformation had attended that Christianity *when* proclaimed in the power and unction of the Holy Spirit. It was not the truth which had failed, but faith and resolution in respect to the truth!

There were plainly all the elements here for a collision of convictions within the Free Church and this occurred at the General Assembly of 1955 which met just a few weeks after the conclusion of the All Scotland Crusade. That a strong debate would take place was probably anticipated on all sides, for it was known that MacRae had brought forward an Overture in the Synod of Glenelg, which had met on 13 April, and that he was to speak in support of it at the Assembly. The last time he had done so, in 1952, on behalf of the Presbytery of Lewis, the Assembly had received it as already observed. The 1955 Overture was on the same subject but it was more specific and there was no escaping its implications with regard to the policy which the Church had virtually approved

1 It was a feature of Professor Finlayson's editorship of *The Monthly Record* that he sought to make it more than a merely denominational paper. In particular he hoped that Graham's preaching would strengthen evangelicalism in the Church of Scotland, where, he wrote, the number of 'men who maintain an evangelical witness in their congregations is put as low as 5 per cent of ministers by evangelicals within the ministry of the Church of Scotland itself' (1955, p 26).
2 Commented on in *The Monthly Record*, 1914, p 2.

in the previous twelve months. As recorded in *The Monthly Record*:

The Synod asked that Presbyteries and Kirk Session should take special steps to ascertain that all persons to be ordained by them fully understood and wholeheartedly accepted in all their bearings the terms of the formula to which they were binding themselves. The Synod also sought that Presbyteries should arrange and convene public meetings for the purpose of emphasising the principles and witness of the Free Church of Scotland, and that Thursday, 16th June next, be observed by the congregations of the Church as a day of humiliation and prayer, with special reference to the low state of religion in the land and to the supineness and shortcomings of our own Church with respect to her distinctive witness.[1]

After MacRae had spoken on behalf of the Overture, in which he referred to the contemporary evangelistic activity of an Arminian character and the danger that Free Church people were being influenced by this outlook, a counter-proposal was immediately made that the Assembly pass from the Overture. It was alleged that to receive the Synod's Overture would be tantamount to an admission of guilt with respect to what MacRae had said in his *Resurgence of Arminianism* and what was implied in the Overture itself. *The Resurgence of Arminianism*, it was claimed, said 'that some ministers in the Free Church were preaching Arminianism'.[2] In the absence of charges against particular individuals, 'all of us would be found guilty of Arminianism . . . all would have to clothe themselves in the white sheet of penitence if this Overture passed'. In the course of the debate strong language was used to express the opinion that MacRae was unfit to be a leader in the Free Church; he was a wrecker and disturber of the peace. One speaker declared that 'He yielded to no one in respect to Mr Macrae as a preacher, but as an ecclesiastic his policy had ever been divisive and disruptive', and he went on to warn the Assembly that by their vote on this overture 'they were electing how the Church was to be ruled for the years to come'. The Church, he thought, needed to be brought to a final conclusion on the nature of the policy she was to follow.

The Rev. Murdoch MacRae,[3] instead of simply seconding the

1 A comparatively full account of the debate on this Overture will be found in *The Monthly Record*, 1955, pp 118–122.
2 It is hard to understand how MacRae could be said to have made such a charge. It does *not* occur in *The Resurgence of Arminianism* and MacRae denied that he held such an opinion. The most that he had said in that booklet was that Arminianism was 'favoured in certain Free Church circles'. Yet much of the criticism which he received in the debate was based upon the allegation that he was making this charge against the Free Church ministry.
3 A native Lewis man – unrelated to Kenneth MacRae. See p 293.

Synod's Overture, was placed under a necessity of defending MacRae's character. 'He always found in the Rev. K. A. MacRae a Christian gentleman who was never known to do a mean thing or take advantage of any one in debate. . . . Men in Mr MacRae's position had been called disturbers of the peace. It was a popular slogan to accuse of divisions. We wanted our own people educated in the Calvinistic system, and if we believed in it we should do all in our power to extend the knowledge of it. Arminianism was breaking congregations into splinters; of that they had experience in Lewis. Had we been as diligent about emphasising our reformed teaching as we ought? If not, we surely could not object to the Day of Humiliation and Prayer. Why was there this sensitiveness on the part of ministers when Arminianism was spoken of?'

When a vote was finally taken on the motion that the Synod's Overture be departed from, it was carried by 53 to 37. It would be wrong to represent this as a vote of censure on MacRae; later in the same week he carried the Assembly with him (by 45 to 38) on the Overture, already mentioned, to terminate the Church's connexion with the Presbyterian Alliance, yet it was certainly a vote against the policy which he believed to be vital for the Church. Perhaps, in view of all that had happened in the previous twelve months, the fact that 36 members of the Assembly voted with Kenneth MacRae indicated more support for his convictions than might have been expected. But it was not enough, and those who took the other side had reason to hope, in the words of the Editor of *The Monthly Record*, 'that this Assembly has mapped the course in which the Church, please God, is to steer for many years to come'.

After remarkably mild comments in his Diary on the events of this long-to-be-remembered week, MacRae concluded, 'It was a sad Assembly, which chilled my heart and filled me with apprehension as to the future'.

I remember when I was a young divinity student being unexpectedly called upon to take the services in the congregation in which I used to worship as a small boy. It was also the church in which the great Dr Kennedy had exercised his ministry. I felt overwhelmed at the thought throughout the day and after the evening service felt greatly troubled, depressed and downcast. The church officer, a worthy man named Alexander MacLean, locally known as Sandy Clunas, was waiting for me in the vestry. He was built on a large size and was especially fond of young men. When I came into the vestry he just put his big arms round me and said 'Never you mind, my boy. As Mr Finlayson of Helmsdale used to say, it is not, "well done, good and successful servant" but "well done, good and faithful servant".'

What is going to count at the end of the day is not success but faithfulness.

K.A.M. in an address given at the
Leicester Ministers' Conference, 1962

19 'The Tide will Turn'

The last eight years of MacRae's ministry constitute the only period after 1912 which is not adequately covered by his diaries. Without explanation, and in the middle of a sentence, the narrative which had been consecutive for so many years breaks off suddenly on 20 August, 1955. Thereafter such diaries as have survived are much briefer in their nature. His change of practice in this regard was probably one of the few adjustments he made with advancing years. For the most part the fact is that the general pattern and routine of his week's work in his late seventies differed little from what it had been thirty years before. Having prayerfully considered the advisability of a move to a smaller charge in 1947, he had come to the conclusion that God meant him to remain in Lewis as long as he had strength. He noted on 4 November, 1960: 'My 77th birthday, how fearfully old I am and how little I feel it! I see others old and tottery yet I regard myself as one of the ordinary crowd who have yet many years to go and whose concern centres on the things of this world. Except for shortness of breath on exertion I feel as well as ever, and as well able to go on with the ordinary duties of life as ever I was. I am not conscious of any inclination to lay down the duties of my lot in preparation for the great removal'. Perhaps some, noting the briskness of his movements, misjudged his age for even after he was seventy-seven he was to have a call from another congregation (Glen-urquhart) which he declined.

Others also noted his physical tenacity. Commenting on his ability to 'carry on', Peter W. Miller, his friend of student days, was to write after his death:

Physically, Mr MacRae was a strong athletic man, endowed with tireless energy, and with his strictly methodical use of time he accomplished more than most in his telling, exerting, impeccable life. Latterly, when he had a long ministry in a very large congregation, his fellow-presbyters used to speak, not without certain qualms, of his doing four men's work. He could fairly have been compared with 'those men of iron' – the Bonar brothers of an earlier Free Church generation. He, like them, had a magnificent natural strength and the wisdom to conserve it. Mr MacRae never spoke, even in his busiest season, of feeling tired, but only sometimes as being too sleepy to attempt anything more at the end of a long day.

This last period of his ministry was marked, however, by a serious illness which interrupted his ministry for nearly seven months in 1957–8. It began with severe pain in the stomach which, after X-rays had been taken, was diagnosed as an ulcer requiring a major operation for its removal. While he awaited this surgery in the Stornoway hospital he suffered an onset of phlebitis which delayed the operation. When, at length, the operation was undertaken, no trace of an ulcer could be found, but he suffered a post-operative pulmonary embolism – the movement of a clot of blood to his chest – and this brought him so close to death that for some weeks his survival was in doubt.

Before the operation, the possibility that his pilgrimage was about to end was clearly before MacRae and his attitude to that eventuality is on record in a letter which he wrote to Kenneth MacLeay of Beauly:

Lewis Hospital
Stornoway
Saturday

My dear Kennie,

You are the best friend I have in the world, with MacQuarrie running a close second, and therefore, considering what may happen under the surgeon's knife or afterwards, I think I ought to send you a message of appreciation of all your friendship has meant to me. We may never meet again in this world, and I would like to tell you that to me there is no home in the world, next to my own, like the lovely home in Beauly presided over by that darling little wife of yours. To spend a few days with you there has been like balm to my spirit and I can never thank you sufficiently for all your kindness and fellowship to me there.

I get my operation – the removal of a stomach ulcer – at 9.30 on Monday morning. Despite my age, prospects (humanly speaking) are excellent. The medical report shows that my tissues are 'young', that my heart and blood are good, and that I have no trace of any such thing as high or low blood pressure, that my constitution is strong, and that I am in very good condition, etc, etc.

These things are cheering and encouraging, but all is in Higher Hands. When I was brought in here I got the text with power, 'He brought me into his banqueting house and his banner over me was love'. And truly this place to me has been Christ's banqueting-house and He has filled me with a sense of His love which transcends all powers of expression. Like Samuel Rutherford I feel that I could head this letter, 'Christ's Banqueting House'. For many, many, weary months – yes, stretching out even into years – I have been in great darkness, but now it has all gone in a blaze of glory which has utterly melted my hard heart. I feel that I could never preach of Christ again, for at the very mention of Him I am sure I

[462]

would break down in the presence of the people. My mind is filled with unutterable peace and I have not the slightest fear or anxiety in the world. I am the happiest person on earth, I don't care whether He takes me or leaves me – only I have a new love for my congregation. The tide is full in.

It is because of this wonderful experience that I think that He surely intends to take me away, but on the other hand there is a verse which keeps saying, 'The Lord hath me chastised sore, but not to death given over'. His will be done.

I am treated here like a king. The Matron, the sister and most of the nurses are my own, and they could not do more for me. Some of the girlies are pure gold. You must never run down the *Léodhasaich*[1] to me after this. There is a very noisy element among them, and they have their own ways, but many of them are of the salt of the earth. Oh to catch them young with sound doctrine and bring them up in the knowledge of the faith!

But I must close, Kennie. Good-bye if we are not to meet again – otherwise loving regards to you both, Yours

Kenneth A MacRae

Another disclosure of the state of his spirit at this time exists in a brief 'testimony' which he dictated to his wife on 16 November. It may be that these words were spoken after the serious complication attending the operation:

I hereby testify that I have lived a long, satisfying and happy life, and now that I come to die I pass on, trusting in the merits of my adorable Redeemer who has taken away the shadows of alienation and filled my cup to overflowing with an unspeakably sweet sense of His love. To Him be all the glory! 'Let all the earth His glory fill. Amen, so let it be!'

To the joy of so many, MacRae was not to die in 1957. The convalescence period was, however, prolonged. For five months Mary and part of her family removed from Ardelve to Stornoway and her presence with her father – to whom she was so closely attached – was an aid to his restoration.

When he was well enough to travel he went to the MacLeays, and Kenneth MacLeay describes his memory of that visit in the following words: 'He came to Beauly for a week after he recovered and when I met him at the Station my heart sank. He was an old man, but after his first sleep here he said he felt "a new man". On the third day of his stay the military step was back, and by the end of the week he had put on 7 pounds in weight. He made an excellent recovery'.

1 Lewis people. As a native of Skye Kenneth MacLeay's comments had reflected something of the traditional friendly rivalry between the two Islands.

By the early summer of 1958 he was back to his full schedule of work in Stornoway and it was in the August of that year that the present writer heard him preach for the first time while on a visit to Lewis. The occasion was a normal Sabbath evening English service in the Seminary. Although a Gaelic service was going on simultaneously in the Church, every seat in the building appeared to be taken, and one of the most striking features to a visitor was the stillness and silence which marked the assembled congregation. In the pulpit MacRae appeared grave, slight and frail – with the exception of his voice which was distinct and strong. His manner was characterised by authority and simplicity. We did not need to hear him preach to know there was no truth in any rumour that he was inclined to hyper-Calvinism, but if any visitor had entered that service entertaining such an opinion he could not have retained it for long. The text was 1 John 3:23, 'And this is his commandment, That we should believe on the name of his Son Jesus Christ' . . . and the burden of the text was persuasively urged upon every individual present. MacRae's pulpit style was not dramatic, his movements and gestures of the hand were comparatively few, but he spoke with the force which belongs to strong convictions and with a clarity of argument which – given the great themes which were his subjects – compelled attention. He seemed to look straight at each hearer and, while he knew that all success depended upon the Spirit of God, he regarded it as his responsibility to employ a manner of speech which was calculated to secure the attention of all. It was said of Kennedy of Dingwall, 'You know when Mr Kennedy begins he takes full command', and this same element was present in the preaching of Kenneth MacRae.

It was his custom on occasion to ask the congregation to remain briefly at the close of a service when he had something to say to them relative to the congregation or the spiritual welfare of the community. This occurred on the evening to which I have just referred, and for some five minutes he urged his people with great earnestness to do everything possible to retain the Gaelic language in their families and church. He believed that there was an important blessing attached to the retention of Gaelic in areas where it was still the predominant language – it would, for one thing, assist in the preservation of values which had no place in the view of life presented so commonly in English newspapers, radio, and television – and he pleaded with the congregation not to let the language fail as it had already done so widely across the Highlands.

One marked feature of the congregational life in Stornoway was the entire absence of any activities or organisations designed for the teen-agers of the church. This matter was so important in MacRae's estimation that it deserves further comment. It will be apparent to the reader of the preceding pages that he was deeply interested in the young; strange though it may seem, it was his very concern for them which made him so insistent that no special activities should be provided for them beyond the Sabbath School. His belief was that the regular life of the church must be such that it meets the *spiritual* needs of all age groups. If it fails to do this in the case of teen-agers, something is seriously wrong, and to propose additional arrangements for them as a remedy is to fail to realise the true nature of the problem.

MacRae deplored the removal of children from a service in order to attend Sabbath schools or Bible classes while the congregation heard a sermon. Nor did he approve of so-called 'childrens' addresses', on the grounds that it encouraged the idea that the sermon was not meant for the young. On this subject one diary entry reads as follows:

'Spoke with some liberty from Mark 4:40 on Christ rebuking His disciples' unbelief. Got in a word against some who would like to see an address to the children interjected into the service, and made it clear I am speaking to the children all along. Children enlightened by the Spirit can understand the preaching of the Word much better than unconverted adults.'

At the same time it should be added that he had no sympathy for the habit of some preachers who seemed to prepare their material with no consideration for the children who would be among their hearers. He made this point in the course of a series of addresses on homiletics which he gave on one occasion in Stornoway on the instructions of the General Assembly.

MacRae's convictions on methods of reaching teen-agers are so little heard or understood today that it is worth while to introduce here his outline of an address on 'Youth and the Church' which he gave in Stornoway at this period. It was from this kind of outline that he gave all his lectures and, as in this instance, the logical manner in which he developed a case made it easier for him to hold his outline in his mind, so that he was never tied to his notes in delivering an address. His main points were clearly in his mind, and in the course of delivery he filled them out with extempore speech.

I THE MODERN IDEA

1. What it is – the segregation of youth – this provided inside the Church so as to keep the youth.

2. What gave rise to it – the drift away from the Church on the part of youth.
3. It takes many forms:
   (i) In liberal churches the provision of guilds, clubs, amusements, etc which all have social contacts.
   (ii) In more conservative circles – fellowships, conventions, etc.
   (iii) With the latter we concern ourselves.

II THE TRADITIONAL IDEA

1. What it was: Sabbath School and Bible Class – the first to give Scriptural knowledge, the second to educate in Doctrine. From there young people passed into the ordinary life of the church.
2. It was an idea which worked well for many a day
3. But there came a time which witnessed its breakdown.

III THE GREAT BREAKDOWN

1. The decay of vital religion was the root cause of the breakdown of the old idea.
2. This decay seen:
   (i) In the preaching of the sanctuary
   (ii) In attendance upon the means of grace
   (iii) In decline of family discipline.
3. The decay of vital religion due to incoming Modernism – the church lost all spiritual power.
4. And naturally the young who were not stabilised were most affected.

IV HOW TO EFFECT RESTORATION

1. The way back is surely the only way to effect a restoration, namely, sound vital preaching.
2. But this is what the age will not have.
3. And the idea of the segregation of youth seems to many evangelicals to be the only answer to the problem!

V WEAKNESSES INHERENT IN THIS MODERN IDEA

1. What happens when these youths are no longer young? Will they fit into the life of the church?
2. Admitted that exercised young people love to get together to compare notes:
   (i) But that must necessarily be upon a very limited range.
   (ii) Enlarge and extend this range and the heart-to-heart talks cease and a different spirit is introduced.
3. Youth is not fit to take the reins
   (i) Impulsive, lacking in experience and in knowledge – apt to go too far, and to go off the rails without realising it.
   (ii) It is a stupendous error to despise the wisdom of the past and this is what youth is ever prone to do.

(iii) We do not know where such an irresponsible movement will ultimately land.

4. This idea makes youth bold and self-assertive:
    (i) Youth is the time for learning and there is much to be learned.
    (ii) Youth leaders are apt to become impatient of any control: the age and experience of their elders are alike slighted.
    (iii) This is not good in any church or congregation.

VI YOUTH MOVEMENT IN OUR OWN CHURCH

1. Features giving rise to uneasiness
    (i) Outside associations.
    (ii) Tendency towards Arminian doctrine.
    (iii) Impatience with purity of worship.
    (iv) No desire to examine our Testimony.
    (v) Some argue that the only thing that matters is acceptance of Scripture as the Word of God, being indifferent to the Reformation testimony of the Confession of Faith for which we stand.

2. The danger of an ultimate split when the battle of 1900 would need to be fought over again.

Conclusion
Nothing can be better than the old Biblical system of a former day which taught that the stated means of grace were for all age-groups.

Whatever anyone thought of MacRae's aversion to the more customary aids for 'retaining' young people in the churches, there was no denying that his congregation – without any youth activities – was thriving with young people. That did not surprise him for he believed that God would honour the maintenance of biblical principles.

There is only one instance in his life, known to us, when he publicly used his own congregation as a witness to the fact that the preaching of the Word of God has not lost its power. The issue did not have to do with reaching the young, although it was related to that question. In June, 1960, a correspondent in *The Scotsman*, one of Scotland's national papers, attributed the decline of religion in the land to what he considered to be a justifiable reaction against the teaching of the Westminster Confession of Faith. To this letter MacRae replied:

FREE CHURCH MANSE, STORNOWAY,
JUNE 7, 1960

Sir, – Mr John F. Ross's assertions (June 4) concerning the Westminster Confession of Faith should not be allowed to go by default. In his letter he calls the Confession a 'monstrous document' and blames it for 'the drift away from the Kirk which we lament to-day.'

The Westminster Confession of Faith is a model of perspicuity, presenting in clear, concise terms – altogether different from the vague, cloudy and indefinite phraseology beloved of the popular theologians of to-day – a wonderfully exhaustive summary of the doctrines of the Word of God and as interpreted by Reformed theology.

As for holding the Confession responsible for the drift away from the Church of Scotland, Mr Ross is entirely mistaken. The drift began over 60 years ago and coincided with the rise and progress of liberalistic preaching from the pulpits of the land. I can remember the time when in Edinburgh one could go into any Free Church and rest assured that he would hear a sermon in full accord with the teachings of the Confession.

Further, it is since the national Church altered her profession of faith from simple acceptance of the doctrines of the Confession to the assertion of her Declaratory Articles and Formula that she believes in the 'fundamental doctrines of the Christian faith' set forth in her Confession, that she has so completely lost her hold upon the people of Scotland. In thus altering her ground in favour of unspecified 'fundamental doctrines' she has evacuated the Confession of Faith of all value as a 'subordinate standard.'

The only teaching that will bring the people back to the Church is the teaching which most of the preachers of to-day have discarded, that is, full-orbed Reformed theology, the Gospel of God's sovereign grace. It has brought the people back before, and it will do it again. – I am &c.

(REV.) KENNETH A. MACRAE

Further controversy followed in the correspondence columns of *The Scotsman* after the publication of the above letter, and this led to a second letter from his pen which was published under the heading 'Free Church doctrines hold congregation':

FREE CHURCH MANSE, STORNOWAY,
JUNE 17, 1960

Sir, – In seeking to controvert my statement that a return to the preaching of Reformed doctrines is the only thing which, under God's blessing, will bring back her lost people to the Church of Scotland, Mr H. McLeod shrewdly avoids the facts upon which I base my assertion and contents himself with the argument that were my assertion correct then the Free Church would have increased in numbers through the years and not have failed, as he holds, even to maintain her ground.

So far as that may be true there are two reasons for it, neither of which vitiates my assertion: (1) the appalling depopulation of the Highlands during those years, and (2) the intolerant, unreasoning prejudice which prevents many outsiders from ever entering her doors, so that she has had no opportunity of making known to them the doctrines of grace. In fact, in the religious life of the land the Free Church has been 'sent to Coventry' for the last 60 years and consequently she has had little opportunity of reaching the outside masses.

But let me adduce a further proof of my contention, and one which lies very close to hand. In this town any favourable Sabbath evening I can count upon a congregation of up to 1,000 – and sometimes over – 80 per cent of whom are young people. I have nothing for them but the straight-forward preaching of the Word of God as set forth in all the confessions of the Reformed Church; and yet they come back every Sabbath, year in year out. Were one of the popular modernistic preachers to occupy my pulpit – no matter how eloquent – I am firmly convinced that ere three months were up he would have no congregation left. The vital element in preaching is the teaching, and that teaching in 100 per cent agreement with the doctrines of God's Word. It is because of this that the Church of Scotland has lost more than half her people, while the Free Church – except for a few isolated cases and apart from depopulation – has kept hers. In other words, Reformed doctrine has kept the people; liberal preaching has scattered them.

Your correspondents have done their best to try to show that the reverse is the case, but they might as well try to prove that black is white. The facts are against them. and the sooner they realise it the better both for themselves and for their Church. – I am &c.

(REV.) KENNETH A. MACRAE

All his life MacRae believed in the importance of seeking to have the Christian position heard in newsprint and he gave more time to this than is customary with ministers. He wrote trenchantly on the proposal raised in the Church of Scotland in 1957 to introduce a modified episcopacy as a step towards unity with the Church of England and, as he believed, through Canterbury with Rome. Scottish independence was to baulk at the bishop-in-presbytery scheme, but MacRae correctly judged the ultimate comprehensiveness towards which the ecumenical movement was moving. In 1960, when a report of the Church and Nation Committee of the Church of Scotland gave its recommendation to a half-day Sunday – with the suggestion that Church halls be used on Sunday evenings for dancing and other amusements as a means of establishing contact with the younger generation – he wrote of it in *The Scotsman* as 'the most devastating blow which the Sabbath has ever received in this land', and urged Church of Scotland evangelicals to reject the report in their General Assembly.

MacRae was, indeed, on many occasions involved in debate over the

[469]

Fourth Commandment. The prevalent religious mood regarded the upholding of that commandment in the Christian era as 'moralistic legalism', and the Westminster Confession of the English Puritans was blamed for Scotland's 'Sabbatarianism'. MacRae viewed the defence of the Christian Sabbath not as an end in itself but as a very important part of the public recognition of God and the authority of His law: if that authority was allowed to fall from the consciousness of the people, and if Sunday work (usually on double pay) was allowed to become an accepted fact, then he saw both spiritual and moral degeneration as inevitable. 'Who hath hardened himself against God, and hath prospered?'

His feelings on this issue are clearly expressed in a letter published after the Farnborough Air Show in Hampshire in 1957. On the opening day of that year's show a plane broke up in the air during a demonstration flight and then fell, with disastrous effect, into the vast crowd.

Free Church Manse,
Stornoway.

Sir, – The press account of the dreadful tragedy at Farnborough may well alarm anyone who has any regard for the moral well-being of the people of this country. The tragedy itself was a pure accident and as such was outwith human control and responsibility, but what alarms is the conduct of the promoters of the exhibition and of the people who attended it in carrying on with proceedings after such a dreadful occurrence. A death at a sports meeting or public function not so long ago would at once terminate everything. Today, no matter what happens – should there be 20 deaths – the show must go on.

In the far places of the earth there are fierce and brutal tribes whom we call savages. Among the most abandoned of these, such a holocaust as took place at Farnborough on Saturday would have aroused more concern than appears from the utter callousness of the English crowd. Next day – the Lord's Day – the crowd of 120,000 had increased to 150,000. Through their midst came a motor vehicle bearing the relatives of the dead to the underground chamber where the bodies lay stretched out awaiting identification, but the show went on and the jets screamed overhead.

The press reports as worthy of remark that one of the injured in hospital expressed his regret that he had missed the show – that was his reaction; no word of thankfulness to God that his life had been spared; no expression of sympathy with those who had been in a moment bereaved; no, nothing counted but that he had missed the show! That is typical of the spirit of today, and it is a spirit which is admired as though it were heroism.

In the same paper there is an account of the hysterical reception in Glasgow on Sabbath night of an American film star on the part of a screaming, screeching mob estimated to number 3,000.

What has come over the British people, once one of the most kindly, cool-headed, steady, and considerate races upon the face of the earth? It is only too evident that their character has completely changed. And why? There must be some reason for such a remarkable change. The answer is not far to seek. History has over and over again shown that moral deterioration is the inevitable result of religious degeneracy. As a nation we have forsaken God, and God has forsaken us. There is more involved in Sabbath-keeping than men realise. Britain, in abandoning her Sabbath, has lost her crown, and it is indeed to be feared that her long pre-eminence among the nations of the earth is speedily drawing to a close.

Yours etc. KENNETH A. MACRAE

In connection with his views on the sanctity of the Lord's Day, an incident occurred in 1956 which led to considerable public comment. In the August of that year the Queen and the Duke of Edinburgh visited the Outer Hebrides and MacRae was invited by the Lord Lieutenant to accept the honour of being presented to them. In his letter, which respectfully declined this invitation, MacRae replied: 'Since the Queen has persistently violated the Fourth Commandment of the moral law of God by attending polo matches upon various Sabbath afternoons; since she has given the sanction of the Crown to the destruction of the Sabbath within her realm, in loyalty to my vows as a Christian, I cannot with a clear conscience accept any honour from Her Majesty's hand'. He also pointed out that the Queen had used the Lord's Day to receive Russian politicians.

When news of this reached the press there was a predictable response in most quarters. His attitude was characterised as 'self-righteousness', 'sheer pompous bigotry and rudeness', and 'stiff-necked self-import-ance'. Yet in one national newspaper, at least, the comment was different. The News Chronicle wrote, 'Real conviction is so rare these days that it commands attention . . . Here at least is a man prepared to stand by his beliefs – and the world can think what it likes.'

There was perhaps no subject which roused MacRae more than what he considered to be the mis-government of the Highlands and Islands of Scotland. In part his warmth on this theme was that of a patriot who believed that the best interests of the people were too often ignored or misjudged, but there was also an underlying conviction that there were harmful spiritual consequences resulting from bad government policies. As an illustration of this, mention should be made of the leading part which he took in 1960 in opposing a government plan to site a N.A.T.O. air-base at Stornoway. He did not contest the need for such a base in the north of Scotland but to site it so close to a town – containing as it might well do a nuclear strike force – was, he argued, an absurd decision. In the event of war the largest civilian population in Lewis would inevitably become a potential target for the enemy.

Of more long-standing nature was his criticism of the government's reaction to the depopulation of the Highlands. The empty straths and deserted homes to be found across the North he could never regard as other than a tragedy. That conviction was deepened by his meeting with many 'rootless' Highlanders of the exile in Australia in 1953–54. Not long after his return, *The Scotsman* published a major article from his pen entitled 'Greatest Cause of Emigration – Persistent Propaganda'. The first paragraphs read as follows:

'Many reasons have been advanced for the present emigration boom, but these are pretexts rather than reasons. The greatest reason of all for the emigration which is depriving Scotland of the cream of her people seems to remain unnoticed. It is the persistent, persuasive propaganda fostered and financed by the Governments concerned, including that of Britain herself.

'As an example of this propaganda, take the meeting which was held in the Town Hall of Inverness recently, at which Canadian films were shown and life in Canada extolled. What wonder, then, that the Press reported that the following morning the Canadian immigration agent interviewed about 70 people. That is why people emigrate in shoals; not because of frustration or labour troubles or anything else at home, but, in plain English, simply because they are allured across the ocean by promises of good pay, good prospects, and an assisted passage, while all the disadvantages are carefully ignored.

'This propaganda has been going on now for generations, and when the time seems meet it is intensified, and the result is such a boom as we have at present. The fever is catching, whole families in a community are caught up in the excitement, and to emigrate becomes the order of the day.

'When these emigrants settle down in their new surroundings it is but natural that they should try to justify what they have done, and they write home glowing letters concerning the great country to which they have come and advise all their friends to follow their example. That, of course, is but human nature. And so this pernicious process, which means the ultimate ruin of the Highlands as the home of the Celtic race, goes on at ever-increasing tempo. It is all very well for Canadians and others to point out the part played by Scotsmen, and especially Highlanders, in the development of their respective countries, but do they ever think of our empty glens and islands, and of the fable of the man who killed the goose that laid the golden eggs?'

He proceeded to argue that the alleged benefits of emigration were far from being the whole picture. From his Australian experience he was able to document 'another side'. Emigrants to that land had not infrequently been surprised to find the purchase price of houses altogether beyond their reach and had been compelled to live in hostels:

'I may state it as a fact that in the 12 months I spent in Australia I had more solicitations for help than I have had in Scotland in all my life. Some of these people have been in these hostels for years and are well-nigh heart-broken, for they realise to their cost that it was easier for them to get out to Australia than to get back to their homeland.'

Finally, he attacked the government-sponsored view that tourism was the Highlands' best hope for the future. 'All this cry about the development of the tourist industry is simply an insult to every High-lander who loves his country. We don't wish to become a nation of flunkeys, to await the pleasure of our masters from the South.' What the Highlands needed was an infusion of capital:

'The cry is raised – "Let the Highlanders help themselves". How can they help themselves when capital is absent, and when all industrial initiative is smothered by huge and preposterous freight charges? Goods from London command the payment of freight at this end. Lobsters, etc., sent to Billingsgate from the Islands have their transit charges also borne at this end! Our Governments all along have refused to protect the interests of the Highland fishermen from unfair competition, with the result that the industry now is at its last gasp. The wonder is that the tweed industry has survived Government interference.

'Millions can go to Jordania and other ungrateful Eastern States, but the Highlands are being slowly killed by studied and deliberate neglect. The only thing that can save the Highlands is the infusion of capital upon a hitherto unknown scale. If poor Norway can do it for the support of her communities dwelling in isolated parts, surely Britain can.

'It is indeed exasperating to see how prepared our Government are to contribute to the transport of the best of our people overseas, while at the same time they give every encouragement to people of alien stock and race to make their home in Britain. It is more than time that our Government were required to send agents among our people to lecture them upon the desirability of remaining in and developing the Highlands, and to make it possible for them to do so by cutting down freights and devoting to the Highlands some of the moneys which they dole out with such lavish hand in sundry foreign lands.'

MacRae knew that if the Highlands had to depend upon tourists rather than upon their own work and resourcefulness, their way of life would inevitably be moulded to suit the wishes of the tourist industry. That industry consistently complained of the lack of facilities for entertainment and dining on Sundays in the West Highlands and Islands, owing to the 'narrow' religious outlook of the inhabitants. Regular pressure was exerted through newspapers and other means to have that outlook changed. To one such published complaint respecting the 'deprivations' suffered by tourists, MacRae replied with his usual brevity and force:

I would like to ask Mr Millar a very simple question: Who is to receive the preference, God or the tourist, when their claims come into opposition? Apparently he thinks that it should be the latter; but he has no right to seek to impose his opinion upon people who think differently and, I may add, more rationally.

Fortunately there are still some conscientious Christians left in the Highlands and Islands. If they constitute a difficulty for the tourist, then the fault pertains to the latter. They constitute no difficulty for those who fear God and keep His commandments.

While thus frequently engaged with public questions it remains to be emphasised that to the end he regarded his own congregation and its spiritual prosperity as his first responsibility. Except for the illness of 1957–58 he never relaxed the schedule of work and preaching to which he had long been accustomed and which continued to be attended with fruitfulness. In a brief diary note on new communicant members, in February 1959, he recorded: 'Nine in all were admitted which I think is the highest since I began my ministry in this charge. To the Lord be all the glory . . . In all 560 communicated. There was a good atmosphere, and at the evening service in the church not a few appeared to be moved.'

An uppermost concern in these closing years of his ministry was to see that he conveyed to his congregation – and especially to its youth – his own understanding of the need of the times. He had always laboured to advance the old theology, seemingly, in the country at large, to little avail. The situation in the 1950's, far from being better than when he began his ministry, was worse, and at times it seemed to him that Stornoway was 'the last bastion of the Reformed faith in Scotland'. In his own denomination he believed that some had lost interest in the fight and others had lost heart; the majority had not welcomed the issue raised in his booklet *The Resurgence of Arminianism*. Confronted with this situation he might have resigned himself to discontinuing such an apparently unequal struggle. That such a temptation occurred to him in despondent moments can hardly be doubted, and even when he was not despondent the question whether such controversy was worth while still faced him and called for an answer. That answer he found afresh in the Word of God. He read again that in a time of crisis in Israel's history Meroz was cursed because 'they came not to the help of the Lord' (Judges 5:23). And, as though a fresh commission from Christ, the words were to ring in his ears through the closing years of his ministry, 'Hold that fast which thou hast, that no man take thy crown'.

The result of this was a stronger commitment than ever to truths which were unpopular in the religious world at large and on these he now addressed his people with a new intensity of conviction. This came through in his preaching and, though his diary entries were now short and intermittent, it is revealed there also. For example, on 22 February, 1959, he wrote: 'I spoke from Ephesians 3:21 on God's glory as the great end of the Church. Pleaded with the young people to take an interest in our Church's testimony'. Again, on 1 November, 1960: 'Spoke from Ephesians 1:1–11 with a measure of freedom and tried to arouse my people to an appreciation of the preciousness of the doctrines of sovereign grace'. At the same time he maintained his practice of giving regular lectures during the winter months and the titles of a number of these lectures speak for themselves: 'Our Testimony'; 'Is it worth it?'; 'Must we lose our Reformed testimony?'; and 'Today's Need for Propagation of Reformed Witness'. In one of these lectures he demonstrated from the following headings that perseverance in their testimony was worth while:

(1) Because the Lord has not forsaken it (2) Because it is buttressed by His promises (3) Because it only survives where it is contended for (4) If we desert the cause He will raise up others[1] (5) Because our children are dependent upon our faithfulness (6) Because He will yet arise.

---

1 In this connection he often warned his people that other parts of Scotland, which were once rich in gospel privileges, had lost Christ's presence because of unfaithfulness.

One striking feature of these lectures was the strong enforcement of practical duties which they contained. 'The tide will turn', he argued in one address, but that did not mean that their present attitude should be simply one of waiting for a revival. There were three principal duties to which they must attend: 'We have to (1) be faithful to our trust – guarding against false charity and the approval of the world (2) diligently declare the truth (3) protest against error'. Each of these points was, of course, elaborated in turn. Similarly in a final series of lectures on Revivals his notes for the third lecture read as follows:

HINDRANCES TO REVIVAL

Introduction: Not that we can hinder – no more than we can the shower of rain – but certain things are unfavourable to revival and grieve the Spirit.

Some of these things:

1. Lack of desire for revival
2. Attempts to *create* a revival
3. Worldliness among professing Christians
   (1) Worldly gain
   (2) Worldly honour and preferment
   (3) Love of amusements
   These grieve the Spirit; hamper efforts of preacher; earn reproach of world
4. Absence of a sense of responsibility
   Lethargy of many no excuse
5. Toleration of offences
   (1) Drink (2) Bad language (3) Gambling (4) Sunday papers
6. Absence of brotherly love
   (1) Cliques (2) Divisions (3) Contentions.
7. Erroneous or inadequate instruction
   (1) Doctrines of men
   (2) Denial of divine sovereignty or of human responsibility
   (3) Not preaching the whole counsel of God
8. Unscriptural practices
   (1) Musical services   (2) Some forms of offerings   (3) Christmas Services (4) Women preachers and elders.

One of the most constant exhortations of MacRae to his people was that they be diligent in circulating literature, both books and booklets. In this respect, as in others, he led by example. He encouraged every effort to spread the doctrines of grace. After the commencement of *The Banner of Truth* magazine in 1955 he personally ordered quantities

of between 150 and 200 copies! When the republishing programme of
the Banner of Truth Trust began in 1957 he rejoiced in it and gave
valuable help and advice on the furtherance of its objectives. As a result
of the renewed circulation of reformed books in the United Kingdom
new contacts were established between like-minded brethren in
different parts of the country and arising out of this a conference was
arranged at Leicester in July 1962. Although then in his seventy-ninth
year MacRae made the long journey by boat and train and gave two
addresses to the forty or so ministers who were present. Most of them
were young men who had never seen him before and who knew nothing
of his long ministry, but his addresses on 'Teaching Essential to
Evangelical Preaching' and 'The Danger of Compromise in Preaching'
were used by God to stir them deeply and to inspire them in turn to
reach others with the same truths. Far from appearing aged and battle
weary he spoke as a man imbued with vigour and enthusiasm. Even the
frailty he had shown in the summer of 1958, when he was still recovering
from illness, seemed to be gone. What he had to say he believed
intensely: the present ineffectiveness of the Church was due to the
absence of truth – let the doctrines of grace be proclaimed, not dryly but
with life, and it would be seen that they had power to work a change.
Sound scriptural teaching was the great need of the day, and when that
came it would surely be followed by the sound of abundance of rain!
In a brief autobiographical reference he said that in his lifetime he had
seen the tide of spiritual religion go far out, as it had done at other times
in the history of the Church, yet it was sure to turn, and just as the
turning of the tide on the shore is almost imperceptible to the eye so
God's cause can quietly begin to come back into its own. It seemed, as he
spoke these words, that others were given faith to see the turning of the
tide as a present reality – only at its beginning, perhaps, but the turn
had come.

Kenneth MacRae was not prone to premature optimism but that is
how he personally felt as he later returned to Scotland. When, back in
Stornoway, he addressed his people on 'The Present Prospects of the
Reformed Faith', he reported that he had seen in England 'a little cloud,
like a man's hand' (1 Kings 18:44). And, reflecting on the Conference at
Leicester, he wrote to a friend: 'The earnestness and spiritual unity of
those young fellows who gathered at Leicester was for me a real tonic
and encouraged me greatly. So far, the movement towards the Reformed
faith may be weak and largely unorganised, but that there is such a
movement cannot be questioned, and in it, by God's grace, there are

tremendous possibilities. Worm Jacob may yet thresh the mountains. May the Lord grant it so!'

While in England MacRae made a last visit to London. As a place the centre of London did not appeal to him but he revelled in its history and was eager to include a visit to the Tower of London amid the engagements of a busy week spent in the capital. It gave him particular pleasure to preach in Grove Chapel, Camberwell, in the pulpit of Joseph Irons whose sermons he had long admired. Perhaps the visit he enjoyed most of all was to Olney in Buckinghamshire, the scene of the ministry of John Newton from 1764-1779. Newton was one of his favourite authors and his commitment to the exclusive use of the Book of Psalms in public worship did not lessen his appreciation of *The Olney Hymns*. After visiting the church and grave-yard, the visit terminated in William Cowper's former home, 'Orchard Side', where, sitting in the poet's seat beside an upstairs window he took the opportunity to write a post-card to Cathie. It was an unexpected place from which to be writing in his seventy-ninth year: that he should be on a preaching visit to England for the first and last time in 1962 was no less surprising. The occasion was appropriate to remember Cowper's words:

> Deep in unfathomable mines
> Of never-failing skill
> He treasures up His bright designs,
> And works His sovereign will

HOLDING ON

Some begin well but have no staying power – soon tire – turn to something else – never finish anything. These achieve little in life.

This should be fought against – and in childhood it can be – for then the man is formed. Determine that you will never be of this class.

Let this be your plan at school and it will ever cleave to you.

It requires patience (Bruce and the spider); It requires grit – hold on (the limpet);

See that you choose the good – and stick to it.

K.A.M. from notes of an address given
to the children at Laxdale School

TUESDAY, 1 JANUARY, 1963

12 *noon, Gaelic*. Proverbs 4:18, 'But the path of the just is as the shining light that shineth more and more unto the perfect day'. Attendance 130.

A quiet beautiful winter day but the hard-packed snow on the roads is now as polished as glass and both walking and driving are very difficult.

SABBATH, 6 JANUARY

11 *am, Gaelic*. Jude 3 – attendance 340. 7 *pm, English*. Job 16:22 – attendance 650.

Felt somewhat hard and unresponsive at both services. Have feeling of disappointment. Wish the Lord would quicken me.

MONDAY, 7 JANUARY

Heard that yesterday's sermons were greatly appreciated, specially the evening one under which many were impressed. Such a result is wonderful, especially since I was troubled with a spirit of hardness all day on Sabbath.

Another beautiful day with frost keener than ever. In the morning our windows were frosted over.

SABBATH, 13 JANUARY

11 *am, Gaelic*. John 3:27 – attendance 300. 7 *pm, English*. Jeremiah 29:13 – attendance 650.

Preached in the morning on the sovereignty of God in the application of the efficacy of the work of redemption and at night on God's promise to be found by those who earnestly seek Him. Felt that the morning's sermon was clearer.

In the forenoon the thaw set in and by night the streets were very slippery. Was therefore surprised at the largeness of the congregation.

TUESDAY, 15 JANUARY

7.30, *Lecture*. 'Attempts to get out of the Bog' – attendance 60–70. Did not enjoy the lecture much. Feel that I am very poor in the art of giving emphasis in speaking where the sense requires it. Felt that I failed to drive home the points of my address.

WEDNESDAY, 16 JANUARY

7 pm, *Melbost.* Psalm 9:10 – attendance 38.

Was ill-prepared for the Melbost meeting, yet received altogether exceptional liberty. Considering the fact that recently I have been feeling in a low, dead, unspiritual frame of mind, the liberty of thought and of speech given me more than surprised me. Surely there is someone in Melbost who draws out of me, for I normally have unusual liberty down there – either that, or perhaps there is something brewing there.

A young girl who was at the Lecture last night was found dead in her bed this morning. It was really tragic and I feel shocked.

FRIDAY, 18 JANUARY

The funeral of poor Isabel MacLeod was the largest I have seen for a long time – the largest and the saddest. Nine of our ministers were present, including two from Skye. The first lift[1] was taken by ministers only. It was pathetic to see a company of boys from her class in the Nicolson among the bearers.

SABBATH, 20 JANUARY

Although got a measure of freedom at the morning service, yet felt somewhat confused, and wandered from my notes quite a bit. Dealt with our need of quickening by the Spirit.

At night spoke of the heavenly rest and the Gospel rest – and the danger of coming short of it. Was enabled to speak with deliberate freedom and felt satisfied with the build of my sermon – but it was too smooth and lacking in power and feeling.

MONDAY, 21 JANUARY

The old man who was buried today is said to have undergone a wonderful change during the last two or three months. God's sovereignty may break in at the end of a wasted life, but death-bed repentances are not given too much credit by the discerning.

A young man today expressed his appreciation of last night's discourse and asked me to explain what an assured hope was. I replied – 'a hope for which you have every reason' – and that seemed to satisfy him.

SATURDAY, 26 JANUARY

How difficult I find it to get preparation time – either mentally or

1 That is, the bearing of the coffin.

spiritually – for the work of the Sabbath! I am disturbed greatly by this lack.

THURSDAY, 31 JANUARY

Today the newspapers are full of lamentations because Britain has been denied entrance to the Common Market, but we are full of rejoicing. The Lord has answered our prayers, and in a most unexpected way, and we have been saved from a connection which in all likelihood would have been fatal to our land.

FRIDAY, I FEBRUARY

Heard tonight of a revival at . . . but got no details. From what I did hear I cannot but feel rather dubious about it. There is a tendency among us to regard a sudden interest in religion, which may be the outcome of a fright, as a conversion and to treat the person concerned accordingly. As McCheyne used to point out, conviction of sin is not conversion and the convicted person may never be converted. Discernment is sadly lacking in this generation.

SATURDAY, 2 FEBRUARY

A beautiful bright winter day. It really is remarkable weather. The barometer has not moved since the 18th of last month, but it has been high since the 27th December. It is snowing tonight in Portree.

SABBATH, 3 FEBRUARY

11 *am*. Matthew 10:31 – attendance 400. 7 *pm*. Revelation 6:17 – attendance 760.

Felt in the morning that I had not sufficient material for my Gaelic service, but enjoyed it very much and kept the congregation till 12.45. I wonder whether having my heads and sub-heads arranged and drawn out, and then to leave the delivery to impromptu speech, is not the better way?

At night spoke on the great day of the wrath of the Lamb. Unfortunately towards the end of the sermon the blurred sight to which I am subject struck me and upset me so much that all my anxiety was to get through my discourse without having to give up. Mercifully it did not affect my speech as it sometimes does, but it shortened and blunted my conclusion considerably. But the Lord may bless it.

MONDAY, 4 FEBRUARY

The glass has continued to fall throughout the day and more snow is not at all unlikely. Rather enjoyed tonight's meeting on the joy of the Lord being our strength.

TUESDAY, 5 FEBRUARY

Got a measure of liberty in speaking at the Lecture tonight on 'The State and Education, as they are in Britain today and as they ought to be'.

THURSDAY, 7 FEBRUARY

I put my car to the garage today so did no visitation – especially since the approaching communion demands so much preparation at home.

SABBATH, 10 FEBRUARY

Enjoyed the morning service very much indeed. At night the Seminary was quite full and it would have been hard to find seats for six more. I rather enjoyed the sermon, but it lacked the sweetness of the morning. Oh for power!

MONDAY, 11 FEBRUARY

On the invitation of the widow, presided at the funeral service of her husband, Murdo Munro, Knock. Felt much moved at the service. About a fortnight ago I met him in the street and I could not but wonder at the warmth and spirituality of his talk. Felt grieved for his widow and family.

TUESDAY, 19 FEBRUARY

The meeting of Presbytery was wearisome – much speaking to little purpose – and we were confined there till 3 o'clock. Before I got through dinner it was too late to go to the Hospital, so I spent the rest of the day trying to catch up on correspondence arrears and other tasks which kept me indoors.

FRIDAY, 22 FEBRUARY

Was saddened today to hear of the death of my dear old friend, Andrew Sutherland, whom I always remember in connection with the Duke Street days of long ago. So the old friends are passing away. I am now the third oldest minister in the Church. I must be getting near the end of my course, but I don't feel like it. I wish I could get some respite from the strain of this huge congregation so that I could have some opportunity of preparing for the great change.

[484]

SATURDAY, 23 FEBRUARY

Today dear Mr Sutherland was buried in Fodderty Churchyard. He was one of the last of the old school, and a faithful pastor if ever there was one. I shall miss him. All the old Glasgow ministers I knew so well in the long-ago are gone now – MacLeod (OBE as we called him), Chisholm, Fraser and now Sutherland.[1] So shall it be with us all. Soon shall it be all over.

WEDNESDAY, 27 FEBRUARY

At night acted as Chairman at a Protestant meeting in the Town Hall. Dr Farrell of USA was the speaker. The Town Hall was packed and an overflow meeting in the Seminary had to be held. There were from 150–200 in the Seminary, while in the Town Hall we had an audience of close upon 800. How thankful I am for such a meeting!

THURSDAY, 28 FEBRUARY

About 170–180 were out at the prayer meeting tonight. Spoke from Psalm 81:10 on the expectation of faith and rather enjoyed it.

FRIDAY, I MARCH

Owing to the long-continued dry weather the heather is ready to catch fire from the smallest spark, and in Sleat there is a fire several miles in length sweeping over the promontory. Another fire is between Struan and Portree.

SATURDAY, 2 MARCH

Fires in Skye are still worse. The drought has lasted so long that the burns are dried up and there is little or no water available to quench the flames.

Such weather for this time of year is unprecedented. Scarcely a shower has fallen here since the year came in and the drought began a few days before that. The situation is serious for Skye. About 1000 sheep are said to have perished and the loss of grass threatens the surviving stock with starvation.

SABBATH, 3 MARCH

At morning service spoke on our need for patience in view of the sad state of affairs today. At night dealt with our great need in connection

---

1 Andrew Sutherland (see p 335n) was the oldest minister in the Church at the time of his death. MacLeod died in 1939 (see p 206), Chisholm in 1957 and William Fraser in 1955.

with the restoration of the Reformation testimony in our land, namely, 'a mind to work'.

TUESDAY, 5 MARCH

The rain has come with a vengeance and today it has not ceased. The wind too is very strong and altogether it is a most unpleasant day.

RELIGIOUS INSTRUCTION IN SCHOOLS[1]

Free Church Manse,
Stornoway
March 15, 1963

Sir,

Lest the views expressed at last week's meeting of the Lewis Education Committee regarding religious instruction in the schools receives any credence in the island I shall be glad if you will kindly allow me space to give some information on a matter concerning which not a few appear to be labouring under considerable misapprehension.

In 1872, under the Scottish Education Act, the Church of Scotland and the Free Church of Scotland handed over their schools to the state upon condition that Religious Instruction as a recognized subject would be carried on according to 'use and wont' for all time coming. 'Use and wont' simply meant that the system of instruction in vogue in these schools would be continued, and impartation of Scriptural historical facts, the memorising of certain selected passages of Scripture and the teaching of Scriptural doctrines through the medium of the Shorter Catechism. To this the state agreed, and 'use and wont' was given place as an intrinsic and necessary part of the Act. The Roman Catholics and the Episcopalians were wiser for themselves for they refused to give over their schools.

For many years the state kept faith with the Presbyterian churches, but as the Scottish Education Department became more and more autocratic and concerned more and more with their centralisation policy, more and more they became disinclined to respect the obligation imposed upon them by the Act of 1872. Little by little they whittled away at 'use and wont' until at last in the Southern parts of the country Religious Instruction became a mere shadow of what it had been. Then when the iniquitous Education Act of 1918 became law, 'use and wont' was deprived of all its meaning and Religious Instruction was left more or less to the caprice of Education Authorities or schoolmasters; while at the same time the upkeep of Roman Catholic and Episcopal schools was made a com-

1 This was possibly MacRae's last major letter to the secular press and it is inserted here both for the importance of its subject and as an illustration of the thoroughness with which he wrote such letters.

pulsory burden upon the public rates. Thus it may be clearly seen that the state has completely broken faith with the Presbyterian churches in Scotland, and the people of those churches whose children are vitally concerned in the matter should no longer remain silent under such cynical and tyrannical double-dealing, but should assert their right to that which the state solemnly and unconditionally pledged them.

And now when these facts have been conveniently forgotten the cry is raised in certain quarters for the abolition of Religious Instruction in Scottish public schools altogether. And why? The teaching of Biblical truth cannot but do good at whatever level it may be imparted. In the days when it was a prominent feature of Scottish education there was no such problem as juvenile delinquency. In view of the sad pass to which we have come as a nation it is very difficult to understand why any reasonable person would wish our educational system to become entirely secularised.

Allow me now to give a few more facts from my own personal experience. When I began my schooling at the Garrison School, Fort George, in 1888 the first hour of every day was devoted to Religious Instruction – and we loved it – and every Saturday, from 9 a.m. till 12 noon the school met for the revision of such Biblical knowledge as had been imparted during the week.

On going to Edinburgh in 1892 we found that there Religious Instruction had been cut down to one half hour at the beginning of each day. But it was taught, and very thoroughly too, and as intensively in the higher classes as in the lower. Thus it was during all my school days in Edinburgh.

During the last 47 years I have covered hundreds of miles in different parts of Scotland examining schools in this subject. I found pleasure in the work and it was a source of gratification to me to find the children so well instructed in Biblical knowledge – to say nothing of the pleasure derived from the kindness and hospitality of the schoolmasters and teachers who so pleasantly received me. But I do say that it is the height of unreason for some serving upon bodies which are under contractual and moral obligation to provide teachers qualified to teach this subject, to demand that, if Religious Instruction is to remain upon the school's curriculum, it should be given by ministers.

It may be of some interest to your local readers to know that the Stornoway Free Church Congregation retained their own school until 1896 when, after many solicitations on the part of the school authorities, the Deacons' Court decided to hand it over. The old part of the Francis Street school building represents all that remains of the old Free Church school.

The introduction of the school chaplaincy system was a gross abuse of power on the part of the authorities responsible for it. For it there is not the slightest legislative sanction. But there is no space to go into that since I have already so far trespassed upon your forbearance. I am, etc.,

KENNETH A. MACRAE

SABBATH, 17 MARCH

Enjoyed the morning service. Felt it easy to speak, thoughts came to me unbidden; felt a warmth in the course of the discourse which was very pleasant, and a melting of spirit which I experience nowadays only too seldom.

The evening service I also enjoyed, but my theme being the unquenchable nature of the Gospel fire, I did not experience the melting which accompanied the more experimental sermon of the morning.

WEDNESDAY, 20 MARCH

Cathie is laid up with what appears to be influenza.

THURSDAY, 21 MARCH

Cathie is much worse today and I did not get out.

7 pm, Prayer meeting. Leviticus 1:4. At the close Rod MacKay read the Financial Statement for 1962 and I gave a summary of what happened in the congregation during the course of the year.

FRIDAY, 22 MARCH

Thankful that Cathie is somewhat better today but I fear that the trouble is now beginning upon myself.

This has been a lovely day but I feel very low in my spirits. I have a stomach sensation which I don't like and it worries me.

SATURDAY, 23 MARCH

Cathie is still very ill and the trouble has so developed in me that it is questionable whether I shall be able to go out tomorrow. I am hoping against hope.

SABBATH, 24 MARCH

7 pm, Seminary. 1 Corinthians 1:21 – attendance 280.

Was prevailed upon to remain in bed till the afternoon. Mr Nicolson took my place in the Church at the Gaelic, and the English carried on as a prayer meeting. I took the evening service in the Seminary. I felt listless to begin with, but ere I was through I felt better. I was enabled to deliver my discourse with clearness. I am very thankful that I was so helped.

MONDAY, 25 MARCH

Cathie had a bad night of persistent and severe pain in the back so that today we had to call the Doctor. For myself I am much better, but still weak and off-colour. I did not go out at all today although within doors I was on my feet all day.

TUESDAY, 26 MARCH

Another day of aimless listlessness. Flu has a depressing aftermath and I suppose I am into that now. But doing nothing in particular does not suit me. It is good to be busy, without being too busy, when it becomes a burden.

Cathie is somewhat better but she is still confined to bed.

WEDNESDAY, 27 MARCH

Cathie is a little better today but still confined to bed. I don't seem to make much progress and I feel pretty far down. Reading of the great Welsh revival of 1740–47 and of the sufferings of the ejected Puritans in 1662. The Lord had great witnesses in the land in those days and He did great things. Would that He would do great things for us again!

THURSDAY, 28 MARCH

Today developed gall-bladder pains which discouraged me greatly. Cathie is better, but her cough is worse and she is still confined to bed.

MONDAY, 1 APRIL

The gall-bladder trouble becoming much worse, I could not get up on Friday morning and have been in bed ever since until this evening. The pain has now gone but I feel weak and shaky and am not fit for much. Fortunately Cathie was able to get to her feet on Saturday, and the Lord has sent help. We have reason for thankfulness.

SABBATH, 7 APRIL

7 pm, Seminary, English. Psalm 76:10. Attendance 550.

Felt very shaky, but felt better as the sermon proceeded. My subject was out of the usual and dealt largely with case of the nation as a whole. I got some force with it but cannot say that I got any melting.

Thankful that the Lord gave me such an opportunity once more and held me up while taking advantage of it.

MONDAY, 8 APRIL

Since this illness overtook me I have done a good deal of reading, particularly bearing upon the contendings of the Reformers and their successors, both in Scotland and England; and I feel the benefit of it. What has been mainly impressed upon me is the necessity of preaching on the needs of our day in the religious life of our land. I fear that as a Church our preaching is too academic, too negligent of the things that are actually happening in Church and nation today. The result is that our people are apt to view these things as they are depicted in the press and not as they appear when the light of God's Word is turned upon them. We are too apt to strive after preaching good and able and popular sermons, rather than the enlightenment and guidance of our people in the perilous times in which we live. Certainly the Gospel is unchanging but the message ought to be delivered in the light of the day in which we live. That note is largely missing.

SABBATH, 14 APRIL

Ventured out today and preached in Gaelic to a congregation of 380 from Hebrews 10:36. Felt weak and at first as though I had tackled something beyond my strength, but the Lord supported me. The feeling of weakness passed off and I was given a good deal of liberty in handling my subject.

At night spoke in English in the Church from Psalm 80:19 and enjoyed a good deal of liberty. Was given an amount of force which, considering my weakness, was wonderful. Felt very done out after it. About 700 were present.

TUESDAY, 16 APRIL

Gave last of series of lectures on 'Into the Bog – Church, State and People – and the Way Out'. Dealt with case of the Church in Scotland today and her only hope as being by way of repentance and returning to doctrines of grace.

THURSDAY, 18 APRIL

I feel quite worried about my health. I am not getting back my strength. I have lost 10 lbs in weight since the onset of my late illness.

SABBATH, 21 APRIL

After yesterday's unsettled day got a warm and sunny day for our baptismal service. How often we get this! God is good to us. Felt weak and unfit for the service, but got through it all right and was thankful. At night the Seminary was full to its capacity after every chair available had been utilised. Spoke from Romans 3:10–12. Towards the end felt that I had gripped my audience. If only the Lord would grip them! Began tonight a series of sermons on regeneration. Dealt with the doctrine of man's total depravity. Felt very exhausted after it.

SABBATH, 28 APRIL

Enjoyed liberty in the Gaelic service and felt part of it very sweet. My subject opened out before me in that way which bespeaks a goodly measure of the influence of the Spirit. Such makes preaching sweet. At night John MacSween, who has just arrived home from Toronto, took the evening service in the Seminary. Enjoyed the service again,[1] although not in the same way as in the morning. Still, for a good day I am very thankful and I trust that the Lord will bless His Word! I spoke more closely to my people tonight than I usually do and I pray that it may have penetrated.

THURSDAY, 16 MAY

Mr MacSween, at present home on furlough from Canada, took the meeting. His discourse was exceedingly able, his matter substantial and solid, and his delivery good. I wish he would remain in Lewis.[2]

SABBATH, 26 MAY

Got unexpected liberty in the morning service, especially in the concluding section. Before going out feared that I had very little, but the Lord helped me and my little became much.

At night dealt with working out our salvation, which I thought might be helpful to young Christians.

After each service asked the Lord's people to pray for the conservative party in the Church of Scotland Assembly when the Report of the Church and Nation Committee comes up for consideration tomorrow.

WEDNESDAY, 29 MAY

7 pm, Melbost. Philippians 3:8. I had so little freedom in preparing this sermon that I lost taste of it and felt almost that preparation was useless. Yet when I entered upon my theme in the Melbost Mission House I got such light upon my subject and such freedom of thought

1 i.e. the service in the church, held concurrently with the Seminary service.
2 John MacSween did remain and served the Point Free Church congregation from 1966 until his retirement in 1976.

that my soul rejoiced in the sweetness of it. This is not the first time I had that experience at Melbost. As a matter of fact I always get liberty there. What is the explanation? Is it someone present or someone praying at home?

SABBATH, 2 JUNE

The beautiful weather still continuing, had a record morning attendance of 530. Again felt that I had very little to give the Gaelic people, but again when it came to the point found I had no lack, and enjoyed the service.

At night the Seminary was packed beyond anything I have yet seen, almost all the spare chairs being utilised. Felt the atmosphere most oppressive, despite the fans, and, not feeling too well, almost feared that the service would be too much for me. However, the Lord sustained me. Preached God's sovereignty to them, and encouraged sinners to apply for mercy to Him who gives salvation sovereignly. May He bless it!

MONDAY, 3 JUNE

Troubled about the persistent pain which I feel internally from time to time. It is different from anything which I have yet experienced. The fear is that it may be something malignant. Is it my last messenger?

SABBATH, 9 JUNE

11 *am*. 2 Thessalonians 3:16. Attendance 510.

7 *pm*. John 3:3. Attendance 900.

Good weather produced good congregations. Had a goodly measure of liberty in the Gaelic discourse, yet felt a little dissatisfied with the build of the sermon. It would take some improving.

At night had largest congregation I have had for a long time, the extra front seat and the side seats on my left being occupied. Preached my last sermon of my series on regeneration. Got a good deal of force with it.

Cannot but feel encouraged by the way in which the people are turning out to these services.

TUESDAY, 11 JUNE

Examined 3 senior classes in Laxdale School in Religious Knowledge.

THURSDAY, 13 JUNE

Examined the Sandwick Hill School this morning in Religious Instruction and was very well satisfied with them. Examined the three senior classes.

MONDAY, 17 JUNE

Finished the school examinations today when I examined 7 classes of the Secondary Department of the Nicolson Institute. It is only too evident that the time allotted to Religious Instruction in the Secondary School is altogether inadequate, for the standard in all classes is very far below that of the Primary School and also of Sandwick and Laxdale.

WEDNESDAY, 19 JUNE

A tiring day trying to overtake arrears in correspondence. Feel that things are getting beyond me. I long for some respite.

FRIDAY, 21 JUNE: KNOCKBAIN

Most favourable crossing. Mr Ferrier met us at Dingwall and got in to Knockbain Manse at 10.15. All so different is this once familiar Manse.[1] It has been put in very good order and brought thoroughly up to date.

SATURDAY, 22 JUNE: KNOCKBAIN

In the afternoon went down to Kilmuir churchyard and took a copy of the details on the stone over Willie MacRae's grave. It is a pretty spot.

Preached in the Church at 7.30 to a congregation of 48 from Hebrews 3:14.

SABBATH, 23 JUNE: KNOCKBAIN

12 *noon*. Galatians 1:4. Attendance 115.

6.30 *pm*. John 3:3. Attendance 280.

Had quite a good day, although I cannot say that I felt anything like power, or even warmth. The Communion Roll here numbers 15, so that the majority of those who communicated were from other congregations.

A very large congregation gathered in the evening, representative of all the surrounding parishes.

MONDAY, 24 JUNE: KNOCKBAIN

In forenoon went for a motor run by Kessock, Charlestown, Redcastle – then back to the main road and on to Avoch, Fortrose and Rosemarkie, then back through Munlochy. The sight of those once familiar places awakened in me many memories.

1 Walter MacQuarrie had now retired and the Rev. Hugh Ferrier was his successor.

Enjoyed the service in the evening and thankful for the liberty given. On the whole this has been a happy Communion.

TUESDAY, 25 JUNE: BEAULY

Mr Ferrier drove us over in the forenoon to Beauly and left us there. I am sorry to leave Knockbain. It is unlikely that I shall ever be there again. I am conscious of a strange drawing to that locality.

SABBATH, 30 JUNE

Enjoyed the morning service better than any which I had while away from home. The Seminary was packed at night and I was favoured with much liberty in my sermon. May the Lord bless His Word to the multitude who listened so attentively to it! This has been for me a good day.

WEDNESDAY, 3 JULY

Got favourable journey by sea and land to Glasgow. Went to 50, Lauderdale Gardens[1] and shaved and washed, etc. Then a car came for me to take me to Partick Highland Church. The bridegroom and best man were both dressed in Highland dress and quite a goodly company were gathered in the church. 4.30 Conducted marriage service – Lewis McLeod Maciver to Patricia Chisholm, 5 Sand Street, Stornoway.

The car then took me back to Queen Street Station in time for 6 pm train to Edinburgh. Spent the night in the old home. Had many feelings as I crept into the bed – an old man – which I had so long occupied as a young man!

THURSDAY, 4 JULY: EDINBURGH–BEAULY

Edinburgh was clouded by a thick wet fog as I left in the morning. So dense was it that from the Forth Bridge I could not see the new road bridge now in course of construction. We did not reach Inverness till 3.5. Kennie MacLeay met me and ran me out to Beauly. It was their communion season there, and Alick MacLeod[2] (Nairn) was with them. At 7.30 he preached a very good sermon in the Beauly Hall from Jeremiah 8:22. I was highly pleased with the warnings he gave against false doctrine. About 44 were present. Very glad to be here again.

FRIDAY, 5 JULY: PORTMAHOMACK

Reached Portmahomack at 12.50 pm. 47 were out at the evening service. Preached from Psalm 32.2 and quite enjoyed it.

1 The home of the Rev. Malcolm Morrison of Partick Highland Free Church.
2 Formerly minister of Partick Free Church, Glasgow. He died suddenly on a visit to the Holy Land a few years later and was buried there.

SABBATH, 7 JULY: PORTMAHOMACK

That things have gone back is only too evident here. The figures speak for themselves –

1949 – Attendances 160 and 78 – 49 communicated.
1958 – Attendances 110 and 115 – 33 communicated.
1963 – Attendances 92 and 130 – 28 communicated.

Enjoyed liberty throughout the service. Outside after the service met Rhea Macdonald. How she has changed! She broke into tears when she met me as she spoke of yon[1] memorable evening in Hilton Schoolhouse.

At night enjoyed liberty in preaching on the Gospel coming in power.

MONDAY, 8 JULY: PORTMAHOMACK

In forenoon called on Angus MacKinnon's[2] widow at Kildary. On our way back stopped to visit the grave of the late George MacKay [Fearn] and his wife. How solemn a thing it was to realise that my once dear friends, whose memory is so upbound with this district, lay there. Such is life! That must come to me too!

Had a congregation of 75 at the evening service. Felt sorry that this communion is over, and somewhat depressed. Wish I were nearer the Lord.

TUESDAY, 9 JULY

Left Portmahomack Manse at 8.15 am with much regret. I am wanted back again next year – but will I be alive till then? Got train at Fearn Station at 8.50. Arrived at Kyle on time. There Mary and the children joined me.[3] We sailed at 3.30 and reached Stornoway at 7.50. Found all well, for which I am thankful.

THURSDAY, 25 JULY: PAIBLE, NORTH UIST

1 *pm*. Isaiah 26:20 – Attendance 38.
7 *pm*. Psalm 80:7 – Attendance 34.
Rev. K. J. MacLeay took the Sollas services and Rev. James Morrison the services in Grimsay.

The day was good although a North wind made it somewhat cold. I suppose this must now be the last place in Scotland in which the 'summer time' is not recognised – at least for church services. Did not feel either softening or power in the services but got a normal measure of liberty.

1 *ie* yonder – in the distant past.
2 Formerly minister of Aultbea.
3 His grandchildren, Kenneth and Mairi, were born in 1952 and 1961. Norman and Mary MacLeod had moved from Ardelve to Portree Free Church in 1958.

Both my themes dealt with the present-day apostasy from the Christian faith in state, church and people.

FRIDAY, 26 JULY: PAIBLE

Was troubled about the suitability of the Question and had no liberty in opening it. I seldom enjoy a Fellowship Meeting owing to my deafness, and this was no exception. But I had my best service yet at the evening service. Kennie MacLeay followed immediately in English without a break and preached for 30 minutes. His discourse was good and warmly evangelical. His prayer was even more so.

SABBATH, 28 JULY: PAIBLE

1 *pm.* John 10:11. Attendance 150, 20 communicated. Concluded 3.35.

7 *pm.* Rev. K. J. MacLeay. Numbers 10:29. English John 3:33. Attendance 170.

Beautiful day. Had a fair measure of liberty at Action but did not feel that I had all my audience.

Kennie preached a warm evangelical sermon although perhaps not very efficiently joined together. I followed with half an hour's English and enjoyed it.

Very thankful for such a good day.

MONDAY, 29 JULY: PAIBLE

1 *pm.* Luke 1:74–5. Attendance 62.

It has been a very happy communion and I feel depressed now that it is over, for probably this is my last visit to Uist.

In afternoon made some visits, calling upon some who were unable to come out to the services.

WEDNESDAY, 31 JULY: STORNOWAY

Tonight Mary and Norman with the children went away. They got a good windless night. We shall miss them greatly, but it was good to have had them.

SABBATH, 18 AUGUST

The day was beautiful and as the people are now back from the moors[1]

---

1 For many years it was the custom in Lewis for people to have summer holidays on the moors where cabins were built for this purpose, one larger hut serving as a place of worship.

the attendances at both ends of the day were much above normal. The Seminary would not have held our evening congregation.

Enjoyed both services very much but cannot understand why I am feeling so weak and done out tonight. For the last while I have been feeling like this once night comes on. I am not well; whatever is wrong with me?

THURSDAY, 22 AUGUST: STORNOWAY FAST DAY

11 *am*. Rev. Murdo MacRitchie, Detroit.[1] Hosea 14:1,2. Attendance 800.

2 *pm*. Rev. Duncan Beaton, Leith. Matthew 29:27. Attendance 160.

7 *pm*. Rev. Murdo Campbell, Resolis. James 4:8. Attendance 1,000. Seminary, Rev. M. MacRitchie.

I never saw such a large attendance on a Thursday until today. All three services were much above normal.

Mr MacRitchie preached a thoughtful and spiritual sermon.

FRIDAY, 23 AUGUST

Question given out by Norman Macdonald – 1 John 4:16. Opened by Rev. M. Campbell. 12 Spoke to Question. Closed by Rev. M. MacRitchie. Attendance 950.

7 *pm*, *Town Hall*. Rev. M. MacRitchie. 7.30 *pm*. *Seminary*. Rev. D. Beaton.

The Town Hall was completely full.[2] In the church only a few seats at the back of the end gallery were unoccupied.

SATURDAY, 24 AUGUST

11 *am*. Rev. M. MacRitchie. Colossians 3:3. Attendance 1300.

8.30 *pm*. Kirk Session.

Had to send to Back for loan of 100 tokens as our stock was exhausted.

SABBATH, 25 AUGUST

11 *am*. *Church*. Rev. M. Campbell. Job 19.25. Attendance 900. Communicants 550. Service concluded 2.35. Town Hall – Rev. M. MacRitchie. Seminary – Rev. D. Beaton. 114 communicated.

1 This appears to be the first reference to Mr MacRitchie since an entry in his Diary for 10 November, 1942, which read: 'The Presbytery met *pro re nata* to interview a promising young man from Back – Murdo MacRitchie – who wishes to go in for the ministry of the Church'. MacRitchie, at this date serving in the Church's overseas Presbytery of Ontario and Western Canada, was to become MacRae's successor in 1966.

2 So many attend the Stornoway Communion from all over the Island that it is necessary to use the Town Hall for additional services.

7 *pm*. Rev. M. MacRitchie. John 3:3–8. Attendance 1350. Town Hall – Rev. M. Campbell. Seminary – Rev. D. Beaton.

MONDAY, 26 AUGUST

11 *am*. Rev. M. Campbell – Romans 13:11. (1000)
7 *pm*. Rev. M. MacRitchie – Romans 8.29–30. Attendance 1200.

At night the church was full to capacity and chairs had to be placed down the two aisles.

It has been a very good communion and enjoyed by all. The atmosphere was good.

WEDNESDAY, 4 SEPTEMBER: BEAULY

Had a very comfortable crossing. Below one could not feel that we were on the sea at all. But the long wait at Kyle, from 4.30 till 6 am, was cruelly cold and the subsequent journey to Dingwall was worse.

Took the Prayer Meeting at Beauly. 26 were present.

THURSDAY, 5 SEPTEMBER

Went in to Dingwall in the evening for a meeting of the Graduates' Fellowship which was held in the Lower Hall of the Town Hall. Seven Free Church ministers, apart from myself, and three Church of Scotland ministers, were present. About 70 were there in all, most of whom were teachers. Rev. McInnes, Portmahomack, gave the first address as an introduction to the study of the parables. I followed with an address on 'Today's need for propagating the Reformed Witness'. It seemed to have been appreciated.

SATURDAY, 7 SEPTEMBER: DRUMCHAPEL COMMUNION, GLASGOW

The evening was very wet, nevertheless the attendance at the church at 7.30 was very good. I preached from Psalm 45:10 and enjoyed it. But I do not feel well. I hope I shall feel better tomorrow.

SABBATH, 8 SEPTEMBER: DRUMCHAPEL

11 *am*. Gal. 1:4 and Table. 43 Communicated. Attendance 110.
6.30. John 3:33. Attendance 320.

The day was good although the evening became rather showery. Had rather a good day. Throughout the whole morning service noticed several who appeared to be very much affected, especially at the Table service.

At night the church was packed to its utmost capacity. Am thankful that I was sustained through it all, for my physical condition is by no means favourable.

MONDAY, 9 SEPTEMBER: DRUMCHAPEL

7.30 *pm*. Acts 16:14. Attendance 200.

Rather enjoyed the service. My malady is in no way lessened and I feel pretty miserable. Yet I am thankful that I have been enabled to discharge this engagement.

SABBATH, 15 SEPTEMBER: PORTREE, SKYE

11 *a.m.* Psalm 45:10. Attendance 53. 12.5 *pm. Gaelic.* Jeremiah 17:17. Attendance 54.

6.30 *pm, English.* Ephesians 2:8. Attendance 95.

I enjoyed the Gaelic service much better than the hurried English service which preceded it. By the time the services were over, rain had come on and the whole aspect of the day had changed. Driven by a strong south-westerly wind the rain drifted up the valley below the Manse in clouds and thus it continued for the remainder of the day. I rather enjoyed the evening service when I emphasised free grace.

MONDAY, 16 SEPTEMBER: PORTREE

Rained incessantly all day long, and scarcely left the house. My malady is worse today.

Called on Rev. Malcolm MacLeod[1] who recently has had a slight stroke. We are all getting near the end of the way.

WEDNESDAY, 18 SEPTEMBER: PORTREE

A perfect day. In the forenoon had a run out to below the Storr Rock and in the afternoon to Penefidhleir. The scenery was magnificent.

The prayer meeting at 7 pm was conducted in English. 34 were present. Spoke from 1 Peter 1:3. John Matheson and John MacPherson engaged in prayer – two of my own boys in Kilmuir days.

THURSDAY, 26 SEPTEMBER: PORTREE

Called on Johnnie Matheson and his wife and had much talk of the old Kilmaluag days.

SATURDAY, 28 SEPTEMBER: PORTREE

My time here is drawing to a close. It has been rather an uneasy time

---

1 Formerly minister at Bracadale and later at Snizort in Skye but at this date living in retirement in Portree.

owing to my indisposition, for I cannot enjoy anything and it is sapping all my energy. Started a new course of treatment yesterday. If it fails I do not know where to turn. I cannot say that I am any better than when I came; I may be somewhat worse.

SABBATH, 29 SEPTEMBER: PORTREE

Enjoyed the Gaelic service. By evening the weather had improved and we had a good attendance at the evening service.

Felt better today than I did yesterday.

THURSDAY, 3 OCTOBER: STORNOWAY

Left Portree with mixed feelings. In a way am glad to get home, for I am weary of my trouble, yet feel sorry to go, for this may be my last visit to Portree.

We left Kyle at 3.30 and reached Stornoway at 8 o'clock after a good passage. Roddie MacLean met us with his car and soon we were home again. All was well before us and we have indeed great reason for thankfulness. The house was very cold, however, and I was glad to get to bed.

FRIDAY, 4 OCTOBER

Dr Macaulay called today. He wishes me to have an X-Ray. I agreed on condition that I would not be kept in the Hospital.

SABBATH, 6 OCTOBER

Owing to operations for the elimination of the woodworm pest the church was closed today and the Gaelic morning service and the English evening service were held in the Town Hall.

11 *am*. Isaiah 46:11. Attendance 450. 7 *pm*. Lamentations 3:48–50. Attendance 680. Considering that the Communion services are going on at Back today the attendance was exceptionally good.

At night the Town Hall was packed to capacity and many were turned away. My sermon was on the modern apostasy and the assurance of deliverance from it by the merciful intervention of the Lord. It was listened to with close attention and I had power to express myself clearly.

MONDAY, 7 OCTOBER: MONTHLY MEETINGS

11 *am*. Attendance 15. 7 *pm*. Psalm 25:9. Attendance 105.

I enjoyed the address on Psalm 25:9 and found ample liberty of expression. I wish that my health would improve.

WEDNESDAY, 9 OCTOBER

1.30. Funeral service. 4 pm. Marriage.

A wild wet day. The outlook for the harvest seems to be becoming pretty grim. It is long since we have had a day without rain. My engagements today suggest the changeful nature of life in this world – some mourning, others rejoicing, I felt the contrast today very much.

THURSDAY, 10 OCTOBER

7 pm. Prayer meeting. Attendance 200. 8.15. Deacons' court. 9.15. Kirk Session. 22 applications for baptism.

A heavy evening, but I took things easy through the day. Despite this, I still feel very far from normal.

FRIDAY, 11 OCTOBER

7.30 pm. Kirk Session.

Met parents desiring baptism, examined three for the first time and dealt with one case of discipline – 22 in all.

The Doctor wishes me to rest, but how can I get rest in this charge?

SABBATH, 13 OCTOBER

11 am. Isaiah 38:19. Attendance 570. Baptismal service. Baptised 17 infants.

7 pm. Philippians 3:8. Attendance 600.

The baptismal service passed off smoothly but I felt weak after it. The Seminary was full at night. I found no difficulty in speaking but I felt rather dry. Feel very pithless now that the day is over, yet thankful for having been upheld.

MONDAY, 14 OCTOBER

Today has been favourable. I hope that it is the beginning of a good spell of weather so that the harvest may be secured.

TUESDAY, 15 OCTOBER

A day of sweeping rain and storm.

WEDNESDAY, 16 OCTOBER

Today has been good but the corn could scarcely have got dry after yesterday's wetting.

Feel coming near to the end of my resources. My condition is definitely becoming worse, and since no remedy seems to effect any improvement, I cannot but fear the onset of a malignant growth.

SABBATH, 20 OCTOBER

11 *am*. Romans 5:5. Attendance 340. 7 *pm*. Mark 5:22. Attendance 420.

The evening turned out very rough and wet. I was surprised that the congregation was so large on such a night.

I feel definitely much worse than I did last Sabbath. My malady seems to be worsening all the time. I fear that I cannot keep going much longer.

SABBATH, 27 OCTOBER

After a week in bed I ventured to take the evening English service in the Seminary. The place was crowded out. Despite the use of extra chairs from the school and St Peter's Church a few hundred were turned away. Spoke from Genesis 7:1 and got wonderful strength. Many waited after the service to bid me good-bye. This nearly overcame me. But what reason I have to praise the Lord for everything!

THE GOLDEN GATES

The golden gates are open in fair Immanuel's land,
The faithful there are gathered on that angelic strand,
'Midst many a glad hosanna life's conquerors enter in
To find that all their conflict was worth this heaven to win.

But shall I see those glories so radiant and so fair?
Dare still I hope to enter from out of such despair?
My arm hath grown so powerless, my strength is sinned away,
Ah, Lord, wilt thou not tell me that even yet I may?

I long to see thy vision, to hear thy voice again,
To feel that touch renew me that waked the dead at Nain;
Wilt not thou send me quickening and yet thy grace outpour
Before the shadows gather and all my days be o'er?

The golden gates are distant, they flash in pearl above,
The saints of God are ent'ring the palaces of love,
The joy song sounds eternal about the golden throne,
Where Christ awaits with longing the coming of his own.

Wilt thou not send to save me, for I am named on thee?
Oh, do not let me perish whom once thou didst set free;
If thou didst save Manasseh and purge his sin away,
Hast thou not power to bring me to heaven's eternal day?

Oh, Lord, I still will trust thee though faint my faith hath grown,
And all the hopes I cherished long since have been o'erthrown,
But still, thou sav'dst Manasseh, and so there's hope for me,
That I shall enter even yet because I trust in thee.

K.A.M.

21 'Soon I shall Serve Him. . . .'

The final entry of the last chapter brought to a conclusion Kenneth MacRae's preaching ministry of more than fifty years and it also marked the end of the regular diary entries which he had made since 1912. His premonitions during the summer of 1963 that he might be incurably ill and that he was preaching in various places for the last time were correct. Yet even with that growing apprehension it never occurred to him to decline any of the many engagements which filled those summer months more fully than has been reported above. And after his three-weeks September holiday with Mrs MacRae at their son-in-law's manse in Portree – where he preached twice every Sunday – he had returned to Stornoway prepared to undertake, in his 80th year, the usual full load of preaching and pastoral duties. On 1 October he said in a letter to a friend, 'I am beginning to question whether the Lord wishes me to stand down. If so, I must not complain, for He has given me a long innings in the Gospel field, but I would like to go on'. That he did 'go on' as far as the last Sunday in October was characteristic of the spirit of resolution which he had so long exemplified.

As the last diary entry reveals, the seriousness of his condition had been recognised by his people when he preached to them for the last time in the Seminary on 27 October. In the week which followed, he went with Cathie by air to Inverness, where he was admitted to the Royal Northern Infirmary for X-rays and other investigations. The Rev. Murdoch Campbell, a friend of many years, visited him there on 7 November and recorded in his own diary, 'Felt the Lord's presence as I prayed by his bedside. A faithful soldier of Jesus Christ is about to lay down his armour'.[1]

On 14 November, in the course of a letter, he spoke of the imperfections of his ministry – 'surely the ministry of one of the Lord's most unworthy servants' – and continued:

The Lord has given me a wonderful field among a most responsive people, and what grieves me more than anything else is that I should have made so little of my opportunity. I longed to be able to lead God's

1 Murdoch Campbell served congregations at Fort Augustus, Glasgow (Partick Highland) and Resolis. Beloved by all, and particularly esteemed for his writings (of which *From Grace to Glory* is perhaps best known), he died in 1974, aged 73. The above quotation is taken from his unpublished diary by kind permission.

heritage into the riches of the truth and to have my heart and mind saturated with the spirituality of the Word, but the many calls incident to the care of such a large congregation made it impossible for me to find the time for the study which such a ministry requires. Consequently I have been mostly skimming the surface and my flock are only half fed. I am therefore amazed as well as humbled that anyone outside my own circle should take any notice of my ministry.

There is only one thing I know I can do well. I cannot lead, but I think I can truthfully say that I am able to hang on. It may arise from natural stubbornness, but I know that popular religious movements, which, despite their lack of scriptural support, carry away so many good people, leave me entirely unaffected. I believe that I can set my teeth and hold on, but that is all I am good for.

I have been very depressed under this illness, but William Bridge's *Lifting up for the Downcast* has been a great help and comfort to me since I came in here. The Lord has been very good to me, although I had little of His presence. For the last fortnight I have had most exhaustive – and exhausting – tests and X-rays, and today I have got the results. The gall-bladder is not functioning properly and it has a considerable amount of inflammation which threatens to become chronic and which is responsible for the pain which I have been suffering, but the other internal organs are all right. The best of the news is that an operation is not necessary and that I can leave the Hospital tomorrow. So there again the Lord has shown His wondrous kindness to such an unworthy sinner.

In spite of prolonged and tiring tests the real nature of his illness, namely cancer, was not diagnosed in hospital. He left there as anticipated on 15 November and, after a further week with friends in Inverness, was able to travel back with Mrs MacRae to the loving care of the home of his daughter and son-in-law in Portree. For three weeks he seemed to improve, but then the symptoms of pain and loss of weight re-asserted themselves, so that by the end of the year the local doctor urged his removal to the Western General Hospital in Edinburgh in order to have the attention of one of the city's leading specialists. Arrangements were made for his departure on 2 January, 1964. On the first day of the New Year he dictated and signed the following words of testimony:

I hereby put on record that since the Lord in His sovereign mercy entered my heart on the lonely summit of Bell's Hill in the Pentlands on that memorable afternoon – 9th August, 1909 – I have sought to serve Him as my only Lord. I have been long in His service here, but I never tired of it. All my grief was that it was so poor, so listless, so forgetful, and so lacking in holiness; but soon I shall serve Him with a perfect service without failure or flaw. The Lord reigneth. Let the earth be glad!

His final crossing from Skye to the mainland was probably the most difficult he had ever faced. So fierce was the storm blowing on the morning of 2 January that by the time the ambulance, which conveyed him by stretcher, reached Kyleakin the ferry men declined to attempt the crossing. After a wait of two hours and a half the men decided it was safe enough to venture. Cathie MacRae, who was probably more conscious of the difficulty than her husband, recorded: 'We left and had to turn back, then out again to move around in circles in mid-channel, then, after a little, we went forward and between two waves drew in to the slip on the other side. How thankful I was to see the ambulance safely up on the road'.

But the difficulties were not over. There was a necessity to cross the Highlands from west to east to catch a train southwards from Inverness to Edinburgh, and in the course of this hurried journey, amidst a continuing storm, the patient had to be transferred on his stretcher from one ambulance to another. The strain was lightened by a number of Christian friends who, at various stopping-places, waited with refreshments and their prayerful good wishes. Not until 10 pm that evening did he finally reach his hospital bed in Edinburgh. The next day he collapsed and blood transfusions were necessary.

From this time until his death Mrs MacRae kept a journal. She intended it mainly as a record of the fluctuations in his illness and for no eye but her own. Jottings of fervent prayers are intermingled with her notes and there are many beautiful expressions of the tenderness of the love which they had shared through forty-seven years. As we quote now from this journal it must, of course, be understood that there are some feelings altogether too personal to be printed here, and yet to pass by this journal entirely would be to leave untold a God-honouring record of Christian experience in that valley of shadows in which the last enemy must be met. Cathie MacRae writes:

10 *January*, 1964. Restless night with pain. Surgeon informed Ken of necessity for having operation.

12 *January*. Ken not so well; suffering pain and other weaknesses. Operation awaits him tomorrow. He is worried. May the Great Physician support and bless him!

13 *January*. Operation delayed till 4 pm.

14 *January*. Ken fairly satisfactory. Saw him in afternoon, very weak, spoke a word or two.

s

15 *January*. Surprised to find our dear patient better – marked change! Speaking strongly and read his letters. Mr F. has good hopes of his recovery.

19 *January*. Ken had walked length of ward – too much exertion. He was in bed and panting like a little bird when we visited at 3 pm. He feels lonely, restless, wanting home.

21 *January*. K. very downcast, said he was 'losing ground'.

22 *January*. Found Ken better – how good to hear that word 'better' from his lips. Had porridge and egg for his breakfast.

27 *January*. Surprised to hear from K. that he may get out of hospital any day now and wishes us to make preparation. . . . Felt a burden descending upon me.[1] After getting home I took my concern to the place where we are invited to make our requests known, and felt truly that my burden slid off.

28 *January*. All arrangements are now ready for K's admission to 'Lyndene' (Nursing Home) tomorrow.

30 *January*. Shocked to see our dear patient so poorly this afternoon. His face and eye-whites were yellowish-tinged. Feel very anxious for my beloved Ken.

2 *February*. Dear Ken much about the same. He related to me a wonderful experience he had while in the Western General Hospital. During the earlier part of his illness – in Inverness Royal Infirmary and in Portree – he seemed to be in darkness, longing for light, longing exceedingly for a promise *for himself*, but none came directly to himself. He said that others had got promises for him, but that wasn't satisfying enough. But one day in the Western General Hospital, probably while praying, he saw himself in a different situation. He was outside, in a wide open field and lying on his back. Gazing up to the sky, he saw the most wonderful light as of a glory very far away. As he looked he felt that someone touched him, and a voice said, 'I am the King's Son, I will never leave thee nor forsake thee – *never*. I am the King's Son.' And Ken went on to relate this: 'The glory which seemed far away came nearer

1 Mrs MacRae was then staying with her husband's elderly sisters, Vic and Ida, at the old family apartment in Warrender Park. She had been ill with a heavy cold that week and it was clearly impossible for him to be adequately nursed in the old home.

until the whole place, yea, the whole world, was filled with it. Oh! it came out of the rocks, shining out of everywhere. Yes, the King's Son! He didn't say I was to be brought out of this illness, yet this scene, with the promise given to me direct from Himself, has changed everything.'

While relating the above to me his face wore a beautiful youthful appearance, almost like a youth of eighteen. He was happy and uplifted. He then lay back on his pillow, weak and exhausted, yet content.

3 *February*. Ken was up when we visited him today and looked extremely frail in his easy chair.

5 *February*. Ken exhausted and dreads the night. 'Oh, the night, the night,' he wearily said, as I was leaving, 'the night is so lonely'. (Gladly would I stay if I could get permission to do so. It takes me all my time to keep back my tears.) I said, 'There are songs for the night, too, my dear. He will compass you about with songs of deliverance. The morning will come before you are aware'.

6 *February*. Nurses got Ken up. He remained in his chair half an hour, looks slightly less jaundiced. He is pining for the hills, rivers, glens, and lochs. He calls out, 'Take me north, take me north, even if I die on the journey, take me north!' Oh! what can I do for my beloved! He could not possibly travel in his present frail condition. May the Most High strengthen him, guide me, and hold me up!

7 *February*. Found Ken looking tired. He was reminiscing with Vic, quite alert in memory, but in my opinion not so well as yesterday; he is terribly weak. What a fight our dear brave soldier is putting up! I called again at night and had the hour with him by myself. He wanted me close to him so that he could speak of the love and sweetness of Christ. Oh my heart was sore tonight to see you labouring to speak on the theme which it was your delight to proclaim in various parts of our land! Among his utterances were the following: 'Beware of self, beware of self!' 'If I had opportunity to speak I would emphasise the excellency of His work – the completeness of it! Christ's finished work is perfect. He has made all perfect.'

He said when a little stronger, that he would like me to get for him a *Banner of Truth* magazine – easy to hold in bed, also Hodge's *Way of Life*. 'Oh', he added, 'some think that doctrine is dry, but I *love* it, I *love chunks* of doctrine, *chunks* of it. It is so full of Christ, full of Christ! (I did, without delay, comply with his request, but sadly I noticed that

[509]

though the thin hands greedily grasped 'Hodge', he could only read a sentence or two, and lay it aside, realising the powers of concentration were gone, or almost gone.)

8 *February.* Dr Willie MacLeod[1] came to see me this forenoon after visiting Ken. He saw a change for the worse and wondered whether we should try to get Ken removed to Stornoway, since he had such a desire to go home. Willie suggests he should travel without delay.

10 *February.* Have had a busy day attending to phone and trying to arrange for our homegoing. Plane is going from Renfrew (Glasgow) to Stornoway on Wednesday. Ken will be on a stretcher in this passenger plane.

13 *February.* Stornoway. Ken said he had 'the best sleep since ——' (I missed his last word) and that he feels better. He told Dr Greig he felt 20% better on completion of his journey than at the start. It is the Communion week and I attended the Seminary service in the evening.[2]

15 *February.* Five people came before the Session tonight, having been brought in under Ken's preaching.

17 *February.* Ken weaker and weary and listless.

21 *February.* Made full and final preparations at manse for dear Ken's arrival from Hospital. Nurse called in afternoon at my request to see if all was right. She thought K.'s bedroom lovely and bright, and so it is. I made up the spare room at the front so that he could get sunshine. Later the Hospital rang to say that as K.'s blood was very low, blood transfusions were necessary, and as the plasma had to be sent from Inverness he could not now be home till Tuesday or Wednesday of next week.

23 *February.* Ken very low in afternoon. I had to put my ear to his lips to hear his broken words. Tom[3] came in and just quoted the words, 'When thou passest through the waters' etc. and left with a heavy heart.

1 A Consultant in Edinburgh Royal Infirmary – the son of Angus MacLeod, once an outstanding Gaelic precentor and highly respected elder in MacRae's congregation in Stornoway.
2 As the manse had been closed for so many months, MacRae had been taken into the Stornoway Hospital at this time.
3 Tom MacKay, one of MacRae's elders and a close friend.

24 *February*. Rev. James Morrison arrived this afternoon and visited his friend. He seemed greatly surprised at K.'s wan appearance. James assured him of his constant supplication for him and Ken's reply was, 'Hang on, James, hang on!'

25. *February*. Norman arrived last night and accompanied Mary to see her Dad.[1] Mary said he spoke quite freely, even had flashes of humour. I am longing to receive him home.

28 *February*. Home to the manse at last!

4 *March*. Haven't had opportunity to write daily notes. Our dear patient goes on much the same day by day. On Monday afternoon he had a rigor and was so weak and flushed after it that I feared the end was near.

6 *March*. Ken very weak today and yesterday but he can still get out of bed wonderfully easily! He feels his strength waning daily, he told me, and said twice today that it was the end, and longs for the fight to be over.

7 *March*. Nurse roused me at 7.15 am to say that our dear patient is very weak and temperature 104°. I went over immediately and I roused Mary. Her Dad rallied before 9 am. Doctor came, took temperature which was down to 99°. Ken asked Doctor what his illness really is, to which he readily replied, 'jaundice' and Ken remarked, 'Isn't it stubborn!'

14 *March*. Ken very ill on Monday evening.

25 *March*. K. has been in much of a steady condition. Temperature normal and pulse strong. A little nourishment is taken and eyes brighter.

6 *April*. K. had a restless and miserable night. Pain and discomfort.

8 *April*. He looked so pinched, but is alert in mind, and today was making arrangements about the car.[2]

1 Mary was at home to help with her father from the time of his return to Stornoway until his death. Norman made visits as often as possible.
2 On this his daughter writes: 'When, by my father's own request, a motor salesman arrived in his bedroom to arrange about the sale of his car, he greeted him with the words, "All my spiritual concerns are safe in the hands of my glorious Redeemer but there are a few temporal matters with which I don't wish others to be burdened after I am gone. One of these is the sale of my car." '

12 *April*. Yesterday Ken insisted on my phoning Mr Nicolson, Barvas (who is Interim-Moderator of the congregation at present) to come in, so that he could give him his desired arrangements for the end. Oh, my beloved, my companion of many years! If I'm spared after you what a lonely world I shall live in! Yet the Lord will not leave me comfortless. He is 'from all mutations free'. May He help me to be submissive to His will.

22 *April*. Ken restless at nights – not so well this week. His voice changed on Sabbath, thick and weak as if losing grip of words, but clear in mind. He took fluids only today. The signs of the great change are ominous. In his weak, whispering tones he quoted these words from John 17, 'Father, I will that they also whom thou hast given me be with me where I am that they may behold my glory' etc.

24 *April*. Our dear one had a good night's sleep. Pulse wonderfully steady, but quite evidently weaker, can hardly speak. Four office-bearers called this evening with a presentation for us both from the congregation.[1] I took them to the bedroom two and two. They spoke tenderly and lovingly while handing over a cheque. His hand was too weak to grip it. Terribly affecting to see the 'soldier' laid so low that he could hardly speak above a whisper. He was moved when trying to thank the congregation through their office-bearers, in a few words. His last message to them was, 'Be ye faithful unto death. Let no man take your crown'. In prayer he said, 'Bless my dear people. Give them a man after thine own heart. Bless my young people'. . . . All were affected as they saw the great change in their beloved minister's face. Downstairs I was also presented with a cheque. How good the Lord is! He does and will provide!

Tuesday, 5 May. Ken's condition much the same for past week. On 3rd May, Sabbath, he became definitely weaker. One afternoon last week he wished me to come close to his side and whispered these words, 'Cath, my darling, I'll be waiting for you on the other side'. 'Yes, my love,' I managed to say, 'but for me it is between now and the other side'. 'Oh', he said, 'the Lord will provide'. Yesterday (Monday), before he lapsed into a coma, he whispered, 'Into thine hands I commit my

---

1 This gift, as later reported in *The Stornoway Gazette*, was a cheque for over £800 to Mr and Mrs MacRae 'in appreciation of their services to the congregation during the 33 years of faithful ministry'. Mr MacRae, it was also recorded, expressed his 'heartfelt gratitude for this token of affection and for the unspeakable kindness of his people down through the years'.

spirit, Lord Jesus'. As I write these words (9.40 am) at his bedside he is lying peacefully – his eyes open and looking upwards (such a lovely shade of blue, clear as the sky on a summer day). I feel sure he is conscious. How thankful I am that he is not in painful agony! He had his long period of pain and discomfort in those distressing weeks and months, now he is free from all pain and awaits an abundant entrance into Immanuel's Land where there shall be no more pain. His eyes appear as if looking intently upward, sightless here, but I do believe he is seeing the King in His beauty and the Land that is not so very far off.

2 *am*, 6 *May*. My beloved Ken passed over the river to the better country tonight at 9.30 o'clock. I had watched by the bedside all day, and was still there when Nurse came, still watching his breathing – which had become more laboured. Suddenly Nurse asked if Mary and her husband were near. She pressed the bell. Vic, Ida and Norman came into the room and almost then the dear sufferer's breathing gently ceased – not a move nor sound of any description, and we knew all was now over. What a peaceful end to a full life! (Thou, Lord, hast indeed let Thy servant depart in peace.) He has gone through the Golden Gates and will join in singing the song of the redeemed for ever and ever. To me, while I gazed upon the beloved dead, the words (so familiar since my childhood) of the Shorter Catechism – 'The souls of believers are at their death made perfect in holiness, and do immediately pass into glory, etc.' – came flashing into my mind full of comfort, so that I could submissively yield him (as it were) into God's hands to dwell with the Redeemer for ever. Oh, what peace and comfort filled my heart! I went to break the news to our dear Mary who stood up well to the trial.

'Until death us do part' – Almost 48 years of happy wedded life is now ended. But nothing shall separate us from the love of God in Christ Jesus.

He was a gentle, tender and loving companion, husband and father, yet valiant for the truth.

'God lives, blessed be my Rock!'

☐   ☐   ☐

Kenneth MacRae was buried in the afternoon of Friday, 8 May, 1964. Prior to the burial the people who for thirty-two years he had regarded as his own, met at their full strength at 1.15 pm both in the Church and in the Seminary. The smaller congregation – some 700 in number – occupied every seat in the Seminary for an English service

while worship was conducted simultaneously in Gaelic in the crowded
Church. In the Seminary the coffin lay out of sight, close to the vestry
door, for it was not MacRae's belief that in the worship of God a coffin
should be ceremoniously placed before a congregation. With the
announcement of verses from Psalm 107, the congregation, led by the
Rev. Kenneth MacLeay, seemed swept by one common emotion of
grief and of praise as they sang to the tune 'Torwood',

> The storm is chang'd into a calm
>   at his command and will;
> So that the waves, which rag'd before,
>   now quiet are and still.
> Then are they glad, because at rest
>   and quiet now they be:
> So to the haven he them brings,
>   which they desir'd to see.

His friend of student days, the Rev. John MacLennan of Lairg read
the Scriptures in 1 Corinthians 15 and Revelation 7, and the Rev.
Murdoch Campbell of Resolis led an awed congregation to the throne
of God in prayer.[1] What abides of that prayer in the memory of the
writer, these thirteen years later, is the manner in which it found its
centre of rest in viewing the death of believers as the fulfilment of a
gracious command, 'Gather my saints together unto me' (Psalm 50:5).
The Seminary service ended with the singing of the last three verses of
Psalm 45, and then, as the other service in the Church was not yet
concluded, the congregation remained many minutes in absolute silence
before the coffin was carried through the tightly-packed concourse of
people to the door. When, at length, the congregations from both
buildings emerged into the bright sunlight, the silence outdoors remained as intense as it had been within. A procession of men, estimated
by newspaper reporters as 1,000 strong, formed its head beside the
simple wooden bier which stood outside the Seminary in Francis Street.
By Highland tradition only males take the remains of loved ones for
burial; consequently those who were not to accompany the coffin – a
vast number of women, children and even infants in arms – lined the
pavements. MacRae had once reflected on the almost military order
with which funerals are conducted in Lewis, and on this occasion,
reportedly the largest funeral ever seen in the Island, it did not fail. With

---

1 Both of these highly-esteemed servants of Christ have since ended their
course, Murdoch Campbell, as already noted, in 1974, and John MacLennan
in 1977, aged 92.

the stillness unbroken save for the sound of feet, the procession moved off, past the manse, past the school – where the children lined a silent playground – towards the cemetery which, a mile beyond the town, lies beside the shore of Sandwick Bay. Twenty-five ministers and scores of men, in turn, accompanied the bier, and such was the length of the procession that when its head was more than a quarter-of-a-mile outside Stornoway the rear was still within the town.

To a visitor from afar it seemed strange that, with such a multitude assembled, no sermon was preached that day in Stornoway nor at the graveside. But there is 'a time to speak' and 'a time to keep silence'. For the majority it was the sermons of days and years gone by which were then being 'heard' again in memory and conscience. 'Pastors and listeners are soon parted', wrote Martin Luther, 'but it is impossible to separate the Word of God from your conscience, which heard the Word'.

Some remembered best his insistent call to his hearers to come to the Lord Jesus Christ. Donald B. MacLeod, writing under the heading 'The End of an Era' in *The Stornoway Gazette*, recalled: 'I was one of the children baptised by him in the first service of baptism he conducted when he started his ministry in Stornoway. The house where I was born is practically in the shadow of the church where he preached all these years. Whether in Gaelic or English, in the big church on Kenneth Street or in the Seminary, his ministry was an integral part of my life . . . In my mind's eye there is a picture of that spare, upright figure standing in the pulpit of the big church on Kenneth Street, a church packed to the rafters with a congregation notable for the predominance of the young. He has closed the big Bible and in that strong voice which reaches to the furthest corners of the building he extends the gospel invitation: "Oh will you not come . . ." '.

There were others who thought not so much of their loss as of the gain of their friend and pastor. Jesus Christ, he had often told his flock, had borne the curse of God's law for them. Among much which he said on that subject the following brief outline on Isaiah 53:9 is recorded on a slip of paper:

Introduction. The rich.
> (i) Death was part of the curse and had to be borne.
> (ii) He was buried among sinners.
> (iii) He went to the grave.
1. It was not too dark
2. He warmed it for His people

3. Don't be afraid to go where Christ has been
4. He rid the grave of its terrors
5. His stay was but temporary.

In that assurance, the men of his sorrowing congregation brought his earthly remains to rest under the green turf beside Sandwick Bay, awaiting the coming of the Lord from heaven. And in the same glorious hope the body of Cathie MacRae was laid beside that of her husband in January 1976.

□   □   □

Tributes to Kenneth MacRae's memory appeared in many of the newspapers of the Scottish Highlands. We close these pages with an extract from a long appreciation which was published in *The North Star*:

What Stornoway and Lewis owe to the self-denying and devoted labours of this great man is known only to God. But as was said of Dr Kennedy and Dingwall, that was only his headquarters. The field of his activity was the whole of the Highlands and Islands – yea, and Scotland as well, for in how many places, and to how many people Mr MacRae was made a very ambassador of Christ, a son of consolation and comfort, will only be known when the books are opened above.

As a preacher of the evangel he had few equals. The pulpit was his throne and his presentation of the cardinal doctrines in language so clear and simple that the youngest could understand was a talent that endeared him to many, while he was not appreciated by all. But wherever he went in the Free Church, north or south, no one could claim the audience that Mr MacRae claimed, and no man in the Free Church was so much loved by the people. But like Daniel of old he often had to plough a very lonely furrow, and pay a price for his convictions; still he was always the Christian gentleman, majestic and calm in debate, ever showing the spirit of his Master who 'when He was reviled, reviled not again'.

The best answer to his critics is the success of his ministry. Everywhere he laboured his memory is revered and cherished, his praise is in all the churches, and surely in his passing we must hear the words of the old oracle: 'Blessed are the dead which die in the Lord from henceforth; yea, saith the Spirit, that they may rest from their labours; and their works do follow them'.

The Manuscript Sources of the present volume[1]

1. Preaching Record, March 1912–March 1913 (pp. 254, notebook)
2. Diary, September 1912–February 1914 (pp. 137, notebook)
3. Preaching Record, March 1913–February 1915 (pp. 328)
4. Diary (now merged with Preaching Record) Feb. 1915–Nov. 1916 (pp. 328)
5. Communion in Arran, 1–5 June, 1916 (pp. 42, small notebook)
6. A daily entry diary for 1916 (published by Wm. Love) one day per page (overlaps with 4 above and fullest where 4 ends)
7. *Letts Diary* for 1917, one day per page
8. *Collins Royal Diary* for 1918, one day per page
9. *Collins Royal Diary* for 1919, one day per page
10. *The Pastor's Diary* for 1920 (very brief entries)
11. *Letts Clerical Diary* for 1921 (4 days per page, filled throughout)
12. Personal Notes, Jan.–July 1922 (notebook, a purchased diary being discontinued, pp. 152)
13. Personal Notes, July 1922–Feb. 1923 (notebook, pp. 153)
14. Personal Notes, Feb. 1923–Dec. 1923 (notebook, pp. 155)
15. Personal Notes, Dec. 1923–May 1925 (notebook, pp. 156)
16. Personal Notes, May 1925–Oct. 1926 (notebook, pp. 156)
17. Personal Notes, Oct. 1926–Dec. 1927 (notebook, pp. 128)
18. *Letts One-Day Diary* for 1928 (page per day)
19. *Letts One-Day Diary* for 1929 (page per day)
20. *Walker's Diary* for 1930 (page per day)
21. *Walker's Diary* for 1931 (page per day)
22. *Walker's Diary* for 1932 (page per day)
23. *Walker's Diary* for 1933 (page per day)
24. *Walker's Diary* for 1934 (page per day)
25. Folio Journal Notebook, Oct. 1934–Sept. 1936 (pp. 183)
26. Folio Journal Notebook, Sept. 1936–July 1938 (pp. 139)
27. Personal Notes, loose-leaf, type-written, 4 July, 1938–26 Sept., 1938 (pp. 22)

---

1 This information is listed in order to give a clearer idea of the extent of the original diaries and also to be a record for the future of the material which was available to the editor at the time this volume was prepared. It is possible that for the few years not covered by this list other diaries of MacRae's will yet be discovered. All here listed is presently in the possession of his daughter Mrs Norman MacLeod, Free Church Manse, Callanish, Isle of Lewis.

28. *The Leader Foolscap Folio Diary* for 1940 (three or four days per page)
29. *Collins Scribbling Diary* for 1941 (folio three or four days per page)
30. *Collins Scribbling Diary* for 1942 (folio three or four days per page)
31. *Collins Scribbling Diary* for 1943 (folio three or four days per page)
32. *Collins Scribbling Diary* for 1944 (folio three or four days per page)
33. *Collins Royal Diary* for 1945 (two days per page)
34. Folio Journal, Jan. 1946–Sept. 1947 (pp. 141)
35. Folio Journal, Sept. 1947–Sept. 1949 (pp. 139)
36. Folio Journal, Sept. 1949–Sept. 1952 (pp. 182)
37. Personal and Congregational Notes, Sept. 1952–Aug. 1955 (large notebook, pp. 205)
38. *Pepys Diary* for 1959 (very few entries)
39. *Collins Paragon Diary* for 1960 (page per day, small, kept fairly fully)
40. *Collins Paragon Diary* for 1963 (page per day, small, kept until October)
41. Catherine MacRae's 'Notes on Ken's protracted illness', Oct. 1963–May 1964 (exercise book, pp. 36)

Index

Eodem die

Praise the Lord oh my soul for this evening! What a glorious time I have experienced. So was His Spirit working in me that ere beginning my discourse I was constrained to beseech the Lord ~~from~~ to keep my eyes from shedding tears. I came very near it however not only in the sermon but also in reading the Word and especially in prayer. I know God was with me for there was no sound or movement even in the reading. The service was in the hall as in the evening the attendance is poor there being only about 60 present. I never entered a place of service in such a condition of spirit before. The words "As many as I love, I rebuke and chasten" had come suddenly before my eyes and had driven home the conviction that my unavailing efforts to find Christ in the earlier part of the day constituted